POWERHOUSE

POWER

Also by James Andrew Miller

Those Guys Have All the Fun
Live from New York
Running in Place

HOUSE

THE UNTOLD STORY OF HOLLYWOOD'S CREATIVE ARTISTS AGENCY

JAMES ANDREW MILLER

CUSTOM HOUSE

An Imprint of WILLIAM MORROW

HarperCollins books may be purchased for educational, business, or sales promotional use. For information please e-mail the Special Markets Department at SPsales@harpercollins.com.

FIRST EDITION

Designed by Leah Carlson-Stanisic

Frontispiece photograph courtesy of Caleb George/Unsplash.com; title page photograph by millicookbook/Shutterstock, Inc.; photograph on Act One by Ken Lubas/Los Angeles Times/Getty Images; photograph on Act Two by Cary Westfall/Shutterstock, Inc.; photograph on Act Three by Al Seib/ The Los Angeles Times/Getty Images

Library of Congress Cataloging-in-Publication Data has been applied for.

ISBN 978-0-06-244137-9

16 17 18 19 20   ov/rrd   10 9 8 7 6 5 4 3 2 1

TO TOM

"Why not gather rainbows while ye may?"

—*Cover Girl*, 1944

CONTENTS

DRAMATIS PERSONAE

The CAA Founders

Bill Haber
Ron Meyer
Michael Ovitz

Rowland Perkins
Michael Rosenfeld

The Young Turks

Kevin Huvane
Bryan Lourd
Richard Lovett

Jay Moloney
David O'Connor

The Money

David Bonderman
James Burtson
Jim Coulter
Stuart Epstein
Rick Hess

Bill McGlashan
Jeff Skoll
Bob Stanley
David Trujillo

The CAA Team (Once Upon or Still)

Abby Adams
Dan Adler

Jay Adya
Steve Alexander

Dan Aloni

Marty Baum

Spencer Baumgarten

Alan Berger

Jeff Berry

Chris Bevilacqua

Bob Bookman

Tracy Brennan

Pat Brisson

Bobby Brooks

Liz Bruyette

Eric Carlson

Sharon Cicero

Sandy Climan

Casey Close

Joe Cohen

Tom Condon

Paul Danforth

Jimmy Darmody

Matt Delpiano

Ben Dogra

Derek Eiler

Ari Emanuel

Todd Feldman

Adam Fields

Len Fink

Richard Fischoff

Jenny Gabler

Lee Gabler

Risa Gertner

Alan Gold

Bob Goldman

Jae Goodman

Marc Graboff

Boz Graham

Micah Green

David Greenblatt

Amy Grossman

Christy Haubegger

Jason Heyman

Shelly Hochron

Judy Hofflund

Rand Holston

Ruth Ann Huvane

Jeff Jacobs

Adam Kanter

Phil Kent

Peter Kenyon

Nick Khan

Bruce King

Tony Krantz

Ray Kurtzman

Rick Kurtzman

Steve Lafferty

George Lane

Hal Lazarus

Michelle Kydd Lee

Philippe Le Floc'h

Rusty Lemorande

Martin Lesak

John Levin

Michael Levine

Rob Light

David Lonner

Joel Lubin

Greg Luckman

Joe Machota

Stuart Manashil

Mike Marcus

Andrea Nelson Meigs

Mike Menchel
David Messinger
Susan Miller
Rick Nicita
Tina Nides
Howie Nuchow
Rich Paul
Laurie Perlman
Chris Prindiville
Rob Prinz
John Ptak
Hylda Quelly
Jack Rapke
David Rone
Leon Rose
Mitch Rose
Mark Rosen
Joe Rosenberg
Mike Rosenfeld
Sonya Rosenfeld
Tom Ross
Steve Roth
Robb Rothman
Mike Rubel
Rob Schlesinger
Jimmy Sexton

Jane Sindell
Brad Smith
Todd Smith
Fred Specktor
Martin Spencer
Ken Stovitz
Tom Strickler
David Styne
Nick Styne
Roeg Sutherland
Rosalie Swedlin
Beth Swofford
David Tenzer
Jessica Tuchinsky
Brodie Van Wagenen
Adam Venit
Bruce Vinokour
Paula Wagner
Bart Walker
Kit Walsh
Eric Wattenburg
Patrick Whitesell
Jack Wigham
Michael Wimer
Michael Wright
Warren Zavala

The Featured Players

J. J. Abrams
Ben Affleck
Mara Brock Akil
Jessica Alba
Herb Allen
Woody Allen
Jennifer Aniston

Michael Apted
Roone Arledge
Rosanna Arquette
Larry Auerbach
Jon Avnet
Dan Aykroyd
Irving Azoff

Diane Baker
Alec Baldwin
Christian Bale
Ginger Barber
Bob Barnett
Drew Barrymore
Kim Basinger
Marty Bauer
Warren Beatty
Kate Beckinsale
John Belushi
Peter Benedek
Annette Bening
Dick Berg
Jeff Berg
Jim Berkus
Chris Berman
Army Bernstein
Halle Berry
Beyoncé
Kathryn Bigelow
Shane Black
Cate Blanchett
Mary J. Blige
David Blitzer
Bill Block
Jake Bloom
Jason Blum
Steve Bollenbach
Michael Bolton
Bon Jovi
Scott Boras
Ernest Borgnine
Chris Bosh
Marlon Brando

Marty Brest
Paul Brickman
James Bridges
Jeff Bridges
Bernie Brillstein
Bob Broder
Matthew Broderick
Edgar Bronfman Jr.
Chris Brown
Bill Broyles
Jerry Bruckheimer
Genevieve Bujold
Sandra Bullock
Ken Burns
Tim Burton
John Calley
Robinson Cano
Mark Canton
Kate Capshaw
Glenn Gordon Caron
Jim Carrey
Johnny Carson
Graydon Carter
Maverick Carter
Dana Carvey
Leo Castelli
Gil Cates
Bob Cavallo
Chevy Chase
Cher
Peter Chernin
Robert Chertoff
Ted Chervin
James Clavell
Bill Clinton

George Clooney
Glenn Close
Lee Cohen
Sam Cohen
Sam Cohn
Chris Columbus
Sean Connery
Martha Coolidge
Francis Ford Coppola
Sofia Coppola
Costa-Gavras
Kevin Costner
Katie Couric
Michael Crichton
Hume Cronyn
Crosby, Stills & Nash
Tom Cruise
Lindsay Czarniak
Bob Daly
Matt Damon
Andy Davis
Geena Davis
John Davis
Martha Davis
Marvin Davis
Roger Davis
Gavin de Becker
Dan Deirdorf
Fred Dekker
Peter Dekom
Freddy Demann
Jonathan Demme
Ted Demme
Lisa De Moraes
Rebecca De Mornay

Robert De Niro
Brian De Palma
Johnny Depp
Bo Derek
Ira Deutchman
Danny DeVito
Dean Devlin
Neil Diamond
Cameron Diaz
Leonardo DiCaprio
Joan Didion
Vin Diesel
Barry Diller
Celine Dion
Richard Donner
Lindsay Doran
Michael Douglas
Peter Drucker
Clint Eastwood
Blake Edwards
Marty Ehrlichman
Jane Eisner
Michael Eisner
Doug Ellin
Larry Ellison
Roland Emmerich
Joe Eszterhas
Chad Everett
Jeff Fager
Tony Fantozzi
Frank Farian
Chris Farley
Will Ferrell
Sally Field
Bert Fields

Carrie Fisher
Ryan Fitzpatrick
Mick Fleetwood
Joe Flint
Jane Fonda
Harrison Ford
Ted Fortsmann
Bob Fosse
Jamie Foxx
Mark Frost
Zach Galifianakis
Sandy Gallin
Alex Gartner
Bill Gates
David Geffen
François Gilles
Terry Gilliam
Arne Glimcher
Roberto Goizueta
Eric Gold
Whoopi Goldberg
Leonard Goldenson
Bo Goldman
Akiva Goldsmith
Roger Goodell
Larry Gordon
Berry Gordy
Sam Gores
Donald Grant
Brian Grazer
Steve Greenberg
Brad Grey
Wyc Grousbeck
Andy Grove
Phil Guarascio

Peter Guber
Marc Gurvitz
Gene Hackman
Hall and Oates
Tom Hanks
Tom Hanson
Ted Harbert
Mark Harmon
Jack Harrower
Patrick Hasburgh
Ethan Hawke
Goldie Hawn
Salma Hayek
Amy Heckerling
Ed Helms
Gary Hendler
John Henry
Jonathan Hensleigh
Katharine Hepburn
Kirk Herbstreit
Marshall Herskovitz
Steve Heyer
Colin Higgins
Masahiko Hirata
Barry Hirsch
Dustin Hoffman
Jan Hoffman
Ron Howard
L. Ron Hubbard
Kate Hudson
Arianna Huffington
John Hughes
Nobuyuki Idei
Bob Iger
Henry Ishii

Doug Ivester

Hugh Jackman

Michael Jackson

Craig Jacobson

Stanley Jaffe

Lebron James

Mort Janklow

Jay-Z

Jefferson Airplane

Jerky Boys

Steve Jobs

Earvin "Magic" Johnson

Mark Johnson

Peter Johnson

Angelina Jolie

Jerry Jones

Barry Josephson

Nancy Josephson

Robert Kamen

Stan Kamen

Art Kaminsky

Garry Kasparov

Jeffrey Katzenberg

Phil Kaufman

Max Kellerman

Don Keough

Irvin Kershner

Callie Khouri

Nicole Kidman

Simon Kinberg

Stephen King

George Kirby

Kevin Kline

Phil Knight

Johnny Knoxville

Paul Kohner

Ted Koppel

Ted Kotcheff

Jim Lampley

Eugene Landy

Jessica Lange

Sherry Lansing

Tom Lassally

Abe Lastfogel

Martin Lawrence

Norman Lear

Heath Ledger

Chris Lee

Brian Leetch

Nat Lefkowitz

Kim LeMasters

Jay Leno

John Lesher

David Letterman

Gary Levine

Randy Levine

Barry Levinson

Steven Levinson

Mike Levy

Roy Lichtenstein

Ed Limato

David Lindy

John Logan

Eva Longoria

Jennifer Lopez

Jon Lovitz

David Lynch

Larry Lyttle

Ali MacGraw

Madonna

Albert Magnoli
Frank Mancuso
Michael Mann
Ricky Martin
Steve Martin
Konosuke Matsushita
Elaine May
Melissa McCarthy
Mark McCormack
Guy McElwaine
Don McGuire
Chris Meledandri
John Mellencamp
Sue Mengers
Burgess Meredith
Barry Meyer
Ellen Meyer
Kelly Meyer
Al Michaels
Lorne Michaels
Jimmy Miller
Rand Miller
Robyn Miller
Milli Vanilli
Yvette Mimieux
David Miscavige
Matthew Modine
Les Moonves
Demi Moore
Tommy Mottola
Rupert Murdoch
Brian Murphy
Eddie Murphy
Bill Murray
Mike Myers

Bahman Naraghi
Nicholas Negroponte
Lynn Nesbit
Paul Newman
Mike Nichols
Jack Nicholson
Christopher Nolan
Bob O'Connor
Carroll O'Connor
Adam Oates
Norio Ogha
Masao Ohashi
Brian Oliver
Mo Ostin
Dave Ovitz
Judy Ovitz
Al Pacino
Manny Pacquiao
Sarah Jessica Parker
Dolly Parton
Alexander Payne
I. M. Pei
Sandi Pei
Anthony Pellicano
Sean Penn
Jon Peters
Pete Peterson
Michelle Pfeiffer
Todd Phillips
Joaquin Phoenix
Nick Pileggi
Brad Pitt
Sydney Pollack
Tom Pollock
Natalie Portman

Frank Price
Michael Price
Richard Price
Prince
Wolfgang Puck
Carlos Quentin
Harold Ramis
Robert Redford
Christopher Reeve
Rob Reiner
Edwin O. Reischauer
Ivan Reitman
Pat Riley
Philip Rivers
Freddie Roach
Julia Roberts
Doug Robinson
Jim Robinson
John Rock
David Rockwell
Felix Rohatyn
Owen Roizman
Ray Romano
Ronaldinho
Bob Rosen
Fred Rosen
Phil Rosenthal
Joe Roth
Claire Rothman
Frank Rothman
Howard Rubinstein
Rex Ryan
Nick Saban
Junko Saito
Adam Sandler

Jay Sandrich
Richard Schaps
Tom Schulman
Shelly Schultz
Arnold Schwarzenegger
Steve Schwarzman
Martin Scorsese
Ridley Scott
Tony Scott
Nell Scovell
Ryan Seacrest
Steven Seagal
Peter Sealey
Jerry Seinfeld
Peter Sellers
Terry Semel
Tony Shalhoub
George Shapiro
Mark Shapiro
Sid Sheinberg
Harvey Shephard
Talia Shire
Mark Shmuger
Lauren Shuler Donner
Brad Silbering
Chris Silbermann
Bob Sillerman
Joel Silver
Bill Simon
John Singleton
John Skipper
Susan Smith
Will Smith
Wesley Snipes
Kevin Spacey

Aaron Spelling

Steven Spielberg

Erik Spoelstra

Jon Spoelstra

Rick Springfield

Bruce Springsteen

Sylvester Stallone

Darren Star

Sage Steele

David Stern

Nick Stevens

Jimmy Stewart

Kenny Stewart

Erwin Stoff

Morris Stoller

Oliver Stone

Sharon Stone

Tom Stoppard

Hannah Storm

Joe Straczynski

Bob Strauss

Meryl Streep

Barbra Streisand

Howard Stringer

Sally Struthers

Donald Sutherland

Kiefer Sutherland

Jessica Tandy

Ned Tanen

Brandon Tartikoff

Tim Tebow

Joe Tessitore

Hank Thomas

Witt Thomas

Tony Thomopoulos

Mike Tirico

Larry Tisch

Steve Tisch

Isamu Tomitsuka

Robert Towne

Roger Towne

Keiya Toyonaga

John Travolta

Steven Tyler

Atsuro Uede

Harry Ufland

Van Halen

Ron Vawter

Gore Verbinski

John Vitti

Dwyane Wade

Mark Wahlberg

Ralph Waite

Bill Walton

Brian Walton

Lew Wasserman

Gene Watanabe

J. J. Watt

Naomi Watts

Elliot Webb

Bob Weinstein

Harvey Weinstein

Jerry Weintraub

Sam Weisbord

Lou Weiss

Audrey Wells

John Wells

Phil Weltman

Tom Werner

William Wesley

Howard West
Fred Westheimer
Jim Wiatt
Robin Williams
Gary Wilson
Oprah Winfrey
Debra Winger
Irwin Winkler
Kate Winslett
David Wolper
Stevie Wonder
Bob Wright

Steve Wynn
Walter Yetnikoff
Jed York
Rick Yorn
Robert Zemeckis
Howard Zieff
Anthony Ziker
Jeremy Zimmer
Sergei Zubov
Jeff Zucker
Alan Zweibel
Ed Zwick

PREFACE

In the spring of 2015, roughly seven hundred agents from the Creative Artists Agency invaded La Costa Resort & Spa outside San Diego, California, for the company's annual retreat. For years, La Costa had served as a go-to spot for well-heeled travelers seeking respite and healthful realignment, but over the next two and a half days, those occupying agents would get to do relatively little relaxing. Having just turned forty, and mindful of the pitfalls, CAA was determined to avoid a potentially debilitating midlife crisis of any kind, so its warlords vowed to use the retreat, the largest to date, to inspire and unify the troops and to fix the company compass on new worlds to conquer.

In CAA's early days, a retreat was just a few dozen people sitting in a circle; now, stadium-style seating in giant conference rooms is the rule. And while all those attending once knew one another well—sometimes too well, considering the dozen-plus marriages between employees who met there and dozens (and dozens) more affairs and hookups—today's CAA has grown so large that excessive intimacy is no longer much of a problem. CAA's reach had grown veritably imperial, with offices in China, India, Switzerland, Germany, and England, as well as Miami, Chicago, Nashville, Manhattan, and its headquarters in Los Angeles. It isn't only a matter of geography: CAA long ago ceased to be a traditional talent agency, and what started out as a television representation business had since spiraled into movies, music, investment banking, advertising, marketing, and most recently, sports.

At the retreat, attendees were fed, feted, and applauded. Most knew better than to take bows either too deep or long, however, because CAA now operates in the most competitive climate in its history, whether it elects to acknowledge that or not. Indeed, one of the subtexts to the retreat was a reminder and a warning that there is no room in today's CAA for those who believe in entitlement or just keeping pace. Veterans and novices alike have seen loyal, long-serving colleagues voted off the CAA island for failing to appreciate that the operating dictum has morphed from "adapt, or suffer." into the more Darwinian *"excel, or die."*

CAA president Richard Lovett, fifty-five, who opens and closes these extravaganzas, has been at CAA since his college graduation in 1982. Two decades into his CAA presidency, Lovett believes his beloved agency competes only with itself, and he is absolutely convinced of its market leadership. Every agency in Hollywood has become expert in defining its greatness, but the metrics Lovett and CAA use are designed to signal universal dominance.

In film, CAA represented more Academy Award winners in above-the-line categories over the past five years than the next four agencies combined. Year-to-year results are also striking: CAA clients, to cite one dominated category, have snared the Best Actress Oscar for ten of the past eleven years (Reese Witherspoon, Helen Mirren, Marion Cotillard, Kate Winslet, Sandra Bullock, Natalie Portman, Meryl Streep, Jennifer Lawrence, Cate Blanchett, and Julianne Moore).

In recent times, CAA clients produced or directed the lion's share of today's major franchise films, from *Star Wars, Harry Pot-*

ter, and *Star Trek* to the Jason Bourne series and the films of the DC Comics and Marvel universes. CAA was responsible for the financing and/or sales of more than eighty pictures in 2015, and arranged the financing for three of the Best Picture Oscar winners over the last seven years: *Birdman, 12 Years a Slave,* and *The Hurt Locker.* Big actor names like Tom Cruise, George Clooney, Will Smith, Brad Pitt, Tom Hanks, and Robert Downey Jr. are all CAA clients.

For television, CAA pulled off the trifecta at that time, representing (that is, claiming clients in the key positions of executive producer, director, and star) the number one show on broadcast TV *(Empire),* the number one show on pay cable *(Game of Thrones),* and the number one show in basic cable *(The Walking Dead).* They declared themselves tops in what might be called "tonnage," too, representing more creators, executive producers, and showrunners in prime time than any other agency. At the most recent Emmys, CAA claimed its clients received 40 percent more awards than the next closest agency.

Katy Perry, Bruce Springsteen, Lady Gaga, David Guetta, and dozens of other artists fill the ranks of CAA Music. *Billboard* has named CAA Music the Agency of the Year for nine of the past twelve years, and at the Grammys, artists represented by CAA won more awards over the past three years than any other agency.

And in theater, lest it be forgot, of the thirty-six plays and musicals that opened on Broadway in the 2015/16 season, CAA boasts that twenty-seven (75 percent) were written, directed, or designed by CAA clients.

Although CAA Sports is one of the most recent additions to the agency's pantheon, *Forbes* named it Most Valuable Sports Agency of 2015, with $6.4 billion in contract value under management. Peyton Manning, J. J. Watt, Dwyane Wade, Sidney Crosby, Cristiano Ronaldo, and hundreds of other athletes and coaches combine with property sales at venues like Madison Square Garden, and numerous big-time sports consulting clients.

In marketing, CAA represents General Motors, Coca-Cola,

Samsung, Chipotle, and Anheuser-Busch, bringing in tens of millions in retainers and commissions.

But CAA no longer operates with undisputed dominance. In recent years, rivals have taken it hard to CAA. There is particular irony in WME's ascendance, both because it was William Morris from which the founders of CAA fled, spending the next two decades grinding their former employer to near dust; and also because Endeavor, which merged with William Morris to create the new titan, was founded by agents who fled CAA during or shortly after its golden years.

No one can say the retreats are tossed together at the last minute; planning for each retreat begins fifteen minutes after the current one ends and includes weighty retrospective analysis on what worked and what didn't. For the anniversary retreat, retrospection went back even further—all the way to the agency's founding. Forty years of CAA history can be conveniently divided into halves that represent two eras of leadership. The first two decades from 1975 to 1995 are known around CAA as "1.0," and the second two, from 1995 to 2015, as "2.0." In recent times, some insiders have taken to calling the years 2010 and beyond "3.0," because 2010 was the year that private equity giant TPG invested heavily in CAA and soon became its majority owner, with 53 percent of the company in its portfolio.

For the first twenty years, the company was run by now-fabled original founders Bill Haber, Ron Meyer, Michael Ovitz, Rowland Perkins, and Michael Rosenfeld. Each was a pioneer in his own way, jettisoning the rules of the ossifying agency trade as the firm grew from tiny start-up to industry dominator. Ovitz was undoubtedly the most indomitable of the Founding Five—and, during the late '80s and early '90s, the most fearsome—but Meyer was equally indispensable.

Let's get this out of the way right now: If, instead of a Mike and a Ron, there had been two Mike Ovitzes, CAA would likely not have become the phenomenon that it did; and if instead of Ron and Mike, there had been two Rons, likewise. The agency needed Ovitz's drive, gumption, and unbridled aggressiveness, but it would likely have been a calculatingly impersonal place without the legion of loyalty that surrounded Meyer, not to mention the invaluable mentoring he did with other agents in which he extolled the art of service businesses. Ovitz was brains and science; Meyer was heart and culture. Theirs was a much-envied balancing act for the first twenty years of the company's existence. Then, exactly midway through its life—1995, the most precarious point—CAA went through a kind of thrombosis, a disturbance in the force if you will, that saw the departures of Meyer, Ovitz, and Haber (Rosenfeld had left in the early '80s, Perkins in the early '90s). When the music stopped, the agency once again had five at the helm: Kevin Huvane, Bryan Lourd, Lovett, Jay Moloney, and David O'Connor. Eventually, a shocking suicide and several secret rounds of corporate infighting would leave only a trio.

Almost any of Shakespeare's political tragedies, or comedies, could serve as road maps to the backstage drama surrounding CAA through the decades. Small wonder then that the 2015 retreat was designed as a vehicle for catharsis, not a time to rehash misfortune, so all forty years could be rolled up into one big happy history. The agency didn't do external celebrations for its anniversary; there was no public-facing element. It was, like most things about CAA, a private affair—reserved for insiders and saved for the retreat.

As part of the scripted program, more than a dozen longtime employees shared memories from the past four decades. Even the valet parkers who'd been fixtures at the agency's I. M. Pei–designed former headquarters got involved. When the company moved in 2006, the new building's owners told the parkers there was no room for them, and instead of abandoning them to history, CAA bosses stepped forward and gave the valets other jobs at the company. The parking troops were greeted like old friends when they strode onto the stage. Varsity clients like J. J. Abrams, director of the new *Star Wars* installment, followed by another J. J., superstar J. J. Watt of the NFL's Houston Texans, shared insights and stories from their front lines. A showbiz panel headlined by actress Eva Longoria and hip-hop superstar Common came next, as well as a panel of digital designers and performers in a nod to both present and future. As custom and rules dictate, CAA used its own agents or executives to field questions and provoke conversation. The agency is proud to trumpet the fact that nobody is ever compensated to attend a CAA retreat, and many a CAAer will offer a snarky reference to the fact that rival William Morris Endeavor paid at least one of their guests, Bill Clinton, for an appearance before WME's assembled throng.

The story that CAA told itself at La Costa was predictably limited and with no small amount of spin. The full story is far more compelling. This book is the product of both years and decades of work. The interviewing process began several years ago, but CAA has been part of the fabric of two prior books, reporting for which began around the turn of the millennium. Those two books—*Live from New York* and *Those Guys Have All the Fun*—were histories of *Saturday Night Live* and ESPN, respectively. *Saturday Night Live* is, of course, a television show, and ESPN a network. Both were born in the '70s and both became world-famous brands. CAA was also a child of the '70s, and while its initials are not as well-known as *SNL*'s or ESPN's, CAA's breadth and scope are far greater than either. CAA may not come close to matching ESPN's economic might, but its universe is far more diverse, and while CAA has been written about through the years, this volume marks the first time the agency has ever opened its doors so wide to an inquiring journalist. The agency made available its entire current leadership for repeated interviews along with almost three dozen current agents, many of whom had never talked to a journalist before. All of them were gracious with their time, recollection, and insight. Most agents maintain that they are members of a service industry in which clients, not agents, are the proper focus. Agents don't want to take credit, at least not publicly, for what their clients accomplish—largely for fear of ticking those clients off. CAA strongly encourages such discretion, so it was all the more remarkable how many present and past CAA employees were willing to be interviewed for this book. Particular appreciation extends to CAA's current senior partners, all of whom spoke extensively. In the end, one of them preferred that his comments be used only for background, a request that has been honored.

To write this book, more than five hundred interviews were conducted, and the words you read are the subjects' own. In some instances, their quotes have been "cleaned up" (removing, for example, the "umm"s and "uh"s and "like"s that accompany most conversations) and certain discussions for the sake of clarity and exposition have been moved or compacted. But otherwise, what you read is as it was told.

Current and former employees of CAA are joined in these pages by scores of men and women who worked at studios, networks, and competing agencies, as well as actors and actresses, athletes, musicians, directors, producers, writers, lawyers, managers, and financiers, all of whom also proved incredibly important as sources.

As was the case with *Live from New York* and *Those Guys Have All the Fun*, both oral histories, *Powerhouse* seeks to be a historical record. There's always a bit of the "Rashomon effect" in the telling (or retelling) of tales, all parties having their own perspectives and agendas, and in typical Hollywood style, many of those involved in the CAA story up to now have spent years rewriting their scripts, artfully obscuring facts, intentionally fogging the view; others have jumped to conclusions and made assumptions without knowing the full story. But every effort has been made here to separate as much fact from fiction as possible.

CAA has played a major role in transforming the entertainment business, and media in general, and in so doing has helped weave the texture of our daily lives. Indeed, lift the curtains of pop culture anywhere on the planet and you are bound to find CAA. And this is its story.

INTRODUCTION

Hollywood's first generation of movie moguls looked upon the growing importance of talent agents about as warmly as they'd embrace union organizing or taxes. At first—very first, before "the movies" were the nation's dominant form of entertainment—agents worked with studio bosses, relieving them of such mounting procedural and housekeeping chores as payrolls, talent scouting, and the matching of available clients to similarly available film projects. It was all very friendly, but as agents developed their own power base, the relationship became adversarial.

In 1925, there were fewer than twelve agencies listed in Hollywood directories, so one could almost empathize with Clara Bow, nationally famous "It" girl, and her professional suffering. Like other actors in pretalkie times, Bow seemed to be on a trajectory toward auspicious stardom, or at least marketable adorability, but also like most actors, she was a resounding flop at managing her own business—that is, the business of herself. No sooner had Bow ascended to "It-ness" in 1926 than she naively signed a contract with Paramount that became a textbook case in stars failing to benefit from their own popularity. The contract paid her less than a third of what comparable performers were earning, and after it expired, it was too late for her to find financial success anywhere. She never attained the heights predicted, and her moment of financial leverage had been wasted.

Movies developed into a huge business in the late 1920s; to consolidate power and maximize profit, smaller production companies began to merge, leading to the creation of eight major corporations—powerful studios that would soon be producing nearly 80 percent of the films released in any given year. Actors were hardly equipped—with information or bargaining skill—to deal with those giant companies, and as a result, the studios were able to develop the famous "star system" that saw many actors controlled, professionally and personally, by the studios that essentially owned them. Those stars had little freedom about which movies they would be in, and their social lives were turned into a constant publicity tour. Unsurprisingly, the notion of actors having advocates to represent their interests became increasingly attractive. No wonder the William Morris Agency, a Broadway institution since the 1890s, but one that had avoided the movies' silent era altogether, ventured into "the movies" in 1928. A few years later, *Film Daily Yearbook* listed more than sixty talent agencies in Los Angeles, with another twenty in New York.

In the 1940s, even stars with representation realized they could fall behind their peers if their agents were not assertive or powerful enough; the profession was so new—despite the moguls' derisively considering it akin to the "world's oldest"—that there wasn't any guidebook on proper care and feeding of talent. Actors found themselves at a disadvantage because so many agents and agencies were still trapped in templates developed when they represented stars of vaudeville and the theater. When agent Sam Jaffe negotiated Humphrey Bogart's new Warner Bros. contract in 1942—just as the great star was ascending—Jaffe's excess of caution not only cost Bogart money he should have made, but also limited his ability to freelance, restricted the number of films he could make, dictated the details of his billing, curbed the influence he had in story and role selection, and affected other items increasingly negotiated by savvier top agents on behalf of top clients.

Major structural changes in the business were under way, however. By the late 1950s, television stole the title of Nation's Entertainer away from the movies. The decline in theatrical attendance meant a monumental shift in the way studios produced films and reduced the cost of exclusive and expensive actors. Afterward, actors and actresses still worked for studios, but the old exclusivities were mostly things of the past. The shift meant that agents were now seen as necessities rather than options or luxuries.

In the 1950s, Lew Wasserman transformed the talent agency MCA into a "packager" that would approach studios with already assembled teams of directors, actors, and writers. With this, Hollywood saw the birth of a new species—film stars who were also independent contractors, with the textbook case being Jimmy Stewart. The star of *Harvey* and many other iconic hits saw his wealth multiply with a single role in Universal's *Winchester '73*. By forgoing a standard salary and taking profit participation instead, Stewart paved the way for actors, directors, producers, and writers to leverage their celebrity at the negotiating table. Similarly, Wasserman cofounded independent production companies for such luminaries as Jack Benny, Alfred Hitchcock, Errol Flynn, and dozens of other MCA clients, allowing them to minimize taxes while exploiting their star salaries and expanding their influence in movie production.

As anyone could have predicted, it was the stars, in particular the television "personalities," who held sway over the American public's imagination and affection. (Not for nothing was *Shower of Stars* the title of a typical drama anthology; the title *Shower of Directors* was likely never considered.) The power of TV was such that a "nobody" could become, virtually overnight, more famous than some venerable holdover from the studio system. Indeed, stardom in movies became less and less bankable as TV created its own sensations. At the same time, major movie stars like Bing Crosby, Frank Sinatra, the independent Mr. Stewart, and many others piloted shows built around them that often then ignominiously flopped. Orson Welles shot a pilot that never even made it to series. Not all stumbled, but television could tame even the biggest egos, with the little screen outgunning the "silver screen" time after time.

In 1962, MCA's dominating presence in Hollywood ran smack into the Department of Justice. Its investigation into the company's "monopolistic practices" resulted in a face-off between Wasserman (whose beloved allies included Ronald Reagan, then in the midst of leaving the Democratic Party and becoming a Republican) and Attorney General Robert F. Kennedy Jr. To avoid criminal and civil penalties for alleged antitrust violations, MCA agreed to divest itself of its talent agency at the same time that the company bought struggling Universal Pictures and Decca Records. Just like that, MCA quit the talent business and created the largest entertainment assembly line in Hollywood. Building on its library of detective shows, westerns, sitcoms, and specials, MCA and Wasserman transformed moribund Universal Pictures into grandiose Universal Studios, owners of the largest and busiest lot in Hollywood.

When MCA departed the representation business, the move solidified William Morris as *the* agency. It had the biggest star clients and the greatest influence on the studios and networks. But perhaps more relevant to this story was the common belief that if you were young and wanted to get the strongest start possible for a career in the entertainment industry, it was the place to be.

That certainly would be the case for five eager young William Morris agents in the mid-1970s.

POWERHOUSE

ACT ONE

I had an agent years and years ago when I was new to New York City and was having trouble finding a place to live because I had two dogs. This person had come to visit me in New York at NBC, and as they were getting into a car on Sixth Avenue, they said to me, "I'm going to get you an apartment if it's the last thing I do." And that was the last I ever heard from them. That's show business right there.

—DAVID LETTERMAN

I

Rebels: 1974–1979

Nothing mattered except states of mind,
chiefly our own.
—JOHN MAYNARD KEYNES

RON MEYER, CAA Founder:

Where I grew up, in those days, there were three categories: you were a jock, a nerd, or a bad boy. I was neither of the first two, and being a bad boy was kind of the cool thing to be. So I created a character for myself. It was an identity.

I hung out with a bunch of guys who did the same thing, and we got into fights. In West L.A., there was a police department—it's still there—on Perdue Avenue, and they were aware of us. Both my parents escaped Nazi Germany in 1939, and though I was born in America, they weren't savvy about American youth culture. My father knew only a little of what was going on with me then, because he was a traveling salesman and was on the road four out of every five weeks. But my mother knew all of it. I got arrested a lot. A number of my friends went to jail. Once I beat up a guy in front of his son. Of all the things in my life, I think about that all the time. I wish I could find these people and beg for their forgiveness; it really shamed me.

MICHAEL OVITZ, CAA Founder:

I was a kid who grew up in the San Fernando Valley, just four blocks from the old RKO Studios, and after my paper route, a bunch of us would go sneak into the studios under a fence. I was mesmerized by what I saw, and that went on for years and years and years.

My dad didn't make a lot of money. He was a liquor salesman. We had a fabulous family life, but my brother and I always had to earn our spending money for whatever we wanted. So from the time I was nine, I worked constantly.

BILL HABER, CAA Founder:

I'm old enough to remember when there were no freeways in Los Angeles. My father was thirty years old when he decided to go to medical school after the Second World War, and we would drive to downtown Los Angeles up to the big, giant general hospital. I was very young. Sometimes we'd go up Pico Boulevard because that's where El Rancho golf course was, and at five in the morning we would pick up golf balls so we could sell them for a dollar each. That money was really important to us at the time. Across the street was 20th Century Fox, and when I was nine years old, I said to my father, "One day, I'm going to go in there."

MICHAEL OVITZ:

I was student body president for a high school of four thousand students. I was also president of my fraternity at UCLA and dedicated myself to being very well organized. I had a huge appetite for getting deeply involved in everything that interested me. In college, I went to work as a tour guide at Universal. There were ten of us— five guys and five women. I soon got hired away by a guy who went to work at Fox helping design their tours, so while I was going to school at UCLA, I was also working full-time at Fox. I didn't go to most classes in the beginning of the semester, but I'd always go to the final exams. I did that for three years, and in my senior year, I decided I wanted to start looking for a job after school. I interviewed at William Morris and CMA, an advertising agency. William Morris responded the quickest.

During the interview, the personnel director at William Morris asked me, "Why do you think you should get this job? There are twenty people in the mailroom, and lots more who want to get in there." And I said, "I can learn everything there is to know about being an agent in ninety days, or I'll give you back all the money you pay me." I knew it was an outrageous and stupid statement, but he couldn't stop laughing. Then he said, "I'm going to hire you."

RON MEYER:

I legally dropped out of school when I was sixteen. I had gone one day a week to what they called continuation school, which you had to be enrolled in until you were sixteen or you would be a truant—whatever that meant.

The army had an active draft at the time, but because I thought I was a tough guy, I didn't want to just go in the army, I wanted to enlist in the Marine Corps, which I did when I was seventeen. It was the best decision I ever made.

When I was in the Marine Corps, I got the measles, and I got put into quarantine. I was in a room with eight other empty beds. Alone. I had literally never read a book in my life. I'm serious, I had *never* read a book. But my mother sent me two books because I was sitting in a hospital with nothing to do. One was called *The Amboy Dukes*, which was about troubled kids in New York's street gangs. The other was called *The Flesh Peddlers*, by a man named Steven Longstreet. It was a novel about a young guy who worked at a fictitious agency, who drove fast cars and went out with beautiful women. I read these two books, and I thought, *Wait a minute . . . why would I be this schmuck when I could be this schmuck?*

So after the Marine Corps, I couldn't stop thinking about being at an agency. I already knew there was show business—I had lived in West L.A., not far from Fox Studios—and I took my one suit that fit me like Abraham Lincoln's suits fit him, because of short legs, you know, and I literally went door-to-door to every agency in town. I didn't know if they were good or bad or who they represented. Some would let me fill out an application. Some would say, "We're not hiring." I'd give out my phone number, but I had no answering machine. I was as unsophisticated as could possibly be. I thought the military background would help me, but I was a high school dropout, and high school dropout worked more against me than the military worked for me.

MICHAEL OVITZ:

Truth is, I really didn't know what representation was, but I knew that I needed to learn the business of artistic people. I'm a frustrated artist—I'm not a writer and I'm not a painter, but I love artists, and I am blown away by how creative people come up with ideas and then turn them into reality. I wanted to get close to them, to understand how they work, and at the same time couple the creative process with the business process.

I didn't want to be a buyer. I wanted to learn it from the sell side, because if I was a buyer and worked at a studio, then I was working at only one place. But if I was an agent, then as a seller, I was able to go anywhere.

RON MEYER:

I was working at a men's clothing store called Zeidler and Zeidler making about $35 a week, sharing an apartment with four other guys at some fleabag place in Hollywood. Now follow this: My mother had a girlfriend whose husband's sister was married to Walter Kohner, who was Paul Kohner's brother. And Walter Kohner was an agent at his brother's company. I had interviewed there, and they said, "We already have a messenger, there's no job." But then, out of the blue, the messenger at Kohner quit, and they called me. They said, "Do you still want the job? We pay $75 a week, will give you a gas credit card, pay your lunches, and you can start Monday." I quit my job, bought a car, and got my own apartment. "Changed my life" is such a complete understatement, I can't even tell you.

BILL HABER:

It was 1965. It was pure providence. I was in law school, sitting in the lunchroom of Loyola Law School, and I happened to glance at the only ad William Morris had ever run in its entire hundred-year history. It was also the only time in my life I had ever looked at a classified ad. And it said "talent agent trainee." So I called them up. Even though I had two children, I left law school—which displeased my parents greatly—and took the job, working for $50 per week in the mailroom, delivering packages.

RON MEYER:

The Kohner Agency was at 9169 Sunset. It was at the beginning of the Sunset Strip, and it was the greatest experience for me. Paul Kohner was an incredible agent. It was a small agency. I knew everyone. I was a kid surrounded by mostly older people.

I cleaned up my act. I hid from everybody I used to know; they dropped out of my life. Once again I was pretending I was something I wasn't—wearing a suit every day, being this hotshot guy, delivering packages, picking up scripts, and driving clients like John Huston, Chevalier, Charles Bronson, Lana Turner, and Ingmar Bergman when they would come to town. I spent six years as Paul Kohner's driver and messenger. It was fabulous.

MICHAEL OVITZ:

When I went to William Morris, I decided that I had to do something that was disruptive. I was in the mailroom with about twenty guys. They'd come in at nine, so I came in at seven. They'd leave at six, I'd leave at ten o'clock at night. Some days I left earlier because at that time I was also going to school at night to get my master's in business. I worked my butt off—reading everything there was to read. I was a scavenger. Those guys were waiting to be fed things; I went looking for things. I viewed the mailroom as an education course, period, and was going to move over everyone very quickly. I volunteered for every job and was very aggressive.

Three months into the training program, I had begun to notice that the president of the company would often come back to the office after dinner when everyone else had left, so I made sure to be there and became the only guy sitting at a desk on the first floor. As I figured he would, he asked if I could do a favor for him. I did the favor so well that he asked me to work for him some more. I kept doing it each night until he finally made me his assistant.

So at the ripe age of twenty-two, I was the assistant to the president of the company. I did anything I could do to show him that I could save him time. If he was opening up a door, I would close it. He gave me a ton of work and let me go until I made a mistake. But I didn't.

HOWARD WEST, Agent:

I saw this young man floating around. His immediate boss didn't come in until ten but Michael Ovitz was already in gear hours before. I would come in very early every day to read my *Wall Street Journal* and started talking to him. He seemed alert, ripe, and aggressive, but in a pleasant way. I said to myself, *He's me.*

MICHAEL OVITZ:

As a young guy I immediately dreamed of running the company. It may have been a fantasy, but it drove me to work extra hard and do things no one else did.

HOWARD WEST:

"Thirsty for knowledge" would be an inadequate terminology for him. I had a lot of teacher and tutor in me, so I didn't mind that he'd ask question after question about all different parts of the business. One day he asked me, "How do you get these important people to return your calls?"

MICHAEL OVITZ:

Howard was my guy there. He spent an unbelievable amount of time with me and was patient when I asked him to explain certain things to me.

ROWLAND PERKINS, CAA Founder:

I went to UCLA and then stayed there for law school, but dropped out after two years and went into the William Morris mailroom. I got promoted pretty quickly to be the head of the mailroom, then worked on the desk of the legendary Stan Kamen, who was one of the most important talent agents in entertainment. After that, I joined the TV packaging department. It was then that I met Mike Rosenfeld, who was working in motion pictures. Mike and I soon realized we were born just twelve days apart.

BILL HABER:

I had a little bit of career advantage early on at William Morris. In the middle of my training period, Vietnam heated up. My wife was pregnant, so I was exempted, but a big chunk of the place was drafted. So there I was, twenty-five years old, running the William Morris talent department.

One of my jobs that I'll never forget was to deliver checks to Elvis Presley on the MGM lot. Once I hand-delivered a check to him on the *Blue Hawaii* set. He opened the envelope and it was the first time I ever saw a check for a million dollars. Elvis looked at me and said, "Why, thank you, Bill." It was the kind of thing you remember for the rest of your life.

RON MEYER:

After almost six years, I knew that there would be no future for me at Kohner, so wherever I could make a contact to get an interview at another agency, I did, very secretly. I met a fellow named Paul Flaherty, who was an agent at William Morris, and he got me an interview with Phil Weltman. At that time, William Morris rarely hired agents from the outside, and I've always been grateful to Paul for getting me in there for an interview. After a series of eight or more interviews over six months with Phil Weltman, Bill Haber, and Rowland Perkins, they hired me as an agent in the talent department. William Morris was the dream job for me.

BILL HABER:

Nobody thought there would ever not be a William Morris Agency. William Morris, we would say, would outlive all of us. In the '70s, they controlled almost everything, and they were the foundation of a business that generally exists on sand. They were a rock; their clients were rocks; and their business was a rock. They were leaders in everything they did.

The corporate culture at William Morris was, by many accounts, largely governed by the rigidly hierarchic boys' club of old-school agents. Seniority dictated power, and the only way to rise through the ranks was a combination of working, waiting, and ass-kissing. Loyalty was king. Cronyism and infighting ran rampant. The television and movie departments often refused to collaborate on projects, and even when they did, any partnership was begrudging, as older Morris executives often refused to break routine in favor of progress. Compensation was based on how much money an individual brought in but also how long the person had been there. Many of the younger generation of agents at William Morris longed for flexibility and were horrified by the deeply embedded culture of obstinacy.

MICHAEL OVITZ:

It was an incredibly rigid, compartmentalized business. Pay scales were incredibly unfair. There was little entrepreneurialism.

RON MEYER:

When I was at William Morris, you felt that you were working for the Pentagon. Everything seemed so big and ominous, and everything senior management said and did felt incredibly important.

MICHAEL OVITZ:

What happened to them is television and movies started to change as movie stars started to consider doing television. All of a sudden, you had people in different disciplines that had always been behind walled gardens working in each other's areas, and William Morris didn't know how to deal with it. We were watching this happen and were mortified by their lack of flexibility. It just wasn't a culture that was workable.

HOWARD WEST:

You had senior executives who had been there for twenty-five, thirty years who should have been working for the post office.

MICHAEL OVITZ:

There were all these cronies sitting on the second floor who just hung out at the business and sucked the profits out of it. They should have let a number of those guys go.

RON MEYER:

Ovitz started before me: We became best of friends very quickly, and sort of a team. It was just one of those things.

MICHAEL OVITZ:

The guys running the business at that time were Nat Lefkowitz in New York, Morris Stoller in L.A., who was the CFO but pretty much the COO, Sam Weisbord in L.A., and the chairman of the board, Abe Lastfogel.

RON MEYER:

It's not like the business today. Top agents were very high profile internally, but if you mentioned their name externally, people might not know who you were talking about. Sam Weisbord was the head of the company, but I always thought he was a nasty, unkind piece of shit.

ROWLAND PERKINS:

Sam was a little weird. He was an older guy, and he used to take out really young girls. They were in their twenties and he was in his sixties. He once told me how proud he was of a conquest: "I went through the whole list of girls I was going out with at the time and very carefully selected one, and I fucked the hell out of her that night and then explained to her that I had gone through the list and picked her out. She was so proud she couldn't wait to tell her mother." I liked Sam, but he was a little strange duck.

MICHAEL OVITZ:

I made an assessment of what holes there were that I could fill as a young guy. What was open that no one had touched? When I went through all the William Morris network sales, most were prime time. There were few dayparts and little syndication. Then I was at a meeting at ABC and found out the network's margins in other dayparts were four and a half times those in prime time, because programming was cheaper. I was in a state of shock. So I started developing clients in that area. I signed a guy named Bill Carruthers who was a daytime director and Jim Young, who did *General Hospital*. I put this whole coterie together. I became very interested in packaging—putting things together rather than just individually handling clients, which turned out to be the base of CAA.

MICHAEL EISNER, Executive:

One of my earliest jobs was in the '70s running children's programming and daytime programming at ABC. I had to go to a lot of game-show presentations where producers would use a little stage and a fake audience to show us their show and then we would decide whether to do a pilot or not. One time I brought my wife, Jane, to watch a run-through, and the show was horrible. As we were leaving, Michael Ovitz was by the door, and said to us, "Hi, I'm Michael Ovitz from William Morris." I think he even exaggerated his title. He was a secretary. He looked twelve but was actually in his midtwenties. He called me later out of the blue—remember, I didn't know him, had never heard of him—and he asked me, "How did you like the show?" I didn't want to say anything bad, so I just said, "Well, my wife loved it," and put the conversation out of my mind. When I got back to New York, I walked into our brownstone apartment and there on the piano was a vase with four dozen roses in it, and a card for Jane that said, "Glad you loved the show, Michael Ovitz." I called him up and started with a joke—"If you ever send my wife fucking flowers again, I will kill you." But then I got serious. I said, "My wife is not involved in any day-to-day business decisions. Do not agent my wife." And that was the beginning of my Michael Ovitz relationship.

MICHAEL OVITZ:

Tony Fantozzi was an agent at William Morris. He took me out for my first big executive lunch and never ordered food, just had four martinis. So Tony says to me, "Aw, this guy Jack Barry. I like him but no one will hire him." I found out Jack Barry was a guy who got caught up in the quiz-show scandals and went and met with him. He was a smart guy who felt he had been wronged by NBC when they banned him from producing after the scandals. I also met his partner, Dan Enright. They were the biggest game-show producers of the '60s, and I liked them both, so I worked my butt off and pushed and pushed and sold a show of theirs to CBS called *Break the Bank*. Lo and behold, Jack Barry's back on the air, not just with a show, but as the host.

I continued to try and sell in a way no one else would. The Smothers Brothers were a giant show on CBS, and when they got thrown off because they said controversial things, I got them on NBC. People in the business couldn't believe these things had happened, but nobody internally said a positive word to me.

BARRY LEVINSON, Writer and Director:

Years before there was a CAA, in the early '70s, Mike Ovitz called me after seeing me on a local TV show in a sketch where I played a roller-skating rabbi from Salt Lake City. He thought it was funny, and at that time he was recently out of the mailroom and had become a very junior agent. He asked if I had an agent, and I said, no, so he became my very first agent. I remember he was very quiet, not the typical agent type who would say, "All right, I'll tell you what we're gonna do." He was much more reserved.

At the time, I was writing on that local show with Craig Nelson and Rudy DeLuca, but pretty quickly after we signed with him, he got me, Rudy, and Craig jobs on *The Tim Conway Show*, and after that went off the air, a bit later, he got us a job writing for Larry Gelbart, who was a producer on *The Marty Feldman Comedy Machine*.

RON MEYER:

When the New York people would come to town, we'd all be at attention. It was a big event. The office would buzz, *The New York guys, they're here*. It was a big to-do of who got included in their meetings and discussions and it always seemed so important. We were never included.

MICHAEL OVITZ:

Lou Weiss was the head of worldwide television for William Morris, and he worked with a guy named Sol Leon, who was a real old-time TV guy. We had three guys who covered the networks: Tony Ford with CBS; Arnold Sank with NBC; and Larry Auerbach, who covered ABC. The five of them were the core of the New York office and sucked out all the overhead and got paid humongous salaries.

BILL HABER:

You had content and you put it on the networks. Period. That was it. The sea change in television hadn't happened yet, but you could tell that the old times were coming to an end, and it was time for new people to take over. But the leadership at William Morris didn't understand that.

TONY LUDWIG, Agent:

I got out of the mailroom at the Morris Agency and became an assistant to Mike Rosenfeld. Rosenfeld had an interesting life. He was an agent most of the time, but at other times, he was secretly at the airport in the San Fernando Valley. My job was to cover his desk and his body of work while he was out learning how to fly. Through Howard West, I ended up meeting Mike Ovitz, who was also an assistant at the time. I would have lunches at Mike's house, which was really a little apartment on Olympic Boulevard maybe two and a half blocks from the Morris Agency. His wife, Judy, would make us tuna fish sandwiches.

MICHAEL ROSENFELD JR., Agent:

My father had grown up in Strawberry Mansion, Philadelphia, and was part of a very creative and talented community there before working on Broadway and then making his way west. At William Morris, he had been responsible for convincing Disney to go with Dick Van Dyke in *Mary Poppins,* and he put together the package for *Barney Miller,* so he had a good career there.

MICHAEL OVITZ:

One day Bill Haber, Mike Rosenfeld, and I were sitting with Rowland in his office on the first floor. That year, we had sold twenty-one prime-time pilots and seven daytime pilots—just us on the West Coast—and Lou Weiss walked in dressed to the nines in his beautifully tailored gray suit, red hankie, red tie, and Gucci loafers. Those were a big deal back then; I mean, who could afford a horse buckle?

He said, "Guys, great year. But we can do better." And Mike, who had sold *Barney Miller* and several other shows, looked at him and said, "Do better?! There's no studio, including Universal, that sold as many pilots as we have." But Lou didn't care about what we had done, he just wanted to talk about what we needed to do in the future.

In a way, CAA was incubated in that meeting. Haber and Perkins were very close and they started talking about how dissatisfied they were, and Rosenfeld and Perkins started talking, too. At the same time, Ron and I began talking to each other about doing something else because we had client lists, which very few people had.

RON MEYER:

Weisbord ran the big staff TV meetings. There was a huge table where the senior guys would sit, and then there was an area behind it where the next tier of agents would sit, and then there was literally a peanut gallery behind those first two rows.

MICHAEL OVITZ:

It was a joke. We were totally disenfranchised; Ron, Bill, and I sat in the last row with our backs against the wall, listening, never saying anything.

RON MEYER:

Steve McQueen left William Morris to go with Freddie Fields at CMA. It was a devastating loss, and right after that, Weisbord made an announcement to everyone that he had just signed the tap dancer Ann Miller, who was then already in her later years. I had been there four years and decided I would make my bones and show them all my stuff. Now, no one at my level had ever spoken—or even asked a question—in a big staff meeting. We were supposed to be invisible. But I said, "Mr. Weisbord, can I say something? We're the greatest agency with the greatest agents in the world and Ann Miller's a talented woman, but we just lost Steve McQueen. We should be on a full attack at CMA. We should use all our resources to sign their stars and not worry about signing midlevel clients."

MICHAEL OVITZ:

The week before, Sam got a memo from New York announcing they had signed Ann Miller. I said to him very nicely, "Ann Miller, huh?" He goes, "Yeah, isn't that great?" The most I could do was not say anything, which was tantamount to saying no.

Ron said, "How could you possibly expect us to compete with CMA when we're signing Ann Miller and they're signing Barbra Streisand?" As soon as he finished, there was silence in the room. No one had ever spoken up like that.

RON MEYER:

Weisbord looked back at me and said, "What the fuck are you talking about? How dare you question me?" After he said, "Fuck you," a bunch of times, I realized I had made this horrible mistake and kept trying to explain myself, but he just kept saying, "Fuck you!" He was a little horrible guy. He wouldn't stop screaming at me. Here I am making $125 a week, that job was my whole life, and I had no money. I had nothing; my whole life was flashing before me at that moment.

MICHAEL OVITZ:

To Ron's credit—as only Ron could do, because Bill and I were much more political—Ron spoke his mind. The good news was that he had that courage; the bad news was he was too emotional and didn't think about how it would affect him in the long term.

RON MEYER:

For the first few weeks after that meeting, a lot of people there treated me like I had a communicable disease. Weisbord never spoke to me after that day. Phil Weltman told me that Weisbord was never going to forgive me and really didn't like me, but Phil said he would make sure I was always okay at the agency.

Phil Weltman served both as head of the William Morris TV department and as mentor to the young founders of CAA back before they left William Morris. Weltman worked hard to make sure young trainees like Barry Diller and novice agents like Ron Meyer and Michael Ovitz rose above the stereotype of the Hollywood agent as a lazy, parasitic vulture. His mission was to keep those mentees on their toes and trained for battle. Weltman made himself accessible at all hours and advised young agents to do the same.

A demanding taskmaster with a strong work ethic, Weltman inspired great loyalty from the agents he tutored. He instilled in them the virtue of professionalism and went against the penchant for compartmentalization—agents acting only on their own behalf—which most Morris executives saluted. He stubbornly demanded teamwork among the younger agents, believing that sharing clients and information would only strengthen the company. Occasionally he would even pass deals over to his young protégés, forgoing credit for himself.

MICHAEL OVITZ:

I was in Morris Stoller's office talking to him at a time when the income of the company took a huge dip for the first time in more than a quarter century. During the course of the conversation, he started to chew the corners of a memo and ended up eating the entire piece of paper he was reading to me. Afterward, I went to his assistant, Walt Zifkin, and asked if Morris was okay. But before he said anything, he took a breath. What I realized was Morris had had a nervous breakdown just because they had one bad quarter. This was such a powerful statement. They were used to a business that was always growing. They had one hiccup and they couldn't pivot. That's when they decided to fire guys who didn't bring in real income.

ROWLAND PERKINS:

I went on a short break for four days, and when I came back, Phil said to me, "Can you have lunch with me today?" We met at the Brown Derby, and he said, "The reason I want to have lunch with you is to tell you my buddy Sam Weisbord called me in his office and said, 'We put you in the computer and you came up wanting.'" I couldn't believe Weisbord had said that to him. How can you say that to your best friend? Then Phil told me he was going to be leaving.

RON MEYER:

Phil called me and Mike into his office and told us he had just been fired. He said Weisbord had told him, "We put your name in the computer and it came up wanting." I will always remember that crazy phrase. Those two guys had started at the company together; they had been best of friends. We could not believe this was happening. As Phil talked, he had a tear in his eye.

MICHAEL OVITZ:

It was really jarring to see a guy like that go from being so tough to being so vulnerable, and it set a lot of minds in motion. Basically they were saying to us, *Hey, you can work here for thirty years, but look at what could still happen to you.*

ROWLAND PERKINS:

Yeah, that really just sort of crystallized everything.

BILL HABER:

It was not acceptable to any of us.

RON MEYER:

Phil was really the person who was the glue that kept that place together. In my opinion, it took William Morris thirty years to recover from the loss of Phil Weltman.

BILL HABER:

There was a bust of Phil Weltman in the lobby of CAA. I never failed to go there and take a moment to thank him for what he did for us and for what he meant to us. We would not have left if Phil was still there; we'd still be working at William Morris.

RON MEYER:

There's no question about it: None of us would have wanted—or had the courage—to leave if Phil was going to still be there. We would have never left Phil. I thought I would spend my career at William Morris.

MICHAEL OVITZ:

The common lore is that Phil's firing caused us to leave, but it's not accurate because even if he stayed, there were so many other things there that were really distasteful for guys like us in our late twenties and early thirties. And remember, Phil was getting old; everyone wanted to propagate that cause and effect because it made

Phil feel good. That said, however, there's no better platform for success than wanting to avenge someone's death, right?

BILL HABER:

In any business on earth—I always say to people—nobody will ever leave you for money, and nobody will ever leave you over titles. People will only leave if they have no loyalty to you.

MICHAEL OVITZ:

It was like a stew, and ingredients just kept getting added. The next thing that happened was that they passed over Rowland to run the TV department.

ROWLAND PERKINS:

Phil was gone, and then so was the promotion I had been hoping for. At that point, my loyalty to the place was gone, too.

RON MEYER:

Once we knew that Phil was going, I tried to convince Mike that the two of us should leave, even though I knew he had a big future at William Morris because they really liked him.

After many conversations, the most Mike would say to me was "Maybe, but not for another year. We should get more clients, and put our business plan together. Then we could go."

MICHAEL OVITZ:

You have to realize at William Morris, there were two kinds of citizens: signers and servicers. Very few people did both. Ronnie and I did both. We went out and signed people and probably had between us seventy clients.

JUDY OVITZ:

I was born in Berkeley, but raised most of my life in Beverly Hills, right down from the William Morris Agency. I went to Beverly Hills High School and then to UCLA, where I met Michael.

MICHAEL OVITZ:

We met when she was seventeen and I was barely eighteen. We were married three years later. Judy and I were the campus couple at William Morris. They loved us. I worked my ass off, and they loved her. She was charming and knockdown dead gorgeous.

JUDY OVITZ:

We had a very good future at William Morris if we stayed, so we were torn. Mike was very happy and we were thought of as the golden couple, and it was clear we were going to succeed after the old guard left.

MICHAEL OVITZ:

Ron took Judy and me to dinner at Chianti and spent two hours selling us on leaving William Morris. I don't think I opened my mouth once. He was talking about only the two of us leaving. We didn't know the other guys were talking to each other. He asked that Judy be there because he had gotten to know her and thought she might influence me.

RON MEYER:

I knew that Mike and I would be good partners, and that together we would be able to push ourselves further than if we were each on our own. I had the street smarts and he had the education. I also knew that if he was going to leave William Morris, I was going to have to make it really convincing.

MICHAEL OVITZ:

When Ron was making his pitch for us to leave, I said it made *sense*, but I didn't say I wanted to do it. I had been told by a couple senior executives at William Morris that within ten years I'd be running the place.

RON MEYER:

My plan was for us to start a company—Meyer-Ovitz, Ovitz-Meyer.

MICHAEL OVITZ:

The Chianti dinner was a seminal turning point. Ron brilliantly sold Judy. He seemed in a hurry. He really wanted out of there. But Ron's a gambler. I'm not a gambler, and I never gamble on anything unless I know I'm going to win.

ROWLAND PERKINS:

At first it was myself, Haber, and Mike Rosenfeld. We had met at my house a number of times and at Billingsley's Steak House on Pico. Nobody from the business went there, it was unchic. We said to ourselves, "As long as we're breaking our butts, let's go and do it for ourselves." Then we found out that Mike Ovitz and Ron Meyer were talking about doing the same thing.

RON MEYER:

Shortly after the Chianti dinner, three other agents—Rowland Perkins, Mike Rosenfeld, and Bill Haber—approached me. Bill was my boss, and Rowland was his boss. Mike and Rowland were senior agents: Rowland in television, Mike in motion pictures. They told me they were also thinking of leaving because of Phil's departure and asked if I would be interested in joining them. I said, I might be, but only if Mike Ovitz was part of it. They didn't know Mike very well, so I said, "Why don't the five of us sit and meet?" I wanted to see what they were going to do, and to make sure they didn't leave before us or screw up our plan.

Howard West was a very close friend from William Morris, and Mike and I had a lot of respect for him. We had stayed in touch with him after he left the agency to become a manager, and then we asked him whether the two of us should go it alone or join the other three.

HOWARD WEST:

I digested the question, then said, "Guys, the industry is ripe for competition. It will embrace you because everyone is tired of the William Morris dominance."

RON MEYER:

Howard told us, "Don't be schmucks, the five of you have to do this together."

HOWARD WEST:

I encouraged them to all go out together and form the new agency. That conversation was the seed of CAA.

BILL HABER:

At the end of every single day, the same five cars were sitting in the parking lot until all hours of the night. Somehow we managed to put those five people in a room and said, "Well, we might as well do this together."

RON MEYER:

It was a much better meeting than we expected. We were all so much in sync that it became an amazing couple hours. It couldn't have gone better. We sounded like the Mitchell Boys Choir.

ROWLAND PERKINS:

The first time the five of us met was at my house in Bel Air in late 1974 to discuss forming a new agency. We made plans to meet again in March, with an agenda to secure a line of credit before making an amicable exit from William Morris. We even planned on notifying Sam Weisbord of our intentions and to stay through the spring to help him set the network schedules.

RON MEYER:

When I was still at William Morris, I had asked Phil Weltman if I could travel to the New York office. There really wasn't a specific reason for me to go, but he arranged it anyway. It wound up being my only business trip to New York. On the first day there, I met Ellen, who was a secretary for one of the heads of the company, and we went out the following night. We had a really great time and liked each other. When I came back to California, we stayed in touch by phone and then she came out to visit me in Los Angeles.

ELLEN MEYER, Manager:

Ron told me, "I'm going to leave with these guys, and we're going to start our own company." I asked him, "Who are they?" and when he told me who they were, I said, "Ron, I don't think it's going to happen. Bill, Rowland, and Mike Rosenfeld have seniority at William Morris; they have profit sharing, titles, and families to support."

Shortly after that, he said to me, "Look, I can't come out and live with you in New York because of this new company, but will you come out and live with me in L.A.?" There was no gray area. Either I stayed in New York and ended the relationship or I went to L.A. to nurture the relationship and see what happened. I decided to go to L.A. and be with him, and just a couple of months after I came out, Ron proposed, and we got married.

RON MEYER:

The truth is, all four of those guys were very well thought of in the company. Phil's leaving really motivated them, but we were all exhausted by senior management constantly talking about their history with Sophie Tucker, Jimmy Durante, and others. They were steeped in the past. We wanted to be about the future.

BILL HABER:

Even though we were all young, we realized that in American capitalism you can't make any real money unless you own your own company. So we realized that as long as we stayed at William Morris, we could never seriously succeed in the entertainment business.

Sam Weisbord would say to me that the highest tribute in his life was that he just bought his first Constable painting, which meant so much to him. I guess we all wanted our own Constables.

RON MEYER:

Early on, there was potentially a sixth Morris agent who was going to join us. We had started talking with Fred Westheimer, who was a good guy.

FRED WESTHEIMER, Agent:

I was working in casting at Fox and I joined there as an agent in the television department in 1970. Ronnie was probably one of my closest friends, and I was very friendly with the other guys. Mike Ovitz and his wife, Judy, spent a lot of social time together with me and my wife, Susie.

MICHAEL OVITZ:

Fred and Ron were inseparable at William Morris.

FRED WESTHEIMER:

One day Ronnie and I were having lunch at Musso and Frank's, sitting at the bar having a salad, and Mike Ovitz came over. We talked about leaving and setting up our own agency. I was intrigued, but at the time I was doing well at William Morris and making good money. Besides, my wife's late father had been a financial genius, and because of his business acumen we were more than fine.

RON MEYER:

Eventually, Fred had conversations with Mike Rosenfeld, Rowland, and Bill Haber as well.

FRED WESTHEIMER:

After a lot of discussion, I decided to remain at the Morris office. There was going to be a meeting at Rowland's house and I told the guys, "I think in all fairness, I probably shouldn't go, because I'm leaning toward staying." There were some very hard feelings because we were all so close, but my wife and I had decided starting a new company just wasn't for me.

MICHAEL OVITZ:

Fred didn't have any choice. Ron kiboshed it. While Ron liked Fred, he didn't think he would be right for our business, so Ron asked Fred and his wife, Susie, to talk things over with him before Fred made a decision. Ron used Fred's wife to get Fred out of it. It was freaking brilliant, quintessential Meyer. He said, "Susie, I just want to make sure that you're prepared not to see Fred for the next five years. Launching this company is going to be really tough. The hours will be long and there won't be a lot of money coming in. I just want to make sure you're okay with all of this." By the end of the conversation she clearly wasn't in favor of Fred leaving, and she thanked Ron. How amazing is that? She *thanked* him.

FRED WESTHEIMER:

If someone was going to say, "Would you make the same decision again?" I don't know the answer. I was very close to Ron Meyer and Bill Haber, and after they left—while I did have good friends—I never replaced the strength of those relationships with others at the company.

ROWLAND PERKINS:

Once Fred dropped out, it was just going to be the five of us, and we were fine with that.

RON MEYER:

It was January, and we decided we would leave in one year after saving money, getting more clients, finding offices, and having assistants ready for us, so that the day we left we would immediately be in business. That one-year plan ended within one week.

MICHAEL OVITZ:

Earlier in the week I had started looking for a credit line we could use when we got started, even though we were probably a year away from being ready. I had bought some minor certificates of deposit for small amounts of money in a high interest market from a guy at City National, and asked him to set me up with someone who would give us a loan to start a business. Period. The next thing I know is that guy at City National Bank told this to the head of City National Bank, who called the head of the William Morris Agency in New York, Nat Lefkowitz, who in turn called Morris Stoller, who was the CFO of William Morris.

ROWLAND PERKINS:

The leak was an accountant in town, Jules Lefkowitz, whose brother was head of William Morris New York. Mike had inadvertently given the information to the bank to find out what kind of credit we could get.

He also knew who the five of us were, so somebody told him a lot of details.

MICHAEL OVITZ:

There's no question that Fred told management, but he wasn't the leak. The real leak was City National Bank. That's exactly what happened, no more, no less.

FRED WESTHEIMER:

I would never do that to my friends; it's just not who I am. I heard later on it was Mike Ovitz who spread that rumor to discredit me.

ROWLAND PERKINS:

It was January 7, 1975. I got back from lunch and the phone rang. It was Sam Weisbord, who says to me, "Are you free for a walk?" He used to walk as part of his regimen around the neighborhood of William Morris and I said, "Sure."

RON MEYER:

I happened to be home that day with the flu.

ROWLAND PERKINS:

Sam and I started walking, and when we got about two blocks away, he very casually said, "It's come to my attention that you and Haber and Meyer and Ovitz are planning on leaving, is that true?" And the only lie I ever told him was "I can't speak for the others, but for me it's true." He stopped dead in his tracks. He was a short guy and I'm six feet. He looked up at me and got as close as possible without making contact, and said, "You have committed treason," then turned and took off for the office. I followed him, and soon as I got in my office I called Ron Meyer at home and told him what had happened. He said, "Okay," and hung up. Then I called Bill Haber and Mike Rosenfeld and told them the same thing.

Mike Rosenfeld was a good man and came into Sam's office to personally tell him he was leaving, but Sam just threw him out. Then Bill Haber went over to Sam, hit him on the shoulder, and said, "Hey, Sam, isn't this a riot?" and proceeded to tell Sam why the five of us were going to try it on our own. Bill just stood there and laughed while Sam sat frozen with his mouth open.

BILL HABER:

Sam was not pleased. The conversation didn't take long at all.

MICHAEL OVITZ:

I had taken a rare break and had gone skiing. When I got back to my house, Mike Rosenfeld had put a note on my door that said, *"You're no longer working at William Morris. Call me."*

FRED WESTHEIMER:

I walked into Sam's office and there were maybe five or six executives there and they said, "Why are you leaving?" I said, "I'm not." They had just assumed I was part of the group.

MICHAEL OVITZ:

Sam Weisbord loved Judy and he loved me, but he looked at me and said, "You've really screwed yourself this time." That's what he said to me. I learned an amazing lesson from that moment. If he'd started that meeting differently, attempted to check his ego at the door, told me he didn't want to lose me, and then offered me an insane amount of money, there was at least one chance in a thousand I would have stayed. Instead, he did me a favor, because instead of being compassionate or even making me feel guilty, he pissed me off. He attacked me and tried to belittle me. There was no way I was going to stay.

After that meeting, Ron and I packed up our things. Rowland, Bill, and Mike had company cars they had to turn in—Ron and I didn't—so we drove the five of us to Rowland's house.

RON MEYER:

Here's the truth: If we had actually stayed for another year at William Morris like we had planned, and during that time, Sam Weisbord had come to me and said, "All is forgiven," I may have actually stayed. There was no way for us to understand whether our leaving was actually going to be real until it actually happened.

ELLEN MEYER:

The bad news was somebody had blown the whistle on the group when they heard about their plans. The good news was, from the moment they were fired, there was no turning back. Now all they had was each other.

JUDY OVITZ:

It was a real shock. We really hadn't made up our mind about whether to leave or not. But now that decision had been made for us.

RON MEYER:

When Phil left and we left, that was the beginning of the end for William Morris.

MICHAEL OVITZ:

If I had stayed, I would have turned William Morris upside down. It wouldn't have been the same company. My guess is it would have looked a lot like CAA, but I may not have gotten all the way to the top there because I'm not sure I could have switched all the fabric.

STAN ROSENFIELD, Executive:

I was working at that time for Jay Bernstein Public Relations, and saw from the beginning how smart they were. They contacted *Variety*, and the next morning on the front page *Variety* reported that "Five key agents have resigned to open their own office." It was "resigned," not "fired," and it wasn't just "five agents," it was "five key agents." It really set the tone for that company's future.

Inside William Morris, the fact that the group left en masse—not to join another agency but to start from scratch on their own—was considered sheer folly by many, with only a few thinking the brave little band of five might stand a chance of succeeding.

Outside the agency, attention centered on the departures of Perkins, Rosenfeld, and Haber because they were venerable senior guys who were well known, enjoyed positive reputations, and had the most to lose. Meyer was less known, but more people were aware of him than Ovitz, who was the most junior and youngest of the bunch.

MICHAEL ROSENFELD JR.:

I was fourteen in 1975. My father gathered the family around our traditional Sunday night dinner and told us he was going to leave William Morris and they were going to start a new agency.

He assured us that leaving was the right thing to do, and that he really liked the men that he was going to form the agency with. My father told my mom, "These are good agents, this will work out." I can still picture him sitting at the table saying the philosophy of the company would be like the Three Musketeers: all for one and one for all.

ROWLAND PERKINS:

We were tossing company names around and I said, "There's a company on Santa Monica Boulevard called 'The Agency,' but what does that really mean, it sounds all about *them*." Then I said, "The other company that comes to my mind is 'Creative Management'—CMA." We realized Creative Artists Agency would be the best name for us—after all, we were going to be agents for creative clients.

RON MEYER:

We sat in a room and started throwing out names. Each one of us takes credit for coming up with the name.

MICHAEL OVITZ:

After we all left William Morris, it was clear that Rowland seemed really shell-shocked.

RON MEYER:

We literally drew names out of a hat to see who would be president, and Rowland Perkins was our first president.

MICHAEL OVITZ:

Rowland was put in charge, and we all looked at him, but he didn't say anything. He froze. I realized that I needed to get things going, so I whipped out my pad, Ron took some of it, Bill took some of it, Mike took some of it, and we were off to the races.

ROWLAND PERKINS:

For the first three days we worked at my house, and then David Wolper, who was a client at the time, said, "Hey, guys, the five of you can come and use a couple of my offices on Beverly Boulevard until you get yourself set up."

MICHAEL OVITZ:

When we got to Wolper's office, William Morris called Wolper and told him to throw us out.

RON MEYER:

He gave us one room with one telephone in it, which we kept for a week until we found office space.

MICHAEL OVITZ:

Every night before we would get together I would go over what we needed to do the next day, prioritize it, and then put the list into a follow-up system I had created. Ron and I came up with the concept of no contracts. I met with a lawyer so we could be licensed with the state, went out and got office space, then did our letterhead. All we did was work.

ROWLAND PERKINS:

We went over to the Hong Kong Bank Building at Wexford and Wilshire and rented five offices, with a reception room and a mailroom, even though we barely had enough money for the security deposit.

JUDY OVITZ:

9100 Wilshire Boulevard.

MICHAEL OVITZ:

It was the last official street in Beverly Hills.

The Creative Artists Agency was officially launched on January 20, 1975, by five equal partners, Bill Haber, Ron Meyer, Michael Ovitz, Rowland Perkins, and Michael Rosenfeld. The founders took out an ad in Daily Variety, *announcing "Established 1975, Creative Artists Agency, Inc." —a sly poke at William Morris, which always bragged that it was established in 1892—along with the agency's new Wilshire Boulevard address and nothing more. It was a strikingly minimalist move given the aggressive and bold agenda for the new company.*

The five men experienced few of the bonds that those who go into business together usually enjoy. These were not golfing buddies, nor a quintet who took annual trips; they hadn't gone to school together, been fraternity brothers, or joined the same country club, church, or synagogue. What they shared, perhaps all they shared, was a desire to be great agents, and the fact that they had escaped from William Morris to do that.

Each was a distinct personality who had his own approach to the business. There were few commonly shared sensibilities. Haber, for example, wanted to be his own man; Meyer wanted to love and be loved; and Ovitz wanted power and to be feared. To complicate the scenario, there wasn't even a single agreed-upon vision of what this new place was going to be. Mike Rosenfeld hoped CAA would be a boutique agency, and Perkins wanted to be free from the pressure he experienced at the Morris office, but from the very first day, Ovitz was consumed with just the opposite: building an entertainment giant and putting the Morris office out of business if he, they, could—eyes flashing, ears smoking.

Whatever their intrinsic differences, there were few blowups among the Five during the agency's formative years—even in the face of such deep disagreements such as how hard they should be working and whether they could survive all being at the same level in the company hierarchy.

Ovitz's drive and agenda effectively quashed any major disagreements. Simply put, there was too much else to do.

RON MEYER:

There were only five of us, so it wasn't like there was a need for a lot of structure.

MICHAEL OVITZ:

Everything was created on the run. Remember, the five of us came from a place that had a seventy-five-year-old infrastructure that we believed was no longer relevant. We didn't want to duplicate it. What we needed most was to generate revenue to pay our overhead, because we were literally doing something I don't think a lot of people have done: starting a business with no investors—and no money.

ROWLAND PERKINS:

We agreed that if we had to, each one of us would carry ourselves for a year without taking any money from the business so all money coming in could go back into the agency. We got a $100,000 credit line at the bank, with each one of us responsible for $20,000, but we never drew on it.

RON MEYER:

My father had died in 1973, with no life insurance and no money; my mother didn't have any money as well. I was making $125 a week at William Morris and had zero assets; I went to a distant cousin and convinced him to loan me $15,000 so I would have money to live off of for the next two years. Had that not happened, I'm not sure what I would have lived on.

MICHAEL ROSENFELD JR.:

My father asked my older brother, who was eighteen, if he had any money in his bank account, and then he asked me if I had any money. He told us, "I'll pay you guys back."

JUDY OVITZ:

We were scared. Starting this company meant we were going to have no money—and we had no idea how long that would be the case.

MICHAEL OVITZ:

My last year at William Morris I made about $50,000 a year, and my last bonus check was only $15,000—even though I earned the agency over $2 million in commissions.

ROWLAND PERKINS:

At William Morris, if you left the company, partners had the right to buy back any stock, because they didn't want to take a chance that we would sell to outside people. So I cashed out.

RON MEYER:

When things blew up and we were fired, Ellen said, "Why don't I take a leave of absence for a couple weeks and come and stay with you? I can help you get things started."

ELLEN MEYER:

Ron took out a loan to live on because there was absolutely no money, so I got a job at Jerry Abrams's company, who was a producer at the time. Then I transferred to the *Mary Tyler Moore* show as a casting assistant and learned a lot about actors and casting there. One thing led to another and I soon started casting on my own.

MICHAEL OVITZ:

Ellen supported Ron. Judy supported me. Rowland had some money put away, Mike said he could make it, and Bill, my guess is, had the first penny that he ever earned—he didn't even own a house, he rented.

ROWLAND PERKINS:

We couldn't afford to hire a lot of help, so each one of our wives came one day a week and acted as the receptionist.

JUDY OVITZ:

We rented furniture and all the wives started answering the phones. The guys were all very determined and Michael was so driven—I just knew this would be successful.

MICHAEL ROSENFELD JR.:

My brother was the first mailroom employee of CAA; he also delivered packages around town. My mom worked in the office; all the wives worked there, and they each took one day of the week, answering phones, doing whatever was needed.

MICHAEL OVITZ:

If it wasn't for the women—Judy, Ellen, Diane, Marilyn, and Carol—there'd be no CAA.

ROWLAND PERKINS:

I was very lucky: two of my clients, Suzanne Pleshette and Peter Lawford, helped me furnish my office. Peter brought in desks and she brought in lamps and a couch.

MICHAEL OVITZ:

Because we left unexpectedly, we didn't get a chance to talk to any of our clients. We each made a list of clients who we thought would switch over to us. The funny thing, is two clients who Ron and I considered friends and were convinced would come with us under any condition—Jack Weston and Kelly Lange—both stayed at William Morris. Several others we didn't know as well came along.

RON MEYER:

The one client I had who I was positive was going to come with me was Jack Weston, a well-known character actor. He was my most important client at William Morris, and he had literally said to me, "I'm with you forever." In those days, he was probably making a couple hundred thousand a year, so we thought we could at least count on twenty thousand a year in commissions, which was a huge amount of money for us. Just as we were starting out, he was in a play in New York called *Steambath,* and we all had to pitch in for me to fly back to be with him on opening night. I saw him, we had a great time after the play, then I flew back. Waiting for me was a letter that had been mailed several days before from him telling me he had decided to stay at William Morris. When I asked him why he didn't tell me anything when he saw me, he said he just didn't feel comfortable talking about it in person. I was humiliated, embarrassed, and very pissed off. This was a huge setback for us, to the point where if we had known earlier he wouldn't be coming with us, who knows, we might not have been so eager to leave. Years later, a friend of his approached me on his behalf and asked me if I would represent him. I said, "Tell him he can go fuck himself. Not if he was the last client on earth."

MICHAEL OVITZ:

For the first year, years, we did meetings every hour on the hour. The first meeting of the day was at 8:00 A.M.—it was just us—and then, starting at 9:00 in the morning, we had people come in around the clock, six days a week. Our last meeting would be at 9:00 at night. When we met with potential clients, all five of us were in the room. We discussed every single client and had unanimity in everything. It was not an edict, but we wanted to do it because we came from a place where clients were signed only by older guys. We tried at the very beginning to be very purist.

All five of us booked every single meeting. Looking back, I don't know how we managed not to miss any, but I remember we didn't even go to doctor's appointments. No one ever left.

RON MEYER:

We quickly divvied up the studios and networks so each one of us had specific coverage. We had very few clients at the start, and we would all meet and try to sign clients at nights and weekends. We pitched ourselves as an aggressive middle-sized agency and built a client list very quickly. When we did sign someone, we started trying to sell them the very next day.

LORNE MICHAELS, Producer:

When I came to 30 Rock during our first season of the show back in '75, Dave Cabot, who was running talent at NBC, called my office and asked if I would meet with these new breakaway agents from William Morris. The Morris Agency had a lot of power back then and it was clear a lot of people wanted the playing field to be leveled. So I met with Mike Ovitz, who it turned out I knew from when he had been around *The Lily Tomlin Show*. During that first meeting, he didn't have anything specific to talk to me about, but he wanted me to know about their new agency, and it was clear I'd be hearing a lot from him.

RON HOWARD, Director:

The first time I ever heard about CAA was when we were doing *Happy Days* and Jerry Paris, who was the director and producer of something like 95 percent of those episodes and was a dominant comedy figure in television, said he got a call from Mike Ovitz, who told him he was leaving William Morris to start a new agency which would focus on TV. Mike told Jerry they were going to be renegades and were willing to gamble on their futures because they were going to be so committed to their clients.

BARRY LEVINSON:

In 1975, Rudy and I were working on *The Carol Burnett Show*, and Mike called and told us he was starting a new agency with several other agents from the Morris office. Then all of a sudden we got a call from someone at William Morris, who told us they wanted to take us out to lunch. We went out to this lunch at Canter's, and there were six agents talking to us about staying at William Morris and all of these things they could do for us. When we left and were walking back to CBS on Fairfax, I said to Rudy, "Did you realize there were that many agents over there at William Morris, none of whom we've ever heard of before now? It sort of scares me that all these guys came out of nowhere." So we obviously stayed with Michael, and we were part of the formation of CAA.

MICHAEL OVITZ:

Our overhead may have been low, but our expenses were incredibly high. All of us were having every meal at restaurants with executives, clients, and potential clients. We were trying to keep things as inexpensive as possible, including staying away from high-priced meals. But then there was the dinner that Rowland put together with Joseph Bologna and Renée Taylor at a very expensive restaurant in Century City. They were hot writers and we wanted them as clients. We all brought our wives, so it was a table for twelve, which was going to be a fortune.

RON MEYER:

Before Joe and Renée arrived, Bill and I said to Rowland, "They picked this place, so maybe they are taking us. Whatever you do, don't reach for the check."

JUDY OVITZ:

We were hoping that because he was a regular there, the waiter would give the check to Joe Bologna.

MICHAEL OVITZ:

It turned out, Renée and Joe hadn't come for a cordial dinner. We had never seen anything like it. She drew a line across the table and said, "This is Joe and me against you." She was really combative. At one point, Bill just said, "What do you mean? We just want to work with you."

RON MEYER:

The check was put in front of Joe Bologna and he just kept looking at it but never addressed it.

MICHAEL OVITZ:

His arm never moved. He just kept smoking a cigar, which he had also charged to the bill.

JUDY OVITZ:

So then Rowland's wife, Diane, takes the check and gives it to Rowland. I was like, *Oh my God*. Rowland was horrified. I think that destroyed their marriage then and there. It was the beginning of the end for them.

MICHAEL OVITZ:

Rowland gives it to Mike Rosenfeld under the table, but Mike hadn't brought his credit card. No one had a credit card except for me, so I took care of it. This was 1975, and the bill was $2,000 and we had no money. It took us two months to get our first commission check—it was something like $950. We framed it and put it on the wall.

BILL HABER:

Six months into the company, I sat with my wife at a place called the Swiss Echo, which is no longer on Pico Boulevard and Overland, and I laid out in front of her $5,000 in hundred-dollar bills, and I said, "This is our first money from CAA."

MICHAEL OVITZ:

Every dime we made went back to the business. I sold a daytime television show called *The Girl in My Life*, and that paid us like $1,000 a week, which covered our rent and phones. Then someone sold a $100,000 TV movie and we got $10,000. We were barely making it. At the time, we didn't even have expense accounts; we were paying our own expenses and deducting them on our tax returns.

JUDY OVITZ:

Thank goodness we didn't have any kids at that time. We were lucky, we only had dogs.

RON MEYER:

In those days, Bill, Mike, and I were very competitive with other agencies, and tenacious about signing clients to CAA. We were extremely effective signers and sellers. We were on a constant adrenaline rush. Every day was exciting.

BILL HABER:

There were people at William Morris who told us we were going to fail. They said, "You just can't go and start your own agency out of nothing. You'll wind up being casting directors." They also spread rumors we had stolen typewriters.

MICHAEL OVITZ:

In '75, the only way you could get any kind of publicity was you had to buy it, right? Mike and I did the logo, which was our three initials titled like it was going forward, and we put it on script covers in really big letters, and then I sent guys out to every doctor's office, lawyer's reception area, and every restaurant to drop them off. The thought was people would see them and wonder, *What's CAA?* We had a blast doing it. Everyone thought we were crazy, including our other partners, but we got a ton of publicity from them.

The agency's main source of revenue was the modestly successful Rich Little game show Rhyme and Reason, *which ran for about a year. By the end of 1975, the company's $2.5 million revenues left each partner a tidy sum of $25,000, but they took no salary and used revenues to pay for overhead and expansion. Revenue was limited to game-show package commissions and some TV bookings. There were no profits.*

STEVE TISCH, Producer:

I moved to L.A. to work for Columbia Pictures in November of 1971. I was twenty-two and was working as Peter Guber's assistant. Peter was head of domestic production. I remember when they left William Morris to start their own agency, and needless to say, it was big news. It was the talk of the town. Most people, especially those under forty, were very impressed that they left the most established place in town to start their own agency, but there were a lot of people thinking they were going to get creamed and wondered how they could possibly succeed.

ROWLAND PERKINS:

I knew we'd survive from the beginning. To what degree I didn't know. I was making the most money of the five of us at William

Morris, but now we all were equal partners, and at the end of the first year we were all making more money than I was making at William Morris in one year. I give Ovitz credit for that. He sold two daytime shows, and once he sold those, there was steady money coming in every week.

RON MEYER:

We went after everybody's clients, and I always felt there was a shot if they agreed to meet you. Even if they didn't come with us, rarely did anyone ever say, "Fuck you, I'm not leaving my agent."

There were a number of times when other small agencies came to us and wanted to merge. We came close once or twice, but it never happened.

RAND HOLSTON, Agent:

I came to CAA in 1983 after leaving a Tiffany literary agency called Adams, Ray & Rosenberg. I brought Stephen King with me, Paul Brickman, who had directed *Risky Business,* and some great writers like Jim Cash and Jack Epps. When I arrived, Michael told me that early on in its history, CAA had almost merged with Adams, Ray & Rosenberg. He said they were all having a precelebratory dinner before the deal was finalized and he got up to give a toast and said, "I'm just so excited about our huge potential together. One day we'll be representing the biggest names in the business, like Robert Redford and Sydney Pollack." And Lee Rosenberg said to him, "Michael, we're going to do great, but let's not get carried away." Michael told me at that next moment, he and Ron whispered to each other, "Let's get the fuck out of here."

Toward the end of 1975, the five men escaped Los Angeles for the first time together, driving about an hour and a half to Lake Arrowhead, where Michael Ovitz's father-in-law had a cabin. The founders thought it would be an excellent opportunity to get away from outside stimuli, talk philosophy, and, most of all, bond. It didn't quite work out that way.

MICHAEL OVITZ:

We never did that again. It was the last time we ever got together, just the five of us.

RON MEYER:

From the beginning, it had seemed to all of us, probably including Rowland, that he wasn't comfortable running things. We would all meet and wound up making a lot of decisions together. At Arrowhead, when it came up that Mike would run things, there was no power struggle. We all agreed.

ROWLAND PERKINS:

I was the first president of the company, and our understanding was that every two years somebody else would move into the presidency but we would all always serve as agents and be equal partners.

RON MEYER:

We decided that there had to be a leader, and Michael was the natural leader in the group. He was aggressive and very much wanted to run the company. He was the right person at the right time to take over.

MICHAEL OVITZ:

No one else ever asked to be in charge and no one ever challenged me being in charge. It was very natural. One of the things that made the company great is that everybody knew their strengths and weaknesses.

ROWLAND PERKINS:

I just wanted to do my packaging. I got tired of having to run the company. We were growing so fast, and Ovitz really wanted to do it, so we let him.

MICHAEL OVITZ:

With all due respect for Rowland, he was working off the William Morris pro forma. I didn't want the systems that William Morris had. I set up systems that were antithetical to William Morris.

BILL HABER:

My job was to put television series on the air that we packaged and to collect a package commission, but in those early days, we were all doing everything we could to get our names out there and find out what was important for our business.

SHERRY LANSING, Executive and Producer:

In 1975, I was the executive story editor at MGM, which meant I bought material to make into movies. So this guy named Bill Haber calls and says, "I'd like to go through the release schedule so I know what's going on." I said, "Great, Susan Merzbach does that for everybody, so I'll set up a time for her to meet with you." And he said, "I don't want to be treated like everybody." I told him, "No, no, I didn't mean to offend you. I just meant she has all the information, and it's more efficient, but I will give it to you now if you want." He said, "I'm not offended, and now I don't even want the release schedule, I'm just going to shower you with gifts." Then he started to laugh and said, "Bye."

The next day, fifty shower caps were delivered to my office. I called him to say that was really funny, but he wouldn't take my call. The next day, fifty boxes of Morton Salts with the little girl and her umbrella were delivered. The next day, I got a bunch of umbrellas. I was laughing every day because it was all so original, and for ten days I received all these funny presents. Susan and I said, this has got to stop; I couldn't even get into my office because of all the stuff that had been sent. So we hired an actor and said, "Put lots of soap in your hair and a towel around you, and go to his office and say, 'The girls throw in the towel,' and throw the towel on Haber's desk." The actor goes to CAA with a towel wrapped around him, and of course the receptionist won't let him through, but the actor was so determined to do his job that he stormed past the door and goes into a conference room where Bill and Mike Ovitz were sitting with a client they were trying to sign. The actor runs in, throws off the towel, and exclaims, "The girls throw in the towel!" And he was stark naked underneath! We thought he would have a bathing suit on. The client looked at him and said, "Wow, this is the coolest place in the world," and signed with the agency. Bill Haber called me and said, "You two are amazing! We must celebrate!"

So he picks a night Susan and I are free and tells us to wait at the MGM gate. This huge stretch limo pulls up and the driver rolls out a red carpet and a man with a violin starts playing as he motions for us to get in. I was making $30,000 a year and had never been in a limo in my life. There was a chilled bottle of champagne inside waiting for us. We knew we were having dinner, but we didn't know where and the driver wouldn't tell us. Then the limo pulls up to the airport, and Susan and I are asking ourselves, *What is going on?* The door opens and the man helping me out of the car says, "Hello, I'm Bill Haber." I had never met him. I said, "Bill, this is crazy! Are we eating at the airport?" He said, "Nope." Then a man in a pilot's shirt and hat comes up to us and says, "Good evening, I'm Pilot Mike," and leads us over to a private plane. I had never been in one in my life. They wouldn't tell us where we were going. We got into the plane and we were in the air for about fifteen minutes before we landed at Van Nuys Airport. They had flown us from LAX to Van Nuys, and it turned out "Pilot Mike" was Mike Rosenfeld. We had a beautiful dinner in the hangar, and then they put me in the limo, which brought me back home. Needless to say, it was the beginning of a wonderful friendship.

MICHAEL OVITZ:

Bill was eccentric. It was part of what made him Bill. He loved the differentiation. He didn't want to be like the rest of us.

JUDY OVITZ:

We were closest with Ronnie. Ronnie and Michael were like brothers then. Two peas in a pod; really, really close. Michael was all business, and Ronnie was the social one. Bill was a little bit quirky but terrific. Mike Rosenfeld and Rowland were good guys, but neither of them wanted to be in charge.

I was really close with Carol Haber and Marilyn Rosenfeld. The five wives would often get together.

MICHAEL OVITZ:

The buyers at the networks and the studios were by and large encouraging of us because anything that could diversify whatever leverage agents had was good for them. It was the competitors, the other people in the community, that loved to talk about how we were going to fail and that the philosophy we had was ridiculous and wasn't going to work. Many in town called us the "TV boys," which was meant in a demeaning way, but we made a decision to joke about it and embrace it. We would walk into a room and say, "The TV boys are here."

One of the things we did at the beginning, in part because we didn't have a large client base, was we made *executives* our clients. We became the de facto adviser to many executives who were working in television and made sure they felt like they could talk to us about their own careers and issues. Haber did this with several people at NBC, and Ron did it with casting directors. This started small, but we never stopped, and in the years to come, we wound up representing almost every major executive in the business. We never asked or received financial favors from them, but we certainly got our calls returned.

For the first year, it was all Darwinian—survival of the fittest, kill or be killed. We had no money, no cash flow. We had a giant behemoth that was organized and well funded in William Morris that was threatening every minute of the day to put us out of business and trying to marshal its army against us. Our biggest film client was Ernest Borgnine. We had no film bookings. We didn't even pretend to be a film agency. We couldn't get any key film guys on the phone—they didn't have the time of day for us.

BILL HABER:

Early on, all five of us were doing the same things, and over time we realized that we shouldn't do that. You have to specialize in the businesses that you're in, and so we realized we had to change the way we were organized.

MICHAEL OVITZ:

We realized that the only way we would do well in the movie business is if one of the five of us did it full time. So at dinner one night—we had these weekly dinners—we decided that Bill, Rowland, and Mike would stay with TV, Ron would split his time between TV and movies, and I would do movies full time.

RON MEYER:

For the first year, all of our series clients were paying commission to William Morris and other agencies, so we were working very hard for them but not getting paid. Ralph Waite from *The Waltons*, Bea Arthur from *Maude*, Sally Struthers from *All in the Family*, Chad Everett from *Medical Center* were some examples. But Everett took out a full-page ad in *Variety* announcing he had joined with us, which was great.

MICHAEL OVITZ:

Sally Struthers was a big client for us. Ron and I signed her together, and it was our entrée to Norman Lear. It was really important to us. *All in the Family* in the '70s broke big-time ground. When we got to Sally, we ended up getting Rob, and then we ended up with Carroll O'Connor; we had three of the four. That was a big deal for us in those days, having the top cast of the top television show.

NORMAN LEAR, Producer:

When they started CAA, *All in the Family* had been on for just several years, and I was bringing out to Los Angeles a lot of actors from New York. I had brought out Bea Arthur to guest-star as Maude, I brought out Rue McClanahan, Sherman Hemsley, Conrad Bain, and many others. It didn't take long for the CAA guys to realize that many of these New York actors had no Los Angeles representation. So early on, Ron, Mike, and Bill will tell you they began coming to our run-throughs and signing as many of the New York actors as they could.

Since all five of the agency's founders had worked in William Morris's television department, most of the agency's clients in the beginning were television actors rather than the highly sought after movie stars who would become CAA's future bread and butter. During their time at William Morris, the CAA founders had objected to WM's television packaging fee of 10 percent of the budget, believing it was "too rich" and "people couldn't afford it." CAA slashed it to 6 percent, and, according to Ovitz, "it increased the volume of our business so we wound up making far more than if we had charged the higher rate."

MICHAEL OVITZ:

Bill and Mike came up with the idea of cutting commissions from 10 percent to 6 percent.

MICHAEL EISNER:

When I was running programming on the West Coast and working with Barry Diller, we had experienced a lot of problems with the agency environment and its expensive packaging arrangements, including hearing that Abe Lastfogel and Nat Lefkowitz, the legendary owners of William Morris at the time, had gone to Leonard Goldenson, the CEO of ABC, to try and get us fired because we were advising Aaron Spelling to make a direct deal with us, thus avoiding the biggest agency. I think Goldenson was proud his "boys" were so protective of the network. So when those five guys left William Morris, I wasn't being vindictive against William Morris; I just thought, *Great, we're going to have a new competitor.* Sure enough, they told me they were not going to hold to the onerous 10 percent packaging fees, so it was in my interest to have them be successful. I brought all five of them into one of our conference rooms and had the heads of development, comedy, drama, movies, specials, and daytime sit there with them. The guys were just getting CAA started and had mostly mediocre clients, but I said to our people, "We're not leaving this room until every single one of their clients has a job with ABC. Every one." Of course later CAA went back to the practice of large TV packages as they should have in their own business interests.

RON MEYER:

At William Morris, I don't think I ever made more than $150 a week. By the end of the second year at CAA, there was no big money, but we were doing fine. I remember saying to Mike Rosenfeld, "If I was given a guarantee that I could make fifty thousand a year for the rest of my life, I'd sign a pact with the devil right now."

MICHAEL OVITZ:

You've got to remember there was no Internet, so we took every chance there was to create an image for ourselves. Because we drove all over town, we got five Jaguars at $15,000 apiece, which was double what a Buick cost or a Cadillac at the time. I arranged a loan with the bank to finance the $75,000 and put up 7,500 bucks. Then we got license plates with "CAA" and our initials. It was a complete show of muscle, which we couldn't afford, but no one knew that, and we had to put on a big show.

RON MEYER:

Today it would seem absurd to go out and get those cars, but it was a big deal at the time. We were really branding ourselves. Mike and I were out every night of the week, entertaining endlessly, going to every premiere, and because of those cars and license plates, people could instantly tell we were there.

MICHAEL OVITZ:

It's funny, when I bought the Jaguars, we all wanted four doors. I wanted us to look like we were old guys who had been around the business and were successful, right? But Ron insisted that his have only two doors. He wanted to look like a young guy.

BILL HABER:

Everybody said, *Oh, they must be successful. They're all running around with Jaguars,* because perception is reality. Then about five years after that, we had a relationship with a place called Hollywood Sports Cars, so Michael, Ronnie, too, I think we all went out and bought Ferraris. I had the most beautiful black-on-black Ferrari 308GTS, one of the most beautiful luxury cars they had, but I would never pull up in front of the Palm or anywhere else because I didn't want anyone to see me in that car. I sold it after just three months and took my son's red Toyota. I was very happy with it.

JAY SANDRICH, Director:

Bob Broder was my agent, and he was leaving to go back to another agency that I had been at but had a problem with, so I said to him, "Because I'm not going back with you, who would you suggest?" I told him I didn't want a big agency, so he said, "There's a new company called CAA and Mike Ovitz is the guy you should talk to," so I met with Mike—this was probably '76—then had dinner with all five of them. They talked about their business, and how they treated their clients. I liked them and signed right away.

Afterward, Mike told me, "Each client always has two of us, and Ron Meyer is going to be working with you as well."

RON MEYER:

Jay Sandrich was a big sign for us because he directed all the *Mary Tyler Moore* shows and was a huge talent, one of the most important television directors in the business. Over the years, we became and remain the closest of friends.

JAY SANDRICH:

As time went on, I talked to Ron more and more, and he really became my agent. In many ways, he became my best friend. He still is.

MICHAEL DOUGLAS, Actor:

I was at William Morris. My agent, Eddie Bondy, a wonderful great character, died, and Ronnie was there and we found out that we shared the exact same birthday—same year, same day. Twenty-five years later, we found out it was literally the same hour. He looked the same way then as he does now: he wears his pants really high with a black sweater, and when he reads, it's really up close to his face. He looks like a Hasid davening.

When Ron started representing me, it wasn't easy. On one hand, I was an Academy Award–winning producer for *Cuckoo's Nest*, which meant some people either hated me or were jealous, and on the other hand I was a TV actor who left a hit show to try and get into the movie business. It didn't go real well; back then, it wasn't easy to make the transition from television to movies. Ronnie and I used to joke about when he was trying to find roles for me, everything was "Jeff Bridges this," and "Jeff Bridges that," so he would raise his hand at meetings and say, "I'm tired of begging for bones for Michael Douglas!" He spent a lot of time with me and was a great sounding board. He also read a lot of scripts so he could find projects that were right for me.

RON MEYER:

Chasin-Park-Citron was an elite small agency that represented twenty of the biggest stars in the world. Because they were older, we sold ourselves as a Chasin-Park-Citron with youth and energy. Our pitch—which was totally honest—was that we were going to be available for our clients seven days a week—anyplace, anytime. We also assured them we would find them the best material and projects available.

I don't know that we were actually putting other agencies out of business, but as far as we were concerned, William Morris was our primary target. There was nothing friendly about our exit, and we pursued their clients vigorously.

ARMY BERNSTEIN, Writer and Producer:

I went to the University of Wisconsin and wrote plays with my fraternity brothers. We did really well, winning some campus playwriting contests and thinking we were kind of cool. So a group of us got together and went to New York to prove it to the world. And after a little bit of alcohol and a little bit of drugs, we wrote a script. A friend of ours got us a meeting with a guy at Warner Bros. who met with us. We handed the script to him and said, "We didn't expect you to be so nice to us," and he said, "Well, maybe you're going be the next big thing." We came back two weeks later and he said, "Okay, now I'm not going to be so nice. I read your script, and it's not bad. It's the single worst script I've ever read in my life. And you should not pursue a career in the entertainment business." We were all kind of devastated. He said, "You must have other things you want to do, right?" One guy said, "Well, I could go to medical school in Grenada," and he said, "Go be a doctor." Another guy said, "Well, I'm in law school right now," and he said, "Stay in law school." When he came to me, I said, "I got nothing." He said, "Well, then you're the one I feel really sorry for." And we left—brokenhearted, our dreams dashed.

I didn't know what to do. I had been reading Thoreau's *Walden* and Somerset Maugham's *The Razor's Edge* and was greatly influenced by the heroes of both of them, men who went to live in the wilderness to find themselves. So I went to Colorado, by myself, and lived alone, with no electricity, no running water, no bathroom, and just a wood-burning stove, for a year, writing.

After that I headed to L.A. and tried again. One day I heard Stan Kamen liked a spec screenplay I had written, and I thought that was the summit. He represented all these big stars of the day, but right before I signed with him, somebody said, "Wait, there's a new company called Creative Artists Agency; you should at least meet them." I met with them, and they were all young and had a sort of madness to them. They made me feel like they were going to make it their mission to represent better than anyone in the world could. I got seduced. So I didn't go with Stan Kamen, I went with CAA.

CAA moved into new headquarters in Century City in September of 1976, replacing its at-capacity small offices in Beverly Hills. In a Daily Variety *article, Ovitz was quoted, "Best of all, we don't owe a dime and we have money in the bank."*

MICHAEL OVITZ:

I saw an ad in *Variety* from an agent named Marty Baum and did some homework on him. He was a legendary movie agent from the old school, and the clients he listed in the ad were amazing. I knew we could be a part of the film business without him, but it would be better to bring him and his clients over to us.

So Marty came in, and said, "You need to meet with Dr. Eugene Landy." Eugene Landy was Marty's psychiatrist. I said, "Why?" He said, "Because he is my mentor, and you can't believe the things he's done for people. I really believe in this guy." So I said, "Sure, I'll meet with him."

RON MEYER:

Make no mistake about it: Marty's arrival was a major event in the development of the agency. He gave us more credibility, brought in more great clients, and helped us establish a beachhead in the motion picture business that we didn't really have up until his arrival.

MICHAEL OVITZ:

As an agent you meet a lot of different people, right? So I'm sitting with Eugene Landy—"Dr. Eugene Landy"—in his office, and it quickly becomes clear to me that he's a puppeteer, a Svengali who is trying to get into the business, and he wants me to pay him.

We started getting into an argument, and he made the mistake of threatening me that he would kill the deal along with other threats. Then we got into a physical confrontation—he got in my face and bumped me, so I pushed him against the wall. I finally got him to back off, and Marty signed the documents.

RON MEYER:

Marty put us in the movie business.

A merger between CAA and the Martin Baum Agency on October 5, 1976, brought an influx of famous clientele, including Peter Sellers, Blake Edwards, Rod Steiger, Angela Lansbury, Cloris Leachman, Sidney Poitier, Richard Harris, Joanne Woodward, Dyan Cannon, Harry Belafonte, and Richard Attenborough. Marty Baum became an equal partner and went on to become the first head of CAA's motion picture department.

MICHAEL OVITZ:

This was a big deal for us to announce Marty, big deal, because everybody criticized us that we weren't in the movie business. Ron and I had just begun to work on the film side, and now with Marty, we had a client list.

RON MEYER:

Marty had been a famous agent and was known as a very tough boss, but he had mellowed by the time he came to us. Marty fit in very nicely, was great, and understood that he wasn't running the company. He liked us and liked that we were young, energetic guys. The situation was attractive for him.

ADAM FIELDS, Producer:

I was Marty Baum's assistant shortly after he started at CAA, and he was The Guy. His client list was an incredible list of blue-chip Hollywood movie stars, including Blake Edwards, Peter Sellers, Sidney Poitier, Rod Steiger, Richard Harris, James Clavell, Carroll O'Connor, Sean Connery, Bo Derek, and Richard Attenborough.

I would see memos from Marty to Mike saying, "I looked at the

deal you're about to make, and there's more you can ask for than five percent of the net. Come see me at lunch." He enjoyed playing the role of mentor to those young guys.

RUSTY LEMORANDE, CAA Assistant:

His Rolodex was massive. It was two large wheels on each end, the size of two large pizzas, and everybody in the business was in there. All of the young agents came to Marty for advice, and he loved being the master. But if they disobeyed him or screwed up, he would chew them out like they were disobedient kids.

Marty gravitated toward packages. With his client Blake Edwards, he would attach everything he could. When I was working on his desk, Blake's pet project was *10*, which was supposed to star his wife, Julie Andrews, and George Segal; George Segal was a really big deal at the time. The project left UA and Orion scooped it up right away. Orion was sort of the film company version of what CAA was, a group of executives that defected and formed their own company and they were outcasts. *10* was a film that nobody wanted and I give Marty a lot of credit; he not only moved it to Orion but when George Segal backed out, the film was effectively dead unless they could replace the cast. Nobody had heard of Bo Derek at that point. I remember the day that Marty said to me, "Go get the Academy directory." At the time, the Academy published two large directories; they were like huge phone books maybe five inches thick on the spine, one for women and one for men. Marty spotted Dudley Moore, who had just been in a Chevy Chase film *Foul Play*, and Marty's the one who said he could be great for the role. He called Blake and said, "You should look at this guy." The rest is history.

BILL HABER:

Marty Baum put his suit on and every day, for more than thirty years, showed up at CAA, where he was always greeted by two assistants. He was not functioning well toward the end, but he was always treated well until the day he died.

RUSTY LEMORANDE:

Ovitz would never say who he was on the phone—not even "Hi, it's Mike." He would just say, "Is he in?" You had to recognize his voice, and we jumped like it was God calling, because we knew that Mike had that authority over you. Marty jumped, too—more for Mike Ovitz than any of his important clients. I always thought that was interesting. Marty had so much more experience than Mike; Marty had been brought in on a pedestal; Mike really turned to Marty for advice on how to handle film deals and, more important, big powerful superstars; and Mike was a kid compared to Marty. Yet Marty was in awe of Ovitz.

AMY GROSSMAN, Agent:

I arrived in late September of 1976, the first female agent at CAA. I was a secretary at William Morris; it did not take long to realize that I would rather be an agent than a secretary. So after about a year, I went into management and said that I wanted to train to be an agent. They said, "No, you seem more like a cheerleader"—which, parenthetically, at UCLA I was. I decided that I wasn't going to get anywhere at that company, and a producer client who met me at a party—his name was Robert Greenwald—said, "The guys at CAA are looking for a secretary, I'm going to introduce you." At that point I knew who they were; they had been in business a year at that time. They were not highly spoken of at William Morris.

I remember Mike Rosenfeld Sr. saying to me, "I'm at a brand-new agency; I don't need another agent right now, I need a secretary. I can't make you any promises, but I will give you a chance." That was a far bigger statement than I had gotten from the Morris office so I left and I went to CAA. I worked for a gentleman named Rowland Perkins. My first day at work was the company's first day in the offices at 1888 Century Park East. I remember I came up the stairs, went into the suite, and Mike Rosenfeld Sr. handed me a vacuum cleaner. I lasted until lunch, then I went down the street to the Hamburger Hamlet that used to be on the corner of Century

Park East and Little Santa Monica and called the Morris office. I was going to ask them for my job back, because I didn't come over to vacuum, but they wouldn't take my call. I can't honestly tell you if they didn't pick up my call because I had gone to CAA and that was the level of animosity at that time, or the head of personnel was just at lunch. Fortunately, my call was not picked up and I slunk my way back to the office. I stayed at CAA for seventeen years.

RON MEYER:

We had a lot of clients who were booking episodic television with guest shots. In those days they probably paid $1,500 or $2,500 for a guest shot on a Quinn-Martin show, or *The Fugitive*, and we depended on a lot of that. When you book something for $2,500, your commission is $250, and even though every penny was always important to us, and the appearances were important to the clients, I realized we should get out of the episodic television business so we could concentrate on the series business and the Movie-of-the-Week business. There was a real robust Movie-of-the-Week business back then, paying actors $25,000 or $30,000 for a two-hour movie. There was money to be made for a certain caliber of talent. This was a big turning point for us, but it meant we weren't going to be able to represent a lot of clients who depended on us just for episodic appearances.

RUSTY LEMORANDE:

You started in the mailroom, and if you survived that, you became an assistant for an agent and that's the big training ground. It's a survival-of-the-fittest system, and it works very well.

MARC GRABOFF, Agent:

I went to UCLA and majored in communications. I wanted to get into the entertainment business and sent my résumé to eight or nine agencies, but I was hoping to get into William Morris or ICM. Neither of them would return my phone calls or respond to my letters. The phone number I was giving out was the house phone at my fraternity house. One day, I'm literally just sitting in that house and someone yells, "Hey, Mark, there's some guy named Michael Ortiz on the phone for you." And I'm like, "Okay, who's that?" I got the phone and the guy goes, "This is Michael Ovitz. I'm at CAA, and today we decided to start a training program at the same time someone handed me your résumé. You've got great timing; come on in and meet."

I went to 1888 Century Park East, 14th Floor, and met with Mike Ovitz and Mike Rosenfeld. It was one of the worst interviews of my life. Mike Ovitz was argumentative and started pushing me from the start. He said, "Oh, I see you're a ZBT," and I enthusiastically said, "Yes." And he says, "I was president of that fraternity at UCLA." I said, "That's great," to which he responded, "I hated everyone and everything about it." I thought to myself, *Okay, this guy already hates me.* So I figured I didn't have much to lose, and—even though it's not my personality—I decided to push back a bit. I didn't get in his face, but I tried to show him I could hold my own ground. I guess I did well enough in the interview because the next day they hired me to start their mailroom. I was the first official mailroom trainee at CAA. There was no formal program set up yet, and there was nobody saying, "This is how you do it." It was really just "Come in, Xerox things, and drive a hundred plus miles a day around town delivering things." One day I had to deliver a $500,000 check to James Clavell, which was half of his option money for *Shogun*. It was the biggest check I had ever seen in my life.

I wound up delivering and schlepping all by myself from June of '77 to November of '77 when they hired Michael Menchel. Then he became the schlepper outside and I was the inside guy.

AMY GROSSMAN:

There was one guy in the mailroom, four other assistants, and the guys. There were probably a dozen people in the company. There was a sense we all had nothing to lose.

I was Rowland's secretary for three months, and in December of that year, Ronnie needed to free himself from representing some of the smaller time actors and actresses who were bogging him down, people who could hack at him all day and make it difficult for him to go out and try to find movie stars. So they made me an agent to take that burden off of him. When they promoted me, Michael gave me some money and said, "Go buy yourself two pairs of Gucci shoes, three business suits, some skirts, and blouses with bows at the neck. That's what you're going to wear."

RUSTY LEMORANDE:

The place was small, and all of us assistants bonded. One weekend a bunch of us went skydiving and when Ovitz found out he said, "Absolutely not. You can't do that ever again." It turned out he was afraid if the plane crashed, the agency would lose all its assistants in one weekend.

AMY GROSSMAN:

When I was at the Morris Agency, my boss got a call asking if a director client, Richard Hefron, was available, but my boss didn't know Hefron's availability because he was represented by an agent down on the first floor whose name was Fred Specktor. At the Morris office, you didn't tell each other stuff—the older agents guarded their clients, and young agents had no upside in working for the older agents' clients. They literally would not be compensated for that kind of work. CAA's setup was the antithesis of that. I could be compensated for what I did in a way that was extremely meaningful. It was really about a free exchange of information. It was a win-win for everybody in the agency, for the clients who were represented by the agency, and I think for the buyers as well.

MARC GRABOFF:

When I first started working at CAA, there was no kitchen, so I would take the coffee mugs from the five partners every morning into the men's room and clean them with a towel in the sink.

Martin Baum's big client at the time was Blake Edwards; the movie *10* was in production, and they brought Bo Derek into the office with her husband, John Derek, for a meeting. The place rolled out the red carpet. I walked into the conference room where they were meeting and asked, "Can I get anybody coffee, water, or anything else?" And John Derek says, "My wife will have hot chocolate." I said, "No problem, I'll go get some hot chocolate." Of course we didn't have any in the kitchen, so I went downstairs to a little stand, bought a packet of instant hot chocolate, and used hot water from the men's room to make it. I brought it to her and she takes one sip of it and makes a face, then whispers something to her husband. Then he looks at me and says, "She wanted Ovaltine, you idiot!" So I had to get in the car, drive around, and find someplace that sold Ovaltine.

AMY GROSSMAN:

I did not find an uncomfortable culture within the company, vis-à-vis gender, but I was harassed sexually, certainly, out in the world. In those days, if you were to receive an unwanted advance from a man, pretty much the only appropriate response was to let it roll off your back. I have a very distinct memory of going to an appointment to see an important television executive. I was nervous; it was a big account for me to start that Bill was trying to extricate himself from—that was the whole process so the guys could move on to new opportunities and have the people under them fill in. I walked into the room and the man behind the desk said to me, "Wow, if Haber had told me what big tits you had, I would have seen you sooner."

MIKE MENCHEL, Agent:

I grew up outside of Philadelphia, Pennsylvania, where my dad had a toy factory. I went to college in Washington, D.C., at American University for two and a half years. I was doing okay, but let's just say other things came into my life then and I was going downhill real fast, so I left and came out to California. I didn't know anybody, I just wanted to get as far away as I could on four wheels.

Budget Rent a Car in San Diego gave me a job where I was responsible for driving cars from the main office to the lot at the San Diego airport and taking the ones that had just been returned back to the main office. I also had to wash them, gas them, and sometimes change their oil. I hated all of it. My sister Susie had moved to Los Angeles, and one day she called and said, "Hey, Mike, why don't you come up to Los Angeles? We're invited to a party at Stockard Channing's house, and there will be movie stars there." I wasn't about to turn that down, and at the party, Susie introduced me to Mike Ovitz, who she knew tangentially because her husband was a root canal surgeon and Mike was his patient. Then I saw him talking to all these movie stars, like Stockard, Dyan Cannon, Sidney Poitier and others. I thought to myself, *This is amazing. They're all listening to him. This guy has some kind of job.* So I went up to him and I said, "I want to work with you." He said, "Do you want to be an agent?" I said, "I've wanted to be an agent for my entire life." He laughed and smiled and asked me, "Do you know what an agent does?" I said, "Yeah, they do what you do." He just looked at me, and it was clearly one of those "don't call me, I'll call you" situations. But at least I was able to give him my number.

Thirteen months later I come home at nine at night from running cars back and forth from the airport and the phone rings. There's a young lady on the other end. She says, "Hi, is this Mike Menchel?" I said, "Yeah," and she says, "Will you hold for Mike Ovitz?" I said, "*What?*" It had been over a year, and truthfully, it took me a couple moments to remember his name. So he gets on the phone and says, "Do you still want to work as an agent?" I said, "I've been waiting for you to call! It's been thirteen months!" He laughed a little bit, and said, "Be up here tomorrow morning at 8:00 A.M."

I left the next morning at about 5:00 A.M. and drove to Los Angeles. I got there so early, the building wasn't even open. I waited and waited, and finally his assistant comes and opens the office and I sat on the couch and waited. Now, it's nine o'clock. Now it's ten o'clock, and I've heard nothing. Now it's eleven. Same deal. At noon, his assistant comes out and says, "I want to apologize to you, but Mike is very busy today. I don't think he'll be able to see you, so maybe you should go home and we'll call you again." And I'll never forget this: I looked at her and said, "Do I look crazy?" She goes, "What?" I said, "I'm not crazy. This could be an opportunity of a lifetime for me. I'm not going home. I'm going to sit here till midnight if I have to." I said, "I'll go out and grab a quick lunch, but then I will be right back. Then I will wait again. He's bound to be free for five minutes." I kept waiting, and at 2:30 the doors blew open and it was Mike Ovitz. He sees me there still waiting, and just says, "Good move not leaving."

I met with him and he said, "I'm going to put you in the mailroom and you'll work your way up from there." I said, "What do I do in the mailroom?" He says, "Anything we want you to do." I said, "I can handle that."

AMY GROSSMAN:

"Buck Slips," as they were called, had our name at the bottom and *Creative Artists Agency* at the top and that's how we communicated. You filled a slip out, folded it, stapled it, and the mailroom or you yourself would run it to the person's office that you wanted it to go to. All the ones that would go to Mike used to come back written in a red felt pen and would say, "SEE ME." So that meant you would go stand at his office door and you would wait for him to turn around and nod—that meant come in. Then you would discuss the thing that you had initially written on that slip or that he had written to you. It was a very personal way to do business; we were all in and out of each other's offices.

MIKE MENCHEL:

I think I'd maybe been there for one day, maybe two, and I got a dispatch slip and it's from Ron Meyer's office. It says, *Pick up a package, UNIBUNG-1 off 1-1.* So I went to Ron Meyer's office and asked, "What is this?" Ron couldn't believe I didn't know what it meant. He said, "Didn't you see these in other mailrooms you've been in?" I said, "I've never been in a mailroom." He says, "Okay. This is a dispatch slip. This means I want you to go to UNI. Universal Studios. Bungalow I. Office II. Pick up a script and bring it back." I thought to myself, *I never would have been able to figure that out.* He said, "You got it?" I said, "I got it, but one more thing . . . where's Universal Studios?" Ron just started to laugh, and that's how my relationship with Ron Meyer began.

Yvette Mimieux at the time was an extremely beautiful actress, beautiful—I mean, truly one of the prettiest women out there. She lived on Stone Canyon in Bel Air. I had to deliver a script for her once. I went to her house and I rang the front doorbell and nobody answered. I thought, *Wow, what do I do now with the package if nobody answers?* So I saw that around the side there was a stone wall covered with ivy with a gate. I went over to it and popped my head over, and saw Yvette Mimieux lying naked by the pool. I said to myself, *Holy shit. That's Yvette Mimieux and she doesn't have any clothes on. Man, is she unbelievably beautiful.* So I'm standing at the gate and I can't help kind of peering—or leering, I guess you would say—at her. Then all of a sudden, a truck comes up and it's a Japanese grocer with fresh fruit. I could see Yvette Mimieux get up and wrap a towel around her and she's walking toward the gate. I froze. I thought, *Oh no, I'm going to be caught looking at her and I don't know what to do.* She comes and opens the gate and I'm standing right there. She says to me, "Why were you waiting? Why didn't you just come in?" My tongue was tied because now she knows I was there looking at her. I had no idea what to do. Then she says, "Can I buy you a peach? This gentleman sells the freshest peaches in California." I said, "Certainly, I'd love one." So there we were, Yvette Mimieux and I sitting together eating peaches.

MARC GRABOFF:

After the mailroom, I did a stint as an assistant to Ron Meyer, who in my opinion was—even back then—the glue that held the place together. I turned out to be a bad assistant, but they liked me and thought I was smart, so Ron and Bill Haber said to me one day, "We're going to put you in a cubicle and you're going to learn to be an agent on your own. Sink or swim," and I said, "Okay." I started by doing things no one else wanted, like booking clients on the *Tonight Show* and the *Merv Griffin Show*, along with some game shows. They were the dribs and drabs of the business. Then I was peddling spec scripts for *Laverne and Shirley* to execs at Paramount. I felt like I was a Fuller Brush man, and I realized I wasn't the back-slapper sales type, and agenting wasn't for me. I like the business affairs side, when everyone's already at the table.

MICHAEL OVITZ:

As part of our effort to sign more clients, we went out and befriended every major lawyer in town because that was where we thought we would get new business from.

DUSTIN HOFFMAN, Actor:

I really didn't have an agent until Michael; I just had a lawyer, Bert Fields. Before *The Graduate*, my phone never rang, and then I felt whenever I had gotten a job, it was because of what I had done on my own. I never got much help from them, so I didn't want one. But then one day Bert said to me, "I really don't know every-thing that's going on. I think you need an agent." He mentioned he knew this young guy who had just started his own agency, and that I should meet him. That was Michael. My wife and I met with Michael and his wife, and we all really got along.

I had just done back-to-back pictures, which was rare for me— *Marathon Man* and *All the President's Men*—and the first picture I did with Michael was I believe *Kramer vs. Kramer*.

BARRY HIRSCH, Attorney:

When Michael was at William Morris, we wound up having a very difficult time with each other over this one deal. He was representing the Krofft brothers on a television show, and I was representing a writer-producer. But after he left the Morris office, he called me up and said, "Why don't we get together and have lunch."

MICHAEL OVITZ:

On the board downstairs at 1888, I saw the name of the law firm Armstrong & Hendler. We were on the fourteenth floor—which by the way was really thirteen, which was my lucky number—and they were on eighteen and I went up and introduced myself to Gary Hendler and discovered that he had taken with him almost every major movie star in the business from his former firm Irell & Manella, which specialized in taxes.

I spent a year cultivating a relationship with Gary, taking him to lunches, to dinners, sending him gifts. I remember I found out he loved chocolate—I sent a barrel of Hershey's Kisses, anything I could do to ingratiate us to him. He was very smart, a Harvard graduate, in his thirties when I met him, but he had every movie star you could think of—Redford, Streisand, Richard Dreyfuss, Sydney Pollack, and Sean Connery.

Gary Hendler's client list would prove to be one of the most important vehicles for upgrading CAA's talent list over the coming decade.

ROBB ROTHMAN, Agent:

When I started at CAA in the mailroom, Michael Ovitz had Sean Connery, who just wanted to play golf, and Robert Towne—those were his only two real feature clients. He literally turned Rob Reiner into a feature director, he turned Penny Marshall into a feature director, and he was signing people left and right. No one has ever had the ascent that he had as an agent. He was the most driven guy. What you learned in TV packaging—putting the elements together and representing the production—he brought to features, and he didn't do it by coming in and assuming the mantle at a big agency; he did it by bringing in all these clients.

MICHAEL OVITZ:

If they were writers, we would get material or source ideas and put them with people. If they were actors, actresses, we'd cover everything that was available for them, and they'd have five people out there working for them. That's how we worked in the first three years—we would walk the extra mile in a business that pretty much wasn't doing that.

RON MEYER:

I loved signing clients and found that I was good at it. I was never great at discovering talent but knew how to take someone who had a good foundation to the next level.

Once we signed someone, we rarely lost them. We always had a very low attrition rate. We were focused, caring, and couldn't have worked harder. If a client was unhappy, we took great pains to show them how much they mattered, and to do everything we could to make them feel cared about. It wasn't difficult, because we did genuinely care. Sometimes clients were unrealistic about what their expectations were; sometimes we were not working as hard as we should for them. In those cases, you had to talk with them and show them you could do a better job. I represented Burgess Meredith and Talia Shire, and found out on *Rocky* the studio was about to go with Lee Strasberg for the role of Mickey and Carrie Snodgress for the role of Adrian. I convinced the producers to read Burgess and Talia. Obviously they each got the job. A funny postscript on this—I always thought Burgess Meredith would be indebted and loyal to me forever for the great job I did for him; instead, shortly after the success of *Rocky*, he fired me because Laurence Olivier was getting roles he thought he should be getting. Call me crazy, but I just didn't see him as the villain in *Marathon Man*. Olivier was tall and statuesque; Burgess was small and gnomish.

ELLIOT WEBB, Agent:

The CAA agents traveled in a pack, and they made great presentations. They were a new breed, and a lot of people in Hollywood wanted to help them because they were tired of William Morris and its monopoly.

BARRY HIRSCH:

I thought it was exciting that those guys would be that entrepreneurial, leaving such an old, established agency. I was entrepreneurial. I went out on my own right out of law school. So the idea of them being willing to take such a huge risk with their careers made them like kindred spirits.

MICHAEL OVITZ:

We used to go to screenings and all go together and walk in together. I know this may sound crazy stupid, but it showed a solidity and it showed a different kind of thought process, that we were a group that worked together, that we weren't just one agent with one client. That was our pitch.

BARRY HIRSCH:

Michael started off our professional relationship by referring me to Barry Levinson, who was then on a writing team doing work for Mel Brooks. It was his way of saying, "Hey, we can do business together. I'll send you clients, and when you get the opportunity, you can refer your clients to me."

MICHAEL OVITZ:

In the course of getting friendly with Gary Hendler, it became very clear to me that Barry Hirsch was very unhappy at his firm. He kept complaining that there were problems in the partnership and that he couldn't get anything done. It was a Friday afternoon and he had gone on and on and on about it, and I happened to leave him and go to dinner with Gary Hendler and his wife. And Gary complained how unhappy he was because he didn't have enough manpower. He didn't have a real equal partner because his partner was not an expert in the entertainment industry, he was just a guy who handled corporate work. So I pitched Barry Hirsch to him, and he responded well immediately. I then called Barry Hirsch and I pitched him Gary Hendler. I arranged for them to have a breakfast Saturday morning at a deli and I went and introduced them, then I left. They talked for three hours, shook hands, and agreed to merge. In two weeks, they put together a firm called Armstrong, Hendler, & Hirsch and overnight basically controlled the legal side of the entertainment business. CAA ended up having two hundred clients with them.

Ray Kurtzman, formerly of William Morris, joined CAA in January 1978 as head of all business affairs and operations. Fred Specktor and Bruce Vinokour, both also formerly of Morris, became agents and executives in the motion picture and television departments, respectively, at CAA in May of 1978. Finally, Steven Roth (of the Ziegler, Diskant & Roth Agency) joined CAA as a partner and an executive in the firm's motion picture division on July 26, 1978.

FRED SPECKTOR, Agent:

I was at William Morris and went to a wedding, where I wound up sitting with Mike, Bill, Ronnie, Rowland, and Mike Rosenfeld. It was the luckiest day of my life. They had left William Morris a couple years before. I looked around the room—there were a lot of William Morris guys there—and everybody from there was unhappy, but everybody who had left there was really happy. I thought to myself, *I better get out of there,* so I called Mike Rosenfeld. He had been my buddy when we worked there together and was actually the executor of my estate.

The guys had already hired Marty Baum, which I thought was a great move for the agency. He was going to give them a face in the motion picture business and represented great clients. Pretty soon after I got to CAA we signed Sean Connery, Sydney Pollack, Robert Redford, and Paul Newman. They were all giants.

RICK KURTZMAN, Agent:

My dad, Ray, grew up during the Depression and was a fairly risk-averse guy, so it was really remarkable that he was willing to give up a sure thing, right? Here he was at William Morris, an established company, getting a real paycheck, with three kids—two kids in college and one still in elementary school—and he gave it all up to go play in the new frontier with those guys. He had shared space with Michael Ovitz at William Morris and they became friendly, and there came a point when he started to feel like he was just a cog in the wheel at William Morris, wasn't enjoying it there anymore, and really liked the new philosophy the guys had at CAA.

There were less than a dozen agents when my dad went over there, and he had to wear many hats. They didn't have enough clients for him just to be a business affairs guy, so he became the guy who was taking care of things in the office while those guys were out signing people. As a lawyer, he was trying to see what problems might occur and implement ways to avoid them. Even though Mike and Ron wanted the final say on most things, my dad really spent the bulk of his time building the infrastructure of the agency. He understood what Mike's agenda was, but he also knew he was going to be the one to create what was necessary for that to happen.

BRUCE VINOKOUR, Agent:

It was October of '78 when I arrived, and CAA was very small—under twenty people. I had been in business affairs at William Morris and wanted to be an agent, but they wouldn't make me one. I was single, living in a small apartment in Westwood, so I left. I got a call from a fellow named Ray Kurtzman, and he said, "You sound outta breath," and I said, "Yeah. I just finished running on the beach." He said, "How'd you like to stop running on the beach and come over here to Creative Artists Agency?" I said, "I don't really know too much about Creative Artists Agency." I remember Ray saying then, "It's a mom-and-pop shop, but I think it's going to explode, and I need someone to work on the television business affairs side." I said, "But, Ray, I really want to be an agent." He said, "Just give me a year. These guys are incredible agents, but they really need help on the deal-making side." I said, "Okay." So I met this fellow named Mike Ovitz and ultimately was hired.

MIKE MENCHEL:

I was the only guy in the mailroom for a while, so I used to work all hours of the night, all hours of the morning. A couple times I used to sleep on Ron Meyer's couch because I just couldn't get home fast enough. One night I was delivering packages and my last package was a script from Mike Ovitz to Sydney Pollack. Sydney Pollack lived out in Pacific Palisades and it was probably 1:00 or 1:30 in the morning when I got to his house, and I'm thinking, *What can I do?* You can't knock on the door at 1:00 or 1:30 in the morning. So I thought I'd leave it in the mailbox. But he didn't have a mailbox; he just had a slot in his house and it was a script; it didn't fit in there. So I thought, *You know what? I'll just prop it up between the screen door and the front door.* So I opened the screen door and all of a sudden the alarm went off. It went crazy. Lights were on and flashing all over the place. There were even sirens. I was freaking out, absolutely freaking out, and the front door opened and a guy looked at me and said, "Who are you?!" I said, "I'm Mike Menchel delivering a package to Mr. Sydney Pollack from CAA." He said, "At 1:30 in the morning?!" I said, "Sir, at any time." He said, "Okay. Thanks." So I said, "Are you Mr. Pollack?" He said, "Who else would be opening the front fucking door at 1:30 in the morning?"

BOB GOLDMAN, CAA Chief Financial Officer:

I joined CAA in 1978 with a starting salary of $30,000. I had come from a business management firm that was handling the agency's financial affairs, and thought I would be there for a couple years, make a few bucks, then take off and do my own investments. Michael Ovitz changed all that almost immediately. He gave me opportunities to do and accomplish more than I could imagine in my wildest dreams. I can tell you Ray Kurtzman felt the same way, but it was even more so with me, because I really wasn't that motivated, and Michael was an incredible motivator.

ROBB ROTHMAN:

I went to USC my first two years, and then when I wasn't going to go to graduate school, it didn't make sense to pay private school tuition. I said, "Okay, I can have fun my last two years." I went to the Harvard of Isla Vista: UC Santa Barbara.

I started at CAA in 1978 and was on Mike Rosenfeld Sr.'s desk. It was a little less than two years from the date I started until I was made an agent. Ovitz called me in and questioned me about a couple of things. He was asking about various clients that Mike oversaw, what they were doing, how much they were getting paid for jobs, just kind of testing me on those clients. It was easy to know that stuff; all the assistants would've known what I knew.

MICHAEL OVITZ:

Marty Baum insisted we hire Steve Roth, who also had great clients.

STEVE ROTH, Agent:

Before I got to CAA, I was with Evarts Ziegler, the most famous literary agent of all. That job, to work with Ziggy as he was called, had come down to me and my lifelong friend, Jeff Berg. Ziggy became a wonderful mentor of mine, and eventually I became a partner. We were called Ziegler, Diskant, and Roth.

With Ziggy I was basically a bookseller and a packager of books. I was very skilled at the art of packaging, which wasn't really big at that time. I sort of put together *Marathon Man* when I was very young, probably twenty-six.

I was most interested in buying Ziegler. Unfortunately, Ziegler didn't want to give up control and I figured I was putting up the money so I wanted control. I had been having these discussions with Ovitz. After the disappointment of not getting the Ziegler firm, I thought, *Well, maybe this is a really good idea.* I had a lot of very good movie clients, directors and authors, and I liked the guys, so we made a deal.

RON MEYER:

Steve Roth was a successful agent from a very prominent literary agency, representing an important group of writer and director clients. He wanted to come with us—and we wanted him—so he was treated as an equal partner with the understanding that we would spend one or two years together, and if everything was working well at the end of that, he would be made a full partner with all of us for the future. If not, we had the right to end the relationship.

STEVE ROTH:

I was a senior partner along with Meyer, Ovitz, and Haber. It was part of my deal. I wouldn't have done it in any other way.

MICHAEL OVITZ:

He was never made a partner. We had it look like he was made a partner, but it was a trial thing, like an escrow.

ADAM FIELDS:

Steve Roth came in and taught Michael so much. Steve was a wealthy kid from Beverly Hills and Mike was a frat guy from UCLA. Steve wore great, cool-looking suits, and had incredible clients. He put Jim Bridges into *Urban Cowboy,* Colin Higgins into *9 to 5* and *Best Little Whorehouse in Texas,* Phil Kaufman into *The Right Stuff,* and Howard Zieff into *Private Benjamin.* He really changed the role of directors or filmmakers being the stars that movies got packaged around.

I remember one day I was walking down the hall past his office and he came running out yelling, "I just got a million dollars for a director. There are no more rules. You can ask for whatever you want now."

STEVE ROTH:

I thought that Ovitz was very dishonest. I never found him to be intellectual. He didn't have a dapperness about him. He always seemed very uptight. He was good in a client signing meeting and he had a wonderful way of manipulating all of his partners around, but I just never found him to be that impressive, and still don't.

MICHAEL OVITZ:

A rich man's son who didn't like to work hard.

STEVE ROTH:

I was pretty headstrong. I brought in all those famous people like Bob Evans into our world, and let's just say everybody was doing too much of everything. Everybody was having too much fun—there were too many girls, and there was too much cocaine.

ADAM FIELDS:

Marty was putting together what was going to be the next *Pink Panther* movie and it was going to be the biggest deal in the history of Hollywood. He was getting Peter Sellers $3 million to do the picture; I don't think anyone had gotten more than a million other than Brando for *Apocalypse*. And he was getting Blake Edwards $3 million not to direct it, because they both co-owned it and they both hated each other. Marty also was representing the writer, Jim Moloney—who was Jay Moloney's dad—the director, and the two producers, one being Peter's wife. It was about a $9 million package. That was game changing for that agency. And every day, without exception, Peter would call, usually at five from either his home in Gstaad or Paris, and would want to talk to Marty for an hour and a half, which meant I couldn't go home. He was either quitting the business or quitting *Panther* and every day Marty had to talk him off the cliff, because so much was riding on the movie, not just for the agency in terms of money but also for the importance to United Artists.

Sometimes Peter would call up and imitate the voice of whoever he was working for, so he would say, "Hey, it's Walter Mirisch or Dan Rissner," and then he would bait Marty into a conversation about himself, Peter Sellers. Marty would rail about Peter, thinking he was talking to Walter or Dan; then Peter would call back twenty minutes later and say, "I hear you've been saying nasty things about me." Then Marty would slam me for not telling him it was Peter the first time, as if I would know when even he didn't know.

Peter was frickin crazy. Now he would probably be diagnosed as a bipolar schizophrenic, but back then he was just nuts. I had a little apartment in Hollywood and he would call me from Gstaad at 4:00 A.M. and ask me to drive by his wife's house to see what cars were in the driveway and write down the license plate numbers. And I had to do it.

Blake also lived in this tiny town, Gstaad. Both apparently drove big Rolls-Royces and always pretended they didn't see each other. There were only two good restaurants in Gstaad at the time, so I used to have to call in the morning to see if either had booked a reservation and then make another one for the other so they didn't run into each other.

RON MEYER:

The five of us made sure to meet every day and we talked about everything and did whatever we had to do to help each other. We stayed close with our agents and always knew what was going on with them. This meant, for instance, if important writer clients wrote an unattached script, rather than sell it directly to a studio, we would put it together with a director and in some cases an actor or an actress, then sell it at a premium. Although we didn't invent it, we did it very effectively and became known as a very strong packaging agency.

ARMY BERNSTEIN:

I had written a previous script that turned into *Thank God It's Friday,* and while I appreciated the success that it had, it didn't personally represent me. So I stayed home and I wrote a screenplay that would reflect more of who I was. People would say, "What are you writing?" and I would say, "Oh, just something personal." I didn't pitch it to anyone and wasn't being paid by anyone because I wanted the freedom and control to write exactly what I wanted. I called the script *One from the Heart*, and when I gave it to Mike, Ronnie, and Mike Rosenfeld, they read it and said, "Get ready, you're going to be rich on Monday. We're going to go out and have an auction with your script this coming weekend. Go home and we'll call you on Monday." I don't think they'd ever done that before.

That Monday, I got a call from the agency at 11:30. One of the partners' wives said, "Please come by after lunch." I thought to myself, "This is going to be either really good or really bad news." I got to the office at 2:30, walked in, and they were all there standing and smiling. They said, "We've sold *One from the Heart*, and it's one of the largest screenplay sales in history." And I said, "Really?" I didn't know anything about prices, but I was thinking maybe I got $35,000, or maybe even higher, like 75 or 80. Then they told me they sold my script for $300,000, which was a bigger number than I could even imagine. I wasn't sure whether to retire or go to Jamaica.

BILL HABER:

I only handled corporations. I wasn't allowed to handle actors. They couldn't put me in a room with an actor. I would say to Ronnie and Michael, "Why can't I handle actors?" And they would say, "You can't handle actors because here's what happens: you sit in a signing room with them, and within two minutes, you start tapping your fingers on the table." They said I was "too transparent." So I only handled companies, and the most important company we had, of course, was Aaron Spelling.

Aaron Spelling was one of the giants in the history of television and, even in the mid-1970s, was known as a creator of hits that could bring a network big ratings and revenues for years. In 1972, The Rookies *debuted and would be on ABC for five years; the popular* Starsky and Hutch *went on the air in 1975; and in 1976, Spelling hit a home run with* Family *and a grand slam with* Charlie's Angels. *He would become one of the most important clients in CAA history.*

MICHAEL OVITZ:

We got a call from Tony Thomopoulos at ABC that Aaron Spelling was unhappy with William Morris, so Ron and I went to see Aaron. Then we went to Bill and said, "Look, you have to do this," and he said, "No, I won't," because they had some kind of dispute when he was at William Morris.

BILL HABER:

At no time did I say I didn't want to do it or that we shouldn't do it. I only said, "I want to make sure I'm the person to do this properly." I wasn't sure that I was capable of having the patience that I thought it might take. I wasn't convinced that I had the temperament to properly represent him and his company. That's the truth of the matter.

We were very thankful that the people who ran ABC at the time made it possible for us to be involved with Aaron Spelling, and I didn't want to fail them or CAA. For reasons that anybody in television would recognize at that time, Aaron was a complex personality. And I had my own idiosyncratic behavior and personality, so it was a question of how we would mix.

Of course in retrospect, it's an interesting discussion because Aaron became one of my closest friends and I miss him every day. I was at his bedside when he died.

Just over three years after CAA's formation, the agency had racked up $30 million in prime-time shows and specials programming at all three television networks.

Long gone were the William Morris–authored theories that the five defectors would fail miserably—or that the Morris office would put them out of business. Nobody in town was thinking the agency would disappear, but at the same time, as the agency approached its fifth birthday, it wasn't in the top tier. William Morris and ICM both had more agents, clients, and revenues. No one at CAA had the pedigree of Stan Kamen at Morris or Sam Cohn at ICM, and although Baum's arrival sent a strong signal to the community that the agency was no longer content with solely the television business, the agency still had its nose pressed up against the movie business window.

Now Ovitz set his sights on publishing. Determined to compete with his rivals in virtually every arena, he took on ICM and William Morris even in the book world where CAA didn't have a traditional publishing department; the only writers it represented wrote scripts. ICM's book department was a continuation of MCA's highly regarded book department, and William Morris had a long list of established and successful authors. So when it came to bringing books to big and small screens, Ovitz decided he would solicit material from all of the other literary agencies—that is, the independents.

And why would these smaller book agents want to deal with CAA after years of dealing with the other guys? Because you couldn't ask William Morris or ICM to peddle rights without actually contacting William Morris or ICM, which meant those agents would be exposing their authors to their competitors. CAA in effect branded itself as a safe harbor. They just wanted to help those author-clients get their books made into TV shows and movies, not to snatch literary clients for themselves. Thus did CAA get into the book business—without getting into the book business.

MICHAEL OVITZ:

Mort Janklow was critical to us. I had read a profile of him in *New York* magazine—one of those five-page profiles, and it was a love letter to him. It talked about how brilliant he was and how his business was dominating the literary world. I called him and asked for a meeting and he said yes.

MORT JANKLOW, Agent:

It actually started back sometime in 1975. My secretary said, "There's a man on the phone named Michael Ovitz, from California, do you know him?" and I said no, so she said she'd get rid of him. But she came back a few minutes later and said, "He's an agent in Los Angeles and he'd very much like to talk to you." I'm not that hard to reach, so I picked up the phone. He said, "I will make this short. Five of us have left William Morris to set up our own shop. We're called Creative Artists Agency. Now I don't want to fool you, we're operating on bridge tables in empty space we've rented, with our wives manning the phones." And then he said, "I'm going to build the biggest agency the world has ever seen in ten years." That was his opening. So I said to myself, *Oh my God, another Hollywood type.* He said, "I'd like to come and see you, but only for a half hour." Then he said, "And I'm only coming to see you." I said, "Well, I'm flattered, come on in," and we made a date for the following week.

So he came in, walked into my office, pulled out a watch and put it on the desk in front of him, and pitched me for a half hour on what they could do for us. Basically, his idea was that even though we controlled a number of big writers at the time, and a lot of these books were being turned into films, we didn't know that ground as well as we knew the literary biz. I asked him, "What could you do for us? We've sold a number of big projects ourselves." He said, "If it's a huge project, it sells itself, but if it's just a good book, we can put you together with the right people and make more complete deals." I said, "Well, it was nice meeting with you, Michael. I've learned a little and we'll be in touch." He said, "This is what I thought would happen; I didn't expect much until you knew us better. How about this? Can I call you every Thursday at ten o'clock your time?" I said, "Sure," and thought I'd never hear from him again. The following Thursday, the phone rang at exactly ten o'clock and it was Mike Ovitz asking, "Got anything for me to talk about?" I said, "No, Michael," and he just said, "Okay, Mort, good-bye." The call was fifteen seconds. No wasted time.

MICHAEL OVITZ:

I went to see Mort in New York and said, "Look, we're going to change the way business is done and we want your books. We won't take your books and we won't charge you anything. We'll give you all of the commission; we just want to be able to put packages together with our clients." But he wouldn't do it. So I asked if I could call him once a week on Thursdays at 10:00 A.M. He probably figured, *What a bullshit artist,* but said fine. For fifty weeks every Thursday, at 10:00 A.M. Eastern, no matter where I was—you could set your clock by it—I called him.

MORT JANKLOW:

He'd call and say, "You know, we just signed Paul Newman. Do you have anything for us? Nope? Good-bye." This went on for months. Finally, I had a project, a new client, who'd never written a book before, called *Chiefs*. That author came to me over the transom, one of the few that did successfully, and his name was Stuart Woods.

I sold it immediately to a division of Mobil Oil, which at the time was in the television business, for a network multipart series. They couldn't get it on, couldn't lick the story, so finally after about nine months I took it back, and just at this point Mike calls, his twentieth call probably. I said, "I have something for you, but it's a wounded bird. Everybody has seen it before it came on the scene. I'd made a deal with the Mobil group to make it into a television series, and they bought it but they don't know what to do with it; they can't make it, so they've just turned around and given it back to me." He said, "Put it in the dispatch bag and get it to me right away."

MICHAEL OVITZ:

Finally, Mort said, "Okay, I'll give you a book." I gave it to several people in the office and then Bill said to me, "This book has been around and passed on." I said, "I think it has, too, but who cares." Bill said, "I agree. I'm going to try and put it together." And to his credit, Bill made *Chiefs* happen. When I called Mort to tell him the book was getting made as a miniseries and asked him how he wanted us to handle the deal, he shit a brick.

MORT JANKLOW:

He called within forty-eight hours and said, "Well, it's a done deal, it's gonna be on CBS." I said, "What'd you do?" and he said, "Well, we did what we always do in these situations: instead of going to the network or producers with the story, we packaged it first." He said, "Billy Dee Williams is going to be the black sheriff, and Charlton Heston is going to play the old white man. We took it to CBS and they were thrilled to buy it." I asked him, "How much did you get for it?" He told me a figure that was about three or four times as much as CBS could have bought it from me a few weeks before. Everybody was very happy.

MICHAEL OVITZ:

Mort's six three and has a hulking big voice. He's a lawyer and a very confident guy. He couldn't believe it. I said, "Yeah, Bill Haber got it together. I'm going to put you in touch with Bill." From that moment on, he started to send us everything.

MORT JANKLOW:

We never had a formal understanding or even an understanding at all of any kind, but whenever I had a property that I thought CAA could add to, I went to him. Pretty soon I met Ron and I met his other key guys—Bill Haber and Bruce Vinokour. They were great. We began to work together on a very frequent basis. At any given moment they had three or four of our properties there, and they did them very, very well. They made them a priority at the agency; they had nobody like me supplying them with material, and what they were getting was the best commercial material available.

MICHAEL OVITZ:

I hired a young girl named Cheryl Peterson and she was our book agent. But what we did that was interesting was all the books that came in galley form we would have printed and change the cover to our agency's red cover. I started flooding people in the movie business with them—two, three hundred copies of every book out to directors and actors and studio executives. I built a relationship with a guy named John Calley by sending him a book a week. Calley could speed-read—he could read a book in an hour and a half—that was one of his great gifts. So I would send him everything. He always respected that we had this flow of material.

MORT JANKLOW:

Mike may be overstating it when he says they wouldn't have been where they were without us, but you could say our contributions accelerated their development and gave them a stronger position in Hollywood. That was valuable for us because we saw that we could place our dramatic rights in the best possible way.

ADAM FIELDS:

Peter was in Paris filming a movie. He calls up one day and he's decided the producer was the greatest guy in the world, and Marty was thrilled and said, "Great." A few days later, Peter fires the guy and tells him to get off the set; Marty just said, "Whatever." A few days after that, at around five o'clock as usual, Peter calls again, railing, "This picture's terrible. I can't believe you put me in it. The director's a bum, he's probably your client"—which he was—and then he says, "You know what we need?" Marty asks, "No, Peter, what do we need?" "We need that producer. Why was I mad at him?" He said, "I don't know, Peter." "Well I'm not going to go back to work until he's here." Marty says, "No problem." He hangs up the phone and says to me, "Where's that producer?" I said, "I don't know. Wherever producers go when they're fired. He's probably in a hotel room with two hookers. I really have no idea." Marty tells me, "Find him, get him to Paris tomorrow, or you're fired." I'm thinking, *Oh my God, if I tell my dad I've been fired as an assistant, I'm fucked and will be taking the LSATs by Friday.* My dad couldn't believe I had taken a job as what he called a secretary, making only $160 a week after graduating with honors from Berkeley.

So first thing I do is call to see when the next flight to Paris is. There's a flight at seven-something, and it's now 6:20. I book the guy's seat, then I call his house, and I get the housekeeper. I speak fluent Spanish and I asked, "Where is he?" She goes, "Out to dinner." I ask where, but she doesn't know. And now I just start calling every fancy restaurant that I had been making reservations at for Marty during the nine months I'd worked for him—not that I'd been to any of them—and I actually find the guy at Chasen's. By this time, it's about ten to seven, and I get him on the phone and tell him, "Look, I've got good news and I've got bad news." He said, "What's the good news?" I said, "Peter Sellers wants you back on the set. You've got your job back!" He said, "What's the bad news?" I said, "If you haven't ordered dessert, don't! Pay the check. You've got to get in your car and drive to LAX right away." He said, "No, no, no—I've got to go home and pack a bag." I said, "You don't have time. You need to fucking go now." He said, "Don't curse at me! Who are you?" I said, "The guy who's going to get you your job back. You're wasting time and you need to go now." He said, "Why? When's the plane?" I said, "In twelve minutes." He goes, "I'll never make it." I said, "You will make it. Just stop talking." Now, there was a pay phone in the basement of our building at 1888 CPE and I had seen on *Dragnet* as a kid that supposedly if you use a pay phone and you put a handkerchief over it and you hang up within three minutes, they can't trace the call. So I called up the airline and called in a bomb scare to delay the plane and hung up. Then I went back upstairs, called the airline, and a recording says, "Flight to Paris delayed." Yes!!

Now I need to call Marty at home and tell him that I found the guy and he's on the way to Paris and that he needs to tell Peter he's coming, but I'm not exactly sure when, as the flight's been delayed—I'm not allowed to call Peter directly. Now I'm thinking, *Do I tell Marty what I did or do I not?* He'll either fire me or promote me.

That thirty seconds seemed like an eternity. Finally I just blurted out, "Look, Marty. I used the pay phone, put a handkerchief over the phone so they couldn't recognize my voice and hung up in three minutes so they can't trace the call, but I had to call in a bomb scare so I could delay the plane. It was the only way I could get him to Paris as it was the last flight." There was a pause, and just when I think he was going to yell at me for leaving my desk without permission, he goes, "All right, well, who called while you were gone?"

He never yelled at me again after that for anything. If I said it was done, it was done and if I said it couldn't be done, it couldn't be done.

In 1979, the company's corporate papers filed with the State of California still had Rowland Perkins listed as president. He hadn't "served" in that function since day one of the agency. No one, particularly Ovitz, had paid much attention to the title for the first four years, but now, in 1979, as the company positioned itself for the new decade, everything was on the table.

MICHAEL OVITZ:

There were three ways to go through the entertainment business in the '60s through the '90s. One was to go for money; one was to go for power; and the other was to go for fun. I decided to go for all three. I wanted money, power, and fun.

RON MEYER:

A few years after we started the company, Mike and I had what we used to jokingly call "our walk in Central Park." We were in New York and went for a long walk and he told me, "I feel like I'm carrying most of the weight here; I've got the most important clients; and I'm the face of this company." And I have to say, at the time, that was all true.

MICHAEL OVITZ:

I remember that walk like it was yesterday. That conversation was me telling Ron that I was really concerned that I was going to get stuck not being able to make the kind of leveraged economics that I wanted to, but he just kept going after Bill. He said he didn't like the way Bill behaved, he was upset Bill used to take off Thursdays to go to Paris every other week, and that he and I were the only ones working seven days a week.

For me, that conversation wasn't about me leaving or threatening to leave. It was how we calculated the money. It was the split.

RON MEYER:

Then Mike said, "I need to be the president of this company and have the ultimate say in its future." He also said he wanted to divide the shares of the company up differently, with him getting more shares than us. He made it clear that if that didn't happen, he would probably leave and do something on his own. I supported his position for two reasons: first, I felt that he was probably right in wanting to be in charge—we couldn't keep having everybody voting on everything—and second, we were all better together than we would be apart. For our future and the future of the company, I knew I had to make this happen.

So I went back to Bill, Mike, and Rowland.

ROWLAND PERKINS:

Ronnie did first talk to me about giving up some of my shares. Ronnie said he, Bill, and Mike Rosenfeld were going to as well. I said, "I want to talk to Michael about it directly." Michael told me he needed the extra shares so he could give them to important incoming agents, and I remember he mentioned Rick Nicita among others. Then I talked to Ronnie again. I certainly wasn't going to stand in the way of our expanding the business, so I said yes.

MICHAEL OVITZ:

I never discussed changing equity in the agency with anyone but Ron, and I certainly never told anyone I wanted more shares so we could give them to potential new partners. From the beginning, all of us were in agreement that the actual ownership of CAA would be only with the five of us. All these years, I have believed Rowland gave back some of his shares because he realized his contributions weren't at the same level as the other partners and that he felt fortunate to stay on for the ride.

RON MEYER:

They were surprised, but I told them, "At this time in our lives, I believe we can make more money being all together than splitting up, and I personally would rather make more money with less shares than less money with more shares." For better or worse, I convinced them.

And so it came to be that Mike was running the company, I

became the second guy, and Bill, Rowland, Marty, and Mike Rosenfeld became our partners.

ROWLAND PERKINS:

It wasn't long before I realized those shares of mine that I had given Ovitz weren't going to anyone but Michael Ovitz, and it made me really mad. Someone suggested I sue him, but I wasn't going to do anything that would divide us all. That wouldn't have been good for our agency. There was just nothing I could do about it.

BILL HABER:

This past November marked my fiftieth anniversary in the entertainment business, and if there was one thing that I could do differently over all those years, it would be regarding the decision to break up the parity of the founding partners' financial relationship. We made a professional mistake. I can't speak for Ron Meyer, but I regret the decision. If I had to do it again, I would have let Michael leave—which, by the way, I don't think he ever would have done. And if he had left, we would have still had a company, maybe just not the same company. But who cares about that? Agreeing to give to Michael some of my own shares is the only professional regret I have in my life.

DAVID GEFFEN:

They started out as equal partners, and Mike kept threatening Bill and Ron that he had to get more than them or he was going to leave. And they wanted and needed and knew how important Mike was, so they allowed themselves to get squeezed—and resented it always. As anybody would, by the way.

Michael Ovitz became president of Creative Artists Agency on August 11, 1979, with hundreds of ideas swirling around in his head, and scores of big plans for CAA and its clients in the new decade to come. Of all those goals and dreams, Ovitz considered two of them to be inalterable. First, he wanted CAA to "own" the

1980s, to become the most important talent agency in the world—and stay that way. Next, adhering to the notion that when the play is over, the actors should leave the stage, Ovitz saw the time coming when almighty MCA boss Lew Wasserman would be exiting stage right; thus Ovitz's second wish was for himself: he wanted to replace Wasserman as the most powerful person in Hollywood.

2

New York-London-Rome: 1980–1985

Every strike brings me closer to the next home run.
—BABE RUTH

CAA, understandably, needed big-name actors to enhance its reputation and ramp up revenues. But the agency also needed success stories to show potential clients and studios that this new gang in town could create stars, and even superstars, just as the older, established agencies did. The search was on. As Haber, Rosenfeld, and Perkins strengthened the agency's television side, Ovitz sought to expand into comedy, hoping to make it a cornerstone of growth. For his part, Meyer went into the ring, almost literally, to chase down none other than Rocky Balboa.

BILL MURRAY, Actor:

Early in my career, I was working for a TV documentary company called TVTV and didn't have an agent. My manager at the time said, "There's this young guy who's an agent at ICM, maybe you could start with him, you know, someone small." So I went over there to meet him, and he introduced me to Jack Gilardi, who was married to Annette Funicello of the Mouseketeers. We sat there in Gilardi's office for a while, and then he stood up and said, "Well, okay, let us know when you get work." I was kind of amused by that.

Three days later, I got the *Saturday Night Live* job and completely forgot to call him back and say I got work. What a drag.

RON MEYER:

Marty had gotten us into the film business when he came over, and we all had made the decision that when the TV business was strong enough that it was generating serious revenues, Mike and I would focus entirely on the movie business, and that's what happened starting late in 1979. Most clients wanted to be in the film business, so we had to make that work. Our plan was Mike would sign writers and directors, and I was going to focus on talent.

SYLVESTER STALLONE, Actor:

It was around '80, and I went to Hawaii. I was walking down the beach, and from out behind a palm tree on the beach steps Ron Meyer. He was wearing an Aloha shirt. The only time I had ever met him was years before, probably '74, when I couldn't get a job, and he was at William Morris. I think I was going for the twelfth lead in *Dog Day Afternoon*. I was probably up for the part of the dog. I hadn't seen him since.

Anyway, he steps out from behind the palm tree, and I go, "Yeah?" and he goes "Hey, Sly, it's Ron," and I said, "Funny seeing you behind the tree here." Ron said, "Yeah, I guess so." Turned out, unbeknownst to me, there was a friend of the family and a person who had worked with me several times as a casting agent who was also friends with Ron. I didn't realize the scene had been set for me.

So he says, "Can I talk to you?" and I go, "Okay." He was very engaging. Ron's voice had this certain tone to it—it's soothing, and it steps into a Svengali-like hypnotic tonal pattern. We started walking back and forth on the beach, for probably two and a half hours, until literally we had made our own tracks, like a tank had been going up and down the beach in front of the Kahala.

BILL MURRAY:

I had become a client of APA, and when they were negotiating my first deal, *Meatballs*, I was sort of telling my agent there what to do. I said, "You've got to ask them for points," and he said, "You don't have the right to ask for points," because people didn't get points back then unless they were some sort of star. But I told him, "You go and tell them I want points," and they gave them to me. Now, they were net points, but they sold *Meatballs* for more than seven times what it cost to make, so the net points became gross points instantly; that was kind of fun. After that, I got taken over by the guy who was the head of the company—a bizarre creature who made as many enemies as friends, and I wasn't happy. That's when this whole CAA thing happened.

MICHAEL OVITZ:

Ron met with Bill Murray but couldn't close it. He called me after the meeting and said, "I can't get this to work. He and I are on different wavelengths. You've got to come in and do your serious business thing with him."

LORNE MICHAELS:

Bernie [Brillstein] called me one day and said, "Mike Ovitz wants to meet Bill Murray." I said, "You know I never get involved in anybody's decision on which agent they should be with; that's not what I do, and I deal with a lot of different agents." Bernie said, "Well, can he come to the show?" So Ovitz called me and I said, "You're welcome to come to the show and just stand around if you like." Billy came to me for a note at some point during dress and Ovitz said, "Can I talk to you after the show?" And they did. Bernie's giant regret until his dying day was that he handed that power over to Ovitz.

MICHAEL OVITZ:

Bill Murray was a crucial part of the comedy strategy I was planning for the next several years, and he was a critical signing. What was also important was the handoff from Ron's efforts with Bill to me. That kind of cooperation never existed in the agency business before, where one agent couldn't close but didn't have an ego about it, so they called in someone else to come in and close. No one did that before in the agency business, ever. They'd keep it a secret because they didn't want to look weak. We had no ego about that shit. We just wanted the client. That is a key part of the DNA of CAA. No ego.

JIM WIATT, Agent:

I started at ICM in 1978, and at that time, the William Morris Agency and ICM were the two significant agencies in town. We had Lee Gabler running the television division at ICM, and Guy McElwaine was in charge of our movie division. Sue Mengers and Ed Limato were there as well, along with Tom Ross, who was running music. Tom and I went to high school together, and he was doing a great job building our music business there. ICM was a very powerful company in the agency world in movies, television, and music.

TOM POLLOCK, Attorney:

The William Morris Agency was in decline in large part because Ovitz had declared war on them.

Even though more than five years had passed since the group escaped from William Morris, the old behemoth was never far from their minds—not even when it came to office stationery. Late one night, as they were recalling the grandiose Morris letterhead with New York, Paris, Rome, and other global capitals imprinted at the top, they decided to take a swipe at the Morris old-timers by putting "New York-London-Rome" on the CAA letterhead, even though no such offices existed. Then they further reversed Morris style when it came to the company description. Morris had been a "Talent and Literary Agency"; but the CAA founders decided on "Literary and Talent Agency," a nod to the importance they placed on writers as the key foundation for their business. Maybe few people noticed this sly bit of subtlety, but the CAA gang did, and that's what mattered to them.

IVAN REITMAN, Director and Producer:

I started in Canada, did a bunch of independent films, the last of which was *Meatballs*. I represented myself, but I had a very good lawyer named Tom Pollock who helped with negotiations and drawing up contracts. I was operating as both a director and a producer, but was more known as a producer, and Tom suggested it might not be a bad idea for me to get an agent because my producing personality was not going to let people take me seriously as a director. Tom said this guy Ovitz had set up a new company, CAA, and I should meet him. Michael was my first agent.

TOM POLLOCK:

Ivan was my client; I had represented him on his *Animal House* deal and sold *Meatballs* for him. He was the hottest guy in town and one of the great things I did for Mike Ovitz was give him Ivan as a client.

MICHAEL OVITZ:

I signed Ivan Reitman right as *Meatballs* was getting done. I went out and tried to get every comedy person alive. I signed Dan Aykroyd, John Belushi, Albert Brooks, and many others, and for the next two years, all we did was put comedies together. Here's the killer: Everyone scoffed at us. We got bad press. Sue Mengers laughed at us. She didn't want any of these people. Old-fashioned and arrogant movie businesspeople were saying movies like *Meatballs* and *Caddyshack* would fail, and that movies with *Saturday Night Live* people in them wouldn't work because, as they said, "Why would people pay to see things they could see for free?!" There was even an article calling us idiots.

I'll tell you when people all of a sudden woke up: They woke up on *Stripes*.

IVAN REITMAN:

Stripes was the first deal I remember that Michael conducted for me. *Meatballs* wound up at Paramount in part due to Jeff Katzenberg, and it turned out to be their biggest hit of that particular summer. So Michael Eisner called me in by myself to have a meeting about my future, and the first thing he said to me was "So what do you want to do over the next five years?" I said, "What do you mean—as a director?" He said, "Yeah, how many movies do you want to direct over the next five years?" I said, "I think, three." I came up with the number arbitrarily. He said, "Okay, you got it." I said, "What do you mean?" He said, "We're gonna put up the money, you'll have three movies to direct, and do you want to produce any that you're not directing?" I said, "Sure. I can probably produce more movies than I can direct, so let's say five," and he said, "You got those, too." "What do you mean, I got 'em? What does that mean?" He said, "We'll pay for them." I said, "Do you mean a put picture?" I was relatively knowledgeable about this stuff, and he was kind of surprised I used the word *put*, and he said, "Yeah." I said, "At what price?" He said, "Well, on the directing"—and I'm not sure these were the exact numbers but they're close—"how about any $7 million budgeted movie you want to direct, you can, up to three over a five-year period, since we don't know who is directing, and we trust you as a producer, let's make it a lower number, at five." At this point, the most expensive I had ever made was *Animal House*, which was $3 million, and *Meatballs*, which was only $1.5 million, and I said, "Well, seven and five, that sounds pretty good." I said, "I'm up for that." We shook hands; I left his office and called Mike, who was probably my agent by this point for maybe a month, and I said, "Mike, I don't know what just happened, but Eisner asked to meet with me," and I relayed the whole story to him, and he said, "Wow. Well, let me see if this is real." He apparently called up Eisner, his good friend, and a couple of days later Ovitz says to me, "I'm not sure your deal is exactly what you think it is. They'll make one and then they will see, so it's a development deal." I said, "He couldn't have been more clear," and he said, "Well, Eisner has a tendency to say things and then he goes back on them. You should meet Frank Price." By that point I had already thought of doing *Stripes*; in fact I had pitched it to Katzenberg at the premiere of *Meatballs* in Toronto. I basically told him the picture I want to do next is *Cheech & Chong Join the Army*; that was sort of the one-liner. I met with Frank Price the next morning at his home, which Ovitz had set up, and Frank said, "What movie do you want to direct next?" and I said, "Well, this *Stripes* movie." He asked how much I thought it would cost, and I said, "I don't know, we haven't really written it, but let's say $10 million," and he said, "Okay, you've got it." He said the same thing

Eisner did and the deal got made immediately. It was a good deal; as a director it was the first time I got gross, 5 percent. Over the years, I became very good friends with both Eisner and Ovitz, and I asked Eisner, "What the hell happened?" and he said, "It's the deal I regret the most," and confessed he did in fact make that deal, but then later that day he bumped into Barry Diller, who at that time was his boss, and Diller pooh-poohed the deal, saying, "He's a young guy; you don't have to give him that fancy a deal, just make a movie with him." But I wasn't going back to Paramount, because once they'd gone back on the deal they'd promised, I was not interested any longer.

I've never asked Diller his side of this story, but Ovitz sort of backed the Eisner version of this. I've never known whether this was a complicated play by Ovitz to get me in fact to Columbia, because for some reason Mike was doing a lot of deals with Frank Price at that moment.

ROSALIE SWEDLIN, Agent:

There was a confluence of factors that really helped CAA catapult to the upper echelons of the agency business so quickly. Perhaps most important was that many of the people running the motion picture studios were people who had come from the television world just as the five founding partners of CAA had done. Frank Price had been at Universal Television and he was now running Columbia Pictures. Bob Daly had come from CBS and was now running Warner Bros. And Michael Eisner and Barry Diller had come from ABC and they were now running Paramount. So the five founders of CAA wound up having stronger relationships in many instances with this new crop of feature executives than agents who had been working in the feature business for much, much longer. It was an enormous plus. As a new agent, I was given several studios to cover, one of which was Columbia Pictures, and because of the close relationship between CAA and Frank Price, we did a huge amount of business with Columbia and I had a lot of success (and fun) covering that studio.

MICHAEL OVITZ:

We all vacationed together—we vacationed with the Eisners four times a year, we vacationed with the Meyers four times a year. They were short vacations. We didn't take long vacations, but we went to Europe with them, and would go away on Washington's birthday together.

FRANK PRICE, Executive:

I had a dysfunctional studio with many financial problems; I couldn't commit more than six months out to anything because I didn't have the money. The stock had been at three dollars a share. But when I arrived, coming from television, I was the new kid on the block for motion pictures, so when I would call William Morris, even though I knew Stan Kamen, he had ten other relationships that came before me. I knew I didn't have a chance with him. The same thing applied with ICM. There was Sue and Guy and they looked at me as the television guy. I had to change the game somehow.

That's what Mike and CAA represented. I could be first with them.

JOE ESZTERHAS, Writer:

When I started, I was a *Rolling Stone* writer and wasn't making much money. I had two little kids, and the way that I first learned about agents actually was an agent in L.A. who was working for Freddie Fields liked some of my *Rolling Stone* pieces. Then Marvin Lassiter read my book *Charlie Simpson's Apocalypse*, which was one of the books that was nominated for the National Book Award. Marvin asked me, "Have you ever thought about writing a script? Because I think your writing is very cinematic." And I really hadn't. As I was growing up I wanted to write the Great American Novel, but I always loved the movies. My dad took me to Fellini movies and many others when I was growing up. So I was broke, bartending, and writing on the side, and here comes this thing out of the sky. And Marvin says to me, "Think about something that you might want to write as a movie."

I wound up doing six months of research on an idea and wrote a script. Norman Jewison read it and told me, "Well, I don't know what the fuck this is; this is not an outline and I don't know if it's fiction or nonfiction, but there's something here." So Norman got attached, and he was really something. He liked me and I liked him very much. He was a very feisty man. He gave me an absolute master class in filmmaking. He took me into all of his meetings, and he had a house in Malibu where I would sometimes stay with him. I saw him one morning walking out on the beach, and I said, "What are you doing out here?" and he said, "I'm looking at the sea, because then I don't have to turn my head around and look at all of those fuckers back there."

Norman and Marvin told me I needed an agent, because if they were really good and they really cared about you, then they could really help you. I was at ICM at the beginning with Bob Bookman. I liked Bob very much, and he was smart and well read. When he left to do some studio gig, I said, "What am I going to do now?" and he said, "I'll think about it," and he came back to me and he said, "You should meet Guy McElwaine. He's one of the premier agents in town, he's got a big reputation, and he represents some of the biggest stars." I said, "What writers does he represent?" and Bob said, "Well, that's the problem, he's never represented a writer," and I said, "Oh, well." But I met him anyway. We had a bumpy beginning—I waited for an hour and a half—but we liked each other right away, and he became my big brother, my rabbi, and we became very, very close. By this time, I'd had a lot of movies made, and I was becoming a hot Hollywood property, because a lot of people had read my scripts, and I was getting a lot of offers.

ROBERT KAMEN, Writer:

I sold my first script to Warner Bros., and because it became attached to an Academy Award–winning actor in the form of

Richard Dreyfuss, it got a little bit of buzz. As the new hot young writer in town, I got passed around to various people at studios, including Jeffrey Katzenberg, who was a junior VP at Paramount. We hit it off, and he said to me, "What do you want out of this business?" I told him, "I'd like to be a major writer." He said, "You can't be a major writer unless you have an agent," and he sets up five appointments for me. The first one is with Michael Ovitz and Steve Roth at CAA. I tell them this idea I have, and Michael Ovitz gets up and leaves the room. I said to myself, *That is pretty fucking rude.* Then he comes back after a few minutes and says, "Okay, you in a room with Jane Fonda and Bruce Gilbert." Now Jane Fonda had just finished *China Syndrome* and was a big deal, and Bruce was her producer. I said, "Look. I don't care if you lie for me; I just don't want you to lie *to* me." At that, Michael Ovitz gets up and as he's walking to the door, delivers one of the classic lines of all time. He says, "I never lie," and he walks out.

I went back to my hotel, and told my best friend Erwin Stoff, who is now one of the principals of 3 Arts Entertainment, "If this fucking guy is lying to me, if I show up tomorrow at 10:00 A.M. and Jane Fonda's not in that room, I'm going to knock his fucking teeth out." I showed up the next morning at 10:00 A.M. and there's Steve Roth, there's Mike Ovitz, and there's fucking Jane Fonda and Bruce Gilbert. She looks at me and says, "I commit." Then I look at Ovitz and say, "You walk on water, right?"

Michael and Steve took me to five studios, and the last meeting was with Frank Price at his magnificent home that Dinah Shore used to live in. It was Rosh Hashanah eve, but Frank is the quintessential goy; he's descended from Aaron Burr, for crissakes. I tell him the story and he says to Michael, "You're not leaving here until you tell me I have the package." Michael says, "Yes. You have the package. Jane will do the movie with you." Little did I know that Mike and Frank were in collusion. So Mike drives me right from Frank's house to the airport and says, "Talk to nobody. I will call you." Then he zooms off in his Jaguar with the CAA license plate. I go home to Colorado with my head spinning.

Four days later, I get a call at 8:30 in the morning from my book agent, Ginger Barber, in New York. I had just sold a novel to Simon & Schuster the same day I had sold that first screenplay. Ginger says, "What's *My Brother's Keeper*?" I really had told nobody about this. So I asked, "Why?" She says, "You're on the front page of the *New York Times*." I said, "What?!" Then she reads me an article about the Hollywood dream but really it's an article about Mike Ovitz and Frank Price and the headline is UNKNOWN SCREEN-WRITER HITS IT BIG. The article said Mike Ovitz sold the screenplay for $350,000 and three gross points. Michael had never told me this. I called him up and first he said, "How did you find out?" I said, "I have a book agent in New York." He said, "What?! You didn't sell the book rights, did you?!" I later found out this was his first big movie package; I didn't even know he was a television agent.

The script never got made, but I formed a relationship with Frank Price, who became my mentor and rabbi. Shortly after that, however, I wrote a movie he did make called *The Karate Kid*.

FRANK PRICE:

Mike and I became friends and were very supportive of each other. I know at one point he called to tell me he was about to lose Sean Connery, and he needed to find him a job. I had a picture that was trying to be put together called *Wrong Is Right*, with a very good director, Richard Brooks, so I approved casting Sean in that. It was a decision I might have made anyway because I knew that I would be wanting Sean Connery at some point in the future, but I really made it because it could help him hold on to to his client. It was in my interest to help build the agency.

STEVE ROTH:

Urban Cowboy was iconic, and unique in so many ways. I read Aaron Latham's piece in *Esquire* and used it to sell a package to Diller and Eisner at Paramount. We got a go movie and there wasn't even a script! We had Irving Azoff, James Bridges, and Bob

Evans attached. I was also able to separate the music part of it because Paramount didn't have its own record label. That record album became its own huge profit center, and as a result, changed the business of packaging. CAA had a piece of the movie and the album, and both did really, really well.

SHERRY LANSING:

The CAA agents were partners. I never felt that they were not on my side, even if I said no, as long as I said no honestly. There was a script called *Neighbors,* which I didn't think was funny. I was newly installed at Fox and put it in turnaround. Months went by. Then one morning I got a call from Mike Ovitz, who said, "Look, I don't want you to be embarrassed but we've just attached Belushi and Aykroyd to *Neighbors.*" I remember getting sick to my stomach, because those two guys were the hottest things around. I was thinking, *Oh my God. This is what a studio executive fears more than anything, that you put something in turnaround and then it becomes the biggest hit.* I was just nauseous. But I said to him, "Thank you for telling me." I thought it was nice that he told me ahead of time so I could prepare myself.

For a year I lived in dread and fear of how that movie was going to turn out, and I was the first person in line to see it. I still didn't think it was funny—neither did many others, as it turned out. I was lucky. But they clearly put that package together.

BARRY HIRSCH:

To Michael's credit, he was the first agent, at least that I was aware of, that embraced lawyers insofar as being part of the original dealmaking process. I think historically lawyers, especially with agents at the William Morris office and a couple of the other agencies at the time, were looked upon as people who caught paper and went over the paper. Most agents trained in those days were really trained to go over contracts. Michael realized that by getting the lawyer involved in the beginning, he could accomplish several things: One, he would nourish the relationship with the lawyer.

Two, he realized that a lawyer might make the deal even better, which would then increase his commission. Three, having the lawyer involved protected him against the lawyer telling the client, "Why did Michael do this when I could have done better than that?" And finally, if the lawyer was involved early on, he wouldn't have to waste his time being involved in secondary negotiable points as well as boilerplate points, which meant he could jump off and move on to do another deal. To my knowledge, he was the first contemporary agent that embraced the lawyer like that.

Michael would call about our clients coming to CAA all the time, and I would tell him very clearly that if that client was someone who was referred to me by another agent outside of CAA, I would not get in the way of that client's choices. Whatever big client wasn't with CAA became a white whale for Michael. He tried to get an A-list actor many, many times, but someone else referred him to me, and I wouldn't violate that relationship. I felt my first allegiance was to the client referral source, and unless the referral source was doing just a terrible job, I wouldn't interfere. But all other things being equal, I referred a lot of clients to CAA.

NORMAN LEAR:

In the late '70s and early '80s CAA was certainly growing and becoming more of a presence in town. I didn't have an agent myself, and I have to say, I don't remember any of them ever asking me to become a client.

SUSAN BOROWITZ, Reader:

I worked for a year at CAA in the early '80s as a reader of scripts and books. There were probably less than fifty agents at the time, and the agency was just taking off. It was a weird place to be for someone who had no interest in being an agent. I'd get to be friendly with someone in the mailroom and then as soon as they were on track to becoming an agent, they'd develop a sort of *Stepford Wives* stare and disconnect. And Ovitz seemed to me at the time to be a sort of overlord. When I was hired, I was told CAA was a family. I just didn't realize it was the Corleone family.

DAVID GEFFEN:

When I was an independent, when I had Geffen Films, I tried to do business with CAA. I tried to have a good relationship with Mike Ovitz. Unfortunately, that never seemed to work out. He'd make lots of promises and never kept them. So I had a lot of problems with Mike Ovitz over the years. I helped him get his first very big star, which was Paul Newman. I would say without question that he was always grateful and never behaved as such.

ROBB ROTHMAN:

The big one was Paul Newman, who had not had an agent—he didn't trust agents—and Ovitz did the most incredible full-court press to sign him. Paul Newman was a car fanatic, and Ovitz went out and got a Ferrari. It was almost like he made himself into his best friend.

SUSAN BOROWITZ:

One day Ovitz called everyone into the conference room and told us how he and Paul (apparently Paul Newman—someone had to inform me since I had no clue) had been racing cars and how much he liked it. This led to an announcement that the entire company was to have a race car outing at Malibu Raceway, where people race go-karts that look like mini race cars on a circular track. It was to be on a Saturday or Friday night. He ended the meeting with a serious and ominous directive: There will be no spouses or significant others invited. "You will come and you will have fun." And then the meeting was adjourned. We all went, but we did not have fun, instead grousing about what a silly requirement the evening was and how we all wished we were with our significant others. I remember worrying a little that he might find out that I didn't have fun.

RAND HOLSTON:

For outsiders, it was intimidating to see these full-page red ad announcements in the trades heralding new clients like Newman, Sydney Pollack, and Redford.

MICHAEL OVITZ:

Redford and Newman were big reasons why CAA grew as it did, and our mantra or joke at the time was that all of CAA was always working on behalf of Butch Cassidy and the Sundance Kid. We were definitely signing major talent for motion pictures. On the television side, the huge turning point for us was *Shogun*. It was monumental for the agency.

TV programming in its first decade had a level of sophistication and artistry that would ironically decline as the medium started to grow. "Golden Age" fare included original dramas every week (most, in fact, "live from New York"); conscientious adaptations of theatrical and literary classics; "educational" programs like Omnibus, Wisdom, *and* Wide Wide World; *and high-minded documentaries like those produced by the legendary Edward R. Murrow and his "boys" at CBS News. Much of that sort of programming went away when the TV audience broadened and the networks no longer concentrated on affluent and educated urban markets, and when film and videotape edged "live" shows out, mainly for economic reasons.*

Even at its best, TV was considered a second-class medium when compared to motion pictures—everything was smaller, not just screen size. Parity with the movies in terms of production values arguably happened with the advent of the miniseries. Roots *established the genre with maximum national impact in 1977, entertaining millions and deepening a dialogue on race in America that still goes on.*

Perhaps even more technically ambitious as a production was NBC's Shogun, *another history-making miniseries that transported audiences to another time and place—in this case, a locale much more remote than eighteenth- and nineteenth-century America.* Shogun, *based on a bestselling 1975 novel by James Clavell, opened the television season for NBC in September of 1980 and was set in feudal Japan of the early sixteenth century, an unlikely setting for an American* big-budget TV drama. The miniseries further stupefied skeptics by breaking one "rule" of television after another—one of them being that you don't have scenes in untranslated foreign languages; much of the dialogue in Shogun was in Japanese with no English subtitles. The entire production was shot in Japan, a TV first, and it stretched out over nearly ten hours on five nights, replacing virtually the network's entire prime-time lineup.

Although every aspect of production was top-notch, there were no big movie stars in the cast to serve as ratings insurance. Sean Connery was offered the lead but declined. The part went to Richard Chamberlain, best known for his TV series Dr. Kildare but soon to be crowned "King of the Miniseries" for this and such later productions as The Thorn Birds.

NBC took ambitious risks right down the line, but the rewards were huge: some 70 million tuned in for the first installment, with the audience increasing through the week, putting Shogun firmly in the blockbuster class beside Roots, which drew 77 million viewers its first night. The final Nielsen tally was a 26.3 average for the week, the highest in NBC history. In addition, the cultural effect of Shogun was immense, sparking renewed interest in Japan and in the Far East generally, and even contributing, many believed, to the growing popularity of sushi in American restaurants. "Pillowing" became for a time the preferred euphemism for sex, just as it was in the film's dialogue.

As had happened in the earliest years of TV, when the medium itself was a coveted novelty, Americans had stayed home in droves to see the show, making it a bona fide national event that cut radically into, among other activities, moviegoing. Television had grown up. It was arguably a second-class citizen no more, and neither was CAA.

BRUCE VINOKOUR:

James Clavell had come to the agency through Marty Baum, but when he came over, Marty let Mike and Bill work with him and put the miniseries together. That sharing of responsibility and the ability to work with people you didn't sign directly was radically different, like breathing rarefied air. At CAA, people had their doors open, were sharing information, and everyone knew to check their ego at the door. In my opinion, this was almost revolutionary. I certainly had not seen anything like it at William Morris.

MICHAEL OVITZ:

Shogun was an uphill fight. There wasn't the giant interest in Asia back then that there is now, and the idea of putting a miniseries on TV with subtitles wasn't something people were jumping up and down to do. As a matter of fact, we had two networks pass. It was NBC that had the guts to do it.

As the agency's financial base became more secure and the partners became more confident, they went on a hiring frenzy that would have made George Steinbrenner proud. The CAA "family" was growing, and though it wasn't the biggest agency in town—William Morris and ICM were still larger and more influential—there was a burgeoning awareness that CAA was the place to be. Agents at other firms were increasingly intrigued, some looking into the possibility of signing on. For CAA, it was open season on both clients and agents at other companies, with the partners themselves openly aggressive about luring both.

RON MEYER:

We didn't grow out of a merger or an acquisition. We grew one agent at a time. In the early years, the people we hired were people we knew, who had some history with us, like Rick Nicita, Fred Specktor, Jack Rapke, and Ray Kurtzman. We knew these people from William Morris and felt confident they could assimilate into our new world. We also had people who came to us wanting to join who we either didn't know as well or believed they wouldn't fit in, so we passed on them. Eventually, Ray Kurtzman would screen everyone and recommend to us who we should meet.

RAND HOLSTON:

No one was hired without getting past Ray Kurtzman. Ray was the heart and soul of the company.

RICK KURTZMAN:

One of my father's many responsibilities was to oversee the training program and hire the trainees (Richard Lovett and David O'Connor among many others). He was the barrier of entry before a candidate could meet with Michael Ovitz, Ron Meyer, or Bill Haber. He never looked to be more than he was, as he appreciated his position within the structure of the company. Yet he became a large part of and helped to create the successful culture. He was a man of his word and brought tremendous integrity both internally and externally. He cared deeply. In my opinion, many people saw him as the moral compass of CAA.

BOB GOLDMAN:

The trainees and other key agents in the company had a very loyal relationship with Ray. No matter what anyone wanted to do, he would think in terms of its impact on the brand, and the CAA brand related to the core business of service. We didn't want that core business to ever be tarnished.

RICK KURTZMAN:

He didn't want to run the company. He knew his place, but he became a big part of the culture there, because he made sure things were fair and honest. He was a man of his word and expected the same of others. I think a lot of people saw him as the moral compass of the place. He was a really smart guy with the kind of depth that makes you want to do the right thing. He didn't take sides; he just cared deeply for the place.

MICHAEL OVITZ:

Ray Kurtzman was, simply put, the best business affairs person I have ever met.

PAULA WAGNER, Agent:

I didn't come at agenting the same way most people come at it. I was the oldest of three girls, and we lived in a little town outside of Youngstown, Ohio. My grandfather was voted the top metallurgist in the country at one point, and he cofounded a steel company. My father was a World War II prisoner of war and an air force captain, and graduated cum laude in economics at Princeton.

My uncle was chairman of the board at a local bank. My family was all business, business, business, but somehow I started acting at the Youngstown playhouse when I was thirteen and realized that was my destiny. I was the ingenue in all the plays being done there and got into the top drama school in the country, Carnegie Mellon. After I graduated, I had a lot of offers from regional theaters; instead, I went out to Hollywood and got an agent named Susan Smith, who was brilliant and driven. She got me a part in the miniseries *Loose Change* and I did a couple small parts in movies, but because I was classically trained, I didn't belong there and went back to New York. I played Maggie the Cat in *Cat on a Hot Tin Roof* a couple of times in regional theater. I was hired at Yale for a *Midsummer Night's Dream* to replace an actress who had left because she was discovered by Joe Papp. All I heard about was this woman was going to be the greatest star in the world. Her name was Meryl Streep.

Then I realized I had five hundred bucks in the bank, had come from a business family, and money became a motivator. I thought to myself, *My whole life has been focused on acting, and I want to be in control of my own destiny.*

So Susan Smith hired me to become an agent, and I loved it immediately. I was now working on behalf of other people, and I woke up in the morning feeling vital and alive. The actors depended on me, and that was absolutely liberating. Somebody at the start said, "You're too pretty to be an agent," but I brushed it off and became even more focused. My secret pact with myself was: *I'm going to make movie stars.*

MICHAEL OVITZ:

When we were recruiting agents, we had our own complete process for it. We'd go around the table at staff meetings and ask, "Have you met anybody who you are competing with that you really like?" That's how we got Rick Nicita, Rosalie Swedlin, and Paula Wagner. We cast the company like you would cast a movie.

PAULA WAGNER:

I was driving a Chevette from Rent-a-Wreck, had virtually no money, but was being as aggressive as possible. I would call heads of studios, and they were stunned I was calling them directly. One day I get a phone call saying, "Hello, Paula Wagner, I'm Fred Specktor from CAA. Would you like to meet for a drink? Your name has come up and we're looking for a lady agent."

I met Fred and Ray Kurtzman and was nervous as hell when I met Ronnie and then Mike. There were only twenty-five people working at CAA back then, but to me, it was the big time. They told me they didn't want any of my clients; they just wanted me. I was hired on October 1, 1980.

They didn't want me to sign clients, they just wanted me to cover opportunities and help Ronnie. He gave me Jane Curtin, Sally Struthers, Bonnie Franklin, John Herman, Judd Taylor, and other television people. There was a director, Jim Goldstone, who Bill Haber represented; coincidentally, I had a small part in his movie *The Gang That Couldn't Shoot Straight* with Robert De Niro. And I had auditioned for Paul Mazursky a million times, so my prior acting background was giving me access in a different way than other agents.

ROBB ROTHMAN:

It was really hard to sign clients if you were a junior agent because the senior guys wanted to be signing people. There was an expression called "Sign and Schmeckle," where the most senior agents signed someone and then turned them over to the most junior agent.

RICK NICITA, Agent:

At William Morris I was the anointed one, in an "only at William Morris" kind of way. At my last bonus meeting with Stan Kamen and Roger Davis, who was one of the top guys at William Morris, they said to me, "We have great things in mind for you. In ten years, you could be the next Stan Kamen." When I heard that timetable, I said, "Fuck that."

I grew up in Larchmont, New York. We were lower-middle class and lived in a small, lovely house that was joined onto other houses. We had one little bathroom for the four of us. My dad was an office manager for a local fuel oil company. It was a white-collar job, but it didn't pay much. It wasn't that my parents never used a credit card; they never had a credit card. I was not in any way poor, but I never thought about money.

There was always a sense I had about what I could do and what I couldn't do; what things I knew would suit me and what things wouldn't, and being an agent suited me perfectly—from day one in 1968.

PAULA WAGNER:

Rick knew me as an actress; I knew him as a hotshot William Morris agent. He represented all the young up-and-coming stars in New York while I was an actress in New York, but he didn't sign me. Rick was married to somebody else, I was married to a set designer—the world-famous Robin Wagner—and about a year or so after we got to CAA, we were both divorced and started seeing each other. Rick's line was "I didn't sign her, but I married her."

MICHAEL OVITZ:

Our strategy and philosophy were interlocked. In interviews we stressed two key issues: First, we all handled everything, we all constantly followed up with each other, and if you didn't want to share and operate like that, you shouldn't be working there. Second, we wanted everyone to know that our business wasn't just a business. It was also a lifestyle. We would be very clear in interviews that if you didn't want to work every day and enjoy it, you shouldn't work here.

It was all Japanese *nemawashi*: reverse concentric circles with top-down American management, which Ron and I provided.

IRVING AZOFF, Manager and Producer:

To me, Ovitz was this kind of preppy, jerky, weaselly TV guy. Ron was my friend, and Steve Roth was really the powerhouse agent for movie directors and writers at the time. His dad owned a company called World Oil—his brother was running it—so he came from a wealthy family. Steve was kind of a party boy, running around with Don Simpson and a bunch of those guys. I remember I would get calls from Ovitz when he couldn't find Roth on like the third day: "I can't find Steven, Phil Kaufman's called me four times, I need to know where he is, why won't you tell me where he is?"

STEVE ROTH:

It was my decision to leave. Part of the reason was Ovitz. I thought he was a bit of a nut, and really didn't want to be in business with him anymore. But even beyond that, my interest was in making great movies, and I came to believe he didn't have as much interest in the quality of the movie as he did just making money for the company. I would go from trying to put Jimmy Bridges together with Bob Redford to make *The Verdict*, to having to deal with *The Incredible Hulk* TV show. I felt that type of work bastardized to some degree the value in representing high-end clients. I'm not trying to be a snob about it, and who's to say if I'm even right.

MICHAEL OVITZ:

When Steve Roth first came over we made a deal that he had to fit in with everybody, but he didn't. It was a nightmare. He had problems that we had never seen before. He was great the first couple weeks, and then crapped out.

STEVE ROTH:

I got an offer from William Morris, after meeting with several of them in a series of clandestine meetings. I was very good friends with Bob Evans at the time, who was quite the power player in Hollywood. Through his close ties to Stan Kamen, it turned out they wanted me to become president of William Morris. They were going through a transition and let's just say they wanted to say good-bye to a certain few from Hillcrest. They wanted me to create an agency of really fine artists. Ultimately, I turned it down, because I realized I didn't want to be in the business anymore. I was burned out. I've been president of World Oil now for over two decades, and I'm really proud of what we've done here. I made the right decision.

JOE ESZTERHAS:

One day Guy told me he was leaving ICM, so I needed an agent. I had met Irwin Winkler and liked him very much, and Barry Hirsch had become my lawyer, and they referred me to CAA. I think the first CAA agent I had was Steve Roth. I liked him, we had fun, he had a great sense of life. He liked to hang out and get down. I think he liked me, and he really worked hard to get me gigs. Then he left one day, and my memory tells me that it was over some disagreement. I do remember in an effort to hold me there—because my connection was really to Steve—Ovitz set up this big meeting in a boardroom, brought a bunch of agents in there, and they put out their whole pitch. The meeting was over an hour. I was very poker-faced and I didn't really say much, and they thought that the meeting was successful and that I would stay there. Afterward, I said to Don Simpson, who was a close friend of mine, "I'm not sure I'm going to stay there; it was a bullshit meeting." So I let Michael know that I wasn't going to stay there, and he called Simpson and said, "Who is this motherfucker to do this to me?" Which I think was an interesting reaction.

JACK RAPKE, Agent:

I was born in the Bronx. My father owned some taxicabs in New York, then had an opportunity to go into a fruit shipping business, so he moved us down to Miami when I was seven. That fruit shipping business turned out to be a disaster, which was followed by a couple more disasters for him in the restaurant business. He wound up as a sales manager for a smoked fish company in Miami. My roots aren't exactly Dickensian, but they are humble.

I was pre-med at Emory University when the Vietnam War was raging, but I didn't really want to be a doctor. I wanted to make propaganda films against the war in Vietnam and realized I first had to learn *how* to make films. So I transferred to NYU film school and was surrounded day and night by people who shared real enthusiasm for film. It was there that I realized my passion was more about films themselves rather than vehicles for propaganda.

To my great surprise, it turned out that I was a very gifted cinematographer. People wanted me to shoot their films and I was getting recognized and honored. I would go up to labs and there would be big-time cameramen who would look at my rushes and be really encouraging. I went out to California with hopes of joining the union for cameramen, but the business manager of Local 52 told me to forget about it. It would be very difficult to get in. One of my friends from NYU who was living with Lauren Shuler, later to become Lauren Shuler Donner, said to me, "Jack, why are you pursuing this cameraman thing? You're great with people, you're good with business, have you ever thought about being an agent?" Another friend from NYU was actually in the mailroom at William Morris at the time, so I got an interview and they told me I could start in the mailroom on Monday. This was two months after the five guys left to start CAA.

Wouldn't you know it, the week that I started at William Morris, after two years of trying to get into a union, I finally received a letter of acceptance into the IA Local number 644 back in New York, so I could work as a cameraman in the city. I had one of those giant career decisions to make: to continue in the mailroom at William Morris for $100 a week, which was $81 take-home, or go back to New York and make $130 or $140 a day. I came to an absolute epiphany that if I wanted to be in the movie business, I had to be in Hollywood.

I was in the training program for two months; the mailroom for three months; a messenger for nine months; and an assistant for a year before being promoted to an agent in the motion picture literary department. I was an agent for three and a half years at William Morris, then left because I was married to a CAA agent, Laurie Perlman, who worked as Ron's assistant, and I got to know the CAA guys through her. They told me that they didn't increase salaries, and I should trust that the bonuses would be higher. I said, "Fine," and we shook hands.

RICK NICITA:

CAA was mostly a TV-based agency, and my coming there was perceived as a strong movie move for them. At my first meeting, I thought, *Okay, I have to figure out what agent represents which clients.* An agent brought up Christopher Reeve and said he was talking to him yesterday and that he was going to turn down a role he had been offered. So I made a note to myself, *Ah, that agent represents Chris Reeve.* But then another agent said, "When I spoke with him a bit later, he sounded a little more into it," so I thought, *Oh, okay, these two guys represent Chris Reeve.* And then another person says, "I think there's an outsider contender here, he was talking about this other script." I remember nudging the person next to me and asking, "Who represents Chris Reeve?" She looked up at me and said, "We do." That was a revolutionary answer at the time. Mike and Ronnie did that. They would involve you in the signing, talk about you like you were their equal—which you weren't—but right off the bat they empowered you. It was great. By the way, it was far less work for them with clients. The clients still could say, "Mike is my agent, but so is Rick." What's wrong with that? It worked perfectly for all concerned.

JACK RAPKE:

At the time, the writers' agents at CAA handled directors, but coming from film school and really wanting to be in the movie business, I didn't want to be involved in development. I wanted to represent directors, be involved with their productions, and when necessary, get involved with writers when directors needed them.

ROBERT KAMEN:

I had finished writing *Taps,* and had a whole bunch of friends over and we were partying, sitting around just doing drugs and stuff. My phone rings, and a guy says, "Hi. My name's Jack Rapke. I'm a new agent at CAA. How would you like to make $150,000 in ninety days?" So I said, "Sure." He said, "I'll call you back." Two minutes later, he calls me back. He says, "How far are you from the Mayfair Hotel?" I said, "It's on Sixty-Fifth Street. I live on Seventy-Seventh." He says, "I want you to go down there. You're going to meet Ted Kotcheff and Jon Peters." And I said, "Okay. For what?" He says, "You did your Ph.D. dissertation on Hasidic Jews, right?" "Right." "You lived with the nomads, right?" I said, "Right." "And you're an anthropology guy, right?" I said right. He said, "Well, it's a movie about a kid and he's in a cult. Just go talk to them." So I got off the phone and thought, *Who is this lunatic?* But all I could think of was if the 150 grand was real, I should go up there. There's Ted Kotcheff, there's Jon Peters, and there's Adam Fields, who was like an assistant at the time. And they tell me this story they have about this kid who's captured in a cult, and deprogrammed—they give me just that, and asked what I thought. I made up a story on the spot, and they hired me right there. I called Jack up and said, "Am I really getting paid $150,000 for three months?" "You'll get the money. How soon can you write the script?" I said, "I can write this in a month once I figure out what it is." And that's how I met Jack Rapke.

PAULA WAGNER:

Because all the agents at the agency were your agent, you had a lot of voices you could listen to, and if you weren't comfortable with your main agent, you could request somebody else. That happened all the time. The key was to keep the clients in the agency.

RAND HOLSTON:

You had to work your ass off—long hours and seven days a week.

MIKE MARCUS, Agent:

In 1972, I had been recruited to leave CMA, which is now ICM. A guy named Mike Levy hired me to join his company, Barton Levy and Associates. I came in to represent writers and directors with Mike, and four years later, Al Barton and Mike broke up the company, and Mike and I wound up merging with Paul Kohner. In late 1980, Mike Levy and I approached Paul Kohner and said, "This company CAA is beating us every time we go head to head to sign a new client. We've got to get a business affairs executive and get more modern offices to protect our future." Paul looked at us, and in his wonderful little Viennese accent said, "What future? I'm eighty-five years old. You guys go off and do it yourselves." So we parted amicably to start Levy Marcus, and in March of '81, Levy calls me and says, "You're not going to believe this, but I was just offered the job as the chairman of the new CBS theatrical films group." I was an orphan. I could have tried to put together what remained of Levy Marcus, go back to Kohner and make it Kohner Marcus, or I could go out and see what else was out there. I chose the latter, and when people heard that I was out there, I was heavily recruited. I had David Cronenberg, who was hot off *Scanners* and was on the verge of being a very hot director. I had John Landis off *Animal House* and *Blues Brothers*; I had Michael Apted off *Coal Miner's Daughter*, and Irvin Kershner, who had just done *Empire Strikes Back*, who was one of Levy's clients but I was close to him and I knew he would be coming with me. I was also representing Richard Marquand, who was hot and would soon be signing to do *Return of the Jedi*.

Jeff Berg and I had lunch. He wanted me to come back to what was now ICM. Gersh contacted me. I can't remember if it was Rick Nicita or Mike Rosenfeld Sr. who approached me about joining CAA, but I was friends with them both. Mike Rosenfeld, even though ten years my senior, had been a member of the fraternity I belonged to at Penn State. They made a big play and couldn't understand why I just didn't say yes, but I was enjoying the flirting.

Finally, just when I was about to go to CAA, Stan Kamen called me, and I think that got back to CAA because next thing I knew I was having dinner with Mike Ovitz. He was very frustrated I wasn't saying yes. He told me, "I can't believe how long this dinner is. It's longer than I've had with most of my clients." I laughed and I think he laughed—I'm not 100 percent sure—but I wound up saying yes and started at CAA in April of 1981.

DONALD SUTHERLAND, Actor:

Ron Meyer came to see me with Mike Ovitz and Bill Haber, but he was the one I focused on. He said they were going to start an agency and wanted me to come with them. I said I couldn't for a while because my agent, Stan Kamen, was dreadfully sick and I didn't want to leave him in the lurch. It was dumb, really. Stan had relegated me to younger agents at William Morris and I was not on his checklist at all, but I was doing what I thought was the honorable thing by staying. It was regrettable, really, because I missed the birthing of CAA.

But in 1981, I was doing Edward Albee's version of *Lolita* on Broadway and Ron came back to me, asking if we could meet. I said the Expos are playing the Phillies, so he said, "Let's go." He picked me up in a long black limousine and we went to Philadelphia. Steve Carlton, "Lefty," pitched. When I think back on it, I can see Ron deliberating, explaining, offering, but, first and foremost, being completely present. He was disciplined and so focused; neat beyond compare, and a very elegant man.

After the release of *Ordinary People*, I couldn't get a look in. Nothing, not a job, not a meeting. Not an audition. Nothing. I was always a hard sell and he managed the selling of me with great acumen, with determination and resolve. For nearly a year, Ron worked to start me up again, beginning with Neil Simon and Herb Ross. He guided my work through ups and downs, lefts and rights. I was filled with admiration for the person that he was, and I fell in love with him. That was back then. I've been in love with him ever since.

JUDY HOFFLUND, Agent:

I started at CAA in 1981. It was about a year and a half after I graduated from college. I had lived in New York for nine months working for a producer, then came to L.A. and took a film class at UCLA and worked for my neighbor who was an agent. I could tell it would be fun to be an agent, and I started reading the trades. What I remember most about them were those big red ads in *The Hollywood Reporter* and *Daily Variety,* saying, "CAA is proud to announce the new worldwide representation of," and they were signing Robert Redford and others—all in their prime.

I had nine months in the mailroom, then nine months working for Ron Meyer, who was my boss out of the mailroom. He had never hired a trainee before; I was the first. Ron is the best guy in the world, and I loved him.

MICHAEL OVITZ:

Every time I went to a public event, people expected me to know everything about everybody. It was tense. I couldn't go out at night to an event and enjoy myself. It was work. Ron could smile and wiggle his way in and out of anything.

ROBB ROTHMAN:

Ron never said much to me, but he was always friendly. The only time he ever got mad at me was when I was in the mailroom and he asked me for a fruit salad. I was in a real hurry and got some canned fruit, and he didn't raise his voice but said to me, "Rob, when I asked for a fruit salad, I meant a real fruit salad." He came into the mailroom an hour later and said, "I'm really sorry, I was just hungry. I should not have yelled at you." I said, "Ron, you didn't yell at me, I was wrong." He said, "No, no, no, I'm really sorry. Go out, buy yourself dinner and give me the check." That's the kind of guy that he was. He was a very good man.

In those early days of CAA, there were a lot of people who hit the skids and had financial difficulties, and I heard more than once that Ron helped them out. But he didn't tell anybody he was doing it.

JUDY HOFFLUND:

Ron was very hard to work for—very demanding, very specific—but he taught me things that I carry with me to this day, like you have to return every phone call every day. Even now, I lie in bed feeling guilty if I don't return someone's call, and I'm not even working anymore.

JAY SANDRICH:

We were on a cruise in the Caribbean—there was me, my wife, Linda, Ron, and several others—and the boat stopped so we could take a tour around this beautiful island. Ron wound up staying on the dock and never got off the phone that was there. He didn't get to see anything that entire day because he was working. But he never complained. He loved to work and took it very seriously.

JUDY HOFFLUND:

Ron was incredibly tolerant with my ambition. I worked crazy hours. I opened and closed the office every single day, and he knew how motivated I was to become an agent. I would regularly close the door and say to him, "Sorry, but when?" One day he told me there was an opening in the television literary area and asked if I wanted to do that or wait longer for a spot in the talent department. I said, "Great, I'll be a TV lit agent." But he also always knew that I hoped to transfer over into his department, talent, which I did six months later. I inherited quite a few clients and took over daily responsibility for Kiefer Sutherland, Phoebe Cates, and others.

In those days Mike gave everybody their bonus one-on-one. I didn't care how much money I was making at the time because I wanted to stay focused on the big picture, which was becoming a top agent in the industry. I put my tiny paychecks in the bank and didn't really care what I got for my bonus. I was making appropriate money for what I was doing, maybe a little bit more than what I deserved. So when I came into Mike's office and he gave me my bonus, I said, "Thank you so much," but he didn't think I was thankful enough. He thought, relative to what people were getting, he was giving me a big bonus. He said, "Judy, I have to say that sometimes you remind me of me; you don't walk around the couch, you go over it. But I've got to tell you, you're a really great girl, and sometimes I feel like you're just going to throw this all away, get married, and have kids." At first I thought, *Oh, he thinks I'm a great girl. He doesn't think I'm a bitch. That's great.* But then another thought started running around my head: *I'm having a financial conversation with my boss. I'm opening and closing this office every single day, which they all know, and working like a maniac to get promoted fast and to advance my career. And he's telling me I might just throw it all away, to get married and have kids?!* I was like, whoa! He had this ability to somehow make you think he was complimenting you, like by calling me a great girl, but he was saying something that was really outrageous.

ROSALIE SWEDLIN:

I started working at CAA on my birthday—August 17, 1981. I had been living in England working in book publishing, doing marketing and author publicity. I would often say to various friends, "I'd like to be the person who finds, nurtures, and introduces writing talent—I don't want to be at the end of the food chain anymore." Someone asked if I had ever considered becoming an agent. I thought about it and decided it might be an interesting career, but my big problem was that I had no clients, so nobody was prepared to hire me and pay me a salary except a very forward-thinking boutique agency, the Anthony Sheil Agency, who wanted someone to represent their book authors for film, television, theater, and radio work, and to exploit their backlist of book titles. I had never considered a career in the entertainment business, but it was an opportunity to try something different and to stay in London. While at the Sheil Agency I got to know several U.S. agents because I would often need American co-agents to represent TV formats and bigger book titles. When I returned to the states in 1981, I wanted to continue my agenting career, and a couple of agent friends who had moved to CAA brought my name up to Mike Ovitz. When I was interviewed by Mike, he told me, "I don't really care who you know or whether you have any clients. If you wind up working here, you'll have all the clients you could possibly handle and you'll get to know everyone. What I want to know is who you are and what you've done with your life." So I talked to him about my work in publishing and my life abroad and two weeks later I got a call offering me the job.

TONY KRANTZ, Agent:

I went to Berkeley, where I was the concert promoter for the student body, and I produced concerts with the Talking Heads, the B-52s, the Buzzcocks, and many other punk rock bands in the day, and I also produced the Berkeley Jazz Festival, which was a four-day event with some of the biggest names in the world of jazz. The year that I did it, the keyboard players alone included Keith Jarrett, Herbie Hancock, Oscar Peterson, McCoy Tyner, and Chick Corea. It was a thrill.

Bill Graham was our competition at Berkeley, and all we could do was promote punk rock bands and jazz musicians because Bill wasn't really interested in those businesses. Bill would later become my first client, by the way, and I packaged the Doors movie, which he produced. It was hard to buy a band at Berkeley, so I learned to really not like music agents. But my parents—both in the business; my mother is Judith Krantz, the author, and my father is Steve Krantz, no longer alive, a producer—said what you really should do is become an agent. They arranged an interview through Mort Janklow, who was my mother's literary agent, and he called up Mike Ovitz and said, "Judy's son Tony is graduating from Berkeley. Would you guys interview him for the mailroom at

CAA?" I got an interview with Bill Haber and Mike Rosenfeld Sr. and they hired me on the spot. I actually tried to negotiate with Ray Kurtzman, who was the head of business affairs and the head of the training program, to avoid the mailroom and go straight to a desk, but Ray wouldn't hear of it. I started in the mailroom at CAA right after graduating in 1981, and spent ten months in the mailroom and eight months on Jack Rapke's desk as his assistant. I never filed a thing—truth is, I didn't know I had to. Jack was a great boss and represented some of the biggest directors in the business.

ROSALIE SWEDLIN:

I believed the type of filmmakers I was interested in working with would expect to have informed discussions about the material, so I would take careful notes in staff meetings about material that I thought would appeal to the people I was working with or those I wanted to try to work with. What was very clear was if you wanted to be a successful agent during the '80s, it was an all-consuming job and you had to have a whole range of skills and relationships.

ERIC CARLSON, Agent:

Nineteen eighty-one was my very first retreat. I'd only been at the company maybe two weeks. I was the lowest guy, I was at the bottom rung of the entire company. Somehow I got to go. What stands out to me more than anything was Michael's closing speech before we all left. It was filled with such passion and encouragement and vision for, not just the company, but for everybody that was even in that room. You could hear a pin drop. He spoke unscripted probably for forty-five minutes, at least. Nobody said a word, nobody looked away, nobody got up and went to the bathroom. On my drive home, I remember pulling over and calling this girl I was dating to tell her, "This is beyond belief. This is going to be the most exciting thing in my life. I've wanted to be in a place like this forever." I remember just floating, driving home that two hours back up to L.A.

MICHAEL OVITZ:

We ran out of space really fast. We kept adding on and kept buying people out of leases. It was really expensive and it was throwing money away, so I started looking for real estate around '81. I always wanted us to have real estate; in the agency business you don't have any assets because every year you start over again. I wanted us to look like we were there forever.

JACK RAPKE:

Bob Zemeckis was in movie jail: *I Want to Hold Your Hand* and *Used Cars* weren't financial successes, and he wrote *1941*, which at the time was regarded as Spielberg's only disappointment. Mike brought him up at a staff meeting, and almost to a person there was a tepid response. I stood up—not literally but figuratively—and said, "I think *Used Cars* is a terrific movie." I made it clear to everyone I believed in Bob, and the rest is history. Of course, Michael took credit for that and a lot of things that happened in the agency that he himself did not do.

RON MEYER:

Sly had just finished shooting *Rocky II*. He was debating whether to do *Rambo: First Blood* and had been offered the role for a great deal of money. Sly's problem was that while he believed very strongly in the book *First Blood* and wanted to do the film, he didn't like what ultimately happened to the John Rambo character in the screenplay. He wasn't my client yet, but Sly told me, "This guy's a hero and not someone who should die at the end." The problem was no one involved in the movie at the time agreed with him. I was convinced Sly was right, and he told me I was the only one who felt the same way. We bonded over that decision. I went and spoke to the producers and the director, and in the end, they wound up agreeing to Sly's way of doing it.

SYLVESTER STALLONE:

I was about to enter into a film called *First Blood*, and even though I hadn't gone with him yet, Ron and I talked about it quite a bit. This is an interesting story, and will give you a little insight into Ron Meyer. My managers at the time were not thrilled by the idea of my bringing Ron on. They said, "You don't need him, you don't need him, he's just there for the money. CAA needs money; nobody's going with them." I told them what was happening at the agency wasn't my concern, and that I liked his personality and thought he was very sincere. I remember him telling me, "All I can say is I'm the best of the worst kind of breed in the world."

I kept being asked by my representatives to stay away from Ron Meyer. They told me, if you offer him money on it, even though he doesn't deserve it, he'll take it. Now, put this in perspective. I was doing *First Blood* and was going to be paid around five million. So it would be a pretty great commission for someone who had nothing to do with the deal itself and had only talked to me about the movie's ending. But I really liked the guy, and he had been really supportive through all those discussions on the ending.

So I decided to test him. I called him and had one of my representatives listen in, but Ron didn't know anyone else was listening. I said, "Ron, I know you all could use a little financial boost, so I'd like to give you ten percent commission on *First Blood* right now." He said to me, "Wow, that's incredibly generous, and I'm not going to lie, I could use it, just let me think . . ." And there was a couple seconds of silence. Then he said, "Thank you very much, Sly, but I'm going to pass on that. I hope there will be other movies where I will have earned my fee, and I get a chance to work with you in the near future. Hopefully, I'll see you down the road." I hung up, looked at the other person who had been listening in, and they almost burst into flames from embarrassment. That was literally the ultimate world-class litmus test, because I don't think anyone else would have passed on half a million dollars when they were desperate for cash. But he did, and that was the official beginning of me and Ron Meyer.

RON MEYER:

Sly was the first major star that I had signed. I was representing important actors like Farrah Fawcett, Kate Jackson, and Rob Reiner; Mike had signed Sean Connery and a couple other important actors, but signing Sly was extremely important for the agency and me in particular. Then *Rocky II* and *Rambo* came out. They were both huge hits, and all of a sudden I was representing the biggest star in the world. Every studio wanted him. He'd go someplace and they'd have to close off the street. I'm serious; it was like when the Beatles came to America in the '60s. We'd come out of places and they'd have police lines you couldn't cross. We'd go into a restaurant and then come out and there would have to be crowd control—people were lined up everywhere. We became great friends and traveled all over the world together. Once we were in Thailand, scouting locations for *Rambo II*, and we were in the remotest jungle area you can imagine along a river where people lived in little houses and small boats. There were no cars, no televisions. All of a sudden, crowds started gathering and shouting, "Rocky! Rocky! Rocky!" It was an extraordinary experience.

JOEL SILVER, Producer:

Sly was royalty. He was so much larger than life. Nobody, nobody, nobody, nobody, was like Sly in that era.

RON MEYER:

Here I was, at the time just an okay agent, who had this whale by the tail. I always said if I could represent just one big star, I'd sign fifty; I would know how to parlay that into building a big business. Once an agent represents a big star like Sly, people believe you know something—even if you don't. He was my calling card. He changed my life, and I've always been grateful to him for it.

Following Sly, we signed Al Pacino, Jessica Lange, Robert De Niro, Gene Hackman, and dozens of others.

SYLVESTER STALLONE:

Ron gave me a script he wanted me to do which was a full-blown comedy. At the time, I'd been so ingrained in doing action films, I said I didn't know if the audience would buy me being so abrasive at times.

RON MEYER:

In the early '80s, I called Sly about an offer I had received for him for a movie that I was really excited about him doing. As I was telling him about it, I knew that he probably wouldn't want to do this film because it somewhat parodied his tough-guy image.

So I called a group together at Sly's house with all the people who were close to him—his inner cirle. I said, "I have an offer for Sly for a movie I think he should do. I think it's an important film for him to do in every way. I don't want someone else to do it, because it's going to be a huge hit." And I said, "I have a copy of the script for each of you to read, and I'm going to call you all in the morning, but I want the answer to be yes. I don't want any second-guessing." The next morning, everybody said, "Yes."

SYLVESTER STALLONE:

Ron told me "Don't change it," but I took the script, and I rewrote it as a kind of compromise, where the guy was action-oriented, but he also had a wry sense of humor and was comedically sarcastic. Well, they didn't like that at all.

RON MEYER:

Nobody wanted his version, so I begged him, "Please, do the original script. This is a movie that's going to be a hit. Someone else is going to do it and you're going to regret it. Please, please, please do this movie." It turned into such a big fight that I was on the phone screaming at him, "Don't be stupid." In the end, he said, "If you mention it again, I'm going to fire you." Then Barry Diller said, "We can replace him."

SYLVESTER STALLONE:

Ron did want me to do the original version, but I didn't think I could pull it off. Then that ship sailed.

RON MEYER:

The movie was *Beverly Hills Cop*, and as everyone knows, it got made with Eddie Murphy, who became a big star off it.

Years later, Sly was feeling bad about something—I forget what it was—and I wanted him to feel better, so I said to him, "I should have fought harder for you to do *Beverly Hills Cop*." He said, "You're right. You should have." There's no moral here; it's just a long story with no punch line.

MICHAEL OVITZ:

Caddyshack, Chevy and Bill; *Mr. Mom*, Michael Keaton, CAA package. *Vacation*, Ivan Reitman, package. *Trading Places*, both CAA clients. *Beverly Hills Cop*, *Ghostbusters*, *Back to the Future*, *Fletch*, *Goonies*, *European Vacation*, *Airplane!*, *Blues Brothers*, should I keep going? We had every John Hughes movie, and made real money on every one of those because there were no expensive stars in his movies; we had many of them anyway.

ROBERT ZEMECKIS, Director:

Everything good first went to Steven and/or Sydney Pollack. That's just the way it worked. That's how it came down from Mike Ovitz.

Legend has it that Dustin Hoffman and Murray Schisgal started developing the idea for Tootsie *back in the silent era. After years of work, Ovitz suggested that Larry Gelbart be brought in to help Hoffman and Schisgal get past hurdles in the story. The trio worked on a couple of drafts while Hoffman discussed the movie with various directors. Ovitz pushed for Sydney Pollack, and despite more than a bit of wariness on both sides—Pollack sensed a one-joke movie, while others pointed to Pollack's lack of comedy experience—it was nevertheless arranged for a single meeting to take place between the three men.*

DUSTIN HOFFMAN:

It was a difficult project; most projects are, but for different reasons. *Tootsie* was an idea that started with me and my friend Murray, and Michael wanted me to meet with Sydney. We met out at the house at the beach. He kept saying he was not inclined to want to accept the job because, he told me, "You're gonna put on a dress and be in drag, and after half an hour, it's going to wear itself out." But he didn't know the throughline of it, the comedy of it, or what the movie really wanted to be about. I said, "I think it's a serious film underneath its comedy," but Sydney just kept on cleaning his kitchen counter. I remember looking at Murray and saying, "Can you put it better?" and Murray said to him, "I think it's about a man who becomes a better man by becoming a woman." And that stopped Sydney in his tracks. He stopped cleaning, and all of a sudden, he was alert, and said, "There may be something here."

Sydney went out to meet with Gelbart and I was waiting and waiting, because as soon as we had the right draft, we were ready to go. Columbia had been standing by us for over a year. I had made *Kramer* for them, and Frank Price was very nice and willing to bet on me. I said during this time we should keep working on the makeup; my goal was to walk down the street and not have people look at me and say, "Who's that guy in drag?" I wanted to be able to really look like a woman. If I couldn't do that, I didn't want to make the film. We worked on hair and makeup for a year, screen test after screen test, and then one day, the projectionist who didn't know anything about the project saw footage of me and asked, "Who's that actress?" So we were finally getting somewhere. But then Sydney called and said he was very disappointed, and that Larry wasn't successful enough on the draft for him to do the film. He sent me the draft and I agreed. We knew we needed a new writer, and I told my lawyer Bert Fields we were in trouble. He suggested Elaine May, and got me together with her. Elaine read the script and she was extraordinary. She hit it on the head; she understood what we were trying to do. She came up with my roommate and that the girlfriend has to have a shithead as a lover, and she has to have a kid, and a father who falls in love, and she said, "I'm telling you right now, you have to have a girl already in your life and I'm going to write her with Terri Garr in mind." She was amazing, wrote it in three or four weeks, and that was it. Whatever was missing, we knew we could correct during shooting.

MICHAEL OVITZ:

Dustin must have seen two hundred actresses for the lead role in *Tootsie*. We had the casting done out of CAA's office. Think about that. You're an actress. Your agent has no choice but to send you to that audition. You walk in and you're immediately treated like a queen. You're offered anything you want, and then you're escorted up to a room where you see one of the two or three best directors in the business sitting with one of the biggest stars in the world in a CAA office with CAA scripts sitting everywhere. It was as low-hanging fruit as you could get.

I put Bill Murray in *Tootsie*. It was last minute. There was a role for Dustin's roommate, and I wanted Bill's box office celebrity to be a support for Dustin.

DUSTIN HOFFMAN:

Michael was certainly instrumental in keeping Sydney interested as long as he did. Sydney was ambivalent right from the get-go, and he was not a particularly collaborative director. I think Larry Gelbart had a phrase for him—"He's the arsonist and the fire chief." And I said, "What do you mean?" And he said, "He always yells, 'Fire! We have to put it out!' then adds, 'Thankfully, I'm also the fire chief.'" He loved to solve problems. Sydney and I were ambivalent right from the beginning. This had been my project; I'd thought of it, with Murray, I gave it the title, and I had also worked with Elaine. When Sydney came on board, he just wanted me to be the actor. I said, "That's not where we are on this. You're coming in as an eleventh-hour director." So Michael had to keep the peace as best he could between Sydney and me.

BILL MURRAY:

Frank Price was running Columbia, and it was Frank's wife's birthday and there was a sort of show-business dinner for her in an Italian restaurant in New York City, and I was somehow invited. It was Katherine Price, Frank, Mike, and I think Judy Ovitz was there, along with Sydney, Dustin and his wife, and my wife, Mickey. We all sat at a big round table and I just remember being funny and having a pretty good time. Then Ovitz left, and I was there with Dustin, who I didn't know at all. I wound up giving him a ride back to his apartment on the West Side—I'm such a square, I drove my car there—and we all laughed the entire way there. And the next day, Dustin gets into it with Sydney about how much he wants me. He tells him, "I want that guy to play the guy."

What became clear to us after was it was Mike all along, just like the guy says in *The Godfather*, "It was Barzini all along." It was always Mike. It was never Dustin. Somehow Mike had a hunch that if you put me in a room with those people that Dustin would go to bat for me, which he did.

They were shooting in that TV studio, and Mike brought me over there to proudly present me to Sydney as the guy. It was classic, because we were in this room with several layers of glass between us and another room where we could see and hear Dustin screaming, "Well, I ain't fucking Robert Redford," which turned out to be one of his favorite things to scream at Sydney. Dustin had just lost it, and he went on a complete tirade, and Sydney was yelling back at him, and their mutual agent was watching the entire thing. Mike was just dying, because he had wanted me to have this nice moment with Sydney, but instead, Dustin is having this total fit. It didn't bother me at all, it was just theater, and sometimes when someone isn't listening to you, you have to get loud.

MICHAEL OVITZ:

Sure enough, in the first preview, without any billing—so no one knew Bill was in the movie—the minute the audience saw

Bill, they went crazy. Everyone started whistling and applaud-
ing. This shit doesn't happen anymore. We put Bill in there for
no money, but he got one point of the gross. He made *a lot* of
money.

*Michael Rosenfeld left CAA in 1982, becoming the first of the original founders
to depart the agency. Under the original buy-sell agreement made by those founders
in the first weeks of the company's existence—and based on a zero valuation of the
company—Rosenfeld was paid $750,000.*

*Rosenfeld had worked hard at William Morris and was a key ingredient of
CAA in its formative years. What he brought to the operation was not just skill
but soul, often serving as peacemaker when necessary among the original five. He
was also, as all the partners knew well, a man obsessed with death, having lost his
father when the "old man" was only in his 50s.*

*Rosenfeld was a big fan of television and movies and a voracious reader with
impeccable taste when it came to judging talent, but from the time the agency was
formed, it was clear that no one would be able to keep up the pace that Ovitz and
Meyer had set. They gave their entire lives to the agency; Haber put in seemingly
thousands of hours, but kept perspective, while Rosenfeld, along with Perkins, simply wasn't going to let his work define his entire life. He may have known so well
that he couldn't keep up with Ovitz and Meyer that he wisely didn't even try. There
were many nights when Ovitz and Meyer would be leaving the office at seven to
go to clients' dinners and premieres and saw Rosenfeld also leaving the office but
going home to his wife and two children. Even during daylight hours, he loved to
escape whenever possible to pilot his airplanes, an exercise not without its element
of symbolism.*

*Rosenfeld saw the business becoming more and more demanding, especially when
one was a partner in the agency. He was the sole architect of his own departure,
and missed by many.*

NORMAN LEAR:
Mike Rosenfeld was a delicious guy, and he became a buddy of
mine very quickly. But he was the kind of guy who if you knew
him at all, he was your buddy.

RON MEYER:

Mike Rosenfeld made the decision to ease himself out of the company. His father had died young, and Mike wanted to spend less time working and more time enjoying himself. So he came to us and told us he wanted to cash out and move on. He was the first of the five of us to leave.

MICHAEL ROSENFELD JR.:

My impression was he was burned out. His own father had died when he was just twenty, and I think he carried that pain with him for a long time. He fell in love with a woman who wound up becoming his second wife, and I think he wanted to start all over. He moved to Sonoma and started producing, but not full-time. He really enjoyed his life up north.

MICHAEL OVITZ:

He contributed a lot and helped enormously with things that were really important to us. I think those initial two years of working around the clock really threw him for a loop. Mike felt incredibly guilty when he would leave early and we were still there. He would be leaving at six or seven, and see us hunkering down for another three or four hours. And we came in on Saturdays. There wasn't a moment we didn't work and I think he got to a point where he couldn't take it anymore.

MICHAEL ROSENFELD JR.:

Truth is, he had wanted CAA to be a boutique agency. I think in his mind when they left William Morris, they were going to keep CAA small. Ovitz put pressure on all those guys. He played offense with everybody, and you were constantly on defense.

RON MEYER:

He was a wonderful guy. He wasn't as high energy or aggressive like the three of us were, but he was a strong agent, and always good to his clients.

MICHAEL ROSENFELD JR.:

My father encouraged me to work here; he thought I could de-velop talent. So I asked him, "Do I have to go to school to become an agent?" He took out a piece of paper and wrote down a number. "What does that say?" he asked. I said, "It says $100,000," and he said, "Well, tell me what 10 percent of $100,000 is." And I laughed and said, "Ten thousand dollars." Then he looked at me, laughed, and said, "Congratulations, you're an agent. As long as you can figure out what your commission is, you're fine."

MICHAEL OVITZ:

Not one of our guys had a contract. We gave out one contract when we started the music business to Tom Ross, and then when it expired in the third year of a ten-year run with us, he didn't even ask for another. We had a very simple thesis at the business: "If you don't like working here? Leave." But we never thought anyone was going to leave.

I begged Mike to stay, but he made it clear he felt it was the right thing for him to do. We gave him the $750,000, which was a lot of money in those days.

RON MEYER:

I think he got better than that. It might've been a million dol-lars, but it was no more than that. It was a number we documented between the five of us that never got revised. It was never based on profits; it was just a number that never really made any sense.

ROBB ROTHMAN:

I had told everyone I was getting married, and Ovitz called me and said, "Look we're in the middle of a writers' strike now. We're not earning any money. You want to take your honeymoon now, you can get a lot of time off because I'm not losing any business. But if you wait and then the strike is over we will have a lot of catching up to do so you'll only get a long weekend. What do you want to do?" I said, "Well, I'm an agent, you're an agent, let's negotiate." I got three weeks, which was phenomenal. But somehow, when I came back, it was like a shift change. People wore ties most of the time; dress-down Fridays had ended. Doors that used to be open were closed. It was just a whole different dynamic.

ERIC CARLSON:

I never went onto a desk. I came out of the mailroom and went straight to being an agent. I think I'm the only guy who's ever done that. What happened was while I was in the mailroom, I wrote a study on all the emerging television markets. It took me three months and was like a thesis. I bound it with all the partners' names on it, then personally handed it to each of them. I said it was a reference guide and included thoughts I had on what we should be doing in the future. Ovitz asked me why I wrote it, and I said, "Because I'm too smart to be in the mailroom; I should be an agent." A few days later, Ray Kurtzman pulled me aside and told me Michael thought I had balls for doing what I did. It reminded him of what he did at William Morris: never accept no for an answer.

Michael promoted me out of the mailroom to agent a month later.

TONY KRANTZ:

In the training program, I had written a paper that was a hundred-page document about CAA and the music business, because CAA was not in the music business at the time. My vision was not to get into the booking of bands because I really didn't love that business, having been the concert promoter at Berkeley; it was really about a different vision, about taking brilliant musical talent and moving them into film and television—say, Quincy Jones producing a movie, a Broadway musical starring Prince, having Ricki Lee Jones score a movie, having Elvis Costello write and produce a movie, taking advantage of CAA's core strengths and bringing music people into the fold into this new kind of music/film/television programming that I really loved.

Fred Specktor was my mentor and sort of supervised the writing of this document. It was, in many ways, the artistic dream of a twenty-two-year-old guy who led with his heart but didn't necessarily lead with the practicality of agency commission. I delivered it to Fred; he gave it to Mike Ovitz. About a week later I was made an agent, not because of that document only, but also because Robb Rothman left the TV/literary department for a smaller agency. It was unheard of that any agent at CAA would ever leave because it was so clearly the place to be, but Robb did, and I had my shot finally to begin my career at CAA.

ROBB ROTHMAN:

I was the first CAA agent to leave and go to another agency. I basically said, "If I stay here, I'm not going to be happy." I was twenty-seven, so if you screw up when you're twenty-seven years old, you have plenty of time to make up for it. When you're in your mid-thirties, it's a lot harder.

I closed my deal with Leading Artists—then called Berkus Handley Stein, which merged into UTA—signed my contract, went home, started calling all the clients, and said please don't call anyone if you can help it. I called Haber, then Haber called Ovitz, who called me and said, "Okay, what's going on?" I said, "I'm going." He said, "Look, come in tomorrow morning, we're going to work this out." And I said, "No," and he said, "Look, I'm not taking no for an answer." So I said, "Mike, I signed my contract and I've gotten legal counsel on this and if you try to stop them from hiring or if you do anything it's tortious interference." Then he starts screaming at me, saying, "I'm going to do whatever I can to make your life a living hell. I'm going to make sure that no one ever wants to do business with you."

JIM BERKUS, Agent:

We took one young agent from CAA, Robb Rothman, and that was a big deal. Then Ovitz called me and made a threat. I just said, "Mike, you do what you do and I'll do what I do." That was it.

I wasn't afraid; it was all smoke and mirrors. But for a long time, Ovitz had a lot of power in this town, and a lot of people were afraid.

ROBB ROTHMAN:

They never really came after me. I think one of the reasons was the agency that I went to had Robert Stein as one of their partners. Now Stein's mother and Ron Meyer's mother had grown up in the same German or Polish village and they were still best friends. I knew Ronnie would never let his mother's best friend's son's agency go out of business.

MICHAEL DOUGLAS:

Ronnie had his mother at every party that he ever had. Sometimes he would bring her even if it wasn't his party. He was so grateful to her for her love and compassion, and she was just a lovely, gracious woman. Much too refined for Ronnie!

Thomas Cruise Mapother IV was nineteen when he started his movie career as Billy in the 1981 film Endless Love, *which was followed the same year with a supporting role in* Taps *and then continued in 1983 with* The Outsiders. *He turned heads in all three films, but it was his level-jumping first leading role as Joel Goodsen in* Risky Business, *released in 1983, that would bring him national attention, launch his stardom, and give birth to one of the most successful and significant careers in CAA history.*

Cruise would spend the next thirty-three years as a CAA client and work with the biggest directors and stars in the world, but it was the early years of his career that were particularly gratifying to those working at CAA at the time.

TOM CRUISE, Actor:

I wanted to make movies since I was four years old, and I had seen a lot of movies. Suddenly I'm in *Taps* and I thought, *If I never get to make another movie again, I'm going to study how they're made.* I was able to go to each department. We had Owen Roizman, who was the cinematographer, and I had known his amazing work from seeing his movies. Harold Becker did a wonderful thing by sharing his movies, and of course I was familiar with Stanley Jaffe's movies. I remember once they knew how interested I was in cinema, Stanley, Harold, and Owen were so generous because they answered all my questions, and I must have asked a million of them. At the time, we had dailies, and they brought me in and showed me rushes of my work and the other actors' work and said, "Listen. These takes are going to be in the movie. So you've got to try to watch it as though you're the audience and not yourself." There were all these wonderful lessons about how to prepare films.

STANLEY JAFFE, Producer:

Originally, there was someone else who was cast for *Taps*, but as we got into rehearsals, Harold Becker started to have doubts about the actor and asked for Tom to be brought back in. He got the part, and the deeper we got into it, the more impressive he was. It became very clear he was something very special.

PAULA WAGNER:

I had just come to CAA. A lot of the movie stars had outpriced themselves in the marketplace. Studios were getting wind of the youth film market and they were using more and more unknowns, so I got this idea: sign all the young top talented people out there I believed in, put them in the best projects, and make them movie stars.

There was an actors' strike, and in that period of time *Taps* got put on hold. I put a few people up for the roles but none were cast. They had done an all-out search across the country, and found a lot of really talented young people. I was assigned to 20th Century Fox, and I met Richard Fischoff, who worked for Stanley Jaffe. He told me about Sean Penn, and showed me a few dailies or photos. I thought he was terrific. I then brought his name up at our staff meeting and said, "There's this young actor named Sean Penn, and I want to go meet him." At that point the philosophy at CAA was sign people who were already established, and there was a good reason behind that philosophy, by the way, which was "We're building an agency—let's bring established actors in." Finding unknowns can be risky because some people make it, some people don't, and when that happens, you've already put in a lot of effort.

So everybody goes, "Who? We don't want somebody unknown." So I let it drop, and then two weeks later another agent, Todd Smith, who had been there much longer than I, said, "I'm meeting Sean Penn." I said, "Well, I'd like to be involved with that because I had heard about him and seen some dailies, and think he's phenomenal." So together we signed Sean Penn.

Meanwhile, Richard Fischoff says to me, "That's great you have Sean, but there's this other guy who you've got to see some footage of—he's amazing. He's going to be a young teen star. He's really got the goods." I brought him up in a meeting and said, "I've got to sign this guy."

STANLEY JAFFE:

Paula called me and said she desperately wanted to sign Tom and said, "If he asks about me, would you mind putting in a good word?" I said, "Of course." I was happy to do it. I always liked Paula.

TOM CRUISE:

Penn goes, "Come out to L.A. and stay with me," so I stayed in his guest house for a couple of weeks. I remember he said, "You've got to check out CAA," because I wasn't signed with any agent.

PAULA WAGNER:

Tom came out to L.A. and was staying with Sean Penn, and Sean told him about me. At the time, I was working with the covering agent on *Risky Business* and was trying to find an actor for it. I met with Tom on top of one of these buildings in Century City, and we had an amazing lunch together. He borrowed a sports jacket—he didn't *own* a sports jacket. I remember that he had this very fascinating intensity in his eyes—and he was warm, polite, and caring. We found common ground—it's important to find common ground—when we talked about our families, and he had played Nathan Detroit in *Guys and Dolls* in dinner theater in New Jersey, and probably ten years or so earlier I had played Adelaide in *Guys and Dolls* in the USO tour. We both had also studied with Sandy Meisner.

As I got to know him, I thought, *This guy is more than a heartthrob. He's going to have a real career. He's determined, he's focused, and he wants to be a movie star.* A lot of the younger people were anti–movie star. They didn't want to be. He definitely wanted to.

I got Sean *Fast Times at Ridgemont High* and *Bad Boys* and it was all very exciting. I had so much faith in Sean to do almost any role, and I really cared about him. During this time, I had also had a lunch with Steve Tisch, the producer.

We went to the Palm for lunch, and he said, "We can't cast *Risky Business*." I immediately said, "Tom Cruise is perfect for it." He said, "Yeah, they won't see him. Nobody thinks he's right for it." It turned out people thought, based on his earlier roles, that Tom was too blue collar to play an upper-middle-class kid from the Midwest. I said, "Steve, I don't ask favors of you very often, but I'd like one now. Just meet him. He happens to be in town. Don't send him to anyone else. I want you to meet him, then tell me what you think, because I really believe in this guy's talent and I believe he can do this role." He said, "Okay, Paula, for you I'll do it."

TOM CRUISE:

I had heard about the project the year before, and remember thinking when I was reading it, *Am I ready for this? Can I carry a film? What's it going to be like having a starring role?* Interestingly enough, I felt at the time that I was ready.

STEVE TISCH:

Of course when he walked into our office at Warner Bros., pretty much all he had to do was smile and then we got it.

PAULA WAGNER:

So now Steve calls and says, "I met him, and we're testing him tomorrow for the lead role in *Risky Business*." I said, "Okay, give me the lowdown. Who's he testing with? I don't want him to go in right after lunch; I don't want him to go at the end of the day; I don't want him to be first." I had a strategy about everything. Steve said, "It's just going to be him and this young actress Paul wants to see named Rebecca De Mornay." Tom tested, and boom, the rest is history.

He wasn't dancing in his underpants in the script, by the way. Tom created that.

TOM CRUISE:

I remember calling Paula and sitting down with her. She wanted to very much take me to lunch and I just remember how warm, intelligent, and beautiful she was. And eventually she just said, "What do you want to do?" I said, "I want to meet filmmakers, and I want to learn and understand all about this art form that I love."

PAULA WAGNER:

I brought him up to the office, had him meet everybody, sold my heart out, and everybody was like, "Okay, take a shot, let's see what happens." This was a new thing, signing these new young actors. Tom was nineteen when I signed him.

TOM CRUISE:

I signed with them and went up to their offices and I remember meeting Ronnie, Mike Ovitz, and Rick Nicita and feeling a real sense of excitement and generosity. As a kid I looked at photos of premieres and read about the old studio system. So I realized if I'm going to do this, I have to teach myself, and I have to find out for myself what it is that I want. I remember meeting with these guys and saying that I wanted to sit down with their filmmakers and study their movies, and CAA had all of those connections. I didn't go to acting class. I didn't go to film school. Film school was every single day that I was making a movie. I wanted to push myself to learn, and CAA gave me this platform and support where I was able to say, "Can I meet Mr. Pollack? Can I meet Mr. Scorsese? If he would give me an hour of his time, I just want to ask him about movies. And you know, I'd also like to meet Mr. Newman." And they would facilitate all of that. Here I am, nineteen years old and having a meeting with Martin Scorsese because of Creative Artists Agency. They knew what I wanted to learn and so I was meeting these people, not just at dinner parties, but at serious meetings about cinema and story.

MICHAEL OVITZ:

One of the first things I wanted to do with Tom was sit in a room and give him a list of the directors he should work with, and I think he wound up working with almost every one of them.

PAUL BRICKMAN, Director:

Cruise's name came up late in the game. We had been casting *Risky* for many months. I can't recall who brought him to our attention. He was on location working on *The Outsiders*. Coppola gave him twenty-four hours' leave to audition for us.

He came to our office at Warners in the afternoon for a reading. I was impressed by his confidence. Once he stopped himself in the middle of a scene, chose a different approach, and started again—a rather bold move for a nineteen-year-old actor. It was apparent to me that Tom had the potential to fulfill two character requirements: he could play both strong and vulnerable. And he could be both naive and sexual. We had read scores of actors. I had many points of reference. I knew there was something special here.

Because he was scheduled to fly out the following day, we arranged an early-morning screen test with Tom and Rebecca De Mornay to take place at Steve Tisch's house. Jon Avnet shot the test with his home VHS camera and deck. (Some of the test is included in *Risky*'s twenty-fifth anniversary DVD.)

I drove to pick up Tom at 5:00 A.M. In the dark, I waited outside a nondescript apartment building in a bleak L.A. neighborhood. Nobody came out. I only had the address; no apartment number or phone number (and it was pre–cell phones anyway). By 5:20, I was about to call it quits. Either I had the wrong address or there was some snafu or the guy was flaky. No way of knowing. I convinced myself to give it five more minutes. At 5:25, I started the engine, thinking about getting some breakfast with Avnet and Tisch. I killed the engine. *Five more minutes*, I thought. *That's it.*

Eventually Tom appeared. I was a little pissed. I thought, *This screen test had better be pretty damned good*. It was.

So it was a really small amount of patience that allowed film history to take its course.

STEVE TISCH:

If Paula Wagner hadn't been as persistent and as supportive of Tom, he quite simply wouldn't have been in *Risky Business*.

TOM CRUISE:

You have to understand, at that point, I thought, "I love making movies. If I could just do this for the rest of my life, I will be so happy." That's how I felt.

SUSAN MILLER, Executive Assistant:

I became Michael Ovitz's executive assistant in June of 1983. Michael had two assistants and one trainee at that time. One was in charge of his phone sheet, which is the agent's bible, and I was responsible for his schedule, writing all his correspondence and buying gifts for executives, agents, and family, including birthdays, babies, and start-date gifts. They ranged from art books to original artwork, Cartier watches to snowmobiles. I coordinated and produced all of Michael's events, fundraisers, movie premieres, his son's bar mitzvah, even Stallone's wedding party to Brigitte Nielsen.

Michael ran his office on a "buzzer system" that was programmed through the phone. One buzz meant place the next call; two buzzes meant pick up the "com line" and talk to him, and three buzzes meant get your butt in his office with a pad and pen ready to go. Every morning, before many of the other agents were in the office, we met with Michael to get our marching orders for the day, but Michael had already started his day on the treadmill at five A.M.

You had to think ahead and anticipate what Michael needed before he asked for it. Follow-up was key, and there were certain rules: Never touch his food; never tell anyone who he was talking to or meeting with; always dress the part, and that meant no open-toed shoes; be kind and respectful; and finally, only lie when your life was at stake.

On my first week there, I got three buzzes and it was the first time I was going to be alone with him. I have to admit, I was petrified. Michael was standing in front of his desk, and I stayed near the door, and then he asked me, "What do you think of this tie with this suit?" I paused for a moment, worried about what I was about to say, but decided to do it anyway. I told him, "Not good." Michael was so happy. He said, "Thank God, someone who is not afraid to tell me the truth."

RICHARD LOVETT, Agent:

In college, I majored in English because I loved to read, but it was when I started managing a band that I became excited about what someone does to help get people jobs. At the time, I knew nothing about the entertainment business. I had read an article in *Milwaukee* magazine about the Zucker brothers. It was astounding to me that they had come from Milwaukee, gone to Hollywood, and then succeeded. And then I went to the movies with my oldest friend and we saw *E.T.* I came out of that movie and decided I wanted to be part of something that evokes such powerful emotions.

I started doing informational interviews in Madison, and going to advertising agencies and radio stations looking for openings. I met a guy who had worked at Leo Burnett and he told me, "You should work at Leo Burnett in the creative division in Chicago; I have a friend there and I'll call him," and it seemed like a sure thing, though I told him I'd never taken an advertising class and knew nothing about it. But I put together a book of ideas and went to Leo Burnett in Chicago in late summer of 1982. I'd been successful at things in the past, but the guy closed my book halfway through and just said, "This is awful." I asked him, "Is there any potential here at all?" and he said, "No." I was on the sidewalk ten minutes later. I had no prospects at all and decided I should go to Los Angeles or New York. I decided to try L.A., and I went and stayed with a friend in Glendale. I started making calls from the entertainment directory and the last call on my first day was to Creative Artists Agency—and they said they weren't hiring.

The sequence of what happened next was nothing I could have ever predicted. I went to see a great-uncle, who had retired and was living in Beverly Hills. He asked me what I wanted to do and I said, "Any kind of training program." He told me he was renting out two apartments behind his building, and in one of them was Don McGuire, who was an actor dating back to the '40s and had written the first draft of *Tootsie*. Don and I hit it off, and then he called his friend Ron Meyer and his agent, Marty Baum, and they arranged for me to have an interview at CAA. I had gotten to L.A. on a Tuesday, and my interview was that Friday at 6:00 P.M. I realized going into it, if there was a test, I was going to be in trouble. If I was asked what a producer does or to name some directors, I would have failed.

I interviewed with Ray Kurtzman, and he said, "Here are the reasons you don't want this job." I was about to say, "I'm desperate, I need a job and I have no possibility of a job," when Ron Meyer came in. I had never seen someone like this before in my life. In Milwaukee, there were no suntans and cool glasses. Ron looked at me and said, "Look, here's what's going to happen. You are going to be dying to go out with a girl. You've been after her and trying to convince her to go out with you, and she's going to finally agree to go out with you. Then ten minutes before you leave for the date, I'm going to call you and tell you you've got to pick up a script for me or do something else, and you're going to have to call her and cancel the date. That's this job." I said, "I'll do anything you want me to do for this job!" We finished the interview and I walked down the hallway and then Ray's assistant Gail Katz said, "Richard, come back!" So I went back into the office and they said, "You can start on Monday." When I was walking out, I asked the receptionist, "Is this a good place? Who are the clients?" She said, "Robert Redford." And I thought, *This place must be great!*

RON HOWARD:

I had been with the same agency that I had been with as a kid actor, but then it got acquired by somebody else, and so I had an agent that I didn't think about much. When I teamed up with Brian, we had the script *Night Shift* and we were trying to cast it. Bernie Brillstein was a big help because we really wanted John Belushi and Dan Aykroyd to do it, but CAA was also important; they were just beginning to become powerful in features. I understood that generationally, there were a lot of people who were represented by CAA that I wanted to collaborate with, and that was really the attraction.

DAVID O'CONNOR, Agent:

I worked for New Jersey Public Television because I was interested in news, documentaries, and politics, and New Jersey is rather deep in politics. Then I realized after two and a half, three years that it was just not a path for me; my strengths and weaknesses didn't match up with what journalism is all about. Another passion of mine was movies, and I had a brother who was working at CBS in Los Angeles, and he was doing quite well. Having grown up in Jersey and gone to school in New England, I thought, *I want to leave the East Coast and try and go into the entertainment business.* So I came out here naively, at twenty-five, just looking for a way in.

Because of my brother I got a lot of entry into the television world and everyone was so nice, but I didn't quite understand the niceness was just a nice way of saying, *Get out of here, you've got nothing to offer.*

RICHARD LOVETT:

I was always ambitious to be my best. I did want to make enough money at some point that I could drop off my laundry to be done, since I was no good at it, but money was never a motivation. If I got to the office and the door was locked, or if I got off the elevator and the newspapers were still on the floor, I was thrilled—it meant I was the first one in. And if I left the office and was the one who turned off the lights, then that was one of the ways I could tell myself I was working as hard as I could. I ate horribly, at Jack in the Box drive-thru because it was open until midnight and most of the other places were closed by the time I was done with work. My two go-to places were Jack in the Box and the counter at Junior's, because for $3.99 you could get eggs, hash browns, and cinnamon toast.

Lovett had been in the mailroom for several months when Rapke called him into his office and asked, "Do you want to be an agent?" Lovett immediately answered, "Yeah!" Rapke said, "I want you to read for me. I'm going to give you screenplays to read and cover." In exchange, Rapke promised Lovett an early "out" of the mailroom. He would jump Lovett over the next person in line when he had an opening on his desk. Lovett took the job seriously, despite the fact that the piles Rapke was giving him each Friday for weekend reading kept getting bigger and bigger. A couple of months later, Lovett went to Rapke's office only to find someone else sitting at his desk as his new assistant. That Friday, when Rapke gave a new pile to Lovett for weekend reading, Lovett drew the line. He told Rapke he had broken his promise and that his reading days were done.

Colleagues would describe the relationship between the two men from that day on as "frosty," "distant," and "troubled." Little did either of them know that a day would come when that lack of a bond would be attached to much higher stakes.

BRUCE VINOKOUR:

Bob O'Connor was then vice president of comedy series at CBS, and he called me to say, "My brother is coming from the East

Coast, and he wants to be in the entertainment business. Bruce, could you do me a favor and just have a cup of coffee with him." Bob said to his brother, "If you want to be in the entertainment business, you should be an agent. And if you want to be an agent, there's only one place to be an agent: Creative Artists Agency." His brother's name was David O'Connor.

DAVID O'CONNOR:

I was living in the downstairs portion of this shitty house down in Santa Monica Canyon and I was painting it to pay my rent. Weekends were really difficult for me because when you're not working and other people are, they get their weekends off, it's all fun and games, but I was stuck painting and constantly being reminded of the fact that I wasn't working. It was becoming a greater anxiety for me. I was also running out of money. After several months of banging on doors, trying to get in to see people, a number of people said, "Go get somebody coffee. Be a runner. Be a reader. Answer somebody's phone. Just get in. Just get a job. Just get started." The corollary was an agency was an interesting place to start because it was the crossroads to everything and a lot of people got their starts in the agency business. And they're the one place that takes people with no experience and trains them. I got an interview with a guy at William Morris named Lee Cohen who was a television agent, and Lee wanted to hire me as his assistant. I said, naively, "Well, am I a trainee then?" Because I was concerned about status and what I was going to tell my parents. He said, "Well, no, that's a whole different track, and if that's the case, you've got to go meet other people here. But I can hire you as my assistant." I said, "All right, well, let me think about that." I was also trying to get in the door at CAA—my brother and several other people said that was the cool place to work. They were the young guys, they were the upstarts. I finally got in to see a guy named Bruce Vinokour in the television department, and we met and talked and he said you should meet the guys who make decisions in terms of the training program here, and that's a guy named Ray Kurtzman and a guy named Ron Meyer. I had no idea who they were.

BRUCE VINOKOUR:

I went to Ray Kurtzman and said, "There's this young guy and he's pretty darn sharp. You should talk with him." And the rest is history.

DAVID O'CONNOR:

So I come in a week or so later and Ray keeps getting called out of the office; I don't know what he's getting called out of the office for, but this took like an hour for fifteen minutes of conversation. I later learned that he was going to see Ovitz.

Kurtzman was probably in his fifties at the time, maybe even a little bit younger, and he's telling me all of the reasons why I didn't want this job and I wasn't right for it. And I thought to myself, *This couldn't be going any worse.* And so then I got done with Ray and my next meeting was Ron Meyer. And that was just the complete opposite. Here's Ron with the most beautiful flowing Jewish locks you've ever seen and he's tan and looking relaxed and he's great and funny and cool and I had no idea he was one of the founders of the agency. Couldn't have been cooler, positive and fantastic. It was a Thursday night, and I walked out the door and I kept looking around the offices and looking at the people, and everybody was young and I came from broadcast journalism, where everybody was old. I walked out of that office thinking, *Gosh, I want to work there. That was a cool place.*

I went back to where I was staying, and kept painting. The house was a piece of shit, but it was right on the edge of Santa Monica Canyon, and the view of the ocean was unbelievable. It was Friday afternoon and I was quitting for the day, then the phone rang and it's, "Can you hold for Ray Kurtzman," and I'm like, "Ray Kurtzman?" It takes him like ten minutes to get on the phone and finally he picks up and goes, "Eh, David you want to start in the mailroom?" I said, "Is that the training program?" and he's like, "Yeah, it's the training program." And without even thinking about it, I shouted, "Yes!" He said, "Report to Jim Kaplan, the head of the mailroom, at 9:00 A.M. Monday." That was that. That Monday, I walked in the door to meet Jim and it was nine o'clock and I had my tie on and Jim takes one look at me and goes, "This is the last time you're coming here at 9:00 A.M. We start at 6:00." So that was that.

Richard was literally the third person I met at CAA because he got in early and it was my first day and I'm being shown how to make the coffee and Fred Specktor's office was right next to the kitchen and Richard worked for Fred Specktor. So here's this bubbly, energetic kid with glasses and he and I had this kind of immediate connection. We started hanging out with each other.

When I started, there were only four guys in the mailroom and I was head of the mailroom by March or April, and then we started taking in what's called "summer campers." And Jay [Moloney] was a summer camper. So here was this lanky, kind of awkward kid who was hilarious. He was just hilarious. So that summer Richard, Jay, and I became friends.

Most young newcomers to CAA started off in the mailroom. Jay Moloney, for whom virtually nothing would be typical, started off in the Ovitz home. He helped out with the Ovitz kids, and obligingly drove Judy Ovitz around town. The mailroom loomed ahead, and Jay eventually served there. When Jay announced he had graduated from USC—forget about the fact that he was a few pesky credits short—Ovitz forked over $10,000 for Jay to visit Armani and acquire a most excellent set of suits. As Jay's father had been a screenwriter, he'd had considerable exposure to show business early in life, but it was nothing like the experience he'd get in the years ahead. Jay may have been the youngest Turk, but he had the greatest enthusiasms and appetites. In the course of satisfying some of those, he would date Sherilyn Fenn, Gina Gershon, and Jennifer Grey, to name just a few. His art collection at the time was unparalleled for someone his age, and he made friends with key artists before they were huge like Schnabel, Dine, Chuck Close, and others.

MICHAEL OVITZ:

Jay was really amazing, the best trainee we ever had without a doubt.

TOM LASSALLY, Producer:

Jay and I met when I was at NYU film school and out here in L.A. for a summer. Jay was at CAA, working as a third assistant to Ovitz. Mutual friends introduced us, and we just had some weird friend chemistry with each other and quickly became great friends. To me, the fact that he was delivering groceries to Sean Connery's condominium was pure Hollywood, the coolest thing in the world. A lot of my first Hollywood experiences were going along with Jay on crazy errands all over the city.

RICHARD LOVETT:

When Jay was a senior at USC, he was an intern on Fred's desk, where I was the assistant. We became deeply connected and close friends. We were like brothers in those days, and so it was with the group of us—Kevin, Bryan, Doc, Michael Wimer, Jay, and myself.

Jay was, tied-for-first, the most charismatic, winning, charming, and funny person you could ever meet. He was kind and big-hearted. He cared deeply about his friends, family, and clients. He loved music and movies and television. He loved artists and they knew it. They felt it.

CAA opened its music department on January 4, 1984, bringing Tom Ross, ICM's co-head of music, over to run it. Meetings between Ross and CAA began in the summer of 1983 at Jimmy's restaurant in Beverly Hills, and in November 1983, Ross told ICM he was leaving. Unique in Ross's hiring was the fact that he'd demanded a contract, something that the CAA founders had been reluctant to provide for other agents.

Early music clients included Fleetwood Mac, Rick Springfield, Jefferson Airplane, Crosby, Stills & Nash, Dolly Parton, and Prince, whose movie Purple

Rain, *adapted from his album, was an early crossover success for the new music division. Released on July 27, 1984, the film went on to gross $68,392,977 domestic.*

TOM ROSS, Agent:

I went to school in Beverly Hills. My father was an entertainment lawyer who had represented Martin and Lewis, Rowan and Martin, Red Skelton, and all four of the major agencies. He was also one of the early owners of the Riviera Hotel. I thought I was going to be a lawyer and went to law school at Stanford for one week for orientation. They handed me all the books and I said, "Wow, that's a lot of reading for the first year." And they said, "That's the first semester." And literally the lightbulb went off and I said, "This is not what I want to do," so I dropped out. And one of our dear family friends said, "Why don't you consider being an agent?" and then I took one of those Minnesota aptitude tests and it said I would be a good Realtor/insurance salesman, so becoming an agent kind of fit.

I grew up with *Daily Variety* and *The Hollywood Reporter*, and showbiz was very common. I went to Beverly High and my classmates were Rob Reiner and Melinda Marx, Groucho's daughter, and Danny Kaye's daughter. Showbiz didn't intimidate me; it was just normal.

I got a chance to interview at the Agency for the Performing Arts, which is still in business. They had me come in but said, "We don't have any openings." I would say that was in September of 1968, and in November, the fella who was running their contemporary rock 'n' roll department, Todd Schiffman, was wooed over to Ashley Famous, a predecessor to ICM. APA was really the only agency that was booking rock 'n' roll for bands like The Doors, Iron Butterfly, and Janis Joplin.

Todd took quite a few acts with him. They called me on November fourth and said, "Would you like to try this? There's an opening." I said, "I'm there." When I came in, there was no mailroom. They said, "Just listen on the phone." On my second day they said, "One of our artists, Jefferson Airplane, is coming to town and you can sit in on the meeting and get a feel for what that's like." So that afternoon, sure enough, the Airplane came in, all kind of grumpy and grizzly. Half sat on the floor. I came in and took a seat on the floor as well and they started talking about the tour that needed to be booked and no more than five minutes after we sat down, the Airplane pulled out a joint and lit it up and it started going around the room. I knew what it was, but also knew if I smoked it, I was going to be fired on my first day; but if I don't smoke it, I'd be seen as a kind of narc and the group would never look at me as somebody they could trust. So I took a few hits and I wasn't really familiar with the quality of San Francisco marijuana at that time. My eyes must have turned purple. I spent hours trying to say, "Oh my God," at least it *seemed* like hours. And so we're getting along, and everybody's talking about cities and what they want to accomplish on the tour, and then somebody opened the door and pulled me out. "Tom, can we see you?" And I was thinking, *Why? Why am I the one they're pulling out of the meeting?* My eyes were purple and they were all bloodshot.

It turned out they wanted me to run up and deliver a script to some movie director up in Bel Air. And I didn't want to make eye contact, so I just looked at the floor. They handed me the script and said, "Go there." I got to the car and said, *I have no idea where I'm supposed to go. I have no idea what I'm doing here. I can't get oriented.* And I just drove around for about two hours. I eventually got there, some big mansion in Bel Air, but the guy missed his flight, so I called the guy who I was shadowing and said, "I'm so sorry. I guess I shouldn't come back tomorrow. I blew it." And he said to me, "Blew what?" I said, "Well, I got the script there late and the guy missed his plane." And he said, "The Jefferson Airplane loves you. They want you to be their agent." And hello, Hollywood!

My dad had represented both the Ice Follies and the Ice Capades, but the Ice Capades had signed Peggy Fleming, and she was about my age. So besides the music, I got to represent Peggy Fleming, which was two different hats, and that wound up playing a big role in my thinking about the future of booking bands.

The old adage in the booking business was "You can never get the popcorn and the peanuts." But the Ice Capades and Ice Follies got a piece of the concessions when they played, because they played weeks at a time. The Ice Capades and the Ice Follies and the circus were the only major accounts that came every year to every major building in the country. They made an overall deal with Peggy because she was a star for fifty weeks a year. So every time she went into a building, she got a piece of the gross above and beyond what they did the year before. And she was the hottest thing in America. I realized there was an open door into what rock bands could take out of a building based on profitability. Remember, the agent's sole responsibility in music was to be the fiduciary of the act against the promoter and the building. My deal was to get them the best, most money out of any situation.

I stayed at APA for three and a half years, and in those years, four or five other agencies figured out that rock 'n' roll was here to stay. Eventually it all spread out.

I went to Associated Booking and I stayed there about three and a half years, then I got an opportunity to go to IFA, which was the Ashley Famous agency that became International Famous. Lo and behold, as soon as I got there—within, I think, six months—IFA and CMA merged and became ICM. The guy that I reported to left and said, "I'm getting out. I'm going to Monterey." I stayed at ICM. I booked every act on the roster. I went crazy, I went to every show, met the whole industry, everyone from Chicago, the Doobie Brothers, Redbone, and Olivia Newton-John. We had Aerosmith, we had Styx, we had the Eagles, the Kinks, Linda Ronstadt, Loggins and Messina, James Taylor. Fleetwood Mac became my pet client, mainly because there was no manager saying what to do.

At ICM I was friends with Lee Gabler. Jimmy Wiatt was a high school best friend; I got Jimmy his job.

JIM WIATT:

Tom Ross was really the reason I even got to ICM at the time, because I was working at a really small three-person agency before I was even working at ICM. At the time Tom was thought of as the most powerful music agent.

TOM ROSS:

I was the department head together with my East Coast counterpart, Shelly Schultz. We built the fort. Every year we hit our numbers, but when it came to our bonuses, there was a different excuse: "Well, you did great, but the film side didn't." "Well, you did great, but the radio division fell apart." After ten years, I was fed up with being a part of a public company and not getting a real major bump in salary or bonuses. I started wondering, *Where can I go? I've now been in the business for fifteen years and I can make a lateral move to William Morris. They would take me.* But I wanted something different.

Sue Mengers was at ICM and she had been promised by Gary Hendler, who was a big entertainment lawyer, that we would get a meeting with Rod Stewart. We got a meeting, but I found out that they were already committed to William Morris. So Sue said, "Tom, you better be good," and it was one of those great days where everything you said clicked. You could see it in the artist— everything they thought they were going to do, I turned around and said, "Why would you do that? That's not a smart idea. This would be better." But they had already committed to William Morris, so that's where they went. The very next day after that meeting, I got a phone call from Michael Ovitz. And what had happened was Gary Hendler called him up and said, "I found your music guy. You should meet Tom Ross."

TONY KRANTZ:

When the music division was getting started, Tommy Mottola, who was one of Mike Ovitz's friends, said to Mike, "If you can get somebody like Tom Ross, I'll give you every act we have." Bob Cavallo and Sandy Gallin said the same thing.

TOM ROSS:

Rumors were out there that CAA might be looking to start a music agency, but everyone thought they would buy somebody. And at that time it was five Ferraris with their CAA initials and you would see them all over town. They had no music department and Michael was very cautious—"Why would I want music?" I said, "Well, you called the meeting. I didn't. But you know, we're providing the cash flow for the agency while various strikes have happened, and ours is quick. Six weeks after we book it, the money is in the book." And over the course of six months, I met with Michael, then I met with Michael and Ronnie, then I met with Michael, Ronnie, and Bill. We used to meet at Jimmy's restaurant, a big hangout of celebrities and film people. Here I was, Mr. Rock 'n' Roll, and they would lead me to a back room and Michael would come in from another door, and nobody had any idea that we were meeting.

I saw this as an opportunity to start something from the ground up. To Michael and Ronnie I said, "The way the business is progressing, the music people are starting to act, the soundtrack business is huge, they're starting to want to have careers outside the music world. What I'm interested in is not having the flash in the pan but building long-term careers, having the best concert department, but also very supportive television film experience." It used to be "Sign them in music and we don't care where they go for film." I said we had to be different. And Michael said, "I will be there, trust me."

I said, "Look, I was the head of the concert department for ICM and you're telling me that I have to trust you. I've been in the business for fifteen years. It's a little late just to, say, go into a deal saying 'trust you.' We're just getting to know each other." We went through a barrage of "everybody's free to leave when they want," but I said, "I'm not looking to leave. I'm looking to stay." We eventually came to an agreement that he would make an exception and give me a contract, which I think was the only one he probably ever did, or at least back then in 1984. After the first year came and went, we sure enough never referred to the contract again. Michael delivered way beyond my expectations.

He would surprise me. I remember he met Stevie Wonder and gave him the handshake, which at the time was pretty rare—the brothers' handshake. And I said, "How did you know the handshake?" And he said, "ZBT." Same handshake.

JIM WIATT:

I wasn't angry. Tom had been a mentor and friend and was responsible for helping me get to a place where I had a career. But it was a big loss for me personally, and for ICM. It demonstrated how powerful CAA was at the time that they could go and recruit the best of everybody, so they became incredibly difficult to compete against. The landscape became far more competitive, not just regarding clients, but also about trying to maintain the manpower you had.

MICK FLEETWOOD, Musician:

Of course we followed Tom. We had been with him at ICM, and it really didn't matter where he was going. He had always been there for us, always rooted for us, and had become a personal friend. We were already connected to him when Bob Welch was in our band, and we thought of him as a team player. He got the pipe dream of what Fleetwood Mac was all about. And when the pivotal moment came, when we were in a state of disarray after Bob left, he got in the trenches with us and played an important role in Stevie and Lindsay joining us. We had many people in the record business telling us we had three bands in one band and it was all getting too confusing, but guess what? That Achilles' heel, so to speak, wound up being the reason for our success, and Tom saw it. The involvement Tom had with the making of that unique lineup was pivotal.

Tom was an appreciator and facilitator. I remember we started to put together the *Rumours* album, and the first time we rehearsed with Stevie and Lindsay he arranged for us to do so in the basement, next to the boiler room, at the ICM building.

ROB LIGHT, Agent:

I went to Syracuse University and had been a concert chairman. I graduated in 1978, went to work at ICM in the mailroom, got promoted fairly quickly, and became an agent there. I actually was offered to go to work at MTV in the spring of '81 because my buddy from Syracuse John Sykes had started MTV, and I turned it down because I didn't really see how music videos were ever going to work on television. But I made the right decision and was at ICM for five years. I reported to two guys, one of them being Tom Ross, who seduced me to come to the West Coast—I'm a New Yorker—and when I came out west, he left ICM to go start the music department at CAA. They were a film and TV agency at the time and he convinced me to go with him. I did, and it was me, Tom, and a gentleman named Hal Lazarus and we started in January of 1984. I was the twenty-seventh agent, and I think the whole company was seventy employees.

TOM ROSS:

Rob became my first hire, and Hal and Rob were my first two guys. Mitch Rose at that time was in the mailroom and said, "If you start a music department, that's where I want to be." And he was one of our early secretaries. Rick Springfield was a client who was huge on a soap opera and would work weekends. So he came with me and the Jefferson Airplane came with me, as did Dolly Parton. I had about ten acts that were coming with me. We hit the ground running. We were booking from January fourth on.

ROB LIGHT:

When we first started it was three agents and we had three clients (Hall & Oates, Christine McVie, and Rick Springfield). We were really starting a new agency, a new music department in an agency that was actually just coming into its own. CAA was on an amazing run in film and TV; they had already picked up a lot of momentum and the cultural energy at CAA was incredibly evident. The team-oriented approach, one of working together and supporting each other for the whole of the company, was tangible. We were an embryonic company, and at that time in the music business, so much of what was happening was so standard and uninspired. There hadn't been something new in the agency space in so long that the cultural newness and embrace of the whole company excited the music industry. And the whole notion of how we operated was so antithetical to every other agency that artists loved it, the business loved it, and we got off to a relatively fast, aggressive start. Tom Ross was a brilliant guy. He was incredibly beloved. And the support we got from film and TV was so unbelievable, it didn't just feel different, it really was different and it worked. We actually felt that support system which no other agency had had.

TOM ROSS:

John Mellencamp hated agents. He had a bad experience with his former agent and Mottola told me, "Look, I'm telling you now, this guy does not like agents. He thinks they're just pimps, so he's going to come in and meet with you, but I don't even know if he'll sit down." So I figured we had to disarm ourselves, and rather than having him come in and we would shake big dicks, we had to tell him we had the smallest dicks in town and it was all about him. And I pretty much did that. We went in and sure enough he was standing. We told him that we work for our clients and it's not about us; that we were the hardest working people; and that we would make him more money on the road because we looked at every single opportunity. At that point, he sat down. Then we went on and on. At the end of it, he committed to us, and after the first tour, he came in and said, "You'll probably never see this happen again, but I want to say thank you. You were right. You delivered."

Neil Diamond, unlike everyone else, could sell out every secondary, tertiary market and obviously the major markets, but he never overplayed. He would play multiple days, but then he wouldn't come back for eighteen months. While they were on the road, Neil would oftentimes challenge a radio station to a baseball game with his crew. Rob Light went out one year and was the umpire for the game against some big city radio station, and Neil was up at bat. I think bases were loaded, three and two count. The guy threw and Rob said, "Strike three! You're out!" And there was just this hush of silence. Neil was pissed. He didn't talk to Rob, and I had to call Neil and say, "We've often tried to get Rob to go to his eye doctor and have his eyes checked. We think there's a problem there and we're sorry if you had to pay a price for it."

We used to have meetings with Prince, and he was quite unusual, to say the least. He would sit in the room with his back to us, and we weren't allowed to make eye contact at any time. We were told, "Do not look at him. If you look at him, you will probably lose a client."

MICHAEL OVITZ:

Prince called me up and told me that he didn't want to record for Warner anymore. He said, "Can you get me out of it?" I said, "I don't know," so I called up Mo [Ostin], and Mo said, "Michael, I'd love to help you. I can't let him out. He's too good." I said, "I'll talk to him." So I went and talked to him. He called me back like a month later and he said, "You know, I decided that I'm not Prince anymore." And I said, "Who are you?" He said, "I'm the artist formerly known as Prince. Please advise my record label that Prince is no longer." I did, and they let him out.

PHIL KENT, Executive:

Prince—four different times we set up an HBO special; four different times he changes his mind.

MICHAEL OVITZ:

Prince was so fricking brilliant. I went to Minneapolis to see him. The guy played twenty instruments, and he had an idea for a movie that I thought was pretty great. Everyone thought I was crazy. The only guy who didn't think I was crazy was Rand Holston. We put *Purple Rain* together, and it was a big hit.

RICK NICITA:

I put him in *Purple Rain.* I was Prince's movie agent and I remember we had a meeting at Warner Bros. Albert Magnoli directed *Purple Rain*; he was pitching the movie and he jumped out of his chair and went down on his knees in front of the executives. They just couldn't say no.

TOM ROSS:

When I started, he had already made the deal for Prince with Bob Cavallo to make a film at Warner Bros.

BOB CAVALLO, Manager and Producer:

Prince demanded, as only he could, he said that he would re-sign with us, but I had to get him a film. And it couldn't be some film where I got him the part of a drug dealer or some jeweler. It had to be a major motion picture studio, and he had to have his name above the title. "Starring me." And he said he would put an album's worth of songs in it.

RICK NICITA:

I got a screenplay together, and CAA started to send it out to directors, but everybody passed. I couldn't get anybody to direct this movie. I tried to get Jamie Foley, who had just made his first motion picture, *Reckless.* And I went to a screening of the film; I was alone in the screening room, and a kid walks over to me and he says, "What did you think?" I said it was good, I liked the editing—for whatever reason I said that. And it turned out the kid was Albert Magnoli, the editor. The kid said, "I went to school with Jamie, I did a student film called *Jazz* you might want to see." So I saw it and I decided, screw it, I offered him the movie. He passed. He didn't have a pot to piss in, and he passed. I said, "Why?" And he said, "It's too square." I said, "I agree, can you fix it?" He said, "Oh, I could do it." He rewrote it and we made the movie.

Now it was a negative pickup deal, so the money to make the movie came from Prince and me and my partner, but we ran out of money, so I went to Mo Ostin. We had a few million dollars in the pipeline from the previous album, so I asked him for a $2 million advance. So we took that money and we almost finished, I was about $700,000 short, maybe $600,000. I went to Los Angeles from Minneapolis to get the money and finish the picture. Warners insisted on a screening, a rough assemblage of all the footage. There were scenes missing, and a lot of those were the comedy in the movie, so they thought it was terrible. But Mike Ovitz thought it was great, truly great. He said, "You've done it. If they don't give you the money"—and he said it in their presence—"we'll get it for you and we'll have it to another studio by tomorrow." And of course they gave us the money.

PHIL KENT:

For the most part, Prince was kept far away from us by his team. One day he woke up and found out he owed Warner Bros. Records an enormous amount of money, we heard maybe $10 million or more—and he freaked out and fired his lawyers, fired his managers, publicists, and business manager. Michael thought he didn't fire us because we were doing such a good job, but Tom said, "I hate to break it to you, but I don't think he knew we represented him."

BOB CAVALLO:

Prince was already about a million-seller. I wasn't going to give people a percentage of something they couldn't contribute to in any way. So there was no agency involved in Prince's career choices. It was only in his personal appearances. And that's only because the law required that I couldn't do it. So if we wanted help, somebody else other than me had to do it, because that's against California code.

Ghostbusters *was released on June 4, 1984, and was a tremendous block-buster, grossing $242 million in the U.S. and more than $295 million worldwide, and also a hit inside the walls of CAA. It was a CAA package, and to make things even better, it was for the agency's favorite studio, Columbia.*

IVAN REITMAN:

I think it was Ovitz who sent me Dan Aykroyd's treatment, but it was Dan who requested that he send it. Dan wanted to do this movie with Belushi back when they were the Blues Brothers on *Saturday Night Live*. When Belushi passed away, Dan had conversations with a number of other actors including Eddie Murphy, and he was also thinking of Bill Murray. By then I'd done these two Bill Murray movies and he knew me; Dan and I go back to Toronto, prior to *Saturday Night*. Like most Aykroyd scripts it had a brilliant idea, all kinds of interesting things in it, but as a script it didn't really work as far as characters and plot. I sat down with Aykroyd about a week after I read it, and I said instead of being in outer space and instead of being about the future—there were a number of different Ghostbusting outfits in his thing—this should take place today, which was 1983, and I think these guys should be regular people that we recognize, maybe working at a university. They get kicked out, they go into business, and lo and behold ghosts are coming to New York and it actually turns out to be good business. I looked at it as a going-into-business story. He agreed, and I'd now worked with Harold [Ramis] a couple of times, and I knew I needed another writer to help balance out Danny's kind of work, so I suggested we bring Harold into it and make him a Ghostbuster as well. I thought that would be a good trio. I called up Harold, who agreed, and literally within a week, Ovitz set up a meeting with Frank Price. By then I had done *Stripes* for Frank and we were pretty close. He called me into the office, and I basically gave him the outline of *Ghostbusters* the way I'd envisioned it, and much like he did with *Stripes*, he said okay.

I think the most gross that anyone had ever paid out on a feature film at that time was 35 percent. We had to figure out whatever the income was going to be, we had to divide it in some kind of proportion, with Bill getting a little bit more than everybody, and Harold getting a little bit less, and Danny and I getting the same. Making everybody happy required an agency of power and somebody that all of us could trust. And that was Mike. He was very instrumental in making sure all of us were happy. Even Bernie Brillstein got a small piece, because Aykroyd had technically sold him his very first treatment for a dollar, and as a result, he didn't have to pay management fees. That was the deal he had made and we all sort of agreed to it. It was something that Harold Ramis was always remarkably angry about.

BILL MURRAY:

That *Ghostbusters* package was mind-boggling. Mike really pulled that thing together, and it was a deal unlike anything else. It was a huge piece of cash. It was ridiculous.

MICHAEL OVITZ:

I had *Ghostbuster* board meetings—Ghostbusters LLC. Bill Murray, Dan Aykroyd, Ivan Reitman, Harold Ramis. We would meet at a restaurant for lunch every three months with an agenda to discuss the business of the *Ghostbusters*, the animated series, *Ghostbusters II,* everything. I ran it like a board of directors meeting and I used Robert's Rules of Order. They loved it.

AMY GROSSMAN:

Our script covers were red with the CAA logo in white. I would take home twelve to fourteen of them each weekend, and there were more to read during the week. Once I got stopped by a cop for rolling through a stop sign, and when he came up to the car, noticed all the scripts in the backseat—and you know where this is going: he had written a script and asked if I would read it in lieu of my getting a ticket. I made that deal on the spot.

TOM STRICKLER, Agent:

I got to CAA after graduating college in 1984 and then I think I was fired like three years later, in '87. I started in the mailroom and did a hard twelve months there. Then I went on to work for Jack Rapke, who at the time was sort of their preeminent directors' agent at the agency. Then I got promoted. And it was almost like a year at each station.

To give credit where credit is due, Jack was a friend and an ally. When your assistant gets promoted, you sort of look after them. They somehow represent you because you ultimately advocated for their ascension through the ranks. Anyway, Jack came by and there was this tiny little review in maybe a column inch from *New York* magazine. He handed it to me and he said, "This could be a movie." Why he was reading this review, I don't remember; it was just a slight synopsis. I read it, and he was right, it could be a movie. So I called the theater in New York—it was off-off-Broadway, and tracked down the playwright, a guy named Bob Harling, and he was excited because I was the first Hollywood agent who had ever called him. I signed him, and then represented the movie rights from the play. This all happened because Jack had helped me. That play was *Steel Magnolias*.

ABBY ADAMS, Agent:

I started in January of '84. David O'Connor was the head of the mailroom, and Richard Lovett had just gotten out of the mailroom and was on Fred Specktor's desk. There were only four of us in the mailroom; I was the only girl. I had never had a car, so my brother leased me a little Honda, and I got a Thomas Guide book.

That June, Ray Kurtzman called me and said, "Dustin Hoffman's wife Lisa is pregnant, and they're going to be in Broad Beach for the summer. He needs a personal assistant. Would you want to do that just for the time he's here?" I said, "Okay." Of course I would have rather been doing that than driving packages around godforsaken places. "But," I said to Ray, "I want you to promise me that I'm not going to have to go back into the mailroom. That

I'll have a desk after Dustin." He said, "Okay, okay." So that's what I did. I was out of the mailroom and had the best summer of my life.

When I returned to CAA, I was on Laurie Perlman's desk. She was married to Jack Rapke at the time, and had signed Madonna—who once asked me to get some Perrier in a bowl for her dog that she had brought to the office. But there was also the time when I was working late on a Friday night and was on the phone with my mother, who was back in New Jersey, and all of a sudden Robert Redford walked up to my desk and said, "Where's Mike?" I had seen him before, but there was just something about him standing by himself at my desk in faded jeans that just made me think to myself, *Oh my God*. Next thing I knew, one of Ovitz's assistants called me and said, "Mr. Redford would like some popcorn."

NELL SCOVELL, Writer:

Abby Adams worked so hard and was so effective at CAA. I often wondered what it must have been like for her to be one of the sole women in that department. Sports were a big part of that culture and one of the primary ways that the male agents bonded. It was strange because my first professional writing job was covering sports at the *Boston Globe* and I would've loved to go to Laker games, but I never got invited. Meanwhile, I had a male writer friend who *hated* sports and felt obligated to go to those sorts of CAA-hosted events. It was a great opportunity to get extra attention from your agent.

Abby was a complete professional. She followed through on everything. And she was extremely supportive of other women. In 1996, the job of executive producer/creator of ABC's *Sabrina, the Teenage Witch* came up after another writer who'd been attached to the project wasn't let out of his previous contract. Abby recommended me for the job and pushed hard to make it happen.

MARTIN SCORSESE, Director:

I had been with my agent and friend Harry Ufland since 1965, and he was at William Morris. So Harry and I went into the '70s together, and he was still sort of handling me at the time I met Mike. The industry had changed greatly after the year that *Raging Bull* came out. It was November of 1980, and ten days later *Heaven's Gate* came out and the studio went down. I was then involved with De Niro in *King of Comedy*, and I was delayed on that. When the film was finally released in February of '83, it was considered a disaster. So it was time to get my career back on line for the picture I wanted to make, which was *Last Temptation of Christ*. That was being pulled together with Irwin Winkler and Bob Chartoff, and a number of other people. That comprised a whole year of 1983, and I must have met Michael in that time. I met with Michael Eisner and with Jeff Katzenberg at Paramount, but ultimately, the film was canceled at the end of the year, pretty much about eight weeks before shooting. It wasn't easy to get a film of mine made.

So around '83, when I found myself in L.A. a lot, there was talk of doing a sequel to *The Hustler*, which to me was rather dubious at the time, because it's a wonderful iconic film. I came back to New York and started making an independent film called *After Hours* in 1984, and that was done with David Geffen at Warner Bros. It did very well, was a highly regarded film in Cannes and a number of other places, and right around that time, in '84 or '85, I remember Paul Newman had sent me a letter about *Raging Bull* saying he saw the film and really admired it. I believe now that Mike Ovitz had mentioned over the years that he had advised Paul to send the letter.

BRIAN GRAZER, Producer:

When Ron Howard and I did *Night Shift*, we pretty much went around CAA to have a meeting with John Belushi and Dan Aykroyd. It was our first movie. Those guys really liked us, but because we hadn't gone through the agency, we weren't getting an answer back, and they pretty much made me invisible to them for a while. Then unfortunately I did the same thing on my second movie, *Splash*, where Ron Howard and I met John Travolta in a little Italian restaurant in the Valley. He wanted to do the movie, but because I didn't go through the agency, I was punished again. But I ended up with Tom Hanks, who became a huge star as well, and the movie was a giant smash hit critically and commercially.

The minute *Splash* opened, I was invited to a bunch of parties I would have never been invited to before, including a big party at Chasen's, where Michael Ovitz came up to me, put his arm around me in front of a bunch of A-listers and said, "We did it, didn't we?" And I thought, *Did we? I know I did. I didn't know we did.* But I realized that wasn't what he was saying. What he was saying was, "Whatever happened was water under the bridge. You're *in*. We want to treat you as a number one superstar client from now on." That's what the arm around the shoulder meant: It's very mafia, and he was the don.

BARBRA STREISAND, Actress and Director:

I was represented by Sue Mengers at the time, and Brian Grazer told me, "I gave her the *Splash* script to give to you," but she never showed it to me. How many other things did she not show me? She had turned me off *Julia*, didn't even tell me Fred Zinnemann was attached, and she didn't want me to do *Coming Home*. And she really didn't want me to do *Yentl*. I remember she did want me to do *Klute*, and also *They Shoot Horses, Don't They?* I thought, *Dance all day? Oy.*

DAVID GREENBLATT, Agent:

I arrived at CAA as an agent in the TV literary department in the fall of '84 from ICM. Ironically, I couldn't get into the CAA training program. About a year into ICM, I started figuring out what being an agent was and realized there were two factions at the company: Jeff Berg's and Lee Gabler's. Lee was the king of television packaging. There were really only three networks at the time that mattered, and he probably had close to a dozen shows on the air. I was in awe of Lee. I thought he was classy and smart and considerate. I didn't really have any real role models in show business, and I thought, *That's who I want to be.*

Berg won the battle and became head of the company, so Lee left. I stayed in touch with him and would lament with Lee how the place wasn't the same after he left. He had started a small agency after ICM and Ovitz threw him a lifeline. A lot of people thought Lee going over to CAA was a great wedge if one day Haber had to go. Lee certainly had the skill set to become the commander of the TV department, but his going over was really about Ovitz wanting to crush the competition. Ovitz used to say, "There's a pie out there and I want it all." To Ovitz it was not Hertz and Avis, where even the second-place company was a huge success. It was just going to be Hertz.

Now at the time, William Morris and ICM were probably bigger agencies than CAA, but every week there was a brand-new red background ad in *Variety* and *The Hollywood Reporter* that would say, "CAA is pleased to announce the signing of," and it would be this big actor or director. It was their way of saying, "We're on the rise, and everybody else better watch out." Seeing all those ads made me want to be there. They were becoming the A-Team. Lee got me an interview with Mark Rossen, who was a TV lit agent at CAA. Mark told me, "David, it's completely different from ICM. It's all about massive communication. If you don't communicate here, you are gone. It is team first or you're out." And he was right. Although there were really good people at ICM, the attitude was *We'll give you some rope and you can hang on to it or you can hang yourself with it.* Nobody was going to help show you how to make it all work.

When I started at CAA, I remember saying to my wife, "I think I found a job for life."

ERIC CARLSON:

Looking at the competition, I didn't know these guys well, but it seemed to be schlubby, like an old archetype of what an agent used to be. We always seemed to be younger and better dressed and better looking, and we moved in packs, at least that's what it looked like to people on the outside. Some people didn't like it, some people did.

DAVID GREENBLATT:

To this day, Michael Ovitz is the most engaging, fascinating guy I've ever met in business. He made you feel like you're the only person on the planet. He made you feel great. When I would sit with him, I would think to myself, *God, I'd follow this guy anywhere. If he was my general, I'd fight to the death for him.*

ARI EMANUEL, Agent:

There was also a Wizard of Oz thing going on behind that cape, because even when Mike didn't know shit, he had everybody believing the opposite. And then he would do these things that were the greatest. He'd come into a meeting and say, "In the next ninety days there's going to be a huge event," and everyone sat there in amazement that he knew about it before anyone else. But it's Hollywood. Shit happens. Of course there's going to be a huge event. And then sure enough, something would happen and he would say, "See this is what I was talking about but couldn't tell you." It was unbelievable. Pure genius.

JUDY HOFFLUND:

Mike was insanely effective in staff meetings, and for the first couple years, I bought it all, you know? My husband would say, "Oh, you're drinking the Kool-Aid," because I would come home and think that CAA was the greatest thing and Mike was the smartest guy, and he would have these expressions that were funny, like, "Well, in thirty to seventy-five days, something is going to happen in our business that I just want you to know I'm forecasting." He never said what it was. Everyone was just looking at him with bright eyes like he was you know, the fortune-teller, like he knew the future of the entertainment business.

DAVID GREENBLATT:

When you think about it, that's such a blanket general statement. You know *something* big is going to happen at Warner Bros. in ninety days. Of course there's going to be something happening in any ninety-day period. They wouldn't be in business otherwise on the levels they were. It could be that they were syndicating *Scooby-Doo*, for all I know, as their something big. But by Ovitz saying that, it gave you the impression he was right in the middle of it, even if he had nothing to do with it. Made you feel you were working at the center of the entertainment universe. You got sucked right into it. It was brilliant.

RON MEYER:

It was very important to Mike that he be perceived as someone who not only knew what was going on, but also that he knew it before anyone else did.

DAVID GREENBLATT:

If I asked Michael to be in a meeting, that was only rarely, because you didn't want to go to that well too many times, he would do it for the team, you know? *Miami Vice* had just come on the air, the hottest fucking thing, and I've orchestrated this meeting with the creator, Tony Yerkovich, to try to sign him. It's Jack, Mike Marcus, myself, Lee. I would say, "Mike, I need you to come into the meeting." So we're sitting around a conference table. Ovitz comes in around five minutes later. He says, "Do you mind if I sit next to Tony?" So I get up, move over so Mike and Tony are sitting next to each other. And Mike starts talking about the vision of what *Miami Vice* can springboard into—he was talking about branding before anyone else was talking about branding. And Tony was very enamored by this conversation—we're all very enamored. Get a knock at the conference room door. It's Michael's assistant, "Excuse me, I'm sorry," hands him a note. "Excuse me, Tony." Takes a look at it. Says to his assistant very deliberately, "Tell Terry Semel I'll call him back, I want to finish my conversation with Tony." His assistant walks out, Michael finishes the conversation. Now, Terry Semel was famously one of the hardest guys to get on the phone in business. I am certain that was scripted. Certain. But it was brilliant, because it made us all feel like we were in the presence of somebody who makes *us* feel like we were really important.

TONY KRANTZ:

The very first thing I ever packaged was a movie-of-the-week based on Joan Didion's book *Salvador* about this war in El Salvador. I was working with a producer named Dick Berg and put together a package with a writer named Ernest Tidyman, who had won the Oscar for *The French Connection*. Shirley MacLaine was going to play Joan Didion. We walked into Harvey Shephard's office, who was the head of CBS at the time, and we pitched it to him and he bought it in the room. And I came back to the parking lot or whatever it was and Dick said, "Now we've got to get the rights." And I said, "What do you mean we've got to get the rights?" He said, "I don't have the rights to the book." And I said, "You're kidding." I was so young that I didn't know to ask the question "Did you have the rights?"

My mother had Joan Didion's phone number in her Rolodex, so I called Joan up and explained the mess. She said, "None of my books have ever been produced in film or television. I'm not going to give you the rights." So I went back to Harvey Shephard and I said, "A huge mistake has happened and I'm very apologetic." But from that, my bosses felt I had an aptitude for packaging and I started packaging MOWs full time. One of them I put together, *Inherit the Wind*, went on to win the Emmy as best MOW a year or two later.

DAVID GREENBLATT:

I was in the TV lit department, and CAA was not a big fan of TV lit. They were a big fan of packaging because packaging [is where] you make all your money. You put somebody on a show for $50,000 an episode, times twenty-two episodes, the client makes $1,100,000 and that's $110,000 in commission. You package the show and you're making, as an agency at the time, probably $30,000 an episode times twenty-two. So one's $600,000, one's

$22,000. So they hated when you sold a writer to somebody that wasn't a package, even though selling a writer to somebody else might have been better for the client's career and in the long run makes them even more of a commodity. Inside CAA it was always about package *über alles*—that was literally a phrase. This was Haber's philosophy.

Before I left ICM, I knew that they weren't going to give me clients, so I made a deal with the receptionist. I said, "We must get a lot of calls for people wanting to send their scripts in here, right?" She goes, "Yeah." I said, "Just transfer them into my office." So after about three months I must have had six or seven piles of scripts. Remember, this is not electronic; people had to Xerox them and mail them in and all that. So every Sunday, I would sit at my house and just start reading scripts. And 99.99 percent of them were atrocious. One day I pick up this script. All I know is an hour and a half later I finish it and I'm sweating and I had never done this before. I looked to see who wrote it and there's his phone number. I call this person up, I say, "This is fucking great. Can I meet you? I want to represent you." And so this kid comes in. He's from UCLA. His name is Fred Dekker. And I said, "I think I can sell this script." And about two weeks later I put $50,000 in this college kid's pocket! So he says, "I've got all these friends that want to be writers and all that." I said, "Send scripts in!" Now I'm at CAA and suddenly I was representing ten or twelve of these guys from UCLA and off this came the director of *The Simpsons*, the writers of *Bill & Ted's Excellent Adventure*, *Men in Black*, *Meet the Parents*, and *Lethal Weapon*, people like Shane Black.

AMY GROSSMAN:

When CAA had signed Robert Redford, it really put us into a different stratosphere. Robert Redford had not starred in a movie since he directed *Ordinary People*, about three years. That was a long time between films when you're that big a movie star. And what was promised to Robert Redford is that you will see material. He wasn't seeing anything. He wasn't getting scripts. He didn't know what was out there. I remember Michael used to come into the staff meeting and very specifically had one very strong quest at that point and it was to find a piece of material that Robert Redford would want to do.

And at the time I was still representing Ron's former television clients; I was not happy. I was representing actors who didn't get a lot of work and they weren't happy people. They were very draining and I would go home at the end of the day absolutely sucked dry from it and it just wore me out. At Christmas the guys brought me in and gave me a bonus check that had a zero on it. I decided, *Okay. Well, I'm going to take it upon myself and do this.* I wanted to be a literary agent, and what Mike did was really, really smart. As the idea of packaging motion pictures came more into play, and more actor and director clients were getting deals at studios, the goal became making sure they had great material. One of the things several of us noticed—both men and women—was most of the guys were not as comfortable sitting down and talking to an actor or director about a story or a script, quite frankly, as what some referred to as the "brainy English-major girls" were: Rosalie Swedlin, Tina Nides, Jane Sindell, and myself once I became a literary agent. So while Ronnie, for instance, was Cher's agent, I got sent out to Cher's house to sit down with her and her studio development person to talk about material. I started walking around the city asking everybody that I knew out in the studios if they had a piece of material that would be good for Robert Redford.

ABBY ADAMS

Ovitz would say, "If you have an idea for Redford, call him." It wasn't bullshit.

AMY GROSSMAN:

I had a very good friend at that time whose name was Roger Towne and he was the story editor at Columbia. Roger is Robert Towne's brother, and Roger was the story editor, which meant he saw all the movie scripts that were on the lot. We had lunch and Roger hands me a script and he says, "Well, why don't you read this. I wrote it." I read it that night and I'm embarrassed to tell you that I did not realize that it was a screenplay based on Bernard Malamud's book *The Natural*. I should have known, but I didn't. I loved it and I started thinking about Robert Redford's career—*The Candidate, Brubaker, Downhill Racer, The Great Gatsby, The Electric Horseman*. And then I said *The Natural*. And I realized in that moment that [in] all of these movies, the title character was the title of the film and each film was the examination of an American icon. And I knew right then when I was sitting there, the baseball player fits under that rubric beautifully. I knew he'd want to do it. And the next day I came into the staff meeting and Michael asked his usual "Does anybody have anything for Robert Redford?" And I raised my hand. I think that Michael might have sent it over to Barry Levinson first because Michael was probably trying to put Redford and Levinson together. And either through Mike or Levinson or Barry Hirsch, the script did go to Bob.

It was very exciting. They made me a literary agent, you know, my life changed with that happening. And I was given, you know, full credit and compensation for that. Half a million dollars? Never earned as much before or since. That's a lot of money to earn in one year.

BARRY LEVINSON

I had done *Diner* and *The Investigators* and a few other things, and then I got an invitation to go to Sundance, because back in those days they didn't have the festival but what they had was these labs where you would get together with other writers, actors, et cetera, and there would be discussions through the weekend about various topics. Redford had invited me to come up there that weekend, and we flew back to L.A. together. On the plane he said, "If you ever get an idea that you think could work for me, let's get together and see where it goes." I said, "Great." I remember laughing about it, saying, *Redford says if I have an idea I should come see him.*

So as it turns out—this is the craziness of the business—I did have an idea for him, and I called him. He said, "Come out to Malibu. We'll have lunch and we'll talk about it." So I went out there and mentioned it to him, and he was very straightforward and said, "No, I don't see that happening, it's not something that appeals to me." So we got off of that, and somehow we were talking about baseball. He says, "Did you ever read *The Natural?* I have a script of it around here somewhere." And he starts looking around for it, and says, "I think there's something interesting here." I took it with me, read it, and called him right after I finished. I said, "I think it's interesting, too. I think it's great."

MICHAEL OVITZ:

We were putting movies together without the studios. TriStar was working out of an office in Century City when we gave them *The Natural.* We just used their checkbook. We brought the script for *The Natural* with Levinson and Redford and Glenn Close attached to it. We also delivered Kim Basinger, Glenn Close, Bill Grimley, everybody in that movie. We walked into TriStar with a full script by Roger Towne and director's notes. There was no guesswork. At the same time we packaged *Places of the Heart* with Sally Field, which won Academy Awards. That was their first release, *The Natural* was their second. Do you understand? *We* were a studio. We didn't go to somebody and say, "Would you like . . . ?" We went to people with movies ready to go. We did all the development work. We did the casting.

BARRY HIRSCH:

Gary Hendler left and became head of TriStar. The first movie he put into production was *The Natural,* directed by Barry Levinson, a client; starring Robert Redford, a client; with Kim Basinger, a client. And Sydney Pollack I think was executive producer. They were all also CAA clients. Michael put the package together and had introduced Barry and Redford, who hadn't known each other. Gary was excited and we were all pleased. Everybody was getting top fees; actually, it was easy more than difficult. But Michael never stopped to smell the roses. He was on to the next one.

DAVID GREENBLATT:

Amy Grossman was a motion picture lit agent, and sometimes being a lit agent means getting one of the toughest jobs on the planet. At the time, Neil Diamond was a huge earner for CAA because of his concerts and he had been in one movie, a remake of *The Jazz Singer*. Amy's job was to service Neil Diamond as an actor, to get him material so we could try to put him in another movie. She was earnest and sincere about it, but at the agency level, the real reason was to keep him happy so he would keep going on tours and CAA would keep getting commissions from them. And this was a big job, okay? Because nothing against Neil Diamond, it's just at that time, no one wanted to hire him as an actor. Whether that was fair or not, I don't know, but she had to try and make a movie happen, which took a lot of time and effort. The point here is even though she had what seemed like a Sisyphean task, CAA still paid her a boatload of money because they realized she probably didn't have a lot of time to do anything else, and more important, Neil Diamond would be out the door if he didn't think a real effort was being made.

JACK RAPKE:

I signed Chris Columbus out of NYU film school. He wrote *Young Sherlock Holmes* and *Gremlins,* then I got him his first picture to direct, *Adventures in Babysitting,* which launched his career.

RON MEYER:

I took every offer for any of my clients very seriously and saw each one as great news. In my mind, when an offer was made to a client, I felt like a miracle had taken place. It meant there was a real role available and it wasn't being offered to another actor at another agency. I would tell my clients an amazing thing had happened: Someone wanted them, no matter who they were. Only one person can do a role, and I always loved it when people at a studio, a production company, or those who were willing to finance the picture wanted my client. Then I would focus on the next two parts that had to take place in order to complete the miracle: The script needed to be good, and my client needed to say yes. If all that was in place, all that remained was the right deal had to be made. Their part of the miracle was over; now it was my job to finish it.

That doesn't mean you always say yes. There were many times when I counseled my clients to turn down offers. I once read an article about Ruth Gordon where someone asked her, "What's the secret to your longevity, how have you survived so long in your career?" And she said, "I never face the facts." I thought that was a very telling line. And she was probably right. If a client really wanted to do a movie that I thought wasn't right for them, rarely did I throw myself in front of a train and say, "You can't do this." I came to believe if a client really wanted to do the movie, but I disagreed, sometimes they would be right and sometimes they would be wrong. And then we would move on. The most important part of this was that I always wanted to tell my clients the truth—what I really believed.

RICK NICITA:

I was never a volume kind of agent. What I call a volume agent is an agent who descends upon every square possible, wants an offer for every movie, and just keeps showing the client how much they're doing. Everything has to be a building block for the next one. I tell every client they're going to be underpaid or overpaid. They're never going to be properly paid. If this one is too little, you'll get too much another time. But if you do great, the money will find you. You're going to be fine. Don't worry about it. You'll get there. I had a client, Kevin Kline, who if he got a big offer I'd be apprehensive about telling him because he was suspicious that any big offer was not a good movie—"If they're offering me that much, then there must be a problem." So I'd have to play down what he was offered.

RON MEYER:

In the mid-'80s, I represented around fifty clients, including Jane Fonda, Cher, Meryl Streep, Whoopi Goldberg, Barbra Streisand, Jessica Lange, Goldie Hawn, Madonna, Michael Douglas, Sylvester Stallone, Tom Cruise, and Warren Beatty. And I was in constant touch with them. It was my life. Mornings, nights, weekends, whenever they needed me. I talked to them professionally and saw many of them socially. I always felt like I had a business and personal relationship with most of my clients.

GOLDIE HAWN, Actress:

My mother used to say—and I say it too except I don't usually say it in Yiddish—"tuches oyfin tish," which means "Put your ass on the table." And that means, "Let's get real. Let's not play around here." And Ron was that way. He was a strong deal maker, but he didn't make enemies. He gave it to me straight.

CHER, Actress:

I'd finished *Mask* and had another agent, but I can't really remember what his name was, so obviously he wasn't that important to me. Then people started saying, "You should meet Ron Meyer. He really wants to meet you. You've got to meet him." And it was coming from everywhere. And so I met him and he said right away, "I'm going to represent you." And I said, "My God, are you like this with your girlfriends?" I've never had anybody rush me like that in my entire life, but I went with him and he's been one of my favorite people since.

PAULA WAGNER:

We tried not to be political with each other, but politics were everywhere. Ronnie Meyer always told us, "You got a problem with somebody? Open the door, go in, shut the door, have it out, and deal with it." We put together movies as a team.

WHOOPI GOLDBERG, Actress:

I hadn't had an agent for that long, but I was going back to California and my agent was really a New York agent. Everybody said, "We've got to find you someone for L.A.," and Sandy Gallin said, "I know the perfect guy." So I went to CAA with Ron and he started dealing with everything for me, even including when I was crabby.

Remember, I was black, or still am. I sometimes forget. Ron said to me, "What do you want to do? What are you interested in?" and he tried his best to explain to me that I had come from having worked with Mike Nichols and then Steven Spielberg; things were going to be different. And suddenly I was in the company of people who weren't aware of what I was capable of, because all they could really see is what I look like. When I started, I didn't really know anything about making movies and Steven helped me so much and made it a joy and a pleasure. Then when I went into a whole other arena as my career went on, I'd be forced to say, "What's going on here?" and Ron would say, "Well, this is the real world. This is what it's like for other folks. You came from rarefied air," and I said, "Okay, I got it."

RON MEYER:

During production on *Jumpin' Jack Flash*, Whoopi became so uncomfortable with the material, she didn't want to even leave her trailer. So the studio called me and I went over to see her. I sat there with her and told her that while I understood why she was so upset, she really had no choice but to come out and go on the set. It was my job to explain the situation to her. I said, "This is real simple. You don't have to come out, you can stay in here and say, 'Fuck you,' but they are going to sue you and take your home away. Your career could end. Even if you think it's a shitty movie, you really have no choice but to live up to your responsibility and finish it. This is really not your choice. You're in this movie, so just make the best of it."

WHOOPI GOLDBERG:

They built a wall that was supposed to be an outdoor wall to look like I was walking across a building, but they built it sort of at building height. I took a look at it and said, "I'm not going to do that!" And they kept on telling me to do it, so I threw my shoes at the producer and said, "Fuck you, I'm not doing that." Then I called Ron and said, "I know, I'm an asshole, but what the fuck?!" And he was real calm and said, "Okay, I will take care of this."

I needed to be protected not only from myself, but from the craziness that was moviemaking in those days. I hadn't been spoken to the way people were speaking to people. I was black, but I also thought that I was an actor, because that's what I'd always been. And suddenly people were touching my hair, saying, "What are we going to do with it?" Ron would say, "Listen, these people don't know any black people who aren't working for them. They just don't know any better. You can't just hit people because they grab your hair and say stuff." Because I would punch people and say, "Get out! What are you doing? Who are you talking to?" My head would explode. But what I came to understand is that they didn't know any better. Ron really kept me from getting into too much crazy trouble.

Fundamentally Ron's a street kid and I'm a street kid. So he understood that there are many ways to deal with stuff. He would be able to say to people, "Relax. Leave her alone so she can do what she needs to do and she'll be fine. But if you're in her face and you're saying stupid shit to her, she doesn't respond well to it. She's not good at that."

RON MEYER:

She went out and finished the movie, and of course she turned out to be right. The movie didn't work, but she was able to continue her career and ultimately win an Academy Award.

FRED SPECKTOR:

As our place got bigger and we started signing more and more stars, sometimes there were delicate situations. We were going to sign Meryl Streep, who was represented by Sam Cohn, and it was obviously a big deal for us. But my client, Glenn Close, at the time considered her her strongest competition. I told Glenn not to be worried, that Meryl wasn't going to be able to do everything, and reminded her that in the end, it's the director and the studio who make the decisions, not our agency. What we do is present actors and actresses for their consideration and we were always going to do that for her. And you know what? She said, "Great." Glenn was terrific about it. She knew we just couldn't beat somebody over the head and force them to hire one of our clients.

RICK NICITA:

I've never had a conflict because I've never—not once—been asked by the buyer to choose one of my clients over the other. My job was to put forth the best options possible. Someone else picks; I didn't. No conflict there.

RON MEYER:

I told every client everything that was going on when a film was being cast. If I heard they wanted a role that looked like it was going to someone else, I would call them and say, "Let me tell you what is happening here. I talked about you for this picture. The director is leaning another way. If you think there's anything more to be done, let me know." I wanted to avoid surprising clients as much as possible.

JOHN PTAK, Agent:

There was a concept at CAA: "Hold the offer." Hold the offer basically means even when you hear that your own client is turning it down, you don't go back to the studio so quickly and let them know that. We may have somebody else at the agency who would be perfect for that and we could flip it to them and position the project for them to get the next offer. Something like that really never happened anywhere else, because the team concept was the bottom line.

RON MEYER:

We were all very good when we had a client who was set for something and pulled out or was offered something else and wasn't going to do it. Before we'd tell the studio, we would talk about it internally and decide who we thought would be best for it and then go to the studio and say something like "Look, you're not going to get Redford, but we're going to give you Paul Newman."

CHER:

I knew Ronnie had other actress clients, but truthfully it never bothered me. I knew that he loved me so much that I didn't think about him giving my work to anyone else. Obviously he could have, and maybe he did, but that wouldn't have really mattered to me anyway. I just loved him.

JESSICA LANGE, Actress:

I was seven or eight months pregnant when I first met Ronnie, living in New Mexico, and basically out of the business. I had left my other agency and was not really looking for an agent. It was winter and he flew in with Ovitz to meet with me. I remember after the meeting, my lawyer, this lovely man Charles Silverberg, called to see how I felt about it. I said, "Well, I don't like the big guy, but I really like the little guy." I thought Ronnie was amazing. He was in a league of his own. I don't think there's ever been or ever will be an agent like Ronnie Meyer. He had this unique talent of being available whenever you needed him. I can't remember ever calling Ronnie and not immediately getting him on the phone. I don't know how he was so omnipotent, but he was able to do it.

RICK NICITA:

We used to say, there were only two times Mike would get really pissed off about calls and clients of the agency: the first was when they would call him—"Why is so-and-so calling me?"; the second was when they didn't call him—"Why isn't so-and-so calling me?" Otherwise, he was fine. It was just a part of the team system.

RON MEYER:

I'm not a schmoozer on the phone; I tend to get off quickly. When people call me, even clients, I'd find a way to say good-bye as soon as I said hello. Some clients liked to dissect and understand everything; others, like Jane Fonda, I could call up and say, "Jane, you're too skinny," and she would say, "Okay, bye."

AMY GROSSMAN:

If you didn't get back to a client in two minutes, for God's sakes Ronnie did, and that was one of the engines that drove us. It felt like you could talk to Ron on an airplane to China faster than you could get on the phone with your own pediatrician.

RON MEYER:

I made myself available twenty-four hours a day, seven days a week—and this was before cell phones, e-mails, and texts. I never took a vacation where I wasn't reachable. I didn't love anybody more than my family, but I did give more attention to my clients.

MICHAEL OVITZ:

When the phone rang, you answered it, no matter what time it was. One time Ronnie was in bed at three in the morning and Stallone called him and woke him up out of a dead sleep. And Sly said, "What are you doing?" Ron said, "Oh, I'm just lying here waiting for your call."

RICK NICITA:

There was a legend that Bill never took an incoming call because he'd want to know what it was about. I still say, "If somebody calls and says it's urgent, don't put through the call." Why? Because you could be caught flat-footed, you won't know what it is, it's never good news. You've got to find out what it's about first so you can return the call and say, "I know, I'm into it." And you never have your assistant tell a client you're "on another line," that doesn't exist. It's always, "I can't find him, he's in the bathroom, at the doctor, or with his kid."

RON MEYER:

I didn't lose a lot of clients. Agents lose clients for a variety of reasons: first and foremost, an agent not getting enough or the right work; second, not having a good enough relationship with the client; third, a client meeting another agent who convinces them they can do a better job no matter what; and fourth, some of these clients just having plain bad luck and holding their agent responsible. Shit happens.

RICK NICITA:

Firing a client was an art. You told them that the agency wasn't really working well for them, that it wasn't personal, and that you knew they would be better served at another agency.

ROBB ROTHMAN:

You'd say, "I've done everything I can. I put you up for all of these jobs, and I don't know what it is, but I'm not able to do it." You would try to make it about your own failings. Sometimes you'd have to say, "I'm just not getting support from my associates here, and if you want to leave, I will totally understand." Often we would call other agencies to take someone on so we could say, "Here's so-and-so's number, call them directly."

RICK NICITA:

Sometimes when a client left, it was a surprise, or at least you would try to *convince* yourself it was a surprise. You tend to know. Jeff Bridges had just stalled out. We didn't seem able to hit the next phase for him and maybe karmically a change was needed. I knew he was going to leave. I felt it in my conversations with him, that the great rapport we had was just seeping away. I remember when my assistant said, "Jeff's on line one," I knew that he was calling to say that he was going. I knew because I knew. And it was a very, very tough call. The two of us were almost weepy. Ronnie always said he would wake up every day convinced a client was going to fire him. That was my day.

LARRY LYTTLE, Executive:

The word from CAA was always "Nobody picks up a check with us." They knew implicitly you'd be beholden to them. Even a minor lunch or dinner—they always went for the check, and more often than not, even if you tried, you had no choice but to let them pay. Beyond the meals, though, were the presents you would get from the agency. You couldn't believe it.

MICHAEL OVITZ:

We put a lot of thought into what we called "start-date gifts"— sending a gift to our clients to wish them well on the start of their movies. Traditionally, agents had maybe sent flowers or something like that. We sent giant baskets filled with things that were edible, practical, and fun. Then Ron and I decided to take it up a level, which was, "Hey, if we're sending something to our client, why don't we just send something to all the actors on the set, even those who aren't our clients and even the director if they by chance aren't our client?" So on the first day of principal, we sent gifts to everybody. Now, if you weren't a client, we sent a smaller gift. You walked into a client's trailer, the basket was humongous, they were like five feet high. We had a company that did specialty baskets, and because you were our client, we kept track of what you liked. I wound up having five people who worked directly for me, and one of them was a woman whose entire job was managing gifts. Come Christmas, she hired three or four more people and had the entire mailroom working for her.

MARTIN SPENCER, Agent:

I was the low man on the mailroom totem pole. And I remember collecting all these packages, putting them in a box, being given a Thomas Guide, and told, "Be back by 2:30." I literally was sent down to my car and told to go deliver packages. Luckily I grew up in L.A., so I at least knew my way around. I came back, got another set of packages to go out—it was either 3:30 or 4:30, I can't remember—and I put up 285 miles on my car on my first day in the mailroom. I just couldn't believe it.

I remember the last package that I had to deliver was to Rick Springfield all the way out in Malibu. I think it was a package from Rick Nicita, and I couldn't find the address—there were no lights on his street, and I just couldn't find it. And I went home that night—I was living at home—walked in the house, I hadn't eaten dinner, and I'm freaking out about this package. I remember waking up Saturday morning, putting on a whole suit and going out and finding Rick Springfield's house at 6:00 A.M. and waiting there to deliver the package. Somebody—I don't know who—came out, and I said, "I'm so sorry. I couldn't find the address last night in the dark, but I wanted to make sure that you had this first thing this morning. I'm really sorry." And they looked at me like, you know, "What are you doing? Why are you in a tie on a Saturday morning?" But that was my job.

ROBB ROTHMAN:

Ovitz's line was "Think Yiddish. Dress British," which wasn't his but he used it all the time. Be kind of crafty but dress with class.

MICHAEL OVITZ:

I always felt that if you were dressed a little bit better than everyone else, it gave you a slight edge when you're in a meeting.

RICK NICITA:

You had to be well dressed. Just pulling on some bad tie to adhere to the code wasn't going to cut it. You had to look good. Soon after, it became a lot of Armani and Zegna.

MICHAEL OVITZ:

In the film business, it was all casual, flashy, very social. We took it to a completely different level, all the way down to the kind of cars we all drove. It was very, very much about a uniform and an elegance. It set us apart.

TOM ROSS:

My body isn't an Armani type, but I got a couple of sports jackets and I wore ties every day for two weeks so I could feel like I was part of the group. Mick Fleetwood came up to talk about a tour, and at that point, I had known him for probably ten years. We're talking, and all of a sudden he says, "I can't talk to you with that tie on. It's not you." I said, "You're fucking right," and ripped the tie off.

ROB LIGHT:

When we first started, Tom and I were trying to sign a band called The Motels—"Take the L out of Lover" and "Only the Lonely." Martha Davis had been a client at ICM and we wanted to sign her. Martha and the band came up to the office and we were sitting in Tom's office, he and I wearing suits and ties. We probably looked a bit uncomfortable because we had never worn suits and ties, but in those first few months we followed company policy and dressed the CAA part. She looked at us and said. "If you're going to be in a suit and tie, I can't sign here." And Tom walked her down the hall to Mike Ovitz's office and said, "Martha, tell Mike what you just told me." And that was the last day that we had to wear suits and ties in the music department.

ROBB ROTHMAN:

Ron Meyer was the only one who could dress casually at CAA. Still, I bet he paid more for his jeans and his pullover sweater than most of the agents paid for their nice suits.

RICK NICITA:

Ronnie never wore a suit, which goes to show you—it doesn't matter.

MICHAEL OVITZ:

I wore a blue suit every day to work. I never created a dress code in the office, but the people that came there all started wearing suits. The only person who didn't wear a suit—and it was kind of the way we set it up—was Ronnie. He wore a sweater and jeans every day and that was his presentation. I wanted a presentation of professionalism for the business. It was great to have Ron as the outsider.

RON MEYER:

As far as agents dating or sleeping with clients, probably the first rule of thumb is: Don't. But since we're dealing with human nature here, I always thought you better be sure that it's a move that your client wants you to make—because if you're wrong, you might have damaged the relationship.

STEVE ROTH:

The office culture was totally different back then. If a company allowed the things today that were done back then, they'd be bankrupt because of sexual harassment.

RON MEYER:

It's important to remember that times were different back then. It sounds so ridiculous today. The working environment was much more like the series *Mad Men*. Shit happens.

I was single and having a really great time. I had a lot of great experiences. We were all guilty. But I never fooled around in the building—that I didn't do. But I'm guilty of everything else.

MICHAEL OVITZ:

Do you want to know what I did that I thought was really smart about all of that? Nothing. I never had a policy about relationships inside the building. I was really loose about those kind of activities as long as it was all consensual. I didn't want to be their parent, and I didn't want to look like I was condoning or not condoning. I was uncomfortable with some of those in the beginning, because I was worried they'd end badly and then I'd lose an agent; they were all good agents.

The weird thing is many of the relationships ended up in marriages. We had a lot of marriages. There were probably more than a dozen.

AMY GROSSMAN:

The hours were certainly long. But it was more than just *Where else was I going to meet anyone?* It all stemmed from the concept behind the agency: your associate is not your enemy; your associate is vital to you.

RON MEYER:

I was married to a terrific woman. Ellen didn't do anything wrong, and we had two wonderful daughters together. Ellen was a great wife and a great friend. It's impossible to overstate how important she was to me in my life; I couldn't have accomplished what I had done over those years without her. I was not a perfect husband and never wanted to hurt her. But after ten years, I felt restless, and wanted something different.

One night I was having dinner at La Scala in Malibu and stopped by a table to say hello to some people I knew, and they were having dinner with Ali MacGraw. When we were introduced, she mentioned she was about to go to London to work on a film in a week, and coincidentally, I was going to be in London in two weeks. I called her before I left for London and we made a plan to have dinner. I left the dinner crazy about her—who wouldn't— and then when I had to come back to London a few weeks later— truth be told, I may have invented a reason—I checked into the same hotel. She had a break from her movie, and we spent a few very intense days together. That's when our relationship started.

MICHAEL OVITZ:

Ron and Ali in London—four days and four nights. He never came out of the room. *Ever.* I got a call every day from him when he was there. He was in heaven. I was envious—and happy to pay the bill.

RON MEYER:

I guess you could say I left my wife, Ellen, because of her. I had been thinking that I needed to move on, and Ali gave me more than enough reason to do so. We wound up being together for a year and a half.

MICHAEL DOUGLAS:

He's a little Jewish guy, you know? And all of a sudden here was Ali MacGraw, the shiksa fantasy of all time.

RON MEYER:

I rented a house on Malibu Road, and when I wasn't with my kids, Ali and I were together constantly. I never represented Ali, she was represented by Sue Mengers at ICM. This was all personal.

MICHAEL DOUGLAS:

Let's just say being with Ali gave Ron a sense of confidence that he's never lost.

RON MEYER:

My phone was constantly ringing, even on weekends. Clients would call me often, and I would call them at least a few times a week so they always knew what was going on. Ali didn't particularly like acting, and she didn't like being a celebrity or being recognized, and here she was constantly listening to me talking day and night about the business. She didn't resent that I represented her competition, but she did resent the fact that my work kept us from having time to relax and really enjoy being together. Sometimes she would ask if we could just turn the phones off for a short time. She just wanted us to have a life. But that was often not possible and created a problem for us.

ALI MACGRAW, Actress:

Handling a lot of superstar clients is an exhausting and often bizarre job. When somebody calls in the middle of the night hysterical because their wig box is missing, you have to have tremendous equilibrium to handle that, not make the person feel like a fool, take care of the details, and keep them from leaving you. Ron did it better than anybody. People adored him.

There are a handful of really superb agents who don't just babysit self-involved performers, but truly make a difference in a client's career, and Ron was one of them. The problem is, it's a full-time job. The clients have to come first, and that annoyed me—which is ridiculous. I could have been a great deal more understanding about that, but it really was a pain in the neck if it's the crack of dawn and somebody's calling up and whining about some movie drama that's going on. I think it's a ghastly way to make a living, but if you're really good at it like Ron was, you must gain some tremendous happiness by changing people's lives so dramatically.

RON MEYER:

On one of our Saturday mornings together, I received a call from an actress client, and it ended up being a fairly long and complicated conversation. As I was talking, Ali got up, and I watched as she started packing her bag. She just couldn't take it anymore. She knew my work had to come first. At that time in her life, Ali needed to be with someone like an artist or musician who could have a more flexible lifestyle. As I continued talking to my client, I watched her take her bag and walk out the door. She was—and is—an amazing woman. I knew what she was doing was best for her, so I didn't try and stop her, but it broke my heart. I loved her.

3

Gyokai wo Shihaisuru: 1986–1988

I'd like to buy you everything
A wooden bird with painted wings
A window full of colored rings.
—JONI MITCHELL

GRAYDON CARTER, Editor:

Right after we started *Spy* magazine, I remember two or three people winning Oscars one night and thanking Michael Ovitz in their acceptance speeches. I had never heard of Ovitz up to that point and so we started asking around. We found out he was super-secretive, much like Mike Milken, the junk bond king. They both used to buy up photographs of themselves. CAA was very secretive internally as well; we were surprised when we learned that even people who worked at the agency didn't know the firm's entire client list. So we decided to start a showbiz column about the industry, and as it turned out, month in and month out, it focused largely on Ovitz—who was far and away the most powerful figure in Hollywood. And it gave him fits. The column, like others at *Spy*, was written under a pseudonym—in this case Celia Brady. Ovitz did everything to find out the identity of Celia. He apparently even hired a private detective to look into what we were up to. When we discovered that almost nobody at the agency had a complete client list—save for Ovitz—we decided to pull one together. We had two reporters work on it for an entire year. When we published it, everyone in Hollywood was astonished. CAA represented everybody. Ovitz had to shut the agency down for a week while the agents reached out to the clients, many of whom were upset. Dustin Hoffman was apparently ticked off that parts that he should have gotten went to Al Pacino and vice versa. A lot of the clients had no idea that their agents were handling that many people.

MICHAEL OVITZ:

When it came out, we thought it was horrible. Ron and I saw the list and went crazy. It turned out it was a big nonevent, however.

GRAYDON CARTER:

Spy was a magazine that worked perfectly without access, so although we seemed to know what was going on out there, we really didn't know the people. Years later, after I came to *Vanity Fair*, Ovitz asked me to have lunch with him. He wanted to bury the hatchet—the one he wished he could have buried in my skull years back. We had lunch a couple of times, and he put on a great charm offensive because he was dying to know how we got all of this stuff.

MICHAEL OVITZ:

The funny thing is, there wasn't much to find out because my life was working, my family, and I collected art. That was it.

SUSAN MILLER:

The phone list was made up of everyone you can think of and more: Dustin Hoffman, Paul Newman, Robert Redford, Christopher Reeve, Bill Murray, Ray Stark, Sydney Pollack, James Clavell, a young Tom Cruise. But what was different about Michael Ovitz's phone sheet was the fact that he was cultivating relationships with high-level politicians, investment bankers, the art world, sports, music, corporate America, and beyond. He wanted it all.

DAVID O'CONNOR:

I got promoted in September or October of '86, but I was already attending all the staff meetings, and talking directly and building relationships with a bunch of clients: Sean Connery, Sydney Pollack, Robert Redford, Bill Murray. Barry Levinson was still very much with Michael. Barry was not very open and welcoming of new relationships, and kind of cold and distant—ironic given what his movies were about.

JOEL SILVER:

I was fortunate to get a lot of attention because I had just produced *48 Hrs.* and then *Lethal Weapon*, which was a CAA package. Ronnie knew me from those movies. About halfway through production of any movie with Stallone, Ronnie would make a point to set up Sly's next movie, because you never know what's going to happen. He created this business where you could buy a "slot" from Sly. Once you owned the "slot," you could then figure out what would be the best movie to make at that designated time, knowing that Sly could get any script in shape to shoot. I had just made *Commando* and *Predator* with Schwarzenegger—B versions of Sly movies—and there was a project I had set up at Columbia called *The Executioner.* I got a phone call from Ronnie, and he said, "I've got to go to Israel. Sly's making *Rambo III* and if you would have dinner with me and Sly, I think I can get Sly to commit to *The Executioner.*" I said, "But I haven't got a script yet," and he said, "Sly will write the script. I'm telling you, if you take this trip to Israel, it will show Sly you're really excited about making this movie with him, and we can try to get him to say yes to *The Executioner.*" So I fucking got on a plane and flew to Tel Aviv on a Friday afternoon.

That night Sly came in with a bunch of bodyguards. We sat down to dinner, I pitched him *The Executioner* and he said, "Sounds good! Let's do it!" Ronnie knew what would happen the entire time. When we finished dinner, I went to sleep, got up in the morning, and flew with Ronnie to London, and then from London to L.A. We talked for eleven hours, and from that time to today Ronnie and I have remained the closest of friends.

SANDY CLIMAN, Agent:

I grew up in the Bronx and graduated first in my class at Bronx Science. That, and four years of research in the neurology labs at Albert Einstein College of Medicine, was my ticket out of the Bronx. Neither of my parents had gone to college. They were career civil servants, but they somehow put me through Harvard College. I believe my mother's entire salary and a good part of my dad's went to tuition, room, and board, and I also worked as much as I could. In the end, I earned two master's degrees at Harvard—from its School of Public Health and Harvard Business School.

There were two stumbling blocks to me being hired at CAA: First, Mike found out I had been fired from my job at MGM, and he didn't like that. When he found out it was just part of a regime change—Freddie Fields had gotten his old partner David Begelman fired—he was okay with it. The second roadblock was Bill Haber. Bill wanted Mike to focus on the core businesses, and it wasn't anything personal against me, but he saw me as a potential big distraction for Mike because he knew my background and could look ahead to the types of things Mike would have me working on. Haber managed to delay my arrival by a year and a half, then Mike just went ahead and brought me on anyway. I was worried about Haber's reaction, but Mike sat me down and said—and he wasn't nice about this at all—"Listen, I own 55 percent of the company," which by the way, only a few people knew at the time, "and nothing is going to happen to you unless I say so."

MICHAEL OVITZ:

Mike Menchel brought Sandy to see me and I gave him a job, but said, "I'm going to pay you five hundred bucks a week, on a week-to-week basis, and I'm going to start to give you things to do for me. If you do them well, if we get along, and if you get along with other people in the business, I will keep you." And he agreed. He sat in my little conference room, and I trained him. It took me a year. The good news about Sandy was he was bright, and he ended up being my right arm.

SANDY CLIMAN:

The entertainment industry is full of complex characters who have tremendously strong qualities as well as humongous flaws. For me, the goal has always been to study good qualities in order to learn what to do, and equally important, to study negative qualities to learn what not to do.

ADAM VENIT, Agent:

I had gone to law school at Berkeley and decided after a year to take a hiatus to work in the entertainment business. I was fortunate enough to get a job in the mailroom at CAA in 1986. The place was really starting to hum. Mike was becoming King of the Universe. It seemed like a big client was being signed every day. It was pretty heady, pretty unbelievable, and very exciting.

The way the mailroom worked was based on seniority, and the senior person in the mailroom told the others what to do. When I was the senior person, the worst thing you could do was tell one of the junior people they had to drop something off or pick something up at Sam Elliott's house on a Friday night. He lived in the northern part of Malibu, almost in Ventura County, which was an hour and a half each way, so your whole night's shot, right? So Friday night comes and I said to Ari, who was in the mailroom with me, "Hey, Ari, I've got bad news. You got to go out to Sam Elliott's house." And he said, "What are you talking about? Lisa Wong's the low man on the totem pole in the mailroom, let her go." And I said, "Well, I'm going on a date tonight with Lisa Wong, not you, so guess what? You're going out there, not her." The funnier part of the story is, the second I was out of the mailroom and could no longer help Lisa Wong, she started dating Jay Moloney.

SANDY CLIMAN:

When I joined the agency in '86, we were signing a major talent each week. Stan Kamen, who had the movie star talent roster at William Morris, was dying of AIDS, and as he withdrew from work, his clients shifted one by one to CAA. The William Morris talent department was falling apart just as a wave of new mini-studios entered the market. It was a seller's market—more movies were being made and talent prices were on the rise. It was the golden age of movie packaging, and CAA was poised to take maximum advantage of it all.

PHIL KENT:

I was VP of programming for a company called Blair Entertainment. A young agent named Eric Paulson was trying to replace himself so he could start packaging in prime time. Eric took me out for drinks one night and said, "Have you ever thought of being an agent? I want you to meet Lee Gabler." So I met Lee, and after that I met Michael and Ronnie together. Then finally I met Bill, who was the official head of the TV department.

They weren't bringing in a lot of people from the outside back then; most of the people were homegrown. That summer, I was hired, Sandy Climan was hired, and John Sykes was hired. We were like the three outsiders all hired in the same summer.

I was brought in to do first run syndication, basic cable networks, HBO and Showtime, Saturday morning animation, network specials—anything that wasn't ABC, CBS, or NBC prime time was me. I was also going to cover the brand-new Fox network.

I represented every client in the agency in my coverage area, so if somebody was doing something at HBO, I would be brought in. I would then keep the primary agent involved. A perfect example, which was one of my worst days, was when Cher had a concert special set up with HBO. We found out that Steve Wynn would give her an extra million dollars if we would move the show from HBO to CBS, and to me it was an easy decision: *Okay, an extra million dollars just so we can run "Live at the Mirage" in the bumpers?* I only made one mistake, I never talked to the client. I didn't think that she would care. I thought she'd be thrilled, but she wasn't. I think Ron had to tell her he fired me.

MARTIN SCORSESE:

I was on a friendly basis with Mike, and at one point he called me and said, "Are you doing *Color of Money?*" I was close with Richard Price at the time, a wonderful writer, and we pulled a story together, had met with Paul Newman, and worked on the script together. He said, "For Vince, have you thought of Tom Cruise?" I said I'd just seen him in *All the Right Moves* and thought he was terrific, and I said, "Yeah, let's do it with Tom Cruise." That's how Mike usually worked. It was not like, "Do it with Tom," it was, "Have you thought of it?" I thought he'd be perfect with Paul Newman. That's how that all came together, and before I realized it, I was sort of in the CAA group.

I believe on the night of the film premiere, afterward Mike said, "Come over to my house, I want to talk to you." So I went over, sat down, and the first thing he says to me actually was, "You know, you can get paid for this." I said, "What?" He said, "Making movies." He said, "I can get your price up." I said, "I've had some difficulties in the past," and he said, "Well, you don't have those anymore, do you?" And I said no. He said, "I'll sign you up."

MICHAEL EISNER:

I don't believe I did much business with Michael Ovitz when I was at Paramount or Disney. The only movie I can remember us doing together was *The Color of Money*, which he sold to me, but we knew the reason we had it was because Rupert Murdoch owned the *Boston Globe* and Paul Newman was furious about something they had written, so he wouldn't make the sequel to *The Hustler* at Fox, which Murdoch owned. Ovitz told me he was doing me a favor giving it to me, but I found out from Frank Price at Columbia that he had passed on it, along with everyone else in town. There was nowhere else for him to go.

At Paramount, and Disney, we were always number one or number two in box office and profits, so it's not like we needed CAA, but they were very good back then. And because we were friends at the time, I would enjoy hearing about his conquests, and he would tell me about the deals he was making. Sometimes I would ask him how he could be involved with such a lousy film and he would say, "We don't smell them, we just sell them." But there were times when I would ask, "How's this movie?" and he would be really honest about whether it was good or not, and he had a pretty good track record—rare for many people, agents included. Here is another point. After I saw a movie on which he gave a review, I almost always agreed with his take. That was important, because later on, when I was going to hire him, I felt like I could trust his taste. But while he was at CAA, I always knew I was the buyer and he was the seller.

MICHAEL WIMER, Agent:

I loved being an agent. The easiest decision I ever made in my life was also one of the most ridiculous—after Harvard, investment banking at First Boston and Stanford Business School; in the fall of 1986 I passed up what I knew would be a crazily lucrative job on Wall Street to start in the mailroom for about $167 a week. Gross. The only thing I loved more than being with a group of smart, creative people was losing myself in a great piece of writing. At CAA, I could do both. I loved it from the first day in the mailroom when I was surrounded by all of those scripts and those bizarre trainees.

My first day, Ovitz came into the conference room to eyeball us. He asked for our schools, and when he heard mine he said, "You're overqualified," to the tune of *you will never make it*. It was a blast. I did runs during the day and read at night. Everything was fun. Hard work with no money makes you poor and bulletproof, so what the hell did I have to lose?

MATTHEW BRODERICK, Actor:

On most jobs—and I'm not alone in this—I usually say, "This is bad. I really shouldn't have signed up. I don't want to do this." One I can really remember is *Ferris Bueller*, which I was very on the fence about. I was just starting out. I had done two plays on

Broadway—these Neil Simon plays where I spoke to the audience, and Ferris spoke to the camera, and I had done *Ladyhawke,* where the character sort of talks to the camera. And I thought, *I'm always going to be like this comedian who talks to the camera. I have to get a real part,* or some stupid idea like that. So I wasn't sure about *Ferris,* thought it wasn't right and I should do something dramatic. At that point I was being offered a lot, too. So I was not at all sure when to say, "Yes, I should take that one."

But Paula and my manager, Arnold, basically would not take no for an answer. I remember either Arnold or the two of them came to New York and said, basically, "We're not going back to L.A. until you say yes."

I'm glad, because they were right. They were absolutely right. I probably have a few movies that I wish I hadn't been in, but *Ferris* was a good one.

JERRY BRUCKHEIMER, Producer:

It was Paula Wagner who played a big role in helping to convince Tom to do *Top Gun.* She had helped launch his career, and when we were getting the movie set up, Tom was certainly on the rise. She really understood him and what was best for him at the time. He wasn't a superstar then, but she knew, and so did we, that he was a talented actor.

MICHAEL WIMER:

I saw that Jack Rapke had the best literary desk, so I started reading scripts and writing coverage for him, and I figured that if I outworked his reading pace, I'd get his desk when it opened up. And when Tom Strickler was promoted in early 1987, I got it. Jack was an awesome teacher—he had good taste, faultless follow-up, and most important, he never lied. That was my single biggest concern about being an agent—I simply wouldn't stick around in a career where I had to lie. Nicita told me that "agenting is the artful presentation of the truth," and Jack showed me that it was possible. What I figured out was that it would be a great career track as well.

That's why I chose to represent directors. I wasn't at all compelled by actors, since most required so much fluffing, and the glitz didn't matter a bit to me. On the other hand, I figured that directors were like field generals who, with so much smoke being blown at them, could smell bullshit a mile away—which meant that they would attach a premium to someone who was smart, strategic, and truthful. It played to my strength. So, although it was not where the highest profile was, once again, it was an easy decision to stay away from the actor business and go with the lit side. The fit was perfect.

STANLEY JAFFE:

The first two pictures Sherry and I did under our deal at Paramount were very small. *First Born* was one, and the second, which I really loved, was *Racing to the Moon*, but they didn't support it. Mike Ovitz called and said, "Let's go to dinner." So we went to the old Spago up on the hill above Tower Records, and he said, "Look, guys. I think you should put aside what you're working on"—what we were working on then was *Fatal Attraction, The Accused*, and a couple of other things—"put them aside, and let me get you a commercial movie—something like *Ghostbusters II*. You'll get a big picture, and then you can go and do these other pictures you're interested in." I remember going back to the hotel and I called Sherry and she said, "I'm suicidal. That was one of the worst dinners I've ever had in my life," and I said, "If that's where we are, we're in trouble." But of course that's not where we were, and we declined Mike's kind offer.

SANDY CLIMAN:

Robert Redford had been with Mike since *Ordinary People* and it was a love/hate relationship. Bob was considered the most important actor in the world and it only made sense for him to be represented by the most important agent in the world. But Bob was intensely independent and bristled at being "packaged" by Mike and the agency. For years, Mike had tried to involve other agents in helping to represent Bob, but Bob had rejected them all as having CAA's interest ahead of his.

One night in '87, I was about to get on the elevator to leave CAA when our receptionist, Liz Bruyette, said to me, "There's a man on the phone for you who says he is Robert Redford." I ran like a banshee for my office. Bob invited me to come down to New Mexico for a reshoot for *The Milagro Beanfield War*, which may have been one of the most difficult periods in his professional life, as the press was lambasting him for going far over budget on his second directorial effort.

Bob picked me up in a Porsche on a street corner and we headed to the remote set location. It was one of those moments where you realize your life has taken a different turn, and I just said out loud, "This is so odd." He said, "Why?" and I said, "I'm just a Jewish guy from the Bronx." He smiled at me and said, "I'm Jewish, too."

ALAN ZWEIBEL, Writer:

I co-created *It's Garry Shandling's Show*, and when that show started taking off, I remember Bernie [Brillstein] one day just calling me and telling me that I was now a CAA client. I didn't ask for it. I didn't petition it. At that time, CAA was the sexiest place in the world, and Ovitz was like God. I said, "Oh. Okay. That's cool." This was a sign of *you've arrived and you're invited to the big party*.

Bernie's relationship with Ovitz was on again, off again. When Bernie would talk about CAA, it would be the way you talked about Ali or some superpower, you know? I remember him dropping Ovitz's name when they got along as if, "Hey, I've got power. Look who my friends are." And when it was off again, there was feuding. Then Bernie called me a few months later and said, "You're not with CAA anymore." I did nothing. I just sat at my desk and answered the phone.

MARTIN SCORSESE:

Mike said, "What do you really want to do? What film do you really want to make?" I said, "Oh, I've been trying to get this film made for a number of years, but it was canceled, called *Last Temptation of Christ.*" He said, "All right, I'll get it made for you." I thought to myself, it's a noble sentiment, *The Color of Money* situation worked out for me, let's see what he can do, and if it doesn't happen it doesn't happen, I'll figure another way. In the meantime, maybe I will do a few films to keep my energy going, and try to find material to work with that I will enjoy. Mike was also very instrumental on that.

BARRY HIRSCH:

On *Legal Eagles,* Ovitz packaged a movie that I'm not sure any of the actors were particularly gung-ho about doing. It became more of the momentum of getting that deal done, and then the actors finding themselves in that package. It was Redford, Debra Winger, and Ivan Reitman. He just put the package together in his own head, convinced the actors and directors, then sold Universal on doing the movie.

MICHAEL OVITZ:

I did *Legal Eagles* because Redford told me for five years that he wanted to do a romantic comedy. I had Rand Holston, John Levine, Tina Nides, Rosalie Swedlin, and all the literary agents talking to their writers for ideas. I put it together with him in mind. I knew I needed a director that could handle Redford, and we had done a development deal with a guy named Steve Gordon who did *Arthur,* which I loved, but he died. So I needed a smart guy, and that was Ivan Reitman.

IVAN REITMAN:

Legal Eagles started as a movie for Bill Murray and Dustin Hoffman, believe it or not. It was two guys and a girl. It was around this period that Bill sort of moved to France and Dustin finally decided to do the Elaine May movie with Warren Beatty, *Ishtar.* So I lost both Bill and Dustin. We had a pretty good script, and Ovitz suggested that I look at it from the other way, maybe two women and a man. He knew that Redford was looking to do something lighter, and he said I should meet with him. I remember flying to his ranch at Sundance and hanging out with him for twenty-four hours. I'd heard all kinds of stories about how difficult it was to get him committed to a movie, particularly in those days where he was at the height of his stardom, but he was very reasonable, had really smart things to say about the script, and after the meeting, I cast it.

MICHAEL OVITZ:

We cast Winger because we wanted a young girl. That was all our doing. It's exactly the way the agency should work. It's our job to get her ideas, material, and offers, so we controlled the casting. Why wouldn't we? That's the way we ran the business. No agency in history had ever done this. Even MCA.

IVAN REITMAN:

I openly cast it. There was no packaging. The only packaging that really occurred was Michael putting me together with Redford. But he was fulfilling two clients' needs: He was fulfilling my need—I didn't want to give up on *Legal Eagles*—and Redford had wanted to do a comedy. I guess at that point I was the most successful comedy director in the English-speaking world, so it just made sense to put us together. It was actually a very good idea, making it more of a romantic comedy than I was originally contemplating. Probably the part that CAA played is that it figured out how to make these deals. As stars got more important and more expensive and had their own corporations, it became harder and harder to put really good actors together in one movie, because everybody had too much. So it was a great fortune to have an agency that could temper everybody's desires, to a point where the economics of the deal made sense.

The movie did fine. It turned out to be more expensive than it should have been because it was the only time I went over schedule shooting, and that was because the two stars got to fighting so much that neither of them wanted to come out. Debra Winger was just probably the worst person I've ever worked with in forty years of making films with all kinds of stars and all kinds of actors. Ironically, she was the one who got all the best reviews when that film came out.

BARRY LEVINSON:

Michael didn't want me to do *Good Morning Vietnam*. I think at that point he was afraid of Robin, who hadn't had much recent success. So he said to me, "Look, you're getting a career that's starting to build, and all of a sudden you want to go make a movie where I'm not crazy about the script, and I don't know how you're going to handle the tone of this, and now you want to go with Robin Williams? Why would you want to bring this on yourself?"

One of the things about our relationship was we could disagree. I felt strongly about this material, I thought it could work. Ovitz said, "Okay, fuck it, you want to do that, go ahead."

MARTIN SPENCER:

Being an agent is not a job, it's a lifestyle. You're working all the time. You're working Saturdays and Sundays. You wake up early and try and read as much as you possibly can. I don't know of any agents that've actually ever read everything they're supposed to read; every time you finish a screenplay, you realize there's one more that you have to read for whatever reason. You had a breakfast at eight o'clock. You had a lunch. You had a drink at six o'clock. You had a dinner at 7:30 and you'd come home by ten o'clock and you'd have to read a script before you went to bed and have to do it all over again. You had to find time to exercise, otherwise you'd be huge. My days started early; I broke off relationships. It was hard to explain to some girls what you were doing and why you were out at night and sometimes why you were at a restaurant with another woman, even though it was an executive from a studio or it was a producer or a young agent. Luckily later on I found my wife: Shareen was not an employee of CAA; she was Rick and Paula's assistant outside of the office and I would see her in the office all the time. She knew what I did and the hours that I kept and it was great. It makes a big difference to have somebody who understands what you do.

SONYA ROSENFELD, Agent:

Mike and I met here as assistants. It's very hard to explain the job of an agent or the way in which our company operates to people who don't work here, so the ability to have your spouse understand that already and have it be a part of his DNA has made our lives much easier to navigate. If you're married to somebody who has a nine-to-five job, and your job is the opposite of nine to five, it's very hard to have your lives mesh.

SYLVESTER STALLONE:

I wouldn't call it a secret society, but agents speak this short-hand, and they live this stuff twenty-four hours a day. You're dealing with a specialist who eats, breathes, and sleeps it; they know the insides and outs, they know who's getting married and who's going to be born, they know where the bodies are buried, and they know where the bodies are going to be buried. They disrupt negotiations to the point that other deals fall apart and they insert their clients in the most political of ways. It's very, very inside and specialized. It requires, first of all, stealth-like maneuvering. But also great aplomb, and being able to be cordial to people who you know are business competitors. There's no question it takes a special kind of creature. It's kind of like the stunt man who jumps off of buildings for a living: this is not normal; common sense says you do not set yourself on fire, but stunt men do it, because they have a certain thing inside them. Agents can be incredibly competitive, I almost align it to really vibrant stockbrokers, commodity traders—they're nuts. But instead of money, they're dealing in souls, in human beings, in personalities, and relationships. It's very fast and the odds change quickly.

ADAM VENIT:

I was working for just a couple weeks when someone said to me, "Listen, there's a stain on the rug in the lobby." I said, "Yeah, well, that's not really what I'm supposed to be doing here." And they said, "Oh, yes, you are." I said, "No, I'm not. I just left one of the top law schools in the country. I'm not doing that," just as Ray Kurtzman walked in. He says, "What do you mean, you're not doing it? Get over there and clean the stain. That's exactly what you're doing here, and if you don't want to do it, then you don't want to be here." So I said, "Okay." He literally handed me a spray bottle and a sponge, and I went out to the lobby and Sylvester Stallone was sitting in the lobby, wearing a big double-breasted suit with wingtip shoes, and one of his big wingtip shoes was pointing to the stain. I had to bow down to him and wipe the stain away to the point where he says, "Want to get my shoe while you're down there?" The beauty of Hollywood is I now represent Sylvester, and we laugh about this story.

MARTIN SPENCER:

On a Friday afternoon—it was like four o'clock—my phone sheet was clear, so I said to my assistant, "I'm going to take off. If anybody calls, tell them I'm in a meeting and I'll call them back Monday." This is before everybody had a cell phone. I went up to Mountain Gate Golf Course and found myself on the driving range hitting some golf balls. I had brand-new golf clubs that I hadn't used yet because I had had an injury and I was feeling pretty good. So I'm on the driving range for about half an hour and all of a sudden I hear this voice saying, "Daddy, isn't that Martin Spencer over there?" I turn around and it's Mike Ovitz and his son Chris. I'm standing on a driving range at 4:30 on a Friday and I'm dead. My heart just stopped. If I could have died, I would have done it right there. He starts walking over to me and he's got this big grin on his face because he knows he's got me. I walk toward him and I say, "Michael, I'm so sorry, I've never done this before. I've never left the office early. It's the only time I've ever done it in my time at CAA." He's just nodding and smiling and the other person on the driving range was a music attorney that Mike knew.

So he came over and started talking, but I was so freaked out because I'm thinking I'm going to go to work on Monday and he's going to fire me. So he said, "Bye, Martin. I'll see you Monday." I said, "Okay, have a nice weekend." The attorney looked at me and he said, "You got busted, didn't you?" I said, "I am in so much trouble, I don't know what to do." I went home, told my girlfriend, and said, "I'm going to be looking for a new job on Monday."

On Monday, he didn't say a word to me. This was in February, and in March or April, we had the company retreat, and Saturday night, five or six agents came up onstage and told their most embarrassing moments in show business. At the end of it Michael took the microphone and said, "Those are all really funny stories. Let me tell everybody in the room Martin Spencer's most embarrassing moment in show business." Then he told the entire company how he busted me on the golf course that day. It was very funny.

AMY GROSSMAN:

Martin Spencer was one of my favorite assistant/trainees, even when he messed up. He was over six feet tall, and I remember he once helped me climb onto the arm of my office couch so I could yell at him at eye level.

SUSAN MILLER:

Retreats in the late '80s were often a time to air out your anger and frustrations, but it had gotten out of control a couple times, so the new rule became: Don't bring up anything negative without out a solution. The retreats were always epic. All of the agents would leave the office early afternoon on Friday before the first group meeting and dinner. On Saturday morning, there was always a team building exercise that was often sports related, and the dinner Saturday night was the more "wild" dinner, with entertainment, games, and a lot of drinking. Then some people would end up in someone else's room, and not by mistake. But Sunday morning—even though many people were hung over, showing up with wet hair and no makeup—Michael would take the floor for his closing speech and the room would be dead silent.

ADAM VENIT:

When I was in the mailroom, Michael Ovitz was God. One of the early jobs you had to do in the mailroom was you had to go into his office, which was locked—the only office that was locked in the morning—and you had to very specifically ritualize his office. You had to pour the water into the pitcher a certain way and you had to make sure everything was set up a certain way. You were told how to do it from the person ahead of you. You were indoctrinated, like it was North Korea and this guy's a deity. So shortly after I got to CAA, as the low man on the totem pole, I went into his office and while I was pouring the water, I spilled it all over. The door opened, and he walked in and saw his desk wet. There was water all over it. My heart stopped for a second, and I thought, *Oh my God*. He said, "What are you doing?" I said, "I'm so sorry." I was thinking this was probably going to be it for me, but you know what? He was really nice about it. He was terse, but not mean. I got him on a good day.

DUSTIN HOFFMAN:

It's like watching your kid grow—you're not aware of it all the time. But if you have friends who saw him when he was a year old and don't see him again for years, they'll say, "Oh my God, look how much he's grown." It's like how you're not aware of yourself getting older. It happens day to day.

At the beginning, Michael was extraordinary, and fiercely hard working. I mean, nobody worked harder than Michael, and I thought that he didn't get enough credit for that. He was always there. He was the glue that held many things together, many times. We had a singular relationship because I was in so early. He said, "Any time you want to talk to me, call, and if I'm in a meeting you're the only one who I've told my assistant I will leave the meeting to talk to." And he did. He treated me in a kind of unique way. We were friends. His kids played with my kids. We had a place at the beach. And we saw each other throughout the years.

MARTIN SCORSESE:

We had the *Goodfellas* script that I worked on with Nick Pileggi, which was at Warner Bros., and I owed them a movie. It was in January of '87. Marlon Brando invited us out to his island in Tahiti. There was some project Brando had in mind, a comedy; he had been talking to me because I had worked with Michael Jackson on *Bad* in 1985. I was with my wife at the time, and Robert De Niro and his wife. On the way out, I had to stop in L.A., and Mike said, "Do me a favor. Go to see Tom Pollock over at Universal, just have lunch, and talk to him about *Last Temptation*." I said okay. I didn't really think much about it because I'd had lots of meetings about *Last Temptation*, with many different people around the world. I had never had any dealings all throughout the '70s with Universal at all; it was usually United Artists and Warner Bros. and one with Columbia—that was *Taxi Driver*. So I said I'll take the meeting, and we did that, and I talked about how I would make the film. The budget was cut way down to hardly anything, I'd make it very cheaply in Morocco or Tunisia, I'd done all the scouting already. The cast was pretty much together, there was no waiting around. So I didn't think anything of it. We left, went to Tahiti, spent two and a half weeks there. When we came back, I had another meeting in California, and *Last Temptation of Christ* had been canceled at Paramount. Aside from budgets rising and complaints going to Martin Davis from Christian groups, the biggest problem, to be fair, was the distributor, UA Theaters, who wouldn't show the film. If you spend a lot of money on a movie, it would be good that it be shown in a theater, so you could understand why they pulled out. In this case, however, Tom [Pollock] somehow had a deal with a Canadian exhibition company called Cineplex Odeon that guaranteed the theaters. Tom felt that the budget was good enough, so we put *Goodfellas* on hold. I had to go talk to Terry Semel and explain, "Please let me go and make this film."

BOB BOOKMAN, Agent:

I was a studio executive for six years, which were by far the six most unhappy and painful years of my career. I was originally at ABC Motion Pictures and then Columbia Pictures. Mike originally tried to hire me back in '77 or '78 when I was at ICM—because I represented Michael Crichton. Around '86, I was going through a version of a midlife crisis: I had a very young son and it was clear by then that my marriage wasn't going to last. I felt that the only time that I had ever been happy, successful, and productive was as an agent, and one day when Michael realized I was serious about it, he said, "Meet me for lunch at Jimmy's on Friday." He always had the first booth on the right, and he ate there a lot. He kind of beat me up in terms of what I was being paid, which wasn't in my opinion all that much, at ICM. He kept lowballing me on the money, and I didn't want to give him the satisfaction of saying yes right then, so I said, "Let me think about it over the weekend." I called him Monday and I said, "When do I start?"

I was charged with running the book department. At ICM, I had actually made the book to film and television department, which had never been handled by one person. But at ICM I was only representing internal material. Since there was no New York literary department of CAA, I needed to have relationships with all of the literary agencies, and then represent their material to CAA clients.

Lynn Nesbit was Michael Crichton's agent in New York, and I got from Lynn the manuscript of a book called *Coma* by Robin Cook. I sent the manuscript to Michael Crichton, first and exclusively. He read it, committed to it, and said, "You're the first person who's ever sent me material I didn't generate myself that I wanted to do." He wound up writing and directing it, with Michael Douglas and Geneviève Bujold.

DAN ADLER, Executive:

I was fortunate to have met the Eisners through a summer camp in Vermont that Michael Eisner is obsessed with. I had one of his kids in my tent when I worked there as a counselor, and so in corresponding with the Eisners on behalf of their son and my responsibility there, I struck up a relationship with them. When I came to L.A. looking for a job, I contacted the Eisners, and it so happened that the day I saw Jane Eisner, the Eisners and the Ovitzes, Michael and Judy, were going that night to see Neil Diamond, who was a client of Michael Ovitz and a close friend of Michael Eisner and Jane. That night I got a message at the house I was staying that I should call Michael Ovitz's office the next day.

I didn't grow up in the business; didn't really know what CAA was until I went for my interview, and didn't even know who Michael was before I went for my interview. I live by a set of principles that matter to me, and I think Michael understood that my loyalty was real but also that my bar was my bar.

I started at the agency in '86. Officially I was in the mailroom for a long period of time, but unofficially I got pulled out of the mailroom relatively quickly, because I came in with a degree of trust from Ovitz based on how I had come in to him, I was pulled in to assist with some projects in his office, and those projects sort of took on more and more commitment and more and more time and more and more responsibility and essentially I was doing it full-time but still officially in the mailroom. I remember thinking to myself as I got out here that *I'll do this for as long as I don't ever have to compromise anything I believe in. And the day I have to compromise what I believe in, I'm out.*

Usually Michael's trainee assistant would sort of migrate into a position, once promoted, of inheriting or taking on a lot of Michael's clients in a transition. But at the point of being promoted, I made it very clear to Michael that I did not want to sort of just do the handoff of the clients, although it was a great opportunity. He said, "What would you want to do?" I said, "Well, I want to produce *Nightline* or do something like that. That's the stuff that really interests me, being all over the place, involved with different things." He essentially said, "Well, let's find a way for you to do some of that other stuff."

DAVID STYNE, Agent:

Dan was an agent but he never really flew the Ovitz coop, as it were. So while I was on Mike's desk, Dan was very much Mike's right hand and was always working on special projects, and if something was really important, Michael called Dan to get it done. But Dan never really had his own clients. He did Ovitz stuff.

DAN ADLER:

Michael's desk was one of the most demanding—and one of the most rewarding—experiences I ever could have imagined. It was as relentless and unforgiving as any work environment could be, with a constant pressure, a zero tolerance for any mistakes, and a state of tension born of the belief that every piece fit into a puzzle and that all of it was part of a bigger plan. It required a balance of stamina, patience, guts, and political savvy, with a constant need to cover your ass—which meant covering his ass!—while focusing on managing internal relationships—i.e., among the various agents—and external responsibilities, especially in terms of clients. In that place and in that moment, one could get caught up in believing that what happened there was all-important. It certainly is the way we all were raised there—yet I remember the other side of that approach coming from Ron Meyer, who in a "we're not curing cancer" kind of statement would try to remind everyone that there was nothing life or death about it all, even if at times you might be inclined to think so, if you listened to some of the yelling going on as agents roared into the phones or as they yelled at their assistants!

On a typical day, the first task was to go through all the newspapers and trade publications. Michael wanted them spread out, neatly, across a big reading space in his office, with the *New York Times*, the *Los Angeles Times*, and the *Wall Street Journal* in one stack, and then *Variety*, *The Hollywood Reporter*, *Billboard*, et cetera, in another.

The rest of that task required taking a yellow highlighter to stories of note, and sometimes even adding Post-its. Of course no matter how thoroughly you tried to complete that task, you'd inevitably omit the one article that Michael would catch, and then he would criticize you for missing it. It was Murphy's Law, I guess renamed as Ovitz's Law!

The next task was to be ready for Michael on the phone. He would call in while driving to the office, and while he was "running calls" with one of the women who worked with Michael for years at a stretch and the males in the "trainee" assistant role, he'd want to run through work in the downtime, between calls. Of course there was a whole system of how all of the folks who worked for him would juggle these tasks and this call process, and another system of how to "clear the line" after each call—as Michael lived in a constant state of paranoia, in terms of people wanting to know what he was doing and in terms of his worries about not letting someone hear something who shouldn't be privy to it. "Is the line cleared?" was a constant refrain, and it led to a whole set of other processes to ensure "security."

Once Michael was in the office, the day took on a different vibe. Although the agency relied on an open-door policy that encouraged agents to walk freely into and out of colleagues' offices, Michael's door generally was kept closed. That was true back at 1888 Century Park East—in one of the trainee-made films that premiered at the annual retreat, there was a recurring shot down the long hallway to Michael's office, where the ominous *Jaws* music played each time the shot was used!—and of course in the Pei building.

Michael would start the day by walking back to the bay of offices where all of his assistants worked, trying to get a quick handle on what was happening and where things stood. He would start by marking up his phone sheet: he had an elaborate system for how to prioritize the day's calls that took into account incoming and outgoing calls, and the daily flow of calls then would be managed by the woman whose job that was—with the trainee assistant stepping in to relieve her at lunch, or earlier in the morning, or late at night, after she had left.

The one piece of correspondence that Michael seemed to enjoy the most was birthday cards. As birthdays approached, we'd review a list of gift suggestions, and he'd choose what the gift should be. I made the mistake one too many times of waiting until the last minute for this task, and I would get yelled at when I did. Once the list was settled, I would bring in a pile of cards, with a list of upcoming birthdays, and Michael would flip through the stack to pull out the one he liked most for each recipient. He would write, usually in a red Magic Marker, some of his best one-liners—including some very raunchy ones—on those cards.

MICHAEL OVITZ:

I had Bob Goldman, Sandy, and Ray Kurtzman. Ray handled the training program, legal, and all the deal making. Sandy was my strategy guy. Bob was my financial guy, like the CFO. I paid everybody well—Bob, Sandy, Ray, all probably made a million and a half bucks a year, and I took care of Dan Adler, too. Sandy was a really important part of the growth of the business because he came in with that Harvard Business School thing, which was new in the entertainment business. He interfaced with almost every senior agent. When they had a client with a big problem or they wanted to go in and do back ends or participation, Sandy modeled all that stuff, too.

At that time, Sandy was as close to Redford as anyone was. He did everything for him, like when Redford wanted to start the Sundance Channel, Sandy helped me create the business plan.

SANDY CLIMAN:

Redford and Mike's relationship was so complicated that Bob often found it simpler to speak with me. He wanted Mike in his life for the handful of times when ultimate clout was needed.

Beginning in the mid-1980s, home video, which at the time was dominated by VHS tape, became the goose that laid the golden eggs for the movie studios. Every year the home video revenue stream grew, and it quickly became larger and far more important than the "ancillary" revenue streams from pay television and broadcast television.

SANDY CLIMAN:

The studios "hid" the home video revenue from talent by only contributing a 20 percent video royalty to gross receipts, making the bulk of the earnings invisible to talent, and their profits soared. At times it seemed hard for the studios to lose money on star-driven films. Knowing this all too well, we modeled the full video revenue and showed our clients what they were missing. We used the leverage of every major talent negotiation to break the 20 percent barrier—moving it to 35 percent into the revenue pot, then forcing the studios to account for 100 percent of the video revenue to talent. Talent knew we understood the game and that we were championing their cause, and this helped us sign a long procession of major stars and directors.

MICHAEL OVITZ:

Sundance was really Sandy. I helped Bob enormously, but he'll never admit it. We gave them a hundred grand for the $200,000 cost to build his theater there. He owned the ski resort and the real estate, so we were giving him $100,000 to build a theater on his property.

PHIL KENT:

I learned a lot about time management from Bill and Ron. One time I walked into Bill's office, and I simply sat down, and he said, "Don't sit. This isn't a meeting. This is just a conversation." He never had chairs at his desk on purpose, so nobody would plop down.

DAN ADLER:

Bill wanted one assistant so he could say that he had only one assistant. Bill loved showing up at meetings in a Volkswagen Bug—it was refurbished and in good shape, but it was still a Volkswagen Bug. But that was Bill. Bill wanted to be that eccentric other guy.

MICHAEL OVITZ:

I wasn't particularly close to Bill. He wasn't as popular in the company as Ron was because he was so quirky. But he was really smart.

PHIL KENT:

Bill was more fun as your friend than as a motivator. Michael was an unbelievable motivator; you felt like you could do anything after talking with him. The only time he ever yelled at me was when I told Barry Levinson his game show idea sucked.

BRUCE VINOKOUR:

There were a number of similarities between Bill and Mike. They were both incredibly bright, both extraordinarily great agents, and both worked really hard. I used to come in on Saturdays around ten o'clock; their cars were already there. When I would leave, their cars would still be there. I once said to Bill, "You're the best agent in Hollywood," and without hesitating or even blinking, he said, "No, I'm not. Mike Ovitz is."

RON MEYER:

I don't think a lot of people understood my relationship with Bill. Perhaps not even Mike. We worked in different areas, but I believed then and believe now that he was probably the best television agent ever. We certainly had different styles—Bill was and is eccentric, and certainly difficult to figure out; I'm probably more complicated, but it's not as obvious. I don't think we ever had a serious disagreement or fight, but while the agency was going through its dramatic growth in the '80s, I wouldn't be surprised if some people thought there was tension among us. There were times then and later when Bill would get so fed up—often with

Mike—and would threaten to leave, I would say to Mike, "Maybe we shouldn't force him to stay." Fortunately, he did stay.

There were times when I went to Mike and said I should be getting a different deal, a different percentage of the agency, but he would just tell me I needed to get it from Bill, rather than from him. I always refused to do that, and it never got resolved.

MICHAEL OVITZ:

Ron and I functioned so well together. Everyone knew he was the only person that could influence me. He was the only guy I listened to.

RON MEYER:

Mike and I were always very much in sync. We spoke so often and were so much in touch that we could finish each other's sentences.

MICHAEL OVITZ:

It got to the point he and I could finish each other's sentences. We trusted each other implicitly. I didn't trust anyone in my life more than Ron Meyer—no one, except for maybe my wife. I have to say that it was something that I never had in my life as a kid, you know? I don't think he did either, by the way.

DAVID O'CONNOR:

Ronnie was much more of a pure talent agent than Michael ever was. He had a real facility for it, had real deep relationships, and was much more personal in the way he did business than Michael was.

PHIL KENT:

I always thought Ron was the glue that held the whole place together, because he got along with everybody.

CHER:

Ovitz was just like, *Look at me, I'm the head of it. I'm the head of CAA.* I had no dealings with him ever, whatsoever. But Ronnie was a real person, a human being. You wouldn't look at him and think he was the head of something.

Ronnie really pushed for me to get in *Witches of Eastwick.* George Miller didn't want me in any way, and wanted to cut my head off. Every time they would call to say, "George is really excited about you being in this film," and blah blah blah, I would call him and he would say, "I really don't want you in this film, but I'm being forced into it now," and I said, "You know what, dude, fuck you. You're not finding me under a rock, I've already been nominated for Academy Awards." He just hated me so, but Ronnie just kept pushing and pushing, telling me it was going to work out. He probably had to strangle George to get me on that set, but I never heard him raise his voice. And it was such a strange thing. Ronnie was right. The moment we started working, he forgot all the horrible things he said about me and we got along just beautifully. I had such a good time on that movie in certain ways—in other ways, no—but in many ways, it was a lot of fun.

MICHAEL OVITZ:

Ron and I played this game that we created very early: good cop, bad cop. I was always the tough one and he was always the one that came in and fluffed people up.

DAVID O'CONNOR:

Ronnie would convince them and cajole them. Michael would pummel them.

PHIL KENT:

Ron only got mad at me two times, in all the years I was there. When Dan Adler and I decided we wanted to represent Garry Kasparov, the world chess champion, he said, "This is the dumbest thing I've seen since Norman Brokaw at William Morris decided to sign Secretariat the horse." The other time I thought I had a really inspired idea. Arianna Huffington, before she became Arianna Huffington, was named Arianna Stassinopoulos, and she was a very good biographer. She'd written a biography of Maria Callas that I was trying to package. I had this idea to have Cher play Maria Callas and lip-sync the original operetta tracks. I thought Ron was going to rip my head off: "She's a fucking rock star. Maria Callas was fucking four feet tall." I still thought it was one of my more inspired packaging ideas, but it got nowhere.

DAVID O'CONNOR:

Ovitz scared the shit out of me and he intimidated me every single day of my life that we worked together.

TOM ROSS:

Magic Johnson and the Lakers were in the playoffs, and everybody in town was going to the games—it was the who's who of the entire industry. I had gotten two floor seats through a major promoter in L.A. that he couldn't really afford, and so I made a deal that they would be Michael's floor seats. When the Lakers went into the playoffs, Michael said, "Listen. I'm getting bombarded by everybody in town. They want tickets. You gotta get me a bunch more tickets." I said, "Michael, it's the playoffs. Everybody wants more tickets." And he said, "Well, aren't you friendly with Fred Rosen? And Claire Rothman?" Fred Rosen ran Ticketmaster and Claire Rothman worked at the Forum. So I called them and they said, "Tom, it's really tough. Don't count on it."

I had tickets for my family, so I gave them to Michael, who gave me this look of *That's it?* It was such a helpless face. And then I found out that he had a conversation with Fred Rosen where Fred said, "You know, these are tough tickets to get, Michael. Everybody is on my case." And Michael says, "I know. I've got extra tickets if you need them." He sandbagged me royally.

SANDY GALLIN, Manager:

There are some differences in the agencies, but I think there's a bigger difference in the particular agent who's looking out for you—and how much they're really looking out for you. Mitch Rose sent me the Milli Vanilli album. They had only released one single, and I listened to the album and I thought, *Oh my God. They are going to be huge! Enormous! Gigantic!* I told everyone in my office, "Find Milli Vanilli. Get them to my house or to the office. I want to meet with these guys. They are going to be enormous."

We found them, met with them, and signed them. They had a horrible, horrible, horrible record deal. So I went to London to meet with Frank Farian, who was their producer, and I told him you've got to give them a new deal. They're working for slave labor. And he said, "You don't understand. They don't sing." I told him, "No, you don't understand. Obviously they sing well enough that millions of people are buying their records and they have had one hit number one record. And the second one is on the way." So again he says, "No, no, no. You don't understand! They don't sing!" And he gets mad and pounds on the table. Diana Ross was in the restaurant, and came over and asked, "Sandy, are you okay?" I said, "Yeah. I'm fine." She said, "Well, you don't look fine. This guy looks like he's going to kill you." She said, "My bodyguards are outside at my car if you need them."

Mitch Rose and CAA evidently had no clue they were the vocals on the record. So I was there screaming and yelling, "They're great singers."

DAVID GREENBLATT:

I had signed a young writer client, Fred Dekker, who had just graduated from UCLA. His goal was to write "popcorn movies." He even had a company called Hollywood Pulp Productions. His idols were Spielberg, Lucas, and Kubrick. But his literary influences were all the pulp detective authors from the 1930s. 1940s. 1950s.

Fred would rave to me about his best friend in college. Someone named Shane Black. I said to Fred that no one has that name. It sounds like a character's name from one of the pulp detective authors that Fred admired. Fred insisted that there really was a Shane Black. And that Shane was the best writer he knew. And all of Fred's college friends were writers. And I continued to not believe him that Shane Black was a real person. I'd met a lot of Fred's friends, but Shane was not one of them. And yet Fred would continually talk about him.

One day I'm in my office and the receptionist rings: "There's a Shane Black here to see you." I say to myself, *Right*. This was just Fred pulling my leg. So I tell my assistant I will go greet this "Shane Black" myself.

I go out to the receptionist lobby and there is this tall, young man dressed in torn jeans, torn sweatshirt, and sneakers that had holes in them. He extends his hand and says, "I'm Shane Black. Nice to meet you. Fred Dekker said I should come see you." I shake his hand and say, "That's really your name. Nice to meet you, too."

Shane had a script with him and asked if I would read it. Fred had been very generous with introducing me to his friends and their writing. They were all very talented. And given that Fred had said Shane was the most talented of all I was very eager to read it.

I read the script that night. It was called "Shadow Company." A great script. Great writing. I knew I could get him work from it. I called Shane, told him how much I loved the script and the writing and asked if I could represent him. Thankfully he agreed.

I started getting him meetings immediately as the response to the writing was similar to my own response. No offers on it, but we did get a job offer for a project at Fox. This was important, as Shane needed the work.

Not long after I get a call from reception: "Shane Black is here for you." He had shown up without notice. I usher him into my office. I ask what's up. He tells me he'd like me to read something he's working on. But he's not sure about it. He hands me the first thirty pages of a script called "The Nice Guys." I read it immediately, while he's sitting in my office. And my world stopped. It was riveting. I couldn't get enough.

I said, "This is fantastic! When can I see more?" He asks if he should keep going and I said, "Fuck yes!" He looks at me and thinks for a second and says, "Okay. I'll keep working on it." I was effusive how much I loved it. He leaves.

Two days later, the receptionist calls: "Shane Black is here." He comes into my office. He looks like he hasn't changed clothes. Or slept for that matter. He hands me another thirty pages. I read them immediately. So now I've read sixty pages of the best script I've ever read. I tell him it is incredible. I encourage him to finish it. Again, he looks at me and thinks for a bit. But this time he says, "I'm either going to finish this in two weeks or you'll never see me again." I said, "Don't put a time limit on yourself. Finish it when you are ready." But he clearly had so much tied up in this. And this affected me deeply. I knew he was serious about never seeing him again.

I said, "If you don't finish it, I'm sure we can get you other work." But Shane, as I've come to know him, is very dedicated to what he starts. And at that moment, he either was going to finish or disappear. And he was dead serious. I told him again how phenomenal I thought the writing was as I escorted him out.

Two days later the receptionist calls and says Shane Black was here to see me. He comes into my office. Now I am certain he hadn't slept all week. Definitely wearing the same clothes. He drops a 130-page manuscript on my desk. I look at the cover. It is now called *Lethal Weapon*. I read the whole thing right there on the spot. And this truly was the best writing I had ever experienced.

I told him to wait in my office. I go into Tony Ludwig's office, interrupt the phone call he was on, and tell him I had just read the best script I'd ever seen. He gets off the phone, I bring him into my office, and introduce him to Shane.

This was on a Friday morning. We had seven offers by that afternoon. We closed the deal at Warners on Saturday.

To this day, it is still the best script I've read. And to this day, people still use it as reference for iconic characters and story-telling.

RICHARD DONNER, Director:

Ovitz was my agent, and you could call and he would always get you to somebody, or get you help if you needed it from the studio. But on *Lethal Weapon*, it was Mark Canton who was running Warners at the time who called me and said he had a script that he thought I would like. I'd never done an action movie, because I thought they were usually extraordinarily gratuitous in terms of the action, but he said that wasn't the case with this script. He said, "This is based on characters by a brilliant young writer named Shane Black, and you need to read it." So that evening I read it, then handed it to my wife, Lauren, who's a producer, and she read it, and said, "Oh, boy. Do it!" So I did.

I called Ovitz the next day and said, "I just got a script from Warners and I really like it," and he said, "Yeah, yeah, we were just about to send you that."

CHER:

I told Ron I couldn't do *Moonstruck*. I was involved with three pictures back to back to back—*Suspect*, *Witches of Eastwick*, and *Mask*. The *Suspect* script was so great—and it was such a crap film—and nobody knew when we were going to be finished with *Witches*, so I just told him, "How can I just go right into *Moonstruck* now?" He said, "Well, I think you're making a mistake, but you need to go and sit down with them and tell it to them directly." Which turned out to be so completely full of shit, okay? Because I then went and sat down with Norman and Patrick, and I was all prepared to say to them, "I'm sorry, I think your script is fabulous, but I can't do it," and the only thing I can remember is waving goodbye to them in the elevator after the meeting saying, "I'm so excited, too! I can't wait till we start." And of course, that had been Ron's plan all along. He even told me, "I knew when I put you back together with them that you would do it." That's how great he was, you know? I didn't even know I was being tricked.

JOE ESZTERHAS:

After Steve Roth had left, Michael had then come to me and was nice to me. He said, "I'm going to be your agent." I knew that wasn't true, because what they always did was have a younger agent handle the day to day stuff. I met Rosalie Swedlin and liked her. I thought she was really smart. One thing that always influenced me was whether someone was well-read, which she was. A lot of those agents don't read, they all bullshit and chitchat, but she read, and she was smart. So I stayed with her for a while. We got along personally, but Rosalie was always a little too interested in actually commenting on what I was writing and making creative suggestions. I'm not good with that with directors and collaborators, let alone agents. Then I was with Rand Holston, and we got along well, and like I said, my career was exploding.

Shane Black and I were going back and forth in terms of these record-setting deals. The topper was probably *Basic Instinct*, because every single production entity except Fox wanted it. There was total madness. The initial offer that I got was four million and I got four to do a piece then called *Gangland* about John Gotti, which never got made. I also got four for a brief outline on a napkin for *One Night Stand*, with New Line. All throughout this time, Shane's prices kept escalating. It was like a war.

BILL MURRAY:

I originally wanted Sydney to direct *Scrooged*, and I had gone to his house to try and talk him into it, but he always had trouble committing to making a movie, so I put all the pressure I could on him. At one point, I had Sydney on the floor of his house and was on top of him, begging him, and his wife was saying, "Bill! Bill! Let him go!" But he couldn't do it.

RICHARD DONNER:

The only movie Ovitz really pushed me on was *Scrooged*. He sent it to me and asked me to read it, and I really thought it was extraordinarily funny and well-written. But I didn't know what it was going to be like working with Bill Murray, and so I mentioned that to Mike and I don't think it was five minutes later that I got a call from Bill Murray saying he was coming up to my house at six o'clock. He showed up at 9:30, and it turned out to be one of the most delightful evenings of my life. He was incredibly charming. After that, I wanted to do the movie no matter what. That was smart, good agenting on Ovitz's part.

DAVID GREENBLATT:

For about seven months, I was selling at least one script a week, $250,000, $500,000 there, $100,000 here. There was a script called *Three O'Clock High*. Did not make a great movie, but I had probably ten bidders on this thing, one of them being Steven Spielberg. I did my duty and I serviced a couple CAA clients. I gave it to Aaron Spelling even though Spelling was a giant TV player but not known for his movies. Gave it to John Davis, John being Marvin's son, who was just starting out at the time. Spelling wanted it, Davis wanted it, Spielberg wanted it, as well as seven or eight other people. So Ovitz comes into my office. Now, usually you go into Ovitz's office. That's like getting called into the principal's office. When he comes to *your* office, you know you're in for some show. So Ovitz comes to my office, he says, "David. *Three O'Clock High*. You've got Aaron chewing me a new asshole, John Davis—I don't need Marvin Davis killing me here. I'm going to marry everybody, okay?" "Well, what about Spielberg? The client loves Spielberg." "Don't worry. I love it when Steven is upset because that gives me a way into him." Now CAA did not represent Steven Spielberg at the time, and it was brilliant because he could tweak Spielberg: "Hey, Steven, if you were here, this wouldn't even be a conversation. But since I don't represent you . . . Now maybe what I *can* do is marry you with everybody . . ." And we ended up marrying John Davis, Steven Spielberg, Aaron Spelling together on this fucking deal.

It did get made; Spielberg took Amblin's name off it because he hated the movie so much. But it was his guy that he had direct it.

CAA was both shaken and stirred on February 1, 1988, when agents David Greenblatt and Judy Hofflund left to join with ICM bigwig Bill Block and form the new InterTalent agency in direct competition with CAA.

"Direct competition with CAA" is a phrase that struck Michael Ovitz as nothing short of obscene. He'd had to suffer through only a relative handful of such departures over the previous thirteen years, but none was more startling to him than this one—especially since it involved the departures of two such highly respected agents. Ovitz considered the move treasonous, though it was Meyer who bluntly declared his determination to put the new agency out of business. In addition to the perceived betrayal, Meyer had been told by knowledgeable people that it was Hofflund—who had been his personal assistant—who had leaked rumors to a prominent columnist about Meyer's alleged marital infidelities.

DAVID GREENBLATT:

I thought Ovitz was brilliant. I said, "I'm never going to be as smart as that guy." So I did an analysis. I was almost four years married at that point. I had just had a kid. Bought a small starter house. And they were just starting to "we want to pay you a lot more money, we're going to defer a lot of the salary so it's paid out over several years." And I said to myself, *This is what golden handcuffs are.* I don't begrudge them that, but I said if I'm ever going to be wealthy, I've got to take a risk because Ovitz, I'm not in his category smarts-wise, but I'm as smart as Bill and Ronnie. I'm not saying I'm as good as they are, but I'm as smart as they are. And, I said, what was the difference between who they are and who I am? They took a risk. They did the setup with the card tables and they left their job or they got fired or whatever the story is, and they started CAA. I said, "The only way I'm going to be wealthy is if I take a risk. And if I take a risk now, I'm falling five foot, eight and a half inches. If I take a risk two years from now, I'll have a bigger mortgage, I'll have a lot more cash that I'm leaving on the table, and I don't know if I have the stomach to do that." And that was it. I knew if I could model myself after their techniques, I could be just as attractive with my new partners, with my potential clients.

JUDY HOFFLUND:

It was a great company. They promoted me fast. They were really good to me, but I wanted to be able to do my own thing. As I got older, it became a bit clearer: I—me, Judy—could never have had the life I wanted as an agent there and been the mother I wanted to be. I needed to be more in charge to be able to do both. I was only twenty-nine or thirty when I left CAA, but I did know that I wanted a family and I knew that would be hard to do. I was always willing to work like a maniac, but I knew I needed to be my own boss.

DAVID GREENBLATT:

When I was at ICM, I befriended a terrific agent there named Bill Block. Bill was always a leader, he had a vision, and he was popular. He was fearless—all the qualities that Jack Rapke had, too. It's ironic that they never worked together because they had very similar qualities. Certainly Ovitz was all of that. And Block came to me and said, "You and I always liked each other. I think there's a big opportunity to start an agency. You and I have these great relationships." Remember I was at the top of the world when it came to spec scripts at that time and I had all these hot clients and all this TV revenue. And I said, "I've got to do something. I want to make a lot of money. I also want to get powerful, but I want to get rich." He said, "Okay, well there's somebody else at CAA who might be interested in the talent side." So I'm thinking, *Okay, wait a second. Bill's movies. I can certainly do TV. And this other person can do talent.* We got all the bases covered.

JUDY HOFFLUND:

I had heard that Bill Block was talking to Marty Bauer and Peter Benedek when it was Bauer-Benedek. I knew Bill a little, just from being out and about. And I said to somebody, "That's kind of a drag. I always thought Bill and I would do something someday." That got relayed to Bill and Bill called me and we met the next morning. Very quickly after that David Greenblatt was part of the equation.

DAVID GREENBLATT:

Bill, I think, was under contract to ICM, but his contract had expired, so he had the right to do whatever he wanted to. I had no contract at CAA. And about two months before we were supposed to do it, Judy Hofflund entered the picture. She was Ron Meyer's protégée. And so she was a young pup, too, just like me, and she was making her mark.

Now what I was dreading was leaving Michael, because his whole thing was about loyalty. And so clearly I was betraying this. But I figured in my head, *I'm doing this for me, I'm doing this for my family, I'm doing everything exactly as you did it, you know? I want to be you. I don't want to hurt you, I want to be you.*

JUDY HOFFLUND:

Bill was going to tell Jeff Berg, and David and I were going to tell Ron and Mike. We had a fixed time in the calendar, which was later in the afternoon. Probably two or three hours before we have this meeting, someone tipped off Ron. I don't know exactly who it was. Ron came into my office and closed the door and said, "Is what I'm hearing true?" And I said, "Yeah. That's what I wanted to talk to you about in the meeting this afternoon." And he said, "Well, get David and come into Mike's office right now."

DAVID GREENBLATT:

Judy walks into my office at CAA, shuts the door, and says, "They know," and I guess I was one of those guys who was trying to avoid the inevitable. I started shuffling papers and putting stuff in files as if nothing had ever happened. And she's looking at me and after a couple minutes she goes, "David. We have to go now."

JUDY HOFFLUND:

David took like twenty minutes to put on his jacket. I said, "Come on, David, we better go! We gotta go to Mike's office." Mike knew nothing because he was on the phone and Ron hadn't spoken to him. Ron, me, and David were all standing on the other side of his desk and he stood up when he got off the phone. I think David said something like, "Mike, we came in here to tell you that we're leaving to start our own agency." And Mike looked like the air had gotten sucked out of him and he fell back into his chair.

DAVID GREENBLATT:

He says, "I want to throw you out the window. Tell me why." I told him why, and he looked at me, I could tell that he was hurt. *I* was hurt. I mean, he was my hero. And I explained it as best I could. I'm sure I sounded like a blithering idiot.

JUDY HOFFLUND:

Mike's first defense was to try to talk us into finding a way to do it in connection with CAA. He said, "I want to talk to you two and Bill together. Maybe we can find a way to do this so CAA is sort of your umbrella company. Would you guys be willing to talk about that?" I said, "Sure, we'd be happy to." I left and went home. David did, too. The plan was we were going to get together with Mike the following day, but his office called and said, "Mike is canceling the meeting. He doesn't want to meet with you guys." That was the end.

TOM STRICKLER:

I was an assistant for Jack Rapke and the guy in the office next to him was David Greenblatt. So because of navigational and geographic configuration in the office, we got to know each other. I'm on this desk for a year, so I begin to get the rhythms of when David comes in, when he comes out, and who he talks to because every time someone calls, his assistant calls out, you know, "It's Aaron Spelling on two." Anyway, you could see by the kind of choreography of his life that something was going on. There were calls that happened where he would shut the door. And he was on the phone a fair amount with Bill Block and Judy Hofflund—something was going on in that configuration. Eventually I made an assumption. Right before a staff meeting—it was sort of an obnoxious thing only a twenty-one-year-old asshole would do—I looked at David and I smiled at him and said, "So you're starting an agency, right?" He went white like a sheet. I kind of smiled at him and said, "Don't worry," and he looked at me and said, "Okay."

So they left and then what happened was an overreaction, and it didn't play well. You were supposed to sign up for the "we hate David, we hate Judy" club forever, and I had no interest in doing that. The other thing was that I told the truth, which I subsequently learned is not the smartest thing to do in corporate America. I was confronted with, "Did you know they were going to leave?" I told the truth. I said, "They never told me, but I figured it out." It wasn't as if he had told me or that he had ever actually ever acknowledged that it was happening. It was just more the navigational direction of what was going on at his office. You could see the tunnel was being built. David was a good friend. I was closer to him than Mike or anyone like that. I wasn't going to sell my friend down the river.

DAVID GREENBLATT:

It was frightening as hell because Michael had the most power in all of Hollywood, more so than David Geffen, more so than Steven, more so than anybody. He didn't necessarily have it in TV, but he had it in the movie business, and the movie business then was still the jewel of media—maybe not the biggest moneymaker but certainly the most visible, most prestigious. He could literally prevent you from getting a job. He could literally get you a job. He had that kind of power.

JUDY HOFFLUND:

At the time, I saw CAA as huge and powerful and nothing remotely close to what we were going to do, or what we were going to ever become. I wanted to keep it more boutiquey but represent big stars.

CRAIG JACOBSON, Attorney:

When they started InterTalent, I was told by several CAA agents that Mike Ovitz, in addition to whatever threats he issued against InterTalent, "asked" his agents to stop doing business with the Hansen, Jacobson, and Teller firm because Tom Hansen is married to Judy Hofflund. So there was a long period of time where most of the rank and file at CAA didn't do business with us.

TOM STRICKLER:

Mike went into hyper jihad mode, because for him, one of the great success stories of CAA was attracting great agents who never left.

DAVID GREENBLATT:

Tom got fired because when I left, he was very supportive, and that was verboten. So we brought in Tom when we started InterTalent.

JUDY HOFFLUND

Probably our combined biggest financial client when we formed InterTalent was Patrick Hasburgh. He was just about to make what ended up being a $10 million, three-year deal at Disney, and he was a star. He told us not even to take a letter of credit out, he wanted to be our big fish and he would help support us financially. Then within about twenty-four hours, Mike Ovitz had taken him to lunch and he decided to stay at CAA. So he went from a guy who wanted to underwrite our company to sitting in my office crying saying he wasn't going to go with us. It was obvious from the beginning that they were going to do everything they could to kill us. Some people had the strength. I really give Kiefer Sutherland a lot of credit. He was a hot actor at the time and he stood by us with lots of strength, even though they put a ton of pressure on him. They were ruthless.

MICHAEL OVITZ:

In the beginning, everyone is going to pull for you. Three years in, people will still be hoping you're there and try to be on your side. They'll want more time from you than you can give them. Five years in, they'll realize you're a force to be reckoned with, and since you're no longer the underdog, and not giving them enough time, they will start to be cynical. Seven years in they'll realize you're not giving them any time, and they'll start to criticize you. And ten years in they're going to hate your guts. And that's what happened.

Everyone else was the enemy. That's how we looked at it. If you weren't with us, you were against us. There was no gray area. We never went after small independents. That's why I never signed Jack Nicholson. Before he came to CAA, Marty Bauer was representing Brian De Palma and Brian tried to sign with us, but we didn't take him. We called Marty and told him about it. A year later, De Palma fired him and came over anyway, so we put together *Untouchables*. We only went after clients at William Morris and ICM—mainly William Morris. Our goal was to break them, and we did; we blew their movie department apart to nothing—to *nothing*. Ronnie and I took Warren Beatty, Goldie Hawn, Chevy Chase; we took everybody. Their last big client was Tim Burton. That's all they were. We did the same thing to Sue Mengers—we took everyone she had: Streisand, Gene Hackman, and many others. From Jeff Berg we took Michael Mann, who was his best friend; they lived *next door* to each other.

MARSHALL HERSKOVITZ, Writer and Producer:

I remember back in the '80s having lunch with Mike Ovitz, which was a big deal for me, because I had just met him, so I was very nervous and excited. It was at Le Dome on Sunset Boulevard. I'm sitting there at the table, and watch Mike Ovitz come in, and it takes him eleven minutes to reach my table, because every single person in the restaurant literally has to kiss his ring. It was an amazing thing to see someone that powerful; everyone had to stop and say hello and do some kind of obeisance to the "great one." At the time, I had been a client for years, but my partner, Ed Zwick, was at a different agency. We thought that made us stronger. When Ovitz finally reached our table and sat down with me, without even getting through, "Hello, how are you?" he went into a diatribe about Ed and what a shithead he was that he led Ovitz on and then didn't sign with him. And I was thinking at that moment this is some illustration of human nature: You couldn't possibly have more than Mike Ovitz had then and what was he thinking of? A person who he thought fucked him over.

DAN ADLER:

At the Wednesday staff meetings, if you mentioned you were about to sign Client X, and Ronnie knew that they were still handled by, let's say the Gersh Agency, he would throw the brakes on it at that point. And quite often, his first call after the meeting would be to the Gersh office, and he would say, "Look, I'm just letting you know that our guys are about to sign Client X, so go save him. If you don't, I'm telling you you're going to lose him." It was his way of being a gentleman, and not beating up on the smaller agencies.

LEN FINK, Executive:

There was a staff meeting a couple weeks before Christmas, and Michael Ovitz stood up and said, "There are probably some agents out there who are very vulnerable at this time of year. Their clients are thinking back on the last twelve months and may not be happy with what happened, so keep your eyes open about those kind of opportunities. But if it's a client who is represented by an agent who only has a couple clients, don't pursue it. We don't need the business bad enough to wreck somebody's life."

ARI EMANUEL:

On one of my first jobs in New York I was listening in on a phone call my boss was having with Mike Ovitz. It was the first time I heard Ovitz, and the first time I ever heard my boss's voice wobble. Ovitz was a genius. He was the man.

I was in the CAA mailroom for about six months, then spent six months at a desk: first David Tenzer's, then Bruce Vinokour's. I would work Monday through Sunday; I was at the office all the time.

DAVID GREENBLATT:

When I was relatively new as an agent there, I didn't pay much attention to the mailroom guys or anything like that. I was too worried about my own self. So Ari becomes the head of the mailroom and he's got a real chip on his shoulder. There was one bathroom at CAA. I'm in the restroom washing up. Ari walks in and says, "You know, that package that you wanted to go out, we can't get it done." With a real attitude. So I look at him, and I said, "You think you've got it made, don't you? Head of the mailroom. Mr. Big Shot. Let me tell you what's going to happen with your life. You're going to get promoted, and you're going to be somebody's secretary. You're going to get their coffee, and then you're going to say, 'Who may I get on the phone for you now?' You're going to schedule their meetings. You're going to have to pick up their laundry, and you're going to have to stay here until ten o'clock at night, be here at six in the morning and work weekends reading their scripts. And maybe, just maybe, somebody will promote you to agent. And you know what kind of agent you're going to be at first? You're going to be covering TV movies for Chuck Fries Productions." And I could just see him wither. To this day we still laugh at this because it was so dead-on. I think that's what lit a fire under him big-time, because that was his vision of hell.

One of the things that we did at InterTalent that nobody else was able to do, Morris or ICM or anybody else—we were stealing clients from CAA. Why? Because Judy and I had worked there. Tom had worked there. We knew their secrets and everybody was intrigued by Bill. It's not like we were denting them; we weren't getting Jane Fonda or Tom Hanks out of there. But we were getting enough clients that we were really their only threat.

You can make a lot of money packaging TV movies, by the way, but it was just not anybody's idea of chic. So Tom says, "I think Ari might be ripe for the taking." I knew they were close, so I said, "Set up a meeting." So I sit with Ari—and again, I had only known him peripherally except for that one incident in the restroom.

ARI EMANUEL:

I loved Bill Haber. Just loved him. Bruce Vinokour was Bill Haber's guy, so I got to see Haber a lot. Then Lee Gabler kind of took over the television department—I think there were some politics going on between Haber and Ovitz. In a way, there was just so much money coming in it didn't matter, but because I was a Haber guy, Lee just killed me when I was an agent. He was just fucking killing me.

PHIL KENT:

Ari was in the mailroom and every now and then would help me at nights with my phone calls after my assistant would leave. He really wanted to work in my area—first run syndication, cable, and all that—and Lee was very militaristic. Lee believed in structure and wanted Ari to be a literary agent. He said, "No, he has to go work in the TV lit department." I said something like, "You're going to kill him, you're going to emasculate him. He's a winner, he's perfect for the rock 'n' roll world of first run syndication. Let him work for me." But they blocked it. They made him work as a junior agent in the literary department.

ARI EMANUEL:

Lee wanted me to service all of these shitty writers—just get them jobs. But then I wanted to sign this new show that had just come out called *The Simpsons*. I wanted to sign Jon Vitti, and a bunch of other great writers coming out of the show. And he would just say, "No. Just service the list." And there I was, had been just an agent for four seconds, and I thought, "Fuck that shit." So when InterTalent was formed, and Bill Block told me he wanted me to be the guy in their new television department, I thought, *Fuck, I can't stand Lee Gabler, and I couldn't stand the politics of the place. I've got to go with those guys.*

PHIL KENT:

Ari was fearless back then. I loved him. I actually have a pretty good sense of who's going to make it in life. I had him picked right up front.

DAVID GREENBLATT:

I said to Ari, "Let's go meet at the bar at Love's barbecue." It was just this horrifically decorated place and you'd go in there and you'd see people in cowboy hats. I knew that nobody would go to be in that bar. It had to be a secret meeting place because the last thing Ari needed was to be seen in public with us and it get back to Ovitz. Besides, I liked operating in a stealth atmosphere. So Ari and I had what I thought was a great conversation and, you know, he was desperate to get out. I knew he was well trained in the CAA ways. I went back to the office and said, "Bill, I just met with Ari. Not only should we hire him, but I got to tell you. I think we will all be working for him one day."

ARI EMANUEL:

It was Presidents' Day weekend, so we had Monday off, and I had told one of my good friends, Jeff Jacobs, who is an agent there, that I was going to be telling them I was leaving Tuesday morning. And on Monday night he squeals on me. It was like an episode of *Entourage*. He fucking squealed on me. He calls me at 5:30 Tuesday morning and says, "I had to tell them." I said, "What do you mean, you had to tell them? Tell them what?" And he says, "I had to tell them you were leaving." I couldn't believe it. So when I walked into the office, everyone—Mike, Bill, and Ronnie—knew I was leaving.

I wanted to tell Ovitz to his face, so I went to his office and said, "I'm trying to see Mike Ovitz." I was told, "He's not going to see you." But I walked into his office anyway. Now, at the time, Mike Ovitz was God, and I was just a fucking street urchin. And he says, "I'm not seeing you." I said, "I'll be back in ten minutes and you're going to deal with me then." When I walk back in, there's Lee Gabler and Ray Kurtzman standing there with him. Ray liked me a lot, so I was calm and said, "Listen, it's been great, but I've got to leave." And then Mike gives me, "We're going to kill you guys and your careers are going to be over." I turned to him, got out of my Chinese chair, Japanese chair, whatever, and said, "Are you threatening me?" And I grabbed the chair with my hands and picked it up and said, "Because if you are, I'll fucking throw this chair right out of here right now. Don't threaten me." I was an idiot. I was a complete moron. You don't do that stuff, but I've been a fighter all my life.

MICHAEL WIMER:

When Strickler left the agency in 1988, I knew that Jack's power and his ego would compel him to promote me despite the pain of having to replace a good assistant. I was up and servicing clients and agents and studios almost immediately. The fun and the money came in by the bucketload. For the next few years, it was just fantastic. There was one weird point, though—my buddy Jay Moloney was Ovitz's assistant and there was a moment that Michael demoted him off his desk. I got a call that Michael wanted me to work for him, so I saddled up. I had a sense that it would be a bad fit . . . I knew that Michael wanted a boy he could manipulate and I was way beyond that, in life-years if not in Hollywood-years. When Ray Kurtzman called me up to his office to prep me before I started for Michael, I saw that he was really uncomfortable. He said, "You have to know that on Michael's desk, you are going to see things in how he handles his life and his business and how he treats his wife that you just won't see anywhere else . . ." He said, "Mike is a genius, but he is sui generis." I remember it because I had to look it up. He was saying that Mike was not like anyone else. . . . Coming from Ray, it was clear what he was saying—*Mike is going to ask you to do stuff and be party to stuff that you are going to find pretty awful.*

I knew that Mike was a genius at agenting, but I also knew that I had enough other options that I didn't need to be on his desk to do well—I just didn't need anything in Hollywood enough to do stuff that was dark or compromising, since I could always go back to Wall Street. I was on Mike's desk for all of four days (but long enough to have a private line installed between our phones that was hooked up for five years!) before I knew it was a bad fit. He needed someone needy, someone with more vulnerabilities for him to manipulate than I had. Someone like Jay. He had more than his fair share, and Mike knew them well—hell, he had installed half of them—and used them all the time.

A 1988 strike by the Writers Guild of America wreaked havoc on the production and scheduling of movies and TV programs, along with hundreds of scripts in pre-production or development. Work could not continue, but the strike stubbornly did, even after federal mediators were twice deployed to hasten a climax.

Michael Ovitz and Bill Haber both had long-standing relationships with the unions—Haber client George Kirby was president of the guild, and Ovitz was close to Brian Walton, then the guild's chief deal maker—but the advantages of those ties were not immediately apparent. The strike began on March 7, but April, May, June, and July 7 all passed with no resolution (when the strike finally ended on August 7, it set a record for the longest such action in history—155 painful days).

As prospects for an early end to the strike grew increasingly unlikely, Ovitz and Haber stepped into the fray. The strike forced the major TV networks to hold off the starts of their fall schedules; instead of the usual late-September/early-October opening nights, new and returning TV series' debuts were delayed until late October and into November (one NBC series, In the Heat of the Night, *didn't start its second season until early December). In the interim, the networks had to rely on a program hodgepodge—reruns, movies, news and entertainment specials, and a peculiar mixture of program-length political spiels and such unscripted (and largely uninteresting) original shows as CBS's* High Risk. *Networks also exploited sports programming, including NBC, home to the Summer Olympics and the World Series. In what then seemed a historic moment, Johnny Carson was able to restart the writerless* Tonight Show *on NBC partly by coming up with his own jokes and serving as his own head writer.*

When the strike finally ended on August 7, 1988, the communal sigh of relief seemed definitely, if not deafeningly, audible, though there was no clarity when it came to naming winners and losers and just what the spoils of war might have been, as well as who got more of them and who suffered the most fatalities and injuries.

LEE GABLER, Agent:

During the Writers Guild strike, I remember Haber saying that everybody's bonuses were going to be protected, that they were going to make sure the bonuses were going to be kept where they should be and "we're going to take it out of our pocket if we have to." I thought, *Wow, that's really magnanimous.* But afterward, when I saw the books, of course they could. It wasn't really that much of a dent.

TOM POLLOCK:

Twins was a groundbreaking deal at the time. It was not Mike Ovitz who made the deal. Ivan Reitman made it with me personally because I was his lawyer before I left for Universal and there was a writers' strike going on. We're five months into the writers' strike and there's no product. Ivan had signed his company up to the interim deal with the Writers Guild that allowed him to hire Bill Goldman and various writers. I agreed to the deal knowing exactly what the numbers were.

What had not been done before is that Arnold Schwarzenegger, Danny DeVito, and Ivan Reitman took no money, so the movie was made for $15 million up front. But they got 35 percent of the gross for a certain period of time and then they took less while we recouped advertising. After that happened, they got more and they eventually went up even higher. They made a shitload of money. It was incredibly lucrative. Ivan, Danny, and Arnold told me that they never made as much money on any other movie as they did on this one.

MICHAEL OVITZ:

Sandy would do all of the modeling to compare to the studio. We had the capability to model as good as the studios, so we knew when they'd say, "Oh, well, we're over budget," and Sandy would say, "No, you're not. Here's our number." We'd fight over his numbers versus theirs.

SANDY CLIMAN:

I brought modeling into CAA for the first time; before that, no one at the agency was thinking about projections, or in other words, a movie's box office potential and all the revenue that followed from the home.

So when we packaged *Twins,* for instance, which was sheer genius and nothing I can take credit for, we were able to have a sense of what it was going to do, and when the studio wanted two of our important clients to give up their fees in exchange for a bigger back end, we could tell them it not only made sense, but it would be terrific for them. Which it was; the back end worked like a charm.

Considering the extensive list of stars, directors, and writers who were counted as clients by CAA in the early '90s, there were bound to be moments of entanglement and disruption pitting client against client within the agency's ranks.

And indeed there were. One of the most notorious was during the fractious production of Love Affair, *a 1994 remake of 1955's* An Affair to Remember, *which had itself been a remake of the original 1939* Love Affair. *This time, Warren Beatty starred with Annette Bening, then his real-life wife, and Kate Capshaw—with a cameo by aging screen icon Katharine Hepburn. The script was credited to Beatty and Robert Towne, legendary big-time CAA client and writer of* Chinatown, *with another major CAA client, Glenn Gordon Caron—creator of* Moonlighting *for ABC-TV and director of the critically acclaimed* Clean and Sober—*brought in to helm. Ovitz had personally recruited Caron to the agency.*

GLENN GORDON CARON, Writer and Director:

I came out to California in '79 and my agent was Elliot Webb, who at that time was at ICM. I'd always been with Elliot and felt this tremendous sense of loyalty to him.

ELLIOT WEBB:

Terry Semel was close to Ovitz at that time and approved Glenn to write *Bonfire of the Vanities,* but Glenn wanted to write it and direct it. That started off a whirlwind romance with CAA because Ovitz had that information and he used it to his best advantage. Glenn was making a leap into motion pictures and I was pretty much in the television business. He wrote and was directing the Michael Keaton movie *Clean and Sober.* I'd go to dailies every day, but Ovitz was feeding him information that I had no way of knowing because I was new to the motion picture business. So I tried to cover it as best as I could, but I had limitations.

GLENN GORDON CARON:

There was a moment when I realized maybe the things I was doing were not really in Elliot's wheelhouse. He didn't really represent motion picture directors, and Michael was saying to me, "If you write good material, we can make all the other things happen. Great actors want to be with great material. Studios want to make great material. That is the glue that holds everything together." And if you look at those early clients that he cultivated, sort of the bedrock of that agency, many were writers.

I had just finished directing *Clean and Sober*—it hadn't come out yet—and I got a call from Jon Avnet. Jon said, "Do you have any interest in meeting Tom Cruise?" I said sure; I had just seen *Risky Business* and thought it was an amazing movie. So I came in and met with Tom and talked to him about an *Esquire* short story that I had read that I thought would make a great movie. We spent about forty-five minutes talking. I'm six or seven years older than Tom was, but in the meeting it was "Mr. Caron"—which was silly, but I left and felt it was great meeting him. I went back and was doing

Moonlighting and Jon called two weeks later and said, "Okay, Tom Cruise has met with ten people, blah blah blah, and you're the one he wants to work with."

I said, "Wow, great." He said, "Let's go over to Universal." So we went to Universal, had the meeting, and sold the movie. I went back to Warner Bros. and I was putting the finishing touches on *Clean and Sober* and Mark Canton called me. He said, "Did you just sell a movie to Universal with Tom Cruise?" I said, "Yeah!" And he said, "How dare you. How *dare* you." I said, "Why? What do you mean?" I truly had no idea that I had done something wrong. And he said, "We've given you your shot, this is your first movie. Is there no loyalty? You go and get that movie back and you bring it here." I just thought, *Oh my God*. So I called Elliot and he said, "Fuck them. Fuck them." I said, "No, I don't want to fuck them. I want them to be happy. I want them to support me." I truly didn't know how to navigate my way out of this, and then my phone rang. The voice on the other end says, "Hi, this is Mike Ovitz." And I said, "Hi." And he said, "I hear you have a problem." I said, "Yes, I do." He said, "Would you like me to solve it?" I said "Yes, please." He said, "Stay by your phone." Two hours later he called me and said, "Okay, I've solved your problem." I said, "What did you do?" He said, "I traded some things. There are some things Universal wanted that Warners had, some things Warner wanted that Universal had. It's all taken care of. Is there anything else you need?" And I said, "God, I'd love two more weeks of editing time on *Clean and Sober*." And Michael says, "Stay by your phone." And less than two hours later he calls back and says, "You have two more weeks of editing on *Clean and Sober*." And he says, "Listen, I'd really love to sit with you and take you out for a meal and talk about representing you." I said, "Oh, I could never do that." And he said, "You could never do what?" I said, "I could never sit with you and have a meal because it would be very unfair to Elliot Webb. I've been with him for ten years and he would just be destroyed if he ever heard." He laughed and he said, "Well, I hope you'll change your mind because I'd love to talk to you." A week later a messenger comes over with a book of coupons from McDonald's. He says, "If you ever change your mind and want to have a meal, Mike." Over the course of the next several months, all of these gag gifts appeared at my office, and finally I said, "All right, let's talk." He basically said, "Look, I love what you do and I want to represent you and most importantly I want to put you in touch with our great clients. You should know Dustin Hoffman. You should know Robert Redford. You should know—" and then he named all these other stars he was representing at that time. And I was like, *Oh my God*, because it meant that I had to go to somebody that I genuinely cared about and say, "I need to make a change." But I felt very strongly CAA was a great opportunity, and I needed to avail myself of it. And I did.

Mike was pretty extraordinary, in terms of those things you looked for an agent to do. He was always prepared. The thing I didn't understand and never got completely comfortable with was the culture where Mike is in your life—and you can get him on the phone—but there are other people that deal with you day to day. I had Rand Holston on the movie side, and Lee Gabler on the television side. I liked Rand a great deal, but he wasn't Mike, and you really needed Mike to make things happen. Sometimes you couldn't get to Mike, which was understandable; he was brokering deals between the Japanese and the this and the that. But I had been spoiled because the person I dealt with every day of my life before was one guy—Elliot Webb.

CAA agents knew for more than a year that Beatty wanted Caron to direct the movie, but unfortunately, once Caron came on board, their arguments were early and often. Beatty didn't like Caron's approach to almost everything during shooting, and their disputes boiled over into the editing of the picture. So what went wrong, and when? Many felt Beatty simply at some point realized he should have directed the film himself, especially with his new wife costarring in it.

What could Ovitz do? He could side with Caron, whom he truly liked and respected and who was, after all, the credited director—but that would mean alienating Beatty, a higher profile CAA client and a bona fide movie star. To make matters even more complicated, Beatty had won an Oscar for directing Reds, had played a major creative role in Bonnie and Clyde, *and lacked no confidence in an editing room—if, indeed, in any kind of room.*

In the end, the fact that Beatty's contract with Warner Bros. gave him final cut approval enabled him to literally "take" the movie away from Caron, preventing him from further editing the film and from delivering his own cut to the studio.

There was a final insult awaiting Caron, who, after originally being given a draft of the script written by Beatty and Towne, then wrote nineteen additional drafts of his own. Caron received a call from the studio, asking, "Didn't you do some writing on the movie?" and when Caron told them he had written all those drafts, they suggested he send them in to the Writers Guild, because the studio received only one draft of the script, the one done by Beatty and Towne. All the scripts were presented to the Writers Guild for arbitration, and Caron, then out of town, was told he needn't bother flying back to L.A. to appear personally during the process. Beatty, however, did show up, and Caron lost having his name on the script and the bonus money that would have gone with that credit.

RAND HOLSTON:

We learned from Michael that in situations where there were issues between our clients, it was only a conflict for us if we weren't transparent. He wanted to make sure we disclosed all the information we knew. You have to tell the truth.

GLENN GORDON CARON:

Warren Beatty had been courting me since he'd seen *Clean and Sober*; Madonna had introduced us. He said, "I want to do a remake of *Love Affair*," and I said, "I have no interest in doing remakes." The truth is, I wasn't even familiar with *Love Affair* as a movie. But Mike kept saying, "Wait a second, here's this enormous movie star—who's also by the way a world-renowned actor—who's picking you. Why would you demur? You know he's right." Having said that, a number of people reached out to me and said, "Do you understand what a difficult and complicated man he is?" Such was my ego that I thought, *How complicated can he be? How difficult can he be? Hey, I've worked with Cybill Shepherd.*

He proved to be extremely complicated.

RAND HOLSTON:

I represented Glenn and had to do what was in his best interest. I told Glenn everything I knew so he could speak to Michael and Ronnie about what was happening with *Love Affair*. In this situation, the movie star is the biggest motor; you can't pretend he's not. Michael was dealing with Warren at that time. Unfortunately for Glenn, the choices were limited.

GLENN GORDON CARON:

He kicked me out of the editing room. There was then a period where I would go every day and sit outside the office waiting to see something. It became clear at a point that this wasn't going to happen, and as my mother was dying, I went back east and kept calling Warner Bros., telling them, "I'd really like to see the movie. I'd really like to know what's going on." And finally they called and said Warren's going to preview the movie tonight, but they didn't tell me where. I was in New York and they said, "Fly to L.A. You'll be taken to Burbank airport. You'll get on a private jet and they'll take you to where the preview is." I said, "Where am I going?" And they said, "We're not going to tell you." I said, "Listen, I have a wife and I have three kids. I've got to know where I'm going." It turned out to be oddly close, but anyway, they ran the movie and I remember thinking the movie was a bomb. On the plane to fly back I was sitting next to Bob Daley, who at that time ran Warner Bros. I said, "Bob, give me two weeks in an editing room, please." He looked at me and he went, "Glenn." He pointed to the front of the plane where Warren was sitting; we weren't speaking at this point, obviously, and he said, "I can't do that. I need him. I need him to do *Oprah*. I need him to do *Entertainment Tonight*." I was so naive about how the food chain worked, and that in the scheme of this whole thing, even though I was the director, I was fairly inconsequential. But I was really dismayed that no one from CAA could do anything. Part of the calculus of being with a superagency is on some level you understand that they have to cleave to the most valuable asset, and at that moment in time, in that universe, he was the most valuable asset. At one point, I called Mike and said, "You've got to help me," and he just said, "Please don't put me in the middle of this."

ROSANNA ARQUETTE, Actress:

I had a great agent who's still my friend who I really loved, Rick Nicita. I went and did *The Big Blue* and he got me quite a lot of money for the time, I think like a half a million dollars, which was a lot for a woman then, believe it or not. Nobody knew who this French director was. They didn't really want me to go do the movie, but it ended up being a huge movie in France.

Nobody had put together you had to pay the tax in France. It wasn't set up in the right way where we understood that or knew that, so all these notices came to CAA in French and I never got them, apparently. I don't know if a secretary just threw them away or something, but what ended up happening was I got arrested at the border for tax evasion in France. I was like, *What?!* It was crazy. And it turned out that I owed them money. I had to go get a tax attorney and it cost me like a hundred and fifty grand. It was a huge thing. I just think it was a communication breakdown and it wasn't really anybody's fault. It didn't feel great, and probably ultimately is why I left the agency.

I was told by Jay Moloney that Ovitz came into an office and there was this life-size poster of me that I think Rick Nicita may have had and he ripped it in half. This sounds so dramatic, I don't even believe it, but it is really what I was told. All I know is that things went downhill from there for me. I think I was put on a blacklist by Michael Ovitz because stuff started happening that was very strange. I had projects fall apart. They were like the mafia.

AMY GROSSMAN:

By the mid-eighties, there was a whole mafia omertà of it all. You were either in or you were out, and if you left, good luck trying to come back.

Kevin Huvane and Bryan Lourd became friends in the mid-1980s while still in their twenties and working for William Morris, although on opposite coasts—Huvane roaming the theater, TV, and movie corridors of New York and Lourd working as a TV agent in L.A.

It was common practice at the agency then for clients to be taken from younger agents, no matter who had brought them into the company, and given to older agents who had more seniority if no other apparent virtues. In addition, Morris agents in Los Angeles were frequently given precedence over those in New York, which hardly worked to Huvane's advantage.

Sensing the need for mutual protection in the hotly competitive Morris milieu, the two young men formed an alliance and a friendship that helped prevent their having clients "poached" by fellow agents.

In his early twenties, Bryan Lourd read a New Yorker article about Hollywood überagent Sam Cohn and from that moment on, knew what he wanted to do. Having come to L.A. from a small town in Louisiana, he didn't even know such a job as "agent" existed, but he knew he wanted to go into show business, and that he didn't know how to sing, dance, or tell jokes.

Among the most influential words of advice young Lourd ever got was from his grandfather: When you get a job, be the first one into the office in the morning and the last to leave at night. Lourd practiced that formula during his first job as a gofer at CBS. He noticed that the first guy to show up in the morning was a security guard—but the second guy was then-network-president B. Donald "Bud" Grant.

Lourd assumed that his duties included attending to Grant's whims and wishes, which he did, bringing the president coffee and the ratings every morning. They became friendly enough for Lourd to ask Grant for career advice, and Grant told him that CBS had discontinued its training program a year earlier, so the thing to do was get out of there—and head for the legendary William Morris mailroom.

Lourd drove to the Morris Agency that afternoon and filled out an application. Six months passed. Lourd had returned to Louisiana when he got the call and a coveted job in the mailroom—coveted even though duties included arriving at 6:30 A.M. to wash out coffee mugs and type phone sheets, the so-called Morning Desk. Then came one of those lucky breaks on which a career can turn. Larry Auerbach, the executive to whom he was assigned, called on Lourd for extra duty when his secretary quit after giving only two days' notice. While Auerbach interviewed candidates for that job, Bryan sat at his boss's desk learning whatever he didn't yet know, rescued from the mailroom—and spared various intermediary upward steps—forever.

Before long, young Lourd was working with Auerbach and making phone calls to Bill Cosby, Marcy Carsey, and Tom Werner as they all planned the landmark '80s sitcom, The Cosby Show, a television classic.

He was hardly an executive or agent yet. There were plenty of menial duties, including being told to get breakfast one morning by Auerbach for a Carsey-Werner meeting about The Cosby Show. Lourd picked up what he thought was an appropriate breakfast—coffee, orange juice, and doughnuts, and arrayed it all at his boss's desk, only to hear the Bronx-born Auerbach scream, "Where are the bagels?! Where is the lox?!"

Following the news-making emigrations of David Greenblatt, Judy Hofflund, and Tom Strickler to InterTalent in 1988, CAA was looking to fill its ranks. Rick Nicita met with Lourd in Los Angeles while Huvane was wooed by Ron Meyer in New York. "I was taught to recognize opportunity when it happened and the lightbulb went off," Huvane reflected years later, crediting his mother for fostering faith in his own intuition.

As a teenager working part-time at New York's Wyndham Hotel (known as affordable to the thespian set) on West 58th Street, Huvane got to hobnob with such theatrical royalty as Hume Cronyn and Jessica Tandy. After graduating from Fordham University, he'd been planning on going to law school, but began to notice that he didn't have many happy friends who were lawyers. So he jumped at the Morris job when it was offered.

During his seven years at Morris, he specialized in theater but worked in all the performing arts. His first client was Sarah Jessica Parker, well before her sophisticated sexpot days; she was fresh from having been the third adorable girl to play the eponymous Annie in Mike Nichols's smash-hit musical.

Though working on opposite coasts, Huvane and Lourd became not just friendly but professionally interdependent. No one mentored or shepherded them through the Morris jungle, so they began to do it with and for each other.

Kevin was the first of the duo to meet Michael Ovitz. When the perhaps inevitable job offer came from CAA, Lourd and Huvane stuck to their pact and agreed to the move only if they could go together as a team. They got their way and joined the agency at the same time.

KEVIN HUVANE, Agent:

Rick Nicita called Bryan, and I met with Ronnie Meyer at the Regency in New York and told them that Bryan and I were a team. They had no idea that we talked to each other every day and that we had made a pact that we would be together for our professional careers. Ronnie loved that.

It happened over a week; I met Michael Ovitz on a Friday. He asked me what my father did for a living, who my friends were, questions like that.

BARRY JOSEPHSON, Producer:

Jay was a catalyst in putting those guys together in a friendship. He could open up any conversation, and talk to anybody at any level. When Bryan and Kevin came from William Morris in New York, Jay and they really hit it off and I remember specifically Jay always saying to me, "You have to meet Bryan and Kevin." I had met them before, but it was Jay who really said these guys are great; one day, they're going to be the future of this company.

PETER BENEDICT, Agent:

We didn't need to peek behind the curtain to know how they were working; my wife was a hot shit writer client there. They were ruthless. She would come home and tell me these crazy stories about sitting in rooms with Robert Redford and Barry Levinson and Jay Moloney. He was Mike's assistant at the time, and he would basically be spying on the meetings so he could go back and report to Mike about what was happening.

MARTIN SCORSESE:

I really got to like and trust Jay. We were making *Last Temptation* and I had spoken to him on the phone a few times, and then finally met him in Los Angeles. Right around that same time, I was starting this business of film preservation and restoration, and Jay, whom I trust, somehow became very enthusiastic about the passion that I felt for the work we were doing. Ultimately Bob Rosen of

UCLA gave me the idea of pulling together a group of directors who had power to form what we call the Film Foundation. And Jay and Mike were the key promoters of the whole thing. Mike got Sydney Pollack in there, I got Spielberg and Lucas. The day the Film Foundation was announced, it was at CAA, with Pollack there, and with letters from Woody Allen and Steven. So the Film Foundation was really formed with the help and guidance of Mike, Jay, and CAA.

TONY KRANTZ:

Jay was a superstar. He was a savant. He was utterly fearless and everyone loved him. He was one of the blessed people to whom it was all so seemingly effortless.

DAVID O'CONNOR:

Richard was launched in the motion picture division right from the mailroom, which hadn't happened before. A trainee usually went into the television group and then they plucked people from television into movies. Then the same thing happened to me. After two and a half years on Ovitz's desk, I had cultivated Jay to replace me and I was launched in the motion picture and literary division. So the two of us were the young guys there—again the first two people directly promoted into the motion picture group—and we were just out there causing havoc. I walked into a motion picture staff meeting on a Wednesday and there are these two young guys they had just poached from William Morris: Bryan Lourd and Kevin Huvane. With a surprising lack of guard on either side, we kind of fell in with each other. When we went out to lunch for the first time, I remember thinking, *They're cool. I like those guys*, and I think the feeling was mutual. Very quickly we looked at each other and thought we all have complementary talents and personalities, so we just started doing stuff together. Then we consciously decided to sign people as a group.

KEVIN HUVANE:

I give full credit to Mike, Ronnie, and Bill. They rewarded teamwork and camaraderie and we spent so much time together and had such a great time, we thought why don't we mix it up and do some business? I'll sign a director with you, and you sign an actor with me. And we had fun with it.

TOM LASSALLY:

Jay was one of the funniest people I've ever met, but more important, had this charisma to him that you just couldn't identify. You could never try and be like him. He wasn't the most handsome, wasn't the smartest person in the room, but he was a star in his own way, and he drove people crazy because he could do so many things with such ease.

There was a moment early on that to me really defined Jay. He wasn't an agent yet, and Madonna, who was a CAA client, was playing Anaheim Stadium. At this time, she was a big music star, but CAA wanted to get her acting career going, so they decided to bring a lot of studio people, big people in the business, to the stadium so they could see her. The agency organized buses to go from their offices in Century City to the stadium, and others followed in their private cars. Jay was one of the people who had to make sure everything turned out okay, and so he brought me. We all got on the bus, got down there, saw the concert, and then after went to the underground parking lot to get on our way home. Jay walks up to the guy at the gate and hands him this gigantic stack of garage tickets for all the buses and cars and a ton of validation stickers, so everyone could get past the gate. And the guy at the gate just says, "Nope, can't do that. You have to take each sticker and put it on each ticket." There were a lot of tickets. I was standing right there, and Jay says, "Look, I have all these important people who need to leave right now. It's really late. Please do it this way," and the guy just says, "No." Jay tried to reason with him once more, but again, the guy wasn't budging. Finally Jay said, "Okay, you've given me no choice," and you know that wood bar that goes up and down that blocks passage to a parking garage? Jay went up to it, grabbed it, pulled it, and broke it totally off. At that moment he made an executive decision that he needed to get these big shots on their way home. He knew that even if that gate would wind up costing a thousand dollars or more, it wasn't worth wasting the time of all these important people. I remember thinking at the time, *I could never do that. What a star.*

4

"Katy, Bar the Door!": 1989–1994

We shape our buildings; thereafter they shape us.
—WINSTON CHURCHILL

MICHAEL OVITZ:

Jerry Weintraub once said to me, "You're going to get to be so powerful that at some point, people will start saying you did things you didn't do and that you were in places you weren't." I laughed at him at the time, but that's exactly what happened.

RON MEYER:

I had the luxury of enjoying being a good cop with a guy who was enjoying being a bad cop. He liked the image of waving a big sword over people's heads, and I liked the image of being Henry Kissinger. Now in reality, Mike wasn't as bad as he was sometimes made out to be, and I wasn't as good as I was sometimes made out to be. Don't get me wrong, I liked being regarded as the good guy, but if anyone mistook kindness for weakness, they would be proven wrong.

JOEL SILVER:

Ronnie and I were in St. Maarten on a boat—it was an interesting group. Jane and Terry Semel, Nastassja Kinski, and Quincy Jones—they were in their room most of the time, so we didn't really see them—my sister Allison, Michael Douglas, and several others. Kelly [Meyer] wasn't there because she was pregnant with their daughter Carson. We decided to go ashore because we wanted to go to the casino, but Ronnie didn't want to do any gambling.

He's had issues with gambling in his past. But my sister says, "I want to shoot craps, can you teach me?" And he says, "Sure, I'll teach you if you want." I was sitting with Terry, who was playing blackjack, and a very good player by the way.

MICHAEL DOUGLAS:

Ronnie was trying to explain to Alison how to play the game, and on the other side of the table was a big Tony and a little Tony. Two guys, wife-beater T-shirts, and they're saying, "Hey, are we gonna fucking play or are we just going to jerk off here?" And Ronnie just says, "Sorry, I'm just trying to explain to her how to play." But those guys keep at him. Ronnie never raised his voice and just said to the guy, "Please give us a moment and leave us alone." But they didn't, adding a "Fuck this," and then Big Tony looks at Ronnie and says, "Fuck you." It was like a light went off. The next thing I know, Ronnie is crawling across the table.

JOEL SILVER:

We heard a big ruckus and I looked over and see my sister is in abject terror; she is just pale. I'm thinking, *Shit!* And I get up and I go over toward the craps table and I actually see with my little eyes—just a second, let me explain something here: There's a Hollywood expression from old John Wayne Westerns: "Katy, Bar the Door." And that's when John Wayne says to the barkeep, "Katy, bar the door. We're going to have a fight here. So nobody can come in or get out"—my friend Ronnie sitting on this guy's chest—BANG, BANG, BANG—hitting him like a jackhammer, with short, quick punches. He's whaling on this guy's face. I mean, he's a marine, for Christ's sake!

MICHAEL DOUGLAS:

Ron is beating on Big Tony, and I mean really beating on him, and then Little Tony starts kicking him in the side of the ribs, but Ronnie keeps punching.

JOEL SILVER:

Ronnie had figured it was smarter to go after the big guy first. In Vegas, there's so much security it could have never gotten to this point, but we were in the Caribbean and things were pretty lax. Finally, they threw us all out of the casino and Terry was pissed because he was winning.

MICHAEL DOUGLAS:

That should give you some sense of how you better not mess around with Ron.

JOEL SILVER:

A few weeks later we were in the South of France on a speedboat in Nice, bouncing along the Riviera, and Ronnie started having a lot of pain, so we went to the hospital. The doctor said, "When did you break your ribs?"

RON MEYER:

As good as it used to feel to be in fights when I was young, I felt that night like I was too old for that kind of stuff anymore, and it really was the last thing I had expected to happen.

BILL MURRAY:

Mike and I were in the Peninsula Hotel, and they have a very nice bar on the roof where you can actually see Fifth Avenue. While we were sitting there, this big guy sits down and starts shouting across the bar at me. And then he looked at Mike and said, "Who's this guy?" and I said, "He's my bodyguard." And he chuckled and said, "No, really, who the hell is this guy?" And Mike just gives the guy this death stare. It was as scary as any bad guy actor I ever saw. Then he looks at him and says, "I'm his bodyguard." And the guy just melted; he was really frightened. It was like when you find out a snake is poisonous or something. I don't know how to describe it, but the guy just came completely apart. He was a big guy, and he just settled up his bill and left. Then we had the bar to ourselves. It was really fun.

At first Ovitz refused to grant screenwriter Joe Eszterhas's (Flashdance, F.I.S.T., Jagged Edge) *request to be released from his CAA agency contract. Typical industry practice is for agents to grant releases to their clients if they are unhappy. During the meeting when Eszterhas announced his intentions to leave CAA for ICM, Ovitz allegedly told him, "My foot soldiers who go up and down Wilshire Boulevard each day will blow your brains out," according to Eszterhas. Eszterhas detailed Ovitz's comments in a four-page missive that circulated through-out Hollywood, with the* Los Angeles Times *calling it "The Letter That's Shaking Hollywood." "I knew when I walked in that you wouldn't be happy—no other writer at CAA makes $1.25 million a screenplay—but I was unprepared for the crudity and severity of your response . . . you said that you would sue me," Eszterhas wrote. " 'I don't care if I win or lose,' you said, 'but I'm going to tie you up with depositions and court dates so that you won't be able to spend any time at your typewriter.' You said, 'If you make me eat shit, I'm going to make you eat shit.' "*

Eszterhas also alleged Ovitz threatened to damage Eszterhas's relationship with his attorney, Barry Hirsch, and with Irwin Winkler (the producer for two Eszterhas films, Music Box *and* Betrayed). *CAA issued a response from Ovitz denying all of Eszterhas's allegations. The* Writers Guild of America *later released a statement that absolved CAA of responsibility for Eszterhas's claims in exchange for CAA's commitment to treat its clients better in the future.*

RON MEYER:

After the meeting, Mike said Joe wasn't going to leave us.

JOHN PTAK:

I was probably the first person to read the Eszterhas letter. This was before I came over to CAA; I was still at William Morris and Costa was one of my clients. Joe had recently written *Betrayed*, which Costa-Gavras directed, and they were good friends. I had a habit of getting into the office early and there on my assistant's desk was an envelope addressed to "Costa-Gavras care of John Ptak"—and it was open. There was a note attached that said, "John, I wanted to make sure you were aware of this." I read it and just thought, *Oh my God.* Sue Mengers heard about it and just went crazy. She said, "You have to let me have that letter!" There was no way I was going to let that thing leave my office.

MICHAEL OVITZ:

We made amazing deals for Joe, getting him millions for his scripts. He had burned through several agents inside CAA, including being very nasty to Rosalie Swedlin, one of our top female agents. We had put him with Rand Holston, and that seemed to be working.

JOE ESZTERHAS:

When Guy told me he was going to come back to ICM and be an agent again, I said, "You've got your first client." He appreciated that, and I liked being able to do something for him, because at this point I'd had some big hit movies and was getting hotter and hotter. It meant something to him that I could help him. So I told Barry Hirsch, my attorney, and he said, "Well, Ovitz isn't going to be happy," and I said to Barry, "Listen, Guy is my rabbi, my brother, he really made my career, of course I'm going to do this." And he said, "Well, you tell Michael; I'm not going to tell him." Barry was not a cowardly man by any means, and I was a little taken aback, but I said, "Sure."

RAND HOLSTON:

The morning of the day Joe sent Michael his letter, Joe and I had breakfast and everything was fine. There was no talk of him leaving the agency.

I was not in the room for the conversation Michael had with Eszterhas, and I firmly don't believe such a conversation ever actually took place. That's not how Michael spoke, and more important, Michael didn't need to speak that way. I question all of it.

JOE ESZTERHAS:

I said to Ovitz, "You guys were terrific, it has nothing to do with any of that, it has to do with my heart," but he just didn't understand that. It was like talking to a man who was suddenly deaf. He kept going back to "Well, we did really well for you," and I couldn't argue with that. I said, "I don't doubt you did well for me, we're talking about something else." It's not like he turned purple and said, "You motherfucker." He was very cool, and the stuff he said about his foot soldiers was said very coldly.

Afterward, I kept hearing from more and more people that he'd used the same words with them. Bernie Brillstein was one, but there were others. Mark Harmon wrote me this really poignant heartbreaking letter about the things they had done or tried to do with him because he, too, was going to leave. One director said not only were the same words used with him during his climactic meeting, but a couple of days later he was driving in the valley and a car drove him off the road. And then there was this tremendous story—and I don't know if any of this was true—about how his secretary wanted to go to Norman Brokaw, and she was killed in a hit-and-run accident near their offices. When *60 Minutes* was desperate to do an interview with me, I called Barry Hirsch and he said, "Don't do this." And I said, "Is this guy really nuts? Is he really capable of nuttiness?" And he said, "Watch your mirrors, check your brakes." My wife and I were terrified. I called Winkler and said, "Listen, is Ovitz fucking nuts? Do I really have to be worried for my life?" and Winkler, who knew him really well, and whose kid had actually been one of his interns, said, "He's crazy like a fox, but don't worry about your life." I thanked him.

RON MEYER:

On occasion, clients had been unhappy and wanted to leave, and most times we were able to address their concerns, make changes, and keep them. We were all very surprised. First, if Joe had a grievance, why would he not have discussed it with any of us instead of going public? He wasn't a prisoner. And second, knowing Mike as well as I did, it's possible that he said those words, *foot soldiers* et cetera, but he would have only said it with a smile on his face and in a joking manner. He would never have made it a serious threat. He was too smart for that. Joe made the proverbial mountain out of a molehill.

MICHAEL OVITZ:

Joe did come to my office and he did tell me he wanted to go to ICM to be with his friend, Guy McElwaine. I said what I said to him, but it was absolutely in jest. I know exactly in the vein I said it. What I said was a joke. He laughed, and I laughed. I thought that was that.

RON MEYER:

I always respected Joe's talent and knew he prided himself on being a maverick. I don't think Joe was ever afraid of Mike or CAA. He probably couldn't wait for an opportunity like this. Mike walked right into that moment.

MICHAEL OVITZ:

If you were a journalist or a competitor back then and heard what Joe was claiming, you said, "Wow!" It was like throwing red meat into a tiger cage. We were a strong talent agency that had stretched the envelope to take our business into a lot of different areas, and we had every client under the sun. I was totally out of control of the message, but no one had anything on me. We were doing too good of a job for Eszterhas and we didn't do anything wrong. It's not like we were involved in some kind of espionage or attempted robbery, but they just killed me. Before Eszterhas sent the letter to me, he sent it to the *Hollywood Reporter* and *Variety*. They both printed it on their front pages. They called for an investigation. I had the guilds calling me to complain about it, which was particularly difficult because the presidents of the Writers and Directors Guilds were our clients. Other agencies saw the littlest, tiniest chink in the armor and tried to drive a truck through it.

JOE ESZTERHAS:

Roseanne Barr wrote a letter to Michael—she was represented at the time by CAA, and this was subsequent to my getting out—and her letter to Michael was nothing but "Fuck you" with all the other words blacked out.

MICHAEL OVITZ:

It didn't go away for six months. The good news is we just powered through it, but it was hard for me. Really hard. Ron stood right next to me, but Bill wouldn't support me.

BILL HABER:

I wasn't in the United States or I would have quit during the Eszterhas fiasco. I was on safari in Botswana, Africa, when I heard about it. It was unacceptable. Unacceptable. That kind of behavior, wherever it came from and whoever was responsible, is infectious. We didn't want other really good, responsible agents talking that way, too. Joe Eszterhas is a questionable character himself, so it's not an entirely clean situation. But I wasn't here. Thank heavens!

MICHAEL OVITZ:

The irony was that Ron had wanted Bill out of the business every five minutes, but I had always said no.

RON MEYER:

Whenever Bill and Mike had a fight—which seemed like every six months—Bill would often tell us or write a letter telling us he couldn't do this anymore and that he would rather go work with the junior blind, where he had worked for many years. So I would say to Mike, "Look, we can't force him to stay, and he should be doing what he really wants to be doing." I wanted Bill to be happy, and if being at the agency wasn't making him happy, then I was supportive of him leaving.

MICHAEL OVITZ:

What Ron and I went through to manipulate Bill to hire Lee Gabler was unbelievable. We had a guy working for us named Boz Graham, an excellent TV packaging agent with fabulous young writers. He disliked Bill and wanted to quit. Tony Krantz hated Bill with a vengeance. So that's when I knew we had to bring in Lee Gabler, because I needed someone between all of Bill's staff and Bill.

DAVID LETTERMAN, Talk Show Host:

Michael Ovitz came to my awareness in a *Vanity Fair* article written about him a long time ago. It talked about the Eszterhas situation and there were people criticizing him. I kept thinking, *Are these people envious? Are they bitter? Are they jealous? Or is he really capable of being walk-in-the-room charming and also scaring Eszterhas out of parking on Wilshire or whatever the hell that was?*

RON MEYER:

Mike and I talked about Eszterhas a great deal. He was embarrassed, and I did as much image control for him as possible. I truly believed that in this case, Mike was unfairly portrayed. Clients and others in town asked about it, and it was a big topic of conversation. I told them all how I felt. In the end, it certainly tarnished Mike's image, and it obviously hurt Mike personally, but I don't think it damaged the agency.

MICHAEL OVITZ:

The whole thing is so stupid. I was watching him in an interview recently, and he hasn't changed. He's still the same weirdo that he was back then.

Western Federal Savings owned a princely parcel of property at the conspicuous corner of Wilshire and Santa Monica Boulevards, as glamourous and strategic a business location as existed in those celebrated "Hills of Beverly." When Michael Ovitz heard the land was available, he flipped, envisioning a showcase for one of his biggest dreams: new headquarters for CAA. And so it was that the bank sold the land to a (less than equally divided) partnership made up of Ovitz, Ron Meyer, Bill Haber, and Bob Goldman.

Ovitz directed Goldman, CAA's CFO, to engineer a series of complex maneuvers with city officials that would hasten the often laborious process of getting permits and permissions. Construction of the (roughly) $20 million project was financed through a bank line of credit, and the partnership in turn gave the agency a long-term lease for the building, so in effect, the agency was sending the partnership a rent check.

While Goldman attended to the science of the project, Ovitz began to focus on the art.

BILL HABER:

The I. M. Pei building is about "perception becoming reality." There's nothing wrong with that.

MICHAEL OVITZ:

There was no doubt we had outgrown our space at 1888; we were adding agents at a very fast clip. Our growth was astounding. But the new building had nothing to do with tight quarters in Century City. Zero. It was part of my plan from day one; I was driven to it, because I have always loved architecture.

I made a list of the top ten architects working in the world and started meeting with them all. But I wanted I. M. Pei from the beginning. I loved his work at the National Gallery in Washington.

SANDI PEI, Architect:

Arne Glimcher is a good friend of ours, and my father's firm had done a design for the Pace Gallery in New York. Arne approached my father and said Michael Ovitz wanted to call him, but he had to give us a little bit of background on who Michael Ovitz was—my father was not very familiar with contemporary or entertainment cultures.

MICHAEL OVITZ:

I had been getting closer to Arne Glimcher and his wife and was blown away by their broad knowledge of aesthetics. I asked

Arne to call I. M. and said, "Please tell him I only want fifteen minutes."

That was always my approach with someone I hadn't met. I'd walk in, take my watch off as I sat down, and say, "Okay, I have fourteen minutes left." With I. M. Pei, I told him I had looked at every building he had ever designed, and that I had this property that I wanted to be a cultural destination. I told him I wanted to put a major piece of art in an atrium, I wanted it to be an icon for the city, and most important, I wanted it to scream I. M. Pei.

Pei said no; why would he say yes? He was in the middle of his work at the Louvre, and the million-square-foot headquarters for the Bank of China in Hong Kong. This was going to be only seventy-five thousand square feet. But he did ask me if I would like to have lunch. I hoped that would happen and had blocked out three hours. We went to Le Bernardin and spent two and a half hours talking about life, art, and architecture, and I think he was in a state of shock at the depth of my interest and knowledge about his work.

Afterward, I would call him every week and go to see him every other week. About a year later, he did what I hoped he would do. He pulled out a piece of onionskin, which I still have, and traced what became the basic outline for the building. We had talked so much, he knew what I wanted, and it was fantastic. But then he said, "I don't have time to do your building; maybe you can use this with someone else." I asked him if he would at least come to L.A. He said he hadn't been there in twenty-five years, and he had never designed a building west of the Mississippi. I asked him for just two days and arranged a weekend for him the likes of which you couldn't possibly imagine. I got him a first-class ticket when first class really meant something and had one of my assistants meet him at his gate and his feet never touched the ground. We put him into a limo, put him up at the best hotel, unpacked all his clothes, and gave him a great dinner party with twelve terrific people, including Michael Eisner, who was running Disney. The next day I took him to the site—which was just a parking lot—and he sat on a chair in a suit for five hours, looking at it. Then he went back to New York.

SANDI PEI:

I was brought in very early; my father thought this project would be a good assignment for me. The project was put on an unusually fast track because Michael was very eager. I knew a great source of travertine in Italy—the Bruno Poggi quarry—and found two amazing samples, which we had shipped back.

When we weren't working, Michael lavished a lot of attention on me and my father. We had an occasion to attend one of his screenings, for the movie *Ishtar,* which was a big bomb, but we met Warren Beatty, Dustin Hoffman, Elaine May, and Mike Nichols. We went to a rather small birthday party for Sean Connery, *Saturday Night Live,* a Michael Jackson concert.

ROWLAND PERKINS:

Before we moved into the building, Ovitz flew Shaolin monks into L.A., and we all marched from our offices in Century City to the new site for a feng shui ceremony. It was classic Ovitz.

ARI EMANUEL:

When we had moved into the new building, you know, the feng shui whatever-the-fuck-it-was building, I looked at that place and thought, *I'm not going to be one of those Hollywood guys who has their license plate read, "CAA this" or "CAA that."* I mean, those guys were sucking down the fucking Kool-Aid. I wasn't that guy.

WOLFGANG PUCK, Chef:

They called and told me they were going to do a lot of parties there. I told Ovitz, "If you're going to do that, I might as well design the kitchen with professional grade equipment, so I can actually use it."

East inevitably met West at the groundbreaking for the building, part Hollywood spectacle and part Eastern ritual in line with Ovitz's burgeoning Asian leanings.

The late grand master Lin Yun was tracked down and flown in for a feng shui ritual. There were also Chinese dragon dancers and a heartfelt tribute to Phil Weltman. There was even a burial of a time capsule marking the occasion and containing such prosaic mementos as a list of employee phone extensions, a copy of the L.A. Times in which the founding of the agency was announced in 1975, and a then-fashionable wide necktie. The ceremony, which reflected the input of cofounder Bill Haber, ended with the release of a flock of doves into the inescapably sunny Southern California skies.

Festivities were followed by a "march of the agents" to another kind of shrine, Jimmy's restaurant, a couple of blocks away, for a celebratory meal.

MICHAEL OVITZ:

We had an opening party at the building with hundreds of top people from the industry. No one had built anything in L.A. like this, and no one had brought in a world-class architect like I. M. Pei. We didn't use any lights, just candles, and you could see the stars through the glass roof. There's a picture of I. M. Pei with Ron on one side and me on the other. It's a perfect metaphor: I was the one who got the real estate, the financing, and the architect, but Ron, who was not involved at all, was the one who got to be charming as he schmoozed Pei.

I could've owned that whole building 100 percent. I could've owned that painting 100 percent. I gave Ron and Bill 45 percent of everything.

TOM ROSS:

Right after we moved into the new building, Michael had a photographer take a group picture of the entire agency in the atrium. I laid down on the floor in front of the group, and I was wearing a purple jacket—not a normal CAA color for sure—and it was one of my thinnest pictures. I had been very heavy, and I know a lot of people were worried about me. They had had an intervention and told me they wanted me to go away and get help, and I thanked them, but said I couldn't go away because of work. So they approached Michael with their concerns and came back to me and said, "Michael wants you around for many years and wants you healthy. He is 100 percent supportive of you going away to get some help." I thought I was going to Canyon Ranch in Tucson, you know, spa, learning, hikes, those kinds of things, but instead they sent me to Sierra Tucson, a full rehab place that had just started a weight-loss division. I was there a month, and one day, I ran into Steven Tyler, who was there for drug rehab and sexual addiction. They arranged for us to spend an afternoon together and Steven said to me, "Man, I don't know if I can do this. I just can't imagine going to a gig and not getting laid or not getting a few blow jobs." I looked at him and said, "Try being an agent for a few years. You get used to it."

NORMAN LEAR:

Mike Ovitz took me down to see the new building when it was less than halfway built. It was a Sunday morning, and we walked around the construction; then he showed me a big space where he wanted a huge mural. I don't want to take credit, but I did talk about how great Lichtenstein would be for the building.

MICHAEL OVITZ:

For the painting in the atrium, there were only two people I wanted: Johns or Lichtenstein. Johns had never done a painting over twelve feet long, but Roy had done a mural. I wanted something that would be in the vein of Mies van der Rohe, who was my idol, and I wanted a Bauhaus-esque feel to it. It's based on an Oskar Schlemmer painting, which hangs in a stairwell at MOMA.

SUSAN MILLER:

I was in charge of overseeing Michael's art collection—lending major pieces to museums all over the world, buying, selling, shipping. The art world is as crazy as the entertainment world.

MICHAEL OVITZ:

Roy was the loveliest man in the world, and I made his deal with Leo Castelli. He moved to Los Angeles with his wife for a month and came in every day to paint. The building was already open, so we were working while he was on scaffolding. I loved it. We were a creative business watching creativity. We invited curators and art school classes to watch him. We created an activity for him any night he wanted, with parties, dinners, and screenings. At one point, Rauschenberg came and helped him.

MIKE MARCUS:

Lichtenstein was out there painting the big mural, and of course, I'm the idiot who goes over to him and says, "Oh, I think you need a little more green right there, Roy." He laughed. I couldn't believe I was talking to Roy Lichtenstein.

MICHAEL OVITZ:

The day he finished, we all watched as he signed his name, then everyone broke into a frenzied applause. Afterward, he came over and did me a favor: I asked him to make a limited edition print of the mural—I only had 150 made and he signed them all—and I gave them to our senior people.

RON MEYER:

The building solidified the terminology "Mike Ovitz's CAA," and I can't speak for anyone else, but I realized then that I would have to subjugate my ego on a whole new level for the company to function properly. If I fought it, it would have been such an unhealthy environment—who knows what would have happened. Not to sound altruistic, but it was easy to do, because I was focused on what was good for the company, and if that meant that Mike was on covers of magazines by himself and Bill and I weren't in the picture, so what.

Having said that, as Mike became more important, we had less fun together. We were still close, but I do believe he started to view me as less than his equal. There were things that I would have in the past been included in that I was no longer invited to, same with Bill.

BILL HABER:

We had three buildings over the course of our twenty years together and they never meant much to me. Once in my career, I had to pick an office, and the facilities people got back to me and said, "You cannot have that office," and I said, "Why not? I'm the executive producer," and they said, "You can't have that office because it's the broom closet."

LARRY LYTTLE:

In a sea of modernity, Bill's office at the I. M. Pei building was decorated in French Baroque. It even had a bidet in his bathroom. He was a big Francophile, to be sure, but this was another of his statements about independence. He never played the game the way others did. Many would call him eccentric; I called him the smartest guy in the building.

MICHAEL OVITZ:

He had decorated his office like it was for Louis the Fourteenth with a freaking gas fireplace. It was a metaphor for how he behaved.

JEREMY ZIMMER, Agent:

The building was a symbol of power and artistry and the best of the best in I. M. Pei and the materials they used. The location was so key, you just couldn't deny it. It was everything you would want to accomplish with a building, and that you would want a building to accomplish for you.

But when we needed more space years later, we wanted to do the opposite of what CAA did, because all we kept hearing from people was "Oh, man, this new building: we hate it"; the clients hate it; and the agents hate it. It's cold, imposing, and just a statement about power.

AMY GROSSMAN:

I hated that building. It was like we were in a glass bowl. But more important, there was a real cultural shift that took place. I felt like I was working at a different agency after we moved in. It was the first time that a hierarchy became visible. Very, very important agents were on the top floor and it went down from there, with accounting and human resource services underground. The open door policy changed too. It wasn't as much fun anymore.

ERIC CARLSON:

You rarely get to identify a specific point in time when a culture changes, but that move was ours. All of these new people were being hired, and I don't know how others felt, but I didn't feel like they had the same mission for everyone to succeed. There were a lot of new people who had different styles of working and communicating, and that didn't jibe well. They weren't as cooperative as people who grew up at CAA; they weren't as helpful. Our gang before really helped each other.

MARTIN SPENCER:

It was a great time for CAA, and a great time to be at CAA. The studios were making lots of movies, we were doing a ton of television, and our music business was really hot. When you looked down to the atrium, you saw clients bumping into each other, and you could tell they loved being in the building because it was so spectacular.

MIKE MARCUS:

For the next four years, it was total power city. It was amazing, and in a lot of ways, you could do whatever you wanted to do in the business.

AMY GROSSMAN:

A lot of memories seem to stem from the conference room on Wilshire. There was intense pressure in our early morning staff meetings. Tuesday mornings at 8:00 were for actor agents, Wednesdays at 8:00 or 8:30 was our entire staff meeting, and Thursday mornings were for the literary department. I remember being pregnant and driving down Sunset and pulling up to the light at Sunset and Doheny to open the door so I could puke. Then I kept going on my way to work. Missing the Wednesday morning staff meeting was like signing your own death warrant. At the meeting, they went around the table and you better damn well have a piece of interesting information to share or it looked like you weren't on top of it. And if you were a "covering agent"—i.e., you were responsible for knowing everything that was going on at the studio you covered—and if someone else knew something—which someone always inevitably did—that you did not know, then you looked like a schmuck. If you performed poorly at the meeting, you would certainly get a dressing down from Mike or Ron.

KEN STOVITZ, Agent:

I primarily did work with writers and directors in the motion picture business my first few years. Then I signed Will Smith. He was on *Fresh Prince,* had the offer of doing *Six Degrees of Separation,* but he had not yet committed to it. He had been at William Morris, and I knew his attorney and his manager, and they were unhappy with what was going on with his representation. They had big dreams for Will, and fully believed that he could be a movie star. Mike and Ron were cool enough to say to me, "If you believe in him, go for it."

LARRY LYTTLE:

I remember being in the CAA suite at the St. Regis Hotel during upfronts when Kim LeMasters, who was at the time president of CBS Entertainment, called Bill Haber with their new fall schedule. It was set to be released that night at seven, and Bill Haber convinced Kim not to release the schedule to anybody but him until the next morning. I was sitting there thinking, *This is incredible. This is real power.* Then Haber systematically let everyone know what the schedule was.

ROB PRINZ, Agent:

I had been in the music department at William Morris in the mid to late '80s and was really into music. The first artist I ever signed was Madonna. I found her singing in a club in Long Island and nobody knew her. I started working with her, but I was in my early twenties and didn't know what the fuck I was doing. I couldn't get her a record deal. But she wanted to act, so I started reading scripts like crazy trying to find something for her, and in the talent department at that time were Bryan Lourd and Kevin Huvane. I read a script that I came across, *Desperately Seeking Susan*, which wound up being her first film. Shortly after I started working with her, though, she fired her manager and hired Freddy De-Mann, who later moved her to CAA.

TOM ROSS:

Madonna's manager was Freddy DeMann, who was a good manager, but his best friend was a competing agent in another company. And every time we would sit down with them and give him our tour, Freddy would run it by his friend, which we really found not only insulting but unfair to our business. We didn't want to show him our best deal for his client and then have them run it by a competitor so they could see deals we found that were much better than theirs. Because back in those days, we had much better relationships with the buildings than anyone else; our volume gave us great leverage. So we finally got to the point where we told Freddy we weren't comfortable with him shopping our quotes. At the same time, he was pissed off that our film department wasn't delivering for Madonna as well as he anticipated. He wanted more movies, she wanted more movies. We told Ovitz that Freddy had been all over town telling people his expectations haven't been met, and asking what could they do for Madonna.

So Madonna was playing the sports arena, and our film people were really upset because they were all the way in the back, and then they noticed that a bunch of William Morris agents were right in the front. Freddy had the front rows pulled for her concert and had filled them with William Morris agents. When Madonna came backstage for her intermission, she was livid. She said, "Who has those seats?!" and we told her, "All of the film department at William Morris. Freddy gave up all the good tickets to them." And she just went apeshit on him, because there she was, trying to feed off the audience, and there were a bunch of old men sitting with their arms crossed in front of them, just staring back at her.

ROB PRINZ:

But the music department at William Morris back then was stodgy, dysfunctional, and disjointed. It wasn't really moving and grooving. CAA was the hot new place on the block and Ovitz had been headhunting me. I remember they started talking to me in the fall of '88 because they flew me out to L.A. and gave me tickets to the Dodger World Series game. That was the game when Kirk Gibson hit that home run. I started there in January of 1989. I think I was just the fourth or fifth music agent. I started working with Madonna and Freddy again. For the next several years, our department always felt new. It felt like the agency business had never seen that type of approach and attitude and energy and level of teamwork and coordination. It felt like a really magical time for our business. It was absolutely the best time in my life as an agent because you felt like anything was possible.

While I was there, I signed Stevie Wonder, Van Halen, and Ricky Martin, whom I helped get onto the Grammys, which was the moment when he exploded. When I saw the pilot of *Seinfeld*, I called George Shapiro and had lunch with him and Howard West at the Grill. There was a deep history between those guys and Ron and Michael from William Morris and I subsequently learned they were not happy with their booking agent. So Jerry Seinfeld was somebody I signed when I was there for touring, along with Céline Dion. We worked with Barbra Streisand on her comeback tour. Back then, we were never booked directly into Europe. There was a sort of a respect between the English agents and the U.S.

agents, so we would never book direct there, they would never book direct here. Eventually that wall went down and I was asked to be the international guy, so I started booking some of our acts directly into Europe. Bon Jovi was doing huge stadium tours, like three nights at Wembley in London in front of 180,000 people.

RON MEYER:

With music, we could cross-pollinate actors, like we did with Madonna.

TOM ROSS:

She's tough. I hid from her. I did spend time with her, but I have to admit, I tried not to. Her manager, Freddy DeMann, was tougher. He was with CAA because it was the right move in terms of what was best for her, but he didn't want to be there. And he would always play us: We'd give him the tour and the deals and then he'd run it by someone else to see if this was really the best deal possible. Finally I said, "We're not giving her the deals anymore because you run them by someone else. Either you trust us or you don't, but we pride ourselves on being the best in the business of delivering talent to arenas."

ROB LIGHT:

We had an incredible run of eight or ten years. We were signing a lot of talent and we hired a great team of new agents. Everyone we were bringing in, agents and clients, were all embracing this culture. And it really was "we're all in this together." Other agencies had always been boutique oriented, where you would have your own office, your clients, and you would have to keep your elbows up so that the agent next to you wasn't trying to take your client. But that was never what CAA was about. So you were going out in teams and we would cover shows together and we would sign together. There was this great energy going on. That first run was incredible.

However hard and cold show business may sometimes seem, there are moments that deeply touch large numbers of people and bring them together in shock and sorrow.

In August 1990, a helicopter crash in rural Wisconsin took the life of CAA's beloved music agent Bobby Brooks, and the loss was devastating to all those who knew and adored him. Celebrated blues guitarist Stevie Ray Vaughan died in the same crash, a tragedy still remembered in painful grief.

ROB LIGHT:

That first window closed when one of our associates went down in the helicopter with Stevie Ray Vaughan, which was a very dark moment for us. One of the few that we ever had.

His name was Bobby Brooks. He represented Eric Clapton and Jackson Browne and Crosby, Stills & Nash. He was a great agent—such a special human being, a magnet for talent and the industry. And really one of the pivotal guys when we first started. Great guy. Just a spectacular, spectacular guy.

TOM ROSS:

If I died and they had a memorial service for me, two hundred people would come, or if Rob Light died, maybe three hundred people would be there. Bobby Brooks knew everyone, and made everybody who participated in a show feel special—from the seamstress to the lighting director; from the sound mixer to even the roadies. We'd go to a show and he'd say, "Wow, beautiful lighting on that song." He was incredible. And he was only thirty-four.

We had an amazing memorial for him at Universal, and twenty-two hundred people showed up. Bill Haber came up to me with tears in his eyes and said, "In all my years in the business, I've never seen anything like the memorial you just put on." That was very touching.

MICHAEL BOLTON, Musician:

Bobby had a way of personalizing everything, and going from the most serious business to just a very friendly, comfortable person to be with.

JACK RAPKE:

Steven Spielberg had produced Bob's [Robert Zemeckis] first two movies: *I Want to Hold Your Hand* and *Used Cars.* Following Bob's success with *Romancing the Stone,* Steven asked Bob, "What is it that you really want to do now?" And Bob said, "I want to direct *Back to the Future.*" The movie was in turnaround from Columbia—they had decided, like they did with *E.T.,* that they weren't going to make it—so Steven went to Lew and Sid and asked them for the financing for the movie. They said yes, and Steven became attached as producer with Bob directing. But Lew and Sid said at the time that they wanted Eric Stoltz to star in *Back to the Future,* who was coming off his success in *Mask,* which was a Universal picture as well. Bob was uncomfortable with that choice, but when faced with either giving up on his favorite project or trying to make it work with Eric, he chose to go with Eric.

After five weeks of shooting, it became clear to Bob—and Steven—that the picture wasn't going to be what they wanted with Eric in the lead role, and so production shut down. It was at this point that the power of Steven as a producer rose to another level. He went to the studio and said they wanted to do the movie with Michael J. Fox, and not only got the studio to hire him but to throw out the first five weeks of shooting. And by the way, because Michael J. Fox was still shooting *Family Ties,* the shooting for *Back to the Future* had to be done at night.

So we made *Back to the Future.* Obviously, it was a giant hit for the time, but no one knew that it would be that big of a hit or that it would be so iconic.

Years pass, memories fade, and people can remember precise things with remarkable imprecision—sometimes as if half glimpsed through fog. Other times, even though their memories seem totally clear, two people can recall one thing very, very differently. We are, each of us, free to create our own private internal narrative for our own personal lives; however, when that internally processed version gets voiced, and its content conflicts with someone else's version, it can all become so visceral, so con-

founding, as to muddle the very meaning of the word "truth." And bingo—that's when "true" and "false" can become almost irrelevant and indefinable concepts.

JACK RAPKE:

The studio decided they wanted to do two *sequels.* Bob Zemeckis had a directing deal on the original *Back to the Future,* which was a traditional director deal in the sense that if there was to be a sequel, he would receive no less than the floor of his deal, so they couldn't do a sequel, hire him, and pay him less than what he got for the original. So I said, "There's no way that Bob Zemeckis is going to direct the sequel or sequels for the floor of the deal. It's not happening." Tom Pollock was the president of Universal at the time and there was a long period of silence. We're sort of marching toward the start date of *Back to the Future II,* and there is still no deal on the back end and no deal on the director fee. I keep on telling Tom and business affairs, "Guys, the clock is ticking and we still don't have a deal." Then it floats back, "Well, we believe we do have a deal." I said, "What do you mean, we have a deal? We've been negotiating. We haven't agreed to a deal." "Well, we believe that when push comes to shove, we have a deal." I said, "Well, that's not the way I look at it." In the meantime, the clock keeps ticking, the fuse is burning down. Now Bob's getting a little frustrated, "Why won't they make my deal? I made a giant hit for them, they want me to do the sequel pictures, why are they doing this to me?" I said, "I don't know. I can assure you that it's not personal, but I can't get a handle on why they're not negotiating this deal in a timely fashion." So we hire Frank Rothman, a litigator who used to be the head of MGM, and he looks through the original *Back to the Future* contracts and he tells me that they could enforce a deal on *Two,* but they have no deal on *Three.* But if push comes to shove and they want to litigate you, they can force you to do *Two* under the original deal.

It's about seven business days from photography. We still don't have a deal and the studio's not talking. So I have a conversation with Bob where I said, "Bob, if we don't have a deal, I don't want you to report to the set the first day of photography." And this is after millions have been spent on preproduction, okay? He said, "What? I'm not going to report?" And I said, "Yeah, because that's the only leverage we have, because they're still not negotiating this, and we're seven days from photography without a deal! I will not let you go to the set." He understood the play and he backed the play—which was not easy.

So the following week, we're about three days from photography, and I say, "Tom, I am going to recommend to Bob that if we don't have a deal, that he's not reporting to the set." This is giant, okay. Next thing I know, Michael Ovitz calls me and says, "What the fuck? Come into my office." He says, "What the fuck is going on? You told the studio that Zemeckis is not going to report to the set?" Now I don't know if he spoke to Lew or he spoke to Sid or Tom, but I said, "Yeah," and I run him through the whole history.

Two days later, Ovitz calls me in and says, "Sid and Lew want to have a conference call with us." So it's now gone to the highest levels. We have a conference call with Sid and Lew. Michael, I think Pollock and Irving Azoff were flies on the wall on speakerphone. Lew gets on the phone and—this is paraphrasing—"Michael, I understand that Bob Zemeckis is not reporting to the set tomorrow night. Is that correct?" Michael said, "Jack Rapke's on the line." And I said, "Yes, Lew. That's correct," and there's a fucking explosion on the fucking phone like Lew is in the back alley of some fucking club trying to get paid for his act. He went thermonuclear in a second. "Michael, I am telling you, I will take every last fucking dollar of MCA's money and sue the fuck out of CAA until CAA fucking goes down, and I will take every fucking dollar that MCA has and sue you fucking personally. Then I will take every last fucking nickel and sue Rapke so that he never makes a fucking nickel in his fucking life, okay?" And then Sid Sheinberg says, "And I will fight the motherfucker that told Zemeckis not to report to the set." And I say, "Sid, that's me. Wherever you want to meet, we go." And Michael's like, "What the fuck?" So I said, "You have every right under your agreement as I read it to have him report on *Two* on the deal we made on *One*, but he has no deal on *Three* and he's not reporting to the set." Bang. Okay, and there goes another round with suing and *Goddamnit* and *How can you fucking do this?* Michael, I tell you, when I looked at him, was a deer in the headlights. I was the one that was fighting in the street. Michael could hardly speak because it was so violent and so intense. And that didn't bother me, okay? Then I said, "Lew, this is exactly what you did with Jimmy Stewart on *Winchester '73*," because I know my history, and there was silence before he said, "I'll get back to you." Two hours later they gave me the deal that I was asking for. Everything.

I think that we actually had the same definition or close to it that Spielberg had on the first one, which would have been first dollar gross on *Back to the Future II* and *III*.

MICHAEL OVITZ:

Lew and Sid called me. I was thrilled to be on the phone with Sid and Lew. Thrilled. Because I knew I'd get a deal done. The whole concept of me telling Jack, "Tell the studio he's not showing up," was to get them to call. Lew did what he always does, started screaming on the phone. Jack came into my office, and I had him pick up the phone. Jack was petrified. He was shaking. He didn't know how to handle this thing. He was way beyond his pay grade. So I let Lew finish, and I said one of the great lines of all time, I said, "Are you done?" He said, "Yes." I said, "Good, let's resolve this. Because I don't want to be the man that gave you a heart attack." And then I said, "Look, Lew, you did this with *Winchester '73.*" Jack didn't even know what the fuck that movie was, it was from my era when I was a tour guide at Universal. It was one of the better strategies I ever did. I enjoyed every second of that call. They couldn't do anything to us.

I had a whole spiel on Jimmy Stewart in *Winchester '73*, and how Lew Wasserman changed the business with him. And that's what I said to him, I said, "This is what you taught me when I was a tour guide." And when I said the line to him about how I don't want to be the man named in *Variety* that gave you a heart attack, and there was no laughter on the other end, I knew I was where I needed to be. And I got it. The deal closed within a couple of hours.

By the way, I had the relationship with Spielberg, not Jack. I had the relationship with Sheinberg, and I had the relationship with Wasserman. What was he going to do? He had no relationship with anybody, except Zemeckis. Who I signed.

That was my meat. I lived for those moments, those confrontations, with a guy of Lew's strength, for me to test my manhood against them. Are you kidding me? And I won. By the way, I won again when I sold his fucking studio.

There had always been a hint of mystery—and a more-than-healthy dose of competitiveness—between the television and motion picture agents, with many in each believing their department was king when it came to revenues.

In television, CAA enjoyed back ends on several lucrative syndication package deals, but the TV commissions on the front end, while they would have been considered big for certain agencies, weren't particularly consequential for CAA in the early 1990s. In the flush economy, CAA's big-time directors and stars were, with few exceptions, the industry's highest paid—many enjoying gross point participation deals. The numbers in film were ginormous. Example: CAA reportedly made more money on Ghostbusters in one year than the entire TV division made over two years. There was a period of time that film was so dominant, it generated roughly two thirds of the company's revenue.

RON MEYER:

Each year Mike and I would spend an entire day at his house deciding bonuses for everyone at the company except the two of us and Bill. The three of us partners were on a formula: Bill and I got the same, Mike's shares through the years had gotten bigger. By the late '80s it was 55, 22.5, and 22.5 percent.

We always made it a point to take really good care of the agents who worked for us. They were all overpaid. We wanted to reward them and also make sure no one else in town could afford them.

We would literally ask each other, "How much could this person get somewhere else?" and we'd give them 30 percent more. There were a good chunk of our agents making over a million dollars in the late '80s.

TOM POLLOCK:

Mike Ovitz overpaid the best agents in town to come work for him. They couldn't get that kind of money anywhere else.

ERIC CARLSON:

When you start to make that kind of money, there's a psychology that goes along with it, that you think you deserve it and more. So when I left CAA, I was making between $600,000 and $700,000 a year, I was thirty-four years old. My dad owned a very successful construction company and he and I used to have these conversations where we'd have this friendly little banter about how much we made that year. I remember at about thirty I started to eclipse him, and he was close to sixty. My dad was not a blue-collar union worker—he was building buildings in Washington, D.C.— and I was making more money. He had five hundred employees, and I was making more money. I thought I was worth every penny of it. It wasn't until years later, and I wasn't making that kind of money anymore, that I was able to kind of put it in perspective. It was a little sick and really not real.

RON MEYER:

But the other part of it was, I would say to Mike, "You know, if we keep on increasing everyone year to year the way we have been, one day we're going to wake up and not be able to afford them anymore." Mike told me, "Don't worry, one day we're going to sell this place, and we need to keep everyone happy until then."

MICHAEL OVITZ:

I also put senior guys like Rapke, Kurtzman, Nicita, Climan, and other senior agents into real estate deals. So if we bought a building, like we bought a building in Beverly Hills, I cut them into it. And they all made money. But I didn't cut in Jay, Bryan, Doc, Kevin, and Richard—they were too junior.

JEREMY ZIMMER:

There was always a sense you couldn't afford to buy a CAA agent, and there was always a sense that CAA, if they wanted one of your agents, would just overpay them by such a staggering amount that there wouldn't even be a conversation.

RAND HOLSTON:

Michael, Bill, and Ron took all of the pain they had at the William Morris agency and promised each other and their future employees that they would do the polar opposite for them.

TOM HANKS:

The legend at the time said that CAA was doing things in a brand-new way. That they were blowing out of the water all the Machiavellian backstabbing for year-end bonuses, which was supposedly standard operating procedures at places like ICM and William Morris. At those places they would be trying to poach clients from other agencies. So CAA wound up with a lot of good agents and clients. But you know what happens though? A CAA actor and a CAA director make a really good movie, and then another actor calls their agent there and says, "Why the fuck wasn't I up for that role? I'm at CAA. I didn't even get a meeting on that." They have to deal with that constant conflict of interest, which never goes away.

BARRY MEYER, Executive:

Between Ron and Bill Haber and to an extent Michael also, we talked regularly about things that worked well for the studio. You talk to them as friends and advisers, and not only as agents trying to sell you talent. At least that's what we did. And it wasn't just me here doing that. I think people knew that there was a special relationship between us and them. Whenever there was anything that CAA really needed from Warner Bros., Ron was the one designated to call me, because we had a lot of history and it was very hard for me to ever say no to him.

MICHAEL EISNER:

When I was at Paramount, I had felt at various times that I should go out on my own, and I would say to Michael Ovitz maybe we should do something together, because I did represent him. But he would always change the subject. It was clear he really liked CAA and that job. As the years went by, however, he began to bristle at California state laws that restricted him as an agent, and when we talked, I could tell he was getting restless. That's when he started doing the investment banking.

BARRY MEYER:

The thing that was so great about Ron is that he never had any illusions about it; some agents call you and you know, whether the star's trailer was five feet bigger or five feet smaller, it became a moral issue for them. Ron never had that attitude about anything. It was all just business. It's refreshing when you're dealing with somebody who has that kind of perspective. And it was that kind of perspective that made Ron the best talent agent I've ever dealt with. Ever. He was better at representing individual talent than any person I've ever met. And I guarantee that if you ask anybody in town, they'll tell you that.

RAND HOLSTON:

We took great care of the clients, not only their careers, but their personal lives—their kids, their wives, whatever they needed. We were 360-degree agents. Whatever was needed, we did it.

DAVID O'CONNOR:

Richard Lovett and I signed Tom Schulman that summer he had *Dead Poets Society* and *Honey, I Shrunk the Kids* that came out with his sole credit on both, if I'm not mistaken, so he was as hot a writer as there was. Richard and I went to the Sundance Film Festival. It was a much less sophisticated film festival at the time and we were just out and about. I didn't even know Tom Schulman was there, but he was with Jeremy Zimmer and he was having an awful time. It was just uncomfortable and awkward. And when he signed with us, he told us this whole story about watching us at the Sundance Film Festival thinking, *Look at how easy those guys are in this community and how much fun they're having,* and he just thought it would be more fun. And we were, we were having a ball. I loved every minute of what I was doing. You know it's that cliché: it wasn't work, it was just fun.

KEN STOVITZ:

Jay and I had listened to these prank phone calls from these comedians called the Jerky Boys at the time. And Mike starts the meeting saying, "Hey, who's into the Jerky Boys?" because Joe Roth had just called and wanted to do a movie with the Jerky Boys. And Jay goes, "Oh, Stovie's got it." I had no idea who they were, other than listening to their stuff, but we so didn't want to disappoint Mike. So the meeting ends and we cold called, found them, signed them, and literally three months later they were starring in a movie that Joe Roth financed when he was running a studio. It was the craziest thing. It could never happen today with the seventeen-person greenlight committees and probably should never have happened, but it did because we were in a situation where we could actually make it happen.

SALLY FIELD, Actress:

Rick Nicita was like a member of my family then, always in my corner. He had a kind of no-bullshit supportiveness and I knew he would always tell me the truth, even if it was something I didn't want to hear. He wasn't going to be blowing smoke up your butt, which is the worst, most horrible, evil thing an agent can do to an actor. You have to know where you stand, and if you don't know the truth, you can get hurt very deeply. I knew he handled lots of women; I never saw myself as going head-to-head with anybody.

RICK NICITA:

If you made a visit to the set, you got bonus points from the client. They almost always appreciated the attention. But if you didn't go, there were major demerits. Fortunately for me, I really enjoyed my clients.

SALLY FIELD:

Rick came with me for a big hunk of the European tour we did for *Steel Magnolias*. The majority of the cast was there and we would ride together in buses everywhere. When we got to Berlin, it happened to coincide with the wall coming down. The bus dropped us off right there, and we got out to see it all happening. Julia Roberts was still somewhat new, and she and I stood there holding hands. Then the soldiers who had once been defending the wall, and who now had sledgehammers tearing it down, hoisted us on top of the wall. I looked at Rick and could tell he was trying to decide whether he needed to get us out of this or not, but Julia and I were looking at each other, thinking, *Holy crap. This is amazing.* There's a picture of Julia and me on top of the wall, and you can see Rick's arm right behind us, making sure this didn't get out of control.

ALAN ZWIEBEL:

My sons played in the same Little League in West Los Angeles as Ovitz's son, and once there was a father-son game. And his son was pitching for the kids' team, and I hit a home run over the fence, and as I'm rounding the bases, I'm saying to myself, *Fuck, what did I just do? This is Ovitz's kid! This is a bad career move.* I got back to the bleachers where we were sitting and I sat down next to Mike and I looked at him and I said, "Oh, God, I'm sorry." And he looked me and he said, "You shouldn't have done that, Alan." Nothing happened but the way he said, "You shouldn't have done that, Alan" was meant to be funny, but it was a little bit of a Michael Corleone thing.

MICHAEL WRIGHT, Executive:

I started acting when I was seven, went to UCLA, got a degree in theater, and then was out there sort of making my way, waiting tables part of the time, and doing summer stock and a lot of work at the Alley Theater in Houston and other regional theaters. I was living the gypsy actor life, making just enough money to get by—which meant probably fifteen or twenty grand a year. I was twenty-one and loving what I was doing, but by the time I was twenty-seven, I was really burnt out.

I was only in L.A. for about three months out of the year at that point because I was basically taking acting gigs anywhere I could find them. I had a small recurring role on *Family Ties* for a little bit, and I was going out on endless auditions. And then I had what I always happily refer to as my Salieri moment: the curse of Salieri is knowing enough to know what great is and recognizing that you're good at something, but not great. I had that moment in the middle of a national tour of a play I was doing and it hit me like a board in the forehead. Then shortly after that tour ended I was at an audition, and as I looked across the room at the people I was auditioning for, I thought, *God, I want to be that guy. He looks tan, happy, and he's getting paid to do something pretty fun and creative.* So I decided to quit acting.

I knew enough to know that this is a business that runs on apprenticeships and mentorships—it's kind of wonderfully old school that way—and I knew that the best opportunity would be to get a job either at a network, a studio, or an agency—a place where I could go pay my dues and get a bird's-eye view of what's really going on and what future jobs might be. So I applied all over town. I desperately wanted a job as an assistant at CBS. I also applied for a job as an assistant in the business affairs department at CAA. I did not want that job, I wanted the CBS job. The CBS people passed on me. CAA offered me this job.

I had been in the theater for most of my life, so I was used to being backstage or in the rafters or in the dressing room. It was very different: Suddenly I was in this I. M. Pei building where all these people were wearing suits and ties and I was like, *Holy shit, where am I?* You can't even imagine the culture shock. I mean literally, two months before I had been doing the umpteenth production of *A View from the Bridge* at some theater in Green Bay, Wisconsin, and now here I was in this place.

I knew right away I needed to get off that business affairs desk because what I wanted to do was go work in development and I wasn't going to find a path to there from that desk. Back then they had this Friday lunch run by this guy who I really liked named Jon Levin. Jon ran a team called the creative group, what Ovitz had envisioned was his own internal development department so he could bring in his top clients and if, let's say, Martin Scorsese said, "I want to make a movie about the mob in New York in the 1940s," then the agents would gather all sorts of material that spoke to that particular interest, then meet with the client and present it. As part of that process they would invite all these assistants to the Friday lunch, feed us, and the price of admission was you had to come pitch a story. Part of the idea was that they were trying to train the trainees and the assistants in the art of pitching and finding stories. To be honest, in my sort of arrogant way I thought, *Oh, man, I don't know what the hell I'm doing here in terms of deal making and this culture, but I'm an actor and a storyteller. That, I know how to do.* So I went to this lunch a few times and they were always pitching true stories, so the third time I thought, *Well, I want to pitch this story for the hell of it.* I told them it was from the *L.A. Times* and it was about this baseball player who was an all-star phenom and who was recruited by this college and was leading them into the championship, but then it was revealed that he had a criminal past, so they had to kick him off the team. But the happy ending was that he got to come back to the team because they made him an assistant coach, and all's well that ends well. They loved it, they were so gracious. I remember them saying, "God, you pitched that so well. It's such a great story." And one of the agents there said, "I loved this for one of our clients," and she says, "Can you come to my office later today and bring me the article?" So I go back to my cubicle and I'm thinking, *I am fucked*, because I made the whole thing up. I just lied. I pitched it like it was a true story, but it really wasn't. So I go up to her office that afternoon and there's a few of them there and I said, "Look, I'm so sorry. I just made the whole thing up." I assumed I'd be fired. I forget which one of them said it, but one of the agents just said, "That's fantastic!" She thought it was so great that I had made it up, and I thought, *Okay, I'm definitely in a different world now.* And from that I got to know Jon Levin and worked with him. I started doing some coverage, and they made me their sort of internal development guy. My job was to come up with original ideas and comb through old unsold or turnaround screenplays and perhaps older books that had never sold. I remember meeting with Coppola, Tom Hanks, Scorsese, and many other amazing clients at the agency. I was meeting fascinating people and learning the business. It was incredibly affirming because up to that point I had been intimidated by this culture, and what I now realized is, *Oh, man, you know what? For most of these people, the ones I really respect and like, the currency that matters most is story.* It is still about story for these filmmakers. If you walk in with a great story, they don't care what your job is or your title. So suddenly I was able to exercise that muscle again.

JASON HEYMAN, Agent:

I grew up in Santa Fe, and I worked on some movies there. I was a PA. I didn't really know anyone in Hollywood, but I got a taste of it. I went to University of Pennsylvania and then did my junior year at USC film school. I also had a full-time internship day job at Paramount working for the head of marketing. When I graduated, I got an interview with Roger Birnbaum at Fox, who said, "When you're starting off, the best place to start is an agency. There's a friend of mine named Jeremy Zimmer who just opened up this company called United Talent Agency. You should check it out." So I sent my resume to UTA as well as CAA, William Morris, and InterTalent. I remember calling UTA and somehow getting Jeremy Zimmer on the phone, and shortly after, I was hired into the UTA training program. That was the summer of 1991.

I was a new trainee, and I had mentioned to a couple of senior agents at the UTA Christmas party that I was a huge fan of Mike Myers and that I thought *Wayne's World* was going to be a big hit. And lo and behold the next morning, Mike Myers's agent Marty Bauer got a call from Bernie Brillstein saying Mike needed an assistant on *Wayne's World*—and he needed someone immediately. Marty said to Bernie, "I have just the guy for you." He calls me in the mailroom. I'm down there making copies. Marty Bauer on the phone. I'm freaking out. He says, "Go get in your car right now and drive over to the Four Seasons. You're going to be working for Mike Myers on *Wayne's World*." My car had been stolen the night before, so I was dealing with that. I got a ride over, walked into Mike Myers's suite, and ended up working with him for a couple months, becoming his right hand through *Wayne's World* as it blew up. I got to know Sherry Lansing, Bernie Brillstein, Lorne Michaels, and Marc Gurvitz, and I mean, it was amazing. And I'm still in the mailroom, by the way! I got promoted out of the mailroom and worked for John Lesher, who was a lit agent at the time. I worked on his desk for about a year and a half, and then when we absorbed much of InterTalent I went to work for Judy Hofflund, who was head of the talent department. UTA had also hired Nick Stevens and Marty Lesak, and our comedy business was blowing up. Jim Carrey was really the catalyst for it, because he was a massive star, and his managers Jimmy Miller and Eric Gold were great friends of the company and really in it with us.

Marty and I really clicked. He had brought his comedy clients with him to UTA, and he and I put together *Half Baked* with Dave Chappelle and then put together *Chappelle's Show*. We signed Will Ferrell when he was a few weeks in on *SNL*. Marty, Brandt Joel, and I put together *A Night at the Roxbury,* and Will just started taking off. UTA also signed Judd Apatow, Ben Stiller, Jack Black, and

Owen, Luke, and Wes off *Bottle Rocket*. UTA also represented Vince and Favreau and put together *Swingers*. All these guys were friends with each other, and they were all working together. It was this amazing environment that we had for years, and UTA was literally in the center of it.

ADAM KANTER, Agent:

When I was in the mailroom, we always used to have to drive people, including wives or kids—usually Mike, Ron, or Bill's. I got called by Mike's office, and was told I have to drive Mike to one of his kid's schools. So I was driving Mike and he was next to me on his car phone. Here I am with the head of the agency, and the entire time we're in awful traffic. I was nervous as hell. He did not want to be late (ever). He was telling me which way to go—"Turn left, turn right"—while he was on the phone talking to his assistant or getting patched through to other people. We finally got up to the school, and there were Judy and his kids, and he said, "All right, out." So I got out, they got in, and there I was, standing alone, fortunately in front of a pay phone so I could call the office to get a ride.

AMY GROSSMAN:

Growing pains were especially tough on those who were there from the beginning and had to transition from the agency being like a family to a corporation. I remember Michael came into the conference room and asked us to vote on whether we felt the company should invest in company-wide personal computers. I voted no, not just because I have always been somewhat resistant to change and was obviously oblivious to the tide of the future, but because I knew computers would be the end of running in and out of one another's offices which made it all so personal and great.

JOHN PTAK:

I was actually pursued by Rosalie Swedlin on behalf of Mike and Ronnie for about a year, and I just decided I had to make the move. The William Morris film department was falling apart. Seven agents had left. Morale was depressing and careers were in jeopardy. I had been at William Morris for fifteen years, and ICM for four years previous to that, with an eighteen-month interlude between the two when I had left ICM in order to try and become a producer. In the mid, early '70s, people really didn't want to be an agent. They wanted to be either a studio executive or a producer. I quickly realized that was what I wanted to do and went back to the agency business at William Morris until January 1991.

I was a literary agent, meaning I primarily handled directors and writers. On an occasional basis I would co-represent performers from Chevy Chase and Daryl Hannah to Gérard Depardieu—my tastes were eclectic.

IRWIN WINKLER, Producer and Director:

I had never had an agent until I directed *Guilty by Suspicion* in 1991, and that was when I signed with Ron.

He was the most honest, straightforward guy I'd ever met. When he called me and asked would I like to be represented, I jumped at it, because he was dedicated to his clients, but more than anything else, agents also have a kind of reputation—either deserved or not—of being black-suited wiseguys. Ronnie is anything but that.

Rain Man, *winner of the Oscar for Best Picture, starred Tom Cruise and Dustin Hoffman and was directed by Barry Levinson—all CAA clients. Originally Bill Murray (another CAA client) was attached to the title role, with Hoffman in the role that eventually went to Cruise. Hoffman, along with Levinson and Mark Johnson (the movie's director and producer, respectively), praised Ovitz during their acceptance speeches, further solidifying Ovitz's visibility and seat of power in the industry. It was another of those movies that took years to make, and one that Ovitz, along with many other agents at CAA, was determined not to give up on.*

MICHAEL OVITZ:

Rain Man was completely done in-house by CAA. We put Barry and Dustin together. We helped with the financing before there was a studio. There was no way this movie wasn't getting made.

PAULA WAGNER:

We're in a meeting and Mike said, "I have this film that Dustin is doing called *Rain Man* and Marty Brest is going to direct it. It's going to be a beautiful film. We love it. There's a great role for Dustin, but now we need to cast Dustin's older brother." *Older* brother, as in somebody older than Dustin.

DAVID O'CONNOR:

Rain Man was one of the scripts I had identified early on. I don't know if I was even an agent yet when I read it, but I remember getting to Robert Lawrence, who was running production for UA, and getting an offer for Marty Brest, Bill Murray, and Dustin Hoffman. Simultaneous offers went out on all three. I remember I had a pretty heavy Friday night.

Eight o'clock Saturday morning Ovitz woke me up by calling me at home and said, "What did you say to Bill when you gave him the script?" and I said, "I told him to read it. I don't remember telling him a specific part," and he says, "Good. Good." Murray was going to play Raymond. And I said, "Why?" and he said because Dustin read the script and he wants to play Raymond. Bill never read the script.

PAULA WAGNER:

We went away over the Thanksgiving holiday to Big Sur, and I read the script. It was beautiful. I couldn't put it down, I cried at the end. I remember saying to Rick, "Tom Cruise has to play this role." When we got back, I went into our meeting and when *Rain Man* came up, I said, "Instead of an older brother, it should be a younger brother." I said, "I think it should be Tom Cruise," and everybody went, "Whaaaaaaaaat?" Except Mike. He looked at me and said, "You do, do you? Hmm . . . interesting." Then Dustin wanted to meet with Tom, so I said to Tom, "I have this crazy idea." Others will probably say Tom was their idea and it probably "was," because the art of agenting is to let clients have the great idea.

DUSTIN HOFFMAN:

When I got *Rain Man*, Michael told me this was not a new script, it'd been hanging around for a couple of years, from studio to studio, and was nothing like the film that was ultimately made. The suggestion had been that I would play the part that Tom Cruise ended up playing, and that Jack Nicholson would play the character I played. First of all, I wanted to play the mentally challenged character. I had seen a *60 Minutes* piece on this ability called autism. Few people had ever heard the word before, and I later found out that the word hadn't been created until 1946. Before that, doctors were very harsh with parents, thinking that parents weren't giving these kids enough love. So I said I wanted to get someone who could develop for me a character who was autistic, something we've never seen before. Whenever I suggested something to Michael, he was always very helpful, so he said fine. He trusted me. And then we had one or two writers, but it didn't quite work the way I wanted it to.

MICHAEL OVITZ:

Marty Brest worked on a script for six months, couldn't get it to work. Steven Spielberg worked on a script for six months, couldn't get it to work, and then we brought in Sydney Pollack, who worked on it for six months and couldn't get it to work. All three were trying to get a movie with a beginning, a middle, and an end.

DUSTIN HOFFMAN:

Once Marty Brest fell out, I think Mike sent it to a few directors, and they turned it down. He suggested Sydney again, and

Sydney and I had a tough relationship from *Tootsie*, so I said I don't even know if he'll consider this. I met with Sydney, and we kind of shook hands and said, "Let's let the past be the past." But Sydney wanted to do a whole different thing with the movie, and again, he was not a collaborator. He'd take something over and make it his own. He was a pilot, Sydney, and he wanted to make the Tom Cruise character a pilot, and it really altered the script in a way I really didn't think it needed. And telling the movie from his point of view, the pilot's point of view, was really making it auto-biographical.

I happened to take my family to Cirque du Soleil. It was the first time that show existed or was being presented in Los Angeles. Our kids were small then, and it was an extraordinary experience. And sitting behind me was a guy with his wife and his kids. He introduced himself to me, and he said his name was Barry Levinson. After Cirque du Soleil we went and had lunch. He told me what he was doing, and I said, "I'm going crazy here with this movie. I wish I could get Sydney Pollack to see it the way I'd like it to work," and Barry agreed to meet with me. He said, "Where do you want to meet?" We both came up with the same restaurant, Paradise Cove off Malibu. I said, "Oh, that's my favorite place." He said, "Mine, too." There was kind of a look between us, and we met a few more times, and I started telling him more about the movie, and he got it. Here's a guy who cons everybody, and he meets a guy he can't con. I said, "Oh, God, would you call Sydney Pollack up?" I later learned that he had this long conversation with Sydney on the phone as he was driving to Palm Springs, and his wife kind of elbowed him and he put his hand over the phone because he was trying to talk Sydney into trusting what existed, and his wife whispered, "You shouldn't be trying to talk him into it, you should direct this movie. You understand this movie." I told Michael all about this and said, "What am I going to do now?" because you can't fire Sydney, and Sydney had to decide on his own whether or not to do it.

BARRY LEVINSON:

Michael was very astute. He called me up and he said, "Listen, Sydney is having problems with the script. Would you read the script, and if it's interesting to you, would you talk to Sydney about his problems?" It did not occur to me, which in fact he might have had in the back of his mind, that if Sydney fell out, he would have another CAA client to step in.

DUSTIN HOFFMAN:

Days passed, and I was praying that Sydney would come back and say, "I've thought about it, but I don't think I can do it." And sure enough, he turned it down.

MICHAEL OVITZ:

When Barry Levinson finished *Good Morning Vietnam*, I called him up and said, "You know, we oughta come back to *Rain Man*." He said, "Good idea." Then he called and said, "I've looked at it, and I know why no one can do this." I said, "Why?" He said, "There's no ending. There is no third act." He says, "I'm going to make a road movie like the old Hope and Bing Crosby movies."

BARRY LEVINSON:

What I told him is what the movie became.

TOM CRUISE:

My sister and I were in a Cuban restaurant, and she looked across the room and said, "Oh my God, that's Dustin Hoffman." I looked over and said, "Oh my God, it is." And my sister says to me, "You should go over and say hello to him," and I said, "I'm not going to do that. He doesn't want to be bothered." She said, "You love his work. If you don't go over and say hello to him, I'm going to get up and introduce you myself." So I got up and went over to the table and said, "Excuse me, Mr. Hoffman," and he said, "Tom Cruise!" I couldn't believe he knew my name. He was in his last week of doing *Death of a Salesman*, and you could not get a ticket, but he invited me and my sister to the show. We went backstage afterward, and he looked at me and said, "One day we're going to make a movie together!" A couple years after that, he sent me *Rain Man.*

PAULA WAGNER:

My participation was Tom Cruise playing that role. Mike packaged it and took the picture through all the troubled waters that it went through. That was Mike. That was genius on his part. What he did was phenomenal.

JOHN PTAK:

The primary pronoun at staff meetings was always "we": "We are doing this; we are doing that." That never happened anywhere else.

SANDY CLIMAN:

Movie budgets were escalating, and *Rain Man* was an early example of a film considered to be highly risky material with a break-the-bank budget. UA wanted its downside protected with a small profit margin of 10 percent before the split with talent; then the studio was happy to give talent a huge back end, which turned out to be great for Dustin, Tom, and Barry.

MICHAEL OVITZ:

I got thanked four times at the Academy Awards that night. It was unbelievable.

JUDY OVITZ:

The Oscars were always very exciting. Of course we were lucky because Michael was the agent for so many who were either accepting awards or presenting them. We always had really great seats, though a lot of times we would just go to Spago and watch it on big screens there. We'd go to the parties after, but a lot of times I'd be sitting at the table alone because he'd have to do the room. I understood.

MICHAEL OVITZ:

It was really difficult for the two of us to go to those events because we had so many clients nominated. Even though we had a lot of winners, we had losers too. Five nominees, one winner; usually we had three losers.

RICK NICITA:

Paula and I went to the Academy Awards many times, and over the years, there were more than several clients nominated. When Al Pacino won for *Scent of a Woman*, he thanked me by saying, "And my agent, Rick Nicita, who urged me to do this part and actually threatened me if I didn't do it 'cause I didn't want to do the part for some reason." The audience laughed.

JUDY OVITZ:

I was very happy the first time someone thanked him from the stage, but I didn't think it happened enough because on so many of those movies, Michael had put those actors into them, and gotten those movies made.

PAULA WAGNER:

Oliver Stone thanked me beautifully when he received his Oscar for *Platoon*. He called me his goddess of film or something. It was a terrific moment.

Rob Reiner had been a client of CAA's for over a decade, and when he and his partners at Castle Rock went into television production, CAA wanted to make sure they got off to the strongest start possible. As a result, it was one of the accounts that Tony Krantz made a priority, and the first year out, the company and Krantz sold nine pilots to the networks, a truly impressive debut for any company, much less a brand-new one.

One of the shows was based on what one executive called a "weird" little presentation out of the late-night division at NBC, featuring a comedian few had heard of. Howard West (who had been so influential during the formation of CAA) and George Shapiro called Krantz and asked if CAA would waive its commission on the show because the budget didn't have enough money to pay the CAA package fee and pay the comedian's managers (West and Shapiro were to be executive producers on the show). Krantz was obligated to take the request to Ron Meyer, who represented Reiner personally, for Meyer's advice and approval. Meyer wanted to be loyal to his former William Morris colleagues, and besides, it was only one of nine pilots and no one thought it had a chance. So Meyer told Krantz that CAA would give up its commissions in the show.

The "weird presentation" was for a show the managers were calling The Seinfeld Chronicles, and it would become perhaps the greatest television comedy of all time, and an asset worth as much as a staggering $4 billion. The loss in commissions to CAA was perhaps as much as $400 million, but Meyer would never regret it. As far as he was concerned, he made it possible for West and Shapiro to be a part of television history—and really, really wealthy.

PAULA WAGNER:

I had people in town say to me, "You are making a huge mistake encouraging Tom Cruise to do *Born on the Fourth of July*. It will be a career ender. It isn't a comedy and it isn't an action film." That was true, but this was about Oliver [Stone]. I trusted him, and Tom had no qualms at all. He didn't take a gazillion dollars up front; as always, if the movie needed it, he would take it from the back end. And he gave Ron Kovic points. The budget started at $9 million, and I think when all was said and done, including John Williams, who came in when he saw it because he doesn't take every film, we ended up at $18 million. Everybody did really well. *Born on the Fourth of July* was the most profitable movie at that time for Universal.

ROBERT TOWNE, Writer:

I looked for Paula's guidance—she always had something interesting to say—but that didn't mean I would agree with her all the time. She knew who the players were, far more than I, and I don't remember if she actually introduced me to Tom, but she made it possible for both of us to get to know each other because both of us trusted her.

MICHAEL OVITZ:

When Tom started to become a big star and got into Scientology, I went to see David Miscavige, the head of the Church of Scientology. But before I did—because I had no idea what Scientology was—I read the book *Dianetics*. I wanted to know the history of Hubbard. I was in the entertainment business; there's nothing that could shock me, okay? I kind of liked it because I love psychology, and I understood what he was saying. It's all Pavlovian. It's stimulus response. The book was a good read, though nothing I would find as a religion. I could see though where actors would like Scientology: They're gypsies, in a way. They don't go to an office, so it grounds them. I decided there were two ways to handle Scientology: Tell them how bad it is and fight them, or just embrace it and try to control any fallout.

So I called Miscavige and said, "I've read everything," and I said, "I love Tom, he's been with us since he's nineteen. He's probably going to be the biggest star in the world. We've got to work together to make sure it all stays chill and cool and his image is right," and he agreed.

PAULA WAGNER:

One of the reasons I think Tom and I worked together as long as we did is that his personal life was his business and my personal life was my business. We were really professional that way.

MICHAEL OVITZ:

I gave the wedding reception for Tom Cruise and Nicole Kidman at the Barker Hangar at Santa Monica Airport. There's an airplane museum and a hangar, and that's where we had the ceremony and their reception. And sitting at the table with me was David Miscavige. By the way, let me tell you something very interesting: When Tom was a client of ours, you didn't hear any criticisms on that, not while he was with us. We surrounded him, and we were so careful.

Walter Yetnikoff was the senior attorney at CBS Records who guided the Sony acquisition of CBS Records, which was a huge success for Sony, both economically and strategically. Yetnikoff developed a close personal relationship with Sony president Norio Ohga, who installed him as CEO of CBS Records and became his key man in the entertainment industry. In 1988, as Sony contemplated buying a movie studio, Yetnikoff, an Ovitz friend, suggested it engage Ovitz as a consultant on this exploration. Sony's other advisers included Blackstone founders Pete Peterson and Steve Schwarzman. Ovitz first tried to steer Sony toward MCA and then MGM/UA, but terms did not work out. Sony finally decided to buy Columbia Pictures Entertainment for $3.4 billion in October 1989; at the time it was the largest takeover of an American firm by a Japanese company.

It was a double victory for Ovitz: He proved that he played a key role in multibillion-dollar deals on an international scale, and it placed CAA in a unique position to do better business with the studio. Ovitz would earn $12 million for helping broker Sony's purchase of Columbia Pictures—the check was sent via U.S. mail by Yetnikoff.

In separate negotiations, Sony considered having Ovitz sell his majority stake in CAA and then take over Sony's two studios, Columbia/TriStar. Morgan Stanley represented Ovitz and the deal fell through. Sony then hired Peter Guber and Jon Peters to run Columbia/TriStar. Ovitz was peeved, both because his counteroffer had been rejected and because he believed they were prodigal spendthrifts. Guber kept it simple. He invited the Young Turks—but not CAA's senior partners—to his Aspen retreat.

DAVID O'CONNOR:

I'm really murky on the details of when Saturdays started. It really started more socially than it did consciously from ambition. We were just hanging out with each other all the time, socializing on a Friday or Saturday night almost every weekend. Some configuration of us. A lot of it revolved around socializing—we would create social opportunities for us to meet and sign clients, be with existing clients, get to know important buyers, producers in the marketplace, just a social setting. It served us pretty well because we were all pretty adept socially, but it just started out of friendship more than ambition.

I remember we signed Matthew Modine, who was a young up-and-coming hot actor at the time. I can't remember where he came from, but we all worked together; it was a group sign. And that became kind of the model.

MICHAEL WIMER:

Around 1991, a private equity buddy of mine from Stanford bought *Premiere* magazine, which was edited by Susan Lyne. In one of her early "Power" lists, the magazine first used the term "Young Turks," mentioning Jay, Richard, Doc, Bryan and Kevin, and myself as the group. Ovitz was on fire when he saw it—he went nuts. He called me on the carpet, as he wrongly assumed that I had made the connection. I'm sure that Susan, who knew the business well, was aware that Jay and Doc and Richard and I were great friends with Peter Guber since he and Jon Peters took over Sony in 1989. It was pretty high-profile stuff, with legendary times at his Aspen home or trips to sets on the Sony plane. Peter was an awesome mentor and buddy, and he couldn't have been a more generous friend. At the same time, Bryan and Kevin were wired into Carrie Fisher's world, and the group of us were the only agents—of any generation—at her high-wattage, intimate parties. What the hell? I remember laughing with Glenn Frey when we were jockeying to use the bathroom after Meryl Streep came out—laughing because Carrie had shouted at her about her "horse stream." Nobody could make her laugh like Carrie. Hell, nobody could make any of us laugh like Carrie did. It was all such a hoot. All six of us were having a blast. But it wasn't true that I had planted us on the Power list.

What was true, however, was that the six of us had started to meet in 1989, on the qt, to discuss how we could be more effective at signing new talent, both in and out of the company, as well as having more of a role in affecting the direction of the company. The problem with CAA was that, in the motion picture department, there was a significant energy gap between the delineated leaders (Swedlin and Rapke in literary, Nicita in talent) and the defacto leaders, which were the group of us. Kevin and Bryan were signing machines. Jay Moloney used his position as Michael's right-hand man to work into the worlds of Bill Murray, Tim Burton, and Martin Scorsese. Richard was outworking everyone and was about to sign Tom Hanks. Doc was running the literary department and had every big writer. I had a huge directors list. We were killing.

ROLAND EMMERICH, Writer and Director:
When we were developing the story of *Independence Day*, I learned that Tim Burton was doing something called *Mars Attacks!* that was a comic book and it was like a parody of what we were doing. So I told Dean [Devlin] that it was fine. We wrote it over Christmas and then sent it to Michael. And Michael really, really liked it. I had said to him, "What should we do?" It was the first time that Dean and I had the same agent. And Michael said, "Well, let's like auction it." And we said, "What do you mean, auction it?" And he said, "Well, can you put a budget to it and attach a director and we will auction the film to all the studios." And that's what we did. And that's what he did, he organized it.

I had just directed, you know, *Stargate*, you know, and like a little bit of a sleeper hit, kind of really hot, but I was with Bill Block and I just didn't click with him anymore. I wanted to change agencies and everything. I called Bryan Lourd, a friend of mine, and I said, "Bryan, I need one of your agents now. Can you approach one for me?" And he said, "Well, I know the perfect guy for you." And it was Michael Wimer. We did that and it was interesting because the night before the auction . . . first of all, he said like, "Let's go out on Wednesday because I hate going out on the weekend because the studios have way too much time." And so we went out on a Wednesday. We met on a Tuesday the night before and he said, "So what's your goal?" And we said, "We talked about it. It's two and a half million in salaries for script, producer, and writing against hopefully two and a half percent gross points." Because we were ambitious. And he said, "Okay, let's start there." And then the first meeting was at Fox and they said, "You are not leaving until you sign a deal with us." Michael took us out of the room and said, "Wait in the conference room." Maybe after twenty minutes he came and said, "Let's leave!" We said, "What happened?! What happened?!" And he said, "The offer is out now against seven and a half gross points with accelerators." And I immediately thought, *Oh my God, this guy blew it. He blew it.* But that evening they signed the deal.

So that was such an amazing deal for two young filmmakers. I had just turned forty-two or so and Dean was like thirty-four. The interesting thing was that this kind of created a precedent. I always credit Michael as the inventor of kind of going out with a script where you have a budget and they have to immediately greenlight you. I did it for *The Day After Tomorrow* and with a movie called *2012.* They cannot back out. It's actually the perfect way to make that kind of big blockbuster.

KEN STOVITZ:

Bad Boys was written for Jon Lovitz and Dana Carvey. I had been searching for Will's hiatus film, so when that fell apart, they went with Will and Martin. No one knew, no one thought the movie had any foreign value. I used to hear that kind of racist comment all the time. He broke every rule and every stereotype. I mean *Bad Boys* kind of shocked people, and then *Independence Day* blew the lid off. Then there was a series of incredible hits like *Men in Black* and *Enemy of the State.* I left CAA when Will asked me to join him at Overbrook. It was a beautiful experience to produce with Will and James and Jada. It still is.

MICHAEL WIMER:

At first it may have been because of the meetings we had. The early meetings, to my taste, were fun and energetic. Jay, God love him, was a ball of this infectious energy. We'd pick clients to chase and internal signs to make and parties to stage. But after a few years, I felt that the tone of the meetings was getting, well, darker. There seemed to be more blood in the water, and the strategies became more about gutting other agents rather than merely signing great clients or putting together great movies. I became pretty sensitive to the fact that the glue that was keeping the group together might be a bit different than I thought. Doc and Richard had a particularly ugly incident with Tom Schulman, who they had signed away from a rival client around the time of *Dead Poets Society* in 1989. Richard stepped on Doc in a way that was pretty uncool. Later on, there were more conversations laced with more venom than I was comfortable with regarding colleagues of ours. It was beginning to bother me. Carrie and I had a conversation about it when she told me, "You aren't like those guys." It was part observation, part compliment and part warning. She was having a fight with Bryan at the time, but Carrie has always been one of the smartest, most prescient people in this town.

RON MEYER:

When Mike realized that there was a corporate world out there and that he was being respected as a businessman more than as a flesh peddler, he found a way to distance himself from us.

MICHAEL OVITZ:

I got paid $12 million for the Sony deal and I turned down running the studio. I gave the Sony executives a list of people, which Peter and Jon were not on, and then when they picked them, I withdrew as a consultant because I could see the writing on the wall. Peter was brilliant, but Jon wasn't an executive, and together it was just going to be a problem. I also didn't think they could handle the whole Japanese side of things.

PETER GUBER, Executive:

A month after the title passed at Sony, Mike Ovitz came to the office and said, "I'd like my fee." I said, "A fee for what?" He said, "For making the deal." I said, "It's the first I've heard of you being involved in the transaction. It's the first I've known of you. So you're peeing on the wrong tree. Go speak to Morita, and if he wants to give you a fee, it's fine with me." He said, "Well, you know how important I am to the business, and if I feel that I'm not being properly handled, I'll be very upset." I said, "Look. I'm not really good at managing anybody's emotions, including my dog's." And that was the last I heard of him.

SANDY CLIMAN:

Mike regularly cited *The Art of War*. While he and Matsushita's number two, Hirata, related well to each other, to succeed we needed to make Mike fully conversant in Japanese culture. To start that process, I bought him Edwin O. Reischauer's seminal book, *The Japanese Today*. Reischauer was the former ambassador to Japan. After briefing Mike on who Professor Reischauer was, I got the two on the phone for an introductory conversation.

DAN ADLER:

The agency always benefited from an incredible staff of readers, who would do coverages of scripts. In addition to the scripts he read himself, Michael always relied on the head reader for a lot of his material. I remember one task that fell far outside of the norm, though: When Michael was heading to Japan for one of the first big—and secret—meetings with Matsushita, he wanted coverage of all of the writings of Konosuke Matsushita, the founder of the company—what we know as Panasonic. So I had to read all of his books and all of his key writings, and provide Michael with a full rundown on what drove Matsushita-san, what he believed, and how he built his company.

MICHAEL OVITZ:

Sandy ran the whole business group, a department with something like eight MBAs in it. I asked Sandy to tell me what other Japanese companies might be interested in the film or media business. What came back to me was, no surprise, companies you'd see if you went to an electronics store: Samsung, JVC, Toshiba, Sony, and Panasonic. That was the list. Then if you went to Europe, it was Philips. Then I asked Sandy to find out which of them had cash on their balance sheet. Sandy went to a stockbroker, pulled the annual reports, then eliminated companies that made no sense. He came back to me and said, "I found one company that makes more sense than anybody else." I asked him, "What is it?" And he said, "Matsushita Electric. They own Panasonic." One number stood out at me when I read the annual report: they had $12 billion in cash. And I said, "Great, give me everything there is to read." We bought every book on Matsushita Electric, including the seven books of the writings of the chairman, Mr. Matsushita. I read them all. And when they had appendixes and other references, we got them as well. Then I sent a mailroom guy to go to the UCLA archives and look at the English-language Japanese newspaper, which I had seen from being over there. We discovered that Matsushita was called by Japanese businessmen a Japanese word that meant "copycat" because everything that Sony did, they copied. And Sony had already bought Columbia. A lightbulb went off in my head and I said to myself, *My God. They're going to want to buy a studio.*

I started looking for ways to get in the door. I discovered that JVC had a young Japanese guy who was educated in America— which was the Japanese way at the time—living in Los Angeles, and his job was to watch Larry Gordon and report back to the people at JVC, who had made an investment there. And lo and behold, JVC was 50 percent owned and controlled by Matsushita, so being a good agent, I started to figure out a way to get on that guy's radar screen. I got Sandy into a relationship with the guy to manipulate him to ask for a meeting with me. Which he did. And I said no. Which is the game: yes is no, no is yes. So for four weeks this guy asked Sandy, once a week, for a meeting with me. And true to his direction, he was told to tell the guy no. The fifth week, worried I was going to overplay my hand, I agreed to a meeting for fifteen minutes.

SANDY CLIMAN:

The first contact from Japan on the Matsushita Electric deal did not come from Matsushita directly, but rather from Matsushita affiliate JVC. JVC legal adviser Peter Dekom helped bring together CAA with the JVC head of audiovisual, Isamu Tomitsuka. For the first meeting, we needed a private and secure place. We couldn't meet at CAA, and we were too well known around town for even private rooms at restaurants or major hotels. So I picked the "Bruin" private dining room at the Holiday Inn in Westwood, a hotel so low-end no one from the industry would ever be seen there. That was the first meeting with JVC. It was Mike, Bob, Ray, and me from CAA, and Mr. Tomitsuka and his Hollywood lieutenant, Henry Ishii, from JVC.

MICHAEL OVITZ:

We exchanged business cards—I had great business cards, one side's Japanese, one side's English; that's how it's done all over the world—and to make a long story short, I charmed the shit out of this guy because I knew everything that was important to them and how to talk with them. In Japan, they don't ask you how you feel. If you have a cold, they don't ask you if you have a cold. If you have cancer, you're not allowed to discuss it. You're not allowed to sit with the soles of your feet toward your guest. You're not allowed to cross your legs. You're not allowed to take your jacket off unless you ask, "Can we all have our jackets off?" I can go through a hundred things like this. I knew how to use chopsticks better than many Japanese. I knew the history of sake.

SANDY CLIMAN:

After several strategy discussions, the JVC team reported back to Matsushita management. Like scouts who are replaced by soldiers, Matsushita took over discussions with us, and JVC was out of the picture, never to be seen again.

Matsushita contacted Ovitz in the fall of 1989 and hired him as a consultant. Ovitz then assembled a team that included New York law firm Simpson Thacher

& Bartlett to represent Matsushita in the United States, as well as Herbert Allen of the Allen & Company investment firm and public relations firm Adams and Rinehart. For its initial meeting with Ovitz, Matsushita sent executive vice president Masahiko Hirata; the firm's decision to send a senior executive showed Ovitz that it was serious about acquiring a Hollywood studio. Ovitz persuaded Matsushita to consider MCA in the spring of 1990.

MICHAEL OVITZ:

This kid wrote to the JVC guys and then JVC asked for a meeting with me, and again, I kept saying no. Then finally the number two guy at Matsushita reached out for a meeting with me and I said it was a pleasure to meet him. I wrote a letter to him, on my letterhead, "Heard a lot about Matsushita. I'm a big fan. I'm an audiophile." Which was true; I've loved electronic equipment because my whole life I've loved music. So I told him, "I know your product line well. I love your amplification equipment and I've always marveled at why you can't make a great-sounding speaker." It hit a chord with him and he said, "I'd like to invite you to Japan." And I said, "I'd love to come, but I'm just far too busy. Thank you." So then four days later, a letter comes. "Would you meet me in Hawaii? I'll host a weekend at the Kahala Hilton." I waited a few days, and I sent a letter back and said yes. I brought Sandy, Bob Goldman, and Ray Kurtzman to the Kahala Hilton for three days of discussions.

I brought them homemade cookies, gifts, pictures of my kids, art, new golf clubs, and a slew of other things. I never talked, ever, about business. So for three days, all we did is discuss golf, Japanese-American relations, electronics, anything that was of interest to them. But they were in a state of shock because I knew their product line better than they did. I had delivered to me every catalog of everything they were making, for domestic consumption or international consumption, and was talking about a new video camera they had coming out, and some of the guys in the room from the company didn't even know about it yet.

SANDY CLIMAN:

The core Matsushita working team was extremely small—Masao Ohashi, who had a background in industrial products; Atsuro Uede, who was a distinguished painter in his spare time; and Junko Saito, a cultured young woman who served as translator. Our side was an equally tight-knit group that included Bob, Ray, and me. Somehow we managed to keep our activities separate from the agency as a whole and secret from the outside world.

MICHAEL OVITZ:

At the end, one hour before we're set to take off, they said, "So if we were interested in looking to buy a motion picture studio, how would we pay you?" That's what the question was. I looked at Hirata, straight in the eye and I said, "Hirata-san, if I provide a service that you find worthy and productive but does not result in anything, I expect nothing but my expenses." And then I said, "But if, Hirata-san, I provide a service that you find worthy and productive, and if the price is to your satisfaction and you buy a company, I will then expect you to take a Brinks armored truck, load it with money, and send it to my house." There was a beat because the translator has to translate. Then he bowed so deep, his head almost hit the table. We shook hands and we left.

BOB GOLDMAN:

We didn't charge them anything up front. We went to them as advisers, much like bankers, and we never talked about fees.

SANDY CLIMAN:

Our trips to Japan were highly orchestrated—even scripted. Mike, Bob, and I would board the ANA flight to Osaka. Mike and Bob would take an Ambien and sleep for eleven hours. During those eleven hours, I would write and rewrite the speeches Mike would give during the next several days of meetings with Matsushita. I would handwrite everything on a legal pad and hand it to Mike as he got off the plane in Osaka.

MICHAEL OVITZ:

On my first trip to Osaka, Hirata walked me into a room ten feet square. On the floor were twenty-five or thirty neat stacks, a couple inches apart, with cover letters on them from every investment bank in the world, thanking them for meeting, talking about their fee schedule, attaching a contract and information about their company, along with research on all the movie studios. Hirata had me look at it; then he looked at me, smiled, and then we walk out the door. He turned every one of them down and took me because I was the only one who asked for nothing, which is how they wanted to do business. They wanted a handshake. I never signed anything with them.

ATSURO UEDE, Executive:

CAA evaluated MCA and other companies for the purpose of Matsushita and advised us on the expected feeling of Mr. Wasserman, how MCA should be operated after merger, who were key persons in MCA, and played an important role to arrange first meeting between tops of MCA and Matsushita.

He [Ovitz] never said he wanted the job. He mentioned that he was taking care of CAA. He didn't want to run the company.

SANDY CLIMAN:

Mike was focused on MCA as a target, first with Sony and then with Matsushita. It might have been a desire to emulate Lew Wasserman, it might have been inspired by his early days as a Universal Studios tour guide, or it may simply have been a desire to develop the massive real estate assets in Universal City. With Matsushita, we evaluated both Paramount and MCA/Universal. Paramount had not yet been acquired by Viacom and it was a smaller target—much more of a pure movie and television play. Plus it was headquartered in New York. I remember driving by Paramount headquarters in Columbus Circle with Mr. Ohashi saying, "I hope we buy Universal because I don't want to be in New York and would much rather have the due diligence in California." MCA had a far broader and more valuable set of assets, and that won the day for the decision to acquire MCA.

JOHN PTAK:

Sandy was Ovitz's briefcase—he was always there and he was the guy who Mike would have in the room to report back to him or to talk on his behalf.

SANDY CLIMAN:

Much of the Matsushita negotiation with MCA was done before Lew and Sid ever met the Matsushita executives. Their first meeting together was at Sid's apartment at the Trump Tower in New York, where Mike made the introduction. Mike had indicated that Matsushita would offer a price in the low $70s for each share of MCA stock. When the offer price came in the $60s, Lew and Sid had felt misled. Things finally broke apart the day before Thanksgiving, and Mike, Bob, and I flew back to L.A. thinking the deal was over. Early Thanksgiving morning, I got a call at home from Herb Allen, who was at the Concorde Lounge at JFK on his way to a family gathering in London. He told me Bob Strauss, Lew's attorney, friend, and confidant, had suggested a compromise price. We were now in closure range. I called Mike, and by Friday we were on our way back to New York to close the deal.

DAVID STYNE:

I started at CAA in March of 1990, and I was a trainee in the mailroom, and then in May of '90 got pulled out of the mailroom to work on Michael Ovitz's desk. Michael had five people working for him at this time, and honestly, it felt like I was working for the president. It was the apex of his power.

I was in the office sixteen hours a day, but on weekends I wore a beeper, and if Michael needed you, he would beep you and you'd call him. I remember getting beeped and then getting on the phone with Michael on a Saturday night, and he said, "Here's what I want you to do: I want you to get in your car, and I want you to go to Mulholland where it overlooks Universal. Then I want you to check out three different viewpoints and pick the best one. Tomorrow morning, you're going to get three limos and go to the Beverly Wilshire hotel at 10 A.M. and pick up the Japanese to bring them to Universal. On the way over, when you get to Mulholland, pull over at the spot you pick tonight and show them the view of Universal below. After that I want you to quietly bring them onto the lot. Have the limos drive around the lot, but don't let anything happen that is obvious." And that Sunday morning, I showed the Japanese what they were buying.

SID SHEINBERG, Executive:

I think we heard officially about the deal two hours before, but I had heard rumors. I heard it before Lew. I was slightly surprised. Among the various companies that were rumored, Seagram's had been one—not rumored out loud, but rumored.

I never specifically reached out to Michael to ask about what had happened, but I spoke to him about his behavior once, hopefully in a civil way. I said I didn't understand why he saw fit to lie to us, and I remember quite vividly his answer. He said, "It was business." I told him, "It's not the way I conduct business."

TOM POLLOCK:

He knew when to flatter and when to scare you, when to use the carrot and when to use the stick. That's how you manipulate people into doing what you want them to do. I don't know exactly how he talked the Japanese into it other than what he said, because they never talked. He told them exactly how great this was going to be.

Ovitz, along with investment banker Felix Rohatyn and Matsushita executive Keiya Toyonaga, negotiated a deal to sell MCA shares for $66, for a total of $6.59 billion. Ovitz and CAA earned $46 million in consulting fees.

MICHAEL OVITZ:

Lew wasn't really wealthy before, at least not like I made him with this deal. He obviously made a good living, but this was real wealth.

SANDY CLIMAN:

For a studio head, Lew took an extremely modest salary, and the payout from his stocks was $300 million, also a relatively small payout for a lifetime of work in a company Lew largely founded. Other studio heads, with much shorter tenures, earned far larger salaries and had highly lucrative stock incentives. Lew took care of the shareholders rather than enrich himself.

We earned the highest investment banking fee in America that year. We were number one on all the lists of deal commissions. Forty-six million dollars in those days was an unthinkably large payday for a single deal.

SID SHEINBERG:

Mike wanted to be the reincarnation, although he wasn't deceased at the time, of Lew Wasserman; even dressed like him. Unfortunately, he missed the point that you have to have a certain character and a certain set of ethics to even aspire to that. Lew disliked Mike Ovitz—I can't even think of three people he disliked—and didn't think he should run the studio.

HERB ALLEN, Businessman:

In terms of learning the business, Michael had no problem learning anything. He's a very quick learner who picks up very fast on whatever he has to learn. Wherever he applies himself, he gets to where he has to be.

The people he worked with the most at the very beginning were at Universal—Wasserman and Sheinberg—to move them to consider a sale. The technical aspects are usually less important. His ability to get deals done was remarkable.

TOM POLLOCK:

Mike was a friend of mine for a long time, but the truth is he didn't really know the inner workings of the business, he's just a really good salesman.

HERB ALLEN:

Michael took CAA to a level nobody in the industry had ever been to. The only person who was close would have been Lew Wasserman with his agency before he ended up at Universal. Mike went miles beyond Wasserman, and Wasserman was the best.

TOM POLLOCK:

The deal closed in the fall, and that Christmas, Universal came out with the biggest failure I had at the studio—a movie called *Havana*, put together by Mike Ovitz with Sydney Pollack, his client, and Robert Redford, his client. It cost $60 million, which was a huge amount of money, and we took a huge hit to earnings within a month after they bought us. And by the way, Michael didn't force me to make it; anyone would have made it. The last film Sydney Pollack had made was *Out of Africa* starring Robert Redford, which was wonderful. I liked the script for *Havana*. What none of us realized is between *Out of Africa* and *Havana* Bob had gotten older and the movie opened with a big close-up of his face on the screen, and while he was still incredibly good looking, he was an older person in a business that is still about younger people.

We had great years, we had bad years—that's the way the movie business works. Eighty-nine was a great year and so part of the price that they paid in 1990 was probably based on "Oh, it's just going to continue like that." And it did: we had *Kindergarten Cop* and the third *Back to the Future* and there were plenty of movies that worked really well, until *Havana*. That shocked the Japanese. And remember, the way accounting works is profits come in over three to ten years, but losses are taken immediately. When there's a big loss, it goes right to the bottom line.

MICHAEL OVITZ:

I still was retained by Matsushita, but I did say to Lew and Sid that it would be really important for them to either use me or get their own expert on Asia and how to handle the Japanese. They decided not to use me and Matsushita was in a state of shock that they weren't talking to me. But I had the relationship with Matsushita, not them. As it turned out, they had a series of issues with the Japanese that arose out of their inexperience.

The Japanese left them alone. The Japanese were actually afraid of Lew because in those days they were very concerned about people connected to the government, and they thought Lew was incredibly well connected. Lew and Sid ran the studio as if the Japanese didn't exist. There was no trust. Wasserman and Sheinberg were so disrespectful in a culture that commands respect. A culture where for two thousand years people bowed to each other, where honor is more important than anything else. And they were nasty to them.

TOM POLLOCK:

Sid and Lew felt betrayed by Mike. They thought they had an understanding with him, and were working more or less on the same side, but they realized that had not been the case.

I talked to Lew many times after the sale, and the last time I saw him before his death, he said to me that selling the studio was the biggest mistake he ever made.

MICHAEL OVITZ:

Sid and Lew screwed up the easiest thing in history. Do you know how easy it was to deal with the Japanese? It was such a pleasure. It was so easy. This is a culture that bows to each other, this is a culture that eats fish for breakfast, this is a culture that has their soup after their meal, this is a culture that eats their sashimi first and their sushi, their rice fish, second. This is a culture that spends forty minutes to make tea, this is a culture that believes in rote education—show me, explain to me—from the simplest all the way up, this is a culture that works under *nemawashi,* which is concentric approvals, until you get to the top, so that the top man is protected. But this is not a culture that you hammer; they didn't understand that.

SANDY CLIMAN:

On the first Matsushita deal, the fee was staggering. I went down to the accounting office at 1888 and personally typed the invoice on an IBM Selectric typewriter—$45 million plus $1 million of unaccountable expenses for a total of $46 million, the highest fee paid to any investment adviser in America that year. I faxed the invoice to Matsushita, and when the money was wired in, Bob Goldman had to quickly figure out how to move it into bonds so we did not have $46 million cash sitting exposed in a single account. I don't think Mike or Bob had ever seen that much money show up in a single transaction.

MICHAEL OVITZ:

I gave Ron a check for $10 million, and then I found out later that he didn't think it was enough. With all due respect, in 1993, $10 million for something you had nothing to do with is a lot of money. I gave Bill $10 million also.

SANDY CLIMAN:

Mike was highly secretive with information, often instructing that we withhold or give partial information rather than the whole story. He would tell Bob, Ray, and me to brief Ron, but only with partial information. We would go to Ron's office, close the door, and then tell him what Mike wanted him to know—and then the whole story. We all knew how to handle information, protect each other, and make sure the right things happened to maximize the opportunities at hand.

Once in a while Mike would ask one of us to deliver a veiled threat to a studio executive to ensure cooperation. I never did. It was counterproductive, and there were far better ways to ensure a proper outcome.

JEFFREY KATZENBERG, Executive:

There is no question that Michael Ovitz is someone who consistently dealt in ways that were destructive, deceitful, and in bad faith. I don't want to characterize it as CAA, because we did business with CAA, and there were many great agents and clients that we did business with there, but pretty consistently, when Michael put himself in the middle of dealings, they were not very fruitful. His power and his impact was enhanced by his ability to set people against one another to utilize relationships, and to put himself at the center of that. That's how he operated.

ALEC BALDWIN, Actor:

I was with an agent and I hit a big pothole in my career. I guess the best way to put it is, I was having a problem with the biggest people in Hollywood, and because I was at a smaller agency like the one I was with at the time, someone once explained to me, those guys who are the buyers were never going to return my agent's call—or they were going to return it really slowly. It's just the way that business works: They're more comfortable working with a certain circle of people. My problem was I needed a tow truck; the other guy I was with was a golf cart. I signed with Ron, and it was one of the best four or five years of my life. I wasn't a Schwarzenegger making them millions and millions of dollars, I was a client in their bullpen, but it was the nicest time in my career. I went with him in '91, and we'd be at Ron's house, my ex-wife Kim and I, and he'd have these dinner parties, and my jaw was almost on the table. It'd be Warren and Annette, and Billy Friedkin with Sherry Lansing, and Joel Silver would be there, and this one and that one. They'd have dinner, very informal, but then they'd show a movie. Some nights, the movie would go on and people sat politely, and sometimes, I won't name names, a couple of really famous people would be yelling at the screen, like, "Whose fucking idea was it to watch this fucking movie?" I'd sit there and look at my wife and be like, my God this is one of the greatest nights—we're really inside the highest reaches of the movie business. If they didn't like the movie they said *fuck you* in ten minutes.

NICOLE KIDMAN, Actress:

Rick was married to Paula Wagner, who I've been really good friends with for years. I'd say Tom brought me to CAA. I was really young—I was twenty-two, I think, or twenty-three. I was with Sam Cohn at ICM, and I got married to Tom and then I sat down with Rick and just really liked him. Rick was a gentleman. I loved Sam Cohn; I think a lot of the agents at CAA would say they loved Sam as well, because Sam was a great agent in this business, but I moved over to Rick because Tom was at CAA with Paula, and then Rick was there, and it was so much easier for me. I thought, *Okay, this seems to be a better fit.* I don't overthink these things, and I'm very much a heart person. I base a lot of things on who I like. I keep it simple like that. I know a lot of people jump around and change agencies a lot, but it's just not my style.

IRWIN WINKLER:

I read an excerpt from Nick Pileggi's book called *Wiseguy* and thought it would make a terrific movie. I called the agent in New York and he said CAA was the co-agent with him and I should call Bob Bookman. I spoke to Bookman and told him I was interested, but he said he already had four or five different offers. So I spoke to Ovitz and told Ovitz I wanted to do it with Scorsese. He sold me the book in five minutes.

MARTIN SCORSESE:

I went back to do *Goodfellas* at Warner Bros. and Mike was very instrumental in helping me navigate the problems with the studio, particularly during post-production. The previews were bad, and the studio wanted me to trim down a lot of the film. They were concerned it played like a comedy, and they hadn't expected that, and it was a very big budget at that time, about twenty-five million dollars. Mike was really the strong man there for me. He came on the set one night—when Terry and Bob Daly came down to urge me to move faster because it was fifteen days over schedule—and Mike brokered a meeting in my trailer. He saw some of the things I was up against, then helped me through previews. At one preview, which was one of the worst experiences we've ever had, the film came up and there was no sound. People were stamping their feet and yelling, so we stopped it. Then there was even more shouting. We were all convening and trying to figure out what to do, and Mike said, "You don't have to do this, you know. You've fulfilled your obligation for a preview. This is it, they don't have it together." I said, "No, let's try this again." He says, "If this happens again, we're leaving." It happened again. We ran out of the theater, and the only place we could go to discuss this was a bowling alley next door. Mike came up real close to my face and said again, "You don't have to do this. If you want to go home, I will take care of this for you." I said, "No, let's see it with an audience." I figured I was out there, we might as well go through with it, but having him there and having that flexibility was important.

KEVIN COSTNER:

I didn't want to have standard deals, and I felt like CAA and Mike would be able to get me away from them. I wanted ownership; and I was willing to be entrepreneurial.

ARMY BERNSTEIN:

One day Kevin Costner came to my house, and was just really down. I said, "What's going on?" and he said, "I have this screenplay, I can't get it made. No one will do it with me." I said, "What is it?" and he says, "It's a Western called *Dances with Wolves,* and it's from a novel. I just love it. I can get some money internationally, but I just can't raise it domestically." I said, "Why doesn't anybody want to do it?" and he said, "Well, it's three hours long, the Indians are going to speak original Lakota Sioux, I'm going to star in it, and I'm also going to direct it. I don't have the money and the winter is coming and if I don't do it now I'm never going to do it. And it's the thing I want to do most in all the world."

I read it, one of the best screenplays I've ever read. I said, "Kevin, if you can't get this movie made, then I don't even want to be in the film business. Let me see if I can help you raise the money," and I literally started to create Beacon Productions that day. I called a friend who I went to college with at the University of Wisconsin, Tom Rosenberg—he had become super successful in the real estate business—and he became my first partner in Beacon. I wanted to go go go, do whatever it took to finance *Dances with Wolves,* but I realized we probably wouldn't be able to get there on time. So I went to Mike Ovitz, who was my agent, and sat down and asked, "What should we do?" He said, "I can get this made," and he set it up at Orion. You see, Michael back then, he could get your movie made. He made things happen. And Kevin became his client.

KEVIN COSTNER:

Michael Ovitz wasn't involved in saying yes to *Dances with Wolves,* but they really had a lot to do with the back end of things. *Dances* started with me and Jim. We couldn't raise any money around the studios, so we met all of these foreign sales guys at the St. James Hotel. The thing that stood out the most was I saw this big cheese plate with salami go flying by, and I looked at Jim and I said, "Who paid for that?" and he goes, "We did," and I asked how much was that and he says, "Seventy-five dollars." You have to understand that was a lot of money for us, and I thought, *Fuck, $75, Jesus Christ.*

I remember going out there and saying to them, "I can't in good faith say I know I'm going to make a great movie. All I can say is I'm going to die trying to make a great one." At that point we raised $9 million. I had made two movies for Orion, *Bull Durham* and *No Way Out,* and they then came to the table for $4 million, so we had $13 million.

Mike had a really enormous amount of clients, and so Sandy Climan was assigned to be with me. Sandy is a really soft backboard for ideas. He's a really good listener who understands things, and he was able to put into terms the things I was trying to articulate. He was able to distill what I was saying and make sure that the deals reflected that. There was no mystery about Sandy, he conducted himself really well. I felt that my asks were honest asks—they were aggressive, but I didn't feel like they were overreaches. So I wanted to make sure Sandy never felt he was put in the position of saying something he felt was fucking ridiculous. Mike was a very effective executive, but Sandy was very easy. That sounds like a weak term, but it's not. It's actually really valuable to someone like myself. I needed somebody to be that way for me.

BARBRA STREISAND:

I didn't really know Ronnie socially back then and didn't really know Mike. Ron and I would talk on the phone because I'm the kind of person who never goes to an agent's office. I've been with Marty Erlichman, my manager, fifty-three years and have never been to his office.

SONYA ROSENFELD:

After I had been an agent for just five years, I was called into the office and Lee Gabler told me, "We want you to be the head of the TV lit department." I was in total shock and wasn't even aware that I was being discussed for the job. And I said to him, "Of course. Yes. I'm incredibly flattered, but how did this come about?" And he said to me, "Your colleagues want you to do it." And at the time they were mostly men. It was Joe Cohen, Ted Miller, Jeff Jacobs, my husband Mike, and other people that I've worked with now for many, many years. They all went to him and said that Sonya should be the next head of the TV lit department. It felt really empowering that it was coming from my peers and especially that it was coming from men.

LINDSAY DORAN, Producer:

My contract was expiring at Paramount and I got a call from someone—I don't know whether it was Mike Ovitz or not—asking if I would be interested in running Sydney Pollack's company. I said, "Sure!" I was so excited. I learned later that Sydney's idea of how to interview somebody was to make them uncomfortable as quickly as possible because that was the only way to get to know a person. I saw him do this to other people later. But I didn't realize at the time it was strategy. So he said, "If you're such a big deal, why haven't I heard of you? People keep telling me how good you are, and I've never heard of you before I met you on this project." Anyway, I must have passed the test. He hired me and made me the president of Mirage. During the negotiation of my deal, Mike Ovitz asked to sit down with me. We met at a restaurant near Cedars-Sinai Hospital at three o'clock in the afternoon, and as I recall, we were the only ones there. I got the sense that this was a regular thing that he did, going to a restaurant when nobody else was there. I didn't know what he wanted, but I thought something had gone wrong with the negotiation and he was angry. But instead, the message was, "I love this man. I want you to love this man. I want to make sure that you're someone who is going to love him properly." It was really emotional. Of course I was going to love Sydney. Who wouldn't love Sydney? I remember telling my husband afterwards that Mike Ovitz seemed to love Sydney like a father and a son at the same time. He told me he wanted to be protective of Sydney, which is crazy and beautiful, really. He said, "Look. I have a lot of clients who were raised Jewish. And I have a lot of clients who were raised Catholic. My Jewish clients are all guilty about their success and my Catholic clients are all guilty about their sins." He said, "Sydney's the only client I have who's guilty about the whole thing."

I remember when he was asked to be in the Woody Allen movie *Husbands and Wives*. He went to New York and he read a couple of lines and Woody said, "Fine. That's fine." And Sydney said, "Well,

I have a question about this character." And according to Sydney, it was really clear that Woody Allen did not want to answer any questions. But Sydney persisted, and he said, "Am I scary? Because I don't know whether I'm just funny or whether I'm really scary when I'm yelling at these women." But Woody Allen wouldn't really address it; Sydney said Woody never liked to talk to actors. So if you look at his part in *Husbands and Wives,* you see he's kind of more violent than almost any character in any Woody Allen movie. It's a very scary performance. It's all Sydney, not the way it was directed. He was capable of being very scary, and yet for Mike Ovitz he was this person who needed to be protected. I did have a sense that he couldn't bear it when *Havana* was a failure—that it hurt him almost more than it hurt Sydney. I knew that one of the reasons he wanted Sydney to do *The Firm* so much after *Havana* was because he knew how much it hurt Sydney to have a failure and never wanted that to happen to him again.

DAVID O'CONNOR:

I had gotten to know Bob when I was Ovitz's assistant, and he would give Ovitz fits. But I got a call one day, an interesting man-behind-the-curtain moment for me. Redford had a company called Wildwood and he was going through presidents quickly. They were looking for somebody, and I had suggested a Warner Bros. executive by the name of Bonni Lee. I ended up placing her in that job, and then I would service the company because I was the lit agent on the Redford account. So I get a call from Bonni one day and she said, "Bob's going to call you directly. He's really frustrated with Michael; he doesn't really want to talk to him anymore, but he doesn't want to leave the agency. He wants somebody who's on the ground, who reads and who can advise him because he's at a critical moment in his career. And it's not Sandy." So I said, "Great." Five minutes later, my assistant says, "It's Robert Redford on two." Bob says, "Look, I'm in town. Why don't you come over tomorrow? Let's meet." I said, "Great." And he goes, "But Ovitz can't know that we're having this meeting." I said, "Well, Bob, he writes my checks, so if he asks me where I am at any given point in time, I'm going to tell him where I am. But look, I service the company and I have every reason in the world to be over at Wildwood's offices." So I went over there and we ended up talking for close to four hours. At the end of it he said, "Well, this is great. I want you to be my agent." I said, "Fantastic. How do you want to proceed?" He said, "Let me talk to Mike." I said, "Great."

I got back to the office and about half an hour later was told, "Michael wants to see you in his office." So I walk up to his office and sit down in front of his desk and he leans back and he looks at me and he says, "You know? I think it's time for you to represent a major movie star on your own, and I think I have the perfect opportunity." I said, "Great! Who do you have in mind?" He says, "I think I can convince Redford that you're the guy, that you're right for him, you know, and that you two have the same sensibility. I also think he'd like you personally." I just said, "Okay. Great. I'm happy. Let me know what I need to do." He said, "I'll work on this and I'll get back to you." I never let on what I knew had happened, but *really?* You've got to manipulate me at this moment in time?

SUSAN MILLER:

I had my son Spencer in 1993. Michael came to the hospital and asked me if he could hold him. As soon as his arms were cradling Spencer, he told me, "I would have had six kids if Judy had been willing."

By this time, I had been with Michael for almost ten years, and he came up with a plan so I could continue working for him: He wanted to build me a nursery at CAA. This was going to be the first time an executive would have a baby and bring her baby to work. Michael took one of the offices and had it turned into a nursery, which was a big deal because every new agent wanted an office. I would bring Spencer and my nanny to the office three or four times a week. I would go have lunch with Spencer, and sometimes even bring him up to my office while I was working.

There was a day I can remember very well, when Spencer was

about to leave, but Michael wanted him to stay and motioned me to bring him in his office. He was on the phone, of course, but in his Armani suit, with his headset still on, Michael proceeded to get down on the floor and play with Spencer and make him giggle.

By the time Spencer was three years old, Michael was insisting on having conversations with him, and would often and secretly give him cash. I would be changing Spencer's clothing and find a $100 bill. Only in Hollywood.

JOHN SINGLETON, Director:

I was at USC as a film student and doing an internship at Columbia Pictures with the hopes of directing my first film. That was my goal. A young development executive named Karen Teischer had a friend named Bradford Smith. Smith had gone to Yale Rep and worked on the original Broadway production of *Fences* with Lloyd Richards and August Wilson, and she gave him two of my scripts, one of which was *Boyz N the Hood*, which I had written when I was twenty years old. Brad Smith was just made an agent at CAA, and he said, "I think this is great material and I want to sign you," which was good for me because everyone else had told me that they didn't understand it. Then he said, "You remind me of a young August Wilson," and August Wilson was my literary idol because I had seen *Fences* when I was eighteen years old, and the Broadway production had won the Pulitzer and Tony for best play. Seeing that had spurred me on in film school to write my first screenplay. So that's why I signed with CAA, because they dropped that fact. Brad Smith set up lunch meetings with people; that was the only way I as a starving student could eat every day—I wouldn't have to pay for lunch.

A lot of people, including the executives at Columbia, were afraid to come on the set of *Boyz N the Hood*, down in deep South Central Los Angeles—not with those Mercedeses and Beemers—so because of that, I had a lot of autonomy. The movie was made for less than $6 million and made close to $100 million. CAA looked like geniuses when the movie came out, and I signed a deal with Columbia to do three more movies. Since the agency had such a big scope, I was able to have meetings with people like Tom Cruise and Brad Pitt at the beginning of his career.

I didn't grow up around anything other than blacks and Hispanics, and Hollywood to me was like this crazy, amorphous lily-white beast. To their credit, I didn't feel alienated at CAA. I tried to encourage them to continue to diversify, but they weren't having it until much later. I tried to get them to sign Ice Cube off *Boyz N the Hood.* They didn't sign him. It was par for the course of business. A certain segment of the industry back then thought all pop culture was white. There's a small section of the business that realizes that the world is bigger than that. But all CAA had to do was sign everybody I put in my movies to see the impact I could have.

One time I went to Ovitz's office, and he was there with Magic Johnson. Michael probably thought I knew Magic, just thinking, you know, we're the only two black people in the building at the time.

MAGIC JOHNSON, Athlete:

I was trying to get somebody to take my career off the court and take it to another level. I asked everybody who was the best in the city to do that, and help me go from being a basketball player to a businessman, and who could also redo my basketball contract. Everybody pointed me in the direction of Michael Ovitz. So I called him and asked if he would take a meeting with me, and he said yes. We had our meeting, and it was really interesting, because it wasn't a long meeting at all. He said, "I have all the biggest actors, producers, directors, and writers in the world. Why should I represent you? Most athletes blow all the money they make and go broke. I don't have the patience or the time to represent somebody who won't listen." I said, "I'm different, I've always wanted to be a businessman." He talked for two or three or five minutes, and then he threw me out. So I went into his office six foot nine and walked out about five foot nine. He really bruised my ego.

He called me back a couple of weeks later and said, "I did my homework on you, and I talked to a lot of people; they said you are serious about becoming a businessman." Then he asked me, "Do you read the newspaper every day?" I said, "Yes." He said, "What section do you read first?" I told him the sports section, and he said, "Wrong answer. It's gotta be the business section." He said, "This is what I'm going to do. I'm going to test you to see if you really want to be a businessman, I'm going to give you all of these business journals to read, and after you do, we'll discuss them. Then I'll know whether I want to represent you or not." So he gave me a hard homework assignment, I came back and he asked me questions, and I answered them. After that, he decided to represent me.

We used to meet at Morton's, and before we went there for the first time, he said, "We're not just going to lunch; I want you to watch and see what happens." So they sat us right in the middle of the whole restaurant, and within the first ten or fifteen minutes, everyone there had made their way over to say hello, and everybody wanted to talk about a deal with him. I said, "Man, it's like everybody wanted to come over and kiss the ring." He said, "I always get the middle table so I can see everybody, and everybody can see me." I took that note.

When Michael Ovitz introduced basketball superstar Earvin "Magic" Johnson to top executives at Coca-Cola, it was clear they were eager to sign the star athlete to a lucrative spokesperson deal. But, typically, the ever-demanding Ovitz wasn't satisfied with what was put forward on the bargaining table, and so his next stop was Pepsi, and by the time negotiations there were complete, Ovitz had secured for Johnson a huge deal to become partners with Earl Graves Sr., the founder of Black Enterprise magazine, in the Washington, D.C., area Pepsi bottling plant. The transaction would prove to be the foundation of Magic Johnson's wealth for years— indeed, decades—to come, and to loom as a landmark of promotional wizardry.

MICHAEL OVITZ:

To be a great agent in those days, you had to be a mini-expert on the beginnings of any subject. I had 250 magazine subscriptions.

I was a strong believer in general knowledge. Every time I went to an event, an opening, a dinner, or a meeting, I was given a short briefing card on one of our buck slips by one of my assistants, and it generally had everything I needed to know.

I never thought anything I did was big enough. During those years, I believed any idle moment was a waste of time. It was critical for me that in the course of a day, I got more done than anyone else. From a lifestyle standpoint, I certainly never stopped to smell the roses.

For ten continuous years, at 6 A.M. each day, Michael Ovitz would face the morning with a diurnal, hour-long, rigorous aikido workout. It got his juices flowing, and it reflected his overall interest in—indeed, obsession with—Eastern philosophy. While other martial arts students would do their hour and wander off, Ovitz began to fixate on his swarthy instructor as yet another potential revenue stream. In one of his cheekiest displays of hubris ever, Ovitz decided he would make that instructor a movie star—and so the career of Steven Seagal was launched.

Ovitz brought Seagal over to Warner Bros., where studio bosses Terry Semel and Bob Daley, along with other key executives, obligingly sat in a soundstage and watched Steven Seagal beat the crap out of sundry guest attackers. It was an impressive display of physical skill and brutality—if not of acting prowess, showmanship, or the speaking of dialogue. No matter; those studio chiefs were wowed, and slick-haired Seagal was on his way.

MICHAEL OVITZ:

Every single day, including Saturday and Sunday, Seagal was my aikido guy. While studying with Seagal I ended up making him a movie star; every day to me had to be a growth day.

At the office, I'd make rounds twice a day, every morning and every afternoon, like a doctor making rounds, to see people's faces, to let them know I was there, and to see if there were any long faces and take temperatures. In the summers, I would send the mailroom guys out and they would buy tubs and tubs of Häagen-Dazs ice cream, put them on a cart, put little hats on, and they'd have scoopers, and go office to office giving everybody ice cream—everyone, the whole staff, not just agents.

After the tenth year, my office was averaging anywhere from two hundred to three hundred calls a day. I had one assistant just doing incoming and outgoing calls.

I never felt that we wouldn't make a ton of money. I didn't worry about financial targets. In the early '90s there was probably about $300 million in revenue a year. The only thing I cared about was overhead. I cared that I could pay everybody more than they could earn elsewhere.

PAULA WAGNER:

I was always well paid. It was commensurate.

TONY KRANTZ:

I was aware that we were paid very handsomely and most of our compensation was paid via our bonus at year-end; perhaps it was 80 percent bonus, 20 percent draw over the course of the year. I had no idea how it was really calculated. I was well liked and I was making a lot of money for the company. Among the young guys I was probably among the highest paid at the agency.

JACK RAPKE:

I was very well respected and very well paid.

JOHN PTAK:

I probably tripled my salary from William Morris 1990 to CAA 1994. By 1993 I was already over a million—not well over, right about.

The phenomenon of so many seemingly competitive actors, actresses, and directors wanting to be represented by the same agency may appear at first to be counterintuitive. Being a big fish in a smaller pond may seem by far the more desired route to success. But CAA's dominance in the late '80s and early '90s changed all that, because much of the agency's power flowed from its fortuitous stranglehold on information. It wasn't just that they advised, or literally represented, many a studio executive in his or her own contract negotiations (often without being compensated), who in turn gave them tomorrow's information today. Executives and producers knew that at some point in a project's development they would want a CAA client, or several of them. It was the very definition of a seller's market.

Then there was the fact few did a better job of "covering" the town and its buyers, of knowing what material was out there and what was happening in the marketplace, than CAA agents in the late '80s and early '90s. CAA's advantage with information, and the fact that the partners insisted on teamwork—in departments and across departments—meant that you as a client ultimately benefited from being in that bigger pond. With its agents working together as a team, exchanging information openly and allied collectively on your behalf, you had more access to what was out there and available. Even when desired opportunities were first submitted to another agency, if and when that other client passed on the material, you'd likely have a much better shot at the on-deck position—your team having queued you up for that spot—rather than having to wait around for the material to wend its way to you. And if you lost something to another CAA client, you at least knew you'd been in the running. The worst fate in Hollywood was to be ignored.

SANDY CLIMAN:

With regard to our agency competitors, CAA was in a unique position. The heads of studios, networks, and technology companies wanted to have a direct line to us. I was discussing a deal with the managing partner at another major agency, and I said, "Why don't you call Rupert Murdoch?" He said, "Sandy, you and Mike can call Rupert Murdoch and he will speak to you. Those guys don't speak to us." And that's how it was, we could call anyone anywhere in the world, and our thoughts were valued and our presence was welcomed. We were perceived as the guys who understood the "secret sauce" of creating value from intellectual property—business wise, savvier, and, most important, able to get things done. We had reach to Bill Gates, Steve Jobs,

Larry Ellison, Roberto Goizueta and Don Keough, Phil Knight, foreign media titans, heads of investment banks, and hedge funds. It seemed as if we could walk into any room at any time anywhere in the world.

BRUCE VINOKOUR:

I recall as if it were yesterday being pulled over to the side of the street by a police officer and getting a speeding ticket one morning while on my way to work. Not because I was going to be late for a meeting, but plain and simple, just because I so wanted to get to work. Bill, Ronnie, and Mike created an environment that was so nonjudgmental, so supportive, and so empowering that it always felt special walking into the offices. They never asked you to give up your individuality; in fact they encouraged it in all of us and then gave us enormous responsibility. All they wanted was for you to give 100 percent and come into the building wanting to do great things on behalf of our clients. To this day, it's still a privilege coming to CAA—that's the environment management today continues to nurture—except I drive a bit slower now.

RICK NICITA:

Everything was hyperbolic, all hyped up, more intense than anywhere else. But it was fun, particularly the camaraderie and the feeling of winning. It was easy to keep score, and we were winning. It's fun to win.

SUSAN MILLER:

Herb Allen's girlfriend at the time—this was around 1994—was making him a private surprise birthday video, so Michael asked me what he could do that would make Herb laugh. We decided to put a long blond wig on Michael, chandelier earrings, and red lipstick. We shot the video from the neck up, and it was hilarious to see Michael dressed up as a woman. The only problem was the lipstick had stained his lips for some reason and wouldn't come off. Michael had a full day of meetings ahead of him. He was pissed, but a part of him somehow managed to think it was funny.

RICK NICITA:

Mike was getting what he wanted and I was getting what I wanted. There would be many conversations where there'd be a decision to make and I'd say to the client, "I think we should take this movie for these reasons," and the client would say, "Yeah, that makes sense, but let's talk to Mike, too, just to get his input on it." So I'd say to Mike, "Client's going to call, she wants to talk to you," and he would say, "What's the situation?" and I'd go, "Ba ba bop, just tell her to do this," and he'd say, "Fine." And we'd take the call and Mike would say exactly what I told him to say, and the client would say, "Mike, thank you. That is really helpful. Absolutely. I'm going to take that picture. Great." It was amusing to me. I didn't give a shit. This game was giving me more than I ever dreamt of in every aspect—lots of work, money, and positive emotions. I have zero paranoia. I have an ego, but paranoia is zip to the point where I sometimes wonder how I got so far in this town.

"Game changer" has become so frequent a term that it is now part of daily discourse, but in 1991, the whole country was enthralled by a conflict that changed not only the late-night television game but also its roster of players.

On his 12:30 A.M. Late Night *show, David Letterman brought a new attitude and new audiences to the all-important post-prime-time world of NBC, and although he kept diplomatically mum on the subject, Johnny Carson was known to favor Letterman as his successor at* The Tonight Show. *That would seem to be the ultimate recommendation, yet somehow, NBC executives chose to ignore it, thereby embittering Carson even as his three decades at the network were drawing to an emotional close. Network executives refused to consult him, Carson said privately, or even to casually seek his opinion on the matter, even though he had brought hundreds of millions in revenue to the network, sometimes making—in tandem with* Saturday Night Live—*the late-night period more profitable than either daytime or prime time.*

As stories began to float in trades and tabloids suggesting Jay Leno was the network's prime candidate for Carson's coveted throne, NBC's treatment of Letterman became a subject of his monologue jokes even by other comics, including those who looked upon Letterman as a comedy god. Finally, on June 6, 1991, NBC announced Leno as the new host of The Tonight Show. *The network made it clear to Letterman that he was welcome to stay put at 12:30, but that hardly appeared as a viable option. Fox had let it be known they would love to have him, and over at CBS, new president Howard Stringer was preparing to go a-courting for Letterman, armed with plenty of inducements.*

What would, could, should David Letterman do? He made what he would later say was one of the smartest moves of his life. He asked a friend to pick up the telephone and put in a call to . . . Michael Ovitz.

MICHAEL OVITZ:

The thesis for CAA that we developed was to be able to play roulette with a chip on every number, odd and even, red and black. We did not have anything in late night, so I asked Jay Moloney to snoop around, and he came into my office and said, "Dave has no agent. He's got a manager and he's really flailing." So Dave came into the office, and when he walked into the atrium, he yelled, "Is the godfather here?" People just started cracking up. He came up and I laid out a complete plan for him in great detail of what I wanted to do. He just sat there and couldn't believe all I was saying because no one had ever protected him. My first choice was to get him *The Tonight Show*, which I told him was most likely not doable. But if we couldn't do that, to get him the show on CBS. And to do that, I gave him the whole strategy of bringing multiple buyers into CAA to the conference room to pitch him. And then Peter Lassally said, "There's a slight problem, he has eighteen months left on his NBC contract." I said, "I'll deal with that." So anyone that came in to the meeting at CAA had to sign a document that said that they realized that Dave Letterman was under contract and that whatever offer they were making him started when his contract ended. I knew, though, that Bob Wright, who ran NBC, would never in good conscience make Dave Letterman sit at NBC and not work for eighteen months. Wright was a real decent guy. And that's what happened.

I had CBS come in, who I always knew was my player. I let NBC pitch him for *The Tonight Show* but they didn't do a formal pitch. I just kept talking to them about putting him on instead of Jay. I had Eisner come in for Disney, for a syndication show, and I had Rupert Murdoch come in for Fox.

HOWARD STRINGER, Executive:

I argued against Rupert and Fox on the grounds that "David, you're too good a person to go to Fox." It was slightly mean, but it wasn't mean-spirited. I didn't have much of an upper hand, but I did have the upper hand of explaining the tradition of CBS to Dave, and I knew in my heart that was the way to go. I said, "You'll be in the great tradition of Lucy, Jack Benny, and Ed Sullivan," and Dave had a great appreciation of the golden days of CBS.

MICHAEL OVITZ:

Dave was a very understated midwestern Indiana mild-mannered polite gentleman. His humor may have been acerbic, but he was not that guy. He couldn't believe these guys were coming to see him. I always started every meeting and then left. I wanted plausible deniability; I didn't want anyone thinking that I was doing anyone any favors, and I didn't want to react negatively or positively, or just sit there and be rude. So I always made the introduction, then I walked out. When I left, people were shocked because they knew I was the guy advising Dave, but I had other guys in there like Lee, Sandy, and Jay who were all smart. I think the only meeting I took was Rupert; Rupert actually had the second-best offer and the second-best shot.

HOWARD STRINGER:

It was never clear to me that Ovitz could get Dave out of NBC. I was very skeptical.

LEE GABLER:

Mike worked his magic—he got Bob Wright to agree that David Letterman and his representatives could take David out and solicit offers for a late-night television show. And I said, "Mike, they have right of last refusal." He said, "Don't worry about it." The next thing I know, Bert Fields got involved in the discussion. He came up with a brilliant element: "If you don't put David Letterman on at 11:35, you owe him $100 million." That's how he got out of NBC.

HOWARD STRINGER:

I think I went to Ovitz more than I went to Dave. Dave is a fairly elusive personality, and I didn't have extended conversations with him. I spoke to Ovitz more because he had access to Bob Wright and to everybody.

MICHAEL OVITZ:

I spoke to Stringer multiple times a week, guiding him through the process, because he had two things he had to do: he had to get Dave convinced he could do it, and he had to convince me that he could line up the stations. They didn't have a late-night spot, but that was their dream.

I knew Larry Tisch didn't want to spend anything because he was all about margins. I laid out the budget and showed him what he could make. I said, "Larry, you've got to look at this as a ten-year investment. Dave Letterman's going to last for ten years." Climan had done a historical ratings study from Nielsen of the time slot—what news did, what special events did—and it was a very simple graph: entertainment outperformed Koppel. But ABC was committed to Koppel, and CBS had zero in the time slot. If you put the cost of the show in and then took the amount of minutes you were going to sell, it was a no-brainer. The numbers were staggering. I got Larry to agree in the room because I didn't want to walk out without him agreeing. I said, "Dave's going to want to know, are you with him or not? Because if you're not, he's going to end up doing NBC, and then you're not going to ever have a CBS late-night show," and that was it.

DAVID LETTERMAN:

I was as low in my life as a person can get without the loss of a loved one. Michael came in with his cuff links and his two-million-dollar suits, and he gave me a career. I will never be able to thank him enough for that. It was phenomenal. It was just phenomenal. There will never be another deal like this in television. After the deal was done, he became like our uncle. He would show up and he would take everybody to dinner. One time he was friends with the Nobu people and we had a big catered sushi dinner. There was no reason to question this man's friendship. None. I've never known anybody like him. I guess you don't know anybody like him for the most obvious reason—there is nobody like him.

Overlooked at the time was a clause in Letterman's contract that not only gave Letterman equity in the 12:30 A.M. hour, but also a rich development deal for a half-hour sitcom. Letterman quickly had an idea for a show, one starring a little known stand-up comic known as Ray Romano.

LES MOONVES, Executive:

Everybody Loves Raymond was great for David Letterman and great for us. God bless him, because you want to know the truth? We would not have produced the pilot if it wasn't for David Letterman. Ray Romano was a stand-up comedian in his midthirties. Phil Rosenthal had never really created anything that worked, but we paid a lot of attention to it because it was Dave's project. Thank God we did.

JEFF JACOBS, Agent:

I started in 1988 and got promoted in 1991. The company creates a real platform for you. Those three letters—CAA—come in the door before you go anywhere.

JOHN PTAK:

Nineteen ninety-one was my first trip to Cannes as a CAA agent, and I got involved with *True Romance*. I knew Tony Scott very well and I had tried to sign him while I was at William Morris. CAA represented most of the cast in that movie, from Tony Scott down to Brad Pitt, but at the time, they really did not have any resources when it came to independent films, and the financing and distribution arrangements. I knew the French producer, Samuel Hadida, who let me make the talent deals as well as represent him in making the U.S. distribution deal for over $8 million. That film really helped me establish credibility at CAA, as I actually got the picture made. I would call up and say, "This is how we're going to do it." It was an absolutely wonderful time because they trusted me.

TONY KRANTZ:

Rick Nicita represented David Lynch, and David Lynch was my favorite director in the world. I thought *Blue Velvet* was a masterpiece. I wanted to be involved with David in any way I could, so Rick invited me into David's life, which was tremendously generous on his part.

David had a prior relationship with Mark Frost, having written a movie that didn't go forward called *Goddess,* which was a fictional Marilyn Monroe movie with the producer who did *Coal Miner's Daughter,* Bernie Schwartz. David was very reluctant to do TV, but I ultimately wore him down, and we ended up having a meeting with Brandon Tartikoff about a show he and Mark Frost wanted to do. They pitched a show about secret agents who were fighting off an invasion of spirits on the isle of Lemur that was like Atlantis, one of those magical islands that was supposed to have existed eons ago. The show was called "The Lemurians." Brandon wanted to do it as a movie but David didn't, so the project died and we were back thinking, *What are we going to do? What are we going to do?* David, Mark, and I would have lunch all the time and we'd go to a restaurant called Nibbler's in Beverly Hills, sort of a Hamburger Hamlet kind of place. David loved it. One day I looked around and said,

"This is your world. You should write a TV series about this, just regular people, your people." Then I screened for David and Mark *Peyton Place*. I got the movie and I said this is what we should do—a big soap opera.

They developed a show that was called "Northwest Passage," and David drew a black-and-white map of a town called Twin Peaks and we went into ABC—because I covered ABC—and pitched to Chad Hoffman, who was the head of drama, and Gary Levine, who is the president of Showtime. The script was undeniable and they ordered it into pilot production.

I negotiated an unusual deal where David and Mark owned 100 percent of the show in partnership with a company called Worldvision, Aaron Spelling's distribution company. They got this huge ownership in return for a fixed deficit contribution from Worldvision. I remember when Ted Harbert, at ABC at the time, came over to our agency suite at the Regency Hotel in New York and said, "We're going to pick up *Twin Peaks*, but," and he said very sheepishly, "only for midseason." I was thrilled because we've got David Lynch on TV. Midseason or not, it was a huge victory for something so new and crazy and wonderful.

The show had time to generate buzz and pre-awareness, and in the last half hour—it was a two-hour premiere—it got a 39 share. The difference between ratings and share is that ratings are based on the percentage of total households in America and share is based on the percentage of those households watching television at that moment. So 39 percent of all the televisions that were on in America then were watching the last half hour of *Twin Peaks*. It was huge.

Brandon Tartikoff famously said when he saw *Twin Peaks*, that the tried and true is dead and buried. And *Twin Peaks*, I would argue, was the first show that made quirkiness and oddity acceptable for TV. Before that the gold standard was *Hill Street Blues*, which was a fully realistic drama. *Twin Peaks* had a dwarf dancing backwards and the Log Lady. That didn't exist in TV, and in many ways, had it not been for the seeds of that avant-garde thing born from my days at

Berkeley and promoting the Berkeley Jazz Festival, where we'd sit at the mixing board at the Greek and watch John McLaughlin and Carlos Santana play the same guitar at the same time, I never would have been inspired to do the things that I did at CAA.

BOB BOOKMAN:

The project that was certainly the most fun, and that I'm particularly proud of, was *Silence of the Lambs*. *Manhunter*, which was based on *Red Dragon*, was not successful, and I guess at the time no one thought a movie about a serial killer could be a successful film. So Ned Tanen was again the head of Paramount, and I had heard there was really negative coverage of the book there. I called Ned and said, "I have never asked you to do this, but on good word, I hear there's a very negative synopsis of *Silence of the Lambs*. All I'm asking is for you to give it to a different reader who you like, with a different sensibility, and let me know what they say." He said that was fair; he called me two days later and said, "Okay, I gave it to the other reader and he gave it a definite recommend, but I'm still not buying it."

So my colleague Fred Specktor comes into my office one day and says, "Gene [Hackman] wants to buy *Silence of the Lambs*," and direct it. Then days later, he comes back into my office and says, "You won't believe this, but Gene is pulling out of *Silence of the Lambs*." I said, "Why?" and he says, "His daughter read the book and says, 'Daddy, you're not making this movie.' " So he's pulled out.

We then got it to Jonathan Demme, and then he cast it as brilliantly as he did. I was actually in the movie, as was Rick Nicita. It's the scene when Dr. Lecter arrives at Memphis Airport in a gurney. The limo pulls up, and Diane Baker is playing the senator, and Ron Vawter plays the Justice Department official with two aides: Rick Nicita and Bob Bookman.

WHOOPI GOLDBERG:

Ron was always honest and never gave up fighting for me, which are just two of the reasons why I love him so much to this day. A friend of mine came over and said, "Do you know about this great role? Every black woman has been auditioning for this thing!" So I called Ronnie and asked, "Do you know about this?" He said, "Yeah, they don't want you." I said, "Why not? What did I do?" Ronnie said, "You didn't do anything. They think you're too well known and that would result in taking people out of the movie." Well, that was the first time I had heard that one. I said, "What about Marlon Brando? He's always Marlon Brando," but he said, "I've used all the arguments. They just don't want you to do it." He could tell I was upset, but I went down to Alabama to make *Long Walk Home,* and two weeks later, I got a call from Ronnie and he said, "You remember that movie they didn't want you for? Well, apparently they hired Patrick Swayze for it, and he said he didn't understand why you weren't there. He thought you would be great for it, and I think he doesn't want to do it unless you do it." My mouth was hanging off the floor. I couldn't believe Patrick wanted me to audition with him, and Ronnie said, "You'll read with him, and then we will figure it all out." I got the part [in *Ghost*], and of course Ronnie had his fingers in there, and had been pushing and instrumental in setting all of it up all along.

RIDLEY SCOTT, Director:

Callie Khouri had written *Thelma and Louise* on spec, and no one picked it up except us. I thought it was great immediately, but because I'm a guy, I don't think they really believed me, that I really got it. We went out to various directors, one of which was my brother, and various other people who for the most part, turned us down on the basis that they had a problem with the women. I said, "That's the whole point. The women do have a voice, and if you have a problem with that, then you shouldn't do the film."

I met with Meryl Streep—the only time in my life—who is wonderful. Then there was Michelle Pfeiffer, who is great. She said, "Listen, I'm having the meeting, but I can't do the film. It's in the wrong time slot, but why don't you come to your senses and you direct the movie?" I went, "Hmm. I had never thought about that." From that moment on, I started thinking about the possibility that I would direct the film. I thought that was quite smart of her, really, because that film could have easily been fucked up.

I'm very difficult to agent for, right? Because my material tends to have no plan. People say, "What's your plan?" I say, "There is no plan." I'm completely random and move from pillar to post a bit like a child in a playpen. There was no real plan for me to do *Thelma*, but it suddenly whetted my appetite and I said to Ronnie, "You know what? I'm going to do it." He didn't say, "Let me know when you come to your senses." Instead he said, "You haven't done that kind of thing before, and you know what? That's the very reason why you have to do it."

GOLDIE HAWN:

That was a movie that I really, really wanted to do. Ron was my agent and set up a meeting for me with Ridley, and I thought it went great.

RIDLEY SCOTT:

Goldie Hawn bought me breakfast, and she was hysterically funny. She made it clear how much she wanted the part.

RON MEYER:

I love Goldie. Through the years, I never had a problem telling actors that they didn't get a certain part, but in the case of *Thelma and Louise*, it was different. She had several meetings with Ridley, and she believed the part was hers, but Ridley told me, "I don't think she's for me," but because I didn't want to hurt her feelings, I ate it: I told her that I didn't think the movie was right for her and talked her out of it. When the movie came out and was a hit, she told me she regretted not doing it, but she didn't dwell on it, and it never affected our relationship.

RIDLEY SCOTT:

Geena Davis had gotten ahold of the script and I met her for tea at the Four Seasons where she made her case. She just had made herself a star by doing a film called *The Accidental Tourist*, and I was impressed by her intelligence and view of the character. Above all, I knew she could be pretty amusing.

GOLDIE HAWN:

I always believe that the part goes to the right person and have never measured my success by what I got and what I didn't. You can't tell someone they have to use you. Ronnie and I both knew this. Oftentimes in the industry, you're looked at as a product. You're looked at as a commodity. I was happy to be a commodity, it wasn't that. I never felt slighted in any way. But when your representatives look at you as a commodity, that becomes a whole different thing. It's all about what you make for the agency. I never felt that with Ron. All actors go through transition periods, and I was going through a transition period. I was getting older and looking at where I was going. I was very systematic. I also am a good businesswoman and I look at myself honestly. I know that women have, oftentimes, a bit of a shelf life. You have to look at your talent, your career, and where you want to go so we sat in a room with Ronnie and several other people, brainstormed this and thought of other ways and other avenues.

RON MEYER:

A few years later, I was able to make a multipicture deal for Goldie at Disney. It was spectacular for her financially and I was really glad it worked out.

GOLDIE HAWN:

That deal Ronnie put together for me was the deal to break all deals. It was unbelievably sustaining, like new blood. It gave me an ability to move forward, to parlay, to create projects that I wasn't even involved in, and I wound up producing movies that starred Julia Roberts and Steve Martin. I don't know another deal that's ever been made like that. It wasn't even an exclusive deal. So even though I was based at Disney, I was doing movies for Universal and Hollywood Pictures. The deal was so good that even *I* felt guilty that Disney was paying me when we hadn't made a movie together.

In the early days of the nascent "New Media" business, the challenge at CAA was to get agents and clients to understand what was looming on the horizon. Technology was out of their day-to-day comfort zone, so "New Media" czar Dan Adler and his team educated them on important changes taking place in the entertainment industry and on the roles the creative community could play in this emerging world. As a result, "new media" became an agenda item at CAA's monthly meetings and even its annual retreats.

Gaming was of particular interest to the agency. New generations of consoles were moving from 16-bit platforms to 32- and 64-bit models. Sega CD was gaining traction, and the Philips CD-i was making inroads. Moore's Law produced new technology platforms at an incredible rate, while developers introduced increasingly ambitious visuals. Electronic Arts was frequently launching sports gaming franchises, even as Virgin Interactive and other companies were busily reimagining what the platforms could do. At the same time, Apple, Intel, Microsoft, Oracle, and others were making large investments into R and D and their own product launches.

CAA believed the key to success for widespread adoption was developing content that would engage consumers, creating stories that would pull in an audience. At the beginning, that meant "interactive gameplay," but too often that resulted in linear stories simply being chopped up. A new level of narrative was reached when wholly original gaming creations made their way to market, with arguably the first real breakthrough being MYST and the world that two brothers from Spokane, Washington—Rand and Robyn Miller—created, producing a game that would end up selling northward of ten million copies.

The gold rush was on, and CAA, along with much of Hollywood, was determined to cash in.

DAN ADLER:

We launched our New Media practice in 1991. At the time, the games business was in its nascent days, with Nintendo moving up to its 16-bit game system and the Sega CD just on the horizon.

Michael—an audiophile at heart—saw great promise in the value of technology and innovation, so Phil Kent and I decided to write a "white paper" that laid out a vision for how the new media world might affect—and be influenced by—the traditional Hollywood media. Michael understood the pitch, and since my day-to-day responsibilities provided me more freedom than Phil's, Michael told me to run with it. This was really Michael's baby; Ron and Bill were usually not involved. Michael really wanted this. It was a new avenue for him to explore opportunities in tech and establish relationships outside Hollywood. And that is just what we did, with a whole new set of buyers to cover and companies to follow—from the growing influence of the hardware and software companies to the burgeoning world of the gaming platforms and developers. It also opened up a whole new topic of dialogue for agents to have with their clients, about something beyond their day-to-day business, which was always a good thing.

One other great launching pad for us came through a relationship we were able to strike with the MIT Media Lab and its founder, Nicholas Negroponte. In one of those great stories of the value of relationships and the reach of CAA, I was able to meet Negroponte through an introduction made by the Peis—Sandi put me together with Nicholas, as it was I. M. who had designed the original media lab building on the MIT campus. Nicholas welcomed us with open arms to the lab, introducing us to many of the key visionaries there. It opened a series of relationships that still bear fruit, and it allowed us to bring some incredible Hollywood talent through the halls of the lab.

I remember doing this presentation in front of agents, repeatedly, and in front of all sorts of clients. I also remember doing it one weekend for the DGA, at their offices, at the invitation of the late Gil Gates, who then was running the guild. It was incredible to see the reaction in that room, as a bunch of DGA members started understanding and appreciating what was happening in this emerging medium.

What became clear from the start, though, was that there was inherent tension and skepticism between the north—Silicon Valley, San Francisco, and Seattle/Redmond—and the south—L.A. and Hollywood. Hollywood at the time didn't have much respect for the brilliance and reach of what was happening up north, and the tech community didn't hold Hollywood in high regard. One effective tool we'd use to wake up the Hollywood people was to show the size of the video-game business—in raw dollars—as compared to the size of the motion picture theatrical business. When Hollywood folks realized how comparable those numbers were—and when we'd show demos of how *Pong* had spawned the early versions of emerging motion-capture technology and photo-realistic games—they started to pay attention. Nevertheless, there was clear value to be built by collaborating with each other, and so we met with many interesting companies—Microsoft, Apple, Intel, Electronic Arts, Nintendo, Virgin Interactive, and Sega, among others. If Michael was going to be in a meeting, that almost always meant we would be meeting with the company's CEO. We met with Andy Grove. Discussions between Larry Ellison and Michael benefited greatly because of their shared values and interests in Eastern philosophies.

I remember meeting with Steve Jobs in the Pei building, when concerns over his being seen there meant that we held the meeting in one of the more unimpressive conference rooms with no windows. And of course we went up to Apple headquarters in Cupertino several times.

Once, when we flew private up to Microsoft headquarters in Redmond, Washington, for a day of meetings, we kicked it off with a dinner in a downtown high-rise, and as we were rushing into the elevator to be on time for our dinner with their executive team, we rode the elevator and watched as Bill Gates was trying to fasten the collar buttons on his shirt.

PHIL KENT:

This is an interesting story and gives you interesting insights into all three of the partners. At the end of 1990, I told Lee I was unhappy and wasn't sure I wanted to keep doing this, and he said, "I think you're just burnt out on this first run syndication area, so I'm going to move some people around, put you under Bruce Vinokour, and you can start being involved with NBC." It turned out to be a huge mistake because I didn't click at all with the scripted series business. So then he asked me to go see a therapist, because Lee thought I had bigger issues than not wanting to be an agent. I agreed, and we didn't tell anyone else about our arrangement. So I saw this therapist for six months, and he said to me, "You know, I'm not saying you're altogether normal; you have some issues, but so does everyone else. There's nothing inherently wrong with you—you just don't like your job. You like to be more in control of your life and the very nature of being an agent is you're always in between the buyer and the seller. At any moment, somebody could completely ruin your week." Then he said, "You can keep seeing me or I can call your bosses and tell them you're like a square peg in a round hole and you shouldn't be an agent." It was the time of year when we all got our bonuses, so I waited until I got my bonus, and when Michael gave me my check, I told him I was unhappy, and he said, "Well, go talk to Lee. I want you to be happy." And I said, *Oh, fuck. I really opened it up now. Michael thinks I was unhappy about my bonus; Lee's going to be furious with me that I told Michael that.* So all afternoon Lee's trying to find me and my young assistant is looking for me all over town. I told him, "Just tell him you can't find me." At the end of day, I finally went back into the office, and I'm thinking, *I'm going to get killed now.* I went in to see Lee, and he takes off his glasses and looks at me. "Let me get this straight," he says. "We're in the middle of a national recession. You're making this nice six-figure salary, and you're upset because you're getting a $375,000 bonus, instead of a $400,000 bonus? Are you fucking kidding me?" And I said, "No, no, you're right. Honestly, I think I'm just not happy. The shrink didn't help at all; in fact, the shrink offered to call you to tell you that I just am not cut out for this."

Lee went and told Michael what was going on, and Michael was furious he hadn't told him before then. Bill Haber thought I was just having an existential crisis and offered to personally pay for an around-the-world trip for me to go and take a little time off. I said, "Bill, that's really sweet of you, but all I'm going to be doing is counting the days before I have to come back and then I'll feel obligated to pay you back." Michael said to me, "You're making a horrible move." He told Dan Adler, "Call your friend and tell him he's being an idiot. Tell him he's shooting himself in the kneecap. Tell him to get his head out of his ass." And then I went to see Ron, and it was so typical of him. He calmly said to me, "You know, there are nights on my way home that I want to drive my Ferrari into the Pacific Ocean, but I don't. It's a tough job. It's not for everybody. The great thing about America is you can do whatever you want to do as long as you are willing to accept the consequences. You don't want to be an agent anymore? Don't be an agent anymore. Go with God." They were all so different in their reactions. When I finally made my decision to go, Michael couldn't accept that I just wanted to leave without having anything lined up. So I mentioned to him, "Maybe I'll look into Harvard Business School." He says, "Great. We'll write that you're leaving to go to Harvard Business School." I said, "Michael, I haven't even applied. You can't say that." He says, "Okay, okay. You're right." Next thing you know, a companywide memo comes out that says, *Phil is leaving the agency to pursue a graduate degree in business.* He didn't mention Harvard in the memo, but for years, people asked me how business school was.

Not since Jaws *or* The Godfather *had there been a movie that screamed sequel so fast as* Ghostbusters, *but for several years after its release, despite it being high on the CAA to-do list, it seemed like an impossibility, which made it even more frustrating for Ovitz, particularly since it involved Ivan Reitman and Bill Murray, two clients he was particularly close to.*

The first big obstacle actually involved Murray and Ovitz himself. Columbia chief David Puttnam had gone so far as to publicly take on Murray and what he saw as a corrupt star system. Ovitz took great umbrage, and the chances for a

Ghostbusters *sequel were a casualty. But the other speed bump was the original group had splintered. There were some hard feelings left in the wake of the original's success. The goddess of triumph had been kinder to some (Bill Murray) than to others (even Aykroyd and Harold Ramis weren't at Murray's level).*

Ghostbusters *had obviously looked like a huge fat hit going in. For once, the dish proved as delicious as it had looked on paper. But in the afterglow, once the last celebration was over, the division of profits among the stars, director, and producers turned out to be extremely unequal, as were the shrieks of pain from Harold Ramis, who as cowriter contributed largely to the film's success (he was also in the cast) but who likely got the lowest payout afterwards.*

Ramis, who once said that the seven months he spent working in an insane asylum helped prepare him for dealing with the movers and shakers of Hollywood, had felt his share of the spoils on the original qualified as lunatic, and was not shy about letting his opinion be known.

Finally, Ovitz was able to orchestrate a sitdown at Jimmy's in Century City with the film's stars, joined by Kurtzman and Climan. At the lunch, Ghostbusters 2 *was referred to affectionately as "economic entropy—money in the atmosphere just waiting to be harvested." The group worked out a new split and was promised an unprecedented economic deal with Columbia.*

Ovitz asked Climan to "model" the movie as the studios had long done, though it was something then rare at the agency level. Financial performance was predicted based upon historic data that linked box office to earnings in home video, pay television, and dear old you-remember-that television.

Climan had studied the studio formulas and developed CAA's own set of equations, giving the agency another edge over its rivals that had not yet developed quantitative financial tools. As it turned out, Climan's model did not differ all that much from Columbia's, and the agency and the studio basically combined their models to come up with the gross percentage.

That backstage story would prove to be one of Ray Kurtzman's finest hours in terms of actual deal making, handing over to those jolly CAA clients a luscious 35 percent of the gross. Plenty of Kissingeresque shuttle diplomacy went into keeping everybody happy; even Bernie Brillstein, manager of the principals, ended up with a prime choice cut.

As an aside, a young Jason Reitman (son of Ivan) was cast in the film as

"Brownstone Boy #2," and Judy Ovitz wound up in the credits as "Slimed Restaurant Patron."

DAVID LETTERMAN:

Michael always had a tiny little spiral notebook with him, and you had to be careful because you would be joking about something, and then Michael would take it out and write it down. You would think, *Oh geez, oh my God.* I remember one time Michael said to me, "Did you get the fruit basket?" And I said, "No," and he said, "Wait a minute, you didn't get the fruit basket?" I said, "I don't think so, Michael." And he takes out his notebook and he writes something down. I said, "Wait a minute, Michael. What did you write down?" He said, "I'm getting rid of the person in charge of gifts." I said, "No no! I got the fruit basket! Don't fire anybody!"

DAVID LONNER, Agent:

I started in 1992 and left in 1996. When I joined CAA, the people who were really on the front line seducing me to go over there were Jay Moloney, who I was friendly with, and Lovett, who I wasn't friendly with but who I was impressed with at the time. When I arrived in the mailroom at William Morris in the fall of 1984, the golden boy trainee about to be promoted to agent was Bryan Lourd. All of us in the mailroom looked up to him and wanted to curry favor with him. The Young Turks were a very seductive bunch, and they seduced me to come over, and coming over from ICM, which was much more of a place where you work with yourself, it seemed like this group of guys were good to join up with. I did bring over certain clients, but they weren't who they are now. For instance, J. J. Abrams was not who he is now. Alexander Payne wasn't who he is now. When I got there, I realized I wasn't going to be part of their clique. And then in year three, Endeavor got formed, and I instinctually felt like I really wanted to go. I was thirty-four years old at the time, I was feeling the entrepreneurial spirit. Ray Kurtzman, my late father-in-law, was upset with the notion of me going to Endeavor because some of the agents that formed Endeavor had left CAA years earlier to form InterTalent, which had been the first time agents left CAA to not only join a competitor, but to form a competitor. I delayed my decision for a year, but I couldn't help feeling that I wanted to do my own thing. I liked the people there a lot, but I didn't feel like my career was on the ascent there the way it was at ICM. I grew up in a culture of individuality, coming from ICM, and then when I got to CAA, doing everything in groups, it wasn't that I wasn't able to do it, it was just that my style had already been forged. I always represented artists from the ground up, so how great would it be to start a company from the ground up?

There were a lot of very talented people there. I think the Young Turks just dominated that generational space. By the time I got there, it was really already their company.

In an unprecedented move, Coca-Cola Company hired CAA in 1992 to advise the corporation on everything from advertising strategy to talent tie-ins.

PETER SEALEY, Executive:

I was a senior officer at Coca-Cola and was on a task force to help the Coca-Cola Company diversify. The company wanted to signal to Wall Street that it was a different Coca-Cola Company. I was one of six internal employees looking at what we could do, and the only two areas that came out that were candidates for acquisition were ethical pharmaceuticals and entertainment. All other industries, all other segments, would dilute the earnings of the Coca-Cola Company. I was interested in the entertainment option.

I was one of two employees sent over to Columbia Pictures to help them integrate into Coca-Cola via the acquisition of Columbia Pictures by Coca-Cola in 1983. I was president of marketing and distribution for North America for Columbia Pictures, and was president of Coca-Cola telecommunications. When we were doing the movie *Ishtar*, God help me, Warren Beatty was going crazy and I had to go to Michael and have him help me with him. Then Elaine May had the inner positive—the film that you were going to actually make the movie out of; you made the negative out of the inner positive—in the trunk of her car driving around Connecticut. If that car burned, we had no movie, it was gone. And Michael helped bring her back under control so we could release *Ishtar*—a truly terrible movie, but that's another story.

In 1988, the Coca-Cola Company decided it couldn't stay in the entertainment business, so they sold Columbia Pictures to Sony. I didn't have a job at that point because they didn't really have anything for me to do back in Atlanta, so I got my Ph.D. under a man named Peter Drucker at the Claremont Graduate University. I did my doctoral work on information technology. Then, on Thanksgiving 1990, Don Keough, president of the Coca-Cola Company, called and said, "Peter, I want you to come back to Atlanta and be head of global marketing for the Coca-Cola Company." He said, "The only burr under my saddle"—exact quote—"has been the fact that Pepsi Cola has been generally acknowledged to have better advertising than the Coca-Cola Company has. I want to correct that before I retire, and I'm retiring in less than three years. So I want you to come back and straighten this out before I retire." I said, "Don, I can do that, but I can't do it with McCann Erickson and a traditional advertising agency. It won't work. It is a factory that churns out thirty-second commercials. I worked with them for five years and I can turn this around, but I can't do it that way." "So how are you going to do it?" he asked. "Well, I'll come back to you with a plan." I saw how the creative process works in the motion picture industry, where the studio was essentially a banker, and the producer and director of the film were the creative forces, so I said to myself, *Why can't I do that in advertising? All I'm doing is producing little thirty-second movies. What if I took that business concept—the producer and director are the geniuses behind superb creative product—and gave them the assignment of creating those commercials, not for a movie, but for the Coca-Cola brand?*

With Don's permission I went to Michael Ovitz, because at that time he was unbelievably powerful in Hollywood.

DAVID STYNE:

When I was on Mike's desk, he brokered the deal with Coca-Cola. I remember Peter Sealey and the executives from Coca-Cola coming up to the third-floor conference room for a dinner and a whole presentation on how the Pepsi Generation campaign had eaten into Coca-Cola's domestic market share. Michael got up and it was just amazing. He knew specifically, innately, exactly what to do, where to target, and what they'd be looking for. I remember being so impressed by his foresight, and his ability to know exactly what these people wanted to hear.

LARRY LYTTLE:

There was an article about Larry Bird years ago, and, the tease was something like, "He's white, he's not fast, and he's not great on defense, so why is he the best player in the NBA?" And the answer was he had this intuitive sense where he saw the play milliseconds before anyone else saw it develop. In the late '80s and early '90s, CAA saw the court that way.

PETER SEALEY:

I told Mike, "I want you to hire a creative director, and I'd like you to produce this campaign for the brand Coca-Cola. It's got to work in every country in the world, and I want that creative director to go out into the film and entertainment community and induce directors to make a commercial for Coca-Cola. A commercial was fun; you could get it done in three weeks' time, it wasn't a movie taking a year and a half, two years. And tell them that for the commercial that gets the most airtime around the world, I will give that director and producer a million dollars."

So Michael hired a brilliant woman named Shelly Hochron to be his creative director and we went out to change the advertising business.

RON MEYER:

Although it made a big difference financially, I was probably more against outside corporate deals than in favor of them. I felt our obligation was to focus on our clients, and not on outside businesses. I was also against getting into the sports business back then because I thought that would take us too far away from our core businesses. In retrospect, I was shortsighted. Agencies today have proven they can take care of their basic businesses and expand without damaging their clients.

SHELLY HOCHRON, Executive:

I was a senior vice president of production at TriStar after working with Peter Sealey at Columbia. I opened up *Variety* one day and saw that Michael had made an agreement with Coca-Cola, and for whatever reason, I picked up the phone and called him. We had met several times through the years while I was in previous jobs. I said, "I just wanted to congratulate you. I know these guys at Coke—they're an interesting group—and I wish you luck with it." Really, there was no agenda other than that. And right then he said to me, "Thank you for calling. Are you happy?"

I wasn't thrilled with what I was doing at TriStar, so I said, "I could be happier." And he said, "Let's talk." So I went to see him and he said, "What would it take for you to come here and help me with this?" And I said, "Well, what are you doing?" Quite frankly he didn't know exactly what he was doing at that time, but many regarded him as the most powerful man in Hollywood and he was interested in what I had to say. He made me feel very special— something he was really good at—so I agreed to take a chance and go work for him at CAA.

LEN FINK:

I was at that point a creative director for Chiat\Day in New York, and we were the agency of the decade. So I had some visibility and a headhunter put me together with Michael Ovitz and I just got along beautifully with him. He had already hired Shelly

Hochron and basically he wanted to put together a group to take a look at Coca-Cola's advertising through CAA's resources. Even though I went to art and film school, I had a tech background and had been working with the Internet, believe it or not, since 1974, so I was extremely computer literate and had some thoughts about what the future of communications was going to be with respect to entertainment, news, and advertising, marketing, and branding. I moved my family to L.A. from New York.

RON MEYER:

Mike will tell you there was a master plan behind the Coke deal, but if there was, I certainly didn't know about it, and to be honest, I really didn't have that much involvement. It was definitely a way to make more money—which we did.

SHELLY HOCHRON:

I felt like a CAA employee. I reported to Michael, I had health benefits, they picked up my life insurance, and I had a car allowance. I was invited to his Rockingham house and always felt like a favored child. If I mentioned to him that I was taking someone out to dinner, I would go there and the dinner would be paid for and there would be a bottle of wine courtesy of Michael. I got flowers from him. I got cards and letters from him. I felt appreciated and I felt respected. And I felt like he knew that I did something that he couldn't do. That was very unusual among the CAA players. Michael said, "I guarantee whatever you're getting at TriStar and then some." When bonus time came around, I was given an envelope, opened it up, and I said, "Huh! That is not what I expected." So I went to Michael and I said, "This in fact turns out to be less than what I was making at TriStar." He was flabbergasted. He said, "Oh my goodness." He took it, ripped it up, told me to go down and talk to Bob Goldman and "Just tell him what you want." I don't really know why he was flabbergasted. I had already told him what I was making, but maybe he didn't understand. I wasn't ravenous. I wanted to be respectful and reasonable.

MICHAEL OVITZ:

Shelly was expensive, I paid her over $2 million, and Len had a good salary as well. I committed to serious overhead, I pulled a guy out of our training department to make him a full-time staff assistant to this group, then I put office space aside. It was all risk. I didn't have a deal, but I knew we'd get it back.

SHELLY HOCHRON:

McCann Erickson was proposing the next campaign round for Coke under the auspices that we were going to consult. I could tell after years of doing this that they were holding back, and even what they were doing was misdirected. I came back to California and went to see Michael and Bill Haber privately and said, "This is ridiculous. This is not going to work under the current guide-lines. They don't want to play with us; they don't feel they have to play with us; I don't want to play with them." Michael said, "Put in writing how you think this should work," so I did. It was hand-written because I was so paranoid about it being distributed, and essentially said, "If you want to make a meaningful contribution and change the way things are done, we need to take over and we have to develop and produce our own material." Michael and Bill said, "Okay, let's do it that way."

Essentially Coke gave Michael a blank check. In the first round, we did thirty-one or thirty-two commercials for Coke. Maybe five or six were done by CAA clients and they were paid enormously well for that—people like Martin Scorsese and Rob Reiner.

LEN FINK:

I had this idea of shooting something in a Coca-Cola bar in a parking garage in Paris. We were a day before we were supposed to shoot in Paris and there was some strike going on and they were giving us a really hard time to get our permits. So I call Ovitz up and said, "I hate to bother you with stuff like this, but I don't have my permits." He said, "I'll call you back in twenty minutes." Next thing I know, I get a phone call from Jacques Chirac's office, and several other people telling me not to worry and they apologize for not having permits for me. That is how much power Michael had in those days. All of a sudden, several VIPs even showed up at the shoot.

SHELLY HOCHRON:

Meanwhile, the whole time we were doing all of this, I was keenly aware that Michael had not negotiated his fee or CAA's fee with Coke.

LEN FINK:

I felt very strongly that we should bring the bottle back, which Coke in the beginning thought was going to make them look old-fashioned, but what I said was: it's easier to be what you are than what you're not, and that we needed to take their iconography and contemporize it and make it meaningful again. Shelly and I were constantly discussing ice cold Coca-Cola and the bottle. We thought, *What are the images for ice?* and we came up with this sort of mass of things, one of which was a polar bear—actually a bear with glasses on.

SHELLY HOCHRON:

I was at home, lying on my bed, looking through *Communication Arts* magazine, and there was a picture of polar bears wearing bow ties. And I looked at it and I thought, *Wow.* I was married at the time to someone who had worked for me through the years in Hollywood, and I wanted to involve him in what I was doing at CAA. So I walked into the living room, handed him the picture and said, "Turn this picture into a theater experience for these polar bears where they're drinking Coca-Cola."

LEN FINK:

We showed it to Michael, and Bill Haber was very much involved. There was going to be a head-to-head battle with McCann

Erickson. We were called to Atlanta for a meeting that had all of the top Coke people in it, and we actually sat in the same room with McCann Erickson while they were there presenting their thoughts on the new campaign. It was me, Shelly, Michael Ovitz, and Bill Haber; McCann brought more than a dozen people.

Ovitz went wild. He went nuts. He just went crazy. He thought we had done such a good job.

PETER SEALEY:

Kenny Stewart, the creative director who did the polar bear commercial, got the million dollars. In fact, he was Shelly Hochron's husband. And I asked him, "Ken, how did you come up with this idea?" He said, "Peter, I wanted to visualize the coldest thing I could visualize for Coca-Cola, and that would be the northern lights in the Arctic Circle. And I said, okay, I'm going to have polar bears watching the Arctic lights and drinking Coca-Cola." And that was the genesis of that commercial, which is just whimsical and beautiful.

In February of 1993, we released the campaign at the Museum of Radio and Television before three hundred people. The thirteenth commercial in, out of twenty-six, was the polar bear commercial. At that moment, the audience changed. It had such an immediate impact. They ceased being objective journalists and became cheerleaders for this campaign. It was amazing. You could literally feel it in the room.

LEN FINK:

At the very end of that meeting, Doug Ivester, a Coca-Cola executive, looked at us and said, "When can you start doing this?" With McCann in the room! I mean it was just so awkward.

PETER SEALEY:

We were going to release it in the fall of '93, but the reaction was so positive we rushed it into production. The campaign was just successful beyond belief.

SHELLY HOCHRON:

I guess you could say to a large extent it came from me so I was emotionally invested in it. When the polar bears became a hit, we got no high fives from McCann. They were humiliated. We had stolen the account from them after their holding ownership for forty years.

LEN FINK:

And the second year, Coca-Cola's polar bears in the United States alone made $42 million in plush toys and pencils, and they sold frames to the polar bear commercials. We didn't get any of that money because it was work for hire.

PETER SEALEY:

In the beginning, Michael said, "Peter, I'm going to do all of this at my cost. We'll decide my profit later." I should have peeked at that. I should have gone, "No, wait a minute," but I said okay. So the campaign goes up and I can't tell you how successful it was. So now I've got to decide how much to pay Michael.

I went through a lot of machinations and I decided to pay him $10 million. I went to my financial guy and said, "Don, I want to pay Michael $10 million. It's a lot of money, but he's worth it. It's a spectacular effort." So I had my accounting people issue a check for $10 million, payable to Michael Ovitz, and I had them put it in the hands of a little toy polar bear and walked it over to CAA. Three days later, I get an envelope from Michael with the same check and a little Post-it note on it. The check is voided and the Post-it says, "Pete. Let's discuss this." He returned the check! And I said to myself, *Oh, Christ. Here we go.* When I brought my accounting guy the check back, he almost fainted.

So Michael says, "Peter, I want to talk to Don about this. It doesn't feel right to me." So Michael went up one step to Don Keough, chief operating officer, and a final step to Roberto [Goizueta], the chief executive officer.

MICHAEL OVITZ:

I don't remember the number for Coke. Honest to God I don't.

SHELLY HOCHRON:

Michael never asked me what CAA deserved for the Coke campaign. I heard he turned away ten. Twelve? That would be high.

PETER SEALEY:

Thirty-one. Thirty-one million. In retrospect, it was worth it. But it was classic Michael Ovitz. You've got to admire the guy.

PAULA WAGNER:

I left CAA in August '92. As an agent you aren't a principal. You're the representative of the principal, and I had decided I wanted to be a principal. I wanted to make movies and start a company. I had been an agent since May 1, 1978, and I loved being an agent, and I was one of a team of people that basically helped create the identity for Creative Artists Agency and made it the premier entertainment company. But on a deeper level, I needed to have something that was mine. I wanted to make my own mark.

MICHAEL OVITZ:

Paula was an actress turned agent at a tiny agency handling few clients with little experience. When Ron and I met her, we knew she could be something special. We hired her and fed her clients to get her started, and she became phenomenally successful.

RICK NICITA:

She left in her prime and they were shocked. It was like, *What?*

PAULA WAGNER:

It felt like I was leaving my family. These were my brothers and sisters.

I had a couple of clients who said they were very unhappy, and one client asked if I would be their producing partner. Tom had always wanted to make movies, so it made a lot of sense because he always had a sense of the bigger picture. And Mike thought that was a good idea.

RON MEYER:

Paula was a great agent, and when she decided to leave to be Tom's partner, we totally understood. No one there was indispensable. You don't ever want to lose good agents, but I immediately took over Tom as well as several of her other clients.

TOM CRUISE:

For a long time people wanted me to produce or direct projects, but I didn't want to do it until I felt ready. When Paula left and we started producing together, I was very excited. And I knew that at CAA, Rick was still there, as were Ronnie and Mike, so I was not hesitant at all.

JOEL SILVER:

We were making *Demolition Man* in '93, and Warner Bros. made a promotional partnership deal with General Motors. There was a guy named Phil Guarascio who was head of GM's brand recognition, I think they called his division Consumer Awareness, and he had a budget of around $100 million a year. He used to give a big check to Ken Burns every few years to fund those great documentaries. One day he said to me, "You know what? We need help with our Oldsmobile brand." In the movie, Sly's character was supposed to drive a cherried-out 1970s Pontiac GTO. He said to me, "We want you to use an Oldsmobile in that scene." So they actually made us, at the GM factory in fucking Michigan, a brand-new 1970 Oldsmobile 442 for the movie. They said, "We need Oldsmobile to be the signature vehicle for that film."

One day this guy named John Rock called me up, he was the actual brand manager for Oldsmobile, and said, "I'm reading about this place CAA. I haven't told anybody yet, but I feel like I can discuss this with you. After like seventy years with Leo Burnett, we're thinking about making a change, and I've heard a lot about what CAA has done with Coca-Cola and maybe they would be a good place for us. Can you see if they would be interested in talking to us?" So I called Ronnie and he says, "I would tell the guy no." And I couldn't believe it. I said, "But it's Oldsmobile! He wants CAA! How can that not be great?" Ronnie said, "I promise you, you'll never get what you want out of this."

So I called Ovitz and told him about it anyway, and he says to me, "I will only do it if I get *all* the GM brands." I said, "Mike. Think about this. This is Oldsmobile. Do well for them, then maybe you'll get Chevrolet or Cadillac," but he told me, "I'm not going to do it for one car. I want all the cars." So I called Ronnie and I said, "How did you know?" And he says, "Because I know him. I live here." Come on, think of it: He wouldn't have the fucking meeting with Oldsmobile unless he got all the GM brands. If they had announced that CAA was going to be the new advertising agency for Oldsmobile, it would have changed the fucking world at that time. He didn't even want to take the meeting.

In the course of redefining the job of agent, Michael Ovitz became a living directory of the most knowledgeable, celebrated professionals available—physicians of all kinds chief among them. Ovitz knew the best doctors to consult and the best hospitals to be treated at, all part of his service to his clients. If a client's son or daughter had an automobile accident, Ovitz could refer the client to the right doctor, the right hospital, and if need be, the right lawyer. He could also recommend the "right" educational institution, be it college or private school. If a studio was hiring an executive and needed to get the executive's kid into a private school, Ovitz knew the heads of each and what buttons to push for admission. All these talents made Ovitz indispensable as an agent, and his expertise was genuinely client-serving, not self-aggrandizing.

RON MEYER:

Mike was very good at making sure all roads led to him. He set himself up very intelligently. He was the guy who could get your kids into the best private schools; he was the guy who could get you into the best hospitals. We didn't know it at the time, but he had a personal press guy, same one as Donald Trump—Howard Rubenstein—and this guy engineered a big *Wall Street Journal* story. One Friday, Mike said to me, "By the way, the *Wall Street Journal* is doing a story on us." I said, "What are you talking about? No one has come to talk to me," and he said, "Oh, they've talked to me." I just said, "Wow, when is it coming out?" And he said, "Monday." When we got the story, it was about him being "the most powerful man in Hollywood." He knew exactly what he was doing. He did have me speak to the *New York Times* once, but that was for a cover story on him for their magazine.

Look, I was proud to be in the building and proud of the company. But I really decided it was Mike's show. At that time, he was the driving force of the agency and I wanted him happy. Besides, I was having the greatest time anybody could have imagined. I mean, please don't let this end.

SUSAN MILLER:

Because CAA represented so many famous actors, fans would often send us letters for our clients, and sometimes crazy people would show up at the office, thinking their favorite celebrity was there. Some time in the early '90s, there was a bomb scare and everyone had to be evacuated from the building. All the agents ran to their cars, where they could continue making calls. Then the bomb squad and fire department arrived. I kept telling Michael we had to leave, but he said, "No way!" He told me he was staying, that he thought it was total bs, and that I had to stay as well. And he was serious.

RICK YORN, Manager:

I worked on Wall Street, then I left to get into the movie business, and I read one of those Ovitz "Most Powerful Man in Hollywood" articles. I was in my early twenties, and seeing Michael out in those days was cooler than running into Tom Cruise. I remember one time seeing him at the Grill, and the whole place was abuzz: "Michael Ovitz is here . . ."

I was dating one of his assistants, and I got invited to the CAA

Christmas party, where he gave out $1,000 in a lottery, and everyone would win vacations and other prizes. I just remember I saw Mike walking around his own party the whole time, by himself, hands behind his back, just checking everything out. He had presence.

DAVID STYNE:

My first couple of years, I was promoted as a theater agent to go to New York. Rob Scheidlinger, who was a lit agent at that time, had talked to Mike and Ron about starting a theater department. CAA had never had one, and there was already somebody from New York, but I was on Rob's desk after Mike's desk, so Mike basically said I want you to go to New York as often as you want, stay as long as you want. I want you to see every show, I want you to meet everyone there is to meet, and you're my probe, I want you to tell me if we should be in the theater business. So I was twenty-five years old and I was single, and I was going to New York eight, ten times a year and I was staying at the St. Regis for a week at a time. It was great. And then I started signing new writers no one had heard about and selling spec scripts, so '93 to '95 I was doing a hybrid of theater and motion picture lit.

STANLEY JAFFE:

When we wanted to put together *The Firm*, we had a couple of possibilities and then I got a call from Mike Ovitz. He said, "Stanley, I can deliver you Sydney Pollack and Tom Cruise." I said great. He said, "You know their deals. I don't want to negotiate it." And then Sydney came and did an amazing thing. He said, "I'll make this for under fifty." And at that time I think Tom was getting fifteen and Sydney was getting like five or six, and we did the whole picture around that.

TOM HANKS:

I was with William Morris for about ten or twelve movies. They were going along fine. Then you get a little bit older, and you start asking questions about the nature of how high up you want to be on the food chain, which is what sort of access do you have to the better material that's out there that goes beyond just your place in the business. I had done *Big* and I had enough successes that made me feel good, but then I felt that I'd hit some sort of wall as far as the material I was getting. I had one very big meeting at William Morris after I said, "Can I get together and meet all these people that supposedly work with me?" There might have been at least a dozen or so, and I said, "Look, things have been going well, but I feel as if I sort of plateaued, I think I'm only seen in one way, and I find myself making some version of the same movie over and over again." I wanted to start a conversation, but I got the distinct feeling that there were people in there that were not allowed to speak, that they were too low on the food chain, and the other agents that could be heard didn't have an original idea. I literally heard, "How about a sequel to *Big*?" So I just said, right there, "If the way I'm feeling is that I'm doing the same sort of thing over and over again, wouldn't the sequel to *Big* be the manifestation of that very thing?"

There's always a certain amount of poaching that always goes on behind the scenes, and back in those days, you used to see Michael around everywhere. He was the type of dude that was always at screenings, always at premieres, always at the charity events. Even though there were overtures that came directly from him, I didn't really respond very much. Because one, I didn't know how to do that, and two, I'd never had any other agent than my guys over at William Morris. But then I actually got a letter from Richard Lovett, a man who had worked at no place other than CAA. It was his first job out of Wisconsin. I felt like I was willing to shake it up and go over to CAA. They'd opened a magnificent building, their I. M. Pei building with the big Lichtenstein in the lobby, and I went over and said, "Okay, I'm ready to go, who is this Richard Lovett guy?" We had a brief meeting, and I've been with CAA since.

AMY GROSSMAN:

I had a fabulous time as a literary agent up until the time that I left. I was thirty-eight and having a baby. I think I was done and I think my *moment* was done. The agency changed. When I started, it was the best thing that ever happened to me, but seventeen years later, when I left, I found Mike's callousness at that point very hurtful. If you knew Mike before Mike was Mike, watching Mike turn into the Mike that Mike turned into was very hard. He bore no resemblance to the man all of us loved. By the early '90s, you couldn't reach him anymore and you felt expendable. Some of it certainly was the growth of the company, and some of it was technological. Once the company went online, while the information may have quickly been going back and forth, the people themselves were not. Once it felt like high school with adult stakes; now it just felt like business. Real business.

RICK NICITA:

Which Michael? Because there were several. Amazing. Smart as a whip. Focused. Best speaker I had ever heard. This was a guy who does not say, "Umm" or "You know" or "Gee." We've all been deposed, right? I read my depositions and I want to kill myself. I take three words, four words, fake left, go right, go backwards, six "umms." He just talks and doesn't pause for a second and everything is so straight ahead. He's charismatic. And he knew, he just knew what the plan was. And he was funny, he got the joke, and gave the joke. There was an open door to his office. Great.

Cut to later in the CAA years: if I saw him walking down the hall, I would duck into an empty office and wait for him to go by. He was just a different guy.

RON MEYER:

There was no real tipping point. We were like brothers. We spoke every day no matter where we were in the world. If we were not getting along, no one but Ray Kurtzman would ever know it.

We made sure to be united in front of everyone else at the company. I always expressed my business frustrations, but as we grew apart it was probably my fault for not discussing my personal frustrations more with him. So instead of letting it out, the anger and resentment just built and built.

MICHAEL OVITZ:

I love Bill. Ronnie didn't. One of the reasons Ron got mad at me is that he felt I should have handled the "Bill Haber problem" and gotten rid of Bill and given Ron Bill's equity.

There's nothing like a presidential visit to drain yet another drop of envy out of your competitors. When Bill Clinton came to CAA's Beverly Hills headquarters on December 4, 1993, Ovitz used the occasion not as a coronation of the president, but of CAA itself, going so far as to make sure competitors were left off the invitation list.

There were over four hundred guests at the $1,000-per-person cocktail fundraiser (for the Democratic National Committee) and 80 people paid $2,500 each, in addition to the hefty admission fee, for one-on-one photo opps with Clinton in the large conference room on CAA's third floor.

Stars who showed up in full glitter included Dustin Hoffman, Kevin Costner, Warren Beatty, and Alec Baldwin, along with such executives as Disney's Michael Eisner and Peter Guber of Sony Pictures Entertainment. And since this was Hollywood, there was, of course, some drama.

Sally Field had to ditch her limo and run six blocks to the building because she was running late and the Secret Service had already shut down the surrounding streets from cars. The Secret Service refused to let Chevy Chase into the building because he had forgotten his ID, which rendered him beyond pissed, so an Ovitz aide was dispatched to authenticate him. And Glenn Close rushed over with her full makeup on from the play she was doing, appropriately enough, Sunset Boulevard.

Partly to offset the notion that the president, making his eighth presidential visit to California, was too friendly to Hollywood and vice versa, Clinton gave a speech in which he chided the industry for relying too much on violent entertainment that may have a profoundly negative effect on young people who inhabit the milieu often depicted in the films—the inner city.

Clinton took pains to establish he was not launching an attack on Hollywood and declared himself a longtime fan of its output. "I love television," Clinton said. "I am a moviegoer almost to the point of compulsion, [and] have been since I was a small boy." He singled out for praise the movie Boyz N the Hood *as a violent film that nevertheless sought to dramatize the corrosive effects of crime on the urban community in a pro-social way.*

MICHAEL OVITZ:

After he was elected, he called me up, and said, "I need a favor." What do you say to the president of the United States when he asks that, "No"? I said, "Of course. What is it?" He said, "The DNC's running out of money. Can you raise us some money?" I said, "Will you speak?" He said, "Yes." I said, "Okay, how much do you need?" And he told me what he needed—I forget how much it was—and he said, "Can you do it?" I said, "Sure, how many months do I have to put this together?" He said, "You have three weeks." And I said, "You have to be kidding." He said, "No, I'm dead serious."

RICK YORN:

Michael was hosting President Clinton at CAA, and I was dating a beautiful girl from Texas, and her dad was a big Clinton guy who put a lot of money into his campaign. So, we went and it was black tie, with major security. And sure enough she marches me right up to President Clinton. I was shaking while shaking his hand. He had this amazing presence. When the president gave his speech, it was a great speech, inspiring, so well done. But I have to say, Michael's speech was even more impressive. And Michael had even more presence.

JOHN SINGLETON:

Everyone in Hollywood was there. I was standing next to Alec Baldwin and Kim Basinger, and then the president mentioned how much he believes movies can effect serious change in the world, and that there's only so much a politician can do. I remember his next words: "Movies like *Boyz N the Hood*." Everyone in the agency looked up at me on the second balcony and gave me a standing ovation.

JUDY OVITZ:

Bill Clinton just loved Michael. One time we were in Paris and we wanted to go to one of our favorite restaurants, and they said, "I'm sorry, Mr. Ovitz, the restaurant is closed." We didn't understand why, but the concierge called us back about an hour later and said, "Mr. Ovitz, it's okay. They said you can come to the restaurant."

MICHAEL OVITZ:

He then asked us for our Social Security numbers, which was really weird to me.

JUDY OVITZ:

So we walk into the restaurant and there's nobody there. We're thinking, "What's going on?" Then Bill Clinton and his party came in and I said, "Michael, Bill Clinton's here." Bill obviously had been told that Michael was going to be there, so he comes over to our table and he says, "Hi," like they were like old buddies. He goes back to his table and we go on with our dinner. When we were done, I said, "Don't you think you ought to say good-bye to Bill?" and he says, "No, no, no, he's busy; we said hello." So we went out and we're walking to our car when one of the Secret Service comes running after us saying, "Mr. Ovitz, Mr. Ovitz! Would you mind staying for a little bit? President Clinton would like to come out and say a few words to you." So Bill comes out onto the sidewalk and he spent a half hour talking to Michael. He just loved Michael.

CAA orchestrated making Michael Crichton's Jurassic Park *into a movie in 1993. The number one film of the year, a critical and commercial hit, became the highest-grossing film released worldwide up to that time (beating out* E.T.*). Crichton had discussed the book, which was originally conceived as a screenplay, with Steven Spielberg. Crichton demanded a minimum fee of $1.5 million plus a* *percentage of the gross. CAA, representing Crichton, bypassed the usual auction process and submitted it to six studios and select top filmmakers. After a bidding war including Warner Bros., Columbia Pictures, and 20th Century Fox, Universal won the rights for Spielberg.*

MICHAEL OVITZ:

Post the first five years, TV was not that important to us. The company went from a 99 percent television revenue business to a humongous music business, and even with that, movies were sometimes as high as 80 percent of our revenue.

LEE GABLER:

I remember Mike coming in and announcing we were representing Steven Spielberg, and everybody's jaw just dropped. That had to be a momentous occasion.

SID SHEINBERG:

There was a period of time when Steven Spielberg—I don't know if he literally, but figuratively—signed with Mike Ovitz. I think the thinking was that he would get access to more important people, books, and other sources. That was a myth because I think that whatever Steven wants, Steven gets.

BOB BOOKMAN:

We submitted *Jurassic Park* to directors first, including Steven Spielberg, Paul Verhoeven, and Dick Donner, and they all had studios that were then bidding on their behalf. And so, to quote the poet Bobby Zimmerman, you don't need a weatherman to know which way the wind blows, and the ideal director for it was Steven Spielberg. That was when he had his deal at Universal. I remember negotiating directly with Tom Pollock.

The partners certainly didn't read books. They might have read synopses of books. I would say the most notable situation like that was *Jurassic Park*, because that was when Mike was signing Steven Spielberg, or trying to.

DAVID O'CONNOR:

More often than not, we couldn't tell if Ovitz had read something or if he hadn't; a lot of agents have that skill.

MICHAEL OVITZ:

When you had the kind of clientele we had—my God, we had Stallone, Cruise, Redford, Newman, Hoffman, Pacino, and De Niro—these guys got movies made. They were all making between five and ten million a movie, and they're doing two movies a year, many also receiving gross points. You can do the math. You couldn't touch that with TV.

DAVID GREENBLATT:

At the time they must have controlled 90 percent of the movie business!

MICHAEL OVITZ:

We had a hundred clients making $20 million a year, and we put together almost 250 films. When you have 10 percent of 35 percent of the gross of many films that come out from many directors, that's a lot of money. We had gross positions in movies like *Ghostbusters*, and we had 50 percent of the gross of *Jurassic Park*. That starts to add up.

SANDY CLIMAN:

Jurassic Park was perceived as a triumph of packaging, but it was really a triumph of how to create value for everyone. Mike represented all the key elements and orchestrated how all the pieces best fit together. Steven Spielberg got a monster hit bestseller to craft into a groundbreaking film. Michael Crichton got paired with a unique genius who could bring the world he created to life with vision and breakthroughs in film technology. And Universal got an enduring franchise that drove decades of value in motion pictures, television, video, theme parks, licensing—you name it. Hit movies are important, but franchises are the grand slam.

PHIL ALDEN ROBINSON, Writer and Director:

Larry Lasker and Walter Parkes and I had always written the role of Martin Bishop in *Sneakers* as our age. Well, it takes ten years writing the script. I was at Kevin Costner's Oscar party for *Dances with Wolves* and Sandy came over to me and said, "I'm working really hard to get Bob in your movie." And I said, "Bob who?" He said, "Redford." And I said, "What movie are you talking about?" And he said *Sneakers* and I said, "For what role?" And he said, "For the lead, for Marty Bishop." And I said, "We really had been thinking of going a very different way from that. Do me a favor, don't send it to him until I can think about this because I don't want to insult him." And he said, "No, no. He's read it. He wants to do it." I said, "Holy cow. Let me call you tomorrow." And I went home that night, it was really late, and I sat up and reread the script, picturing Redford in the role to see if it would work. And much to my amazement, it was the best version of the movie I had ever imagined. It was just a revelation to me. At this point it was almost eight or nine years of working on the script. I now saw it in a whole different way. It was more poignant, it had more gravitas, it was funnier. Just in every way it got better. First thing in the morning I called Walter and Larry and they agreed and I called Tom Pollock and said, "We got to do this." And he was very excited. It happened very quickly at that point.

MICHAEL OVITZ:

When people started losing to us, they started passing rumors that we didn't pay full commission, like we took 5 percent or 2½ percent, and we'd get clients calling and potential clients' business managers saying, "So-and-so will come but they want the special deal." We used to laugh about it because we didn't have a special deal. Nobody. No one. Aaron Spelling, Spielberg, Kubrick, all paid us. We asked for one thing: loyalty to the company and 10 percent if you're a client. And we never, ever took less than 10 percent from anyone except in music and in TV packaging. So all these rumors that Sue Mengers spread around—"the boys take less than 10 percent"—we never did. Ever. None of us. Ron and I held that line. I remember I signed Al Pacino and he called up and said, "I'd like the 5 percent deal," because William Morris told him to say that to us. And I said, "Al, we'd love to handle you, we don't have a 5 percent deal. When you're ready to pay what everybody else pays, call me." He came back and paid us, and stayed with us.

In the early '90s, Paris-based Crédit Lyonnais was the seventh largest bank in the world. While the bank was growing, it acquired many smaller and more regionalized banks. One such bank was based in the Netherlands (renamed CLBN or Crédit Lyonnais Bank Nederland) and did a lot of film financing, which seemed at first glance to be rather normal for a midsize European bank.

That all changed when during a routine audit in 1991, the bank discovered a rather large loan to an individual who clearly did not have the profile or credit to obtain such a large loan (Giancarlo Parretti, who was known to the bank and otherwise had big political connections in France and Italy). That loan was made for the purchase of MGM film studios.

The president of CL, François Gilles, ordered an investigation into the loans and during that process discovered that MGM was hemorrhaging cash and teetering on bankruptcy. After a couple of years of sustaining the studio with periodic cash infusions, Mr. Gilles flew to New York in 1993 to interview a number of investment banks to advise CL on what to do. All the banks told them to liquidate and take a 50 percent loss on their investment.

Mr. Gilles, through their mutual accountants, KPMG, met with Michael Ovitz and got a totally different recommendation that was counter to all the previous meetings he had.

Mr. Ovitz told him to not shutter the studio and lay off 1,200 people, particularly in light of CL's growing operations and ambitions in the United States. He advised them to bring in a new management team, to kick-start the dormant United Artists, and to add some fresh cash. He also said that CAA would handle it all and ensure them a flow of films from all agencies and suppliers, and then CAA would help sell the entire business at the highest possible price.

Ovitz recruited the respected Frank Mancuso to oversee everything and then they hired John Calley to revitalize UA.

Both labels quickly attracted a lot of talent and projects and started to turn around.

Several years later, Ovitz did assist in selling the studio and his promise to CL and Mr. Gilles was fulfilled 100 percent.

While this was all taking place, Ovitz and CAA were accused by rival agencies of a conflict of interest by being in a position to both buy and sell talent. Additionally, concerns were raised over CAA now having access to the books of production companies Crédit Lyonnais had invested in (which they never had nor did they ask for), allowing them to see the numbers behind deals. The odd thing was that the main accuser, Jeff Berg of ICM, was the largest supplier of clients and product to MGM and UA.

BAHMAN NARAGHI, Executive:

I was a senior executive at Crédit Lyonnais in 1993, representing the bank's interest at MGM. Ovitz told us Terry Semel was his first choice to take over MGM, but we also knew he had okayed Sandy Climan to recruit former Paramount head Frank Mancuso as a backup. Ovitz was asking for Semel to receive a significant equity stake in the studio—something the bank's number two Gilles was not going to accept, but Gilles went along with the negotiations on Semel to satisfy Ovitz even after he had decided on Mancuso.

SANDY CLIMAN:

Mike thought he was going to be able to make Terry's deal, but I knew from Bahman that the chances were slim, so I kept Mancuso engaged about the opportunity during the weeks of negotiation between the bank and Terry. In the end, Semel was given a new deal by TimeWarner CEO Jerry Levin to stay at Warner Bros.

BAHMAN NARAGHI:

As soon as Terry was out of the picture, we hired Mancuso. That deal was much easier to make, and he went on and revitalized MGM, and, along with John Calley, restarted UA.

SANDY CLIMAN:

We placed Frank and his team at MGM, we received another multimillion-dollar fee, and we were able to further cement CAA's role as a key corporate deal maker in Hollywood.

MICHAEL OVITZ:

I knew when I was negotiating for Terry to come over to MGM that he was either going to get a great deal there, or [Jerry] Levin would hear about it and he'd get an even better offer to stay at Warners. Let's just say he nearly doubled his deal when he stayed at Warners. As an agent, I knew what he was doing, but as his friend, it was fine with me.

MIKE MARCUS:

I left because I was offered the opportunity to run a major movie studio. I became the president and chief operating officer of MGM. I had been an agent for twenty-five years, had packaged major movies, and I was good at putting together movies. I had a lot to do with putting together *Mrs. Doubtfire*; I had a lot to do with putting together *Ghost* and *American Werewolf in London,* and it was my idea to bring Terry Gilliam into the *Fisher King* mix because I knew that Robin liked him and was interested in the script but wouldn't commit to it without knowing who the director was.

When Mike Ovitz called me into his office and said, "Look. Mancuso called. He wants to talk to you about possibly running MGM." And I said, "C'mon, Mike. What do you really want to talk about?" He had to tell me three times before I was convinced that he was telling me the truth, but when it sunk in that I could actually do that, I thought, *Well, I've accomplished everything that I wanted to accomplish. Why not?* He said, "Look, I don't know if you ever thought about doing that. If you want to do it, at this age it's a good idea, because if you wait too much longer, you'll never get a shot. On the other hand, you're one of the most present people that we work with here and I don't want to see you go. I like working with you. So it's entirely up to you. I'm not going to help you or push you in. It's up to you."

It's a good thing my interview with Frank Mancuso went well, because if it hadn't, it would have been rough going back to being an agent. I mean, look, in the history of the world, how many people have run a movie studio? I was twenty-five years in, I had done virtually everything you could do as an agent and it seemed like I should give it my best shot at the time. After all, the movie business was still the biggest game in town, and always challenging.

KEVIN BACON, Actor:

It felt like a downward slide from *Footloose*. At that point in my life, I was really just looking at leads because that was what I thought I was supposed to be doing. And Paula said to me, "I remember seeing you," actually before she represented me, "in a lot of theater in New York," because that's really where I started, as an Off-Broadway stage actor. I was doing edgy character stuff, not trying to really carry things. In some cases it was a major role, but at other times it was just darker, edgier, sometimes funny stuff, like gay hookers and junkies. And she said, "I think you need to get back into that in the movies. Don't just focus on leads." And at that point I rethought what kind of career I was going to have and what kind of an actor I was going to be. I started thinking less about the size of the role. There were three things that suddenly I took out of the equation. One was the paycheck; second was the size of the role; and third was the size of the movie. The first thing Paula suggested was that I go and sit with Oliver Stone. He had a part that she thought I could do in *JFK*. She represented Oliver as well at the time. And he asked me, "Can you be transformational with this part?" And I said, "Sure." So he said all right and gave me the part. I didn't even audition for him. It was one of those special times when I could actually feel a change within myself, like *Okay, this is what I need to do, not all the time, but this is the type of actor that I want to be. I've been a character actor pretending to be a leading man. That can't continue.* And I have Paula to thank for that. Afterward, the tide changed and that led to *A Few Good Men, Murder in the First,* and *River Wild.* The movies got better, and the parts got better.

ALEC BALDWIN:

You need to realize that the agency is going to do what's in the interest of the greatest number of clients or the most important clients. I was very practical; I knew that five other guys had to say no before I got the part. Dustin Hoffman once said to me, "Alec, we're all in line; some of us are just in a shorter line." It was a very wise statement, because that competition between performers to get scripts and parts is very real and very aggressive, even to people at his level. The biggest stars in the world, when I came into this business there was Nicholson, De Niro, Pacino, Hoffman, and Michael Douglas—a lot of great movie stars, and they were all jockeying to get material. That's something that never changes. The preciousness of good writing, it's very tough to come by.

KEVIN BACON:

There's always two ways of looking at it, right? One is, you can get lost. At a big agency, there are a lot of names to service. The other possibility is what you always hear from people who work for big agencies, which is that they have amazing access, and that their top five guys can't do everything, so you're going to see it once they pass. I think your feelings about which one you believe change and shift.

MICHAEL OVITZ:

De Niro wanted to develop Tribeca when no one was down there. I took De Niro once to Matsuhisa on La Cienega. There was a private room that you could enter from the parking lot behind the restaurant, and I used that room at least two nights a week. Then Bob called me and said he wanted to go back another time. We wound up going back three times in like three days.

Bob had an undeniable and clear vision about Tribeca. He saw the opportunity first. He was way ahead of everyone. I put Sandy on this, introduced them, and he and I made a deal with Nobu for them to open up Nobu Tribeca.

SANDY CLIMAN:

The budget could not accommodate Bob's cash acting fee. While we could preserve his back-end gross profits, I had to convince Bob to take a significant reduction in up-front cash. To do this, Sherry agreed that Bob would not have to work the full run of the filming schedule—only a few weeks bunched together, leaving him free to pursue other activities. Unfortunately, this was not how the schedule actually worked out, and Bob was working pretty much the full production schedule. When this became clear to Bob, he was furious and called me. Late that night, Sherry Lansing called me to an emergency meeting with Bob at the Nikko hotel in Los Angeles, which was doubling for the Vegas casino in the film. At the meeting, Sherry, line producer Mike Tadross, Bob, and I reworked the schedule as much as we could. Sherry was charming, Tadross was the consummate production master, and I made Bob's case and fought tooth and nail for him. Nobody was happy, but everyone walked away with a deal they could live with. And that is how the movie business runs.

SHERRY LANSING:

It's a gift if they put together a package—they've done your work for you. But that doesn't mean that you have to say yes to the package, and so you can't be intimidated. I remember once Mike called me and he said, "Are you okay?" And I said, "Sure, what do you mean?" He said, "Are you feeling well?" And I said, "Yes." And he said, "I don't know. I'm sort of worried about you." And I said, "Well, what do you mean?" And it was because I had not liked the package! I started to laugh. I said, "Mike, that's not going to work. I don't have a cold. I don't have a disease. I just don't like what you're selling." How brilliant that when Redford was in a cold period, they didn't even think of cutting his fee—just let him work for scale with a big back end, because that, you know, wouldn't hurt him. Then they could maintain his fee.

When producer Sherry Lansing was trying to set up Indecent Proposal, *a sexy drama about infidelity, at Paramount, executives insisted that while the studio did want to make the picture, it would do so at a price—a modest price, in modern filmmaking terms. Even so, there were talks with Warren Beatty and then Tommy Lee Jones for the older male lead and Nicole Kidman, Sophie Marceau, and several others for the pivotal female lead, none of whom would come cheap. After months of searching, no suitable lead could be found—at which point CAA put forth Robert Redford, just coming off* Legal Eagles, *a picture that did not live up to expectations, and* Havana, *which handed Universal one of the largest losses in its history. CAA was determined to get Redford back into the big leagues, and* Indecent Proposal *looked like an ideal comeback vehicle, but the only way the deal would work was for Redford to defer his usual up-front fees and agree instead to a percentage of the back end. It was a gamble for the actor—an especially big gamble if the movie were to tank. Lourd and O'Connor wound up sitting with Redford during rewrites.*

Now cut to April 7, 1993—opening day for Indecent Proposal, *starring Demi Moore, Woody Harrelson—and, up there next to them on theater marquees, Robert Redford. And how did the gamble go for him? Final worldwide gross for* Indecent Proposal: *$266 million. Redford's estimated share of it: a hugely decent sum north of $30 million.*

ALEX GARTNER, Producer:

Tom Schulman and I set *Indecent Proposal* up at Paramount and we spent approximately a year developing the book to screenplay with writer Amy Jones. Someone slipped Adrian Lyne the script, and after he read it, he expressed interest in coming on board as director. Then we were told Sherry Lansing would like to come on as producer. This began CAA's larger involvement: They already represented Tom Schulman and Sherry Lansing, and I became a client as well. CAA, along with attorney Alan Wertheimer, renegotiated Tom's and my producer deals to executive producers so Sherry could be the sole producer.

The casting process was robust and Adrian explored and tested all sorts of amazing actresses and combinations with well-known or star actors, but Paramount was insistent on not paying full star quotes to keep the budget under control. This caused a couple of actors to pass, so when the focus went to Robert Redford, CAA and Paramount crafted a "creative deal" that I recall was SAG Union minimum on paper but may have included an advance against his back end. No question, it was a great bit of agenting and the beginning of this kind of deal becoming much more frequent. It ended up being a great bet for all involved. We got our actor and he made more than he would have otherwise when the movie worked.

Rowland Perkins had been the most senior of the five young agents from William Morris who joined to form CAA in the first place. He was in many ways— ethnically perhaps not being one of them—built for the traditions, pacing, and culture of the famed Morris office; laid-back, these traditions definitely were not. When word of CAA and the five founders pirouetted all over town, Perkins's was likely to be the first name mentioned, the one that most enhanced the pedigree of the new operation. The irony was that he never fit in at a company where he was one of the owners as much as he did working for someone else. Ovitz was like a tsunami washing over him day after day; the agenda and pace at CAA were brutal, and though Perkins loved the business and was known as a gentleman in many corners, he lagged a bit behind from Day One. No matter. His presence at the new shop, and his validating decision to leave with the other four, gave the initial liftoff its rocket fuel, and Perkins would spend his remaining years at CAA always trying to avoid making waves and always diplomatically yielding to his younger and less experienced cohorts. When he left, there would be no door slamming, no shouted threats, not even a raised voice. It would be a graceful good-bye, and thus a farewell befitting an uncomplicated man in an awfully, and increasingly, complicated world.

ROWLAND PERKINS:

I left because I didn't want to be an agent anymore. I was really tired of it. It wasn't just a job, it was a way of life, and enough is enough.

MICHAEL OVITZ:

Imagine being John Henry Rowland Perkins the III locked in a business that was 90 percent Jewish in those days. When we left William Morris, it was a very difficult transition for him. We were loyal to him; there was never a year when he brought in as much as he made, but we were happy to carry him for close to twenty years.

ADAM VENIT:

Jon Lovitz was the first client I signed, and I signed Lisa Kudrow through an introduction he made for me. He also introduced me to the world of *Saturday Night Live.* I became a regular at the show, and wound up having a really good career representing people from that show. Jon started to get kind of hot, and I was a young agent trying to do my best. One day he had offers to do the movie *North* with Rob Reiner and a movie called *Jimmy Hollywood* with Barry Levinson. Both directors were Ovitz clients. As a young agent, I would avoid interaction with Ovitz: You didn't want to have a problem with him. Ovitz called my office, and I was so nervous. He said, "You got the offers, right," and I said, "Yes." He said, "I like *Jimmy Hollywood* a lot. Barry's movie is the right movie for him to do. What do you think?" I of course said, "Yes, absolutely." Ovitz says to me, "Let me know when he reads them," and he called me six hours later and asked, "What's going on?" I told him Lovitz hadn't read the scripts. He said to me, "He needs to read the scripts." There was a lot of pressure. Of course, the next day, Lovitz called me and said, "I want to do the Rob Reiner movie." It was tough and scary. I thought, *Oh my God. What am I going to do?* I kept thinking it over and over, but finally I had to call Ovitz. I said, "Mr. Ovitz, Jon really likes Rob Reiner's movie. He wants to do *North.*" He asked if there was anything I could do to convince him to change his mind, and I just said, "I'd be happy to ask him to reconsider." But he said "No, Lovitz has to make the right choice for himself." He never killed me over it.

MICHAEL WRIGHT:

I learned most of the lessons I learned at CAA from Kevin Huvane, Bill Haber, Jon Levin, and Bruce Vinokour. Those were my real sort of mentors there, really excellent men. I remember sitting outside of Kevin's office rolling calls with him. Richard Lovett was in the office next door and I was throwing a baseball back and forth with Richard through his door, and then Bryan Lourd was next to Kevin in the office on the other side. It was a pretty heady time. These guys were on fire. And it was fun to be a part of that.

Then CBS offered me a job, and [with] hesitation I said, "Yes, I want this job, but I need to go talk to Mike Ovitz," and on their form I disclosed I had a $10,000 loan from CAA. So, three days later, I was in a meeting with the TV department at the Aaron Spelling offices and at the end of the meeting Aaron said something like, "Hey, Michael, can you hang back? I want to talk to you about something," and Bill Haber says, "No, he has to give me a ride back to CAA." And a hush fell over the room, because I was not in the business of giving Bill Haber a ride, so obviously something was up. So then we drove back in my little crappy car, because I certainly wasn't driving one of those fancy cars at that point like the rest of those guys had. And I remember Bill saying to me something like "You've really disappointed Mike." And I kept trying to go see him and explain it to him, and he wouldn't see me and I went from feeling fine going to work every day to within a day I was a pariah. I knew that it was time for me to move on, I wasn't meant to be an agent. I knew that being an executive at CBS was a better fit for my skill set. And I was actually worried that I was not going to get the job at CBS because if you piss off Mike Ovitz, then that was not a smart thing to do back then.

Bill Haber and Kevin Huvane helped talk him away from being mad, because he was *really* mad and he wouldn't see me. My last day, I went to see him and he looked at me and he basically said, "We fast-tracked you and made this not easy for you, but made

CREATING A NEW ERA: When CAA was formed in 1975, Michael Ovitz was the youngest—and least experienced—of the founders. In 1977, the agency's leadership gathered for a rare group photo. Top row, left to right: Marty Baum, Ron Meyer (founder), Michael Rosenfeld (founder), and Steve Roth. Bottom row: Bill Haber (founder), Ovitz (founder), and Rowland Perkins (founder). *Photograph by Judd Gunderson. Copyright © 1995. Los Angeles Times. Reprinted with Permission.*

WOMAN POWER: The first staffers at CAA were the founders' wives who took turns as assistants, including from left: Carol Haber, Ellen Meyer, and Judy Ovitz.

STABLE OF STARS: Along with Paul Newman, Robert Redford was one of the most important clients in the company's development. Later on, the Redford-Ovitz relationship would get complicated. From left: Ovitz, Tony Thomopoulos, Redford, and Judy Ovitz. *Photograph by Peter C. Borsari/© Borsari Images*

DAWN OF THE DIGITAL AGE: In the mid-1980s, CAA began exploring beyond the boundaries of Hollywood. One example: In 1988, Microsoft CEO Bill Gates (left) met with CAA's Sandy Climan, aka "Ovitz's briefcase," at the company's Redmond, Washington, headquarters.

JOB HAZARD: Meyer spent a magical year and a half with Ali MacGraw; what finally came between them was not another man or woman but Meyer's telephone, which got more of his attention than MacGraw did. Meyer's life as an agent was a 24/7 proposition; the calls never stopped, and the relentlessness of agent life proved too much for the famous actress, who wanted better balance in their lives together. *Photograph by Peter C. Borsari/© Borsari Images*

SWEPT AWAY: When Meyer first got a glimpse of Kelly Chapman on Sunset Boulevard, he was instantly a "goner," removing himself from the dating market so he could woo and then wed her. They would go on to have two children together, remaining married to this day. *Photograph by Firooz Zahedi*

TRAITORS IN THE MIDST: Meyer and Ovitz exploded upon learning early in 1988 that two CAA agents were leaving to join expatriates from other agencies to launch InterTalent, a new competitive agency. As if the apparent disloyalty weren't enough, the AWOL agents—David Greenblatt (middle row, second from right) and Judy Hofflund (middle row, third from right)—were considered two of CAA's best, making the wound that much deeper. Meyer felt most grievously betrayed; he'd not only trained Hofflund, but was told Hofflund had leaked gossip about his personal life to one of the trades. CAA declared war on the new agency, vowing to bring it to its knees. *Photograph by Lloyd Segan*

BOLD STATEMENT: CAA employees gather for a 1991 company photo in the atrium of their lauded and derided I. M. Pei–designed haute headquarters at the corner of Wilshire and Santa Monica Boulevards in Beverly Hills. Roy Lichtenstein painted the building's towering mural while the office was open for business.
Photograph by Henry Groskinsky/The LIFE Images Collection/Getty Images

HAPPY FIFTIETH, MARTY: CAA's client list in 1992 was long and prestigious, but Martin Scorsese (left) remained an Ovitz favorite. Ever the matchmaker, Ovitz (right) brought Jay Moloney into the great director's orbit and the two men became friends. *Photograph by Phillip Caruso*

HAPPY THIRTIETH, JAY: If Ovitz had been forced to choose a successor in the early '90s, he wouldn't have had to think long about it. He viewed Moloney as his heir apparent, until he began to understand the torment—and ensuing problems—eating away at his protégé. From left: agent Jessica Tuchinsky, Moloney, actress Uma Thurman, and Bryan Lourd.

BENCH STRENGTH: CAA's Jack Rapke was one of the most powerful and well-paid agents in Hollywood, in large part driven by his incredible client list. Later, believing he was betrayed by Ovitz, and unable to take control after Ovitz went to Disney, Rapke left the agency to partner with Bob Zemeckis. From left: Michael Mann, Harold Ramis, Marty Brest, Jerry Bruckheimer, Rapke, Jim Cruikshank, Brian Grazer, Zemeckis, James Orr, and Chris Columbus.

UNITED AND HUNGRY: "Young Turks" became the most overused label in Hollywood during the 1990's, as five colleagues formed their own power base through friendship and strategic thinking. Originally there was to be a sixth, Michael Wimer, but he bowed out for personal reasons. From left: David O'Connor, Jay Moloney, Kevin Huvane, Richard Lovett, and Bryan Lourd.

LAST HURRAH: CAA's three remaining founders—Ron Meyer, Michael Ovitz, and Bill Haber—celebrate the agency's twentieth anniversary in 1995. It would be their last year together.

LONGTIME FRIENDS; SHORT TIME COLLEAGUES: After more than a year of on-and-off discussions with Michael Eisner (left), Michael Ovitz became president of the Walt Disney Company. The appointment was doomed from day one. *Photograph by Peter C. Borsari/© Borsari Images*

IN TOM WE TRUST: Paula Wagner (right) started representing Tom Cruise when he was nineteen, and the two would eventually become producing partners and even run United Artists for a time. Cruise has been represented by CAA for more than thirty years. *Photograph courtesy of Paramount Pictures*

WHAT AGENTS DO: CAA booked clients Ann and Nancy Wilson of Heart to pay tribute to Led Zepplin with a career-boosting performance of "Stairway to Heaven" at the 35th Annual Kennedy Center Honors, Kennedy Center Concert Hall, Washington, D.C., December 2, 2012.

BRAND THIS: CAA's marketing team, which creates campaigns for brands like Coca-Cola, Cadillac, and Chipotle, celebrates their third and fourth Grand Prix victories at the Cannes Lions International Festival of Creativity, making them among the best marketers in the world. From left: John Kaplan, Todd Hunter, Jae Goodman, David Messinger, Tony Fur, Angie Sun, Jay Brooker, and Jesse Coulter.

SIGNING SPREE: Nick Khan (left) has been one of CAA's most aggressive agents, luring clients away from other agencies and aggressively seeking—and often getting—more money for his clients, including former NFL quarterback Tim Tebow.

GAMESMANSHIP: CAA opened its sports division in 2006, initially raising fears inside the building and becoming the object of ridicule outside. But sports chieftains Howie Nuchow (far left) and Mike Levine (far right) have clawed their way to having the last laugh. Sports is now the number one generator of revenue of all departments at the agency. From left: Nuchow, Greg Luckman, Paul Danforth, and Levine. *Photograph courtesy of the Golden State Warriors*

THIS TIME IT'S PERSONAL: In the aftermath of a dozen CAA agents defecting to United Talent, the antagonism between the two agencies (not to mention between others) is as prickly and tricky as it's been for decades. The *Hollywood Reporter* commissioned illustrator Taylor Callery to create this image which appeared in the magazine on April 8, 2015.

SHE'S THE BOSS: Sonya Rosenfeld, with fellow agents Andrew Miller, Grant Kessman, and Ryan Ly at the 2015 Emmys, runs the TV literary department and has been at the company for more than three decades. She met and wed her husband, Mike Rosenfeld Jr., who also works at CAA; it's one of more than a dozen intra-agency marriages.

ID REQUIRED: Having started as small-scale get-togethers, CAA retreats now draw more than seven hundred colleagues annually. At the 2015 edition, agents Michelle Weiner, Steve Lafferty, Frank Jung, and Risa Gertner take a timeout.

ROYAL OPPOSITION: Ari Emanuel (left) and Patrick Whitesell serve as co-CEOs of WME/IMG, CAA's toughest competitor in its history. Both agencies appear headed to public offerings but are pursuing different strategies. Is there enough room on Wall Street for both? *Photograph by Brigitte Lacombe*

CAA LEADERSHIP, TWENTY-FIRST CENTURY: In an industry of dynamic change, and under new owner TPG, long-termers struggle to adapt and prevail. From left: David O' Connor (who left CAA in 2015), Richard Lovett, Steve Lafferty, Kevin Huvane, Rob Light, Mike Rubel, and Bryan Lourd.

CASH EQUALS TRUTH: In 2010, when private equity giant TPG first invested in CAA, many believed the course and culture of the agency would change. Some still do. Either way, CAA now has stronger financial DNA and a big appetite for ambitious future investments. David Bonderman (left) and Jim Coulter are TPG's co-chairmen. *Photograph courtesy of Epic Imagery*

this possible." And I said, "I appreciate that, I know that, I meant no offense. But I'm just not meant to be an agent, it's not what I do. And so this opportunity was a great one and my mistake was that you heard about it before I could tell you, but I was on my way to tell you, but I would have told you what I'm telling you now, which is I want to go to a place where I can really be my best." He basically said, "You're making an enormous mistake. You could have done so well here." He didn't make it personal, he looked at me like he thought I was an idiot, to be honest. He was looking at me like I had so disappointed him. He seemed to genuinely believe in his heart that I was making a mistake and I couldn't make him understand, *I don't want to do what you do.*

JACK RAPKE:

I don't think Michael wanted anybody to succeed away from CAA because it would then send the signal: *Oh, there is life after CAA.*

MICHAEL WRIGHT:

But here's the thing, and I said this to him at the time: I was a nothing. I was a baby agent, barely producing enough revenue to cover my salary, which wasn't much. And the decision I made was a decision of the heart. It wasn't calculated, it wasn't strategic; I was just really trusting my gut. And I was right, by the way. I found, for better or for worse, my right path in this business, and as it turned out I was pretty good at being a creative executive.

I think those four years were like going to grad school. I learned a lot. I think when people try to categorize it one way or the other, they're just being dishonest. It was a combination of amazing great things and some dark shit, too. I mean like anything, right?

RAND HOLSTON:

Forrest Gump is a movie I am extremely proud of. I represented Wendy Finerman and Steve Tisch, the producers.

STEVE TISCH:

Gump was '94 but we set up the project at Warner Bros. in '85—a nine-year development gestation period.

It didn't hurt that Ovitz wanted *Gump* to be made. Hanks and Zemeckis were clients. When the head of the most important talent agency in the business at that time says he wants to make something happen and he's very passionate about making something happen, it's a lot of wind in your sail.

RAND HOLSTON:

We had to restructure the deal more than once. The studio decided it wasn't willing to make the picture for what had been previously discussed, and when they gave us the new number, it was clear the only way to get the film made was taking the principals above the line—Bob Zemeckis, Tom Hanks, Wendy, and Steve—to take less cash up front, and we made sure they were able to get more gross points on the back end. This turned out to be a really good deal for all of them.

ROBERT ZEMECKIS:

The studio was going to shut the movie down if Tom and I didn't give our fees back. This was something that they do all the time: There's forty-eight hours left before you shoot, and they say you've got to take X amount of million dollars out of the budget. So we said, "How are we going to do that now? We've got to start shooting in forty-eight hours." And it comes back, "Well, you guys are just going to have to give us back your fees."

STEVE TISCH:

Sherry made her appeal, which was very focused and basically said, "Here's why the movie won't get made, here's why the movie will get made. To get this movie made, to cut the budget from X to X minus Y. We've done all we can working with the production department. I'm still over budget, I want to make this movie, and to cut a significant amount out of the budget—which is the only way the picture will be green-lit by me—you, Tom Hanks; you, Bob Zemeckis; you, Steve Tisch; you, Wendy Finerman, have to not take any money up front, no producer's fee, that's going to come out of the budget. And if you agree, your back end will be enhanced, but basically I'm asking you to be my partner in this movie." I don't remember who all said yes, but I said yes. I honestly don't remember if Ovitz was at that meeting.

SHERRY LANSING:

I remember so vividly having a meeting with Bob Zemeckis. I was sitting in a chair and he was sitting on a couch in my office and I said, "Look. I hate to bring this up, but would you consider deferring?" And without missing a beat, he said yes. And he said something like, I know what happened to Robert Redford because he had deferred and made so much more money off of *Indecent Proposal* than he would have if he had gotten his salary. And I remember thinking at the time—I had deferred on *Indecent Proposal* when I was a producer also. You would never ask someone to defer who was the sole support of three children and needed the upfront money, but if you could afford to do it, deferring certainly worked out for many people.

It was great for us that Bob Zemeckis agreed to defer, and one of the smartest decisions he ever made. He wound up with much more financial success that way.

DAVID GEFFEN:

Mike was a very good agent, but you know, there's one thing you can say about agents in general, and particularly about those who are really good. And that is that they are incredibly full of shit and very good at it.

RICK NICITA:

I never felt Mike valued me enough, frankly.

AMY HECKERLING, Director:

I was at another agency for a very long time, because the person had seen my student film and wanted to handle me. So we were together for a very long time, but at a certain point I kept feeling like I was banging my head against the wall. I would write something and it would be in development and even though I'd had a film, *Fast Times at Ridgemont High*, that cost nothing and made tons of money, it seemed like it didn't get me anything like all the guys were getting, you know?

I was afraid of CAA because of Mike Ovitz. He scared me. He seemed scary. Showbiz scares me anyway. I'm easily intimidated. My ex-husband had been with them and I always felt like he followed whatever was the cool thing to do. I always felt more of an outsider in everything and so I felt like "I don't belong with the cool people." I mean, that's not where I sit in the lunchroom. But at a certain point I felt like, gee, maybe I should explore other possibilities. Michael Wimer, Ken Stovitz, and Richard Lovett came to my house, and I told them, "You're the in crowd, that's not where I live." And they're like, "No, no, we're the nerds. We're the nerds." I just didn't believe it because they were just too cool and cute and well dressed. And you know there were articles in the press about CAA and the Young Turks running around Wilshire Boulevard, but they sent me a gift basket, and it was to prove that they were nerds. It had pajamas with feet on them and a Brady Bunch quiz book and crazy stuff to say, "We're not cool. We're not the cool kids." And part of me just went, *Please.* But the other part was like, *Wow. They're trying. That's so sweet. You know?* So I was like, *Okay. Why do you always have to run away from what everybody else is having?* Why not try it? So I said okay.

At a certain point I went in to pitch a TV idea at Fox and they said, "No, we want to do something about cool kids. When other people come in to pitch stuff, it's always about the outsiders. How come everybody always pitches the outsiders? We want to do something about the in crowd." So I wrote a pilot based on a character I had always had floating around in my head which was the opposite of me. Somebody that was positive and wasn't afraid the world was always going to take them down and assumed things would always be great. I found that type hilarious. When I joined CAA, Ken Stovitz asked to see everything I had been writing, and I showed it to him, and then he called me up and he said, "This is too good to be a pilot. This is a movie." So he got to the TV people, had everybody talk, then he made that happen, ultimately in the form of *Clueless*. He got to Scott Rudin, and when Scott Rudin read it, he liked it. And then we went from everyone in town passing on it to a bidding war. The fact is that Ken Stovitz refused to give up in the face of everybody telling him we're not doing movies with stupid teenagers anymore because *Airheads* did badly, and the genre has passed because nobody wants to do female characters and all these things that people would say were the rules of the day. Ken just ignored them all and fought and banged against all the walls until they came down.

As frantic as the pitching-and-developing seasons can be at TV networks, it's really not always about the latest hot new concept being feverishly shopped around. It might instead be a golden oldie rustin' on a shelf in a musty script library. Agents, to be sure, very rarely write pilot scripts, or star in them, direct them, or produce them, but what they can do is bring one to life. The big cliché that says agents have no taste and care only about "The Money" simply throws too many smart and creative talents under the bus. In the case of the mammoth hit ER, *a towering NBC tentpole from 1994 through 2009, the brilliance was in seizing an almost magical moment in time. Michael Crichton, already acclaimed for* The Andromeda Strain, *was on top of the world after the earth-moving success of* Jurassic Park, *and that was when CAA agent Michael Wimer, who represented Crichton at the agency, seized the moment and took a walk to the script library. He found out that, incredibly enough, a studio had tossed* ER—*Crichton's motion picture script for a new kind of medical drama—into the discard pile some time in the mid-1970s. He realized that the very element that made Warner Bros. pass on it as a feature—a never-ending stream of stories pouring through the emergency room doors—made it perfect for the world of television. Together with colleague Tony Krantz, the two artful archivists would lead the way, with*

CAA, NBC, Warner Bros., and Steven Spielberg's Amblin Entertainment all striking gold.

BILL HABER:

Tony Krantz is the finest packaging agent I ever worked with.

LEE GABLER:

When I think of *ER*, I give Tony Krantz the majority of the credit.

BILL HABER:

The development of *ER* and the setting up of *ER* at Warner Bros. was 100 percent Tony Krantz's work. From the beginning of it being on to its success, it's all 100 percent Tony Krantz's work.

MICHAEL WIMER:

In 1993, after the fabulously successful opening of Steven Spielberg's direction of Michael Crichton's *Jurassic Park*, Ovitz made it clear he wanted more from this pairing, but not everything was possible. We had previously signed Michael from a small agency, and we stuck to our then-traditional gentleman's agreement that we would not mine Michael's backlist away from them. This approach at CAA was originally developed by Ron Meyer, but it wasn't contractual and it certainly did not apply to large agencies. We just wanted to make sure we didn't destroy a one-client agency when their golden goose came to CAA.

Tony Krantz came to me and asked if there was any existing Crichton material we could use. I told him that we could not use any of Michael's TV material, as it was the province of the previous agent. I remembered, however, that our agreement did not prevent us from using a dormant movie script in the television world. This would prove to be a critical piece of information.

Michael had a couple of those in his library, and the one that made the most sense was a project over at Warners that he had written almost twenty years earlier, inspired by his years as a physician.

TONY KRANTZ:

I had read a script written by Michael Crichton called *ER*. I hadn't really thought much about it. It popped into my head in a creative meeting—literally, popped into my head: what about that script that I had read five years before . . . *ER*? That script sat on the agency shelf for thirteen years. Called it up from the library, reread it over the weekend, and I said, "This is a TV series." It was a script that Michael was going to do as a movie with Amblin and Warner Bros. This was after the success that they had had with *Jurassic Park 2*; they were the biggest people in the entertainment world, Michael and Steven. Bob Bookman represented Michael Crichton, so I went into his office and said, "This is the idea: do this as a TV series. Can we convince Michael Crichton?" Bookie, to his credit, put me on the phone with Michael Crichton, and I convinced Michael Crichton that if I could get thirteen episodes on the air, he would let me try it as a television series.

It was owned by Amblin, but at Warner Bros. on the motion picture side. Tony Thomopoulos was running Amblin Television. So I went to Tony and I said, "Let's try to pull it from the movie side of the company and do it for television." Michael Crichton wanted a showrunner because he was insisting on doing no work on the series. Coincidentally, I represented John Wells. John had an overall deal at Warner Bros., as luck would have it. I called up John and I said, "Here's the situation. Let me send you the script." He read it, said, "I would love to do it." And Michael Crichton, Tony Thomopoulos, John, and I had a breakfast where John was truly inspiring and Michael said, "John can be the showrunner." Then we had to make the deal with Warner Bros. It was the hardest deal I had ever made to date because Michael Crichton was insisting on 100 percent parity with Steven Spielberg, who was the biggest director/producer in the world. What Steven got, Michael insisted on getting too, with one exception: that Michael's services on the series would be contractually zero—he would get paid the Steven Spielberg deal but be obligated to do nothing. Outside studios were still supplying exclusively to networks, so if you are Les Moonves, not only are you making a Steven Spielberg deal, which is mega, but you're making two Steven Spielberg deals in one show. It was an unbelievably difficult deal.

LES MOONVES:

I was running Warner Bros. television at the time and Tony Krantz at CAA was packaging it along with Tony Thomopoulos, who was running Steven's television company. And they called us for one reason—we had John Wells. John Wells was a producer exclusive to Warner Bros. So he was a CAA client; they wanted to keep it in the family. I think it was Tony who said, "I got this script I want you to read. It is twenty years old and was written by Michael Crichton, and he and Steven had worked on this script many years ago. We think it would make a great TV series, and we're sending it to you guys because it's John Wells." So I read the script and it was sensational. You could tell it was written twenty years ago and it was written for Boston because it mentions a Celtics player, but they didn't want to do it in Boston because *St. Elsewhere* had been in Boston. They decided to be in a different city, so they picked out Chicago. Crichton said he was going to do no notes on it—that was sort of the deal—but he ended up doing sort of a nice polish.

BILL HABER:

It was phenomenal. Elements were being put together with people that I never ever believed would work together, or that the deals could be made. And Tony Krantz did that.

MICHAEL WIMER:

Television in those days was not a terribly sexy business and was looked at very much like a demotion for a feature player.

Michael's earlier feature work had not been anywhere near the level of success of *Jurassic,* and he was wondering why on earth I was pushing a television move when he was still enjoying the glow alongside Steven. Ovitz didn't know the underlying script and television only made it onto his screen when a show like *ALF* would syndicate. Otherwise the television world was all Haber's. Fortunately, I knew exactly how to get both Crichton and Ovitz to support the move. First, I told him how much Crichton made as a novelist (it was simple—but big—math) and I gave Mike the per-page number. Then I told him that Michael would have to do almost no work to the script—it was a minor adaptation and we could get someone else to do it—which I knew Crichton would reject when I told him the huge value of "created by" rights. Which was exactly what happened. But the real capper was that we could deliver this piece of business to Steven's television business with almost no investment whatsoever by Steven. Ovitz quickly agreed. Crichton was in.

TONY KRANTZ:

Fox network existed at this point, but they didn't program at ten o'clock, and *ER* was a ten o'clock show. They had passed on the script anyway; ABC didn't want to do it, I actually forget why; and CBS had a show called *Chicago Hope* with David Kelley, so they had their big medical show that year. I had one buyer, NBC—but they didn't know that. NBC president Warren Littlefield called me up Sunday at my house and said, "Okay, I've read it, we're interested. Let's take the meeting." The basis of a meeting was that they had to agree to thirteen episodes up front if it went well. Don Ohlmeyer, Warren's boss, was at the meeting, and he had a scowl on his face the entire time. He didn't say a word. NBC passed on the thirteen-episode deal and offered six episodes subject to a creative meeting that they still wanted to have. We had that meeting a week later where John Wells was spectacular and answered every possible question they had, but I got a call the following day where Warren said, "We'll only order a two-hour movie." I said, "Warren, you said thirteen, then it went to six, and now it's a two-hour movie?" And I, a young agent, said to the president of NBC, "You bought that piece of shit *Viper* and you're not going to do *ER* from Michael Crichton and Steven Spielberg, who are the two biggest and best names in the entire entertainment business?" And he said, "Yup." My wife was standing next to me and we thought I was never going to work at NBC again because I was so direct with Warren Littlefield. So I called up Michael Crichton and he said to me, "Tony, it's a two-letter word, and it begins with N." And the show was dead.

I was taking a road trip with a buddy through Appalachia and I checked in with my office on a pay phone—I had a message from John Wells. Michael Crichton had called him from his vacation in Hawaii. Maybe he had mellowed out or something, but he said, "Let's do it." It was within two days of it being too late to make the pilot for NBC. But we made the pilot, and it tested through the roof. There were some editorial fixes that NBC suggested which Warner Bros. embraced to sort of make NBC the "saviors" of the show. Les was brilliant at making all of this happen, with the testing and managing the whole enterprise and network notes. And then I got a phone call from Warren Littlefield the night before the network was set to announce the schedule. This was in the era where Thursday night at ten was the ultimate slot—*Hill Street Blues, L.A. Law*—and Warren says to me, "Tony, I'm not going to tell you where the show's going to get programmed, but it is going to be a workhorse for NBC for years to come and I just want to thank you for putting it together."

LES MOONVES:

Casting the show was great fun. There are different stories about George Clooney, but the truth is I had him under contract for four straight years. We kept putting him into things that didn't work out, and then I sent him two scripts at the same time. I sent him the *ER* script and this other show called *Golden Gate.* I said, "Tell me which one you want to do." And the other one, *Golden Gate,* was a bigger part, but he said, "This *ER* script is fabulous. I really want to play this role," so that's how that ball rolled down the hill.

And by the way, *ER* to this day was the best pilot I have ever seen in my life. From start to finish it was a brilliant piece of material. CBS had *Chicago Hope* and they were going to be competing against one another—they were both going to be on Thursday night at ten o'clock, but they both were premiering on Sunday night. I remember waking up early Monday and looking at the overnights, which meant something then. The *ER* number was huge. It became number one right away and stayed there for many many years, and it received the most expensive license fee NBC ever paid.

MICHAEL WIMER:

The show was a success from the beginning and it went on to become the most nominated and most awarded show in broadcast history. It got Michael on the cover of *Time* magazine and was one of the biggest television successes at CAA. The TV guys even made me a plaque that said MOTION PICTURE TV AGENT OF THE YEAR, a bit tongue in cheek because in those days, nobody crossed over!

TONY KRANTZ:

After five years, the option that NBC had to continue to license *ER* was coming up. The perfect storm was at hand: *You are going to lose the rights to the biggest show in America unless you pay up.* That created a scenario where Warner Bros. made a landmark deal with NBC where they split all the show's revenue 50/50. The license fee went up to $13 million just to Warners and CAA's package commission remained proportional to that. So that meant the commission was 3 percent of the license fee plus a deferred 3 percent, plus 10 percent of the back end. Three percent of the $13 million license fee every week is $390,000 in commission times 22 episodes for another six or seven years, plus 10 percent of the back end: $200 million. I mean, the biggest movie star in the world was making $20 million at the time. That's a $2 million commission. $200 million was a whole other kettle of fish. It's possible that CAA's total take from *ER* was about $300 million, or more, it's hard to say. And that money keeps coming in to this day, raising the tally.

LES MOONVES:

Those package fees were huge. ICM was kept alive for many years because of two shows: *Simpsons* and *Friends.* They had packages on those and they made a lot of money. *ER* made a phenomenal amount of money for CAA. But you know what? They actually earned it.

One of the reasons I was brought to CBS is because I had been involved in *ER* and *Friends,* two shows that helped make NBC number one.

MICHAEL WIMER:

Many years later, I received a wonderful note from Michael, which should give you a great sense of who he is. For quite a small amount of work, he was about to receive his first participation check, somewhere north of $30 million. That was a gigantic amount for anyone in the feature business, even for Steven, who received the same check. He asked me what was customary to give to those who had worked on the show for the many years without points. I told him there was no custom whatsoever, and to my knowledge no one had ever even raised the question; most folks just cash the check. But Michael talked to Steven and John and they decided to host a sit-down dinner for the *ER* crew—with waiters delivering a covered plate underneath which sat a check to each and every person who had contributed to the show. That was one of the most satisfying moments of my career.

TONY KRANTZ:

I was making over a million a year, but I felt I deserved a little bonus at least for having put together *ER.* That seemed reasonable to me, I mean, it was the biggest show on television. At CAA, such a request was very controversial. Finally, after a lot of wrangling, they paid me $125,000, which was about $67,000 after taxes.

TOM HANKS:

I think everyone comes to a project with *this could not have happened had it not been for me, or us, or an idea I had back in 1967.* The reality is, these things bat around for a very long time, sometimes they are not made, sometimes they do get made, but to give any sort of individual credit for making it happen is usually a mistake.

Look, here's what happened: A movie sits around for a very, very long time, and it lacks whatever that chemistry is to either move it up the food chain so it gets closer to getting made, or it actually gets made. I had met Eric Roth on another project, and I thought the guy was a genius, and I actually tried to get this other script made that he had written. I wanted to be in a movie like *The Postman,* which he had done a draft on, which got made much later on by Kevin Costner, but I actually had a meeting with Terry Semel testing the 800-pound gorilla theory. I said, "I want to be in *The Postman,* and here's why," and I had about a fifteen-minute explanation. And Terry said, "Great, go find somebody else who wants to go make the movie." That's what the requirement is.

Bob Zemeckis didn't make *Forrest Gump* because CAA said, "Hey, Bob, we have your next movie for you." That's not the way it works. *Forrest Gump* had drifted around a long time, and there had been other actors connected with it and other directors that dabbled with it. If you add up the direct circle of people who at one point had said, "Hey, this might make a good movie," it was probably triple digits, but nothing happened with it. Nobody can make it happen until a playmaker says, "Okay, this is going to be our next movie." Bob Zemeckis stood up and said, "Okay, I'm in. This is it." And it's at that moment that they tried to start making the deal, which was not an easy thing to do. Paramount squawked about everything. There were a million budgetary things which had to happen, and it was the beginning of a very long months-long process, during which at any time the movie could have fallen apart, which it didn't, because it had a filmmaker like Bob. That's the way he works. Once he decides he's going to make a movie, he starts making the movie, and everything else has to somehow work out.

DAVID LETTERMAN:

Ovitz calls me up and says, "We're gonna be down in the Caribbean and I know you're coming. Do you mind giving my son a ride?" And I said, "Well, no, I'll be happy to give him a ride." So we're going down there and I'm being a wise guy with the young kid, and I said, "Look, do you have any money?" And he says no, not really. And I said, "Do you have to ask your old man for money?" And he says, "Well, yeah." And I said, "That's ridiculous. I'll tell you what I'll do." And there was a bottle of Tabasco sauce on the table. I said, "You drink this Tabasco sauce, I'll give you a hundred bucks." So the kid opens up the bottle, and he drinks it. He just drinks the goddamn hot sauce and I thought, *Holy shit. What if I poisoned Ovitz's son? Oh my God!* And the kid just kind of barked and coughed a little bit, stuck out his hand, and I give him a hundred bucks.

RON MEYER:

By 1990, Mike and I were in year fifteen of a ten-year plan. After the first ten years, we said we would sell the company, and we'd run a studio or do something else. For ten years, we talked about that, but we never did it. We had offers to be bought, some for cash, others for stock, but Mike always said no. Looking back on it, I believe Mike never wanted to leave his position of being the most powerful man in Hollywood.

SANDY CLIMAN:

I said to Ron, "Watch out." It became very clear as the agency went on that Michael had a different agenda. Michael's very intelligent, and with his hubris, ego, and talent, he saw new worlds to conquer, including the corporate world. One of the interesting things about the industry back then, and to a degree still to this day, is that production and talent were on the West Coast, but it was all financed by the East Coast. There were very few people who could link the two. One of the reasons Michael was able to become the most powerful man in Hollywood was that he was successful in both areas. He could dine out in New York and tell the most sophisticated bankers and investors all these Hollywood stories they would love.

ANDREA NELSON MEIGS, Agent:

I went to Duke Law School, and during my second year, I clerked for the Los Angeles district attorney's office. They offered me a job after graduation, but I wanted to do entertainment law. But then I thought, *If I go straight into a firm, I'm going to be sitting on the sidelines and doing briefs for the next eight years. If I go to the DA's office, I will be in a courtroom immediately, which will get me great experience which I will be able to segue to a boutique firm.* But after three months, I decided I didn't want to stay that long, and a woman I went to law school with was Michael Ovitz's assistant.

She said come to work at the agency. It's not practicing law, but you'll be dealing with contracts and be in negotiations. I had to have a hard conversation with my parents about starting all over again in the mailroom. My dad was supportive but made me promise that I would pass the bar so I always had that to fall back on. I started in the mailroom in '95 and stayed at CAA for eleven years. I worked for Fred Specktor, Joe Rosenberg, and then

Patrick Whitesell; then I became an agent. My first client was Cedric the Entertainer, and I later worked with Halle Berry and Jamie Foxx.

SANDY CLIMAN:

Bill Gates and I had discussed for several years when the personal computer would begin to play a meaningful role in entertainment, and in 1994, Bill felt the time finally seemed right for Microsoft to make its first major foray into the world of interactive content, along with entertainment audio and video. Bill gave his personal blessing for CAA and Microsoft to form a partnership, and he dispatched CTO Nathan Myhrvold to come to L.A., where we negotiated a $50 million joint venture. But when I brought the deal to Mike, he was livid. He told me the deal was meaninglessly small, and he wanted $500 million from Microsoft, $500 million from Condé Nast, and $500 million each from two cable giants for a total capitalization of the new venture at $2 billion. It was a very tough discussion. Both Bill and Nathan could not understand Mike's overreach and seemed flabbergasted.

LEN FINK:

Chiat\Day did the Apple "1984" commercial, so I sort of knew Steve Jobs through that. So I flew up with Sandy in Michael's plane, and we went to Pixar and we're in a meeting with just me, Sandy, who's a visionary, and Michael. This is when Jobs was forced out of Apple.

So Jobs was there and he's got the storyboards for *Toy Story*, and at one point Jobs says, "I'd like Len Fink to leave now." I basically got kicked out of the meeting. Jobs either remembered me or did research about who was going to be at the meeting. I think he was going to talk about some proprietary software, because I'm known as having a tech head.

Michael, being protective, was like, "Why are you asking him to leave?" And he was pissed. The way I got around it was I said, "Steven, I'll go excuse myself if somebody can arrange it so I can see what the progress is on the stuff that you're doing for us at Pixar."

I don't know why Michael didn't buy Pixar.

MICHAEL OVITZ:

We were minting money—it was unreal. I had this investment banking thing going. I made *Institutional Investor* four years in a row as doing one of the top ten deals in the country, and I personally was one of the top investment bankers in the country, four out of six years. I had the advertising thing going. We were doing M&A: Imagine wanted to go public, we were doing it with Allen & Company. I made a deal for Joe Roth to go to Disney, and sent a check for a million dollars over without even asking. We were getting paid in every direction for everything.

TOM ROSS:

I felt like I had died and gone to heaven. It was the greatest experience of my life. I felt I was on the A-Team. Every year when we had our retreat, Michael would throw out this list of accomplishments that the agency had pulled off in the past year and it just empowered everybody to go, "Wow." At that time, you could name everybody in the room.

RON MEYER:

I was just living the life. I was making more money than I'd ever dreamt of, I was popular, I was going out with great-looking actresses, I mean—fuck, *don't let this end.*

There are very few guys whose ass I couldn't kick, physically. Don't just assume that because I'm a nice guy I couldn't just grab somebody by the throat and fuck him up.

MICHAEL DOUGLAS:

There's a dark side to Ronnie. There's a dark, dark side, and I felt it as a fellow Libra. I think he struggles with that, but always tries to do what's right.

So who was this Ron Meyer guy anyway? In the early 1980s, as Ovitz was emerging as a major force and grabbing up much of the oxygen in many a room, Meyer was able to have his own larger-than-life narrative, even if he didn't quite see it, or want it, just that way. He was an average-sized guy who everyone said had a heart of gold, but wait: He enlisted in the Marines, his body was festooned with tattoos, and he was known for having beat the living crap out of men almost twice his size when situations called for it.

His wavy brown mane got almost as much attention in Hollywood as his client Farrah Fawcett's flowing 'do, and while he'd rather wear anything but a suit and tie, when he did get dressed, he'd cut quite the swath.

Between marriages, Meyer went off on sybaritic tears through Hollywood and the rest of the hemisphere—a challenge to sheets that made Warren Beatty's romps look practically papal.

A final cogent coda to the growing Meyer legend wasn't, as you might think, Meyer becoming a besotted Hemingwayesque boozer. No, it was gambling that ensnared Meyer and caught more than just his fancy. Soon Meyer was overindulging with style and skill, sometimes tucking more than $100,000 into his pocket on a single evening at the poker table, or betting on sporting events, and that was back in the 1980s and '90s when, as they used to say, a hundred grand still amounted to something.

Then, as it must to all gamblers, losing came to Ronnie Meyer. Several times, Meyer faced huge daunting debts, once in the hole for several million dollars. And this wasn't to some casino on the strip. The "guys" Meyer was on the hook to only swam in the deep end of the pool.

Meyer was forced to swallow his pride and ask Ovitz for an advance on his earnings, the operative word being "ask," since Ovitz controlled the company. Ovitz said no, but did offer to put Meyer on "an allowance" to help him curtail future gambling losses. By this time, Ovitz was fearful for Meyer's safety.

When time came to pay the pipers, Meyer himself went forth to meet his debtors, at night no less—standing bravely or foolhardily and telling them he didn't have the money yet. He didn't have the money "yet"! But all his years of negotiating finally paid more than 10 percent: He left that meeting alive, both legs operative, genitalia intact. He was even granted a stay, and it would be the late giant of producing, Ray Stark, who would wind up lending the money that kept Ron Meyer in one piece.

PATRICK WHITESELL, Agent:

I went to Luther College in Iowa, lived in San Diego for a couple years, and then moved up to L.A. because I wanted to be in the business. I decided I would get started in a mailroom and interviewed at CAA, ICM, and InterTalent. I saw that it was going to take longer to become an agent at ICM and CAA—three, four, or maybe even five years—because they were much bigger. But at InterTalent, which was smaller, I thought I could get through it faster. I also liked the idea that even though they were a boutique, the agency was started by people who had left the big boys, so they knew the game. This was late 1990; InterTalent was where I met Ari [Emanuel] and we formed our friendship.

My thesis proved right. I made it from mailroom to agent in about a year. I loved it there. We were competing for movie stars with the big agencies, but much to my chagrin, they sold the agency. I went to UTA because that's where all of the talent people went, signing a three-year deal. That was the height of dysfunction at UTA—it was a horrible culture. So after being an agent for less than three years, I'd been in one unstable situation and one shitty environment. CAA started chasing me to come over; initially it was Kevin Huvane and Bryan Lourd, but then it really became Rick Nicita.

When we were at InterTalent, CAA was trying to put us out of business every day of the week. They were our fiercest rivals. So it was kind of surreal that I was talking to them. Ari was at ICM and we were still friends and he said, "You should probably go to CAA, because you're going to build an actor business and there's no more stable place. And Mike Ovitz is king of the world."

TONY KRANTZ:

We would have retreats and in the early days there would be forty agents or fifty agents. We would sit around in a circle in the ballroom of a hotel and people would speak up and it was incredibly meaningful to me—incredibly emotional, frankly. The retreats were inspiring. I remember in one of them—I was a young agent, maybe twenty-seven—I said that part of the reality at CAA is that it is a collective and that sometimes individual agents need to also get "kudos and glory" for the work that they did. And there was a hush in the room. Nobody ever said that at CAA. Nobody would ever be so brazen as to say that an individual *wanted* kudos and glory for doing what it was that we did as part of a group. But people came up to me ten plus years later, and they remembered that comment because they were all feeling it themselves. It was real, and I gave voice to a bit of a third rail at the agency.

MICHAEL WIMER:

Ron knew that Mike was going to ask me to perform a loyalty killing and that I would leave the company before doing that. He'd gone to see Mike and got me off the desk immediately. Interestingly enough, a few years later Mike did ask me to do that killing. We were at a retreat at which Rosalie Swedlin had been savaged by the full group. She was about to explode and Mike pulled me aside and asked me to publicly put a knife into Jack: "You have to go after him, you have to take him down," he said—and I didn't. Another one of those momentous decisions—and at face value, it would seem to be a difficult thing to say no to your boss, especially Mike. But this was another easy one. Why? Because screw him.

TOM ROSS:

Michael and Ronnie both were tough. I mean, I would go to dinner with them once in a while at Spago, and for the first twenty minutes, they'd go through our list of superstars, and ugh, the things that they would say, you know, like, "What a goddamn asshole. I can't take him anymore." *Whoa.* It was pretty tough. But they built Fort Knox.

SANDY CLIMAN:

When I joined CAA we did everything possible to stay out of the press—to be the "behind-the-scenes" power brokers. Early on

Mike asked me about outreach to the financial community. I told him that my friends on Wall Street did not know who we were or who he was. He internalized that and set about ending that anonymity. That's when the press started. At first the press was a huge positive, but it then became a complication with hidden liabilities. The issue with Ron and others was that the articles became more and more about Mike, and less and less about CAA. Mike was named the most powerful man in Hollywood. All of a sudden a talent agent engineered himself to the top of the list. You had a *BusinessWeek* cover story—wait a minute, *talent agents are in* BusinessWeek?! The last time a talent agency was profiled in a top-tier financial magazine was during the breakup of MCA. A studio head friend of mine boarded the Boston–New York shuttle one Sunday morning to be greeted by rows of passengers all reading the *New York Times Magazine* cover profile of Mike. Through the rows of seats, all he said he saw was the cover photo of Mike. At this point, we were all very worried we were headed in the wrong direction.

MICHAEL OVITZ:

Ronnie and I signed most of the big clients in the business. No offense, but Kevin Huvane didn't sign Meryl Streep; he didn't know her. I gave Kevin Huvane Meryl Streep as a client, and his whole frigging present client list is based on the fact that he represents Meryl Streep. She's the core of his whole list.

What made the company work is that Ron and I were always pushing clients down the food chain. If I signed someone, I put another agent on the phone with them as early as I could. Ron did the same thing. We were fearless about that, fearless. This hadn't been the norm in the business ever before.

BARRY JOSEPHSON:

Inheriting those clients was everything. Certain other agents there had a group of clients but never grew their list because they were not getting clients from Ronnie and from Mike. They weren't receiving clients from the top guys, but these Young Turks were. It was also that they really wanted it bad; they loved the business, they loved being agents, they loved representing talent; and they saw, very specifically, a future for themselves.

Jay was representing Tim Burton, Martin Scorsese, and Bill Murray. These were cornerstone clients.

TOM LASSALLY:

As much as people may think he lucked into things because he worked for Mike Ovitz, Jay had an incredible eye for talent and was truly passionate about the clients he was working with. Jay signed Leonardo DiCaprio when Leonardo was brand-new. I was an executive at Warner Bros. at that point and we had just put him in *This Boy's Life*. He was just a kid, but Jay immediately saw Leonardo's talent. And when he saw talent, he worshipped it.

BILL MURRAY:

Jay was a star. Jay was really something. He was the star of those Young Turks. Those guys would go on vacations together, and he would set it all up. He would say, "Guys, we're going to raft the Colorado River. We're going to Easter Island, or some other crazy thing." He would set everything up and they would go together and have these amazing adventures together. These guys had a lot of fun, and Moloney was the guy that really made that happen. He had the ability to laugh at himself, which, you know, for a young guy in that business was unusual.

TOM LASSALLY:

We all went on many trips together, including Guana. Our friend Andrew Jarecki's family owned this island there, and for like four or five years in a row we went there for Memorial Day. It was quite a group: Jay, Richard, Bryan, Doc, Barry Josephson, Gavin de Becker, J. J. Abrams, Peter Guber, Eric Eisner, and some years even more. They were the greatest trips ever.

TOM ROSS:

Michael loved Jay. Jay would go to New York, stay in Michael's apartment, and have wild rock 'n' roll parties. All these fine pieces of art would get moved onto the bed and we would hear these stories about how he had to spend the next day fixing up the apartment so Michael never had a clue what had happened at his apartment.

ROB LIGHT:

Jay had a great relationship with everyone in this town. I mean, he was just a soft-spoken big teddy bear of a guy. He was really instinctual about artists, so people just loved him.

MICHAEL WIMER:

My next momentous decision, like most of the previous ones, came dressed in a pretty simple moment. I had started dating a girl in the television department named Sharon Cicero. She was great. We had been dating for a while and I realized that this was different. In the spring of 1993, I took her up to the Biltmore on one of our getaway weekends. While we were out by the pool, I got a call from one of the guys saying so-and-so was leaving his agency and we needed to have an emergency meeting to deal with it. In that minute, it was crystal clear. I looked over at Sharon while she slept and I said, "Can't do it. Go on without me." I knew, right then, that it was one of those huge decisions. Things were beginning to feel "off" in those meetings . . . what I wanted from the group of friends at the beginning was now at odds with what that group was becoming. Frankly, I had never taken any joy in killing anyone, and I didn't need it. I had friends, stories, my future wife, money, and success. If I was going to choose between going down that road or starting a family, it was an easy choice. I pulled out. It was the right move and I didn't have a moment's regret when Ovitz later gave the company to the guys. They deserved it.

RON MEYER:

When those guys started evolving, there was no stopping them. I used to say to Michael when we were all there, "We have to make them partners. We have to do something or you're going to wake up and have those guys compete with you. They will exhaust you."

TOM LASSALLY:

Jay had a very challenging childhood with very little supervision and an alcoholic father who was not there for him. He was a kid who bounced around and ran around and was a little bit of a wild man. He was raised by wolves. His life at CAA gave him structure and he looked up to Mike Ovitz. Yes, Michael was tough on Jay, but he was tough on everyone. Ovitz was good for Jay. He taught Jay discipline and hard work and gave him a place in the world, goals, and lots of things he never had. It would be hard for anybody to say Ovitz didn't do well by Jay.

DAVID O'CONNOR:

Jay and I were sitting at Richard's house in the room where he watches TV, and the other guys were in the kitchen. We had called Michael and he said, "Where are you guys?" and because he lived right around the corner, he just came over. Bob Goldman was with him. We never quite understood what Bob Goldman did.

So as I'm hearing his car pull up in the driveway, I look over at Jay, and suddenly his nose starts to bleed spontaneously, just gushing blood. I go, "Holy shit, Jay—you know, your nose is bleeding." He ran to the bathroom and he's got tissues shoved up his nose just as Michael's walking in the house. I looked at him and said, "Jay. What the fuck is going on?" And he says, "Oh, nothing, I've got these polyps in my nose and I've got to have a procedure done." But his behavior was really erratic and he was really wired up in this meeting, acting kind of crazy. That was when I first realized we had a problem with his coke use, at that moment. All of us looked at each other and said, "Wow. Something's wrong here."

Ron Meyer was in his office with one of his many protégés—CAA agent Kevin Huvane. On the phone was actress Demi Moore. The news was good, and Demi told Meyer how grateful she was for the help. "Kevin did all the heavy lifting on this," Meyer told her. "He's the one that deserves the bulk of the thanks."

Elsewhere, CAA agent Jay Moloney had just gotten off the phone with one of the agency's superstar clients, director Martin Scorsese. Moloney was bouncing off the walls, telling Michael Ovitz and several other agents gathered Scorsese had told Moloney how much he loved him and how much he loved working with him. It was, Moloney said, "The greatest phone call of my life." Ovitz took all Moloney's unbridled enthusiasm in, and then said to him, "Yeah, and I can take him back with just one phone call." Moloney's face went flat.

ACT TWO

When I moved to L.A., one of the first things someone told me about the industry—with a Talmudic hand on my shoulder—was "Be careful. You're entering a business where most people don't root for their friends to fail, they root for their friends to die."

—STEVE TISCH

5

The Prince of Denmark:
January 1, 1995–August 15, 1995

If you wait by the river long enough, the bodies of your enemies will float by.
—SUN TZU

Nineteen ninety-five. It would turn out to be the most tumultuous year in CAA history. Although there had been hints along the way suggesting change was imminent, few could have guessed that the next eight months would be so dramatic.

In the previous decade, CAA had recalculated the entertainment industry's power equation in profound and even shocking ways. Soon that ecosystem would be jolted, buffeted, and transformed yet again.

The year started off normally enough—which for Ovitz and company meant going their own independent way from what other agencies were doing. CAA's motion picture, television, and music divisions were humming along, as was the investment banking arm, and now there were two more significant items to be added to the list, once again, both high profile: the pursuit of an NFL franchise and a bold if risky effort to marry telephone companies with video. This second new brainstorm, to be called Tele-TV, would be headed up by then-CBS President and Welsh-born Howard Stringer, later to be Sir Howard after he was knighted by Queen Elizabeth II in 1999.

ROGER GOODELL, NFL Commissioner:
In the mid-'90s, when Michael was still at CAA, I was an executive at the NFL primarily working on trying to get stadiums built in communities, and trying to keep teams from relocating. It was within that context that I first met Michael.

He had real vision about bringing a team to Los Angeles, and he wanted to deliver what he thought the community needed—which was a great stadium, a great facility, and a great architectural piece. He also wanted to create an entertainment destination so he could capture the magic of Los Angeles, which is the entertainment capital of the world.

Michael's plans really worked from a creative standpoint, not just the way he looked into the future, but the way he pulled the past into it. He did research—he had books and books, and he brought in architects who were completely different from anyone who had designed a stadium before, like David Rockwell. Now who would have ever thought about bringing him into a stadium? Michael did, so it could be more than just a stadium in a traditional sense; it became a living space, a place to entertain. He was ahead of his time.

STEVE TISCH:

My father had bought 50 percent of the New York Giants in 1991, and Mike got in touch and told me, "I'm interested in owning an NFL team. Can I talk to you about this?" I said, "Of course." I liked, and still like, Mike Ovitz, so I didn't feel that was much of a quid pro quo.

ROGER GOODELL:

I use the word *relentless* for Michael, because he is. When he gets hooked on something, he becomes relentless. He's just completely engulfed in it. It's focus on steroids. Michael would have brought a similar benefit to us at the league in the way we market, and in the way we look at many other things. He looks at things differently than you or I look at them. To you and me, that's a bottle of water. To Michael, it's something else. I believed his vision for a new team was correct, but he also needed to have the money and needed to have a team. Those pieces don't always come together in exactly the right way. Maybe because he was the most powerful man in Hollywood and able to make things happen on his time frame, he thought he would have a certain amount of control. It may have been difficult to realize things are a lot more complicated in the NFL. We have to get three-quarters of the owners to approve anything of significance. He had to buy a team, or at least get an option on a team and find out how he was going to acquire them. He also had to find a stadium that was financeable, one that followed all the rules. That's where the frustration came in. At that point in time, I want to say the expansion team was somewhere in the $500 million to $600 million range—not including building the stadium. That's a serious commitment, by the way, and a lot for Michael to swallow. Well, that's what it takes. It takes someone who has that kind of capital to invest and make that come true. I think that was just slightly out of reach, which is where his frustration came from. He just didn't have the resources. He couldn't control all of the pieces.

Then again, the teams that were then selling for $500 million back then are now selling for $2 billion. So his vision really was right, and if he could have made it work, it would have really worked.

SANDY CLIMAN:
The idea behind Tele-TV was pretty simple—the giant cable companies were talking about getting into the telephone business in competition with the Regional Bell Operating Companies, or RBOCs, which were the seven "Baby Bells" created from the antitrust break-up of the AT&T system. The RBOCs were huge businesses, with a virtual monopoly on local telephone service, but their profits were government regulated. If the cable companies sheared off even 10 percent of the RBOCs' business, the phone companies could quickly turn unprofitable. I had the thought that we should bring together three RBOCs which covered major media markets into the telco version of a broadcast group to compete with the cable guys in providing television service. I walked into Mike's office with two maps of the United States. In my left hand, I had a map with hundreds of dots covering the country, representing the scattershot nature of cable operators. In my right hand, the map showed the seven RBOCs, whose service footprints blanketed multistate regions of the country. I said, "Let's put three

of these RBOCs together into a TV service." We initially selected NYNEX, which included New York City; Ameritech, headquartered in Chicago; and San Francisco–based Pacific Telesis, which also included most of Los Angeles. After we launched Tele-TV, Michael Eisner had Disney launch a competitor called Americast. Eventually, we had to replace Ameritech with D.C.-based Bell Atlantic when Eisner convinced Ameritech CEO Dick Notebaert to shift from Tele-TV to Americast.

DAN ADLER:

Michael's Tele-TV pitch relied on a fundamentally visionary approach to how TV-quality programming could be delivered over twisted-pair copper—and a lot of sizzle. I remember weeks of preparation for the big pitch meeting that took place in the screening room of the Pei building. A lot of focus was on how the idea of a "program guide" could become something much more than the scrolling text screens that cable guides of the day were offering, and to make that point, we enlisted the help of our client Robin Williams. As was always the case with him, a couple lines of direction resulted in a riff that was one of the most memorable one could ever dream of seeing. Robin essentially took on the role of "navigator," and to really drive that home, the idea was to have him come out of the ocean, walk up on the beach, and then let his brilliant mind capture the spirit of what this new world could be. And so a few hours of production on the Venice Beach resulted in one of the most magical pieces of content imaginable. We also had David Letterman record a top ten list that was equally powerful and memorable. Needless to say, the room was blown away by the substance and by the sizzle.

SANDY GRUSHOW, Executive:

I had a very close working relationship with Barry Diller while at Fox, and we remained in close contact even after he departed the company in '91. In '94, after I became the president of Fox network's entertainment division, Barry called to inform me that he was planning to make a run at CBS and that he wanted to introduce me to Howard Stringer, who was chairman of CBS at the time and who would be staying on if Barry was successful in his bid. Howard and I immediately started talking about working together at CBS. At exactly the same time, CAA partner Bill Haber whispered to me that he had a really interesting opportunity for me to consider: three telcos—Bell Atlantic, NYNEX, and PacTel—were joining forces in an effort to get into the video delivery business and CAA would be helping them to navigate Hollywood. Turns out Barry did not acquire CBS and Howard decided to leave CBS. Howard then called to tell me that "Mr. Ovitz had put me on his magic carpet," and that *he* would be joining the telco venture as chairman and wanted me to join him as president. After a quick consultation with Barry, I agreed to do so.

SANDY CLIMAN:

Bill Haber targeted CBS head Howard Stringer as founding CEO for Tele-TV, and Mike and Bill put on a full-court press to recruit him. Howard would call me daily asking, "Is this the right thing for me to do?" I told him, "Howard, you really don't like working for Larry Tisch. If this works out, it's great—you make history. If not, you have a guaranteed payment of $20 million from some of the largest and most stable companies in America."

HOWARD STRINGER:

I wish I'd stayed at CBS, but I was with Barry Diller all the way through the potential sale and was with him on an airplane when that deal fell through. At that point, I thought it was time to leave, and Tele-TV was an exciting, entrepreneurial opportunity. But it was a very difficult thing to do after thirty years.

DAVID LETTERMAN:

When Howard left, the network really went into free fall for a while. He was a real gentleman. I don't know about this "Sir Howard" bullshit, but he would come by and say hello, much like

Ovitz did. Mike and Howard always checked in and made sure everything was okay. Then Westinghouse owned it, and the guy running the company never showed up. I was a real punk about it, and even talked about it on the show, but you know, I was a different person then.

SANDY GRUSHOW:

From the beginning, the telcos were focused on delivering interactive television. They were doing tests, but the platform was far from ready to be deployed at scale. And so they needed an interim video delivery strategy. They decided on a microwave-based technology called MMDS. It would require people to have tiny antennas on their property.

LEN FINK:

I was trying to get these telco companies to understand what they could do. I said, "Your phone is something that, as things develop, people are going to carry with them. And it could carry preferences, it could have things that connect you to what now are called applications." And I said, "It could be an entertainment and news delivery system." Then I held up drawings of a controller for television that was a touch screen. I said, "You can touch these things on this screen, turn down the temperature in your house, and watch the news." Later, Bob Goldman at CAA went to Ovitz and said, "This is really a huge idea and we should try to copyright the intellectual property." I don't know whatever happened about that. But we were basically talking about the iPhone in 1995.

SANDY GRUSHOW:

On my very first day on the job in early '95, Michael Ovitz introduced the three telco CEOs, Ray Smith, Phil Quigley, and Ivan Seidenberg, to Michael Armstrong and Eddie Hartenstein of DIRECTV. Howard and I were both in the room, and even though I would later come to question how much Michael actually understood about the telcos' intentions, to his credit, on this day he was trying to convince them to abandon MMDS and acquire a satellite company, which, I believe, could have been had for under $1 billion. After Michael and Eddie left the room, the three telco CEOs summarily rejected the idea. They were committed to MMDS. Well, it turned out that MMDS was a highly flawed technology and we all witnessed the explosive growth of DIRECTV in the ensuing years. Michael had it right. Who knows how the media business would have evolved had they followed Michael's suggestion?

SANDY CLIMAN:

The failure was the timing. We were too early on the merger of telecom and video.

LEN FINK:

The technology was behind. I kept saying, "It has to be as good as television or we're going to have a problem." There were problems with cost as well. Bell Atlantic had this set-top box that was, I thought, just too expensive, but there was an incredible footprint between those three companies, and we had the content. This was content delivery. We basically had what Netflix was; we just missed it.

HOWARD STRINGER:

I listened to a podcast a couple of weeks ago that said if the telcos had stayed with Tele-TV, they would have had Fios a lot faster, and it would have been a very bright thing for them to have done. But it would have taken too long; it took ten years anyway. It was a piece of technology way ahead of its time, and yes, we did make money, but that wasn't the most important issue.

SANDY CLIMAN:

We made an enormous amount of money on Tele-TV because the fee structure was heavily front-loaded, with the largest payment of all due to us in year one. I had sold that schedule of fees to our three RBOC partners, telling them that the true "heavy lifting" was in the first years. It was not an easy sale, but it did protect us from any of the pitfalls that could have later undermined the venture. The full Tele-TV fee to just CAA alone would have been over $50 million in five years, and we earned over a third of that amount before the team ended its operations.

Ovitz was getting restless. He didn't want to keep doing anything he had already done. Meyer was getting restless, too, but was torn. On most days, he dreamt about getting out from under Ovitz—a big part of him had just had enough of what he believed was his cohort's obsession with secrecy, control, and autonomous activities ostensibly on behalf of CAA, but most certainly to the benefit of himself. The original "one for all and all for one" had become for Meyer only the latter. But on other days, the agency business itself bothered him a lot more. He had been doing it for twenty-five years and sometimes believed his best chances for a major change would be via Route Ovitz.

RON MEYER:

Something was happening. You could feel it.

MORT JANKLOW:

Michael was never a backslapping part of the Hollywood community. That was not his style, nor did he see that as his role. He was a really serious business executive and could have run any media company in the world and done a great job. He knew how to create incentives for people; he knew how to keep a little bit of distance so that people didn't lean on him personally more than they had a right to; and his judgments were very good and very sound.

Then things started going off the rails.

MICHAEL OVITZ:

I was forty-nine, about to be fifty. I had been working steadily full-time since I was seventeen. I was burned out.

MAGIC JOHNSON:

I felt Michael's pain. We had become good friends, as we are today, and I only wanted the best for him. One day I said to him, "Why don't you run a studio?" He said, "Earvin, I don't have to run a studio. I run them all now anyway."

BARRY HIRSCH:

Sometime toward the mid-'90s I noticed Michael started to behave like he didn't like what he was doing. He also shared those thoughts with me. He didn't like those late-night phone calls from clients. That's when he started to look elsewhere. He was more than tired; he was just disenchanted with what he was doing, and so I think he gave more and more to the Young Turks.

PETER GUBER:

It was very seductive to any human being to be at the center of all of those activities, and that's where Mike Ovitz was at that time. And when the other opportunities came his way, difficult questions came along as well, like Who will I be when I give it up? What will I be when I take this new job? Will I be a second banana to the person who's the first banana? How will I be looked at in the community?

BILL HABER:

For any agent, the minute you become more important than your client, your company is finished, because an agent is never himself or herself—there's no such thing as Ron Meyer; there is only Farrah Fawcett. The minute it becomes Ron Meyer and not Farrah Fawcett, it's not a company anymore. The nature of the agency business is you represent other people. It is never about you. Michael had become the most powerful man in the industry—so high profile, so important, and so successful that he came to be more than the company.

SYLVESTER STALLONE:

The odd thing was, Mike Ovitz was the low man on the totem pole when they got that group together. He was doing syndicated television on a low level. Ron was senior; so was Bill Haber and those other guys. But there's an aspect to Ovitz that makes him different. The scent of power appealed to him, and it emboldened him. This was not the way they went into business. It was never *Mike is the leader and we're all following*. It was quite the opposite. That was probably what blew Ron's mind. He was thinking, *I wouldn't have gone into business if I'd known it would be this*.

PETER GUBER:

Ron was in an abusive marriage with Mike. That's exactly what it was. And he was a victim, but he was also an enabler. I'm not faulting him for that, and I'm sure he recognized this as well. An enabler, right.

JOHN PTAK:

Primarily because of Crédit Lyonnais, I had spent a lot of time traveling with Mike, learned an awful lot about him, and got to really like him. Truth is, I thought he was rather shy. But during the period when he was getting so much attention, he started walking through airports with sunglasses and baseball hats, and Sandy Climan and I would be running flank.

RON MEYER:

I had said to Mike for years the good thing we did was bring other agents into our clients' lives, and that led to the bad thing we did, which was give up control over the clients. I kept saying to Mike, "We have to have an exit plan." I would say Mike and I were in the twentieth year of a ten-year plan that we would turn the agency over. I said, "We're going to burn out being agents. We're working seven days a week, twenty-four hours a day. It's got to stop."

RICK NICITA:

One day I was sitting in Ronnie's office and his assistant said, "Ovitz on line one," and I saw Ronnie wince like he had just been punched in the stomach. It was so palpable, I just thought, *Wow.* It was like somebody had just hit me over the head with a hammer because in the previous few months, things hadn't seemed the same. When I saw Ronnie wince like that, I knew things had really changed.

BARRY MEYER:

For better or for worse, CAA is the story of something that came together because of good relationships and fell apart because of bad ones.

HOWARD WEST:

Michael's aggressiveness was always more feared than respected. There were a lot of people who respected him, a lot, but more feared him. Ultimately you pay a price for that; ultimately they dislike you; and ultimately they want to whack you.

SYLVESTER STALLONE:

Mike Ovitz carried a heavy hammer, and he swung it like he was Beverly Hills Thor. He went around smashing people, sometimes I think just for the fun of it. He did things to me that I thought were beyond unfair. We got into sort of a business with art, and the person he hooked me up with turned out to be a disaster, and had me spending a great deal of money on art that turned out to be—well, I don't want to get into it because of the lawsuit, but it just wasn't good. The next thing I know, he's throwing an engagement party for them at CAA, a building that I basically put tons of money into with my commissions. I told him, "I find this to be really offensive. You know how much these people hurt me, yet you're celebrating them?" He said to me, "What do you want me to do? Cancel it? Throw them out? And embarrass yourself and me all over the city? Would that make you happy?" I believe that was the last time I talked to him for many, many years.

Is he beloved? That's a rhetorical question.

TOM ROSS:

Michael never let me down. I learned more from him in my first two years working for him than I had in the fifteen years before that. He was the greatest manager I've ever worked for, and he set a new standard for how agents were treated, regarded, and compensated.

IRVING AZOFF:

Ovitz had wanted to be the most powerful man in Hollywood, and now that that was happening, I'm of the opinion that he started believing his own press and getting kind of egoed out. There was definitely no love lost between Ovitz and Wasserman and Sheinberg at Universal.

SID SHEINBERG:

I considered Michael a friend, but where I come from in Texas, friends behave a certain way toward friends. With Mike, you weren't exactly sure who he was representing. He discussed with me the possible sale of his agency, something I don't think he was doing with many others. I thought he had a wonderful business, forgetting for the moment the way he conducted it.

DAVID O'CONNOR:

Jay and I were in and out of his office ten times a day because of the amount of contact we had with his clients. He always kept us in the fold, but I remember many times when either one of us or both of us would walk into his office and say, "Michael, what's going on here?" People were calling us incessantly saying, "You know he's fucking you, right? He's leaving. He's going to leave." But he would always deny it to us.

JUDY OVITZ:

Michael always had great visions of what he could do, but he was getting frustrated because there was so much more he had to give and felt his hands were tied.

MICHAEL OVITZ:

I didn't want to be in the service business anymore. I felt it was time for a change.

DAVID O'CONNOR:

I had been working with Sean Connery, and at one point, he made it official. He took me to lunch and said, "You're my agent. When Michael's doing this or that, you're my guy." And he was very clear about what he wanted from me.

Arne Glimcher wanted to direct this movie called *Just Cause* and his film career was almost a creation of Ovitz because Arne was one of the most important art dealers and Michael had built this incredible art collection with Arne's help. Michael was hell-bent on getting this movie put together for Arne, and so he committed Sean Connery to the movie. The problem was, Sean Connery didn't know he was committed to the movie, he just thought this was a script in development.

On a Friday, we got a new script for the movie, and we all read it over the weekend. The plan was to call Sean on Monday, and Ray Kurtzman was going to be on it as well, because he was very involved in Sean's deals. Ray was getting increasingly unsettled about our legal situation because as far as Warners was concerned, Sean was committed to the movie and they had already spent $10 million on preproduction, and Ray didn't want this to be a liability for us. The call was supposed to start at 9:00 A.M. and Sean is very punctual, and sure enough, at 9:00 A.M. he called and said to my assistant, "What's going on here? I've got a call scheduled; get these guys on the phone." So he hangs up with my assistant, and I'm supposed to call him right back, but Michael is not around. I can't get Michael. But there's no delaying a call with Sean, so Ray and I get on the phone with him, and he says, "Well, did you read the script?" And I said, "Yeah," but I didn't want to talk about it until Michael was on the phone. Then Sean just goes off on it. Says the script is a piece of shit, and he's just ripping it apart. We're now ten minutes into the call and he has now completely talked himself out of this movie.

Sean always called me "the boy," and a couple minutes later, Michael finally gets on the phone, and the first thing out of Connery's mouth is "Well, me and the boy both agree that this script is a piece of shit and this is not a movie for me to do," and I was ready to pass out. Michael says, "You know what, Sean? I'm sorry I'm late. This isn't the time or place for this conversation. Let me call you back." And you could tell he was pissed as he hung up. But I didn't have a chance to refute anything that Sean said. And now I'm still on the phone with Sean, and he starts yelling at me. I mean, screaming. "This is exactly what I was talking about, boy! You have to stand up to him. You have to tell him that this is not a movie that I should be doing and you have to stand up for me now!" Meanwhile my assistant hands me a note which says, *Michael wants to see you as soon as you are off the phone with Sean.* So I get off the phone with Connery and walk to Michael's office. What usually happens is he'd been on the phone and you'd have to wait in his office until he was off the phone. It could be ten or fifteen minutes. But in this instance, as soon as he saw me, he said to whoever he was on the phone with, "I'm sorry, can I call you right back?" And he gets off the phone. He looks at me, takes off his headset, and is so fucking pissed that he throws it down on his travertine desk and it shatters all over the place. I even got hit with the shrapnel from it, right? And he comes around his desk and he gets right up into my face, and he's bright red. His veins are popping out of his neck and his forehead and he starts screaming at me, "You don't know what the fuck you're doing! You're a fucking amateur! I don't know why I fucking pay you and you're done with Sean Connery! You're off the Connery account! Fuck you! Get the fuck out of my office!" I thought I was almost fired.

So I was kicked out of the Connery business, and he did wind up doing the movie; then Sean asked for me to be brought back in and I had to go to Miami and referee between Sean and Arne. I later found out that Michael had gotten Sean to make the movie by not commissioning him on the movie.

MICHAEL OVITZ:

We had accomplished everything at CAA we thought we could accomplish. There wasn't anybody really left to sign. Bill saw the TV packaging business being squeezed, and we thought the movie business was going south in terms of what we could control. It had been our main source of income for many years; we had close to fifty clients who were making more than $10 million a year; and contrary to what some people thought, we were getting a full 10 percent on all of it. We were able to pay our people a ton of money because of this, but I was petrified that if that pie shrunk, it would be a disaster for all of us.

SID SHEINBERG:

I remember on many occasions saying to him, "You've got a business where you invest nothing other than your overhead and yet you get a percentage of the gross. Why are you so anxious to get into the movie business? This is a tough business." I think his answer basically was "But I don't own anything. I don't own a copyright. I don't have contracts with talent. My business can go away." I can't tell you that I'm totally right, but I think he felt upon occasion that agents were not regarded as the class acts of management. My wife was once an agent, so I never felt that way, and of course Lew Wasserman made his career essentially as an agent, not as a studio head.

BILL MURRAY:

It seemed like he was in Japan as much as he was anywhere else. He managed to pull off all those big corporate deals—and they were great—but at a certain point they got so big, things couldn't really get any bigger.

MICHAEL OVITZ:

I saw a bunch of young guys who I was overpaying who thought I wasn't paying them enough and the more time I spent time with these corporate deals—not just doing the M&A work but advising people after as well—the less connectivity I had with my important clients. That meant that the younger guys I had shared these clients with were having more and more contact with them. And people were talking in their ears, rabble-rousing them up. Don't kid yourself; I knew this. It just wasn't a recipe that sounded like a lot of fun.

RON MEYER:

After Frank Wells died, and Jeffrey [Katzenberg] left the company—this was late '94—Mike told me Eisner had offered him a job at Disney, but that he didn't want to accept it because of certain conditions. I said, "Why don't I take a shot at Eisner and see if I can make this work?" The truth is, at that time, I was more than ready for Mike to leave. So I called Eisner and we went to a restaurant on Melrose and we sat there for five hours. Eisner told me, "I want Mike to spend a year learning about Disney. I want him to go all around the world. I want him to spend two months in China and two months in France." He also said he would be open to being co-CEO or co-chairman. I don't remember the entire list of things Mike gave me, but Eisner agreed to everything Mike had wanted except for one situation: If there was a decision where they disagreed, Eisner would privately have the final say. I went back to Mike, who mulled it over for a day or two and then decided to pass.

EDGAR BRONFMAN JR., Executive:

The first time I ever heard from Mike Ovitz was around 1985. He called and told me his father worked for one of Seagram's distributors in Southern California, and according to Mike, management there was forcing him to retire. He said they'd even taken his office away. So I said, "That doesn't sound like the way our distributors normally behave, but let me find out what's going on."

So I actually called the guy who ran my U.S. sales operation at the time and I said, "Look, this guy Dave Ovitz, he's on the Thrifty Drug account and evidently they're trying to get him to retire. Make sure he stays there as long as he likes and that he has an office. When that's done, call me back." He called me back an hour later and said, "Dave Ovitz is in his office for as long as you want." And I said, "Thank you." I called Mike and said, "Call your dad. He's in his office." He said, "I don't know how to thank you," and I said, "You don't have to thank me, I'm happy to do it." And he said, "Well, no, no. I want to thank you. Would you like to meet Martin Scorsese?" And I said, "I'm always happy to meet somebody, but you called me for a favor, I know who you are, I admire what you've done, I'm happy to do you a favor." The next time he came to New York, he called to see me, and from then on, he made it his business to be my friend. There was no salesman like Mike.

MICHAEL OVITZ:

When my dad was about sixty-five, I was worried about him retiring and just sitting around the house. He had no hobbies, no interests, no education—he was old school. So I went to Edgar Bronfman Jr., who he worked for, though I had never met him in my life. I said, "I know sixty-five is your mandatory retirement age, but I would forever be grateful to you if you kept him on. I'll pay you to pay him. I'm afraid if he retires, he'll die." Edgar couldn't have been more gracious; he kept my dad on for another seventeen years, never took my money, and I ended up representing him in the acquisition of Universal.

EDGAR BRONFMAN JR.:

Here's the coda to the father story: So I give Dave Ovitz his job, effectively forever, in the mid-'80s, and then in 1995, I'm told Dave Ovitz, who was then in his mid or late eighties, not only can't drive to work, but he's effectively blind. I called Mike and he said, "You're right, we should do something about it. We'll retire Dad. I get that. But could you do me a favor?" I said, "What's that?" He said, "Could you keep him on the payroll just for a dollar a year so he can continue to get his medical benefits?" I could not believe he was saying this. And I said to him, "No, Mike. It's time for you to take care of your dad."

In February 1995, Michael Ovitz and Herb Allen dispatched Edgar Bronfman Jr. on a secret mission to Osaka, Japan. He was to meet with top executives at Matsushita Corporation, whose management had sent out feelers to Ovitz expressing frustration in dealings with Lew Wasserman and Sid Sheinberg and wanted to explore selling the studio. Ovitz and Allen made a presentation outlining potential buyers, and the one that surprised the Japanese the most was Seagram's, the legendary Canadian-based distiller, owned since 1923 by the Bronfman family. Edgar Bronfman and his brother, Charles, had run the company for decades, but now Edgar Jr. had been given the keys to the family car, and he had set out to re-create the company in bolder, livelier ways.

EDGAR BRONFMAN JR.:

Mike had been pitching for us to do something together for several years, and in February of 1995, he called me and said, "Would you be interested in having a private conversation about a purchase?" The discussions started to get serious pretty quickly. I knew I wanted to divest in DuPont; I thought it was going nowhere and it did indeed go nowhere. Matsushita came in, so it looked like I sold DuPont to buy MCA, but it wasn't planned that way.

CHARLES BRONFMAN, Executive:

When you have a family-controlled business, which this in essence was, there's a lot of freedom, and my problem was during this whole Hollywood episode, it was my brother and my nephew on one side and me on the other side. I was against everything. I was against the purchase of Universal, and I was against the sale of DuPont to pay for it. But I didn't want to start a family war.

Matsushita had given us very clear instructions; we were not allowed to talk to Lew and Sid. I felt badly because they were getting bashed with rumors that Seagram was buying them and they didn't know anything. They didn't call us, and we couldn't call them.

EDGAR BRONFMAN JR.:

Sunday, April 9, 1995, my dad and I called Lew and said, "We signed the deal—can we come have lunch with you tomorrow?" So the four of us had lunch. Sid and Lew were in rare form—I mean, they were screaming and yelling and browbeating and saying basically, "You have to announce a management team this afternoon. You can't leave the studio hanging out there." This just went on and on. It was clear to me that my dad was not going to help. He just sat there and listened and was like, "You wanted this deal, you handle it."

So, finally I said, "Guys, I hear you. We come here with the greatest respect. You've built an unbelievable institution. All we want to do is make it better, and we'd like your help to do that." I said, "We don't have a new management team today. We're not going to announce the old management team today. There really are only two alternatives as I see it: Stay and help us get a new management team, which is what we'd really like, or you can decide you can't do that. I don't have a third alternative." At that point, we decided that my dad was going to go up to Lew's office and I was going to go to Sid's office. Lew was telling my dad, "I'm fine, I just want to make sure Sid's okay."

In his office, Sid started to realize that things were what they were and he moved from me as the enemy at that moment to Matsushita. Now he's yelling at me about Matsushita, how horrible they are, how they've made his life misery. Then he tells me a story about how he and Lew flew all the way to Osaka but they refused to see him, and they just had to fly back. Then he said, "I wrote a letter to the chairman of Matsushita," and he's screaming, "How could they not see Lew Wasserman?!" Now during the negotiations I had heard about this letter—I had never seen it—but I know that Matsushita thought it was the ugliest, angriest letter they'd ever seen in their lives. Anyway, so Sid's banging on the table and he says, "I sent that letter, and do you know that to this very day I have not had the courtesy of a reply!" I said, "Sid, I'm the reply." He looked at me, smiled, and said, "I suppose you are."

I never negotiated with Mike about coming to run MCA until we had a signed deal with Matsushita. But it was always part of the gestalt that we should buy something and he should run it. He talked to me about TimeWarner too because we were then shareholders. It was always his goal, to run something.

RON MEYER:

Mike had big plans for Universal. He was going to move many of us from CAA over there. He expected me to join him. Although I never said no, I wasn't sure it was the right thing for me, and I'm pretty sure if he had gone, I would have wound up staying at the agency. I knew I could lead the group at CAA, and I was *the* leader of all those guys because they trusted me and liked me, but it was Mike's company. We were partners, but Mike had always been the boss and the figurehead of the company.

Bill had no interest in running the company. I wanted to reconfigure the company and do it differently. I also knew that if Mike left and we didn't go, there were going to be a lot of other possibilities for Bill and myself.

PETER GUBER:

When Ron was at the agency, he spent a lot of time between the devil and the deep blue sea.

EDGAR BRONFMAN JR.:

I very much wanted Mike and Ron and Bill. I thought they would be a great crew. They built a great company; they were entrepreneurs who could do it again. The trio was important to me because it was taking the founders of CAA and putting them at MCA. Getting all three was more of a coup, frankly, and it had more management depth than just Mike: Ron was going to run film; Bill would have television; and Mike was going to run the overall show. We'd deal with music and publishing and other stuff later.

BILL HABER:

Michael was going to run Universal. I flew in by helicopter to a meeting where we broke down how we were going to run what was in those days the biggest entertainment company in the world. That sounds like fun, doesn't it?

EDGAR BRONFMAN JR.:

Nobody wanted Ovitz. I mean, Lew hated Ovitz, Sid hated Ovitz. They certainly didn't want to see their legacy being run by Mike.

I started negotiating with Mike for the three of them to come in, and the package he wanted was huge—about $250 million— but what really started to work against my relationship with Mike was his level of paranoia—"Are you on a landline? Where are you? Who's around you?" Oh my God, it was crazy.

MICHAEL OVITZ:

It was actually more than $250 million, because I was negotiating for all of us. The whole package was between $400 million and $450 million, which would have included Ron, Bill, Sandy, Ray, and Bob, and maybe Jack.

TOM ROSS:

He was very paranoid. When he traveled, he thought his rooms were bugged. It got to be very intense. It was obvious that there were other things on his mind, and that he wasn't really dealing with the agency or his clients the way he used to.

JACK RAPKE:

For a number of years, Michael always had this sort of amorphous vision of taking the agency and the agency's assets and sort of blending that into one of these bigger media companies, and he always alluded to the fact that I would be part of that.

When I heard that Michael was negotiating with Universal, I confronted him and asked him if he was going to keep his promise and take me with him. He said, "Well, maybe not initially. Some people will have to stay at the agency to stabilize it after I leave."

At that point, the gauze came off my eyes, and I saw it all very clearly. I told him, "You're going to fuck me on the equity you promised. You promised we were going to do this together and that you were going to give me the studio and now you're going to fuck me on that too. You told me to say no to other opportunities, even though you knew I really wanted to run a studio. I guess ultimately I have to take responsibility for my own actions, but you have just wiped me out—emotionally and psychically. I am going to look for my exit."

TOM ROSS:

While rumors were circulating that Michael was in talks to run MCA, I had gotten a call about running RCA records. I called Michael's office and we set a meeting, but he had to cancel it. I kept trying to get in to see him, and then I ran into him in the hallway and said, "I really need to sit with you," and he said, "Yeah, yeah, we'll do it." Then a couple days later I got a call from him and he was livid. He said, "Everywhere I go, I have to hear you're going to RCA. You do know I'm RCA's consultant, don't you?" I said, "Michael, I have an opportunity to go there and I need to sit with you to see if this is something that I should take advantage of." So we sat down and talked, and he said, "If you want to run a record company, you can do it from here. The sky is the limit."

I said, "Michael, I need to explore other opportunities. I don't want to feel like I've already peaked. There are other things I may want to do. You already have your beach house." And with that, he opened one of his desk drawers and said, "Is this about a beach house?" It was as if he was about to throw a set of keys at me, but I said, "No, it's not specifically about a beach house, but it is about my financial future." He said, "Tom, have I ever disappointed you?" I said, "No." Then he said, "And that day will never come."

Ovitz had a well-deserved reputation as one of the savviest and fastest deal makers in the country. And the man was a veritable process freak. But that was trifling compared to the value he placed on decisiveness.

Yet now, with Universal his for the grabbing, he chose instead to audition for the role of Hamlet. The usual ferocious clarity was nowhere to be found. Meetings and moments that appeared to be critical got sucked into a whirling quagmire. It was the wrong kind of spin and proved predictably dizzying.

BILL HABER:

Michael had the right to ask for $250 million. I didn't begrudge him that.

EDGAR BRONFMAN JR.:

One day I was talking to Mike about the $250 million and I asked, "Is the equity you want going to be split the same way as CAA? 55 percent, 22.5 percent, 22.5 percent?" He said, "No." So I said, "Well, how's it going to be split?" He told me, "Ninety for me, six for Ron, four for Bill." I said to myself, *I've got to get out of this.*

JOEL SILVER:

There's an expression around Hollywood that I actually think was coined by Allen Grubman, a New York music business attorney, "It's not about the money . . . it's about the money." Money colors everything, and now it was about the money.

EDGAR BRONFMAN JR.:

One of the moments when I was alone with Ron, I said, "Ron, it's none of my business, but I asked Mike what the split was and he told me 90 percent, 6 percent, 4 percent. I just want to make sure that you know about that and know that's not how I'm splitting it, because if this deal works, I don't want you pissed at me like I somehow fucked you over. I've had nothing to do with creating that split." He said, "No, no, no. It's Mike. That's the way he is. We'll fix it."

To me, Ron was like a battered wife. He was just in this thing for so long he couldn't see. I thought just the opposite: Any guy who would do that to his partners who built the business with him after twenty years of success was going to do the same thing to me if he could.

RON MEYER:

He took care of himself; the deal he was making for me probably wasn't great, but Mike's attitude was always he needs more than I do anyway. I was poor my whole life, and was making more money than I ever imagined. At CAA, I didn't want to kill the goose that laid the golden eggs.

SANDY CLIMAN:

We were in Edgar's New York town house—Mike, Bob Goldman, me, with Edgar. We were done negotiating Mike's deal to head Universal, and Mike had finally said, "Yes." But Mike just kept going without a pause. He was very intense and was bringing up point after point. Finally, Edgar stopped him and said, "Can't we just take a minute and enjoy this moment?" But Mike couldn't.

RON MEYER:

When Mike was negotiating with Edgar, I really thought it was going to happen.

EDGAR BRONFMAN JR.:

Then we started having conversations about how the business was going to run—what his role was going to be versus my role, and that's when I realized he had absolutely no idea how corporations worked. Zero. I was like, "Whoa." One time it was around treasury and I said, "Mike, the treasury function is at corporate," and he said, "Well, I need my own treasury function," and I said, "Mike, if you say you need your own treasury function, you don't even know what a treasury function is. You can't have two treasury functions." He said, "Whatever you have, I have to have." I didn't realize how little he really knew—not that he wasn't smart, he just didn't know. But he was more invested in making people believe he was a genius than actually letting people know that he was brilliant about certain things but completely not educated about other things. He didn't have the vulnerability to say, "Hey, I don't know about this. Teach it to me." He couldn't be vulnerable with anybody about anything. There were huge pockets of things he just didn't know about how to run a company.

SANDY CLIMAN:

Even though Mike had agreed with Edgar in New York to the deal, Mike continued to wrestle with whether leaving the agency was the right decision for him. The staff already knew that we were in discussions for Universal.

IVAN REITMAN:

I was very close to Mike through the negotiations with Universal. He told me Edgar just kept offering him more and more, and what the offers were. I had kept telling Mike, "Just say yes. This is the best deal I've ever heard of, and at some point he's going to lose patience." He was the worst agent for himself as a client.

PETER GUBER:

All change is anxiety provoking—good change or bad change. How you handle that anxiety can shape your clarity around a decision. I think what happened was he had second thoughts about leaving the agency, so his process lacked the clarity that he brought to other people's processes that he managed. He was not his own best adviser, right? It shows you, when you have yourself as an agent and you're the client, you have a fool for a client.

JOEL SILVER:

Terry Semel, Ronnie, and I had dinner at Mike's house the night they were going to finally close with Edgar. They had been negotiating for months and they were intending to lock it up that very evening. The deal was the greatest in the history of man; it was ready to go, and Edgar was ready to sign off. When we were having dinner, Mike said he was going to tell Edgar that the only thing left to be resolved was a substantial cash increase because he wanted Seagram's to pay his taxes. And Ronnie said, "Mike, we're going to lose this," but Mike just said, "I know what I'm doing." Terry and I left; Ronnie and Mike stayed and got on the phone with Edgar. So I heard from Ronnie afterward that Mike did say, "If you find a way to cover the taxes, we'll close the deal," and Edgar was very disappointed.

RON MEYER:

I was in the room at the Century Plaza Hotel when Mike and Edgar Jr. shook hands and closed their deal, but there were still a few open points. I said, "Mike, you're losing them, you've pushed this too far. They've said yes to everything you want," and then I told him, "If you keep asking for more, you're going to make this deal go away." The negotiations continued, and during that time, I heard that Mike and/or his lawyers brought up some new issues.

SANDY CLIMAN:

We were all at Mike's house. Mike, Bill, Ron, Bob, me— debating the pros and cons. Once again, it seemed like decision time on Seagram and Universal. If Mike went, we all went. Given what had gone on at the agency and knowing Ron's state of mind about his own future, I saw little choice but for Mike to take the deal. Finally, Mike asked Ron and Bill to join him upstairs in his bedroom for a private chat. They came back down and Mike said, "We're not going. Not taking the deal."

MICHAEL OVITZ:

I was planning on taking around fifteen people with me from the agency. It could've been fourteen. And that's when I went upstairs and I realized: *What am I doing? I'm taking the whole senior management team out of the business. Why don't I just stay with the business since at least we're in control of it?*

CHARLES BRONFMAN:

I didn't follow the whole process, but I did know Edgar Jr. wanted to hire him and apparently they had agreed on compensation. A few of us heard about the compensation, and it was totally out of the realm of possibilities. I called Edgar Jr. on the weekend and said, "We can't do that." So that was that.

MICHAEL OVITZ:

It became very clear to me that Edgar, who I kind of liked, was not in control of the business and that his father and his uncle were in control. Because they halved the offer they made us. They cut it way down, and they cut the equity way down. I said to Ron and Bill that I felt I couldn't trust us going in there and having complete autonomy.

EDGAR BRONFMAN JR.:

I realized that I had just agreed to buy a movie studio among other things, and I couldn't just tell Mike Ovitz to go fuck himself. If CAA—the largest agency in Hollywood—blacklisted Universal, there would be a crappy outcome. I had to get Mike to turn it down. So I used my uncle, who Mike knew was the least enthusiastic about making a deal with him, as an excuse. I just kept backing up the numbers. I just kept saying, "Mike, I really want you, but Charles is driving me crazy about this, I really can't do this or that," until he finally said, "Fuck you, this is ridiculous. I'm not doing it." I said, "Mike, please reconsider," but he said, "Forget it."

RON MEYER:

It could have been his; he fucked that up. He would have owned a piece of Universal.

TOM POLLOCK:

That Mike Ovitz ultimately talked himself out of the deal that Edgar offered him shows, in my opinion, how little he understood about the business. Ovitz had wanted language in the deal about how much interference Edgar could have, and that was idiotic. With Lew and Sid gone, and Edgar, who many thought was not the brightest individual in the world, Mike Ovitz could have run Universal with a free hand. He might have run it badly or well, but he would have had a free hand.

JACK RAPKE:

So he blows the deal. Now he comes back, humiliated, embarrassed. By this time, everybody knows that he was negotiating to leave the agency, even the clients know. It wasn't *"Is* he leaving?"— it was *"When* is he leaving?"

LEE GABLER:

Michael came into a staff meeting and said that he was staying. The place stood up and applauded. I said, "Okay, we're moving forward, everything is good."

SANDY CLIMAN:

Over the years, every time Mike flirted with a deal to leave the agency, it was secret. If the discussions became known later in time, usually years later, there was both plausible deniability and the reality that we had not left. With Seagram and Universal that changed. When Mike had gotten up in the CAA theater and admitted to the agents, "They're talking and we're listening," he put the company in play, and we were never going to put the genie back in the bottle. The sense of lifetime security at an impenetrable fortress evaporated in an instant. Days later, the same group assembled in the theater to hear Mike say he had turned down the job and was staying at the agency. What Mike said he saw was wild applause and visible relief. What I saw was my friends clapping, but they were ashen—some angry that they had been excluded from the group going to Universal, some feeling betrayed, some sensing that this was the beginning of the end for the CAA to which they had pledged their undying loyalty.

DAN ADLER:

The sort of unassailable CAA truism is nobody really had contracts there and yet nobody really left. That culture certainly started with the partners themselves—Michael, Ron, and Bill—but it was most embodied by Michael. There had been many rumors, particularly around the Sony era, that Michael would leave to run Sony, but Michael vehemently denied all of them. But that summer, there were rumors that were so strong, Michael was forced to stand up at a staff meeting and say that he was indeed negotiating to run Universal. As it all kept playing out later in the summer, *Newsweek* hit the newsstands and the story said Michael was leaving. Very early that morning, a memo went out announcing an all-staff meeting, at which Michael stood up and said, "I'm staying." On one level, it was a great relief, but on another, it was an enormous blow. It was sort of like the father who'd gone off and had an affair, then acknowledged he had the affair and came back and said, "Never mind, I'm still here. Don't worry about it." I think part of the CAA code, that covenant of sorts, was broken by what had happened with Michael's Universal dance.

SANDY GALLIN:

It was like Ron was in an abusive, horrible marriage. Instead of partners in bed, they were partners in business. He used to call me up and tell me, "You can't believe what Mike did."

RON MEYER:

Barry Diller offered me a job once at Fox, but it was a quarter of the money that I made. I had another offer, from Stanley Jaffe at Paramount, but neither were good enough jobs for me to leave CAA for.

When the Universal deal didn't happen with Mike, I realized that he was never going anywhere. I had always hoped that Mike would leave and I could stay and reconfigure the company and do it differently. But in the end, I realized Mike was never going to leave unless I did. He was in the position he wanted and making all the money he wanted.

I knew that it was time for me to separate with Mike. We were a marriage going bad. It was then that I told Mike and Bill that I was going to be leaving the company. I told them that I didn't know when I was going to leave, but that I was probably going to open up the Ron Meyer Company—that I wasn't going to be an agent somewhere else, and I was just going to put a shingle out and figure out things from there. I said I would let them know my timing.

IRWIN WINKLER:

Ron and I discussed it a lot at the time. He felt at this point in his life he was ready for a new challenge. The offer that was made was very generous. But I think the most important thing was he just felt it was time for him to move out of the agency business and find something new. Don't forget, there were a whole bunch of Young Turks like Bryan Lourd and Richard Lovett who really wanted to take over.

JEFFREY KATZENBERG:

Ron and Bill were the salt of the earth, and they were in business with a maniac. The two of them were really, really decent, honest brokers, and people you could trust and partner with. So when Ron was considering moving on and leaving the agency to take an executive job, we for sure talked about it, and I encouraged him.

DAVID GEFFEN:

Ron is a very good friend of mine. We had gone to a screening, then he was dropping me off at my house, and I said to him, "You can't stay an agent for the rest of your life." And he said, "I'd leave it tomorrow for the right job." I said, "Well, what would be the right job?" He said, "I want to have a job like John Calley's job at Warner Bros.," which we both understood was a job where he wasn't the top guy but he was a very significant guy there and he came and went as he liked, he dressed the way he wanted. I understood exactly what he meant. So I said, "Okay, if there's ever an opportunity for a job like that, I'll see what I can do."

EDGAR BRONFMAN JR.:

When the deal with Mike fell apart, he got himself on the cover of a magazine and basically humiliated me. It wasn't just that he said, "I'm not doing that." He pissed all over me, which really pissed me off. Then I got a call from David [Geffen]. At that point, he hated Mike and liked me—then, not now. David told me that Ron was going to call me. I'd gotten to know Ron through the process of negotiating with Mike, but Mike never allowed me to spend much time alone with Ron. So when Mike and I stopped negotiating, I had one observation and two motivations: my observation was that CAA was like a tanker. Mike Ovitz was the tugboat and the tanker went where the tugboat went, but Ron was the rope that attached the tugboat to the tanker. So I knew when Ron called me that I wanted two things: to get Ron and to fuck Mike the way he was trying to fuck me. I'm not saying that was the right motivation, but I'm telling you those were the two things that were in my head.

DAVID GEFFEN:

What happened was, Edgar called me up and told me that he was having problems closing the deal with Mike and he wanted to talk to me about it, so he came to my apartment in New York. He explained the deal and how Mike kept on asking for more and renegotiating to try and make it better. He told me his father had finally lost patience with it. He felt he had gone too far and wanted to go in the other direction and make it less than what was on the table at that moment.

And I said to Edgar, "You know, you're going to have nothing but trouble with Mike. This is the way he is." And because I knew Ronnie wanted out, that Ronnie hated being an agent and was fearful he'd never get out, I said to Edgar, "I've got the perfect guy for you." He said, "Who's that?" I said, "Ron Meyer. Ron Meyer is the guy you should get. Ron Meyer is a guy who you can work with; who you can trust; who isn't greedy and everybody loves him. And he knows everybody." So he said, "What would he cost me?" I said, "Send me a contract and Ron will sign it. He won't negotiate it at all." He said, "Are you serious?" I said, "Absolutely. Whatever you send me he will sign."

I called up Ronnie and I said, "Ronnie, it's here. I can make a deal for you to become president of Universal." And Ron said, "You're kidding." I said, "No, I'm not kidding, and I think we can close the deal." I said, "I told him that whatever he offered you, whatever that was, there'd be no negotiation. You'd sign the contract as it was." He said, "Count on it." And that's how it happened.

MICHAEL DOUGLAS:

Edgar Bronfman Jr. was an old friend of mine, and I followed all the steps that happened with Ovitz until the straw that broke the camel's back. I encouraged Edgar to call Ron; I said, "Edgar, you really need a Ron Meyer. You need someone who's talent friendly." Steven Spielberg had a strong hold in there, but it was not a talent-friendly studio and it desperately needed somebody like Ronnie to kind of bring it back around.

DAVID GEFFEN:

It was really immaterial to me what would happen at CAA. Ron was my friend. I was interested in doing the right thing for Ron, and what created the opportunity for Ron was that Mike Ovitz was a pig. He was unable to say "done deal." Because had he said "done deal," the deal would have been done. Mike wanted out of the agency business and was trying to get out, but Ron walked away with his job because Mike was greedy. That's the whole story. Mike fucked the whole thing up.

EDGAR BRONFMAN JR.:

I really wanted to be the anti-Sid. For so many years, Universal had been a factory; a difficult place to work; and a studio of last resort for many people, other than Steven. I wanted it to be the opposite. I wanted to be leaning forward into talent. I first thought Mike was very talent friendly, but I came to understand from the negotiations that he wasn't at all, that it was Ron who had the relationships. Michael had a few—Sydney Pollack, Martin Scorsese, and a couple of others—but Ron would give the company credibility in town; he had tremendous talent relationships and respect. People were loyal to Ron because Ron was loyal, but no one was actually loyal to Mike. Mike had behaved like he didn't really want to make a deal except on his terms.

Ron called me at 6:00 A.M.; he was also in New York. He said, "I'm in my bathroom because I don't want to wake up my wife." Then he says, "L.A. is calling me; can I call you right back?" I said, "Ronnie, how long are you going to be on the phone? I'd rather you didn't call me back because the phone is going to wake up Clarissa." This was so long ago there weren't cell phones. He said, "Call me back in ten minutes," so I said, "Fine." Fifteen minutes later I call him. He said, "Please don't tell anyone, but this is why I have to get out of the agency business." I said, "What happened?" He said, "Hugh Grant just got arrested for getting blown. We had to bail him out."

RON MEYER:

A few days later, Mike came back to me and said, "If you feel that strongly about it, go see Edgar, get the offer reinstated, and tell him I will accept that last offer." So I went to New York and made a very strong pitch for Mike. But Edgar made it clear that under no circumstances were they going to reinstate the offer to Mike. He literally said, "There's no way that's going to happen." And then Edgar looked at me and said, "But we would like you to take the job." One of the things that had happened since Mike had blown the deal with Bronfman a few days before was that David Geffen had been kind enough to say very good things to Bronfman about me. David is a really good friend, and obviously his words were meaningful. I said yes right away.

EDGAR BRONFMAN JR.:

Ron knew how to make a deal. I was really happy to have Ron.

RON MEYER:

I went back to the hotel and called my wife to tell her. Then I had to call Mike. You can only imagine that conversation. I remember it like yesterday. Mike said, "So how did it go?" and I said, "Not the way you would expect. Edgar said under no circumstances would they offer you the job again, but that they wanted me to do it." Mike asked me, "So what did you tell them?" I said, "Mike, I told them yes." So immediately Mike said to me, "You stole this job from me." I told him, "No, Mike, you left it in the trash can and I retrieved it," and then the conversation ended.

BILL HABER:

Ronnie was at the end of the parade with the shovel, and Michael was the elephant. After a while, Ronnie got tired of it.

MICHAEL OVITZ:

Bill is bright, he's rough, he's eccentric. When he was at William Morris, he gave pop quizzes to the agents. He is a brilliant guy if you gave him a script to read, but he's not progressive: nothing changed from William Morris to CAA. Ron and I bookended him and kept it working. I tried to keep him there because I was petrified to lose whatever that magic was that we had. But in retrospect, I should have let him go, because Ron might have never left the agency if I did that.

RON MEYER:

If I really thought Mike was going to leave at some point, I would have stayed and waited. But I finally realized it was all bullshit. He just wasn't going to leave. He was making the money he wanted.

BILL HABER:

I'm not discussing his ethical basis or his own personal moral compass; Mike was a smart guy. Very smart, and he drove CAA to be something extraordinary.

Throughout my whole life, and to this day, I say: If something's difficult and you don't have an answer, go to the truth. No matter where it takes you, go to the truth. Not Mike Ovitz; he makes up the truth to get to where he needs to go. He'd betray me in a minute. He has an art collection worth hundreds of millions of dollars. I've been in the house—it's one of the most beautiful houses on Earth. Mike Ovitz built that. He did what he had to and built that himself. I'm a different person. My wife and I met teaching mentally retarded blind children. The founder of Foundation for the Junior Blind is the godfather of my children. And to this day, when I see a community in Lebanon of fifteen kids from Syria living in a tent in the snow, and that's all they have? It's very hard for me to lie about a television show. You know what I mean?

IVAN REITMAN:

I don't know what Ronnie's deal was, but it was way less than Michael had negotiated. Ron was the real workhorse; it was clear Mike relied a great deal on Ron. But Ron saw the writing on the wall, so he made the next smartest deal, and he actually said yes to it. So Ovitz was miserable. And by then all these so-called Young Turks, this next generation, no longer trusted their boss and wanted their piece of that agency, and they represented all the up-and-coming clients. I think he saw that writing on the wall, he was always really smart about that.

MICHAEL OVITZ:

You have to understand how important the Ron relationship was to me. It wasn't just the business side of it. There was nothing I didn't trust him with. I know he didn't think I treated him the way I should have, but I thought I did and I loved him like a brother. Never in my life before, during, or since have I ever trusted anyone like I trusted him. Ever. Ever. I told him everything. So when he left, I was shocked, so devastated that I didn't know what to do. I had never made a plan without him. I went into a deep, deep introspective state.

What had happened was antithetical to what we preached, and was a great lesson about communication. That's what makes it so interesting. I wasn't communicating to him what I felt, and he was doing the same with me. In their final moments at the company together, the head preachers of communication didn't communicate. Then he told me he thought we had lost communication a year earlier, which I didn't see at all. But I was running all over the world.

RON MEYER:

Leaving was very emotional for me. After Mike and Bill, the first person I told was Michael Douglas, who was not only my client but my dear friend. Then I called Sly. The next afternoon, there was a meeting of the entire company, and I stood in front of everyone and told them I was leaving.

Several employees would say later they could remember seeing Michael Ovitz get teary-eyed only twice—once when President Clinton came to CAA, and the second time was when he had to address the staff after Meyer left for Universal. He didn't want anyone to see how upset he was; he quickly exited the room.

RON MEYER:

That afternoon I called every single one of my clients and told them I was leaving and who I thought would be the best agent for them going forward. I also spent a lot of time briefing those agents on my clients. To this day, I have remained friends with all of my former clients.

JESSICA LANGE:

Ronnie called and told me he was leaving the agency to run the studio. We talked about who he wanted me to be with, but it was all very devastating, because I understood immediately—just instinctively—that I would never have another agent like him again. I knew that period of my life was going to end and that things would shift dramatically. And you know what? They did. The years I was with Ronnie were the best of my career. After Ronnie left, I really felt like things floundered after that.

I keep asking him if he will quit Universal and come back and just represent me for the last couple years before I retire. I don't think that's ever going to happen.

DONALD SUTHERLAND:

Was I surprised that he moved on to make room for the Young Turks? No, it seemed like a normal evolution. Bureaucracies get old. Stagnate and die. Regeneration seemed the only way to sustain and continue success. Was I surprised he became the head of Universal/NBC? I guess, a little. He is not aggressive in the way I perceive the people who pursue those positions to be. He was offered it and he took it. In a business where loyalty is not a benchmark, he is a sublimely loyal man. He expects honorable loyalty in return and I have seen disloyalty hurt him deeply. He is an astonishing creature in the zoo that is the movie business. Everyone who's worth a pinch of salt holds him in esteem. I'm trying to think of something bad to say about him. Something negative. I can't.

WHOOPI GOLDBERG:

I was devastated. Because I knew what it meant: Nobody would care for me the way that he did. It wasn't a bad breakup, it was just a breakup. He broke up with me. I understood that he had to go, but I just thought, *Oh my God, nobody's going to care as much.* And you know what? I was right.

ALEC BALDWIN:

If you're Leo DiCaprio, and you've got Marty Scorsese on your side, that's a nice thing to have. Otherwise, you need someone in your corner who's going to send you scripts and think about you. I always felt that when I was with Ronnie, he was in my corner, and when we were together, I did a whole bunch of studio films, including leading roles. Above all, he was no bullshit and had many great lines. Once he said to me, "Hey, man, just sit back. As time goes by, they forget how much they hate you."

SYLVESTER STALLONE:

That was very, very traumatic. He called me up and said, "I'm going to move on to another job," and then he got so choked up and I couldn't understand what he was saying. I've never heard a man cry that hard in my life. It was overwhelming, and it became almost the sound of grief. Then I became swept up in it, and we sounded as though we had just witnessed someone we love pass away. It was that heavy. Truly. He could barely get the words out, and then of course that emotion is quite contagious, so I was swept up in it. We were realizing that with all of the laughs and glamour and good times and money stripped away, what was really at the core of that relationship was something really much, much more profound than I believe either of us had experienced. I've only felt that way one other time in my life.

Then I wrote a poem to him about how when two mountains meet, they can see one another and while they no longer will be joined, they'll still be within each other's view. It was pretty heavy.

KEVIN HUVANE:

Ronnie knew that his place here was making sure that people felt valued. Michael is very smart business-wise, he really is, but Ronnie's combination of the heart and the brain was a great one.

FRED SPECKTOR:

I had been in Santa Barbara and walked in the door of my house as the phone started ringing. It was Ronnie. He says, "How do you like being Stallone's agent?" I said, "What are you talking about?" He said, "Well, I'm gone. I'm going to Universal Studios." I was taken aback and could just say, "Oh." I was sad because he was a good friend and I loved working with him. But I don't blame Ron at all. He saw a fantastic opportunity, and I think he felt he had run his course as an agent. He had been a great agent, and now he wanted to try something new. If the job had been offered to a lot of people, they would have done the same thing.

KEVIN HUVANE:

When Ronnie left, I was pretty devastated because to me he was the heart of that agency and he really cared about us; he really loved us. After Ronnie told us, Bryan, Richard, Jay, Doc, and I sat with Michael, and he said he was staying.

RICK NICITA:

I was at home, and the phone rang. I picked it up and it was Mike, but he sounded different. There was no "Hey, Rick." He just asked, "You hear from Ronnie?" and I said, "No. Why?" And he said, "He took my job," and hung up.

JUDY OVITZ:

That's when Ron lost me as a friend. He turned around and took the job that should have gone to Michael. The moment that Ron left, it was just a matter of time before Michael left.

IRVING AZOFF:

Michael and I were never close, but Ron and I were. I socialized with Ron and I hung with Ron; we've been friends forever. Ovitz was a business relationship; Ron was a business and a personal relationship. If you said to me what's the prototype agent—who has the ability to really be involved and understand the social relationship side of agenting—Ron would be number one on my list, and I don't know who to put at number two.

SYLVESTER STALLONE:

Ron Meyer could have been president of anything. He has this incredible gift of being embraced by everyone—not liked, we're talking loved. If there's such a thing as the Hollywood deity, he's it. I know that sounds a bit weird, but there's nothing that anyone says that's bad about him. But I do know he's also incredibly tough and has a wellspring of ferocious energy when he wants to let it loose. The man was a marine. Watch out, or he'll hit your beach.

RON MEYER:

There are things Mike gets credit for doing at CAA that he doesn't deserve and things he probably doesn't get credit for that he does. But for sure, he pushed us all further than we would have pushed ourselves. I would have happily settled for so much less in my life than I ended up with, and Mike is really the one responsible for it.

MICHAEL OVITZ:

I made some really stupid mistakes that I could've easily have fixed with Ron. Part of what we were great at was that he balanced my insensitivity. We both had the same feelings, but our behavior looked opposite. As sensitive as I was to creative people and creative issues, I could sometimes be insensitive to those around me.

Ovitz had famously been known for never taking a sick day, but after Meyer left, he spent the following week out of the office. And when he called in, staff members

said he didn't even sound like himself. He was clearly depressed, people said; they
were worried about him and told him they didn't think it was a good idea for him
to go to Sun Valley, as scheduled, for the annual Allen & Company Sun Valley
conference, the pinnacle event for media moguls. But Ovitz said he wanted to try.

JACK RAPKE:

Ovitz was virtually catatonic after Ron left. We would go into meetings with him, people would ask him a question, and Ray Kurtzman would have to answer because Michael could barely talk. I would go in and have a conversation about a piece of business and Michael would sit there and not say a word.

RICK NICITA:

Mike was a zombie. Seriously, I'd walk in his office and he'd be staring out the window. This was not a guy who would stare out the window. It was awful to watch.

LEE GABLER:

I don't know if he was clinically depressed or not, but clearly he had a problem.

ARNE GLIMCHER, Director:

I was in touch with him consistently during that period of time. We were already best friends. His greatest shock was the betrayal by Ron. I mean, he adored Ron. Before I came into Michael's life, Ron was his best friend. It was an astonishing betrayal, and he was incredibly depressed about it.

BARRY HIRSCH:

Certainly Ray Kurtzman helped him at the end. He was Michael's conscience a lot even before Ron left, and when Michael wanted to do things that would've been hurtful to others, Ray was in his face saying, "You can't do that. You can't do that." I think Michael respected and appreciated it on the one hand, and probably got angry over it on the other hand. After Ron left, Ray was the one who really saved him. And, if I recall correctly, got him to a psychiatrist very quickly.

SANDY CLIMAN:

Mike went to Sun Valley and he was face-to-face with Ron and Edgar fresh from the announcement that Ron would be running Universal. Mike totally froze. We were all petrified for Mike's well-being. After Ray was on the phone with him, he said to Bob and me, "I've never seen him like this. I'm sending a plane for him now. He has to get out of there." Ray got him home quickly and safely.

MICHAEL OVITZ:

Without Ron, I had no buffer with that whole next level at the agency, and frankly, I knew—I'm not an idiot—where that would go. They'd want to be my partner. They'd want to divide up what stock Ron had. They'd want to throw out Bill and then they'd turn on me. I knew that. I had Jay Moloney starting to show signs of flipping out; I had Ray Kurtzman getting older; I was giving Jack Rapke bonus checks for millions of dollars when he wasn't signing that kind of business, just handling my clients, and a bunch of other people who wanted more and more and more. It was a fucking mess.

Then one day, Jay came into my office, slammed his fist on my desk, and said, "We want to see the books." I was totally startled and had no idea at that time he had a drug problem. I tried to be calm and said that at the right moment, depending on a series of events that might or might not occur, I'd let him know. That evidently wasn't good enough for him and he started to come toward me. I went into his face and told him, "Get the fuck out of my office," and at that point, he knew better than to continue.

Of course he didn't know what it meant to see the books. He had no idea. None. Zero. He bought me a gift afterwards, a beautiful watch. It was his way of apologizing.

LEE GABLER:

It was pretty gutsy to walk into Ovitz's office and say, "We want a piece of the company." Forget Jay being on whatever he was on at the time. Those guys handled it great. It was a great poker play.

MICHAEL OVITZ:

They did put him up to it, without a doubt. They didn't have the balls to do it themselves. He came in all worked up to do it because they couldn't look me square in the eye. It was an awful moment.

That's the difference between me and them: Everything I did was calculated and strategic, and all of their decisions were done strictly out of emotion.

DAVID O'CONNOR:

We felt that we were representing the vast majority of the important clients and we felt like we were the engine room. We were also the people signing a lot of new business. People on the outside were saying, "Ovitz is going to leave, and then what are you going to do? You'd better figure out your response." And people were also in our ears saying, "Why don't you guys go start your own thing?"

MICHAEL OVITZ:

The minute Ron left I was stuck in a position of either firing those guys and trying to do it on my own, which I could have done, or trying to work it out somehow, but before he left, Ron had made it clear to me—and I agreed—that Bryan, Doc, Kevin, Richard, and Jay wanted the whole company. It was going to be a shitfest either way. But it was easy for me because I didn't want to do it anymore.

LEE GABLER:

The Young Turks threatened Ovitz that they would leave and told him they had financing and would walk out the door.

MICHAEL OVITZ:

They did the opposite of what I had taught them to do. They were really nasty to me. I really worked hard for those guys. I gave them everything. I gave them money, I gave them clients. I wasn't holding their hand the way Ron did, but I was there for them; I killed myself for those people. I really did. I probably would have never left if they embraced me.

BARRY HIRSCH:

One of the things about good deal making is intuiting or figuring out where the other guy is vulnerable. And Michael's way of figuring that out was to kind of play the little boy: "Please help me." That was at the beginning, and then he got much more forceful toward the end. In his own way, he was pretty psychologically astute, except about himself. *Introspection* is not a word in his vocabulary. Michael's success made him more unhappy than happy.

You can have all the money or all of the art in the world, but if you don't have family and friends, there's not much to life. When I think about it, I become sad about it because I cared about him.

TOM LASSALLY:

Those five young guys had banded together. They knew they could have more influence that way, and the first time there was a rumor that Mike might be leaving, those guys wanted to be able to challenge the future.

MICHAEL OVITZ:

Twenty years of four guys out in a field, bending over and picking cotton from crack of dawn till dusk. When you have no clientele, it's hard to sign clients; when you have a ton of clients, it's really easy to sign clients. At the end of the day, clients, whether they're Matsushita or Spielberg, were our business. But when I am selfless and let Jay Moloney in on every single thing that Spielberg is doing, there's some moment where you think, *That's interesting. He may control the relationship.* Which he didn't, but it makes you uneasy.

BILL MURRAY:

I guess I shouldn't have been surprised when I heard that he was leaving. Michael had these relationships with all the major guys out there, and some of them were real monsters and not pleasant people to be with or deal with. And he'd be in a position where he had to like haggle for me or haggle for one of his other clients, and it was just hell for him. But he always kept it together. Once a year—and it was usually toward the holidays—we'd be on the phone for probably an hour and he would let his hair down. He would pretty much go all the way around Hollywood, like he was looking out his window, and he'd go from one studio to the other and go off on those guys. It was really, really funny—much funnier than any pissed-off actor could be about a studio—because he knew these people better than anyone, and he had them by the throat in terms of who they were as people. I would laugh so hard. He'd really let it fly, and I felt so good for him that he could just let go.

RON MEYER:

We had known for some time that the young guys were restless. Everybody saw how hungry they were, and we had had to consider the possibility that they would ultimately go out and start their own agency. I had always said to Mike we ought to make them our partners, and that if we didn't, we could wake up one morning to find they had left with a lot of our clients. He just said, "I'll take care of it, don't worry, we'll be gone before anything like that happens."

MICHAEL OVITZ:

We assumed they'd do to us what we did to William Morris, and the only thing we thought would keep them was to help them sign clients and to pay them inordinate sums of money. If you're twenty-eight or so and you're making a million bucks a year when a million bucks a year is a lot of money, you probably aren't going to think a lot about going somewhere else.

I don't know if they ever thought about leaving, or that people and clients would go with them. I have no idea. But after Ron left, I did know two things: I didn't want to go on the defense at that stage in my life, and I didn't want to stick around and find out what they were going to do.

RICK NICITA:

Mike and Ron—they weren't about to get cowed by anyone, much less younger guys. Then you might say, *Well, why would they leave?* Because doing this thing of client representation, agenting at this level of intensity, altitude, responsibility is tough. It's 24/7. You're never off duty. You always have this low-level anxiety, this hum in the back of your head that your clients are going to leave you. You're always functioning like something bad is about to happen. Every agent comes back to their office after lunch and says to their assistant, "Who called?" And there's a part of them that's in a crouch going, *Did anything bad happen?* That's really what they're asking. They're not asking, *Who called?* They're asking, *Did anything bad happen?* If the answer is "Three calls. X, Y, and Z," then the answer is "Nothing bad happened." But you can't do that for that long. It will kill you.

SANDY GALLIN:

Most people can only stand being an agent so long. And then you have to do something else or you want to kill yourself.

MICHAEL EISNER:

I followed everything going on with Michael Ovitz and Edgar Bronfman. I knew he had been "overasking" and then saw him on the cover of *Newsweek* the day after they had told him they no longer wanted him to have the job. He had basically blown himself up.

MICHAEL OVITZ:

Eisner was pressing me hard. This was the second time that he was pressing me to go there. I had a better offer from Disney before the Universal thing. The year earlier he had tried to get me to go there. I have a picture of him and me and Frank Wells with mouse ears on at the Disney commissary.

MICHAEL EISNER:

The moment I decided to make Ovitz the [second] offer was when he was at the Allen & Company conference in Sun Valley. Ronnie had gotten the Universal job and was being carried around on a throne. Michael Ovitz called me from there, and I don't want to say he was catatonic, but he said he couldn't leave his room and was clearly very upset. He asked me to get him out of there, and I thought to myself, *If he's able to confide in me in his moment of darkness, I think I can trust this guy.* Trust was always my issue with Michael Ovitz. I needed to know he could move from being an agent, where success and failure were wrapped around his 10 percent, to being a good executive where the total bottom line of each project mattered, where the sum of the parts added to return on equity and profits.

MICHAEL OVITZ:

So Eisner walked me around Sun Valley and I was so engrossed in the discussion because he caught me at a moment that I was receptive. I kept saying let's keep walking because it's so beautiful up there and he kept saying, "Let's sit down." That night, in the middle of the night he went to the Sun Valley Emergency Room and he had a heart problem. He couldn't walk, he couldn't breathe.

We shared the same internist for twenty-five years. I knew what was really wrong with him. He was supposed to be working only three days a week.

MICHAEL EISNER:

Michael Ovitz made CAA, got the most unbelievable deals for his clients, and changes the business. He was maybe the best agent I've ever seen. He was extremely charming and did his homework. He didn't scratch other people's backs when they scratched his back, so he made enemies. There's a whole lot of misinformation out there about his coming to Disney. You have to remember, a series of really important things happened in a very short period of time. First, Frank Wells died; second, I did not have a heart attack, but I did have a bypass operation; third, we bought Capital Cities-ABC, doubling the size of Disney; and fourth, Jeffrey left the company. I was chairman and CEO and added president to my title, because there were certain people inside the company vying for the president title who I did not want to get the job. That doesn't include Bob Iger, who I did not know well at the time. We just bought ABC and he was off handling it.

JUDY OVITZ:

Through the years when we traveled with them there was always talk about the two Michaels sharing Disney together, but nothing ever happened. Then Michael Eisner got really, really sick with his quadruple bypass and we were in the hospital with him the whole time. I was holding his hand when Jane would take a break. We were all really, really close. After the whole thing with Universal happened, Jane pleaded with Michael to say yes, and I think that was part of what really spurred Michael to do it. He knew the agency was in an upheaval because of Ron's leaving and so he finally said yes, thinking that they were both going to share Disney.

MICHAEL EISNER:

I know a lot of people believe I had tried to hire Michael Ovitz around the time of my illness because I wanted to turn the company over to him if something happened to me, but here is the truth: I was in a precarious medical situation for a very, very short time and needed a bypass. I was somewhat unexpectedly about to have an operation, was on morphine, and woke up as I was being wheeled into surgery. My wife and sons came into the operating area, and I said, "I've got two things to tell you: First, I want to be buried aboveground, like in a mausoleum. And second, the only person I want to succeed me is Barry Diller."

ARNE GLIMCHER:

They were two families that lived together. They went together on holidays in Europe; all the kids were together. They couldn't have been much closer. Eisner thought he was dying. He had had heart surgery; Michael slept in the hospital room for a week with him. I know because I talked to him from the hospital room. There was nothing he wouldn't do for Eisner. It was a very close relationship.

MICHAEL EISNER:

Intellectually, I wanted to get it done and believed I could change him, that I could make him worry about the bottom line. My fantasy was that he would be collaborative, that he could go out and be as charming with our internal executives as he was with movie stars. My fantasy was that he would help me around the world, because I didn't want to travel that much anymore, and he loved to travel. My fantasy was that he would meet with the likes of Chirac in France and other world leaders, and do all of the great stuff for Disney that he did for his clients. I had zero fear he would be a threat to me at Disney: I knew how he had pushed the others aside at CAA and gotten control of the agency, but there was no way he was going to take my job or shoot me in the back. Disney was doing great, and the board knew everything that was going on.

SANDY CLIMAN:

With Ron gone, Mike was faced with a choice he found unenviable—stay at the agency with new partners who had previously worked for him, or go to Disney and basically restart your life as number two at a studio with a new set of players. From my conversations with Michael Eisner, he knew Mike was in a weaker negotiating position than in prior times when Mike had been courted by Eisner to join Disney.

MICHAEL EISNER:

A week later I said we should continue our conversation about him joining Disney. I made a deal with him that was a tenth of the deal that he'd been talking to Universal about, and it was an absolutely normal deal. We put in place a bonus plan that was reasonable. The only thing we did in the deal, which came back a little bit to haunt me—although it ended up being meaningless— was usually if you lose your job, you have to exercise your stocks within sixty to ninety days. But he convinced my lawyer, because we weren't going to make up the money he was going to lose from leaving CAA, that he could hold his stock for the term of his option, which was four years. I thought it was a bit of a peculiar request, but a couple people involved told me it made sense; he was just protecting himself. He was not allowed to bring anybody with him apart from his secretary. In our discussions I said, "We have a very good company. I don't want anybody other than you." And then he called me and says, "You gotta buy my Rolodex," and I asked, "What is your Rolodex?" He explained, "I've got a really complicated computer Rolodex and I need it." I'd said no to every-thing, but I said okay to his Rolodex.

So we made the deal. Sid Bass came over and we had a drink in celebration and then flew back to Los Angeles to meet with two key executives at Disney. I had decided that the CFO wasn't going to report to him [Michael] because I just didn't want to give up the financial control of the company at that point. And then the gen-eral counsel said he wouldn't report to him. When I told Michael Ovitz both executives were going to report directly to me, he said, "I won't take the job then," and I said, "Okay." He went upstairs in our house, then came back down and said, "You know what, I will do it." At that moment I was thrilled, but I have to admit over the next period of time I was slightly disappointed I didn't back out. In hindsight maybe in the very back of my mind, in my unconscious, I thought, you know when a bride says she knew when she was walking down the aisle it was going to be a mistake, but continued on anyway? I wonder now if I was that bride.

SUSAN MILLER:

When Michael was discussing going to Disney with me, we were standing in his driveway at Rockingham, and I asked him what his title was going to be. He put his arm around me and said, "I will run the company with Eisner. We will be equal." He asked me what I thought, and I said I didn't understand how that was going to work, given they were both type A personalities who wanted to be in control, and that it would either be fantastic or the worst experience for us in our lives.

EDGAR BRONFMAN JR.:

When Ron left, Mike went into a chasm. Eisner didn't know that Mike had no choice. Mike would have gone there for a dollar.

RON MEYER:

After I left, given Mike's deteriorating relationship with the group that had taken over, Mike probably had no choice but to take the Disney job. It was not a surprise to me.

TOM POLLOCK:

Mike left because he knew there are good agents and there are old agents, but there are no good old agents. Eventually you get shoved out. There was no way for him to make a name for himself. It wasn't so much the money, but he wanted to run a company like Universal or Disney and be thought of not as an agent. Because agents are looked down upon. He wanted to be Lew Wasserman; he wanted to do what Lew Wasserman did.

IVAN REITMAN:

Mike was the right agent at a time when the agencies had enormous power because of the money that was coming in. If you controlled some of the biggest stars in the world, you had enormous leverage over the studio, and he used some of that leverage on behalf of his clients. So it was a wonderful time to be a successful movie director. Having him represent you was a great thing. He had the best group of people and probably the most leverage. But it was already starting to wane, and I think he just got bored by it. He had too much power, his head got really big, and I think he lost perspective. The negotiations with the Bronfmans were the first bad, bad sign of that, and the next bad sign was when he finally took the job with Eisner.

I remember I was at Arne Glimcher's Athens house. My wife and I were there alone—I don't even think Arne was there at the time—and he called me up on Sunday morning and said, "Hey, look I've got to tell you, it'll probably come out today or tomorrow, that I've decided to go and work with Eisner over at Disney." And I said, "Are you taking over for Eisner?" and he said no, with him. As co-chairman? And he said, "Well, no, under Eisner." Then I was quiet. He said, "You seem to be very quiet." And I said, "I'm not so sure it's such a good idea." He got really pissed off at me; he told me everyone else thought it was great. He was pissed that I wasn't supportive. In fact, he didn't talk to me for two weeks. I didn't even know what happened later that night, the supposed famous meeting that happened at Eisner's house where all the guys under Eisner said flatly they were not going to report to Ovitz. The deal was done at that point, as you know. It just didn't feel right; it didn't make any sense. It was an act of desperation.

I think Eisner offered him the lifeline, and he took that.

SUSAN MILLER:

I was in Hawaii on vacation and Michael called me the night before and said, "Guess what? We're moving to the Valley!" I came back three days later and started getting us ready to move over to Burbank.

DAVID O'CONNOR:

Jerry Bruckheimer had a weekly pickup hockey game; every Sunday night a group of us would get together and we'd play. This was going on for many years and then finally, somewhere along the line, somebody had the great idea: "Let's take this show on the road. We're going to go to Vegas for the weekend, we're going to grab a couple of pros who often played with us, and we're going to go have a great time." That was the first year of it and we had a great time. So I was in Vegas and Bryan Lourd called me and said, "We're supposed to meet with Ovitz at nine o'clock in the morning on Monday morning. Do you know what this is about?" I said, "I don't have any idea. Is he calling to tell us that he's leaving?"

So we show up Monday morning, I'm in the office, it's probably eight o'clock, 8:30. We're all there. We're actually in the same area in the building and we're kind of speculating about it. I'm hanging around my office and the phone rings. I'm supposed to have lunch that day with a guy I went to college with named Andrew Greenebaum who was in Disney strategic planning at the time. He calls me and it's 8:58. He's on the phone with my assistant and I hear my assistant say, "Yeah, I think you're still on for lunch," and my assistant says, "You're still on for lunch?" and I go, "Yeah, why wouldn't I be?" And through the phone, through my assistant, he says, "Well, given the news, are we still on for lunch today?" "Andrew, what the fuck are you talking about, the news?" And he says, "It just came across the wire that Ovitz is going to Disney." This is literally two minutes before I'm going to walk into the room. I'm like, "Our lunch is canceled. I'll talk to you later." I walked down to see Bryan and Richard and Kevin and said, "Here's what this meeting's about."

MARTIN SCORSESE:

Mike called and told me, "I'm going over to Disney and I'm taking you with me." I immediately said, "All right." But it was a little unnerving, and the idea of him leaving did feel kind of funny because his advice was important to me, and I didn't know what this was going to be like. I also thought, *If you were so powerful, and you had changed the industry the way Lew Wasserman had done back in the '50s, what can you do after that will compare?*

In the room that Monday morning was Jack Rapke, Lee Gabler, Ray Kurtzman, Bob Goldman, Sandy Climan, Tom Ross, Kevin Huvane, David O'Connor, Jay Moloney, Bryan Lourd, and Richard Lovett. (Rick Nicita was in Italy on vacation.)

DAVID O'CONNOR:

Michael comes in, sits down, and says, "It will be announced today that I'm going to become president of the Walt Disney Company."

KEVIN HUVANE:

He came in and said, "It will be announced that I am now the president of the Walt Disney Company."

We were all just shocked. I don't think any of us were expecting it.

DAVID O'CONNOR:

There was sort of this silence around the table, I'll never forget this, and Richard in his inimitable way says, "Michael"—I have no idea where he's going with this by the way, I look at him like, *What are you going to say now?*—"Congratulations! That's fantastic!"

RICK NICITA:

We had taken a villa in Rome, in Trastevere, just gotten there on Sunday, and on Monday I call to check in and I get a message that Mike wants to see everybody and I go, "No can do"—here I am, you know? The next thing is I get a call from Martin Shafer, who ran Castle Rock. I return the call and he goes, "What do you think of that?" And I go, "What do I think of what?" He goes, "Ovitz." And I go, "What about him?" Martin Shafer ended up telling me, because I returned my call too fast. I flew back that night. The vacation was two days. I flew back from Italy Monday night. Yeah, nightmare.

DAVID O'CONNOR:

It was all very fast and traumatic and crazy—one of those situations where you just had to put one foot in front of another. There wasn't a whole lot of hand-wringing. It was like, *Okay, so now what?*

KEVIN HUVANE:

I was actually a little foggy until we quickly shifted into "What are we doing?" mode.

JOHN PTAK:

We'd have these Monday morning staff meetings and usually he'd come in and his jacket was off. In this case he came in and he was wearing a suit, and he hadn't taken his jacket off. I turned to Glen Meredith sitting next to me and I said, "Uh-oh!"

Michael Ovitz had been taking care of other people and their problems for twenty-five years, and while that taking-care-of was primarily for profit most of the time, there was also this: Michael wanted to be the one in control, the one giving marching orders instead of having to march—and the one who delivered the goods when people were in need. And they were. And he did.

But now, following Meyer's departure from the agency, things had fundamentally changed. For the first time, Ovitz was the one in need, and his world couldn't pivot fast enough for him. Yes, he was able to work out an exit strategy with his dear friend Michael Eisner for what seemed like a big new job, but there were many moments when he was the one who needed advice—well beyond the legal counsel he was getting from Ron Olson, his lawyer.

One clear example was his farewell speech to the company. He didn't really think it through, and no one stepped in to help. He had always been able to deliver strategy and agendas and tough-love motivation and then have Meyer step in and complete the other side of the proverbial coin, the equally proverbial heart of the matter. In what had to be one of the biggest moments of his professional life, Michael Ovitz failed to comprehend completely what his soon-to-be-former employees needed from him, and what his legacy almost demanded. He was oddly unemotional, never mentioning how much CAA had mattered to him, and failing to say even that he was sorry to be leaving. He didn't play the coach and give everybody a bolstering, rah-rah "don't worry, everything will be all right." In short, he didn't let the room know he was human, something they would love to have heard. It was clear Ovitz had already moved on in his mind to Burbank—or else that he didn't have the presence to convey what he was really thinking. It was thus that twenty turbulent years came to an unemotional close.

JUDY OVITZ:

I wasn't there in the building when he made the announcement he was leaving, but he told me about it after. He was so torn. He felt terrible. It was horrible.

TOM ROSS:

I was in shock, even though we all knew something was going on. I was in a unique division, so my vision was that Michael leaving was not really going to affect what I did and what my department did, other than how it was all going to play out for the entire agency.

When Michael and I had talked about my desire to run a record label, he had said to me, "Well, you know, there may be something coming up." So I thought he was perhaps going to take me with him to Disney as the head of records; I thought I was part of his mythic group that wherever he went would be in business together. It turned out, I was quite naive.

MICHAEL OVITZ:

It was bittersweet. I was excited about this new job and becoming a buyer, but I felt like I left my family behind.

KEVIN HUVANE:

He talked to us, left, and then went out of the conference room and went to the elevator.

DAVID O'CONNOR:

I hadn't even gotten back to my office from the theater and I remember seeing him with his assistant going down the elevator to his car. And I was like, "Holy shit."

Michael Ovitz headed out of the CAA building on his way to the Disney Studios and a live interview with Michael Eisner at which it would be announced that Ovitz was becoming president of the Walt Disney Company. At that moment, eight men hastily gathered in a second-floor conference room: senior executives Lee Gabler, Jack Rapke, and Tom Ross, joined by CAA's own version of the Gang of Five: Kevin Huvane, Bryan Lourd, Richard Lovett, Jay Moloney, and David O'Connor. If any of them thought about looking for a wall safe where a CAA succession plan might be stashed, they could forget it. There was no plan.

It was an uneven bunch in terms of vintage (roughly twenty years separated youngest from oldest) and of salary. The five Young Turks each made just over a million dollars a year—a lot of money for anyone their ages. The bigger salaries rested in the four-man senior group. As head of music, Tom Ross was pulling in about $2.5 million a year, and Rick Nicita and Lee Gabler were both around $3 million. Jack Rapke, at over $4 million a year, was making four times as much as the brash young guys he suddenly found himself standing with.

There was history too. Rapke and Lovett had disliked each other from practically day one. Veterans said Lovett couldn't forget how Rapke had, he felt, lied to him, offering his assistant slot to someone else after Lovett had spent countless extra hours reading scripts for Rapke.

Neither Rick Nicita nor Tom Ross had visions of running the company, but Rapke thought he was clearly entitled, as did Lee Gabler, who believed revenues coming in from television were the most important and dependable stream the agency had going.

While the senior contingent was split, the Turks were a solid force of one, totally united, and ready to do whatever it took to exploit this once-in-a-lifetime opportunity.

One obvious metaphor that comes to mind is the Supreme Court, a group of nine known for ideological blocs and warring factions. Some of its most important decisions were five-four splits. Would there now be just such a schism at the newly reconfigured Creative Artists Agency?

DAVID LETTERMAN:

I've never known anybody like Mike Ovitz. There is nobody like him. He was such an overwhelming positive force, and in show business there are not many positive forces. He put me back on my feet. It's comparable to my heart surgery, for God's sake. You know, the heart surgery where they take the heart out of your chest cavity and they run it down to the gift shop. I don't know what they do with it. But they rebuild you. Well, that's what Ovitz had done to me. When I found out he was going to Disney, I just thought, *I don't know if I want him going to Disney. Wait a minute, Michael, what about me?* What I really regretted about it was that by going to Disney, he was no longer going to be the guy. And he was the guy. So I selfishly thought about myself first and how much I didn't want him to go, but then secondarily I thought, *Who's going to be* the guy *now?*

6

Partial Sid: August 16, 1995–2001

Generally speaking, envy, resentment, revenge, and self-pity
are disastrous modes of thoughts.
—CHARLIE MUNGER

Once Michael Ovitz's departure from CAA became public knowledge, the earth in Hollywood started to quake. The Los Angeles Times *quoted "one top entertainment executive" as predicting, "The agency business is up for grabs. You no longer have one guy driving all movie deals. This should be good for everyone in town and bring down costs, which have gotten out of control." Others disagreed.*

Inside the halls of CAA, a titanic internal power battle was under way. With no plan of succession in place, and with no consensus among the nine anointed agents, it became clear that decisions had to be made—and be made quickly. At the top of the list was agreeing to a management structure. The gang of nine quickly learned that Ovitz had set up a "transition committee," adding Ray Kurtzman, Bob Goldman, and Sandy Climan to the not-so-merry band now trying to figure out the agency's future.

Nobody knew which of a dozen possible scenarios would erupt. One, two, or even three of the most senior partners could have left, and while the Young Turks had seemed unified prior to the explosion, there was plenty of Hollywood precedent for allegiances ending once the seat at the head of the table was actually there for the taking. There were no contracts holding anyone in place, and most important, no shared vision for the company's future, other than making as much money as possible. Who, what, and how were all contentious elements.

Young Turk or venerable veteran, these men (yes, not a single woman) were no strangers. They had all worked together for years; everyone was well aware of the others' strengths and weaknesses (more than they understood their own). The battle in which they quickly became embroiled was a generational struggle for power, yes, but also a clash of egos, personalities, and testosterone, all manifested in formidable, very serious ways. All of them were well versed in finding middle ground—it was the nature of their business when cutting deals for their clients. But this was different: This was about the throne. This was no squabble; this was war.

When a private company goes through upheaval at the highest levels of its management, fewer rules apply than if the same thing happens at a public one—and much more secrecy comes into play.

Welcome to Hollywood's game of Power Musical Chairs.

RICHARD LOVETT:

There was no succession plan. Nothing was obvious. It wasn't clear to anyone who was going to lead the company, or even who should stand up in front to address it. We didn't know what things were going to be like or what they were going to feel like.

Ovitz had strong and specific opinions about the Young Turks. He had been analyzing them individually and en masse for years and, if needed, could have written voluminous analyses of each Turk's strengths and weaknesses. And while he acknowledged and appreciated Lourd's diplomatic nature, Jay Moloney would always be first among equals in Ovitz's mind. Jay was a natural for the agency world, Ovitz believed, who could show his clients all the love they needed, yet at the same time do all the fighting necessary with buyers in negotiations. Above all, he saw Jay as the true leader of the group, and the right leader (one day) for CAA. Even after Jay had burst in on Ovitz and demanded to "see the books," it took Ovitz only a nanosecond to give Moloney the benefit of the doubt and believe that "the others" had put him up to it.

Those "others" were protégés. Moloney was the heir apparent, the Ovitz favorite, and the only one to fit tight within the "loves him like a son" category. He may have been the most formidable personality still in the building—with an all-star client list to boot. It was all the more ironic, then, that just as the Young Turks were going to battle for control of the agency, Moloney's drug issues turned him into a painful sideshow. To complicate matters further, Moloney's doctors were recommending that he have open heart surgery to correct a congenital heart defect. He was going to need the surgery sooner or later; they advised him it was better to have it when he was "young and healthy." After consulting with his inner circle, Moloney decided to go ahead with the surgery in the hopes that it would restart him and essentially serve as his rehab. Moloney had the surgery soon after Ovitz's departure in August, and his recovery went well, but by November, he had relapsed once more and was back to rehab—taken out of the picture.

Many believed that Moloney's position of influence was overstated, that much of his perceived power emanated from his being so closely attached to Ovitz. On his own, however, they felt he rarely projected power and was often considered to be something of an innocent. So who knows what might have happened if a healthy Jay had been a vital part of the equation at that precipitous moment. The Turks would still have been the Turks, but it's hugely doubtful that all else would have remained the same.

MICHAEL OVITZ:

For years, Ron and I had supported, guided, groomed, advised, shrinked, directed, and heavily compensated all of them. It was clear to us that Jay, Richard, and Bryan had the best qualities to lead the company into the future. We figured Jay and Richard could also handle the operational issues that were so important, and Bryan could act as an ombudsman, which would be needed to fuel and oil the massive number of key relationships that would touch the agency. We were also concerned about potential client departures and keeping clients happy, and it had been clear to many that I had given Jay my key clients who were the marquee names of the company, so he was well prepared in that regard.

SANDY CLIMAN:

The Young Turks were agitating for ownership; the old guard senior agents were being simply forgotten. I went to Lee Gabler's office, and he completely unloaded on me. He was furious that Mike was in discussions with Richard, Brian, Kevin, Jay, and Doc, and had not even spoken with him. Lee said, "I'm out the door. I'm leaving." I said to Lee, "Mike is here finishing things up. Walk down to Mike's office and tell him there is no deal until he makes a deal with you, Jack, Rick, and Tom." And that's what Lee did, and that's how the two factions that inherited the new CAA were fused into one ownership group.

LEE GABLER:

I don't have any particular dislike for Mike Ovitz at all. In fact, I respect what he accomplished. The only negative thing I'd ever say about Mike Ovitz is that his decision to leave—which he had the right to do, and I wished him well—didn't include a succession plan.

Bob Goldman knew I was really ticked off, and so Mike invited me to his house in Brentwood. We sat down at his bar and each had a drink. I told him how frustrated I was that he had left without an exit plan. He never answered. But we buried the hatchet.

MICHAEL OVITZ:

There was a plan, and it wasn't hastily put together. It was the nine guys who were generating the largest share of income and handling the most important clients, mostly either signed or developed over the years by Ron and myself. It was the head of the TV department, the head of the music department, the five Young Turks, and Jack and Rick. That was the core of the upper end of the company. We didn't want to leave the business to any one individual.

TOM LASALLY:

Those five young guys banded together. They knew they could have more influence that way, and the first time there was a rumor that Mike might be leaving, they wanted to be able to challenge for the future of the agency.

MICHAEL WIMER:

When Mike left, he didn't have any choice but to leave the company to the group, or he knew that any of the key players not in it would leave. And he also knew that it really wasn't his problem.

It was more of a problem for Jack Rapke, Tom Ross, Lee Gabler, and Rick Nicita.

A year earlier, Ovitz had told Gabler he was thinking about giving the Young Turks a piece of the agency's profits (not its equity) and Gabler told him: "Close your eyes, and now imagine Tom, Rick, Jack, and I all gone."

RICK NICITA:

It shouldn't have worked out because it wasn't much of a plan. As a matter of fact, it wasn't a plan at all. But whatever it was, time was critical. We needed to make decisions fast. There was no "Well, we'll take a couple of weeks." No one even said, "Let's take a couple of days."

ANDREA NELSON MEIGS:

When Michael left, there was just disbelief. People were saying to each other, "Is this really happening?" Everybody was whispering and doors were closing all over the place. Outsiders were saying, "The walls of CAA are going to crumble," but I didn't think that.

LEE GABLER:

You have to remember, Michael controlled everything. Michael was the first and last word and no one challenged him, which was the reason why the company was so successful. When all this happened, people started to think about what they were going to do, and if there really could be life for CAA after Michael.

KEVIN HUVANE:

Was there an option for the five of us going somewhere else? There was always the option that people would fund us. We knew it would be harder to stay and make it work, but the challenge of that was also a good one for us. There was some initial panic because it was so unexpected, but we rallied. We were already a team, so we didn't have to learn how to be one.

JACK RAPKE:

At that moment, everybody could have gone their own separate ways. There was definitely a possibility that the five young guys could have gotten financing from somewhere and formed their own agency. They weren't going to take my clients, but they could have taken others.

ROBERT ZEMECKIS:

No matter how dark or painful the news was, Jack always gave it to you straight. In a business where everyone is dishonest and lying all the time, Jack, no matter what, always told the truth. And that gave him great power.

KEVIN HUVANE:

Tom Cruise, Meryl Streep, and many other clients said the same thing: "It's fantastic—don't worry about it," because we were already their agents. It wasn't as if we were just taking them over.

I remember that first Friday night Warren Beatty and Annette Bening invited the five of us to their home for dinner and told us, "Don't worry about us; we're staying." We could breathe again. We knew it wasn't going to be a disaster.

RICK NICITA:

I certainly didn't know up front there was a dinner that Friday night. They could have said let's bring everybody. Not really their style.

TOM ROSS:

It was pretty much expected that the department heads would move up the ladder and run the agency. That's been the precedent for the industry; we were the heirs apparent. What wasn't apparent was the five Young Turks coming in and looking at us like we were four old jerks.

ARI EMANUEL:

Lee, Jack, and Rick could have had it. They didn't understand the power of the CAA brand back then. They should have fucking jammed the young guys who didn't even have any real money to start something else. That's where Richard, Kevin, and Bryan were geniuses. They did the reverse. They jammed the other guys, and I give them credit for that.

LEE GABLER:

It was very unpleasant and really ugly. There were raised voices for sure, but it was sad because some older guys didn't have the intestinal fortitude to stand up and say, "This is what we're going to do, not this." And I blame that on Jack and Rick. Tom was a great asset and was ready to do what needed to be done.

TOM ROSS:

Lee and I were very tight, but not Jack and Rick. We were friendly, but there was no common ground.

MICHAEL OVITZ:

I didn't know what any of them really thought of each other in their heart of hearts. Remember, we were in a cutthroat, highly competitive business that was one giant game of separating presentation from real feelings in order to get things done. By spreading it out amongst all of them we mitigated the risk of a bad transition, and it allowed them to make the decision and handle all the internal jockeying issues that we knew would pop up in a transition of leadership.

JACK RAPKE:

We had a younger generation that was coming up right behind us and was very aggressive. We had a very, very mature group of clients. I personally was never threatened by this because I had an incredible client list.

RICK NICITA:

Even though there was this committee of nine, those five were running it. It was about math. There weren't even swing voters. It was just five to four.

TOM ROSS:

It was like many Supreme Court decisions: five votes to four.

JIM BERKUS:

They boxed out Nicita, and even though Rapke had had a lot of power, he was severely diminished without Mike.

KEVIN HUVANE:

We knew we needed to give respect to Lee Gabler, Jack Rapke, and Rick Nicita because they had been there a long time and they were the generation ahead of us, but there was no doubt that Richard should be president. It was an easy decision. He has a skill set that is remarkable, including being incredibly organized.

LEE GABLER:

I got a call from Bob Goldman, who said, "How would you feel about Richard being president?" And I said, "Is that a comma or a period?" He said, "Well, no. Richard would be president, you and Rick would be co-chairmen, and the rest of the guys would be managing partners." And I said, "I don't care about the title. What I do care about is how the company functions." By that point, I knew the young guys would have walked if Richard wasn't in a position of responsibility.

JACK RAPKE:

I thought I should have been the guy, but I didn't have the votes. And I was pissed off for what I had been put through with Mike—which nobody knew.

LEE GABLER:

I could not have worked with Jack as co-chair of the agency. Jack's ego was not something I would want to handle. The direct answer is no.

MICHAEL OVITZ:

Jack was pissed at me because he thought we should have left him in charge of the whole business, but we knew the young guys wouldn't work for him. Ron and I decided that if we put him in charge, the business would implode.

TOM ROSS:

I was shocked when Richard wound up becoming president. Absolutely shocked.

DAVID O'CONNOR:

Richard really wanted it, and he also had the skill to stand up there and be the face of the company. None of us had that skill. He's a very good writer and a very good speaker, but it wasn't like he had his own vision or strategy for the company. We were still a group.

FRED SPECKTOR:

To this day, Richard Lovett was the best assistant that I have ever had. I've known Richard from the beginning of his career and better than anyone else in my opinion. I never dreamed Richard would be the president of this company, but I always knew he was a leader. He was a leader even among the trainees.

LEE GABLER:

I don't want to boost Richard up as a great manager, which he's not. One of the things he never understood—and Bryan told him this—is that being able to administer, and being able to guide and to direct people, is an asset and an asset that you can't buy. You either have it or you don't have it. Ovitz clearly had it; I felt fortunate to have it. But Lovett didn't have it.

What I should have done is called a meeting with the television department and said, "I'm going to go after the presidency and I can't tell you if I'm going to get it, but if I don't get it, I'm going to leave and I'd like to take all of you with me."

Hindsight's terrific. The biggest word in the English language is "if."

STEVE LAFFERTY, Agent:

Lee came to me early on and said, "I'm going to be one of the managing partners and we're going to figure this out. It's going to be a very good thing for all of us." We then reached out to the other senior members of the TV department to do everything we could to cement our group and shore up problems as they emerged. We were basically the same company, but the three very formidable leaders had left, and people don't like change.

KEVIN HUVANE:

We all thought Richard becoming president was all of us being president because we knew we were one unit. We so trusted him that no one worried about having a title. If Bryan had become the president, I would have been happy with that, too.

TONY KRANTZ:

I had been totally scooped. Those five guys took over the company because they had strength in numbers, a client list, a vision, and they were also the core of the motion picture division, which was the lead dog of the agency. In TV, we didn't ever think that way. It was years later that I learned that TV had leverage due to the money it made.

TOM ROSS:

They were rude and indignant. They were young and impetuous and made it clear that they could leave and go out on their own. Bob Goldman clearly had given them the keys to the bank, but we didn't know it. They gave us no credit for having built, managed, and expanded the departments over the years.

LEE GABLER:

Those five guys didn't want us there. They could control Rick, they didn't care about that. There was no doubt in my mind that they didn't want any of us involved.

They did not want us as part of the company. I sat in a room with them and I watched it all. They orchestrated Jack getting pushed aside and they absolutely did the same thing to Tom.

RICK NICITA:

Jack abdicated a lot and was not happy, but I was in no more favorable a position than Jack. The young guys were so close, and finished each other's sentences, and were so culturally connected that it was an impossible bond. Jack, Lee, Tom and I—we were just four guys who were vaguely the same. Those guys were real pals, they hung around and came up together. They were a link. The four of us were "Hey, how are you doing? See you later." And what became five was because nine minus four equals five. Five just became mathematics at the end.

JACK RAPKE:

It was ridiculous. I didn't work all my life so I could be voted out of the agency at some point in the future. That fucking made no sense to me. So what do I do? I call Peter Chernin. And I said, "Peter, I'm not going to go forward with this. I want to be a producer. Let's talk." And he was game. I tried to make a deal. My attorney was gone, on holiday. All of this was happening very quickly.

RICK NICITA:

Jack felt that he should've been made the king. A combination of healthy ego, significant achievements, maturity, résumé, and most important, Ovitz had made him promises over the years and had kept him from going elsewhere by saying, "You're my man. All this shall be yours one day," that kind of thing. Well, guess what, he was one-ninth. It was now a baseball team with five younger player-managers, and he could wake up any day and be in left field, right field, or who knows. Jack smarted from that from day one—from day one.

JACK RAPKE:

So now I start to consider what I want to do with my life. Do I take this moment to actually step out of the agency business, which I had been considering for several years, notwithstanding reaching the pinnacle of my success?

Remember, being an agent wasn't my dream. My dream was not to represent the people who made movies, but to be one of the people who made movies. I think what made me such a successful agent was that I always approached it as a filmmaker. I was always focused on what was best for the movie, it wasn't just about selling the client. I had opportunities over the years to go into the studio system and Michael begged me not to do it and even talked me out of a couple of those situations in the eleventh hour. I had brought him in because I knew that I would need his cooperation if I was going into the studio business and didn't want him to have a vendetta against me.

With all due respect to the younger guys—and I really say this sincerely—I think they are terrific agents, they really are, but for myself, if I had an absolute choice, I would not have chosen them as partners. We were put together as partners.

DAVID O'CONNOR:

Jack disappeared for a period time during those first ten days, and what we found out was that he was negotiating a deal for himself, if I'm not mistaken, at Fox as a producer. And we were all wondering where the hell he was.

JACK RAPKE:

I wasn't gone for ten days. I was up in Canada and was gone three or four days. I didn't want to break a promise to my son. That was more important to me.

Everybody had to make decisions quickly, and I couldn't make the deal at Fox then, so I just said, I'll stay. It was just a matter of biding my time. I felt I had an obligation to my clients.

DAVID O'CONNOR:

He came back at the end to say he was in.

JACK RAPKE:

This will sound bad coming out of my mouth and it will sound like hubris, but it's not meant to be that way: They recognized that I was the single best deal maker in that agency. I knew the accounting, I knew the law because I worked very close with all the attorneys. I knew where the money was. I knew what was important. I could see the forest from the trees, you know? And that comes with experience and wisdom—even though at that point, they were still young and felt they knew it all.

Once the dust-up had settled, there were eight partners. Richard Lovett, president; Lee Gabler, Jack Rapke, Rick Nicita, and Tom Ross, co-chairmen; and Kevin Huvane, Bryan Lourd, and David O'Connor, managing partners. Anyone concerned that Lourd—often regarded as the most powerful of the entire bunch— would be peeved at "only" being named a managing director needn't have worried. Lourd was the designer of his own kind of clout, one marked by its governing principle: The less you know, see, and hear about me, the better. *He didn't need a title to tell him what he already knew; that he'd be playing a critical, if not the critical role, in the future of the company.*

DAVID O'CONNOR:

In ten days we figured out a management structure for the agency going forward, including making Richard president—which was controversial given his youth and the fact that those senior guys were sitting there—and we also completed our exit transaction with Ovitz, Ronnie, and Bill.

RAND HOLSTON:

Michael, Bill, and Ron were extremely generous with the new leadership when they left. They made a net deal, which was about $200 million. The nine guys' salaries were predetermined. They could pay all their employees whatever they wanted, and at the end of the year, after every expense was paid, whatever was left over would go to pay down the $200 million. People thought it would take five to seven years to pay it off, but there was so much money coming in from what had happened under Michael, Ronnie, and Bill that it wound up taking less than five years. The new leadership was very fortunate they had been so generous.

MICHAEL OVITZ:

I knew what I was going to ask for in terms of a buyout when I took the Disney deal. Bob Goldman and a lawyer at Munger, Tolles helped me put that CAA exit together. They accepted it. There wasn't much negotiating. We asked for a very, very light deal. It was about $175 million divided by the three of us.

We left them everything and didn't take residuals. We left it all with them. I mean *Jurassic Park* is in its fifth iteration right now. We gave them the commissions so they could operate. We also left them a certain amount of working capital so they didn't have to borrow it. We took the money in installments, and we didn't charge them interest.

DAVID O'CONNOR:

We arrived at a structure for the transaction that, truth be told, was really advantageous to us and probably disadvantageous to the owners given what they had built and the value they had created. It was a sweetheart deal. Under the circumstances we had such little risk, and in retrospect, when you actually think about it, we had no risk at all.

MICHAEL OVITZ:

I did what I felt I had to do at the time. There's nothing I could have done differently without disrupting the place. Could I have asked for a royalty? That's probably the only mistake I made. I should have said, "In success, I want a royalty." But it didn't matter to me; I did just fine.

DAVID GEFFEN:

Mike made a very bad deal for the three of them when he sold the agency. By the way, he was the sole person doing this. Bill and Ronnie were not involved; Mike did this. When he sold the agency to them [the Young Turks] for less than the accounts receivable, it was an incredibly stupid deal, incredibly stupid. But what can I say? If Mike Ovitz was smarter, they each could have kept 10 percent of the agency under the agency rules, the guild rules. The guys that were left would've been thrilled to death to get 70 percent of that agency.

RON MEYER:

I had left CAA on a Friday and went to work at Universal on Monday. There was no time to work out a complicated exit arrangement. There was a very low dollar amount buy-sell agreement that had been established from the day we went into business, but what happened was soon after I left, we threw out the buy-sell agreement and took a buyout from receivables.

RICK NICITA:

In retrospect, I think it was a real generous deal on their part because we owned the agency without having to pay anything for it. We also got to keep our healthy salaries. I don't think I quite realized at the time how lucky we were.

DAVID GEFFEN:

Mike presented himself as a brilliant businessman, but in fact he was not. Not at all. But you know, Bill and Ronnie went along with whatever Mike wanted. They always did.

MICHAEL OVITZ:

Any outsider that has a brain will tell you at that moment in time, those nine guys were the luckiest people in the world. They were inheriting twenty years of our working a lump of clay over and over again into a priceless piece of art or a racehorse in its prime, fresh off a victory in the Kentucky Derby.

We started with no money and built an incredible company. They didn't have to start anything. It was the opposite of starting from scratch.

ARI EMANUEL:

They got handed the company. They took over a huge company that had huge cash flow. Their only costs were manpower and fucking travel and dinner expenses.

MICHAEL OVITZ:

We had a four-year schedule. The first year we didn't take anything. There was a point in the fourth year where they accelerated the payments by six months. There was nothing wrong with that; it just proves we left them in a great position.

DAVID O'CONNOR:

We paid them off ahead of schedule.

LEE GABLER:

We paid them back faster because we made more money than we thought we would.

ARI EMANUEL:

In 1995, CAA was a fucking monster. A fucking monster. And don't forget, there was no competitor. William Morris was not a competitor. With all due respect, ICM was not a competitor. We had all bailed out of that fucking place. Everybody was leaving there. So they had really no competitor of any size and scope.

RON MEYER:

After Mike, Bill, and I left, I was not worried for those guys. I didn't think they were going to be in any trouble at all. They did exactly what we thought they would do and what they should have done. The competition wasn't good enough to go and beat them. With all due respect, there just wasn't a real threat out there. And financially, the amount of receivables coming in gave them a huge cushion. So those guys were set up very well and had been integrated with the clients of the agency and were well prepared to represent them. Every one of them could comfortably say to a client, "You know us. Give us a chance. Let us show you what we can do."

JIM WIATT:

When Mike and Ron left, we put together a team to recruit their clients. We discussed it at every staff meeting and spent a lot of time making our best efforts. I thought we had done a pretty good job building ICM at the time—keeping it a viable player—and now we wanted to take advantage of the opportunity.

JASON HEYMAN:

When UTA started in the early '90s, it was as hot as an upstart agency can get. Sandy Bullock, Jennifer Lopez, Michael J. Fox, Mike Myers, Drew Barrymore—and CAA stole all of them, one after the other after the other. UTA agents weren't trained to poach. We didn't spend every waking hour trying to figure out how to make other agencies' clients unhappy.

JEREMY ZIMMER:

Michael changed the entire agency paradigm, those guys were only created because Michael created the playbook. I'm not saying they wouldn't have been successful agents but he basically gave them the whole playbook and said, "No, no, no, this is how we do this and this is how we walk and this is how we dress and this is how we talk and this is how we eat and this is what we do. This is how you threaten and this is how you woo." He did the whole thing. He was incredible.

In the aftermath of Michael Ovitz's departure from CAA, just about anybody in Hollywood with a triple-digit IQ heard, firsthand or remotely, about how much the Young Turks resented and even hated him. To faithful Ovitz believers, to agnostics in the battle, and naturally to Ovitz himself, the animosity simply didn't make sense, especially because he had given the go-ahead for them to be hired.

Ovitz was also the guy who had shared his biggest clients with them, giving them the kind of exposure and airtime that 95 percent of the agent community in Hollywood could only dream about. He was the guy who paid them generously, over a million dollars a year in their late twenties. And finally, perhaps most important, Ovitz was the guy who relinquished the keys to the castle, a castle drowning in dollars, but who didn't give them to Rapke or Gabler, but instead created a nine member leadership group that he knew would function or malfunction like the Supreme Court—there could be five to four decisions all day long for years.

So where did the anger come from?

It's too easy and pat to say this was about sons separating from their father. We're not going to go all Luke and Darth Vader here. (Okay, maybe just for that second.) They thought he had lied to them; they quickly realized how many relationships they had to repair all over town; and they believed AMG was a direct assault on their business. In fact, there is evidence to suggest all three may have been at least partially true. But that still doesn't account for a seemingly deep-seated hatred. As one friend of the successors said, "They just couldn't control themselves" when it came to trashing Ovitz. What made all this so overdetermined?

Two elements come quickly to mind: First, Ovitz was a painful reminder to them of things that they had to do once they took over, things that stood in contrast to the carefully crafted brands each of them had created for themselves and for the brand they had collectively created for the group. Put a Young Turk on an operating-room table for dissection and you would find a thick Meyeresque exterior and a tangle of Ovitzian muscle and tissue inside. The Turks prided themselves on being charming, affable, and well liked, all hallmarks of Meyer's DNA and qualities Ovitz didn't appear to give a damn about. CAA's now former leader kept the quest for power and battle out-front, and his sensitivities, including hiding his profound desire to be liked.

The Turks went from social club to strategic signing club to power chess players' club—and then they took a step they didn't have to take, the "Reject or Destroy Anybody in Our Way Club." And ironically enough, if they hadn't added the last agenda item, they might not have reached the Promised Land. So there's that.

Part of the resentment toward Ovitz, then, had to do with their looking into a mirror and being forced to admit that they did learn some really useful tactics from this guy and they did have to do some of the things he had had to do. Such is the baggage that comes with power. Lourd is charming beyond belief; Lovett will suffocate you with such words as "culture," "loyalty," and "teamwork"; Huvane fuels such loyalty among his clients one could believe they would go on a hunger strike for him if he asked; and O'Connor is the guy you dream about having as a college friend, and then friend for life. But make no mistake: These guys could be killers. They have as much cunning and need for control as Ovitz did. They just may have been smarter about how it manifested itself in public.

The second reason for such resentment against Ovitz was because he could play the ultimate ace up his sleeve whenever he wanted. They knew he had taken The Big Risk. Along with Meyer, Haber, Perkins, and Rosenfeld, they had thrown caution to the winds and put their young families in financial jeopardy when they started the company. They built it; the Young Turks just came. The Young Turks were prodigal sons, with the agency functioning like the trust fund a rich kid gets when turning twenty-five. Yes, they had made their hard-earned contributions, but they hadn't built the place from the ground up. So in essence, it was like Ovitz was saying to them, go ahead, keep clients, keep agents, and don't let the place burn down, but it will never be like starting a company on a card table with a phone. Now who wouldn't be envious and possibly bitter in the face of that?

DAVID O'CONNOR:

One of the amazing things about the process that we went through is we began to understand all the lies that had been told for a long time, like Rapke and Nicita thought that they owned a piece of the building, and that wasn't true.

RICK NICITA:

None of us had any idea Mike had a jet, that's for sure. That was a big discovery.

DAVID O'CONNOR:

I remember getting on the plane and seeing matches that said "Ovitz" on them and I said, "Hey, Mike, is this your plane?" And he said, "No, no, no. They just put that stuff out there because I'm a frequent customer," and some other bullshit excuse. I had no idea what was going on.

RICK NICITA:

We always said we could never have a plane. Everyone would have wanted it, and what do you say when De Niro says, "I need the plane Saturday," and you find out it's already been promised to Pacino? What a no-win nightmare. But I remember we got a note from Sally Field that said she was firing us, and I said to Mike, "I better go visit her; there's a plane that I can take to Idaho at 4:30," and all of a sudden Mike says, "Go to the Santa Monica airport and you can get on a plane in two hours." I said, "How is that?" and he just said, "There will be a plane there." I thought he chartered it. So I flew to Idaho and was able to convince Sally to stay with us.

RON MEYER:

They talked about "the plane," but the truth is, it was none of their business. They were employees. They got paid well—more than they would have anywhere else—and if there was a plane that they didn't know about, tough.

MICHAEL OVITZ:

They were annoyed? Why were they annoyed that it was a CAA plane? Who cares if they were? The young guys were being paid over a million a year. They brought in nothing near that, and the other older guys in charge were making more than twice that.

They've spun this yarn that is completely untrue. Number one, they told people that Ron and I ran the company into the ground and they saved it. We handed them the most extraordinary stream of bookings. We left them with *ER*, with *Jurassic Park*, with *Ghostbusters*, with everything you could think of, just streams of income and client flow. And secondly, I did have an airplane that Ron and I used, and no one else. And that was none of their frigging business! It has nothing to do with them. They didn't start the company.

If people knew that we had a plane it would have bankrupted us because all of our clients would have wanted to use it. We would have had to buy a fleet of airplanes. Flying private is all anyone cared about. It's why Cruise bought an airplane, Schwarzenegger bought an airplane, and so many others. By the way, Sydney Pollack also had a plane and we shared pilots and maintenance.

LEE GABLER:

I remember that at one of the meetings we had after Mike left, we were going through financials and we were able to count on *ER* bringing in more than sixty million dollars in the years to come. I believe it wound up being close to one hundred.

It was really an eye-opener in terms of the amount of money they made. Their whole thing was they were always being magnanimous to their people and giving them great bonuses. I'd bought into it, I'd drunk the Kool-Aid, but when I looked at the books I came to the realization that of course they were being generous—they were making a fucking fortune. Not that they didn't deserve it—they'd built it—but they were making a ton of goddamn money, so they could afford to be generous. I forget the exact numbers, but if you told me Mike was taking over twenty a year and Ron and Bill were each taking more than ten, I would say, "Yeah, I believe that."

RAND HOLSTON:

The back ends of *Golden Girls* and *Empty Nest* alone were just huge. They were some of the biggest contributors to the agency's bottom line in CAA's history.

RICK NICITA:

I wasn't pissed off about what Mike had been taking for himself. What mattered to me then was if I was being taken care of, and as far as I was concerned, I was. He was a damn genius. He made that thing, and he made me. How could I ask for more than that? What did I care what he got?

DAVID O'CONNOR:

The new executive compensation committee was Richard, Bryan, and Lee.

LEE GABLER:

Bryan and I were put in charge of the compensation committee, which did two things: it meant that television and film were both represented, and it solved the generational problem, making sure both sides felt they had a seat at the table. The comp committee controlled the agency, and we had to agree unanimously on any decisions that were made. Richard was running the agency as president and obviously had a lot to say in the motion picture area, and in terms of acquisitions, but Bryan, Richard, and I had to agree on bonuses for everybody, including ourselves. So there was a check and balance system put into place. The titles weren't the most important thing; the power was with the comp committee.

We went in there when we took over and broke down the salaries and Jack was making a lot more than I was, and Rick was too. Jack was making four. Rick was making three, Tom and I were making two and a half, and the young guys were making around a million.

DAVID O'CONNOR:

The five of us were making just over a million dollars, but Lee, Jack, Rick, and Tom were making a lot more money.

LEE GABLER:

They did not jump salaries right away. We kept things the same for a while and then we brought the younger guys up to two and a half. Jack and Rick stayed where they were and then we all got the bonuses to equalize.

What surprised me the most was the fact that television was as dominant as it was in profitability. I never paid any attention to that before. Motion pictures grossed more, but that department cost more to run. At the end of the day, net profitability is what really counts.

KEVIN HUVANE:

I only remember working. Every minute of your day was filled with something. We had almost three hundred employees. We had led departments, but we had not led a company. It was like learning a new language. We were really good agents, and now we had to learn how to be really good businessmen. I had never looked at a spreadsheet before, and I remember thinking, *Oh my God, we spend that much on fruit?!*

LEE GABLER:

When we were struggling to figure everything out that first year after Michael, Ron, and Bill left, Bryan and Kevin would go to New York and get full-blown suites, and when I complained, they said to me, "Well, you can do that." I said, "I don't want to do that. I don't need to stay in a fucking two-bedroom suite for a week, along with a twenty-four-hour driver. I don't need that, and I want to put that money in my pocket and the pockets of others." I finally said to Bruce King, our CFO, "I'm not paying for any of that," because I was overseeing the books. We were worrying about being able to pay bonuses to people at the end of the year, and you don't run up $250,000 of bullshit expenses when you can give that to people who are working their asses off. But at some point, I just said, "Fuck it. They can do what they want."

TOM ROSS:

There was a rude awakening for many of us. We began to realize the young guys didn't appreciate all the people who had kept the agency afloat for years and years with their clients. They came in and made it seem like it was all about them; they didn't want to have anything to do with what occurred in the past, particularly anything that was connected to Michael and Bill.

LEE GABLER:

They favored people who they shouldn't have favored. They also would put people in charge of departments like you would change socks. You would look at their choices and think, *What are you doing? This guy can't find his face.* And then six months later they would change it all again.

MICHAEL WIMER:

After Mike left CAA in 1995, I had gone up to Dick Donner's house on Orcas Island. I'm a pilot and Dick had offered his and Lauren's house while I got my seaplane rating. So here I was, doing takeoffs and landings on Lake Washington, when I received an emergency call through air traffic control. What the hell? So I land the plane in the river and taxi to a dockside restaurant, then I tie up my plane. I call the office. It's Ken Stovitz. And he goes, "They fucked us, they fucked us, they fucked us. We're Sophie's other child!" And I had no idea what he was talking about. Then he said, "It's going to be the five of them and not us." I had no idea what "us" he was talking about since he and I didn't overlap in any area. I wasn't surprised at all, but rather I was thinking, *On what planet do you think you'd be included in this group, dude?* His misreading of his power was gigantic. I got a great sense of what lay ahead for the company if he thought he should be on the board. Yikes.

DAVID O'CONNOR:

Somewhere in the November time frame Ken Stovitz called a meeting of everybody who was not a managing partner in the theater at like 7:30 in the morning to ostensibly talk about the fact that the nine of us were anointed, and that we were making decisions about bonuses and everything like that, seemingly without any kind of endgame or outcome in mind. And we got wind of this, I would guess, the day of the meeting.

KEN STOVITZ:

After Ron and Michael left, I thought it was important to talk about what was going to happen, and I was vocal that we should all talk about it. I thought it was a rare opportunity for us to all be in it together, so we could all talk about the succession plan, and everyone could be involved in having a piece of the company. I called for a meeting, and Richard and Bryan asked me to not have that meeting. Then the whole company had one. At that meeting, I stood up and said what I feel many people wanted to say. I think the analogy I used was that at the time United Airlines was owned by all of the employees, and I said, "Why can't we be like United Airlines? Why can't we all own a piece of CAA? Some would be entitled to a greater share, but why can't everyone, from the first kid out of the mailroom to the most senior agent, be all in it together?"

They never really gave the suggestion a chance. I think the meeting was orchestrated in such a way that they didn't have to. My rule of thinking was that CAA had always been founded on the concept that we were all in it together and all represented our clients together, then why wouldn't we put our money where our mouth was? Why don't we share in the reward together? We'd all be incentivized.

DAVID O'CONNOR:

We debated long and hard about whether or not to fire Ken Stovitz. We decided not to. We sat down and had a series of difficult conversations with him. I actually, of all of us, was the closest to Ken before the whole Ovitz thing, but he went off the deep end over what ended up happening here. He never really recovered from it. I think he just felt ultimately destroyed by the fact that he wasn't part of the management team.

The management group decided to have an emergency sort of

off-site within a matter of weeks. We ended up going to the Beverly Wilshire Hotel and we all sat around and aired our various grievances about our being anointed to run this company. We made it very clear that all of us had various options and that we opted to keep everything together. But if people didn't want it to be kept together, we would be perfectly happy to go all on our merry way. It was kind of cathartic and it gave everybody the opportunity to air their concerns about our leadership and at the same time send the message of "You don't like it? Then the whole company's going to fall apart." We came out of that dinner mostly resolved to stay the course, at least for the short term. But if things were tipping in the other direction between then and Christmas, my guess is we probably would have concluded that it was time for us to leave and start our own thing.

KEVIN HUVANE:

One moment I can still remember is after Michael left, the valet guys came up to me and Bryan and asked if they were still going to have jobs. It was sort of heartbreaking. They asked us if we were staying because they thought if we weren't, there wasn't going to be a company. We loved those guys; they were the first people to greet you, and were the most welcoming group, and set the tone for building. At the moment, I think we both realized in a deeper way just how many people were now depending on us, and that we needed to make this work.

We would say to each other all the time: "We have to lead by example." The template that was put in place by the founders was a good one for us to follow, which is reward teamwork, treat people kindly. I reminded everybody every day that when they walked into the building, they had to smile. I know it sounds silly, but when you smile, you send a signal that everything is good, because if our colleagues were looking at us and if we looked worried or concerned, they were going to be worried and concerned. We had to make sure that people felt everything was going to be fine.

Our first hire was someone to run our foundation for philanthropy. We wanted to make the statement that while all this was challenging, it was also an opportunity, and we could do it in a way that was reflective of who we were as people.

MICHELLE KYDD LEE, Executive:

I grew up in a little town in Maine. Both of my parents were teachers and service was a big part of my childhood. I worked for United Way, the MS Society, and a variety of different nonprofits, before moving then to Los Angeles when I was twenty-four and doing affordable housing fundraising in Venice, California. Just before coming to CAA, I was doing refugee relief in Bosnia and Croatia, which was a completely random thing to do, but I was very, very taken with what was going on when that part of the world was at war. I went with a friend and we worked in the camps providing infrastructure to college kids who were coming over to be social workers in the refugee camps.

RICHARD LOVETT:

Michael had his own leadership style and understanding of power. My partners and I had different ideas, and I wanted to express them. My goal was to promote and support the work of others, and I was not pursuing my own profile.

MICHELLE KYDD LEE:

When I returned to Los Angeles, it was strange, because I was still focused on the war over there. I went on a trip with a bunch of folks in Jackson Hole, Wyoming, and one of the people in the group asked me, "So what do you do?" I said, "It's hard to explain." But he was really curious, and kept asking me. After I told him he said, "You should come work at CAA." I had no idea what that meant, and when I found out he was an agent, I thought, *Well, that's odd.* I went back to visit my family in Maine and was on this remote island and started getting these phone calls from CAA. What I didn't realize was that Michael Ovitz had left CAA and the guy I had met in Wyoming was Richard, who had just become president of CAA—and now he's calling me in the barn of our farm.

I said, "Congratulations on your new gig," and he said, "Thanks very much. I think you should come work for us." I remember I said, "Doing what?" And he said, "I'm not sure," and that's how it all started. They told me, "Build your business. Bring your expertise to us. Learn our culture, learn our ways, and then figure out how we can best benefit from having you as part of us and build something that's never happened before." I was a nonprofit girl at twenty-nine years old with a backpack coming into a company filled with people in suits who in my mind had it all figured out.

DAVID O'CONNOR:

The top priority was to hold the clients to the business. There were a lot of forces out there who would have loved to see CAA break up. There was such enmity for what the agency was and had become.

LEE GABLER:

A client can smell the sweat on an agent when they're nervous about losing them. Agents do silly things that they never did before, like calling them on a weekend and saying, "How's it going?" when they hadn't done that for the past ten years. People do things that are very, very obvious and transparent when they are frightened, and that's what was taking place.

RICK NICITA:

Meetings, meetings, meetings. Tom, Nicole Kidman, Al Pacino. It all became one big blend, and a bunch of us would take the meetings with agency clients. I remember a big meeting with Dick Donner to keep him there. I had nothing to do with Dick Donner, who was very big at the time, but I was at that table.

KEVIN HUVANE:

I had Tom Cruise, Brad Pitt with Bryan, Demi Moore, Meryl, Nicole Kidman, Geena Davis, and then I became Glenn Close's agent. People didn't realize how much we were already established as their agents. Their lives didn't change.

RICK NICITA:

For every client who said, "What are you guys going to do? Are you guys all right? Are you going to be able to represent me?," there was a "You've already been my agent. I've trusted you. Mike was great, Ronnie was great, but you're the one who read that script and you're the one I had breakfast with that morning, et cetera. So if you're telling me that you're still going to be able to pull it off, then let's give it a go."

Remember, nobody signs on for a thousand years. Another agent rule is "Every client is leaving you. The only issue is when." Every client is out the door; it's just a question of if it's going to be a long walk or a short walk, but they're all leaving. Whenever you see an obituary of an agent, it says, "During their career they represented X, Y, Z." And some of us play a game and go, "Okay, while they were active agents: left him, left him, left him, left him." But that's just how it is. Occupational hazard.

DAVID O'CONNOR:

The first client to leave, I'm reasonably certain of my facts on this one, because it was a client that I was involved with, originally, was Steven Seagal. Which, if you know Steven, is perfect— of course he's going to be the first client to leave. But there was a drumbeat of several clients. I know Costner was a big one in there.

KEVIN HUVANE:

They were talking to us on a daily basis and we had a history with them, so we weren't starting over. There were some exceptions. Annette Bening had only spoken to Ronnie, so it was a total start over, but she had also remembered that I had seen her in her play when I was a young agent in New York and contacted her. At the time, she had already signed with an agent, but she knew that my interest was genuine going back to before she had even done a movie, so that was a very easy transition.

I think Bryan and I were very closely identified with being able to handle the talent part, keeping clients, signing clients, and we knew to keep the company going, we literally had to be on top of that.

STANLEY JAFFE:

A lot of people thought Mike and Ronnie had a hold on their clients, and that many of them would be poached after they left the agency. I too thought they might be in trouble, that they would be fighting an uphill battle. But I've got to give Richard and his partners all the credit in the world—they were under attack, they fought back hard.

RICK NICITA:

I want to say Stallone and a bunch of people left. We always felt we were on the brink of it, but it was a testament that we didn't lose more. Part of it was because the opposition didn't get their act together. The other agencies dropped the ball; they were terrible. Nothing had changed. They didn't adapt to the situation.

I still don't understand how we really stayed as good and smart as we were. I think they couldn't show the team effort that, even in our weakened state, we still showed. They were unable culturally to show it, and it still became the same ICM singular agent trying to sign a given client that they hadn't signed with before. Whereas CAA had the whole management group saying we will take care of you.

ROB LIGHT:

I don't think that we felt that there was a feeding frenzy for our clients in music as much. Not that we weren't part of the bigger company, but Tom was a big personality, and most of the music clients, even though they touched film and TV and other things, their touring business didn't change. Ronnie and Mike not being here didn't impact them day to day.

DAVID O'CONNOR:

There were so many holes in the dike and only so many fingers. I hate to mix metaphors, but we were jumping on loose balls. I remember Richard and me meeting with Marty Erlichman and Barbra Streisand, trying to hold her. And then we met with Dustin Hoffman and tried to hold him. It was crazy. The ones where we had the relationships with, like Redford, Connery, Bill Murray, and Marty Scorsese, there was no problem at all.

DUSTIN HOFFMAN:

In a sense, I was relieved when Michael left, because as he was getting more important and more respected, he was not that close to my work as he had been in the past. I will always believe he was the best agent I ever met, and I introduced him to many people—I think I introduced him to Spielberg—and they all went with him, and they would thank me for bringing them to Michael. He was just head and shoulders above other agents. But at a certain point, he wasn't aware of what I was doing like he had been in the past, and I was getting word that another agent would be handling this, and another agent would be handling something else instead of him. Sometimes he would tell me to call so-and-so, and I was hearing another agent suggest parts for me. I finally said to him, "Michael, I really think I should leave. I know we haven't stopped being friends, but you're in an entirely different position now. You're not just an agent anymore, and I need an agent." He said he understood, and asked me not to leave until he left. I didn't want to embarrass him, so I think I stayed another year. That's why when I heard he was leaving, I felt relieved—I realized I could finally leave myself.

He did suggest an agent at the agency that should take over for him, but we just didn't have a rapport. That's the guy who runs it now, I think.

TOM CRUISE:

I was in post-production on *Mission* in England when Mike had left, and I spoke with him. I love Ovitz and I love Ronnie, and I loved the opportunity to work for them and how they set things up for artists. That support we felt was incredible, and I never really had an agent outside of them.

Then, I spoke with Kevin and Bryan. I never thought about leaving. I knew them. I'm a pretty loyal guy. Once a friend is a friend to me, they're a friend, you know?

MATTHEW BRODERICK:

The whole agency was so associated with Ovitz and his personality, at least for me. It was very disconcerting when Mike and Ron left. Ovitz was never really my agent, but there was always this feeling that if you had a real problem, you could go see Don Corleone, and he would fix it. I had always felt very taken care of. So when they left, there was a period of, *What's this going to be?* But it worked out. Bryan Lourd was very good to me.

TOM HANKS:

Ovitz and Meyer leaving didn't mean that much to me. I always felt like I was just Richard's client.

DAVID LETTERMAN:

It was very hard for me when Michael left. He had been such an overwhelming positive force, and in show business, there are not many positive forces.

DAVID O'CONNOR:

I have no proof of this, but one of the things in retrospect that really pissed off Geffen, Katzenberg, and Spielberg was that we had heard they thought Ovitz leaked a DreamWorks story to the *Wall Street Journal,* and they never forgave him. I'm convinced that Spielberg stayed as a client with us as a fuck you to Michael, because nobody dealt with him other than Michael. He was the only point of contact, and when we all kind of jumped in and tried to hold on to him, his message to us was "Don't worry. I'm with you guys."

KEVIN COSTNER:

After Mike left for Disney, I didn't have an agent for five years. A lot of agents came at me, and I think one of the really big mistakes I made—because I probably didn't have the best access to material at that time—was that I should have just gone with Patrick [Whitesell] right away. I was just tired of how political things had gotten at the agencies and how much in the news agents were, with all the intrigue, so I just backed away from it and worked with a lawyer.

ALEC BALDWIN:

I went to UTA for a year, I went to Morris for a couple of years, and then Matt DelPiano, who was on Ronnie Meyer's desk as his assistant, became my agent at CAA, and he's been my agent ever since. I've enjoyed working with Matt.

RICHARD LOVETT:

We were able to retain the vast majority of our clients; some big names did leave, but most stayed. And our agents stayed. Neither of those things were guaranteed, particularly given the shocking events that had set this transition in motion.

From the beginning, Bill Haber had been both insider and outlier, a sharp-eyed, boldly spoken contradiction. His eccentric behavior and idiosyncratic tastes set him apart from the other founders going back to the creation, and yet few could dispute his high level of intelligence and keen moral compass.

One by one the original founders had left, and the last man standing? Haber, all six feet, two inches of him.

BILL HABER:

I was sitting there by myself; Ron and Mike had both left. As much as the Young Turks loved me, and I them, they wanted to move on with their own lives. I knew I couldn't sit there indefinitely, but had I wanted to stay there, they probably wouldn't have allowed me to stay. I didn't blame them. Life moves on. Life moves on to another generation. I had to be smart enough to know that and move on with my own life.

Then there was a full-page *Los Angeles Times* article in the business section with a picture of me, announcing that I was about to take over Sony America, and it was true; I was going to do that. But when I saw that picture of me in the *L.A. Times,* I realized that I didn't want that life or that profile. I don't need people to know about me. I'm the only producer in the history of Broadway that no longer has his name in a *Playbill.* I don't care about it. It doesn't mean anything to me. I have nothing to prove to anybody.

Through my relationship with Sally Field, I secretly arranged a meeting that even my wife didn't know about, actually, in Westport, Connecticut. I went and had lunch with the head of Save the Children, Charlie MacCormack, and liked him.

I had a meeting with Boutros Boutros-Ghali for UNICEF and they had offered me to take over the warehousing division of UNICEF. It wasn't close enough to children for me. And so I said to Charlie MacCormack, "Here's the deal I'm going to make with you at Save the Children: You can't pay me. I'm going to pay you. You can't give me a title; I won't take a title. I want the smallest office in the building. Now can you make that deal?" And he said, "Yeah, I'll do it," and he told the board, "Well, we'll have this showbiz guy for six months." The next day I took all of my clothes and moved to the Westport Inn and called my wife and said, "We're moving to Connecticut." I've been there ever since.

KEVIN HUVANE:

I will never forget Bill Haber when we went into his office after he said he was leaving to go do Save the Children, and it was one of the most touching moments I've ever had here because he said, "I need to go. It's your time and you should grab it. You're going to do great." I remember him adding this: "You'll make this place even better than we did." He was so gracious.

BILL HABER:

I think they were very well trained in the process and the genetics of running a successful agency. In many ways, they were better prepared than we were when we started the agency. Are there some who I wouldn't go to Hawaii with on vacation? Yeah. But they're mostly good, decent people.

PETER BENEDEK, Agent:

Lee Gabler was a very good agent, but he wasn't Bill Haber. Between Witt/Thomas/Harris and Aaron Spelling, Haber controlled ABC and in many ways was as significant as Mike Ovitz. He just didn't want the attention Mike wanted. When Haber left, things changed dramatically on the TV side. It became more of a level playing field. I was going after CAA clients in the TV space as soon as Bill left.

Around that time, I got on an airplane and Dick Wolf was sitting next to me and all he did was complain about CAA all the way to New York. Then about a month later, I got on a plane coming back from New York and Dick Wolf was sitting on the plane next to me again. Total accident, and all he did was complain about CAA the whole time again. When I got back to work, I walked into my partner's office and said, "We're going to sign Dick Wolf before the end of the year." And we did.

RICK YORN:

Ted Demme was on a call with his agent at CAA, Harvey Weinstein, and Bob Weinstein about a Miramax movie. They were having some issues with the movie, and the agent was trying to get heavy with Harvey. Mike was already at Disney, and Harvey said, "Hey, Mike Ovitz doesn't work there anymore. I don't give a fuck what you say."

BILL MURRAY:

There certainly was a huge vacuum because he controlled the center and made people who didn't like each other and didn't trust each other sit down together. Mike would say, "Okay, we're going to solve this. We're going to figure this out today. We're going to come to an understanding and make a deal." That's an unusual skill that I just never really saw anyone else have like he had. When studios had disputes—they were like the Jews and the Arabs sometimes the way they fought—it really was good for the whole town because it meant tens of thousands of people worked. Mike could know that on a Friday afternoon at Christmastime, fucking fifty thousand people were working because he made those sons of bitches bury the hatchet.

SHELLY HOCHRON:

When Michael left, it was a bit strange. You have to understand that none of those young guys had had anything to do with what I had been doing with Michael. We had been operating in a completely separate sphere. So I wasn't surprised Bryan kept asking, "What are you going to do, what are you going to do?" We thought about it a lot—me, Len, and Jack Harrower, who I wound up marrying by the way—and we decided to enter into a partnership with Disney because we determined that remaining affiliated with Michael was in our best interests.

RISA GERTNER, Agent:

I came over to CAA from UTA in January of '96. I was representing a number of very high-end writers and a few directors, but I always wondered what it would be like to represent more substantial directors, and I wanted to be in the business of putting movies together. The thing that struck me right away was the level of generosity of spirit, meaning that people were so kind to each other here. That was so different from where I came from.

From the start, I never felt like this was a man's world here. There was already another generation of women who were in very strong positions, and the guys running the company at the time were clearly comfortable with women in leadership roles. I was made the head of a department very shortly after I got here. And everybody I hired then were people I had met with; almost always, Richard and Doc didn't meet those people until after they were hired. They were incredibly deferential.

ADAM VENIT:

CAA had signed Brad Pitt and Leo DiCaprio right around the same time. Brad Pitt was basically signed by Kevin Huvane, Bryan Lord, and to some degree Jay Moloney, off *Thelma and Louise.* Leo was signed off *This Boy's Life* by Jay and Bryan and Kevin. Jay was the lead, and I was brought on to be the young agent on the team, and because Brad was older and hotter at the time, I wound up really doing most of the work for Leo because he didn't get as much attention from those guys.

I left CAA because Doug Robinson, who now works for Adam Sandler, said, "Look, these guys got the agency from Ovitz and company, and we're never going to own it. Don't you want to own something one day?" He told me about Ari and David Greenblatt, who had started Endeavor and really wanted to start in movies. They basically had TV agents and wanted us to come over. We had Chris Farley, Adam Sandler, Wesley Snipes, and Will Smith. I really owe him that to this day.

When I left to go to Endeavor, I was going to resign on a Monday morning, but I was out with David Lonner and his wife, who was Rick Kurtzman's sister, and she basically told on us the day before. Richard Lovett found out and we had to drive to his house and resign. It was me, David Lonner, and Doug Robinson.

When we got to his house, he was very upset. He started by saying, "I'm really hurt," but then went from "I'm a nice midwestern guy from Milwaukee" to being kind of a jerk. He was yelling, telling us, "How dare you do this! This is not going to end well for you." And I remember saying, "We're going to an agency with four people. We're like a pimple on your ass. What's the big deal? I was hoping you would actually feel happy for me," and he just said, "I'm going to destroy you." I was surprised he was so mean, and the yelling was definitely not cool. It wasn't the way I would have handled it.

I was so naive, I hadn't told any clients, which in retrospect was really stupid. The only one I told was Adam Sandler, who I'm close to personally. So after this stupid meeting, I had to start calling my clients. Chris Farley was in rehab and I couldn't reach him, and I couldn't find Leo. That night was the premiere of *Romeo & Juliet* that he was in, and my new partner says, "You've got to go to the premiere." I was emotionally exhausted at that point, it was late, but I went to Grauman's Chinese and found myself standing at the curb next to Bryan Lourd, who was also waiting for this poor kid to come out of his limo. When he did, we both stood on both sides of him, and we sat on both sides of him at the party. It was the most uncomfortable evening for everyone—mostly for Leo. In retrospect, what jerks we were for ruining his night; it was just the craziest thing ever. He left CAA and didn't come to us either. He never took an agent after that.

ABBY ADAMS:

My brother had died; my dad had died, and I thought to myself, *Do I really have it in me to continue?* Apart from my personal sadness, it just wasn't as much fun anymore. This had less to do with CAA itself and more about the corporatization that was taking place in the entertainment industry. One of my favorite parts of the job—patiently grooming writers—was not as realistic as it used to be, and I wasn't enjoying the other work nearly as much. I was feeling like it really wasn't something I wanted to kill myself over, particularly being a mother. It's very hard to have a balanced life and be in that business as a woman especially, and I didn't want to be in a position where I wasn't going to see my child for twelve hours a day.

ADAM VENIT:

Back then, I already had kids when a lot of those guys didn't, right? And I remember one day I was going home for my twins' birthday party at 6:00 P.M. And they said to me, "Where are you going?" I told them I was on my way to my kids' birthday party, and I remember it to this day. They said, "You're going home at six o'clock? Really?"

And I had to wear a suit and tie every day at CAA. I hate wearing a suit and tie. I don't think I do as good work in a suit and tie. I always said, "God, I want to be Ron Meyer," and he didn't wear suits. So after Mike left, I started to dress a little more casually, and one day Richard said to me I should be wearing a suit and tie. I didn't want them to tell me how to dress.

LEE GABLER:

There was no consistency; that's the rub that I had with Richard. They would bring people in knowing full well they just were antithetic to the culture. He would bring this person because they had important clients. So what if they don't fit in with what the culture's all about. But the culture's not the most important sort of thing, it's the only thing. If you lose that or if guys don't have that, you have a problem.

PATRICK WHITESELL:

There was a Friday in August, I was in the hallway and had a suit on, but no tie. Richard passed me and said, "You've got to wear a tie to work." In my head I was thinking, *Are you fucking kidding me?* Bad culture play, if you ask me.

DAVID GREENBLATT:

Jack got the biggest shaft of all. There's never been anybody with that list of directors ever.

JACK RAPKE:

Some of the young guys were now talking to my client list with more frequency, and I was waking up with problems I should have never had. I always tried to stay ahead of the curve and take a global view of my business. That's how I pushed myself to stay on top of my game. They couldn't do it. So I was now spending hours cleaning up shit that if they hadn't gotten involved, I wouldn't have had that problem. And while they were talking to my clients, they were sending me some television director who wanted to get into the feature world.

LEE GABLER:

Jack freaked out; he wasn't going to be "the guy," and he left. He just walked out. No notice. He just walked out. One day he came in and he said, "I want to follow my film career," and he left.

JACK RAPKE:

I have a son, at the time he was just a young kid, and I was reading some of his creative writing and I thought it was very, very good, and I started to think, *Gee, wouldn't this be ironic that my son would have to complete his father's journey in Hollywood where I was only an agent and the son was the one who actually made the movies and television?* And I don't say that disparagingly. Could I live with that? That basically my son was completing my own journey? I didn't want my son to complete my journey. So I called Rick and said, "You better convene everybody." We met at Rick's house, and they begged me to stay six months—"six months so that we can have more of a toehold with the client list?" And I said, "Guys, you've had years to develop relationships with the guys that I have. I'm going to move on. I don't know exactly what I'm going to do." I knew if I went to become another agent in another place, I was going to take all of my clients and they all would have come, but it's not what I wanted to do, so I told them, "I'm not going to go into the representation game." I didn't want to be a manager because I didn't want to be conflicted with regard to making movies because they have to support their client rather than be an objective producer. And you are not recognized for an Academy Award if you are a manager/producer. I wanted to cut and be pure because I was about the films, always. I wanted them to know that. Further, because we were still struggling to pay debt back and everything, I went away without invoking the clause that they had to pay me for that year. They paid me probably $300,000 pro rata. Ray Kurtzman wanted to do that. I didn't want to put any stress on them. I probably could have had it paid out over time. I didn't want to stress. I was out. I walked out at the top of my game with class and dignity and elegance.

ROBERT ZEMECKIS:

Jack proposed that we start this production company and we become partners, and I thought it was a really good idea. I loved working with Jack and I thought Jack had a lot of wisdom and knew about the business and it would be, and I believe I was right, a really close and good working relationship.

I've never asked Jack any of the details of what happened. I know that he was deeply hurt, but I think he's come to accept the fact that he was just lied to by these guys from Day One.

ROBERT KAMEN:

Typical Jack. He calls me up one night and doesn't sugarcoat anything. He says, "Babe, listen. I got to tell you something. I'm not your agent anymore." I said, "Are you firing me? I don't understand." And he said, "No, no, no. I'm going to go work with Bob Zemeckis. We're going to do a company. You're cool, right?" And I said, "Not really." He says, "Well, I'm doing it anyway. So I'll be in New York next week. Let's have dinner." And that was it. It was very Jack. But we're still best of friends.

PATRICK WHITESELL:

Ronnie leaves and goes to Universal, and Michael leaves to go to Disney, so within the first year of my being at CAA, the reason I went there—stability—is just gone. I did see, though, that with the top guys gone, there was going to be movement. I realized this is all creating a massive opportunity because everybody would be moving up a level.

LEE GABLER:

I could have worked with Tom Ross, and I could have worked with Bryan Lourd. Forget about Kevin and Doc; forget about Jack and Rick. The only two people I could have worked with were Tom and Bryan. The others I wouldn't cross the street for.

JEREMY ZIMMER:

We were aware that there was a public facing group of nine, but the real group was just five. They were letting a lot of the group pretend.

TOM ROSS:

We would have board meetings and I think at one point I said, "You know, if you're going to treat us like monkeys, at least put some bananas on the table." They were always riding Lee big-time, saying, "How come we don't have this package? How come we don't have this?" They were meddling in all of our businesses, and Rick was too naive to see it. They were all over his client base, all over his territory. And then I started finding out they were meeting with Clive Davis and people in my area. That's when I started to think, *They're working against us.*

FRED SPECKTOR:

When Ron left—and even when Michael was gone—my attitude about my own career was I didn't want to have another job. I never thought about leaving. This was where I was going to work for the rest of my life. Call it being Pollyanna, but I just love the DNA of this place.

Michael Ovitz stayed just fourteen months at Disney. After twenty years of autonomy and unquestioned power, there hadn't been a single day of either for him in his new job. The disparity between his days at CAA and Disney were almost violent.

MICHAEL EISNER:

Very quickly there were negative signs. Bob Iger had called me and said Michael Ovitz had made some deal with somebody that he didn't even tell me about; then he made a deal with Scorsese to make *Kundun* and didn't even tell me beforehand. It was not a good start.

But I thought this was growing pains for Michael, a learning curve for Michael, adjusting to the corporate world for Michael. I tried to get him to sit with our general counsel and with our CFO. He wouldn't even sit with them. He wouldn't admit that he didn't understand corporate finance. He wouldn't spend time with Steve Bollenbach, the CFO. In the end, he just couldn't do the job. It wasn't about getting Tom Cruise $20 million a picture anymore. But he wouldn't come across the bridge. People say agents can't cross the bridge, it's simply not true. Lew Wasserman crossed the bridge just fine.

EDGAR BRONFMAN JR.:

Universal had done a deal before I got there with Scorsese, and he had just made *Casino*. Ron saw the picture, and I said, "How is it?" and he said, "It's great. And it's forty-five minutes too long." I said, "Well, get him to cut it." He said, "He won't." I said, "What do you mean, he won't?" He said, "He's Marty Scorsese. He told me he's not going to cut the movie. It's the movie he wanted to make. He's not cutting a minute of the movie." So I said to Ron—knowing how he would respond—"Well, then, let's end the deal. Let's not be in business with people who have no interest in us. We're putting up all of the money for their movie. If they don't care how we come out of it, let's not be in business with them." Ron said, "Edgar, it's Marty Scorsese. You can't start out trying to be a talent-friendly studio by firing Martin Scorsese," which I knew. So I said, "Well, maybe I can't, but Ron, I don't understand why we're in business with people who ask us to have total regard for them while they have no regard for us."

Then we just got so lucky on his next picture, which was about the Dalai Lama. With Seagram's, we had a huge spirits and wine business in China, so I was like, "I'm not doing this. I don't need to have my spirits and wine business thrown out of China." Then Marty went to his old agent friend Ovitz, who by now was at Disney, and not only did they make that movie, they also took his deal. I was like, "Go with God." We didn't make another movie with Scorsese while I was there.

JUDY OVITZ:

Our first experiences at Disney were not good ones. It's not the happiest place on Earth.

MICHAEL OVITZ:

I had a guy that I had made a deal with that was so weak he could barely walk up the stairs. He was working three hours a day. He had a quadruple bypass. But we just conflicted the minute we started.

SUSAN MILLER:

I knew the minute we arrived at Disney that we were screwed. There were only a couple execs who welcomed us; everyone else it seemed was too busy trying to figure out how to get rid of us. We had left a privately held company of approximately three hundred people and arrived at a public company with thousands spread out all over the world. When we were there just a couple months, Sydney Pollack, one of my favorite people, called and asked me, "Susan, how do you like Mousewitz?"

JUDY OVITZ:

He had had a meeting with all of the heads of Disney the first night, and these department heads said, "I'm not reporting to you." And then Eisner didn't back him up. Didn't say a word. He probably enjoyed it. Michael came home to me and I'll never forget: He said, "We're screwed."

MICHAEL OVITZ:

I never wanted to spend more than five to seven years at Disney, ever. It was never my intention to be there long term.

DAVID GEFFEN:

As good an agent as Mike was, he was not a good partner. And he was incapable of being a partner, as was demonstrated when he went to Disney with his closest friend in the world, Mike Eisner, who fired him. He can't be a partner. It isn't within his makeup.

MICHAEL EISNER:

He wouldn't be fired. I would say to him, "Michael, this is not working, I really think we have to part ways," and he would reply, "What time is the theater?" I couldn't even get him to have a conversation about being fired. Then finally Gary Wilson, one of our board members, was on their shared yacht and told him, "You're being fired." At this point, he had the opportunity to go to Sony. I met with Nobuyuki Idei in his room at his hotel in New York City. I knew Sony loved Ovitz. Basically I was presenting to them a solution: They could give Michael what he wanted, a CEO job, and that was something I could not offer. I would not hold him back. While he was packing to go back to Japan, we discussed a deal that was right out of baseball trading, out of free agency, and would have been so great, avoiding negativity from anybody and giving Ovitz a second chance and ridding Disney of the thorn. I said to Idei, "I know you want Michael Ovitz. He's not going to be CEO of Disney, because I'm not leaving. He can be yours. So if you want him, it is okay with me." Then I went to Michael and said, "Michael, you're gone. I think you can, however, get this job at Sony." So he flew to Japan to meet with the top leadership, and the first thing he does in the meeting with them is ask for complete autonomy. First of all, you never ask for autonomy. It may be something you get by establishing a great track record, making smart decisions, and providing leadership, but you never use those words. Second, you certainly never ask for it from the Japanese. It was the stupidest thing for him to say in that situation, and it killed any chance of him going there.

Here's the worst part. I finally, finally got him to leave. We were in my mother's apartment in New York and settled it. I wrote the press release. It was rather nice. Our board approved it as it had approved his severance package. Under the circumstances, he even liked the release, but before I had even called the board to say all was completed, he had hired a PR guy and was talking about how much money he got and how he took us to the cleaners. Luckily for me, nobody thought then, or thinks now, that I made a mistake firing him.

ARNE GLIMCHER:

Michael isn't the guy to take the second-man position, but he took the second-man position and would have the first-man position when Eisner decided to retire. Well, Eisner got well. When he knew he wasn't going to keel over and die, he didn't need Michael anymore. I think he was an incredibly ruthless man. The friendship didn't mean a thing, or it didn't mean a thing at that point. So Michael got hit in the head twice by people who were incredibly close to him. I think his best friends for years had been Ron and Michael Eisner—and they both betrayed him.

In the aftermath of his brutal departure from Disney, Ovitz sought to reconnect with the man that got away. Now, in his proverbial Hour of Need, he wanted to reestablish the ties he had with Ron Meyer, to revisit and reinvigorate the close friendship he had missed so much. But, in life and business, game plans can take sudden detours, and this one would prove to be a Malibu doozy, right off the famed Pacific Coast Highway.

EDGAR BRONFMAN JR.:

Ron and Kelly were going to build the Charlie Gwathmey house on Paradise Cove. They showed me the land and the plans. I said at the time, "Ron, you're going to spend way too much money on the house for this piece of property. The property is just not that great a property to build a house like this." He said, "Well, I love it." Right after that, I was having lunch with Berry Gordy. I'd known Diller forever and I used to stay at his house in Malibu, which was next to Berry Gordy's house. They had an adjoining fence, and even though I'd never seen Berry Gordy's house, I knew the land and the property. And Berry said to me, "You know, I'm going to sell my house in Malibu," I said, "Really?" He said, "Yes," and I said, "Is it on the market?" He said, "I'm probably going to put it on the market in a week or two." I said, "Berry, do me a favor. I think I know who needs to buy your house. Let me make a call." So I called Ronnie, and I said, "Ron, I've never seen Berry's house, but he's going to sell it; you should buy it and put Charlie's house there." So he called Charlie and asked him to come out and take a look at the property to see if indeed he could put that house effectively on this piece of property. I had called Ron on Thursday or Friday, right after my lunch, and Charlie came out to look with Ron on Monday.

JOEL SILVER:

Mike came to see me at my family's house in South Carolina over the Christmas break and we took a walk around the pond. He started crying—which we all knew he could do on cue—and told me he needed Ronnie back in his life and asked if I could help make things better between them. After he left, I called Ronnie to say, "You've got to sit down with him. He's crying. He wants things to be better." Ronnie said, "I don't buy it, but I'll meet him for lunch and see what happens."

RON MEYER:

He said, "What can I do? How can I ever make it up to you? Will we ever be friends?" You know, the usual Michael bullshit. I said, "Look, Mike, I don't know." But as I always do, after seeing him for a while—it's like sort of having a brother, or someone you're so involved with in a big part of your life—I was getting a soft spot once again. And he said, "Let's go and take a walk." After I said all the shitty things I could say, we took this walk and he said, "You know, I can't believe I don't know your son. I want to know your baby boy. And did you ever build that house that you were going to build?" I was like, "We're debating right now, Kelly and I, what to do." There was no house; it was just a shitty property. And I said, "Berry Gordy's property." He didn't blink. He kept talking about the weather, the cars, us, didn't say a word.

EDGAR BRONFMAN JR.:

Ron and Mike had this makeup lunch that Mike had scheduled on Sunday. Mike was saying, "I'm going to move to Aspen," and

Ron says, "I think I'm going to build this house," and tells Mike the whole story.

MICHAEL OVITZ:

I was in Malibu at a coffee shop with Ron, and he told me he'd bought a piece of land to build on, but it wasn't big enough, so he bought the piece of land across the street as well. I said, "What? With a public road running through it?" And he said, "Yeah." I said, "No offense, but that sounds pretty dopey." He said, "Well, I saw this other piece in Paradise Cove that Berry Gordy has, but it's too big and too expensive." I was taken aback and didn't know what to say in response, because I had discussed that exact piece with Berry some time prior and was interested in moving off Broad Beach, where I had a small beach house.

RON MEYER:

At that time it was outrageously expensive for us or for any-one in Malibu, and Edgar said he would loan me the money. I said, "You know what? Let's just do this. Let's do it." So that was Sunday. Monday morning I call Bob Goldman—he still was my business manager, and told him I wanted to buy some land. And he says, "What property?" I said, "Berry Gordy's." He said some-thing like "Really?" I said, "Why?" He said, "Mike bought that property."

EDGAR BRONFMAN JR.:

I mean, what else do you need to say?

RON MEYER:

At first a part of me actually believed he bought it for me, to make peace. I didn't think it was possible he bought it to fuck me. I called Mike and I didn't want to say, "Did you buy this for me?" but I did ask him what was going on. Then he told me he had an option on it. I said, "If you had an option on it, why did you just nod when I said I was thinking about buying that place? Or say,

'I have an option. You can't have it'?" He said, "Well, I was so shocked by it." I said, "Mike, this is bullshit. What the fuck have you done?" He said, "Let me get back to you."

MICHAEL OVITZ:

After Ron changed his mind and decided he did want the property, I needed some time to figure it all out. Maybe I was still bitter about our breakup and his consistently saying hurtful things about me all over town. I know he thought I stole the land from him, but you cannot steal something you already have.

RON MEYER:

There was no option. He doesn't know the truth from a lie. He just doesn't.

MICHAEL OVITZ:

I did give the land to him—for what I paid for it—and he built a beautiful house and is living in it now. He spent $5 million on the land and the house is stunning and probably worth $50 or $60 million or more, but the story of me not giving him the land is still told as if he never got it. It's actually hurtful and funny at the same time, but then again, we are in Hollywood, actually Malibu, so lore trumps facts all the time.

RON MEYER:

I. M. Pei or his son Sandi was going to build the house for him. There are houses on both sides, separated by hedges. It's a nice wide property, a great property, but they said to him, "For what you want to build, Mike, this is not palatial enough." So that's when Mike decided to sell it. Bob Goldman called me and said, "Do you still want the place?" I said, "Yeah." And that's what happened.

If Malibu is a dream land of ultimate escape, Hollywood can be a veritable trap, a place where even the best of times can become the worst before you know it. Chris Farley, in many ways the rotund successor to John Belushi at Saturday Night

Live, had everything to live for, including a nascent movie career and a ton of talent. But private demons pursued him and made Hollywood his personal prison of excess.

DAVID O'CONNOR:

I knew Chris really well and was the senior guy involved with him, but I had less day-to-day contact with him than Adam Venit and Doug Robinson, so when those guys left, we had a fight over Chris.

Beverly Hills Ninja was coming out and there was a lot of press around it and there was a reporter who was following him around. Chris was trying to stay sober, but he goes to this Sky Bar, and I got a call from the reporter the next day. He said, "Chris ditched me at the Sky Bar." And I said, "Were there women involved?" and he said, "Yeah. He left with a couple of women." So I figured, okay, maybe it's the hooker thing again. Whatever it was, he disappeared. He wasn't returning phone calls—we literally had no idea where he was—but we tracked his credit cards and found out that he was in Hawaii. So we cut the credit cards off—Marc Gurvitz, his manager, had some sort of power of attorney privilege of some kind—so Chris would run out of money. Pretty soon he called Gurvitz, and Gurvitz said, "Where are you, what are you doing?" and he begged to have his credit cards reinstated. Gurvitz said, "No, here's what's happening. I'm sending somebody on a plane to Hawaii right now. They're going to pick you up and they're going to bring you back. And then we're going to talk." So the guy goes, picks up Chris, and brings him back on the plane.

As soon as he got off the plane we went to Bernie's office. The three of us sat with Chris and he was detoxing like you can't believe—just sweating, and he looked horrible, beyond horrible. Chris was crying and it was very emotional. Then Bernie looked at him and said, "Kid, I've seen this movie before. It's John Belushi. If you continue doing this, you are going to die. I guarantee you. You're going to die. You are going to die. Do you understand? Hear me now: You are going to die unless you change something. You have to get yourself together." And we sent him off to rehab that night.

Those guys tried to sign him when he was in rehab. Adam Venit was desperate to get him back.

ADAM VENIT:

I loved Chris. When I left to come to Endeavor, he was in rehab and literally unreachable. He didn't come out for maybe six weeks, and when he came out, Gurvitz told me, "Look, he loves you, but it's too much for him to make a decision right now." So he didn't come to me, and it was really painful. It really hurt, because Chris and Adam were the two people I was closest to. I think it hurt him too. In November of the following year, he called me and was crying. He said, "Venny, I'm so sorry it's taken me so long to call you. I miss you and I love you. I'm coming to you now." It was one of the most meaningful moments of my professional life. I said, "That's great. I'm so thrilled." He said, "Come see me in Chicago," and I said, "I'll be out there in a couple weeks." He died before I got there.

TONY KRANTZ:

I ran the prime-time television department where we developed shows and kept the core television enterprise moving forward at the agency. In truth I didn't have any real authority inside the company to effect things beyond running the creative packaging division. And so when the company changed hands and I looked at the ongoing musical chairs that was happening, I went to Richard and said I'd like a little more authority within the television department. It wasn't about more money, it was about just a little more growth and to be impactful in the running of the company in a way I thought I could help with.

LEE GABLER:

Tony comes from a very successful family. Tony wanted recognition. Tony wanted kudos—his words, "kudos and glory"—and so he aspired to that. He worked with people, and he worked with me; I didn't have a problem with him. He didn't run off half cocked. But Tony absolutely wanted acknowledgment for what he was involved with, and wanted somebody to pat him on the back. So in that respect, Tony didn't fit in the way everybody else did.

TONY KRANTZ:

Lee didn't want to make it work with me because he looked at me as "the other"—I was the son of Judith Krantz who grew up in Beverly Hills and went to Berkeley and was not adopted; Lee was adopted. He saw things in this skewed way, and at the core, he just didn't like me, and now that he was in charge, it was his time to do what he wanted to do. He looked at me as somebody who was a potential threat and who had been loyal to Bill and Mike.

I would have stayed at CAA had Lee been willing to share power in the most minuscule of ways. Richard wanted to make it work with Lee and me. Lee didn't want to make it work with me, so I knew it was time to make a life change or be forever unhappy. I wanted to live my life with no regrets, so I knew it was time to start to look elsewhere and I knew I would never want to be a competitor to the agency I loved.

LEE GABLER:

He went to Richard and Richard said, "You have to talk to Lee." That sums up Tony: Don't deal with the guy you have to deal with—go around. He had run the packaging department for a while, and the reason that it wasn't as successful as it could have been is because Tony again separated himself. He was not capable of getting everybody to feel that it was one for all and all for one. He was more of an isolationist and it wasn't working. There was a tremendous amount of resentment. I didn't demote him but stayed more involved than I would have.

TONY KRANTZ:

Mike Ovitz was the king of CAA, so he could command his subjects in whatever way he wanted. Richard, Bryan, Kevin, and the others were building a company that was multipronged, more complex, and more ambitious. At that time it was all about the actors, it was all about the motion picture directors. It was all movies—or so we thought. I think Richard did not really understand the deep inner workings of TV or the nature of Lee's managing structure and the toxic dynamics within them. So you know what? He's not going to be able to say to Lee, "Do this or that." And at that time of a company in flux, it wouldn't have been the right move for Richard to rock the boat. Stabilizing the company was the right move for him to make.

LEE GABLER:

He was not going to achieve what he wanted to achieve at CAA and that was being the number one guy on a pedestal. He wasn't going to, that wasn't going to happen.

TONY KRANTZ:

My wife and I were in San Francisco, on line to see *Ransom*, the movie that Ron Howard directed and Brian produced. And she said to me, "Why don't you partner with your friend Brian Grazer?" And I had just packaged a show with him that we had sold to ABC. Imagine didn't have a television division and I thought it was a great idea to start one up. So I called up Brian on Monday and he was instantly interested in it. I'd never met Ron Howard before. A week later, the three of us found ourselves in Michael Eisner's breakfast room, where Michael wanted to create the next Carsey-Werner. Imagine Television, which didn't exist, would be that.

LEE GABLER:

I talked to Brian Grazer. Brian Grazer just said, "I'll do what you want."

TONY KRANTZ:

We took a long time to negotiate that deal. I kept it hidden from CAA, but before this, I had met with Richard to say, "I want to start looking to do something else." I wouldn't go down the road on anything without their knowledge that I was out there in the world looking—but I knew Lee would try to kill whatever I was trying to make happen, so I kept the Imagine deal quiet. By the way, it took me a year to have the courage to have that initial discussion with Richard, because the culture at CAA was one where if you had a conversation like that, you had to be prepared, at least in my thinking, to be fired that very moment. Maybe we were all brainwashed by golden handcuffs and fear, but that's what I thought. And as somebody who had essentially created his self-worth from a business point of view in the world of CAA, I literally bled CAA red. I had literally never been inside another agency. I didn't have social friends at any other agencies, either. I was all about loyalty to CAA. I had grown up there from the mailroom. For me to say I'm open to looking at something different—not to be a competitor, but something different—it took me a year to have the courage to say that to them.

Then it was time to announce the deal with Imagine with me as partner and CEO. It was a Thursday and CAA still didn't know about the deal. I gave interviews to Joe Flint at *Variety* and Lisa de Moraes at *The Hollywood Reporter*. They asked about everything that I had done about packaging *ER* and *The West Wing* and *Twin Peaks* and *90210* and all of these different things they had learned about. And they were going to run a front-page story, both trades, with my photo that next Monday. I had never been in the trades before—it was verboten to speak to the press. There was a huge culture of restraint as it related to the press at CAA. I walked into Richard's and Lee's offices and said I'm going to become the chairman of Imagine. Richard was cool and was actually happy for me about it. Lee decidedly uncool about it. He felt blindsided. He *was* blindsided. But it was a choice that I had made for my own self-protection and because I knew Lee would try to kill it.

Saturday happens, Sunday happens, and I'm at my house and I get a phone call from Lisa de Moraes. She said, "Lee's called me and he's disputed everything that you've said. He said that you didn't do anything that you did." So I took her through everything in detail. She said, "I believe you. We're going with the story." And she warned, "You should know that he's called Joe Flint to say the same thing." And I didn't have Joe's number. So I'm sitting there on a Sunday afternoon, my backyard by the pool, the sun is out and I, panicking, call *Daily Variety* and the recorded voice says you've reached the mailbox and "if you know your party's three-digit extension, dial it now. Otherwise leave a message in the general mailbox." I dial out of the blue *275.* "You've reached Joe Flint's office"—I swear to you. And I say, "Joe, it's Tony. Call me, here's my home number." Out of the blue—275. There was a guardian angel over me and I literally picked those numbers from thin air, one try. And Joe calls me up, we have the same discussion, he goes with the story.

LEE GABLER:

Tony doesn't work well with others. He cooperates, but he needs that ego boost in order to continue.

TONY KRANTZ:

Lee blackballed me for a decade by not allowing CAA to be in business with me. These were my dear friends, who were not allowed to talk to me. That's why I became a client of Endeavor and Ari, and those guys embraced me. We made *24* together, which made them a hundred million dollars or more in commission, and it was because Lee Gabler didn't like me, plain and simple. Now I'm back as a CAA client and loving it.

In the weeks and months following Ovitz's departure from CAA, few would have expected CAA's music department head Tom Ross to still be at the agency more than three years later. He had turned down several significant offers through the years to stay alongside Ovitz, and there was nothing about the transfer of power in 1995 that he could stomach. But in 1998, Ross had given a speech at the Pollstar convention that railed against SFX Entertainment, a business run by Bob Sillerman that was undergoing a series of purchases consolidating the ownership of regional music promoters, along with amphitheaters and management companies.

The New York Times *characterized the moves as "the biggest transformation"
in the history of the rock and pop concert business. Ross had been so outspoken
against Sillerman's concentration of power that after the first five minutes, some in
the audience believed he was committing professional hara-kiri. And that's basically
what happened.*

*On November 8, 1998, it was announced Ross would be leaving CAA after
fifteen years. No one said publicly that there was a link between the SFX contro-
versy and his termination, but no one in the industry believed otherwise. Ross may
have been naive about the consequences of his campaign against SFX, but he was
one of the most well-respected and dedicated chieftains in the modern music agency
business, loved by his artists and by many colleagues—even competitors.*

*Taking over the mantle at CAA music would be Ross's protégé Rob Light, one
of the first hires Ross brought in when he started the music department in 1984.
Ross asked to continue working with CAA in a consultant role, and Light agreed
to push for Ross to be kept on as a consultant, but the partners never offered such
a role. Instead, in exchange for a severance payout, Ross was saddled with a
non-compete clause.*

TOM ROSS:

It was November. I was going to go to Nashville and they said,
"Tom, you've got to come back to L.A. Don't go to Nashville."
And I said, "Well, I'm already in New York." "No, no, no. You
need to come back. There's an emergency. We really need you
here." And so I came back. Mike Rubel, Bryan, and Richard were
there and they just told me, "Tom, you can't work here anymore."

There was a side factor: Bob Sillerman from SFX. I felt he was
an enemy of the agency system, and they were going to bypass the
agents. They were going to go direct to the acts and make their
deals and leave us in the cold.

BOB SILLERMAN, Promoter:

I never met Tom Ross. What happened was that on his own, he
gave an interview that said that "Sillerman thinks that by owning
all of these promoters, our artists are going to work for less." He

was severely mistaken and he was being vitriolic about it. And it was quite surprising because not only had I never said that, but it's never a good idea in business to expect people to make less.

TOM ROSS:

The Sillerman thing was a problem, but it was a problem that during the Mike Ovitz days he just would have fixed. I was very outspoken about not letting him control us. I believed it was going to shrink the playlist of radio. It was going to shrink the opportunity for our artists to grow, and would result in the same acts on the same stations in every city across the nation. And we come from a business where each territory broke acts: Van Halen came from L.A. Bruce Springsteen came from New Jersey. Philadelphia was Hall and Oates. Chicago and Atlanta had their cultural bands, and all of that was going to stop. The other agencies were saying, "He's right. They're going to go around us." They knew I was messing with a tough guy, but I was protecting our business.

SFX sent one of their L.A. promoters, Brian Murphy, to the office and he met with Richard Lovett—I don't know if he met with Rob Light first—and said, "I'm sending a message that we cannot have Tom doing this. It's not acceptable and you gotta get rid of Tom Ross." And that started the ball rolling. And they went on a witch hunt.

Rob said, "If you want to start anew, I'll go with you." I said, "Rob, I don't think I have it in me. We built Fort Knox. Now we're going to tell people it's not what we thought and start all over again?" I said, "You put in too many years, I put in too many years. The only thing I want your confidence in is 'I built this, this is my design.' I want to walk in this building and hold my head up high." Ovitz may have orchestrated people out, but he always got them set up properly when he did so. Not this crowd.

Every time we had our yearly retreat, there was always a salute to Phil Weltman for giving them the opportunity and guiding them. And I felt that I needed to be recognized as the architect of this department and I should be a consultant. And Rob said, "Absolutely!" And I said, "Well, they don't want to give it to me, but if you insist, Rob, they will have no choice. I need you to stand up to them and say I won't do this without Tom Ross being a part of it." And he basically said, "You got it." And I never even heard from him.

We used to joke that Rob was Broadway Danny Rose from the movie because he would always say, "I'll be there, don't worry. I'm covering it." But unfortunately on this one, he never followed through. That's when I started to listen to others who told me he must have been much more involved in my exit than I ever thought.

LEE GABLER:

Rob was not in a position to throw him under the bus, but Rob played, in my opinion, Richard against Tom. Rob certainly sidled up to Richard.

Tom Ross came to me and said he couldn't stand Richard Lovett. He just said, "I'm done." He and Richard were always in each other's face. Tom just said, "Why don't you just buy me out?" And that's what took place, we worked out a settlement for Tom.

TOM ROSS:

I was like Mike Ovitz in the music world, and was referred to as "überagent Tom Ross." After five years, we were owning Nashville, and we were far ahead of the other agencies. I was loved, and I loved my colleagues and so many others in the industry. I did my damnedest to make things happen, but more and more of my time at CAA had become about managing the division internally and dealing with the record companies, the business managers, and the lawyers. I got less and less involved with the clients, which may have been part of my ultimate downfall. But someone had to manage the company.

ROB LIGHT:

Tom's a brilliant agent, always had a charm and grace that was a magnet for talent. At the time we started CAA, he really was the most respectable agent in the business. And he bought into Mike's DNA and culture. And it was just such a different face and such a different energy to a music business, we just took off. And we, you know, for fourteen years he was unstoppable—unstoppable.

One of the things that I've always loved about this place is it's incredibly horizontal. It's not vertical. It's not hierarchical. There was always this sense of a natural progression of leadership. We had an incredible team that worked with me, so it wasn't like, "Oh my God, the whole team's going away." And there was that run of every agency calling all the key clients going, "Are you happy? Are you going to go?" But I think because we were so closely knit and had been together so long I never thought it was really going to fall apart. I never was worried. You know, there's always going to be one or two people who are going to take advantage of it and go, "I'm out of here," but I don't think we lost but one or two clients in the whole transition. And that was a testimony to how close-knit the group was.

MICK FLEETWOOD:

It was shocking and we were definitely upset. There was real sadness that our relationship ceased to be. I don't know ultimately whether Tom truly, truly knows that all of us in Fleetwood Mac have a gigantic amount of respect for him. Tom would have been a great manager for Fleetwood Mac. He was so invested in us professionally and personally, it was really like a divorce.

STEVE JENSEN, Manager:

Tom Ross is the most influential music talent agent of the twentieth century. I've known him since 1975, when he lured me away from serene Northern California to start a career in Los Angeles. Tom always had the intuitive faculty for sniffing out promising talent, and a keen sense for navigating the politics in Hollywood. The combination of recognizing an artist's potential and leading the charge to help them realize their dream is a rare combination, and was just one of the reasons Mike Ovitz, Ron Meyer, and the other CAA partners entrusted Tom with the mandate to build the music division at CAA, which still thrives today.

ROB PRINZ:

The years that I got to be there when Ovitz was there were fantastic, but after Ovitz left, there were promises that were unfulfilled and I was feeling disappointed that the place was growing in a direction that was taking me away from what I loved to do. It was getting so big and splintered, and I was being pulled into so many meetings and having to do so many things that I didn't feel were relevant for my core business. And that was on top of financial stuff being promised and not delivered on. So when other opportunities came along, it just felt like the right time for me to go.

Ultimately, it's a relationship business. I'm fortunate enough to work with Jerry [Seinfeld] and Céline [Dion] for twenty-five years each. I went to UTA for a while, then I came over to ICM, and they have stayed with me. The first time I saw Jerry after I moved here, he was getting off a plane somewhere and started making this funny announcement, "ICM's here! ICM's here!" He doesn't care where I am. He's loyal and he's the King.

In January 1999, Michael Ovitz—along with Rick and Julie Yorn—founded Artist Management Group (AMG). AMG focused on client management with an eye toward utilizing its roster of directors, actors, and producers toward creating digital content. Ovitz recruited CAA agent Mike Menchel to his new company, who brought with him CAA client Robin Williams. The Young Turks had more than bristled at the formation of Ovitz's new company, but the hiring of Menchel and the taking of Williams jolted them to Defcon One. CAA issued a decree that anyone who signed with AMG for management would be cut by CAA as a client.

MICHAEL OVITZ:

AMG was started to try to be the first real digital production company. We made deals with Sprint and Verizon to program mobile telephony. It was my idea that we would manage, not agent clients; we had no license. We would hire all of these great producers and then turn them loose on normal TV, but also when they had downtime, we'd have them doing digital. I was fifteen years ahead of my time; it's exactly what's going on right now.

We were trying to make digital content. We had an interface we designed that looked like the Apple TV homepage. My meetings in those days were with the CEO of Verizon, the CEO of Bell Atlantic, the CEO of PacTel, the CEO of Sprint, the CEO of Dish, the CEO of Hughes. My goal was not to be in the traditional side of the entertainment business; I wanted to be in the revolution that was coming. I was early, but it didn't matter. I wanted to be in there. I didn't want to be representing people. If I did, do you think I wouldn't have called Spielberg and all my old clients? I didn't. I didn't do any of that stuff, but I got tarred for it. I had a whole staff of development people, CAA didn't. We were paying money for content. I had $100 million of inventoried television writers—that I put up the money for.

CAA decided that they didn't want me in the business at all—forget that I really wanted to be a producer; I could care less about being a manager. They had everyone go out and tell everyone that I was a horrible person and I was competing against them. I had no interest in competing with them—that would be a fool's errand. If I did, I would have set up an agency. And all their bullshit "they won't work with us"? We had a ton of CAA clients we were paying money to. It was bullshit. They took our money.

BOB BOOKMAN:

CAA said you can either be represented by AMG or you can be represented by CAA. Everybody except Michael Crichton and Marty Scorsese stayed with CAA.

MICHAEL OVITZ:

Anybody that we got as clients *had* agents. I think only Leo DiCaprio didn't have an agent. The big thing they used against us was Robin Williams. Mike Menchel was one of the first people I hired at CAA, when he was like nineteen or twenty. He was very unhappy there, and he wanted to come with us, and when he came, I should have told him to leave Robin Williams at the agency, but he didn't because Robin wanted to go with him. And Robin had two managers, that was the problem. He couldn't keep an agent and a manager, something had to go. So he decided he didn't want CAA, and that's the only client we had that was like that. They used that like it was some cardinal sin. We had five hundred clients at AMG, and probably a hundred under contract.

MIKE MENCHEL:

When Robin came over to AMG, it was simply a natural, obvious move. He was my client, he had been with me and Mike, and that's where we were. I literally cannot remember even having to ask him or it being anything we had to even think about. It was totally seamless, and there was absolutely no drama involved in the decision at all. Now, it created drama. I mean, I'm not stupid.

PATRICK WHITESELL:

I was running the talent department and started getting calls from ICM and William Morris, but I didn't even listen to them. I had brought Matt Damon with me from UTA; then I signed Drew Barrymore, and then Christian Bale and Hugh Jackman. Things were rolling; business was good. Then I got a call from Rick Yorn, who said, "Hey, come out to my place. On the qt, I've got something you should hear." So I go up to Malibu, and Julie Yorn is there, and so is Mike Ovitz. He says, "I'm going to start AMG and want you to be our next partner. It's going to be Julie and Rick and me, and I want you to be in it." And when I left there, I was thinking, *Fuck, I'm doing this. He's still Mike Ovitz and his plan sounds unbelievable.* Then Ron Meyer called me and said, "I was his partner for twenty years. You can't go into business with Mike Ovitz." I said, "How did you even know I met with him?!" We talked about Mike's business model, and as I asked Ron more questions—heard his answers—a lot of stuff just didn't make sense to me. So I called up

Mike to tell him I wasn't going to join him, which was a very hard, scary call to make. And he goes, "You've got to have breakfast with me." Then Richard Lovett hears about it and says, "Mike Ovitz?!" Because at the time, those guys had let everyone know that they hated him. So Richard got very tight about my possibly going, but I had already decided I wasn't going to do it.

JILL SMOLLER, Agent:

At my first staff meeting at AMG there was a guy who had to give a report and you could tell he hadn't followed up on several things. Now instead of just saying, "I didn't do it," or "I don't have it," he kept going. I was thinking, *If you get caught with your pants down, take them off and take the hit, but don't pretend that you took care of something when you didn't because all that's going to happen is you're going to get bled.* So in a room full of people, Michael just bled the kid into the wall and took him down as far as he could go instead of just taking one good shot at him. Like, how much do you have to humiliate somebody? Very quickly, I realized, *Oh, this is what this is going to be like.* I found it fascinating because I've grown up around brothers. I've also played professional sports and know what it's like to play tennis in front of a bunch of people in a little outfit and potentially suck. If the worst thing that happens to you is that somebody is trying to humiliate you, okay, take your shot. But that kind of environment does not breed productivity.

MICHAEL OVITZ:

We had a very good business we put together, but CAA worked overtime to hurt us. And Ron spoke against me. It killed me, because I always thought we had a relationship that would supersede all of that.

BARRY LEVINSON:

He went to Disney, it didn't work out, then he forms his own company. I left CAA to go there, and there was all this friction between CAA and Michael, but I did feel an allegiance to Michael, because of all our years together. It was a long relationship. Then at a certain point, it was clear that this company was too dysfunctional. Whether it was a good idea or not, it was too dysfunctional. It was a point in time when he was obviously sensitive, and I was suddenly being extremely critical of the company. That started to sour the relationship in such a way that the whole relationship came to an end.

JILL SMOLLER:

I don't think there were a lot of people in town who were looking for it to succeed. Certainly I don't think anybody had counted on the lack of goodwill there was in town for him. There was so much ill will that many people in town were trying to make sure the company didn't succeed. At the end of the day, it wasn't a good environment internally either. So nobody was rooting for it inside or out.

SANDY GRUSHOW:

The most profound experience I ever had with Michael Ovitz was when he got in over his head financially at AMG. It's funny. As a relatively young executive in Hollywood, when you encounter someone who was once known as "the most powerful man in show business," you assume that person is like Oz, all knowing, and it was a bit shocking when you discover otherwise. Michael Ovitz was clearly an extraordinary agent, but it turned out that he didn't really seem to understand the inner workings of the television business. Everybody who understands the business knows that if you're going to start a studio and make exclusive writer deals and deficit multiple TV series, it's going to get very costly, especially if you don't have a preexisting library that's throwing off revenue. I just got the sense that he had never done the math.

SUSAN MILLER:

When Michael started AMG, he asked me to meet with Jay and he looked fantastic. He had been clean for three months. I told

Jay I wanted the best for him and that I didn't think it was a good idea for him to come back to work in the industry at that time, or maybe never. I really didn't want to work with him, because I was so worried what might happen, and I told Michael about our talk, but at that point for Jay, money was an important issue. He had someone negotiate a deal for him to come over, but they overplayed his hand. Michael didn't make the deal, and I remember Michael telling Jay, "If you want to come back, you're going to have to prove yourself and earn everyone's respect again." Unfortunately, there was a very unhappy ending. Many people tried to blame Michael for what happened to Jay, but Jay was bipolar and in my opinion, his painful ending would have happened if he had been a stockbroker and never met Michael.

For Lovett and the new ownership, the immediate focus after Ovitz had left was on the representation of talent—keeping clients, signing new ones, and trying to re-sign recent defectors. They saw many of Ovitz's "ancillary" businesses like invest-ment banking and advertising as distractions. They were now in charge, dammit, and CAA 2.0 was going to be about making their stars happy and placing them in as many movies and television shows as possible.

But by the summer of 1999, the dot-com bubble was continuing to expand, and many of the agency's clients were increasingly interested in what was happen-ing on the silicon screen. The partners realized there were significant revenues to be found in the digital world, and they joined a long list of others in Hollywood who invested in idealab!, the high-profile incubator launched by California tech entrepreneur Bill Gross in 1996. Dan Adler, who'd built the agency's new me-dia practice back in the days before "new media" meant much of anything, was brought back to the agency in late June of 1999 (his only requirement being that he wouldn't be called an agent), and he was charged with managing the idealab! joint venture and rebuilding the new media department. Adler and his team took meeting after meeting with a who's who of the client list, many of whom wanted to be a part of this gold rush even if they had no specific ideas of how they would be involved. That meant trying to find the right opportunity and crafting the right deal, be it in making a game, creating digital content, helping a client actually join a start-up, or even launching their own company. CAA began representing a range of technology-centric companies who wanted to break in to—and leverage—Hollywood and its high-profile talent.

By the end of that year, the department was growing aggressively; key executives from the outside were hired, along with the promotion of some key trainees from within. In less than a year, the department had fifteen agents, and as they grew out of space in the Pei building, the agency continued its commitment by building out a floor in an office building across the street, allowing the new media department to work in space—and with a dress code—more reflective of a tech start-up than a talent agency.

It was a great mix until the bubble's burst, at which point some of the new media resources (and team) morphed into the marketing practice while others left.

DAN ADLER:

In many ways, what we did in new media was the most perfect example of how collaboratively CAA functions. If I went in and asked an agent if I could get together with their client about a particular idea or project, they inevitably would get on the phone and make the introduction for me. In other cases, after we'd make a presentation to one department or another, agents would reach out with ideas and with introductions. Although the primary agent might join these meetings, there were at least as many cases where I would—or some set of the new media team would—be the only CAA person with the client. I always marveled at the willingness of agents to open up their relationships, and I've always believed that this fundamental lesson—that more smart people working on a particular team would always yield better results—remains one of the magic elements of CAA. Rather than protecting and defending relationships, CAA shows that the adage of "the total being greater than the sum of its parts" really does hold true. Over and over again, I saw how a willingness to share a relationship and to empower a colleague helped to strengthen the primary agent's relationship with his or her client, rather than to take away from it in any way.

Jay Moloney had all the requirements to be a superstar among Hollywood agents; that fate seemed, in fact, inevitable, and he'd made tremendous progress by the time he was twenty-five. He was not just well liked but loved madly by those with whom he came in contact, partly because he took such an apparently genuine inter-est in their professional lives and in their personal pursuits of happiness. He once went right up to Meryl Streep at a party and said to her, "You should definitely be one of my clients!" Streep looked at him and said, "Why should I?" To which Jay exclaimed, "Because it would be great for me!" Streep couldn't help but smile and laugh.

Known for the extremes he'd go to in helping a friend realize an ambition or live the dream, Moloney went to extremes in his affair with cocaine as well. Yet the young man who'd been spoken of often as the heir apparent to Michael Ovitz was headed for disaster, and all the people he'd helped along the way—a considerable, auspicious number—could not put Jay Moloney together again.

He formally left CAA in 1996, with the hopes that taking time away from the agency to travel and get healthy would present him with a new start.

TOM LASSALLY:

Jay didn't have substance abuse issues for most of his life. He would drink a little bit, but it wasn't an issue in his life on any level until he was at Morton's one night and somebody said, "We should do some coke." I wasn't there for that moment, but Jay told me about it later. We were at the farmers' market one day and Jay said to me, "Someone once said to me you're only as sick as your secrets, so I just want you to know, and it's no big deal, that I did some drugs." I said to him, "Jay, I only took one psychology class in college, so maybe I'm off base here, but if you're telling me this, maybe it's because you've got a problem." He said, "No, no, I'm fine, I just want to tell you everything. You're my friend."

RICK NICITA:

It was the temper of the times. Everybody was flirting a little with disaster. There was a lot of white powder floating around.

TOM LASSALLY:

People loved Jay. Some resented him because he was so success-ful and so young, but there are no villains in this story. Everybody was supportive.

BARRY JOSEPHSON:

He had a remarkable unflappable, really joyous personality. If you were a journalist, he was so curious about what you did. If you were an actor, he was so curious about what you did. He wanted your experience to be better. He saw himself as a catalyst to improving someone else's life and livelihood and career, so no matter what someone told him, his brain was half listening, half thinking how he could engineer more success, more growth, and he knew how to put the pieces together. He'd clock things very early. He believed in Tim Burton so much. He represented Johnny Depp when he was a boy. When I was making *The Professional*, Natalie Portman had the biggest crush on Johnny Depp, and so I said to Jay, "It's her birthday next week. Do you think you could get Depp?" And at her birthday celebration in walked Johnny Depp. That's what Jay was all about.

JEFF JACOBS:

I met my wife here. She worked for Jay, who was a force of nature and an incredibly generous man. After we got engaged, he personally paid for her bachelorette party and came to our wedding. There's a beautiful photograph that he bought us as a wedding gift that still hangs in our living room. He was an impactful person in my life and my wife's life as well. He was really a flaming star of talent, and there are things that I do as an agent today that I learned from Jay Moloney.

PETER GUBER:

Jay Moloney was a force of nature. My children, my daughters, they were all friendly with him. He would come to our ranch. He would go on trips. He was like having a little brother or another son. We did no business; it was always, "Oh, let's go see Bono" or "Let's go on this hike" or "Let's go see this thing at the museum." He was insatiably curious. He had a flair for life that was fun to be around. He had an intense loyalty about friendship. You always felt a sense of joy being with him. And I loved him—that's the right word. I loved him. One time I thought to myself, when my daughters were growing older, "He'd be a good guy for my daughters." There's no higher praise from a father. But I didn't know the dark side.

RICK NICITA:

I was never connected with Jay. It's not like we were adversaries, but he had a way of doing things that I didn't understand. It was always about brinkmanship. He would promise the client anything and everything; then he'd call the studio and say, "I need this from you. I'm going to be fired by my client if you don't do this for me. I'll owe you." So he would make a promise and then beg to get it. I didn't believe in doing either of those things, but I guess it worked for him to an extent.

DAVID O'CONNOR:

Michael's a very complicated guy. I don't mean this entirely in a pejorative sense, but he's a very manipulative guy and he would find your weak points and he would just manipulate them. In retrospect, Jay had a fragile psyche. His dad was an alcoholic, his mom was really troubled, and he came from a fractured household—I don't even know all of the details, but he did have kind of a fucked-up background. I think that in Michael he found a role model and a very important presence in his life that he never had before. It was a very powerful relationship.

BILL MURRAY:

Mike was giving Jay a lot of greatness, a lot of great impressions, a lot of information, and a lot of knowledge. And he felt like he had to bust him on it sometimes, you know? Because you could love Jay to death. You could love him like crazy, he was so much fun. But at the same time, you couldn't make it too easy for him. He had to earn this. That's just human nature. Mike gave him a lot, but if he gave him everything, it wouldn't have meant anything.

ADAM VENIT:

Jay was the heir apparent to everything. As Mike became more and more important, Jay did all his business. He was the one who really spoke to everyone for Mike. It was unquestioned.

BARRY JOSEPHSON:

When Mike was still at the agency, Mike was very kind to Jay, but he was also really tough on Jay. Unfortunately, Jay always wanted so much more from that relationship than he got, and I don't think he ever realized he wasn't going to get it. He wasn't Mike's son. And when Mike left, as much as Jay wanted to become independent and grow up on his own, he wasn't prepared for it.

TOM LASSALLY:

Once Jay did coke, once his body chemistry got exposed to that drug, you could snap your finger and it was just like *that*. I'm not a doctor, but from that moment, Jay used substances to try and regulate himself. *Oh, I'm too this? Now I've got to do* this. It was that way for three years. But he really couldn't regulate himself—his body chemistry was too wildly affected by the drugs.

RON MEYER:

I had no idea Jay was doing cocaine. It was the furthest thought in my mind. Jay was such a squarehead boy, and boy is the best way to describe him. There was nothing manly about him.

If Mike or I knew there was a drug problem with Jay, we would have put him in rehab. No question about it.

DAVID O'CONNOR:

I'm telling you, I was as close to Jay as anybody, and this drug problem came out of nowhere. When we were going through it, we kept looking at each other like, *How could this be possible?*

ADAM VENIT:

He knew how to use his power well, but then he started to become a little erratic. Then one day he didn't show and went missing; then three days later he came back with two black eyes and looked beat up. The story was he was driving his Saab convertible and on the corner of Hollywood and Highland or somewhere near there, someone mugged him, took him to a motel, kidnapped him for four days, and beat the shit out of him. There had been carjackings at the time, so people were panicked. Only much later did everyone realize it was a complete fabrication and he was just on some bender.

TOM LASSALLY:

Many people—and I certainly don't blame them—simply don't understand addiction. They say, "Well, why doesn't somebody just stop?" When Jay was at his worst, Ovitz was on his way out to Disney, but his illness wasn't about a father figure leaving. I don't personally believe that. It was only much later into our friendship that I realized that Jay was bipolar. Jay was always up and down. Jay was manic and could go up to Sharon Stone at a party and say, "I'm twenty-four, I want to sign you."

BARRY JOSEPHSON:

He loved being amongst artists, he loved being amongst writers and directors and actors and musicians; he had a real passion for talent and he was the kind of guy that could walk right up to a table, he didn't care who was sitting there. He was like a heat-seeking missile; if he saw talent that he loved or whose work he liked, he'd walk right up and say, "I can do a better job than your agent. Your agent's not doing enough for you and I can do better." He would piss off a lot of other agents when he did that, but everyone else loved him.

TOM LASSALLY:

Those were the type of things that made him a star. But he could also get depressed, and I mean depressed. Only later did I realize that his highs were too high and his lows were too low. Once we drove cross-country because he was just so depressed.

DAVID STYNE:

As I recall, one of the first, if not the first, clients to put us on notice was Robert De Niro. And we, Richard, and Bryan organized a meeting to basically re-sign Robert De Niro and Jane Rosenthal to the agency. It was in the third-floor conference room at the old CAA building and there were fifteen of us in this meeting, representing every facet of the agency at that point. And as he's listening to everybody's pitch, you know, he's got that expression on his face that you've seen in the movies a thousand times. He's looking like, "So what have you got for me?" You know, he's doing that thing. Everybody in the room was on their game that day, from talent department, to motion picture lit, TV to theater to new technology, everyone—literally God would have signed with CAA that day. It was as good a meeting as you could possibly have. After that meeting, we didn't even need to, we knew we'd nailed it. You could just tell we'd won Bob over. Jane was smiling. It was a big deal, it was just a huge confidence and momentum builder that we could do this and that we were gonna do it.

What was such a wild dichotomy that day was Jay Moloney had just come out of his first stint in rehab. I was sitting right next to Bryan Lourd and Jay came in and sat right next to him right before the meeting started, and I heard him say to Bryan, "I fucked up again." And after the meeting, I remember it was like this crazy kind of pulling in two directions, where we had re-signed Bob De Niro, and the whole company was going to be marching in this new direction, and it was really sad to see that Jay was slipping again, and it was kind of the beginning of the end. Unfortunately.

MARTIN SCORSESE:

Jay was with us all the time, a very good friend, but I never noticed anything untoward or awkward. We checked in with each other every day on every project, even for little problems like I can't get the actor to stay an extra half-day. Every possible thing I could think of, I was working with Jay on. He called me once and said, "I just want you to know, I'll be gone for a few weeks, I'm doing some elective surgery. Everything's fine." I thought that was unfortunate, but it was elective surgery. But apparently it may have been for rehab. I just couldn't sense any big change.

TOM LASSALLY:

Jay was always up for rehab. He never gave up, and once it [his drug use] was out in the open, he never denied it and never lived a fake life. He would go to rehab, get out, set up his new system, and say, "Here's my program." It would all be set up and then *boom*. There would be a huge slip. He went to many different rehabs. He went to the Mayo Clinic. He went to Minnesota. He went to Israel. He moved to Guana and they took his passport away so he could just live there for a month and meditate. I visited him in Oregon and at some of his other rehabs on family days, and he would often say, "Now I'm good. If I can do this for thirty days, I'm sure I can go back to work." And there would be another explosion. He just couldn't stop. He tried everything. He was always ready to try. But he would then slip and slip.

BARRY JOSEPHSON:

We all tried. We did an intervention with Jay that Bryan helped to orchestrate with a psychologist, and Ovitz came to that, which was important. I lived with Jay for two weeks in his house, there for him all the time; I chased away drug dealers twice because the problem is, once you devolve into that world, even when he was striving to be drug free, they were preying upon him because they knew he had a lot of money. He had this modern pad in the Hollywood Hills and there was a Chuck Close painting on the wall and modern art throughout the house. He was living alone and one of the top agents at CAA—they knew. He tried everything: different lifestyles, different places to live, and no matter how hard he was trying, it wasn't a winning cause.

MARTIN SCORSESE:

I was making another push at Fox to get into their vaults to restore or preserve whatever they had, and I got ten minutes with Rupert Murdoch, and Jay came with me. It was raining and Rupert was standing there in his raincoat and Jay and I talked to him about the quality of the films he owned, asking for a systematic appraisal of their elements. Afterward, Jay came over to my house, and we talked for a while. He did seem more sad. It was clear a lot had happened.

TOM LASSALLY:

I literally remember going running one day thinking of the music we were going to play at his funeral. I just thought, at some point, he's going to get tired. My daughter was about two at the time. Jay hadn't shown up at my wedding because he was so messed up, and he wasn't there when she was born. There were a lot of moments that were important that he couldn't handle, and that was fine. But I remember thinking one day, *My God, who knows what's going to happen to Jay. He may never know my daughter.* So I called him one day and told him to drag himself out of bed and to meet me for coffee. He was superdepressed, but I asked him to please come just so he could see my daughter. We went to the Starbucks on North Beverly, and I don't think he was wasted, just incredibly depressed. But he met my daughter.

The next day, he hanged himself.

BILL MURRAY:

I felt such incredible pain when he died, and so did Mike. All of his friends were a wreck over it. I think there was great remorse about how they tried to handle it as a group. But it's not like anyone had the skill. You can't really fix a person. It's a terrible, terrible feeling.

TOM LASALLY:

Jay had lost his will to fight. He had fought the fight. He had tried everything.

BILL MURRAY:

I always think about Moloney's funeral service, which was really a lot of fun. I got to speak for fifteen minutes, and it was fun to make jokes, stick and stab, and be really wicked, because that's exactly how Jay would have liked it, you know? I stood there and said, "As I stand here and look around this room, I see the faces of so many people I recognize, and people I know, and I see so many people who really should be the one who is dead instead of Jay."

TOM LASSALLY:

Then he looked out into the eyes of various people and said, "Like you, and you, and you, and you, and you." It was the biggest laugh of all time, and a great moment of letting out all the suffering. I did one of the eulogies, but the one I will always remember the most was Bill's. Jay would have loved that joke. He loved Bill Murray; they had a truly special relationship, and Bill was so good to Jay. The entire memorial service was amazing, and Jay would have loved the fact that so many people had shown up.

JESSICA TUCHINSKY, Agent:

I remember Kevin and me trying to figure out where he was going to be buried. We chose Hollywood Forever Cemetery, next to Cecil B. DeMille, overlooking Jayne Mansfield with a good view of the outdoor movie screen. We knew he'd be happy in his afterlife.

BILL MURRAY:

Fuck, I miss him to this day.

There'd been many an inflow into the ranks of agents at CAA, but outflows were far less frequent, especially self-initiated ones. The system that Ovitz and Meyer had created—making it financially prohibitive for competing agencies to steal away their agents—had been holding up rather well since their own departures in 1995. Yes, there had been an initial, if somewhat limited, exodus in the first year of CAA 2.0, but the lineup had since stabilized for the most part.

In the year 2000, however, the always tricky and emotional issue of partner-

ships reared its head, with the Young Turks trying to determine what might happen to partnership architecture in the near and distant future: Would other agents have real equity? What about voting rights on key matters? Bottom line, was there a real role for anyone outside Lovett, Huvane, Lourd, and O'Connor? Irony of all ironies. The Turks were now getting asked the very same questions they had asked—and demanded be answered—of Ovitz and Meyer.

In the aftermath of the '95 departures, the Turks had promised to create an ownership structure, something that was far easier to pledge than actually do. The issues surrounding its formation were delicate, but ones they wanted to control. Bruce Ramer, a highly regarded attorney with a client list through the years that included Steven Spielberg, George Clooney, and Clint Eastwood was brought in to help construct a plan. What surfaced was a "Membership" program whose agenda was fourfold: first, to limit dilution of equity; second, to protect the agency from any single or small group of agents who might threaten or pull off an exodus; third, to serve as a retention vehicle; and fourth, to create more of an "equity culture." The membership program became a tiered partnership program with compensation tied to the performance of the company overall. Those who "belonged" also received an exit benefit—as long as you left and didn't compete—which was one times the average of your compensation of the previous three years. For the Turks, it was two times.

For the first few years, the program worked, due largely to the fact that revenues were really strong, but when revenue growth began to slow down for a while because overhead grew and margins decreased, membership compensation by formula also went down—a punch in the gut especially for high performers in their prime. It also disincentivized investment in new areas. Challenging economics had revealed the program's deep flaws, and a series of philosophical debates about partnerships once again surfaced, even amongst the Turks.

It all either started from or came back to square one—whether or not the inner circle of CAA was going to be a fluid one and grow as new leaders emerged. But the dirty little secret plan of the Turks was how could they keep the richest amount of cash flow (aka big money clients) with the least amount of dilution. There was a specific dynamic attached to the challenge. Inertia would keep young agents and more senior agents at CAA without much of an issue, except for extraordinary circumstances. The demographic in between, those in their thirties and early forties, was the rich target zone. So veterans like Rob Light and Steve Lafferty, neither of whom they wanted to lose, were easy, especially because they operated in their own areas, music and television, respectively. Things got way more complicated inside the motion picture department. That was Turk-owned territory. There, agents like Josh Lieberman and Michael Wimer were lifers who started in the mailroom. Cut them and they bled CAA's signature red; no need to worry. But the one guy who was the least covered by seniority, inertia, cultural connectedness, or an overly integrated client list was Patrick Whitesell, already regarded by many as having a wide open future, and who just happened to have two aces in his hand—a pair of young, movable stars in Matt Damon and Ben Affleck. To make the situation even more unstable was the fact that Whitesell had a less than profound relationship with Lovett, Lourd, Huvane, and O'Connor. The combination made Whitesell attractive to nearly every other significant agency in town. In yet another ironic twist, the Turks tried to counter this in an almost Ovitzian manner, spreading word that they had given Whitesell a fair number of clients to manage in addition to the ones he walked in the door with, like Damon and Affleck, and even with those two, the Turks believed—and were not above declaring—that they had played a significant role in the blowup of Damon and Affleck's careers. Several of the agents there at the time talked about the resentment and hesitation the Turks had about having Whitesell come into the inner circle as there was a question as to whether or not he had really earned it and whether he was selfless enough to be a leader. Nevertheless, they recognized he was a solid agent, and even though they knew he was going to be the most difficult all-star to keep—either through kinship or cash—the potential risk of losing his clients was worth an attempt.

For a while, the Turks danced a dance and bought time, which as it turns out, worked against them, allowing Whitesell to ultimately believe that the promises made to him of special treatment were just smoke, mirrors, and manipulation. He decided to head straight for the nearest exit. Not only would Whitesell be one of the most significant losses in the agency's history, but his departure would eventually set off a major upheaval in the business, giving birth to CAA's strongest competitor in forty years.

PATRICK WHITESELL:

That fall, when I went into my year-end bonus meeting, I was expecting to just see Richard as in years past. But it was Richard, Bryan, Kevin, and Doc, and I asked, "What's going on?" And they said, "This is a great day!" They gave me a great bonus, told me how happy they were with me, and said, "We want you to be one of us." I said, "What do you mean?" They said, "We want you to be our partner in the company. It will be you, Rick, us, and Lee Gabler." I said, "Holy shit, this is great." And then Richard said, "But here's the thing: We have another year of paying off Mike, so we can't change anything right now. But we'll have it paid off in a year. All we ask is that you don't talk about it to anyone, and in a year from now we'll make this official."

ADAM VENIT:

Richard was the type of guy—and I have no problem saying this publicly—who said all the right things but there was never anything behind it. And he would promise things and then nothing would ever really happen.

PATRICK WHITESELL:

Right around this time, Ari, who had set up Endeavor, called me. We had remained friends, and he said, "Dude, you should really come here. You can help us start a movie business and build it from there." I knew how smart he and his new partners were, and they had a killer TV business already in place that you need when you're going to start a new agency—it's the backbone financially. I said, "Well, that would be cool, but the time is not right for me. The guys here want to make me their partner." And I remember Ari saying, "Fuck, if they're going to do that for you, that's pretty awesome." So the entire next year I worked my ass off and go in to get my bonus. Once again, I got paid well, but then I asked, "Hey guys, what's up with the partnership, you know, being one of you guys?" And they said, "Well, we did get Mike paid off, but we have some restructuring we need to do, so give us until January and we will get back to you." I was a bit confused, but said okay. January comes and I say to Richard, "Richard, what's going on with the partnership?" And he says, "Yeah, we're almost there, we think we have something together and we'll come back to you in the next sixty days." So now I don't hear anything until April or May, right? I've been waiting over a year and a half, and he says, "We think it's going to be you and Beth Swofford." And I said, "Beth Swofford? You told me it was just going to be me. This is the first time I'm hearing about another person." I left the meeting, and thought, *Beth's a great agent, she's killing it, she's doing really well. Why would I begrudge her getting something?* But something didn't seem right. I just said to myself, *Bonuses come in October, and I'm not going to say a fucking word until then. It's just five months. I will wait and see.*

LEE GABLER:

They overpaid a lot of people because they were afraid they were going to leave, and made a lot of accommodations—this was on the motion picture side. None of that occurred in television or music. When Patrick Whitesell threatened to leave, Richard—and I'm sure he got the other guys to agree—wanted to make Patrick an equal partner to the rest of us on our level. I never would have approved that. If they gave him papers and he signed it, I still would have said no. And it wouldn't have happened. Patrick? An equal partner? Patrick had as much commitment to CAA as a stray dog.

PATRICK WHITESELL:

That October I get called up to Bryan's house. They said, "We're going to do this all properly; we don't want to do it at the building." Richard and Bryan are there and Richard tells me, again, "This is a great day. I know it's taken a lot longer than we originally said, but we're going to give you this partnership agreement. Take a look at the document. This is all very exciting. It's going to be you and twelve others." I looked straight at him and said, "Okay, great," and left, thinking to myself, *You've got to be fucking kidding me.* Then I read the document over the weekend, and it was all bullshit. It was just a shitty profit participation program where you get X amount of points and there was a net pool. In addition, I would now have a noncompete clause for the first time. It was a joke. I was beyond being offended.

I went into the office on Monday and told Richard, "I am not signing this. First off, I was told it was just going to be me. Then you added Beth and now it's twelve. I don't know what the fuck that is. And second, why would I ever sign this? I'm actually better off right now, I could leave at any time, I don't have a contract and have leverage with you financially. This is insulting. I am never signing this."

So then Kevin talked to me and Bryan talked to me, trying to sell me on the agreement. They said, "You're a leader, and this will be a big step for you. Maybe we can tweak a few things." At this point I just said, "Stop. You know what, Richard? Let's you and I have lunch." And there I said, "Put the contract aside. What do you see my role being here as this company evolves?" And he says, "Well, I think what we do is hopefully you take over for me and you run the motion picture business. Bryan and I are working on some things and we need to be freed up in order to do that." At this time, Richard was literally running the motion picture business every day. But the big thing that he never said was "You know, when I leave . . ." Everybody else at some point talks about when they are going to leave. He wasn't. So now I was really pissed because (a) I've been lied to and (b) I was being played by people who are supposed to be your partners, who you are supposed to trust.

When I left CAA, I said, "Richard, here's the thing: if I stay, I will never be one of you guys. You guys grew up together. Even if it were just me, and not twelve others, it would be like a basketball team with four seniors and a freshman, me. And you guys are never going to graduate. This is always going to be your team." I finally understood that and was okay with it. They were peers and deserved to run the company in whichever manner they desired. I would always be an assistant coach at CAA. I realized I wanted to be the head coach.

That entire partnership episode made me unhappy for nearly two years, but it really was a blessing. It got me thinking: *What is it that I really want in my life?* If they had made me a partner when they first told me, I would have signed the deal and it would have been the worst thing for me. I realized then that what I really wanted to do was bet on myself, take all the risks, and build something with Ari that would compete with them. I knew they were the star talent agents, and I was younger and they would come after me with everything they could, to try and steal every client I had. At that time, I had Ben Affleck, Matt Damon, Christian Bale, Joaquin Phoenix, Drew Barrymore, Kate Hudson, Jessica Alba, Hugh Jackman, and Jennifer Aniston, who ironically was the first person to say, "I'm leaving with you," but was the one who wound up staying.

MICHAEL WIMER:

After Patrick Whitesell left in 2001, Richard and the guys gave me a simple one-paragraph letter stating that I could, at any time with no requirements, join the board with Richard, Bryan, Kevin, and Doc. It was signed by Michael Rubel, CAA's attorney, and my lawyers said it was completely bulletproof. I never took them up on it. If the boys had a knife with my name on it, I never saw it. I'm aware of what happened down the line, of course, but I am pretty happy that I made the decisions before someone else did. Many years later, when I was talking to Doc, wondering why on earth the guys couldn't just keep it fun and happy and energetic for all those years, especially since we had so damn much money and success, he said something really prophetic: "You can't imagine why they did what they did because you just aren't built that way—you don't think the way they do." Carrie was right. Thank God.

STEVE ALEXANDER, Agent:

I was at CAA twice. I was there '88 through '91, I left to become an independent producer, and then came back in '95 and stayed until 2007. I was brought in by Lee to bolster the TV talent department, but the clients I wound up signing really brought me over to the motion picture side. One of the first clients was Heath

Ledger. Lee was a very specific kind of boss. I really liked him, but because he wanted things to go a certain way, we had a lot of challenges. I felt caught in between the motion picture side and the TV side; finally there was a moment where it sort of broke down, and Lee and I had it out.

After that, I was unhappy enough that when Patrick left to go to Endeavor, he called me and said, "I know your situation over there. I've been a party to it. You know, you should be a part of this." I went over to Endeavor to kick the tires and got into a real negotiation. They tripled my salary in writing. I left with a closable deal. But the timing was such that there was a CAA retreat coming right up, so I thought I would use that as a gut check before I made up my mind about going to Endeavor.

That Friday I went to the retreat, we went through everything, and I did my thing. I talked about my clients like Heath and Johnny Knoxville. On Saturday, right after lunch, we in the talent department gathered in a big circle. We had a minute of calm before the session was supposed to start, and I was pouring myself a Diet Coke when I looked over at the door and saw Kevin standing by the door, motioning for me to come over. Immediately I thought, *They know. The jig is up. It's over.* I walked through the door and sure enough, there was Kevin and Bryan and Richard. They said, "What's going on? We hear you're going to Endeavor, that you've already made a deal." My heart was beating so fast, but I did cop to it. I said, "I haven't gone all the way yet, but it's doable." I wound up airing all the problems that were going on with me. We walked around the golf course there for about an hour. I was under a lot of pressure. They basically said, "We'll take care of you, and match the deal you've been offered by those other guys." I knew part of it had to do with the fact that Patrick had just left and they didn't want it to start looking like there was going to be a bunch of people following him. I ended up recommitting to stay at CAA, which in retrospect was a mistake. It was hard to recover from that. From then on they looked at me as someone who could leave the company at any time. I just should have gone then.

DAVID STYNE:

John Hughes was obviously a huge client for CAA, and he was represented by Jack Rapke. I think Jack Rapke was in Hawaii or on a boat somewhere and literally got a fax from Jake Bloom that John Hughes was discharging the agency, and Jay had said to Jack, "I'm sorry John made me send this to you on Christmas Day." He was terribly sorry. So anyway, John Hughes left and then John Hughes came back to the agency and was represented by Rand Holston, and Rand made that deal for John to write and produce *101 Dalmatians.* This was a huge fucking deal at Disney, I can't even imagine how much money John Hughes made, because he had a huge gross position. I'm sure he made more than $50 million. Anyway, John Hughes left the agency again, and I think he signed with Jim Wiatt, who was at ICM at the time. So Jake Bloom I guess called Richard Lovett, probably in 2000 or 2001, and says, "Hughes wants to come back, put together a group and you've got to go fly up and see him in Illinois." So Richard, Bryan, me, Michael Wimer, Jenny Gabler, and Brad flew up private to John Hughes's farm in Illinois. He was great, we go through the cows and the whole fucking thing. Then at a certain point John Hughes leaves and comes back with this titanium briefcase. And he opens it up, and he says, "There are fifteen completed screenplays that I've written in this briefcase that nobody has ever seen." Because, you know, Hughes was, like, famous, he could write a screenplay in a weekend. He was just a mad genius. And so he says, "What I'd like to do if it's okay for you guys, let me tell you about some of these and I want you to be honest and tell me what you think." So he starts pitching us these movies, and he's like the greatest pitcher of all time. He was pitching us these whole movies. So the first one—yeah, we like that. Second one—yeah, we like that. We literally listened to five or six whole movies pitched, and every one is like, "Yeah, we think we could do something with that." So after that, he says, "So, this next one is about a woman, she's in a hospital in Chicago, she has an abortion, but the abortion is dumped out in the alley at night, and it's like a partial abortion, and it lives.

And this little baby boy kind of grows up in the alley, and he's like this street urchin. And I call this one *Partial Sid.*"

Partial Sid, like Sidney. So Bryan Lourd and I just looked at each other, and it's like this moment of truth and we go, "No, we don't think that's a good idea at all." And Hughes goes, "I am so glad that you guys said that, because Jim Wiatt put me with one of his agents at ICM, and I pitched him *Partial Sid,* and he said 'John! That is genius! Johnny Depp *is* Partial Sid.' " We all just started laughing, and because we were honest, he came back to the agency.

7

Bar Hopping: 2002–2009

In a world of diminishing mystery, the unknown persists.
—JHUMPA LAHIRI

The Young Turks were motion-picture people. When they stepped into the sand-boxes of television or music, they did so briefly and with a stubborn diffidence, and then back they went, scurrying home to the comfort zone of the movies. Not that there was anything wrong with that. But now one could almost feel a certain sympathy toward them because their beloved movie industry was changing right before their eyes. The ugly truth was that it had become much harder to get a movie made, and as a result, they were faced with their second major learning curve: The first was when they had to figure out how to be owners and leaders and run the business. Now they realized they would have to spend more time exploring alternate pathways for revenues.

One Turk in particular, however, was relieved, even excited, and became very interested in where the business was going to be five or ten years ahead. He started spending fewer days with traditional duties and pursuits and began devoting more of them to exploring the future. In theory, that move made sense, but it was also a risky one. Looking for new opportunities can be worthwhile, but when that journey cuts into duties associated with bringing money into the company, it becomes a dangerous one. Now there was a fissure in the family.

And then there were the other agents—and clients—who would get caught up in the changes as well. The old rules were gone. The agency was shifting in subtle and not-so-subtle ways. The bar was higher for survival than in the past. And if you couldn't pull that off, you might be told, "We entered your name into the computer—and it came up wanting."

DAVID GEFFEN:

I don't think it takes much to be a very good agent. I think it takes charm more than it takes intelligence. You're a hand-holder. The way an agency really works is not that the agents go out and find jobs for most of these people. They just answer the phone. There are casting directors, and directors, and producers who are deciding who they want for a picture. They call up an agency because they represent a particular person they want. If that person's not available, they say "What about so-and-so?" It's not like they're really out selling other than at the lowest level of casting. Other than that, they're just picking up their phone. If you have Julia Roberts, if you have Paul Newman, if you have people like that, the phones are ringing all of the time. Everybody wants them. It's only at the lower levels where you're calling up and saying, "There's this new actor, he's in this Broadway show, and he's going to be a big star." That's when an agent is selling. It doesn't take a whole lot. Being an agent is a job in which you have to constantly sign every client you have. Because everybody's going after them, just like they're going after everybody else's clients.

It's a tough job; you have to service these people, and you're constantly blowing them. And you're dealing with people who fundamentally are insecure. That part of the job is tough.

ANTHONY PELLICANO, Private Investigator:

I didn't care for agents, period. I had no liking whatsoever for Ovitz, period. Didn't like the guy at all. I attacked him a couple of times in the very, very beginning, but then had absolutely no contact with him over the years until 2002. Why didn't I like him? Because of things that he did to some celebrities and other people. He was just a piece of shit at the time. Didn't like him, didn't want to have anything to do with him, and I don't think he liked me either. He also was dealing with a guy by the name of Gavin de Becker, a little piece-of-shit wimp who used to scare the shit out of the clients that he represented by instilling fear in them. I did just the opposite. In other words, if you were a client of mine, I didn't make you weaker, I made you stronger.

I was more than a private investigator; I was a problem solver. When people become celebrities, they develop problems. They develop drug problems, they develop marital problems, they develop social problems, they develop monetary problems, et cetera. Let me give you a for instance: A guy goes out with a woman a couple of times; she gets pregnant and demands money either to abort the pregnancy or she'll go forward with the pregnancy. A woman gets involved in a business deal that goes sour. A person calls up a movie star, and says they want to make a movie with them; the celebrity is very kind to them but doesn't commit, and then all of a sudden their name is bandied around and attached to the movie, and they get sued. Or many, many times a tabloid newspaper attacks them, and I would have to defend them and counterattack. For instance, a guy is becoming an action star and somebody says he was giving somebody a blow job on his balcony. You know, things like that. I can go on and on.

I was in the very bottom of what was going on in Hollywood and I had to protect these people and they paid me money to protect them. Whatever you can dream of, I probably did, and then some, but it was always for the benefit of the client.

You have to understand that I was extremely hard-boiled. I was no-nonsense. I was a man of honor who only cared about keeping his word and doing what he was supposed to do. So I didn't care who was carrying the guns on the other side, whether they be somebody of Michael's status, Eisner's status, or whoever the big shot was at the time. I didn't give a fuck. All I cared about was taking care of what I needed to do. If you came to me and I decided to work for you—which took a little doing, too—and I said yes, that was it. No matter where you were or what you did, I did what I was supposed to do for you. And I always won.

The majority of clients that I got came through business managers and through lawyers, not through agents. Ron might have mentioned my name from time to time to people who got in trouble, but he never directly gave me a client, ever. He wouldn't call me up and say somebody got into trouble and alert me to it. He wouldn't do shit like that. If the client asked him to speak to me on their behalf, yes, that would happen, but Ron never called me up and said, "Listen, I've got a celebrity who's strung out on drugs and he needs this and that." Lots of other agents did. Ron Meyer is probably the most honorable man I've ever met in Hollywood and he has stayed honorable throughout all of the years that I've known him. He's like me in that he gives you his word, he's there. He's 1,000 percent a friend and he has shown that friendship in so many ways. He is my kind of guy, if you understand me. He is not a bullshitter. He has always stood by me 1,000 percent.

RISA GERTNER:

My kids are twelve and ten, and I had them on my own. To say that the partners were supportive was an understatement. Bryan Lourd was involved in picking my donor with me. They all came over right after my baby was born.

I think one of the biggest misconceptions of this company is that everybody is the same. That's hardly the case: You have two owners of the company who are gay, I'm a single mother, and we have great diversity. It couldn't be less of a cookie-cutter group of people.

I came over to CAA from UTA in January of '96. I was representing a number of very high-end writers and a few directors, but I always wondered what it would be like to represent more substantial directors, and I wanted to be in the business of putting movies together. The thing that struck me right away was the level of generosity of spirit. People were so kind to each other here; coming from a place where people were so nasty to each other was a big change.

From the start, I never felt like this was a man's world here.

There was already another generation of women who were in very strong positions, and the guys running the company at that time were clearly comfortable with women in leadership roles. I was made the head of a department very shortly after I got here, and almost always, the people who I met with and hired didn't meet with Richard and Doc until after that had happened. They were incredibly deferential.

JASON BLUM, Producer:

In the early '90s, I was producing at a theater company called Malaparte that Ethan Hawke was the fearless leader of, and that's where I met Bryan. I then went to work for Bob and Harvey in 1995 and had a fancy title, but I was still really a junior executive. Bryan and I didn't have much occasion to speak to each other for business at that time, but every so often, when I was in a pinch, I would talk to him and he was kind enough to guide me through some of the big turns of my life. One of the key turning points in my professional life was when I quit Miramax in 2000, moved to L.A., and began producing a bunch of independent movies. I was very frustrated; no one saw me doing it, and some people lost money. Harvey and I had maintained a good relationship and we had a conversation about me going back there and I was pretty set on doing that and that was one of these moments where I talked to Bryan. He said, "I want you to meet Brad Grey before you move back to New York. You should just see what they're up to." At that point in my career I thought the holy grail was a fancy first-look deal at a studio with all the bells and whistles. That meeting with Brad Grey turned into such a deal less than a month after we met, and Bryan was right smack in the middle of it all.

Bryan essentially represented me for ten years and I didn't pay him a dime. He was always saying, "I believe in this kid." That's a significant thing to do for a year or two, but to do it for ten years is extraordinary.

And then I basically got *Paranormal Activity* from CAA. They sent me a rough cut of the movie on a DVD. They were kind of hip-pocketing it, and there was a deal for it to go straight to DVD or straight to video. What happened next is a long story, but I basically went to them and said, "Let's not sell this to home video. Let's see if we can get a theatrical release." Now it took me three years to do that, but the significant part of the story is the way I was introduced to *Paranormal Activity* was through CAA, and I have never been happier to write a commission check in my life.

SIMON KINBERG, Writer and Producer:

Around 2000, I was a graduate film school student at Columbia and I wrote a script in my first year that a professor of mine named Ira Deutchman, who was the founder of Fine Line, read and liked. He sent it out to L.A., to different agents, managers, and lawyers to represent me, and actually executives as well, to try to sell it with him attached as the producer. That was my first round of coming out to L.A., and in those meetings, I met Martin Spencer, who was a CAA agent at the time. I signed with Martin and went back to school and started working.

MARTIN SPENCER:

Simon Kinberg was introduced to me by a young executive who was working for Jordan Kerner at the time. We were having lunch at the Palm and he said, "There's a guy named Simon Kinberg—he's still in college in New York—and he wrote this script about digging up bodies in New York City at the turn of the century. Basically rich people died, they were buried, and then grave robbers would dig their bodies up and ransom them back to the families." I read the script, loved it. I met Simon and we got along really well from the start, and I began to represent him. The first deal that I made for him was to do a rewrite on *Elektra 2005* at Regency, and after he turned it in, I got a phone call from Lauren Schuler Donner where she told me she thought he did an amazing job. She said, "Not only did he rewrite the script, but he restructured it." She kept saying "the structure is amazing." From the start, there was never any doubt that Simon was going to be a huge success.

SIMON KINBERG:

My thesis project for film school was the script for *Mr. and Mrs. Smith*. CAA did just the thing they're famous for: they took that movie from a pitch that literally every studio passed on, sold it to Summit, and then helped build it from the ground up—a pretty top-to-bottom CAA package, though I'm not sure who represented Angelina at the time. Actually, they initially put it together with another client of theirs, Nicole Kidman, playing Angelina's role, but when that version of the movie fell apart—and Nicole dropped out of the movie for scheduling reasons—they held it together.

MARTIN SPENCER:

The Saturday after *Mr. and Mrs. Smith* opened, we knew it was having a huge opening weekend, and there is nothing better than calling your client the Saturday after their movie opened. I told Simon, "Congratulations," and it was a great moment, particularly since we had started working together when he was so young.

Simon is a huge basketball fan, and I called him the afternoon of game one of the NBA finals, and said, "What are you doing tonight?" We had a great time that night. Then I called him the next morning and said, "And what are you doing tonight?" We wound up going to the finals on back-to-back nights.

SIMON KINBERG:

I felt from the beginning that Martin believed in me and saw something in me—whether he did or he was just trying to convince me of that, he did convince me of it. I felt that confidence from the agency early on. Maybe six years later, I had dinner with Martin and he said that he felt like I could transition into being as successful a producer as I was a writer. And that felt like a shift in perspective for me.

TOM STOPPARD, Writer:

It never occurred to me not to have an agent. It's less to do with finding work than with negotiating contracts. I couldn't do any of that myself, and wouldn't want to spend my time on it. As a playwright, there's no work to find—only inspiration. In between plays, the agent is the conduit for offers of film work.

SARAH JESSICA PARKER, Actress:

I'm Kevin Huvane's oldest client. I'm not his *oldest* client, but I am his longest-term client. We've been together for thirty years and grew up in the business alongside each other. We lived together in New York. When I had to be in L.A. for work, Kevin said to me, "Live at my apartment!"

I handed Kevin a really important job, and frankly he's never really let me down. He is really a source of enormous stability in a business that doesn't typically cultivate stability. I've been acting for a long time, but I was becoming a young adult and making decisions on my own, and he came to me when he was at William Morris, took me to lunch at the Russian Tea Room, and talked to me about what he knew of my career. He worked a lot with clients in the theater at that time, and it was a really big deal for me to have a conversation with the next level of agent.

Kevin has a lot of strengths. He's enormously respectful—he was raised like a classic Irish Catholic boy—and he has a real sense of paying dues and working hard. He also has an enormous belief in his decision-making process. He is somebody with the courage of his convictions. He is not afraid of anybody and can't be intimidated. When he arrives at a decision or point of view, he believes in it, and I have found that to be really helpful. For me, it's the best kind of counsel.

Sex and the City is the perfect example. He called me up and said, "Darren Star reached out to me. He's written this pilot and tells me he wrote it with you in mind—you were in his head when he was writing it. I'm going to send it to you. I've read it. I think it's really good. You should meet with him." And I said,

"Really? I feel like I've got it all right now. I can do a play, then do a movie, then do a play, then do a movie. There's a lot of flexibility. What could be better? Do I really want to go back to making a television series when I'm maybe held hostage signing a long-term contract?"

I met with Darren and there were a couple concerns that I had—like I really wasn't keen on doing nudity and language issues—but Kevin continued to say to me, "This is different. You have never done anything like this before. No one's ever done a part like this. Do this." And I did.

After the pilot was done, I sort of forgot about it and went on with my career, but then it was picked up and I was faced with this commitment and said, "Kevin, I don't want to do a series. How do I get out of this?" He said come sit down in a room with me and Lee Gabler, and they asked me what the problem was, and I said, "I'm scared of doing a series." They said, "What scares you about this?" It was no longer the artistic stuff; it was more the idea that I wanted a strong producer who I knew I could rely upon, and they just figured it out. They brought on this great producer who I adored and trusted, and I arrived on that set day one of the first official season and never looked back. I loved every single solitary day of that experience, and I am fully aware that I would have never done it had it not been for Kevin.

TOM HANKS:

I have no idea who else Richard represents. I even make jokes about who else he must represent. He's never told me. He always laughs and says, "I only have your picture up here on the walls."

SARAH JESSICA PARKER:

Back then, Kevin hadn't cornered the market yet on female clients the way he has now. There are times that I only discover that he has a new client that in ways you might argue is competition for me but I just simply don't see it like that. There's no good that's going to come of that. That's the way it is. I believe the more work he does with female clients, the better informed he is going to be. I can't compete with Sandra Bullock. That's just never going to happen. She's Sandra Bullock. Meryl Streep? She occupies a space all of her own. The list goes on and on. I'm not really like any of them, I'm just not. I know it looks on the surface like there's a lot of overlap, but I don't see it that way. I genuinely mean this with all my heart: I have no sense of competition with his other clients.

RICK NICITA:

There's some heavy chases with clients for roles, but not as many as you'd think. It's just constant nudging. It's constantly not letting them bail out, not getting near the exit door. With Al Pacino, on a picture called *The Recruit*, he had been doing his, "I'm not so sure, maybe yes, maybe no," and I said to him on the phone, "I am going to now hang up on you and I'm going to call and accept the role." And he said, "No, no, don't!" And I said, "I'm going to. Right now, talk to you later." And he said, "No! no! Don't do that!" I hung up, called, and accepted the role. I called him back and said, "I did it. Just accept you're doing this movie." And he said, "Thank you. Thank you, Rick. Thank you very much." I knew he was going to say that. And he got a big payday.

When Naomi Watts was offered a role in *The Ring*, which really was a big picture for her—I was at a Wesleyan board of trustees event and I was on the phone with her and said, "Say yes to this. I'm not letting you off the phone until you say the word 'yes.'" And she said, "Uh . . ." And I said, "Yes, say yes." And she goes, "Uh . . . yes." And I go, "Great. Good-bye," and hung up. To me, that happens more than the client saying, "Oh, I want it so much." That doesn't happen very much. They're scared to expose them-selves. It's not an intellectual decision. They're scared. They're very, very vulnerable. They can go out and make an ass of themself, or do something that's going to set their career back. Sometimes it's easier not to work.

NICOLE KIDMAN:

I didn't want to do *The Hours*. I was in Australia and was really sort of down. I thought, *Oh my gosh, I can't do this movie, I can't find the strength to leave my parents at this time, to go off and do it.* At the time, I was having this weird relationship with my own drive and my own ambition. Part of me just couldn't be bothered, and I know that's almost blasphemous to say. So I called Kevin and told him, "I can't do it, I'm sort of depressed and I've got to just stay here." And he said, "You make that plane, you get over there now, and you do this role." And after he got done talking to me, I thought, *Yes, okay. I should go.* Thank God, he talked to me like he did, because I would have just curled up in bed and stayed there. Instead, look at what happened with that movie. I need tough love sometimes.

He's always been there for me, for now, well over two decades. I think he has a lot of female clients who he has that kind of relationship with, and I remember when we were doing *The Hours*, Kevin represented Meryl, me, and Julianne [Moore], and we were all on *Oprah*, singing his praises. He fights for women in the industry. Kevin is known to be ferocious in terms of his protection. He can be like an Irish street fighter. I respond to that, I love that. At the same time—and he would hate me saying this—he's a pussycat. He had this incredibly soft, gentle side. Either way, he's an incredible negotiator, as everybody knows.

DOUG ELLIN, Writer and Director:

When we went to sell *Entourage* to HBO, the character of Ari didn't really exist. There was an agent, but at that point it was based on some version of Jeff Jacobs, my agent at the time. I first met Jeff when he was a counselor at the camp I went to when I was twelve, and he was what I knew best of as an agent. At the pitch meeting, it was me, Jeff, Steven Levinson, and Ari, who was there because he represented Mark Wahlberg. I had never even heard of Ari before this, but as soon as the meeting started, Ari said three or four things that just blew me away. The guy was unlike anyone I had ever met, and I remember I looked at Jeff right there and said, "This character is changing to Ari."

JEFF JACOBS:

Sometimes a single assignment can change a client's life. Tim Van Patten played Salami on *The White Shadow*, and has been a client and friend since before he directed an episode of television. Tim had directed thirty-five episodes of *Touched by an Angel* and *The Road Home*, and we fought hard to make sure the creator of a new drama and the production company behind it understood how great and talented he was. All we did was get Tim to the door, then stood back and watched him kick it in—with his talent and passion. So Tim got a chance to direct episode nine of this new series with a character actor who had been around for a while, and did a fantastic job. His career went off on an entirely new, higher level. Since then, he's won multiple Emmys, multiple DGA awards, and been nominated more than you can imagine. He also directed the *Game of Thrones* pilot. Oh yeah, the series? It was called *The Sopranos*.

MICHAEL BOLTON:

It's a team. Unless you have a manager who has a background as an agent, everyone is contributing in his or her own way, and you don't want to have any one person always in the driver's seat. There's wisdom in working with people who are smarter than you and more experienced than you in their areas of expertise, and taking advantage of their accumulated life experiences. I never want to walk into an agent's office and feel this person's not as smart as me.

EMMA BANKS, Agent:

I think you try to have an area of expertise around you. So it goes back to the teamwork ethic of the company and the fact that everybody will work together. I don't need to know everything on my own, but I know whom to ask in the company. If I want to know whether a brand deal an artist gets offered is a good one,

I have a wealth of experience within the company of people who do that for a living. Everybody is just a phone call away. I work in London, but we're all on a direct dial system that means I don't even have to dial America. It's just four digits and I'm through. It's that simple.

DAVID STYNE:

Michael Mann had wanted my client John Logan to rewrite a Western for him at Disney that Bill Broyles had written, and I said to Michael, "You know, I think John would be better for *The Aviator*," and Michael ended up hiring John to write that. While John was writing *The Aviator* for Michael—and for Leonardo, who was attached to play Howard Hughes—Michael directed *Ali*. After he was done with *Ali*, Michael intimated he didn't want to direct another biopic, and was looking for another kind of movie. I knew there was a Howard Hughes project with Kevin Spacey attached at MGM, and there was also a Howard Hughes project with Chris Nolan and Jim Carrey at Warner Bros. and Castle Rock. So I said to Michael, "Look, I know you've said you don't want to direct another biopic, but I want you to know if we don't move on *The Aviator*, I think we're going to get beat." I went on—treading very carefully—and suggested that he produce *The Aviator* instead of directing it. It didn't go over that well initially, as I'm sure you can imagine, but then Michael came back with his short list of directors, and Marty Scorsese was at the top of that list. We gave the script to Marty, he read it, and committed to it. Michael wound up producing it, and I believe he had first dollar gross, so it worked out great for everyone.

When Coke came back into the CAA fold in 2002, the agency's marketing arm was a consultative service. Jae Goodman was hired in 2006, and at that point there were four or five clients, including Sprint, Delta, and Coke paying a range of fees. Goodman was hired to build a creative team that would work alongside the strategic marketers already at CAA, but would also expand beyond insights and consultation and into the creation of actual content that would complement ad campaigns. Under Goodman, along with marketing co-head David Messinger, the marketing division would see exponential growth in the years to come.

LEE GABLER:

There were two individuals who were handling Fox in 2002, and they were talking to Peter Chernin, who was the head of Fox Television. They were trying to sell a summer show and Peter just didn't want to do it. I think one of his comments was "I'm not going to put on a musical show. I'm going to put on fire-eaters and circus acts," because it was a low-budget season. And in a conversation that was had with people at Fox who will remain nameless, word got back to Murdoch about *Pop Idol,* which was a big hit in England, and why weren't they doing it on Fox? The next thing I know, Fox is now talking about a summer series with not six episodes, but eight to fifteen.

Steve Heyer was the head of Coca-Cola at the time. We were at the Winter Olympics in Salt Lake City to meet with Coke about what was in development, and Steve said to me, "What's on the horizon? What should I be looking at?" I told him about *American Idol.* Forty-eight hours later, Coke was in.

It was a big deal, paid off well for Coke. And us. That was a package. Millions of dollars. Millions.

DAVID MESSINGER, Executive:

We knew that there was talk about bringing this show *Pop Idol* to the United States and saw that there was an opportunity for Coke to become a part of it. And to be something more than an advertiser, to have a role in the show. That's what was really so revolutionary about it. Many people will talk about the very strong integrations that Coke has had with that show in a variety of different ways. There's been the Coke red couch where contestants sit and talk to Ryan Seacrest. Then of course, the Coke cups that sit on the judges' table. Coke even does a number of retail programs where people every season can win a chance to go to the *American Idol* finale.

JAE GOODMAN, Executive:

CAA's experience with Coca-Cola in the '90s established a beachhead for the brand Creative Artists Agency in the world of marketing. That relationship with Coke ended, and then coincidentally or not, Coca-Cola was the first client of the new incarnation of CAA Marketing. There are fundamental differences between the two eras: CAA 1.0 was built specifically to create ads, whereas CAA Marketing 2.0 would never assume that a TV commercial is the most effective brand solution.

We are a complete marketing services organization. We look like an ad agency, but our focus is on making brand entertainment that draws an audience, rather than ads that interrupt an audience. Our mission statement is that we drive business results for corporate brands through content, culture, and influence. Just like an ad agency, we have creative professionals like me, marketing strategists, account managers, and content managers who know how to get virtually every form of content made.

In 2006, when our group was created, the partners who run CAA had the foresight not to take talent agents and convert them into a marketing practice. They went and sought out people who have experience working in the marketing world who would be a good cultural fit for CAA.

We service our corporate brands by creating solutions for them. Those solutions may include talent, and when we do include talent it's often CAA-represented talent, but it's also often talent represented elsewhere. We represent the brand's interest and help the brand find the best talent for the content we're creating.

DAVID STYNE:

We signed a writer named Anthony Zuiker, who wrote a spec script called *The Runner*, which was about his experiences growing up in Las Vegas and being an inveterate gambler by the time he was fifteen or sixteen, and how he had to basically go to work as a runner for a high-end bookie to pay off his debts. And we sold that spec script to TriStar, to Chris Lee for like 750 grand, and then found out that Anthony Zuiker had optioned the script to another producer and didn't tell us when he became a client. But anyway, after a couple of years, taking a couple of feature assignments, and after a couple of failed pilots, Anthony wrote the pilot for *CSI*. When we signed Anthony, he was literally driving a tram at the Mirage making $8 an hour. And he created *CSI* and *CSI* became *CSI* 1, 2, and 3. This was Jerry Bruckheimer's first network play, and via *CSI* Jerry became an incredibly successful TV producer, in addition to his feature business. Steve Lafferty told me CAA's back end was probably $40 to $50 million from *CSI*. The economics just aren't like that anymore, even in network television. That was like the last huge home run.

AMY GROSSMAN:

When I was a literary agent at CAA, I got to work with any-one who was in the agency; I spent my time looking for material as opposed to representing clients. But when I was younger and actually representing clients, I made it a point to work as hard as I could for them, even if they weren't having much success. Sometimes those situations were the most compelling. Mark was my favorite example. One day I was told an unknown actor had just come into the office, but when I saw him, he was hardly un-known to me. I knew it was Mark, because when he had been quarterback at UCLA, I was a cheerleader there. We began work-ing together and got to be very close—platonically—and I saw firsthand how much self-belief and fortitude he needed to survive because it was really tough for him. A lot of people look at *NCIS* now and think of Mark Harmon as one of the biggest television stars in the world, but for me, I can't separate the many years when no one would even see him for a role. One year, as a thank-you, Mark gave me a silver whistle with the word *Coach* engraved on it. I still have it.

In 2005, CAA opened its Beijing office, sending an aggressive signal out onto the global stage and declaring anew its sense of manifest destiny. It was also a fitting way for Richard Lovett to mark his tenth anniversary as agency president; he felt more determined than ever to expand CAA in ways that few of his competitors could even imagine.

As one office was opening, however, another was closing—or at least being transformed, changing in ways that would further differentiate CAA "2.0" from "1.0." The glittering edifice that I. M. Pei had designed as a gateway to Beverly Hills still glittered, but the agency's success had rendered it obsolete, if glamorously so. Construction was well under way on a new home at 2000 Avenue of the Stars in Century City, slated to open in January of 2007. Though lacking perhaps the panache and prestige of Pei's showpiece, the new quarters had ample room for the high-profile agents CAA had seduced away from competitors. Indeed, CAA had recently stolen nearly a dozen high-profile agents from its competitors, including Jason Heyman (with client Will Ferrell), Martin Lesak (with client Tony Shalhoub), and Dan Aloni (with client Christopher Nolan) from United Talent; Spencer Baumgarten (with Pirates of the Caribbean director Gore Verbinski) from Endeavor; and Todd Feldman (with director Todd Phillips) from William Morris. They joined previously poached agents, including ICM's Bart Walker (with Sofia Coppola), Nick Styne (with Cameron Diaz), and Tracy Brennan (with Kate Beckinsale), as well as William Morris's Hylda Queally (with Kate Winslet and Cate Blanchett). Unlike the Pei building, which Ovitz had been the majority owner in, the new building would not be owned by the agency or any of its partners: they were signing a fifteen-year lease and CAA would be taking roughly 180,000 square feet of what would be an 800,000-square-foot giant.

Growth, however, like almost any other accomplishment, tends to bring new problems of its own.

MARTIN LESAK, Agent:

At the time CAA was this big, very dominant place, and UTA by comparison was smaller and younger, even though we had incredible clients. As much as I think our size made us somewhat vulnerable to CAA, it was also a cultural thing. We were really more builders of clients and agents than we were poachers. Our mentality was to grow the talent and make them stars, especially in comedy, which was not an area that CAA had really excelled in. UTA was earning a reputation for comedy because the agency understood the relationships between the clients and all the op-portunities that existed, and the studios were just waking up to the box office potential of comedy. It was a great time for UTA; we were a place where great talent was really flourishing. I think CAA saw what we were building, and they made it their mission to go after it, not to create their own, but just to try to take it from UTA. So suddenly your clients are being hit on all day long and you fear that they'll eventually leave you. It's not an easy po-sition to be in, so as much as you feel loyalty to your agency and all the opportunities that came with UTA at the time, you get worn down, and after a couple of years you find yourself starting to think, *Hey, maybe we really do have to be at this place,* out of self-preservation.

MIKE RUBEL, CAA Chief Operating Officer:

In 2003 or 2004, if you were to look at an org chart—though we generally don't have org charts—you would have seen motion picture, television, and music. You also would have seen commer-cial endorsements. But at that time I would have said to you that 95 percent of our clients, buyers, and competitors were within a ten-mile radius of our Los Angeles office. Nashville was our only other office, and we were very, very focused on traditional motion picture, television, and music work.

RICK NICITA:

At CAA in 1980, we could all sit around a circular table. Once we turned the corner on the new century, if you had to put us all at a table, it would have to be as big as Texas.

BOB BOOKMAN:

The company became so big we had to leave the I. M. Pei build-ing. Say what you will about the impracticality of it, and the atrium being a tribute to Mike's ego, it was a great building to work in. It was organized horizontally, there were all these great passageways, you saw all this activity, and if you looked over the rails, you saw people waiting for meetings. There was just something magical about working in that building. Then we went into that new building and on the very first day someone christened it *The Death Star*. And it was like *The Death Star*.

GENE WATANABE, Architect:

CAA had basically outgrown the headquarters that they had built in Beverly Hills. As a young architect, I was well familiar with where CAA was located, and it was a beautiful building. We had designed the new office building as a speculative development, not knowing who would locate there. We had the building 90 percent designed before we started talking with CAA and a commitment was made. Following that, pretty significant modifications were made to the interior of the building, with some modest modifications made to the outside.

When we were first developing the concept for 2000 Avenue of the Stars, it was made very clear to us that the building needed to be subservient to the two towers behind it, and that's because at the time it was the same owners. The owners of the Century Plaza Towers wanted to make sure this new building on Avenue of the Stars in no way would block the views or diminish the presence of the landmark Century Plaza Towers.

One of the exterior changes involved is where CAA's main entry is located today. There's one small appendage that's two stories high and projects onto Avenue of the Stars. That particular space had a great deal of appeal to CAA, considering CAA's clientele, it would be a bit of an inconvenience for them to mingle with the public in the main building lobby. A celebrity or well-known person coming through a major office building could be annoyed by an autograph seeker or paparazzi. CAA felt that location would be ideal to create their own entry, their own lobby, off the main motor court. That way their clients would never have to intermix with the main public and other tenants of the building.

The marble came straight from Italy, very close to where Michelangelo quarried his marble for the statue of David. It comes from a very specific area in Italy that is well known for variations of white marble. It's called Forte dei Marmi.

BOB BOOKMAN:

You ever been to Rome, the Piazza Venezia that Mussolini built out of marble? I felt like it was a tribute to that. It was so impersonal.

MIKE RUBEL:

CAA had been a client of mine for more than a decade before I joined the company. The senior lawyer within the organization, Ray Kurtzman, and the senior finance person, Bob Goldman, were migrating towards the next chapters in their lives, and I had more than substantial institutional knowledge of CAA as my corporate client. After more than twenty years in private practice, joining CAA seemed like a great opportunity. I came over initially as general counsel and migrated over the years to a quasi-chief operating officer. We're short on titles, but I try to keep the trains running on time across a wide range of geographies and practice areas.

LEE GABLER:

I was never in favor of opening an office in Beijing; I didn't get the metrics of that or, for that matter, spending money on satellite operations.

DAVID STYNE:

There was a partners dinner at Bryan Lourd's house, where it was announced that because CAA had bought into sports and other new businesses to open up new revenue streams in light of the film business shrinking, and because we were moving into this new building, the partners were going to need to take a 10 percent haircut this year and a 10 percent haircut in the next year. People were just kind of looking at each other, and then Rick Kurtzman said something to the effect of "You know, it's really exciting that the company is growing so fast, that we're getting into all of these new businesses, but it feels like a lot of what made CAA feel special, that unique company culture, is getting lost in the mix." And then Kevin Huvane said, "Hey, Rick, what we had was really great. But that was then and this is now." They were basically saying this is a different animal now and everybody who's here better get hip to what needs to happen or it won't be good for you. I thought it was a very defining moment. It wasn't the old CAA anymore.

KATIE COURIC, Journalist:

Bob Barnett represented me when I was working in Washington for local news and then when I went to the Pentagon. When I became co-anchor of *Today*, things were going great, and after the first three or four years, I had an opportunity to go the next step salary-wise because I was also getting calls from people like Don Hewitt, production companies like DreamWorks, and studios like Warner Bros. expressing interest in me. Bob Barnett is a great lawyer, but he doesn't take offers from other networks, weigh them, and figure out how to negotiate against them. So I thought, *Gee, maybe it's time for me to get more of a full-service agent rather than just an attorney.*

LES MOONVES:

I needed a big change here, a big splash. We'd been through all the stuff with Rather, and Katie was a big deal. Was it expensive? Yes. Did I know it was going to be expensive? Yes. Did I know it was going to be that expensive? Probably not.

JEFF ZUCKER, Executive:

For Katie's first renegotiation as anchor at *Today*, she hired Alan Berger, who was my agent. I was producing the show at the time, and the feeling was that Bob Barnett, who had done several of her previous deals, was in a difficult position because he was doing a lot of business with NBC and wouldn't want to alienate them if things got tough. CAA didn't care if they alienated NBC. Bob wasn't happy Katie went with CAA, and he never really talked to her again.

KATIE COURIC:

I interviewed a lot of agents, including Mike Ovitz when he had his management company, AMG, and others. I felt most comfortable with Alan Berger and I knew CAA was a powerful agency. I thought it would also be helpful for me to be at an agency that represented a lot of other well-known people who I may want to interview. Alan did a great job for me, and I do feel like I got a considerable jump in salary that I might not have otherwise gotten.

LES MOONVES:

When we were trying to bring Katie over here, there wasn't a whole lot of negotiation. We learned we were going to have to match what she was getting at NBC, and we didn't think they were bluffing. I knew what she was being paid and knew it was a big number. But you know what? We decided we needed to do it.

JEFF ZUCKER:

I think it would've happened without CAA. I offered her more money to stay at NBC—by the way, in the hindsight of her career, she should have done that—but she had a singular thing in her head that she wanted to do and I understand that. So CAA was helpful in making that move. They're really good at making the deal, and they're really good at making you money. They're not as strategic at positioning you.

RICK YORN:

The number one thing that's different is that when Mike was steering the ship, they would take care of their clients in a way that just doesn't happen anymore. It was a different time.

LES MOONVES:

At CBS for many years there was the "57th Street Divide." You had CBS News on one side of the street, and across the street in the BMW building was *60 Minutes*. When Katie came in, the idea was that she would do *60 Minutes* pieces, and she did do some. But that's Jeff Fager's ballgame over there, and he gives out stories as he sees fit. Would she have liked to do more stories? Probably, but that wasn't a CAA issue. It's not the agent's job to work within the company once she has a deal in place.

ALAN BERGER, Agent:

In the third year of Katie's tenure as the anchor and managing editor of the *CBS Evening News,* we learned that upcoming budget cuts would involve significant layoffs, including several members of the staff of the *CBS Evening News* team—from senior level producers to young associate producers—all key contributors to the production of the daily newscast.

Katie met with CBS News president Sean McManus to discuss their situation and how she could fight for her colleagues and save their positions. When it became clear that financial pressures required going forward with the cuts, Katie decided—in consultation with her personal advisers—to take matters into her own hands.

Katie voluntarily, and quietly, agreed to cut her CBS salary by over $1 million, creating a savings to preserve the jobs of her associates on the broadcast. Katie insisted on two conditions for the unprecedented self-imposed give-back: One—the money would be directly used to pay for her staff so that they would not be terminated. Two—this would be done quietly with no public or private acknowledgment or announcement about her gesture.

This act exemplified Katie's appreciation of and commitment to her team. We went to Sean McManus and made the offer on Katie's behalf and these individuals remained employed—with the individuals involved never knowing what had happened.

NOAH OPPENHEIM, Writer and Producer:

How I got to CAA is a fairly interesting story. I went to Harvard and wrote, and became editorial chair, for the *Crimson,* which is the student newspaper. During my senior year of college, Phil Griffin and Chris Matthews were driving from New Hampshire back to New York a week before the 2000 presidential primaries, and because of a snowstorm, they had to pull off I-95 in Boston, and they stopped at a bar in Harvard Square and started talking to undergrads there. Phil wound up following them to a party in the basement of the newspaper building, and picked up a copy of the paper and read a column I wrote. He asked, "Who wrote this article?" and they pointed to me drunk in the corner. They beckoned me over, and Phil asked me, "How would you like to come on MSNBC next week and talk about the election from the perspective of the youth vote?" So the next week I went on MSNBC with Chris, and after that, we started talking about what I was going to do after graduation.

I wound up going directly to *Hardball*, and got promoted very quickly to the point where I was sort of running *Hardball* when I was just twenty-two. Then we discovered Joe Scarborough, and I worked on *Scarborough Country* after Joe left Congress. But soon thereafter, Jeff Zucker asked me to go to L.A. to work on the Dennis Miller talk show, which was a tall order. On my first day, Dennis said to me, "Nice to meet you. This is going to be our last conversation. If they want to cancel my show, let them, but I have no intention of listening to you." I clearly needed some guidance to help me through this impasse, and Rick Ludwin, an executive at NBC, introduced me to Alan Berger at CAA, who has helped me enormously ever since.

TOM HANKS:

An agency doesn't operate the same way any longer. It's all gone. The industry used to be so flush with free money that it was almost impossible to do wrong, even with a crappy movie, because here's why: home video—and by that I mean the VHS cassette. Every movie, every mom-and-pop chain rental store had to buy at least one copy—two or three if they wanted to make sure they could always have something for their customers. So that meant two or three copies times how many video stores were there across the country, half a million? Suddenly the VHS business was bringing in big money. So the studios were all going through this vast expansion, making new buildings with glass and steel everywhere, tearing down back lots, and in some cases even sound studios. The money was pouring in. And then it all stopped.

MICHAEL WIMER:

I was married in 1995. We had our baby daughter in 1997. Eight days later, my wife Sharon was diagnosed with Hodgkin's lymphoma. My friends in town and at CAA could not have been more generous. I took off six months to raise Sarah; Sharon was on radiation and chemo, so she couldn't be around a newborn. We celebrated remission. Nine months later it came back and we moved to City of Hope for a stem-cell transplant. The next couple years were safe enough to adopt my boy Luke. Along the way, I left CAA in 2005 after an inspired meeting with Peter Guber. I realized that I'd rung all the bells I'd wanted to ring and staying there longer would just be about money, and that was never my thing. I went on to start a feature and TV career, which have allowed me to spend more time with my family. Unfortunately, the sickness came back and devastated us all. Sharon made it through two harrowing double lung transplants. I got to be there for both. She ultimately passed away a few years ago. If there are any thanks to be given, it's that I was lucky enough to have the time to be there for my family throughout those years.

CHRISTY HAUBEGGER, Executive:

I was adopted by a tall blond family. I'm a Mexican-American and grew up in Houston, Texas, then went to the University of Texas at Austin. I got a rather marketable degree in philosophy, and when I realized I didn't have a lot of skills, I felt fortunate to get into law school at Stanford. One of my professors encouraged me to take a class of his on corporate governance and social responsibility. I was there more for the social responsibility piece of it, and I was surprised by how much I enjoyed the corporate side. So I took some business school classes there and had this amazing and horrifying realization that I was in the wrong school.

When the 1990 census was tabulated, there were 26 million Latinos in the U.S., which was about the size of the entire population of Canada, and there was a cover of *Time* magazine announcing the "decade of the Hispanic." Apparently that was rescheduled, but it was a big news story. When I was younger, I always read teen magazines, even though they made me feel really unattractive and left out, and for a class project I decided to write a business plan for a Hispanic magazine that was based on *Essence* magazine. I never thought I would have the opportunity to do such a thing, but the professor said it was a really good idea and told me, "You should really think about doing it." Something about being in Northern California and coming out of Stanford made me think I could be an entrepreneur, and I put my law degree under my bed and lived on love and ice water for a couple of years while I put together a magazine business. I ended up finding a joint venture partner in *Essence* and launched the magazine that was called *Latina* in 1996 with this rising young star named Jennifer Lopez on the cover. I wound up selling it to a private equity fund, and it's still in business. I sold because I wanted to move beyond print, to tell our stories and change our images all over. I wanted to figure out where else that could happen. I had an opportunity to work as a producer on a couple of films, including *Spanglish*, which was directed by Jim Brooks.

I met Richard Lovett and Michelle Kydd Lee socially at the end of the '90s, and Richard later said to me, "You should come work here." I met a couple other folks here, then went back to Richard and asked him, "What would you want me to do in the Latin market? What's your goal here?" Richard said—and this is a fairly exact quote—"We don't know what the business is, but we're pretty sure there's a business and we're pretty sure you'll figure it out." I said, "Okay."

Somebody here once said to me, "CAA likes to hire great athletes because we figure we can teach you the sport."

MICHELLE KYDD LEE:

When you're introducing yourself to people in the world, those three initials are incredibly powerful, although I spend a lot of time in Washington, D.C., and sometimes when I say CAA, people think I'm saying CIA; that gets a little tricky.

In our community, many of us were public school educated, and yet in the span of one generation, many of us are now sending our kids to private school. So now there is a disconnect in many ways with the public school system, which is why we made sure that our people are constantly going into our public schools, mentoring kids there and giving them the opportunity to learn more about our industry. After Katrina, we were incredibly active in New Orleans, and still are. We've been at the White House and active in Mrs. Obama's initiative to support troops, veterans, and their families.

SONYA ROSENFELD, Agent:

I was in a conversation with an executive who was close friends with a client of mine. This person had been talking directly with my client about doing something together and I kept saying to him, "Just remember, he has this other obligation which is already a deal, and so if it goes forward, it's going to be something that he has to do." They kept talking and talking, and sure enough, the day came when he had to move ahead with his signed deal. I had to call the executive and say, "Remember that thing I've been telling you about? It's now happening. So he's not going to be able to engage with you in this new project that you were talking about." Well he started going crazy, screaming at me, and I was sort of shocked because it wasn't as though this was the first time he had ever heard about what might happen. He called me a liar, and then started calling my client a liar, which really pissed me off. And then he said, "Honey, listen . . ." And I go, "Did you just 'honey' me?!" And he goes, "No, I didn't!" And I said, "Yes, you did! Don't honey me!" He was all flustered and got really nervous, then we hung up. We had never met in person, but we were actually at the same event the following week, and someone pointed him out to me, so I walked over and I said, "Hi, I'm Sonya Rosenfeld, and I just wanted to introduce myself." He said, "Oh my God, I'm so glad you came over. I felt so terrible!" He sent me flowers the next day, and now we're good friends.

When CAA executives finally decided in 2006 to enter the world of sports, they chose a very particular strategy and path. They could have made a hair-raising acquisition, formed an alliance, or rushed out to hire not necessarily even an agent, but an established high-profiler like Dick Ebersol to figure out how to conquer the athletic world. Instead, CAA elected to grow something from their own garden and, despite reports to the contrary, to do it relatively cheaply.

Tom Condon joined CAA Sports in April 2006 as co-head of its football group, along with agent Ben Dogra. The arrival of Condon marked a major development for CAA's sports representation as Condon and Dogra's combined clients numbered close to seventy-five of the top players in the NFL. A former offensive lineman for the Kansas City Chiefs left his position as lead football agent at IMG where he was one of the league's top agents.

As a player, Condon was elected to the NFL Players Association's executive board, and in 1982, he got a huge lesson in the business of football when that position put him inside the negotiations during that year's players' strike. Condon went on to become president of the NFLPA from 1984 to 1986. Condon earned a law degree from the University of Baltimore during the NFL off-seasons. After leaving the NFL, Condon went on to run his own small agency before joining IMG in 1991. IMG chairman Mark McCormack died in 2006. He had barely gone and Condon and Casey Close were still adjusting to the change when IMG president Peter Johnson announced that he, too, was leaving. Both Condon and Close had key man clauses in their contracts relating to Johnson, both of which were exercised. They ended up coming to CAA, and effectively their entire division and all their clients followed. IMG was suitably, severely shaken. With that, IMG was no longer in the football business and no longer in the baseball business. A couple months later CAA hired Pat Brisson, the head of IMG hockey, and he came over too with his group and his clients.

RICHARD LOVETT:

In 1997, I called Bryan from New York and said, "We have got to be in the sports business." Bryan said, "That might be true, but we've got lots of work to do back here. Get back to L.A. We've got to stay focused on what we're doing." Which was exactly right at the time.

We needed to enter sports not only at the right time but at the right level. As time went on, we did have an important insight as a consequence of specific conversations with IMG over many years. After Mark's death, we formed a version of a joint venture with them. In a short period of time, we learned that we were much more aggressive in our work. We certainly realized if they are the best in the business, and we are more aggressive at what we do, we believe we can compete and succeed.

DAVID O'CONNOR:

The design from the very beginning was that the Trojan horse in the sports business was going to be the athlete representation side. We all knew that we were going to be building something a lot larger and more diversified than just representing a bunch of athletes.

BRODIE VAN WAGENEN, Agent:

Our baseball and football divisions effectively transferred overnight from IMG and started the CAA Sports Group. Tom Condon and his football group, Casey Close, Jeff Berry, and I on the baseball side, all came over. We turned the CAA sports lights on in April 2006. Before that, CAA Sports didn't exist.

TOM CONDON, Agent:

I had been at IMG and ran the football division there for fifteen years. Peter Johnson, who was the COO, had hired me, and I had a key man clause in my contract that if he left, I had a sixty-day window to explore other options. In January of 2006, Peter left IMG, just two and a half years after Mark McCormack had died, so things were really changing at IMG. I realized that the business had changed a great deal; athletes were now celebrities, and I wanted to look at places where my clients would have more opportunities for exposure and marketing, along with post-career possibilities. I met with two other sports entities, and then met with Richard Lovett and Mike Rubel. After I got to know them, I knew I had found what I was looking for.

DAVID O'CONNOR:

Around 2004 or 2005, there was a shift in my role. Quite frankly, I was getting a little bored with the movie business, so I intentionally reduced my client load and transitioned them to other agents in the office. I wanted to be involved in some of the larger moves of the agency, and had already been involved with many of them on a strategic level. I spent an enormous amount of time with sports building that division out.

MIKE RUBEL:

We started it in the talent space, and so we were representing athletes and with agents who had spent their career representing athletes. And so it started with the feel of "We know how to represent talent." Still, it was the largest initiative that we had undertaken. It wasn't as obvious as adding theater. It wasn't like adding Beijing, which was a Mandarin-language film business, but it was still living in the film space. It wasn't like adding London to our existing international music business. We were already doing music internationally. Not to that scale, but we were dealing with the same buyers for the same client.

And so there was a period of time where people wondered, "Gee, how is this impacting the overall economics of the company and how is this impacting management's attention?" and there was a moment—not a day, because it wasn't the first day that people asked that—but there was a moment where people were trying to understand what is diversification. What are the implications that diversification will bring? And it kicked off with sports, not generally with these other somewhat more obvious additions.

TOM CONDON:

We're looking for clients who are intelligent, have great character, and have great passion for the game. And those people seem to play for a very long time. And typically they're also able to take advantage of the resources and the platform that we have here at CAA.

BRODIE VAN WAGENEN:

I grew up in Southern California and was a baseball player. I ended up going to Stanford University to play baseball and obviously get a decent degree. I was a three-year starter at Stanford, and the track record is that if you're a starter at Stanford, you're going to get drafted to go make your way in the minor leagues. In March of 1995, the year before I was graduating, and about sixty days before the draft, I had to have total shoulder reconstructive surgery. It's funny how fortune happens. I was probably never good enough to be one of these players who never had to work for a living in a real job; getting an earlier crack at it I think really helped me in my career.

My first job in sports was working for the Chicago Bulls during the peak of the Jordan-Pippen years on the marketing side. During the dot-com boom, I did some work in new media on the brand side, before going to IMG and becoming a baseball agent in 2001. Mark McCormack passed away, Betsy McCormack, his widow, ended up selling the company to the Fortsmann Little Group— and the culture at IMG really changed. They started transitioning to business outside of the more traditional talent representation side and it just wasn't the same group of people.

JEREMY ZIMMER:

What they did was, they analyzed very intelligently that the movie and television business were going to come under a lot of powerful headwinds, and it was going to be harder and harder for them to continue to grow. So they needed to diversify and sports was the spot to diversify in. They saw Mark McCormack had passed away, thought there was a real opportunity to go in and consolidate the sports representation business and be in sports what CAA had been in entertainment. And I think that was a smart and logical strategy. But I think they did it so fast and over-paid so much for it and I don't know that they necessarily got everything that they thought they were paying for. That doesn't mean that it won't ultimately come together in a good way but it feels like they got way out over their skis financially.

CAA co-chairman and partner Lee Gabler left the agency on May 2, 2007, to join David Letterman's production company Worldwide Pants as a consultant. Gabler had been with CAA since 1983, and served as the head of CAA's television department from 1989 to 2005, when he had given over day-to-day responsibilities for running the department to Steve Lafferty.

STEVE LAFFERTY:

Lee started talking to me in 2003 about his eventual plans to leave the agency within the next few years. He was very methodical in the way he went about things and set me up early on as his number two. I was the deal maker and problem solver while he set the overall tone and direction. He dealt with all the personnel issues and the policies of the overall company. We worked on many clients together from David Letterman to Aaron Spelling, John Wells, and Witt-Thomas, to name a few.

LEE GABLER:

It was no secret that Lovett and I didn't like each other, which was the main reason I didn't want to stay any longer. It was time for me to get out of there; twelve years was enough.

It was a very hard time for me. I was always asking myself, *Why am I here?* Under Richard's tutelage, the agency was getting involved with a lot of things they shouldn't have been involved with to the point where it was no longer a talent agency. It had become just another conglomerate. As a result, there were so many new people now part of the agency that it became impossible to continue the culture we had, or even to build a new one. It certainly wasn't the company I joined, or one I wanted to stay at.

But any notion that I was fired is 200 percent inaccurate. At the end of the selling season every year, usually in August, I had lunch with Bryan Lourd, and in 2006 we went to lunch, and he said, "What do you want to do?" and I said, "To stop in a year." We talked about who might be a candidate to take my place; I told him Lafferty should be the one who should do it, and that all of the clients basically were handled. I said I would take the next year to make the transition, and that's exactly what I did. I also said, "If you want me to consult for two years after I leave, I'll do that. But if you don't, that's no problem—no harm, no foul." During the course of that next year, they felt that because I wasn't going to be functioning at a sustained level like I did before, they wanted to adjust my bonus at the end of the year, which I felt was ridiculous, but I said fine. Then when I was getting ready to leave, they asked me if I would extend a little while longer, to make the transition into the new building. They said it would be easier for everybody if they saw me make the move over to the new building with them— change, but familiarity, and all that. I didn't particularly care to do that, but I agreed, and stayed an extra six months. I don't know why people thought I was fired. If I was, that was the longest firing in the world.

STEVE LAFFERTY:

In the management transition, I didn't want to upset the apple cart and tried very hard to give the appropriate amount of support. Meanwhile, I think Lee had a lot on his mind about how much longer he wanted to run the department, when was the right time to start shifting his life post-CAA, and so on. Lee had bought a beautiful piece of land in Santa Barbara and was building a house where he was planning on moving sometime in the future. He passed the torch over to me in March of 2005 and we went into a new phase in the CAA TV department.

LEE GABLER:

The biggest arguments we would have were about their desire to give certain people bonuses they didn't deserve because they were worried about them leaving or they were trying to persuade them to play a certain role. It wasn't until I left or was leaving that they started axing people, changing deals. I knew eventually it was going to turn to that.

STEVE LAFFERTY:

I grew up in an entertainment family. My mother was a radio and voice-over actress; my father was a producer/director of live radio and television. In 1947 or '48, he was directing a radio show when some executive walked into the control room and said, "We're doing a TV shoot down in studio X, can somebody help set us up to do it?" My father replied, "I'd love to do that," and that's literally how he got started in television. He would go on to do shows like *Person to Person* with Edward R. Murrow, producing the interview with then presidential hopeful John F. Kennedy and his wife, Jacqueline. He produced and sometimes directed many diverse types of programs from variety shows like Danny Kaye (which won an Emmy award its first season), to Andy Williams, game shows, and dramas. My father directed several *Twilight Zone* episodes—some of his most cherished work. Later in the mid-1960s he went on to be head of West Coast programming on CBS and helped develop *Hawaii Five-0, Mission: Impossible, All in the Family, M*A*S*H*, and the *Mary Tyler Moore Show*, among many others. He then went on to run Late Night and MOW/Minis at NBC and ultimately finished his career producing a number of TV movies, including *An Early Frost*, for which he won a Peabody.

Because TV was really something that I felt I knew a lot about, I decided to go to law school and try the business side of the TV business. My first job was working with Grant Tinker and Arthur Price at MTM in a junior business affairs job. Over the next ten years, I did stints at Taft/Hanna-Barbera and Viacom/Showtime. While working at Viacom, I decided I wanted to switch sides and start representing talent. I felt I could make a much greater impact on things if I worked on helping talent get the deals they deserved—not something companies were particularly generous with. So I went out and got the only job I could find in a talent agency, which was the head of Business Affairs of Triad Artists, a newly formed mega-agency grown out of the merging of three smaller agencies. They were really terrific, and after a time they allowed me to rep writers and actors even though I was head of biz affairs. In 1990, Bill Haber and Lee Gabler hired me to head the TV Business Affairs group that reported to Ray Kurtzman. Ray was a legend, and his guidance in navigating a very tricky set of relationships was invaluable—teaching me the tenets of being patient and that most problems basically solve themselves—if you don't work them into even bigger ones!

Early in 2007 CAA recruited three sports deal makers to run CAA Sports: Howard Nuchow, former president of Mandalay Sports Entertainment (the mini-conglomerate run by former Sony co-head Peter Guber), where he ran baseball operations and was involved in acquiring the New York Yankees' Class A affiliate in Staten Island, New York, and the Yankees' AAA affiliate in Scranton, Pennsylvania; David Rone from Fox Sports, where he served as executive vice president; and Michael "Vino" Levine, former president of Van Wagner Sports Group, a sports media sales firm representing close to two hundred MLB, NHL, NBA, and college teams. (Van Wagner Sports sold signage sponsorship at athletic facilities, annually negotiating deals generating over $200 million.) The experience of Levine, Nuchow, and Rone signaled an expansion for the young CAA Sports department into a full-service business not just for athletes, but teams and brands beyond the borders of a traditional talent agency business. There was a non-rousing chorus of, "Hey, who are these guys?" in some corners, not surprising because of their relatively low profiles, but CAA didn't mind if expectations were low or if equal parts criticism and skepticism surrounded the new effort. And the trio in *particular wasn't ruffled by competitors who were already disregarding them; they were convinced they would have the proverbial last laugh.*

PETER GUBER:

Richard didn't call to ask me about Howie; Howie called to ask me about Howie, which was the smart thing to do. Howie called and said, "This is an opportunity that I want to take on. What do you think?" Howie had been with me ten years as the president of our company, and I enjoyed him and I was very close to him. I was not thrilled he was going, but—I mean, why would I be thrilled when the president of my company was going to go and leave?

After some drama, I came to the realization that this was part of life—people move on—and I was supportive. I was especially supportive when I found out he was going to have a partner, Michael Levine, because Michael's dad was like my roommate and best pal in law school. So I knew he wouldn't be alone in the mix, and that he would have a compadre.

BRODIE VAN WAGENEN:

In January or February of 2007, Howie and Vino came on board, and for the first time, we had leadership and a sense of where our growth would be coming from. They brought vision.

TOM CONDON:

When Richard hired Mike Levine and Howie Nuchow as the sports division co-heads, that allowed us to spend more time on the field with our client players like we were prior to when we came to CAA.

RICHARD LOVETT:

We had a unique opportunity to build a sports business from scratch. There is no greater challenge than to be the defending champions each year as we have been in movies, television, and music, but what an opportunity it was to be the challenger and have a blank page. In finding leaders for our sports business, we wanted executives in sync with our culture, people of great character. We wanted to start with a new generation, and we were looking for charismatic, high-energy, ambitious people. We overachieved in having the good fortune to hire Howie and Vino.

HOWIE NUCHOW, Executive:

I started as a sports management major at the University of Massachusetts, and I was fortunate to do an internship with the New Jersey Nets, where one of my responsibilities was to pick up a guy named Jon Spoelstra at the airport. Jon Spoelstra is arguably one of the greatest team marketers in the history of sports. Commissioner Stern loved him, and he was one of the great team marketers in NBA history and did a lot of great things with the Portland Trailblazers. So when I was graduating college, he said to me, "You should apply for a job at the New Jersey Nets." He was also doing something called the Hawaiian Winter Baseball League that he was launching, and I said, "Aw, the Nets opportunity sounds interesting, but I want to go to this Hawaii thing that you're doing." He said, "Apply for a job at the Nets." I said, "Really, Jon, Hawaii seems to be my thing. I think I could do great things with you." Then he looks at me and says, "Again, why don't you apply for the Nets?" I was about to say something else, but he just said, "Howie, stop. I'm going to be named president of the Nets and you should apply for a job there."

They hired twenty-one young people to sell tickets around New Jersey and that was my first job, but I never looked at it as just selling tickets. I looked at it as *he's using the Nets as a platform to do all these other revenue-driving things* that he was doing, and I caught on early to that. So I did that for several years even after he left the franchise.

Peter Guber had always wanted to get into sports, and he knew Jon Spoelstra. Jon told Peter, "I think there's a guy who could buy into your theories of minor league baseball, and he's crazy enough to leave his job." He was right. I thought if I was around somebody like Peter it would be much more interesting than going through the regular NBA ranks as a young vice-president. I worked with Peter for ten years. We wound up running franchises that were the crown jewels of the industry, and I just loved it. One day a former intern of mine who was working for Richard Lovett called and said, "Will you meet with Richard Lovett and talk to him about the sports business?" And that was the first time we had ever met.

MICHAEL LEVINE, Executive:

I grew up in North Tarrytown and Chappaqua, New York, and then went to Cornell University, where I studied history and painted houses during the summer and played a lot of lacrosse and basketball. Really didn't know where my career was going to go—thought maybe I would teach, thought maybe I would coach. Somewhat luckily and serendipitously between my junior and senior years in college a friend of mine from school got an internship application for a job at CBS Sports. I rustled together a résumé and a transcript and wrote an essay and met a nice human resources woman who sort of manufactured a job for me in the media relations department at CBS Sports. Proofreading press releases and working with the media that was covering sports television was a really interesting position to first see the sports business. I got exposure to on-air talent, I got exposure to sports media. Working on weekends and the following fall on the *NFL Today* set, I realized that I was not going to do well in live television; I didn't like the atmosphere in the trucks—it was so tense and fast that I just preferred being in the office and working with the talent. I went back to school, and got hired by a brilliant guy named Art Kaminsky, who owned a sports management company called Athletes and Artists. It was a small firm that represented a lot of hockey players in the NHL, a lot of retired athletes who were now on-air television personalities. We represented Al Michaels and Dan Deirdorf and Chris Berman and Mike Tirico and Bill Walton and Brian Leetch and Sergei Zubov and Adam Oates in the NHL. And I loved that part of the business: I loved working with the athletes. I loved getting to know the on-air broadcasters. And I wanted to win for them. So I gravitated toward the part of the business that was sort of limitless, which was trying to come up with opportunities for the athletes and the talent to try and secure endorsement opportunities or speaking appearances or extra revenue opportunities for them. Because I was a young twenty-one-year-old who no longer got a report card, it was nice to sort of be able to measure my success through the amount of money that I was making for the clients.

That company merged into the Marquee Group, which was a sports management, sports marketing, sports events, and television company that was meant to go public to try and challenge IMG in the mid-'90s. And that then rolled up into SFX Sports Group, which Bob Sillerman owned after he had sold SFX Broadcasting. We went from being this mom-and-pop representation firm to being as big as any company in sports with the possible exception of IMG. We bought ProServ, we represented Michael Jordan. David Falk was the CEO and my boss. And it was a blast.

The talent that was accumulated within SFX Sports Group was really impressive. They had an incredible roster of executives and agents. But they were all set up to operate strictly in their own lanes for their own earn-outs and their own personal successes. So what could have been murderers' row ended up imploding because there was this battle at the top for their own personal agendas and their own financial rewards.

I stopped at about 2000, joined a guy named Richard Schaps who owned a company called Van Wagner Communications. I essentially was hired to help build a sports business for his billboard company. They owned some assets in sports that we turned into Van Wagner Sports Group, and it became essentially a national sports media sales organization selling a specific piece of inventory for eighty teams in college sports, all the NBA teams, and all the major league baseball teams: the rotational signage behind home plate and underneath the scores table in basketball and the All State field goal nets in college football. I was out of the agency business and loving it.

I was in constant communication with Howie. I would have a deal that was falling apart and he would calm me down, and he would have personnel issues and I would sort of talk him off the ledge. We'd swap budgets and we'd talk each other through these things. And even though we hadn't worked together, there was a lot of trust and a real professional friendship that we developed.

HOWIE NUCHOW:

Richard knew the landscape was shifting. He said, "This company has to diversify."

MICHAEL LEVINE:

I knew nothing about CAA other than Michael Ovitz's role in the Dave Letterman move from NBC to CBS. I mean, I knew the prestige of CAA but it was definitely a perception of mystery because of what I thought I knew about Michael Ovitz. I had never heard of Richard Lovett. I had never heard of Bryan Lourd or Kevin Huvane. I didn't know about any of them.

We were negotiating our deal and they said, "What titles do you guys want?" And for the three of us, it didn't make sense any other way for us to be anything but equals. It would just eliminate any kind of discomfort or imbalance and we could all be all for one and one for all. We didn't realize at that time how much of a fit that was with the Young Turks and the CAA way. But when they heard it from us, they were thrilled.

JEREMY ZIMMER:

The way they approached it, just overpaying all of the agents, just paying so much money to get into that business so quickly to become dominant so quickly—it felt like it just tilted from being this very well-organized organic machine that would bring in agents from the outside but quickly compressed them into the machine so everything pressed smoothly, and suddenly it's this whole other thing with a massive distraction going on and suddenly it became a whole other management piece. And people got distracted—and at the same time, the headwinds from the business that they were in were very real. And rather than sort of move away from it, in my opinion, they needed to work harder at it, as opposed to now focus your attention on a more potentially lucrative business. They had historically made so much money from first dollar gross players that when the first dollar gross business came under attack, their revenue got hurt a lot worse than, say, our revenue because we weren't so based on first dollar gross. We had come up built on television packaging and television revenue. So I think that that shift in the business was really hard for them.

MICHAEL LEVINE:

I think that we both shared a perspective about the sports industry and it holds true today: We believe there are lots of great marketers in our industry. And we think that there's a scarcity of sellers. And we said if we're going to be in this, in order to win we've got to be able to sell anything and everything that we're doing. Because to me that was the missing link at SFX: We had all these great properties, we had all these great athletes. We had all these great media properties, but we had too much and we didn't do a good job of selling any of them. So as a sales organization we were a mile wide and an inch deep. And we felt at CAA if we could really sell the clients of the agency that we were going to build at CAA sports, then we were going to win. We were going to limit the amount at first so that we could prove that we would win, and if we succeeded, then the clients would come.

We knew that the money was big in transactions having to do with teams. We knew that the money being spent by the networks for media rights was growing rapidly. And we knew the sponsorship business real well, and that there was a lot of money and margin there. So Richard and Bryan and Rubel understood that stars matter and that athletes were stars. The DNA of the company is to represent talent, and that was going to be no different in CAA Sports. It was the very essence. We needed to have agents who were the best in class but also were more ego-less than some of their competitors and could work as a part of a collective team.

PAUL DANFORTH, Executive:

Vino and I have known each other since we were in our early twenties. When CAA was recruiting him, he called me to ask my opinion. I remember it like it was yesterday. It was right before Christmas and he said, "I think this thing's getting real. What do you think?" We talked for over an hour and a half, and at one point I just said, "You have a chance to go and build something with an incredible brand behind you. This is a once-in-a-lifetime opportunity. You need to do this." And then I was taken aback, because he said, "All right, if I'm doing this, then are you going to do it with me?" I wasn't expecting that question. I had been at the Mets for so long, and I had just spent an hour and a half telling him he should take the shot. I said, "We're thirty-five years old. Let's try to build something special."

MICHAEL LEVINE:

Paul Danforth came to CAA and was hired by us after being the chief revenue officer for the New York Mets, helping to close the CitiField naming rights deal, the Anheuser-Busch and the Pepsi deals in the new CitiField.

When we were hired, we were in our mid-thirties. And I remember Bryan sitting with me at the Mayrose Café, where he was interviewing me. We were having breakfast. He's like, "If you were to go back and redo Van Wagner Sports Group, you know, would you do it the same way?" And I just said, "Of course not. I made so many mistakes along the way." And he said, "Why don't we do it over? Why don't we start over and do it again? And let's avoid those mistakes together?" And honestly? That was a moment when

I felt that I could absolutely work for these guys. They understood from the very beginning.

HOWIE NUCHOW:

We knew we were going to do this well. There was not one doubt in our mind. And Richard knew that we knew that, and he was betting on it.

Each division in the agency business is likely to have its own set of senses and sensibilities; such was certainly the case at CAA. The motion pictures division was sometimes referred to as the Ivy League, strictly cream-of-the-crop, while the TV division was scrappier, and the music division? The "wild ones," naturally.

When Sports entered the CAA biosphere in 2006, some members of the team already had bull's-eyes on their backs because many of the veteran agents elsewhere in the agency weren't enthusiastic about adding them to the mix. It didn't exactly help that those agents and others were warned repeatedly of agency-wide belt-tightening as a result of start-up costs for the new division (although estimates on some of those costs proved to be wildly overblown or, in some cases, just plain inaccurate).

The Sports guys had their own culture, and to put it gently, it didn't blend seamlessly with any of CAA's existing ones. One tiny moment of proof came on the last night of the first CAA retreat after Levine and Nuchow had come aboard. Sports agents were letting loose like crazy, and just as things were closing down, a couple of the boys hopped over the bar, grabbed a big bottle of rare wine—a bottle greatly prized by the owner, incidentally—and started enthusiastically passing it around. It was actually rather harmless, frat-boyish "fun," hardly noteworthy perhaps except for the stunned and hostile reaction it provoked from others in different divisions of the agency.

To them, it looked as though these rookies were overstepping their bounds— almost as if a freshman U.S. senator were trying to wrest control of a bill, or give a big rabble-rousing speech too early in his first term. The Sports guys didn't care. They were determined to have a great time and to let their work, and its results, speak for themselves. And did they ever.

MICHAEL LEVINE:

We did some evaluatory work for the International Olympic Committee, which is really the crown jewel of TV rights. It was pretty heady, investment-banker-like, McKinsey-consulting-type analysis that we did. That wasn't like just, "You got this much and now you should get this much." It was an evaluation of the entire media rights landscape and why the Olympics had such a prominent place in that landscape.

DAVID O'CONNOR:

That was more of a prestige thing. I can't even remember what we got paid on that. But you know, the Dodgers paid us $12 to $14 million, too. The Rangers paid us the same amount of money. The baseball deals were big ones.

JOHN SKIPPER, Executive:

It has always puzzled me slightly when major sports organizations believe they need a third party to advise them how to sell their media rights.

After advising the IOC in advance of the London-Sochi Olympics, CAA Sports moved on to a fully American icon. The New York Yankees became the department's first large institutional client when, in October 2007, it closed a stadium sponsorship deal for the new Yankee Stadium that would open in April 2009. In total, CAA sold over $700 million in sponsorships for the Bronx team. Sponsorship partners included AT&T, Delta, and Pepsi.

HOWIE NUCHOW:

It was the biggest piece of inventory available. Before we were in Randy Levine's office, Randy basically stood up and said, "Guys, if I give this to you, we completely put you on the map. So how are you going to make this work?" And we're all kind of like just, "Put us on the map? Are you serious?" It's basically the definition of the map. Because it was the biggest thing that was going to show. It was something that was going to be outside of athlete rep.

MICHAEL LEVINE:

It was the first time that the Yankees ever hired outside. There were so many different competitors, everyone in our space, essentially every company.

HOWIE NUCHOW:

I remember it as fifty-one—and they were all coming at us.

MICHAEL LEVINE:

You've got to realize for the three or four or five years prior, Howie was a partner with the Yankees on their two sort of most valuable minor league franchises. And at that same time period, I worked with their head of sales on brokering a dozen to sixteen sponsorship deals for their own stadium from my old company. Paul Danforth was the chief revenue officer for the New York Mets and competed with them for fifteen years. There was a lot of familiarity with all of us over a several-year period. And I think they liked us. They trusted us.

HOWIE NUCHOW:

Also it was the halo of what CAA was. That wasn't lost on Randy and the guys. It wasn't like we were three guys across the street. We were a part of this big company that they had heard about.

RANDY LEVINE, Executive:

We knew those guys, particularly Mike from when he was with the Mets. They're good guys. But you know, we have our own sales force and they're terrific. We did the deal with them because we knew them, it didn't matter that they were at CAA. At the end of the day they assisted and were helpful, but do they deserve credit for it? No, our guys and our team deserve the credit. That's not taking anything away from those guys, it's just the facts about what happened.

MICHAEL LEVINE:

The meeting was at the old stadium, and Michael Rubel was with us and Richard actually came with us as well. At this point we had spent several weeks going through this and we believed we were getting the business, but it was the moment we were officially given the nod and we were retained, and it was pretty telling to the two of us that Richard and Rubel were there to sort of show that support.

HOWIE NUCHOW:

After they congratulated us, we shook hands and walked out across 161st Street and we went over to Stan's Sports Bar, which is an old New York Bronx institution.

MICHAEL LEVINE:

And Rubel had gone there when he was younger. It was like three o'clock on a Wednesday afternoon; there was no team, no game. We bought beers and we toasted and it was a "hey, we've made it" moment. I actually went behind the bar, bought the second round of beers. I bought the four of us Stan's T-shirts that we still have because we knew this was going to be something to look back on. Those beers, as Will Ferrell once said, "when it hits your lips," that's a great feeling and a special moment.

We sold $707 million worth of sponsorship and put the Yankees in a position to be able to maintain their leadership position for a long period of time.

RANDY LEVINE:

They assisted us in three deals, AT&T, Delta, and Pepsi—only two of them were commissioned, and then we decided not to renew them. Not because the guys are great guys, because they are, but we didn't want to give the impression that they played instrumental roles in the new Yankee Stadium because that would be an overexaggeration and unfair to our guys here.

Raymond Kurtzman was born the same year as the talkies. It was 1927, and as Jolson triumphed in The Jazz Singer *at Grauman's Chinese, Ray Kurtzman came to life in another part of Los Angeles, and he'd never stray far from that city of his birth, attending first UCLA for a BA in marketing and then USC for a law degree.*

It was a full half-century before Ray joined CAA, making him one of the original twenty. He had started quietly in the business, first at Allied Artists Pictures, then up the ladder to Mirisch Pictures, and finally, Columbia. He learned all there was to know about the movie business and then, generously, he shared that knowledge with anyone who'd ask.

Technically he was head of business affairs for CAA, but he was prized as much for his heart as for his brain, unofficially the go-to guy forever being gone-to, regardless of the topic.

For years he mentored the founders on the rules and regulations, the ethics and the scruples, and the bad and the beautiful. He was Obi-Wan from Star Wars *and the High Lama from* Lost Horizon, *known for having the proverbial "gruff exterior," even growling like a lion on occasion, but ever the pussycat on the inside.*

He died of Alzheimer's complications in April of 2007. What memorial could be not only a fitting but a living one? The question is easily answered: not that far from the place where he was born, not that far from where Jolson, projected on a screen, sang miraculously to an amazed audience of first-generation moviegoers, there now stands the private Ray Kurtzman (CAA) Theater.

Yes, "CAA" is part of its name, much as Ray Kurtzman will always be part of CAA.

RICK KURTZMAN:
Here's a seventy-nine-year-old man who basically had been out of the business for seven years—hadn't been at the center of things for a long while in a business that changes all the time—and when

I walked out to give my eulogy, I saw there must have been 1,000 people there. I mean, it was crazy.

I guess Michael Ovitz doesn't like going to funerals. He wasn't there.

MICHAEL OVITZ:

I asked Rick Kurtzman if I could speak. And he said Lovett said no. I found that odd, since I'd been friends with Ray from the time I was twenty-three years old, and we'd worked together almost my entire adult career, and Rick Kurtzman was like family to me.

He clearly asked Lovett, because you could hear in his voice how uncomfortable he was. There was no one closer to his family than me. When Rick was in high school, I would take him on day trips and weekends with me like he was a son. I hired him and trained him from the time he was a kid to be an agent. And Rick displayed absolutely no courage in suggesting to Richard that I speak. I felt that was fascinating.

ANDREA NELSON MEIGS:

When I left CAA it wasn't because of some big blowout, but it was traumatic for me. All of my mentors had gone away. Ray Kurtzman had passed away; Patrick Whitesell had gone to Endeavor; Joe Rosenberg had left the business; Fred Specktor now worked for his former assistant, Richard Lovett, and the Young Turks who had taken over.

I was in my review meeting and we were going over numbers and I thought their bonus numbers for me were low for what I had brought in. So I asked for a reconsideration of my bonus, because my guys were doing well. Cedric was making five million a movie, Jon Voight was making five million, Beyoncé was making five, Chris Brown had a two-million-dollar quote, and I had showrunners who were on the list of the top fifty, with two shows on the air. I had asked several people who were about the same level what they were getting and it was clear that I was nowhere near what the other guys were making. I wasn't even at the low end of what the men were making. And my request to reevaluate was met with "This may be a good time for you to look elsewhere." I was shocked; then I thought it was a joke. I thought that the next day they would say, "Let's talk about this further," but instead I got a call from one of the partners, who said, "I'd be happy to help you look elsewhere. Is there anyone I can call for you?" And I thought, *Wow, this is real.* I didn't feel like I had a go-to person. So here I was, a dual degree, successful female African-American agent with a client just nominated for a Golden Globe, now looking for a new home. Once again, this was a reminder *we just had to be better* to get a shot.

When I left, pretty much all of my clients came with me— Beyoncé, Chris Brown, Mara Brock Akil, Mary J. Blige, and others.

BART WALKER, Agent:

I went to Harvard Law School and started my career in San Francisco as a lawyer. I read a *New Yorker* profile of Sam Cohn, the legendary ICM agent and it was eye-opening. I learned he meant so much to the worlds of theater, books, film, television—everything that I cared about. I couldn't believe that a person like him existed and that he had this life and career. So I moved to New York to become an entertainment attorney, and believe it or not, three years later, a job opened up at ICM in business affairs working with Sam Cohn.

Sam was famous for discouraging his clients from having relationships with lawyers; not surprisingly, many of them didn't. Today many clients have agents, managers, lawyers, and business managers; the committee involved in making decisions is pretty spread out. But with Sam, the committee was just Sam. He was the guy making the decisions. And all I did was Sam's deals. For a young lawyer, it was amazing. My first assignment was to work with Bob Fosse and negotiate with the Shuberts. But this job was limited—it was a legal job in an agency. The clients were great, but it was a tough job and Sam himself could be really rough. I decided this job was a stepping-stone, and not something that should last.

I wound up leaving ICM and worked for an independent production/distribution company for several years, but then that company ran into difficulties with a new owner. I called Sam. The warmth in our relationship started as soon as I had left ICM, and I knew I could trust him. I said, "This is not going the way I thought it would, what's your opinion?" He said, "You should be an agent, but you have to move to Los Angeles." I met with Jeff Berg and the senior team at ICM in L.A. and was there for eleven years.

I kept running into Bryan Lourd at award events I was attending with my clients. At some point we just decided, "Let's get to know one another," and we went out for a drink. The management structure at ICM during this time was Jeff Berg, Nancy Josephson, and Ed Limato. It wasn't something I felt comfortable with and I was very impressed with the way Richard, Bryan, Kevin, and Doc managed that place. They were so attentive to everything, and the focus, the tenacity, the professionalism there was really different. So I went over to CAA.

CAA, like all the agencies, is very active now in independent finance and distribution. I like to think that I create a structure for my clients' films that originate with the filmmaker. For example, on *Lost in Translation*, Sofia Coppola and I raised finance from Japan and built the finance structure from that foundation, with different licenses for different countries. This centralized her control—she owned the copyright and had full creative control. From a business point of view, this created a real economic upside, as all the rights and territories were uncross-collateralized, creating different potential streams of revenue, so a success in the U.S. or France or Japan would pay dividends without reference to how it does in the rest of the world.

Once I was at CAA, I began to see that the intimacy with my clients that I had always valued wasn't so valued there. It seemed that once the artist became a client of CAA, the individual agent was a bit faceless. They set it up so it's the agency that represents you and the client has a lot of interchangeable parts. Well, I didn't want to be an interchangeable part of a big company that somebody else owned. I want to be close with my clients and a passionate advocate for them.

I see a continuum for any agent. There's the artist on one side, and the world of finance and distribution on the other side. At CAA, most of the successful people are in the middle; I have always placed myself more at the artist's side.

STEVE ALEXANDER:

Heath and I were very close. By the time I would drop my son off at his school in the morning, we may have already talked two or three times. So when I hadn't heard from him that morning, I began to think something may be wrong. I got into the office, started doing work, but kept looking at my phone, waiting for him to call or at least text.

We had a rule at CAA that you couldn't bring your device into meetings so you weren't distracted. But I was so concerned about Heath that of course I brought my BlackBerry into the meeting. I set it down on the conference table in the meeting and just kept staring at it. About forty-five minutes into the meeting, my phone finally rang and it was my friend and Heath's publicist, Mara Buxbaum. I could tell immediately something was very wrong in her voice and she asked me if I knew about an address on Broome Street in New York, and I said, "That's Heath's apartment." As soon as that came out of my mouth, she started crying. She said she had gotten a call from the coroner in New York saying that they've responded to a call at that address.

I left my stuff in the meeting and walked back to my office, in total shock. I remember booting up my computer and his death had already been reported online. This was so totally unexpected. It was a perfect storm: he had been sleep deprived, and he was dealing with some things that he really didn't have experience with. It was a terrible accident. Then the phone started to blow up and other agents who were leaving to go to Sundance were stopping by. Bryan Lourd popped his head in to tell me how sorry he was and was extremely supportive. He then said, "Do whatever you need to do." I left and flew back East with Kim Ledger, Heath's dad, who had flown in from Australia right away. We went to Heath's apartment, crossed the police line, as it was basically a crime scene. When I came back to L.A., people were reaching out to me, but I didn't come in to the office for several weeks.

Amy Pascal called and said, "What can I do to help? I always loved Heath." She offered all the resources we would need to have a memorial for him, and gave me a soundstage. There were over three hundred and fifty people there, studio presidents, directors, and colleagues. A few people spoke, and when it was my turn, I couldn't shorten my thoughts, my memories of him, so I spoke for what must have been thirty minutes. It was a terrifying, amazing experience. I felt completely naked up there, but it wound up being really cathartic.

In July 2008 it was announced that CAA partner Rick Nicita would be leaving the agency to become co-chairman of Morgan Creek Productions. Nicita had been with CAA for twenty-eight years.

RICK NICITA:

There was no inciting incident, nothing like that. I wish it were that exciting. Ronnie and Mike and Bill left in 1995, and I left in 2008. That's thirteen years of "The New Thing." I was with CAA without Ron and Mike basically as long as with them. I had plenty of the new.

When I left there were five owners of the company: myself, and, in no order, Richard Lovett, Kevin Huvane, Bryan Lourd, David O'Connor. What we called the board was a little bigger, but the ownership of the company was the five of us. They were and are terrific guys, really smart, very ambitious, in the very best sense of that word. But from my point of view, they had one flaw that was unforgivable and uncorrectable: they were all thirteen or fourteen years younger than me, and they almost always saw things in a different way than I did. There's no other way to put it. As a result, I was very conscious of figuring out a path to the exit door—which they didn't seem concerned about at all. They were very nice about asking me if I was sure I didn't want to stay on longer, but we all knew it was time.

I had been thinking about leaving for at least a year or two. I always knew I was going to be leaving at some point, but I never really stopped to deal with it. I'd been an agent for forty years, and after a while I was sitting in Wednesday morning staff meetings, which I'd been going to since 1968—at CAA and elsewhere—and somebody would talk about, "So-and-so's available," and a calendar like in a movie would run through my head, flapping through the years. *1971, 1983, 1996, 2000, and so on.* I'd sit there going, *Wow, am I just going to keep doing this? Why am I doing it? Am I doing it because I want to do it? Am I doing it because I'm scared to even think of not doing it? Am I doing it by rote force of habit?*

I was offered the head of William Morris at one point, but I didn't want to deal with it. A couple of opportunities were vaguely discussed about producing, and studio stuff, but I wasn't ready at the time. But then that final year or so, I didn't really know how to go about it. How can I even check things out? I felt constricted, and then it was like having tunnel vision, and something came into my vision: the Morgan Creek situation. I've always had a combination of naiveté and confidence, which sometimes can work, sometimes not. I just thought, *What the heck, I'm going to do it, what's the worst that could happen?*

JACK RAPKE:

It wasn't Rick's lifetime dream to leave the agency business to go run Jim Robinson's company.

RICK NICITA:

It wasn't about more money. What did I really want? I wanted to have my health; I wanted people to treat me with respect; I wanted a good glass of wine; and I wanted to be with my beautiful wife.

NICOLE KIDMAN:

I was devastated when Rick left. I asked him, "Why?" I tried to convince him to stay. What I enjoy about life is the longevity of relationships, navigating through a long journey together if the person is honorable and decent and willing to do it. Obviously I'm not a masochist.

I think if you're committed artistically to a path, then you'll stay the course, and if you're not, you won't. That's what Rick really understood about me artistically. He knew I have really strange taste. After I won the Academy Award, I really wanted to make *Birth*, which some people couldn't understand. They even said to me, "What are you doing?" But he was always supportive, and even joked, "You're not crazy, you're just idiosyncratic." And he was right.

Kevin and Rick were a balance for each other, so when Rick left and I was with Kevin, it took me awhile to move on, and then he set me up with Chris Edridge and that subsequently has been a really strong relationship, too. But the main person is Kevin. He's always been there, for now well over two decades.

I had a terrible knee injury on *Moulin Rouge*, and then subsequently I was doing *Panic Room*, and I had to pull out of *Panic Room* because I just physically couldn't continue. It was pretty bad. I'd shot for two weeks on *Panic Room*, and he just told me, "We'll get through this," and we did.

I think so much of a relationship between an agent and an actor is finding the true essence of what the actor is trying to do, and then helping formulate that path for them. That's probably why I'm very loyal to Kevin, because I know the path I forge is windy and weird, and that's not for everyone. I'm slightly naive, and kind of wide-eyed. I was raised in a very Catholic family, and my father was very moral with a strong social conscience—so I have what you probably would call a moral approach to playing out my professional decisions. I'm not so much talking about what the film is about, because I don't believe I'm moral artistically all the time, but more in terms of the code I use when I either accept or pass on roles.

In 2008, CAA's Rick Hess was an executive in charge of the agency's Film Finance Group, increasingly finding himself, often in tandem with partner David O'Connor, involved in multifaceted transactions from private equity, hedge funds, and wealthy family offices to fund slates on movies. For example, CAA had put together for producer Jerry Bruckheimer a financing fund that was north of $300 million from Barclays, and even though it was discontinued after the crash of 2008, Bruckheimer was still able to walk away with roughly $20 million for development. Add to that a massive deal for Chris Meledandri to start a subsidiary group at Universal and it became clear that there was a full-service investment bank advisory group to be formed. Hess called his friend Bob Stanley, who ran Merrill Lynch's Sports and Entertainment group, and said he wanted to take a page out of the Goldman Sachs playbook, and before you could say the word "fees," Stanley and a few of his key operatives at Merrill were on the way to CAA.

But with CAA Sports fully engaged in the athlete representation business, the idea now was to construct a Chinese wall between agents representing players and bankers who could concurrently represent the team's owners, among others. The result was an independent company named Evolution Media Capital (EMC). Hess and Stanley became full-time employees of EMC, which CAA had a 49 percent equity position in and EMC management had 51 percent.

EMC got out of the starting gate very quickly, generating fees through numerous engagements across media and entertainment, but its fattest fees came from Sports Media Advising from Pac-12 and the Dodgers, the latter garnering EMC a tidy $13 million. When Nolan Ryan let it be known that he wanted to buy the Rangers, EMC advised him on the deal; the resulting $4 million "advisory fee" turned out to be essentially an appetizer for the media rights deal that EMC would then negotiate for Ryan, with those fees coming in at $10 million.

DAVID O'CONNOR:

Rick Hess and I dreamed up this idea that we could start a boutique investment bank as a sidecar to CAA's business—leveraging

CAA's network of relationships and bringing real strategy and real banking chops to a pretty unsophisticated organization. And so we just did it: EMC.

We created an off-balance sheet film fund for Jerry Bruckheimer. It was several hundred million dollars; we got Barclays bank to invest in Jerry's film business, which gave him co-financing power with Disney. Unfortunately what happened is we made that deal, the crash happened, and the guy who authored this at Barclays ended up leaving and the new CEO looked at this and he called me up and said, "We got to get out of this." So we made a settlement. Jerry still came away with some real money, and it was a hell of a deal at the time. Really groundbreaking.

RICK HESS, Executive:

I was working at Propaganda Films when Bryan Lourd reached out and asked me to join the agency. He wanted me to help build the international film practice. I knew it would be a great opportunity—and it's hard to say no to Bryan, so I said yes immediately. But one problem—I wasn't an agent, but I was at an agency, so I needed to represent someone. I decided to do something totally off the wall and represent the money, the investors— the buy side, as they say on Wall Street. Traditionally, Hollywood didn't treat outside investors so well, but I thought if we helped them finance better movies, we could—to quote one of my favorites movies—help them help us. Perfect virtuous cycle—by building healthy companies for strong financiers such as Jeff Skoll and Bill Pohlad, they would flourish to finance more movies for our clients. This could only happen at CAA, where culture focuses on sharing information and collaboration, and where there are so many clients that had the power to drive the financing of a film. With everyone's help, we were paid real fees and retainers as movies were made, so it actually became an interesting business, which has scaled today under the leadership of Roeg Sutherland and Micah Green to become the industry leader by far.

As we were doing larger and larger deals requiring capital markets expertise we began to intersect more with the Wall Street investment banks, and it became quickly apparent that we had relationships, insight, and industry knowledge that even the largest investment banks didn't have. Along with CAA, our partner in all of this was Bob Stanley, who ran the structured finance group at Merrill Lynch focusing on media deals, and he was seeing things inside Merrill that concerned him, so we took the leap together and in 2008, when many banks were pulling back from media, we launched our own boutique media investment bank. We called it Evolution Media Capital, since our goal was to play an integral role in the evolution of the agency during an exciting time. CAA was uniquely positioned to be the launching pad for this, based not only on its profound depth of industry knowledge, but also based on the collaborative culture that allows information to flow seamlessly. I believe what differentiated us from the very beginning was not only our unique partnership with CAA that brought our clients a perspective that other banks couldn't bring, but it was also our desire to think like principals. This meant we had to be creative partners for the agency and clients, as was the case in helping launch Illumination for Chris Meledandri. The sports business soon started scaling and we had taken off—advising teams, leagues, and media companies alike.

DAVID RONE, Executive:

The Sports Media Advisory business was certainly an integral part of the growth of CAA Sports both when it sat directly in CAA Sports and more impactfully, once it became part of Evolution Media Capital. As a team, our sports media group, led by Chris Bevilacqua, Alan Gold, myself, and Jay Adya, was successful in winning numerous engagements throughout the period of 2009–2011, the most prominent of which were the assignments for the International Olympic Committee, the Pac-10/Pac-12 Conference, and the San Diego Padres.

ALAN GOLD, Executive:

I worked for the NFL for many years as the head of business affairs for NFL Enterprises and negotiated the deals involving NFL Sunday Ticket, NFL International, and NFL Films. I joined the company in 2008 and Jay Adya was our first hire. Jay is extremely talented and he became a partner a couple of years ago in recognition of everything he has done for our clients and the company. EMC currently has over twenty employees split between our offices in New York City and Los Angeles.

JAY ADYA, Executive:

Before I came to CAA I was a co-founder of a sports focused internet start-up, and before that, I was a management consultant for many years. First, a McKinsey spinoff called Mitchell Madison Group and then later Deloitte Consulting. I'm also a recovering business school graduate from Columbia.

This topic of media rights is something you can't minor in, you've got to major in it, and at the end of the day, if someone says you're tough but fair in a negotiation, that's as high praise as you're going to find.

DAVID O'CONNOR:

Probably one of my proudest accomplishments while an agent at CAA came about when Rick Hess and I were looking at the animation space. We knew that there was a lot of money in family entertainment, but nobody was really paying much attention to it, and a lot of studios didn't have a family entertainment strategy. While there was lots of money floating around, outside money was looking to get in. But there were very few people who could actually run the business, who actually had expertise in it.

While all of this was going on, my really close friend from college Chris Meledandri called me up. He had created 20th Century Fox Animation and his deal was coming up and he wanted help and some perspective on what he should be asking for. So we sat down at lunch and I said, "Wait a minute, Chris, you don't know how valuable you are." I think Fox was paying him about a million bucks a year, and he had created the *Ice Age* franchise for them, which was billions of dollars of value. I said, "Here's how we're going to negotiate with Fox. On a separate track, we're going to create a company that you're going to run. We're going to get off-balance sheet financing and we're going to align you with another global distributor." At the time we had at least three studios that would be great strategic fits. But he didn't want to be an employee, he wanted real ownership. So we created parallel paths. On one track was the Fox negotiation, which I told him would take a year, and they would give him a 15 percent increase. They would grind it out and play hardball. I told him, "At the end of the day, they're not going to pay you anywhere near what you're worth. But on this other track, we'll create this opportunity to change your life, for you to have something of your own." I remember having a meeting with Mark Shmuger and David Lindy, who were literally in the first day of their new jobs as co-chairmen of Universal Studios, and Bryan, Richard, Kevin, and I met with them in their first official meeting and I pitched them the idea of being in business with Chris, and they said, "Yes. We want you to do it." It took probably well over a year, but ultimately we created Illumination. Universal came in and financed the company 100 percent. They wanted to clean up their balance sheet because they were about to sell to Comcast, so we got paid an investment banking fee for $4 or $5 million, and then on top of that we've commissioned every movie that Chris has done. Chris got a very, very, rich deal, probably the best producing deal there is. The truth is, on *Minions* he'll probably make $80–$90 million. To date he's probably made hundreds of millions. And he's got *Despicable Me 3*, and *The Grinch Who Stole Christmas*.

JOE MACHOTA, Agent:
I was four eleven going into my senior year of high school and was obsessed with the Tony Awards since the age of nine, so you

can imagine I was a very popular kid. I always loved the theater, which led me to New York City in 2001, when I was in the original company of *Mamma Mia*.

The theater division started here in 2002, when Bryan and Kevin brought George Lane over from William Morris. That's when they opened up the New York office, which first concentrated on theater, commercial endorsements, and music. Three years later, I started as the first theater floater in our New York office, and then worked as George's second assistant, who was in charge of house seats. I knew at that point I had to get promoted because *Jersey Boys* had just come to town and was the *Hamilton* of its time. You couldn't get a ticket and everybody wanted them. Not available was not acceptable. Nine months later, they told me I was going to be one of the first trainees out of New York. I was thrilled. By the next retreat, I was promoted to an agent.

It's been a thrilling ride. It is a nonstop job. Almost every evening there is a client function—either a preview, an opening, screening, premiere, or client meeting. I'm a big believer in 90 percent of new business happens after office hours, so there's an edict in our department that you should be out every night. That's where you find new business and you meet new people. We are all trying to be in the right place at the right time, to create new opportunities for our clients. To be able to do what you love—I'm the luckiest man in New York City.

ERIC WATTENBURG, Agent:

When I came to CAA, one of the things they kept telling me about was how culturally this place was not like anywhere I'd ever worked. I'd only worked at two other places, William Morris and then a small agency called N. S. Bienstock. They kept saying, "The first principle of CAA is if we all help each other, good things are going to happen." And I kind of thought, *There's no way this is possible*, because William Morris was a place where everybody was looking out for themselves. You could literally have a colleague in the office next to you working at cross-purposes with you on business, and that would not be uncommon. Here that is unacceptable and not tolerated and would never happen. I think that kind of sums up the difference. What I'm most proud of in our department and with our success is that we operate extremely candidly, ethically, and transparently, and we have the highest quality long-term relationships with the entire community as a result. And I know that has yielded better results over the long term. No question about it.

MIKE RUBEL:

By 2009, people saw the level of success that CAA Sports was having from representing athletes to representing the Yankees for sponsorship for the new Yankee Stadium and then Madison Square Garden, to representing the Pac-12 and the Texas Rangers for their media rights, to building an investment bank that represented the buyer groups of the Padres and the Rangers.

All of a sudden, the people who criticized or misunderstood us started saying, "Maybe these guys know what they are doing."

Following the Yankees deal, CAA property sales was retained by Madison Square Garden to sell top-level sponsorships for the arena. In October, Delta signed on a signature-level sponsorship partner at the renovated arena, a deal valued at $6 million per year. JPMorgan Chase would sign a marquee deal valued at $30 million a year. And there were more. And more.

At the time, few in Hollywood—even at CAA—realized the potential that sports held for the agency and its future, although such was not the case up in San Francisco.

Meanwhile, back in Beverly Hills, Endeavor—founded in 1995 by Ari Emanuel, David Greenblatt, Rick Rosen, and Tom Strickler—while never as large as CAA, was blessed with personalities who made it far more than just another blip on the CAA radar. The agency had a swagger that was much larger than its footprint, and this made rumors of a merger all the hotter. Endeavor had brought the word "entrepreneurial" front and center to clients and potential clients by promising them not just jobs but that virtual companies would be built around them. The relatively feisty firm had made inroads into

CAA's television business and, particularly with the arrival of Patrick White-sell, had managed to establish an impressive beachhead in the motion picture business as well.

Finally, after weeks of anxiety and speculation, a merger was announced, on April 27, 2009, between brash young Endeavor and crusty rusty Old Ironsides—aka William Morris.

The actual day of the first combined WME meeting was, some would later recall, "surreal." The matter of which building would house which offices was settled fairly quickly when Endeavor's quarters dominated as the meeting place of choice. Matters of detail—like who would design the combined companies' new logo—tended to come down on the Endeavor side. In some circles, the action was seen not so much a merger of two companies as a much-needed management upheaval at William Morris.

"Upheaval," indeed, and it would be a long while before a creative calm settled in. Nearly two hundred and fifty agents were let go the first day, and months of instability would follow. Initially, the new ruling board was nine members large, with Jim Wiatt of William Morris in the top slot, followed by co-CEOs Ari Emanuel and Patrick Whitesell of Endeavor and David Wirtschafter of William Morris. The clash in sensibilities could be most readily seen in the behavior of those at the top in both agencies. It was obvious that not all of these personalities, colorful or bland, would survive. Employees including executives spent much of their time surveying their coworkers and wondering, or coldly calculating, who would live (stay) and who would die (be trampled in the merger). Tension was palpable everywhere.

Many believed Wiatt was essentially flogged by his own troops, and before anyone could scream, "Entourage," Emanuel and Whitesell were installed atop the newly formed agency. The event further suggested less the melding of two existing agencies than the ceremonial branding of a new and much larger one. The biggest change for the newly united partners in matrimony was cultural, at least initially. For the previous several years, the William Morris Agency had been perceived as virtually the William Moribund Agency, its vital signs evidencing more than mere trace levels of acute enervation. The merger brought about a much needed cultural resuscitation to the workforce, and then soon thereafter, there were several high-profile firings that transmitted an even stronger signal: It doesn't matter who you represent; if you're not willing to be on the team, and practice with the others, you're a goner.

It was a merger designed to come barreling right at the heart, soul, gut, and spirit of CAA, a boldly and openly declared war. Its extreme aggressiveness may not have been wholly a function of Ari Emanuel's presence on the mothership, but that can't have helped.

The fight was on.

ACT THREE

I'm always baffled by "Hey, it's only business." I've never operated that way. I take everything personally.

—NICOLE KIDMAN

8

Cool Summers: 2010–2016

It will never rain roses: when we want to have more roses,
we must plant more roses.

—GEORGE ELIOT

ARI EMANUEL:

Here was the turning point, the very end for them: about six or seven years ago, Richard Lovett went out and said, "We're going to represent everybody. We want 100 percent market share." It was like he took Studio 54 at its height—when you couldn't get in because it was so exclusive—and just said, "Fuck it, we're letting everybody in." Some people freaked out, but I said, "This is the greatest day of our lives! Do you understand this! This guy is taking Tiffany's and turning it into Sears. Hallelujah!" We have won because he doesn't understand what this business is about.

Look closely at CAA's revenues since its founding, and you will see a stream that has grown without interruption—even throughout 1995's upheaval, guild strikes, and myriad changes across the entertainment industry. Their business, and that of some other agencies, can be likened to the proverbial iceberg: Above water, movement on the client front; wins and losses at award shows; and hits or misses with product. But beneath the water line is a foundation of stability and predictability that often is underappreciated by those assessing the industry. Open just a few envelopes in the CAA mailroom more than three decades since the founders unfolded their card tables, and you would find commission checks from the Blake Edwards estate for his directing services on 10 back in 1979, along with checks for film and television projects involving hundreds of other clients. And that would be before you got to the bigger dollar pile from the Jurassic Park, Mission:

Impossible, *and* Back to the Future *franchises, or* ER, Dynasty, Melrose Place, 21 Jump Street, *and dozens more. Once an agency gets a foot in the door on a client's profit participation for a movie or television show or is the direct recipient of a percentage from a movie or TV package, there can be a long, long, trail of money pouring in.*

It had taken the Young Turks roughly five years to get their bearings following the massive upheaval of 1995. As they'd rounded the corner on a new century, it turned out Ovitz's explorations with advertising, investment banking, and technology were prescient. The business was changing; new paths needed to be forged. Coincidentally, Lovett, Lourd, Huvane, and O'Connor believed they had the foundation to grow both their footprint and the agency's range of representation, hence the move in the next several years into marketing, offices abroad, and sports.

But that was hardly enough. They wanted more. Since the company's founding in 1975, financing needs were largely limited and flowed from a straightforward line of credit at a local bank. Such borrowing was rarely used—even during the company's initial lean years—because the partners kept putting as much money back into the agency as they could. Through the decades, there had been minor teases with mergers, a few potential acquisitions, and invitations to be acquired, but nothing got close to the serious stage.

The notion of seeking an outside investor in CAA was something that had been discussed for several years, and in 2010, the agency finally met the right bride: TPG Capital (the initials originally stood for Texas Pacific Group), one of the world's premier private equity firms.

JIM COULTER, Co-chairman, TPG Capital:

Essentially, we are an investment firm, and what we do is a particular type of investing, often referred to as private equity. At TPG, we manage approximately $75 billion of equity assets or largely equity related assets. If I were to give it a headline, I would say we invest in change. We find companies or industries going through a moment of evolution, and we put our capital and creativity to work to help them through that period of time. This theme runs through a whole series of different types of investments—from Uber to turning around Continental Airlines, to our investments in health care after the passage of Obamacare. And it's this idea of change that was one of the governing principles in our appearance as an investor in CAA.

DAVID BONDERMAN, Co-Chairman, TPG Capital:

The long and short of it is, the entertainment industry has been totally dislocated by what's going on around it, and any time you have dislocation like that, you have opportunity. We've been in and out of the media business since the mid-'80s. We had MGM, and we were twice in the cable business.

DAVID O'CONNOR:

When we started EMC, our investment bank, one of the things it led to was a relationship with David Bonderman. Rick Hess and I were in a meeting with him and we wanted to start a principal investing vehicle alongside our investment bank, and, being naive and unsophisticated about how these things work, I said, "David, let's start a fund together." And he said, "Well, I can't do that because I can't do fund-to-fund investments, but one of the things I could do is actually buy a piece of CAA and you guys could take the proceeds and put them into a fund and we could co-invest." That ultimately led to the idea of bringing private equity in and monetizing some of CAA.

JIM COULTER:

There's a general misconception about what private equity firms do in their portfolio companies. Our relationship with each company is bespoke. When a company is in a crisis, our people may go in and help run it, but there's a tendency to think of private equity and our type of investing as buyouts, particularly leveraged buyouts. That's actually a relatively limited part of what we do at TPG.

DAVID BONDERMAN:

We were intrigued by CAA because they're in the middle of the ferment that's going on in this industry, but they've been brokers instead of principals, and we think they have plenty of opportunities to be principals.

JIM COULTER:

In early 2010, members of my team met with the senior team at CAA with the understanding that they were considering taking in outside capital. They wanted to evolve their business and take advantage of investment opportunities in the marketplace and were looking for someone who might partner with them to invest capital. The team at CAA was very self-aware and realized the investment skill set was something that was not as developed in CAA as it was at a place like TPG, so having a partner that, if you will, were experts at investing would add to their DNA.

Having been around the entertainment industry from time to time, I was familiar with the brand. But given the hypersensitivity to privacy at CAA, I couldn't have told you how large they were or the extent of their activities. From the external side, you see pieces of CAA, whether they were at awards dinners or industry lists in terms of their activities. I was aware they were important and large, but not very aware as to what CAA was in its entirety.

DAVID BONDERMAN:

If sports weren't part of the agency, I think we would have still been interested in an investment, but not at the same price. Sports is a fast-growing, dynamic business.

JIM COULTER:

One of the challenges in the investment business is what I'll call uncommon wisdom. Common wisdom is what people think about a situation; it's usually not that valuable because it's something everybody sees. What is valuable is if you find uncommon wisdom, which is where you see something that the rest of the world sees one way and you see a different way. So when I first ran into CAA, my reaction was actually common wisdom that Hollywood agencies might be difficult to invest in, because they're people businesses, and maybe not great stewards of capital.

What surprised me is the deeper I looked, the more uncommon wisdom showed up, and things that I might have expected to be true weren't necessarily the case. In 2010, when we first looked at the company, their sports business was still new, still in start-up phase, and still in cash flow negative. We looked at that business and could say, "Here's something that represents a breakout opportunity for this business." Concert touring was a much bigger business than I would have expected from the outside, and the strength of the TV business was stronger than I would have expected. The stickiness of CAA's businesses and the resilience of their businesses were much stronger than I expected. The light went off for me that this is not only an agency; it is a content play because of their extraordinary access to a very large pool of content. As the value of content increases around the world, an investment in CAA would be the most diversified and interesting way to be in that marketplace.

Talks between CAA and TPG began in March of 2010. In October, TPG acquired a 35 percent stake in CAA for $166 million. The deal valued the agency at nearly $700 million, and included $500 million for future capital needs.

The new CAA board was composed of seven directors from the agency and three from TPG. The CAA members were Lovett, Lourd, Huvane, O'Connor, Rubel, Lafferty, and Light. The TPG members were cofounder Coulter, TPG principal David Trujillo, and the then-CEO of eBay, John Donahoe.

BOB BOOKMAN:

David Bonderman spoke at the first retreat after they bought a minority interest in the company, and he was talking about all the things that TPG could do for us. The first example he gave was Ryanair. You know Ryanair, right? It's an ultra-low-cost European airline where once you buy your ticket, everything else is extra including using the bathroom. And he was saying, "We're trying to get regulatory approval on short-haul flights so that passengers can fly standing up," which obviously means so they can jam more people in, and I'm thinking, literally, at that moment, *He's confusing the agents at this company for passengers on one of his airplanes, not the aircrafts themselves.*

The other example he used was some big hotel chain they bought, and he puts this diagram up about how they were maximizing the way housekeepers cleaned rooms. It looked like a Venn diagram done by Sol LeWitt, and I was thinking, *This is a metaphor for how we should be working, and if that's their mind-set going in, nothing good will come of this for me.*

DAN ALONI, Agent:

I'm not a guy who's good at walking into someone's office at the end of the year and having them tell me, "You've had a fantastic year and this is what we're giving you." It's way too subjective. So I was one of the very, very few people at CAA who had a contract. Typically, when you go to a large agency, you get a contract for two to three years, especially if you're more senior, and then you switch over to the bonus structure. I had a contract for three years, then they extended it for another three years at my request. And when that contract was up, they made an offer to extend for another three years. They claimed I was the highest contracted person in the company outside of the four lead partners when they asked me to sign another extension. I said I wanted to understand where I fit in within the future of the company.

David O'Connor had pulled out a piece of paper previously and said to me, "There's a new board, an interim new board that's going to happen and you are on it," which is one of the things that I had talked about with them from the beginning when I had started at the company. Soon after, part of the company was sold to TPG. Anyone who understands business knows you wouldn't create a new board if you are about to sell a percentage of the company. They then came to me and made an offer for more money than what I had been paid the previous three years in a guarantee.

BOB BOOKMAN:

When the first tranche was announced, Richard made the point of saying that everybody was getting a check for something—*even if you've just been here a week, you'll get something.* But I didn't feel what I got was compensation for all the time and commitment I had given to CAA over twenty-five years.

MARTIN LESAK:

CAA was supposed to be this hyperinclusive company where everyone was supposed to be a part of the "family." We were told that the TPG deals were all about growing the agency, but even after the first deal went down, there was a different feel to the company, and people started to question what was really going on. It definitely changed the camaraderie, and you could sense that the culture was starting to splinter. It was slowly turning into a company that was all about the bottom line.

DAVID BONDERMAN:

What you have to figure out is, whether in the context of the company that is partially owned by the people who work there and partially owned by people who don't work there, how to effectively grow. How do you scale and expand while protecting and preserving the original ideas that made the business special?

BOB BOOKMAN:

We went from a company where everybody knew everybody, to the kind of company where it was, "Who are you?" There was a retreat where when you arrived you got your name tag and your lanyard, along with a list of ten people on a card. And I asked, "Who are these ten people?" because I didn't recognize any of them, and was told, "Oh, they're colleagues of yours, you have to track them down and get a fun fact about each of them." That was how impersonal it had become.

In the world of physics, when two spatially separated events occur at the same time, the question of whether they are absolute is a function of witnesses' time frames, a phenomenon known as the relativity of simultaneity.

The marriage of CAA and TPG arrived at a time when the CAA partners were still grappling with a radically changing media landscape and trying to get their own house in order financially. People believed TPG had summoned a series of budgetary reviews, but just as Noah started work on an ark before even a drop of rain, some financial controls were put in motion before TPG had to request, or insist upon, a single one.

One affected area, expense accounts, may sound trifling, but not in the representation game. So it was that modifications in CAA's travel and entertainment policies brought about changes in the culture as well. One example: For years the opulent St. Regis Hotel in New York City had served as a virtual dorm for CAA agents traveling on business. No more. New regulations were put in place prohibiting midlevel and junior agents from bunking there. Limits were also placed on dining allowances for midlevel and junior agents no matter what the city.

ADAM KANTER:

They did start to get more conservative with expenses. We had this meeting where they gave you a number and said, "Here's your monthly number for meals and entertainment."

MIKE RUBEL:

At the 2014 retreat, we commented that some out in the audience probably assumed any particular change in an expense policy was TPG related. All companies have expense policies and modify them from time to time—"Blame management, not TPG."

It would soon turn out CAA wasn't the only agency making big decisions about private equity. In May of 2012, Silver Lake bought a 31 percent stake in WME for $250 million, and Egon Durban, its managing partner, became part of the agency's executive committee. Silver Lake had hit a grand slam when it made a big-time gamble on Skype, buying 65 percent of the company in 2009, and then selling it approximately a year and a half later for a profit of more than two billion dollars.

A few weeks later, ICM publicly announced that it had done the near opposite, buying out the Michigan-based Rizvi Traverse Management company. The stock repurchase was the culmination of an internal war within ICM pitting chairman and CEO Jeff Berg—who lost and would soon exit the agency—against Chris Silbermann, ICM's president. (While he kept his leadership role under the new arrangement, Silbermann, in an effort to highlight the partnership concept, declined to take the title.) Ironically, it had been Rizvi Traverse's money that had allowed Berg to purchase Silbermann's previous company, the Broder Webb Chervin Silbermann Agency.

For ICM employees, the buyback could be seen only as a way to put years of instability and difficulties behind them at last. After the buyback, it was "their" company, and "they" could experience firsthand its triumphs and hardships. When discussing the new sense of ownership, Silbermann paraphrased ICM client Thomas Friedman: "In the history of the world, no one has ever washed a rental car." Friedman of course was talking about democracy, but Silbermann had used it to rally the troops during the buyback battle.

The new ownership culture for ICM was wildly praised internally, not only because there was a new level of incentivizing going on, but also because there was now cash available to make acquisitions the partners themselves wanted to make. They finally had control over their own destiny and no longer had to worry about cash being distributed or there being some financial engineering that they'd have to live with so that outside investors could boost their own returns. Or as a senior leader said, the agency had gone from mostly mercenaries to primarily patriots.

CHRIS SILBERMANN, Agent:

We may be smaller, but here at ICM, there's nowhere to hide. Here everybody is close-knit, everybody works together, and if somebody's not doing something they're supposed to be doing for a client or a colleague, it's pretty obvious. You can hide your ass off at CAA. You can hide at William Morris. You can even hide at UTA. As a result, there are so many mediocre agents at those companies.

On March 25, 2010, Michael Rosenfeld Sr., one of the original five founders of CAA, died at seventy-five after spells of poor health. Although Rosenfeld was the first founder to leave the agency—a mere seven years after it began—colleagues said that Rosenfeld's warmth and fellowship continued to be felt years into his absence. To the ever-chattering Hollywood world, however, the most intriguing aspect of Mr. Rosenfeld's passing wasn't who showed up for his memorial service but, rather, who didn't.

MICHAEL OVITZ:

No one called to tell me Mike had died, not Ron, not any of the guys running CAA, and I'll give you a better one: Mikey Rosenfeld Jr. didn't call me either and I mentored him like he was a son. But Nikki Finke wrote this unbelievable story basically saying how dare I not show up to the funeral. The reality of it is that I didn't have a clue. How would I have known? I had stopped reading the trades in 2001. I wasn't connected to any of those guys anymore. I was off in another world, Silicon Valley, and no one up there knew who Mike Rosenfeld was.

RON MEYER:

Mike Rosenfeld was a good agent and a solid guy in every way. People trusted him, he had great relationships, and while he wasn't as aggressive as Bill, Mike, and I was, he always got things done. He was really the heart of the company.

BILL HABER:

Michael Rosenfeld Sr. was always haunted by his father's young death at thirty-seven. It shadowed him always. It forced him into an early retirement and presaged his own early death. We understood that and lived with it through his career.

Only a handful of full moons following the death of Michael Rosenfeld Sr., Marty Baum died at his home in Beverly Hills, California, on November 5, 2010, at the age of eighty-six. Integral to the survival of the fledgling agency, CAA's early merger with Baum and his varsity client list enhanced the pedigree of the founding five, and the affection of multiple generations.

RON MEYER:

Marty brought with him great clients, and made deals for his clients that no one else could make. But it's nearly impossible to calculate just how much of a difference he made to the entire agency. Marty was *the* game changer for us.

MICHAEL OVITZ:

Marty was our first major decision and our best major decision. His client list put us into the movie business the day he walked in the door; his advice kept us from making countless mistakes. Marty let us tap into all of his long and deep experiences as an agent and producer, and his presence at the company gave our younger agents exposure to the roots of the old entertainment business that were so important for the future. The history of film and television sets such a wonderful foundation for current opportunities, but can sometimes be hard to find or difficult to unlock. Marty Baum did all of that—and more—for us.

RICHARD LOVETT:

Near the end of his career, Marty was the only agent working who had started in vaudeville and had gone through every chapter of the development of the modern television and movie businesses. He provided one of our great company ritual moments each year. During the last dinner of each year's retreat, we would start chanting Marty's name and clapping, and then he would speak in front of the company and tell remarkable stories of his amazing career.

SANDY CLIMAN:

There was a memorial for Marty at CAA in the Ray Kurtzman screening room, and it was very interesting. Mike, Ron, and Bill were there, and sat together which got a lot of attention. There was even some comment by Richard about that from the podium—in a nice way—but having everyone there together seemed quite uncomfortable.

When ESPN aired a live special called "The Decision," on July 8, 2010, millions watched as LeBron James announced he was leaving his hometown Cleveland Cavaliers to sign with the Miami Heat. The move, teaming LeBron with his fellow "Big Three" superstars Dwyane Wade and Chris Bosh, ushered in a new era for the Miami team. The Heat would go on to reach the NBA Finals in each of the next four seasons, winning titles in two of them.

The signing of the Big Three was one of the grandest moments in recent NBA history, and it signified a major foray into the NBA for CAA. At that moment, the agency represented James, Wade, and Bosh, along with Miami head coach Erik Spoelstra. Wade and Bosh had signed with CAA in 2009 after agent Leon Rose suggested to CAA sports chiefs Howie Nuchow and Michael Levine that their agent, Henry Thomas, be brought into the fold. As for Rose, he had been planning this "Big Three" moment for years. Looking back now, his intricate chess moves, planned and executed far in advance, have to be admired even by competitors.

LEON ROSE, Agent:

I was an attorney in a law firm and I had my own company, Rose Professional Management. When CAA approached me and they told me that they were getting into sports and showed me all the resources my clients and I could take advantage of, it was very intriguing. I realized this broader concept of representation was where the business was heading, and so for me and my clients, I felt that it would certainly be the right move.

PAT RILEY, Coach and General Manager:

This was such a huge undertaking—the first time in the history of free agency that an opportunity like this had come along. For years, the players had single agents, but then those agents started to pair up with multimedia companies like CAA so they could be an arm for endorsements and other things that happen off the court. It was a real coup for CAA.

LEON ROSE:

When I did LeBron's second contract with Cleveland—the extension in 2006—I recommended to LeBron we do a three-year contract where he could opt out after the third year, because it guaranteed that his next contract would be under the existing collective bargaining agreement. It also was shorter, which would keep the pressure on Cleveland in order to build the best team they could, and it gave him flexibility in regard to getting out of his contract. Dwyane Wade and Chris Bosh, who were also in the same position, took three-year deals as well. So that's what led to all of those guys becoming free agents in the same year.

HOWIE NUCHOW:

Erik Spoelstra's dad gave me my first job, so Erik's the only client I handle myself, out of respect for his father who gave me everything.

I was with Spo in Miami the first time all of the Big Three were coming into the office as members of the Heat. Dwyane, LeBron, Chris, and some others all came pouring in. It was basically all CAA guys there in this small area getting ready to go in and have a group meeting with Pat, Spo, and a few others. That was one of those moments when I just said to myself, *Wow.*

MICHAEL LEVINE:

The players were in control of their own destiny at that moment. The friendship between Dwyane and LeBron existed long before 2006. It was and still is a real friendship. We didn't make them friends, but that summer, we had the ability to help them communicate in real time, help them evaluate the possibilities, and to talk through the potential upside of being together. At the end of the day, they themselves decided it would be fun to play together, and so that is what they did. It was a great decision that led them to win two championships and reach four NBA Finals in four years together.

DWYANE WADE, Athlete:

It was a one-stop shop. Everyone they wanted was represented at the time by one company, under one umbrella. So everyone could sit down and talk and figure this thing out together. It was one of those times when it all worked; I know I was happy, and the CAA guys were all terrific.

HOWIE NUCHOW:

You could make a case that there was more money out there for them on their own, but they were willing to give up that money, and we were supportive of that in every way. Pat Riley said, "It took an agency like yours to make this happen." From the beginning we made sure we were going to only support the players' wishes and never think about commissions in this process.

PAT RILEY:

CAA had a lot of impact on the deal. Howie allows his agents to work in the best interest of their clients, but I'm sure he had a lot of influence behind the scenes, and we were able to have all three players come to an agreement.

Even as CAA's representation of athletes continued to get the lion's share of publicity for CAA Sports, it was EMC, the agency's majority owned advisory business, that was gradually and methodically piling up deals.

In 2011, EMC advised the Pac-12 athletic conference on its latest TV rights negotiation, garnering the conference a twelve-year, $3 billion deal with Fox Sports and ESPN. The deal, announced on May 4, was the largest TV rights contract in the history of college athletics.

In that same year, EMC was hired by what would become the new ownership group of the Philadelphia 76ers. On October 18, 2011, a deal to purchase the Philadelphia 76ers was approved by the National Basketball Association's Board of Governors. An ownership group headed by private equity investor Josh Harris, managing partner of Apollo Management, L.P., and including the Blackstone Group executive David Blitzer, paid $300 million for the team in a purchase from Comcast-Spectator. This time, EMC acted as buy-side advisers to Blitzer, helping to analyze media rights and other opportunities in line with the purchase.

DAVID BLITZER, Executive:

The Sixers was our first real effort at investing in a team. I had started by looking at the ownership landscape and talking to people in the business who I trusted. Michael and I have been hanging out closely for years. I'm a passionate sports guy, and I've only had one job, and I love that job, but I love sports and the business of sports. So I've always been jealous of Michael. In many ways, what they're doing was my dream. They're working and making money in sports.

MICHAEL LEVINE:

Blitz and I have been friendly since we met as kids playing sports against one another and really became close during college when he lived at UPenn with two old friends of mine. Our wives and kids are friends, we've shared Yankee tickets since the new stadium opened, have always loved going to sporting events together, and have battled in our fantasy football league for over fifteen seasons.

DAVID BLITZER:

Philly was losing a significant amount of money. I did love the sport. I did love the city and the team, but it also had to make economic sense. We were very diligent about the economic model, which came back to my initial relationship with CAA. It wasn't just, "Okay, let's write a check because it's a cool thing to own a sports team." I remember calling Michael and asking, "Please give me the lay of the land: ownership, dynamics, players, where this team is going, and most important, from a value perspective, talk to me about media rights."

I also wanted them to think about really interesting passionate people that have some brand out there in the market and invite them into the ownership group, and CAA came up with Will Smith, who is now one of our co-owners.

It wasn't long before a football stadium was part of the mix. When the San Francisco 49ers announced they had reached a deal with Levi's (which was represented *by the Wasserman Media Group) for the naming rights to their new home in Santa Clara, California, it was the result of CAA and the 49ers having pitched the stadium to thirty-two companies around the world over a two-year period. At the time, the deal ranked as the third-most-lucrative stadium sponsorship in American sports history. When the paint was dry, CAA had sold more than $650 million worth of ancillary deals and would be collecting hefty commissions on them for the next eighteen years.*

JED YORK, CEO, San Francisco 49ers:

Once we had a vote passed in 2010 in the city, and were approved for the loans from the league, CAA was one of the first calls we made, because we knew they'd done a great job with other venues. They definitely have a different style and brought a bit of swagger to our team; it was fun working with those guys.

PAUL DANFORTH:

We like to partner with people who need help as they go through a transition. The 49ers are a great example. They were a tenant at Candlestick, and after playing there for more than two decades, they were making a move into a new stadium, and they hired us to help them find a partner for it. The stadium was privately financed so they needed help funding construction, and that meant sponsorship. We worked with their chief revenue officer and sponsorship team to try to maximize value. We work on a retainer and a commission basis.

We sat down with them and shared the story we had developed for them. We said, "Let's not just talk about this as a new building. Jerry Jones built the biggest building because that's Jerry Jones and it's Texas, but with Silicon Valley nearby, let's make this the smartest stadium in the world." We had done research on all the companies in the San Francisco area and tried to determine how they could help the 49ers and their fans have a better stadium experience. We met with hundreds of companies. I was on an airplane every week. We thought when we started the project that the sponsorship would go to a tech company, but it wound up being Levi's, because we realized if one tech company bought the naming rights, it would have potentially scared other tech companies away from partnering with the stadium. What we figured out was there was a lot of interest from the tech sector, so we had to figure out who could live with who. We did an Intel deal, a SAP deal, a Citrix deal, and a Brocade deal—all companies in technology, and all that could live with each other.

On May 23, 2011, Time Warner Cable announced the hiring of David Rone as president of TWC Sports. Nuchow and Levine would continue to co-head CAA Sports following Rone's exit. A few months later, the division looked to match its sales capacity with the creation of a corporate consulting practice.

GREG LUCKMAN, Executive:

I head up the corporate consulting division of CAA Sports. We identify and negotiate strategic partnerships on behalf of brands. We focus our efforts on advising companies such as JP Morgan Chase, Emirates Airlines, and Bose, amongst others, in their sports marketing investments. While our clients may be in different categories—financial services, airline, beer—they are all looking to have a conversation with their consumers. We agree on a scope of services and then operate on an annual retainer basis, not commissions like most of the company.

When brands are looking for the types of services an agency can provide for them, we answer them by tapping into the whole power of the agency. That really is our secret sauce. We're very fortunate because of our connectivity and where we sit in this world of pop culture. We recommend and manage the right marketing solution for them, that could be a sponsorship of an event like the U.S. Open Championships in New York, an NFL partnership—if the objective is to gain scale and reach more people nationally—or it could be an endorsement deal with an athlete like when we brokered a deal between Bose and J. J. Watt.

On November 30, 2011, with the announcement of Jimmy Sexton's move to join CAA from SportsTrust Advisors, the CAA Sports presence in the NFL added an additional forty players and thirty pro and college football coaches. Sexton's clients included coaches Rex Ryan and Nick Saban and quarterbacks Philip Rivers and Ryan Fitzpatrick. With Sexton's addition, CAA Football now boasted representation of about 150 NFL players (in 2011, there were approximately 1,700 players in the league), a third of whom had played in a Pro Bowl, and just under half were starting quarterbacks in the league. Nine of the last thirteen of the NFL's most valuable players were in the fold as were nearly a hundred first-round draft selections—more than three times as many as CAA's next closest competitor. Sexton joined the ranks of Tom Condon and Ben Dogra as the leading agents of CAA Football.

JIMMY SEXTON, Agent:

I had my own company, Athletic Resource Management, and had been in the business since 1986. At one time, I was representing more than twenty NBA players, and probably double that number of NFL players, along with many coaches.

It was great growing the business, but I got to a place when I wanted to offer more to my clients. They weren't just players anymore; they were celebrities, entertainers, and businesspeople. I believed CAA gave us a platform to present our clients with a lot more opportunities.

Being in the representation business in sports is amazing. You meet young people in college and watch them progress through their careers and lives. You get them a rookie contract all the way through their veteran contract, and all the while, you watch them develop and mature, not just as a player but as a person, and you're able to help them realize goals they had set for themselves. To me, that's the most satisfying part of the business. At the same time, there are certain clients you have who aren't able to make it, and if they don't know that, you sometimes have to be the one to tell them. Let me tell you, those are really, really rough days.

We don't abandon our clients after they are done playing. We like to catapult them into the next phase of their lives. We always tell our guys, "You may play ten years in the league, but you're still going to be in your early thirties, and there's a good chance you could live longer after you quit playing football than you lived before you even started. You've got a lot of life left to live." So we stay with them, and help bring them into broadcasting and marketing and endorsements. All things we do incredibly well here.

Represented by CAA agent Tom Condon on the field, J. J. Watt, a star player for the Houston Texans, arrived in the NFL as part of the 2011 draft. Off the field, through his representation at CAA, Watt signed deals with an array of companies that included Papa John's, American Family Insurance, Reebok, Gatorade, Ford, and Verizon.

PAUL DANFORTH:

Our overall talent sales group is composed of salespeople who focus on football, baseball, hockey, tennis, and those people roll up into me. Our ideal scenario is for our athletes to share as much as possible about their goals, and how hard they want to work off the field, because quite frankly, some great athletes don't want to dedicate their time to doing commercials; they only want to focus on playing their sport. But in the case of J. J. Watt, he wants to be the face of the NFL. He works really hard. We were on a commercial shoot a few years ago with Yahoo! and I remember he was asking the director, "How do I get better? Tell me. I want to learn!"

We also may have clients who have gone through financial ups and downs, so their desire to work off the field changes. Some athletes aren't concerned about the brands they want to be associated with, but others, like J. J., are. He only wants first-class brands and will turn down other opportunities. We show our athletes all offers that come in for them because we want them to be part of decisions. We will always offer our opinions, but the final word is theirs. We've hosted meetings in our offices and elsewhere for brands to get to know our clients and have a chance to hear them tell their own story.

J. J. WATT, Athlete:

I definitely have a very active business life now. I told these people at CAA what my vision was, what the goals were, and how hard I was willing to work to accomplish what I wanted to do, and then they put me in the right avenues for success.

I want to make the absolute most out of this opportunity, for however long it lasts, because I know that when it's all over, it's over. I believe that if you want to be considered a high quality person, you have to associate yourself with high quality people, and if you're going to endorse products, they've got to be high quality products. Now it's kind of gotten to the point where they really don't bring me any other kinds of opportunities.

Once my football career is over, I'm going to go either one of two ways: The movie and TV thing does interest me, I can't lie about that, so that could be an option. Or, the way that I think is most likely, which is I'll go back to Wisconsin and coach high school football, and just be a small-town regular guy as much as I can. I'm fortunate enough to have made enough money in my career already to where if I wanted to just settle down back in Wisconsin and live a normal life, I will be able to do it.

As studios increasingly focused on the production of tentpole films and blockbusters, often left to fend for themselves were mid-budget adult dramas, films that could be made for $60 million and below. Increasingly hard-pressed to find financing for these projects, CAA—along with many of the other agencies—recognized the need to fill a gap that the studios had created. The agency's film financing department was hardly new; John Ptak, and later Rick Hess, among others, had been involved in raising money to get movies made. The group was now headed by Roeg Sutherland and Micah Green.

Sutherland joined CAA in 2001 in the mailroom; Green joined in 2005, from the film sales business Cinetic. CAA's film financing department consists of twelve staff, eight of whom are agents. Films put together by CAA's film financing department in recent years include: 12 Years a Slave, Black Swan, The Butler, American Hustle, The Imitation Game, *and* Looper. *In 2015, the department was involved in the production of more than seventy films.*

ROEG SUTHERLAND, Agent:

The nature of the business has changed dramatically to the point where every motion picture agent in this building has to help put movies together in order to help create the most possible job opportunities for clients. It's no longer just about finding jobs for clients. We all are passionate about doing the work to make films happen for our clients, which is a good thing, as it's really the only way we can be successful.

MICAH GREEN, Agent:

Our goal simply put is to enable the production and successful release of as many great films each year as is humanly possible. We do this without regard to whether the major studios want these movies to exist or not.

One way we do this is by acting as strategic adviser to film investors and funded production companies. We work confidentially on behalf of very well-capitalized investors to find the strongest projects available, and to assemble them with the very best talent we can find, with rational budgets and well-considered distribution plans.

Here, before clients lock into a project, before they have decided exactly what their movie is going to be, we have conversations about their vision for the project, and where it can fit as a commercial proposition within the marketplace. We try to answer several fundamental questions before we begin pitching it to investors. How can it best be realized in the film business as it exists today? Is it likely to be fast-tracked through a studio's internal development process, or can we increase the film's odds of getting made by keeping it independent through development and packaging and presenting it to studios as a complete package or even as a finished film?

TOM HANKS:

A lot of times actors and directors end up shepherding their own work up the food chain, but Richard Lovett shepherded *Cap-*

tain Phillips into my hands from the get-go. *Captain Phillips* didn't exist in any other place except in the minds of the studio with me playing Captain Phillips. He got heard on that. Those things do kind of happen.

RON HOWARD:

The studio system is shrinking, but there are so many other ways to get projects going at an agency like CAA. They have relationships with financiers, companies, and distributors. It's about trying to find that intersection point between what their client base, their talent, has to offer and what the marketplace will bear. I think they do it well, and I think they continue to do that thing that I care about the most, which is to allow a person like me to be able to connect with talented artists I want to work with.

MICAH GREEN:

Beginning eight years ago, we cultivated a community of investors, ultimately creating a class of high-end financier-producers that did not exist previously. At that time, we saw smart people with money and taste who wanted to succeed in the entertainment business, but few people on the inside of the business were truly looking out for them in a meaningful way.

Sometimes we can help an investor understand up front that their financial agenda cannot be reconciled with their creative interest. It's better to help an investor avoid making an expensive mistake than to enable a short-term victory of a movie getting financed at the cost of a very public failure which could chill the entire market.

What was customary for independent financiers a few years ago, and is still the norm at studios, is that the studio options the underlying material for the film, and then controls the project for the duration of a term, which can be several years or more. What is most challenging about this is that this shift in control occurs prior to a commitment to actually fund the project's production.

A project can therefore be held up or killed entirely if the film-maker finds herself or himself at odds with the studio over creative or financial choices that arise during development or packaging. Our agency has worked to change that norm, particularly within the independent realm, encouraging financier-producers to work alongside talent as collaborators rather than gatekeepers. The companies we advise have been great partners in this respect, and have really helped transform the nature of the relationship between filmmaker and financier. Their approach is often to attach to a project at an early stage and fuel its development and packaging. They work collaboratively to arrive at a package and budget that the filmmaker is happy with and which they feel comfortable greenlighting. At the same time, most of these companies are determined to play the role of facilitator for artists and not to risk being perceived as obstructionist, so where they find themselves out of sync with a filmmaker, they will generally let them take the project and move on to other financiers rather than hold up its production.

ROEG SUTHERLAND:

Black Swan fell apart in preproduction. That was probably one of the most challenging movies our department has put together, but it was obviously worth it. When you are close to production and an issue arises with the financing, we are going to do everything we can to make sure that movie happens. In the case of *Black Swan,* the initial financier failed to come through with the money they had committed, and we had only days to replace them before the movie would have shut down. Fortunately, we were able to convince Brian Oliver at Cross Creek to step in quickly and co-finance with Fox Searchlight, which saved the day. *12 Years a Slave* was initially set up with RiverRoad, but the budget was high and RiverRoad was not comfortable greenlighting it without a big domestic deal in place. Luckily we were able to get New Regency to take that on just a few weeks before production.

TOM HANKS:

Here's the thing. Agents lie to you every day. There's been plenty of times when this person wanted to get material to me or vice versa, or I was trying to get in on something that might have already been established, and there's just no guarantee it's going to work out. But all of that can be superseded by a secret meeting between yourself and a filmmaker. And just because an agent says it's good doesn't mean you're going to want to do it.

JOEL LUBIN, Agent:

I came to CAA in 2004 from William Morris, and am the co-head of motion picture talent with Jack. We have about thirty-five to forty agents in our department.

JACK WHIGHAM, Agent:

I also came in 2004, from Weil, Gotshal & Manges, a big law firm back east. Joel and I happen to be best friends. Joel has a wonderful analytical brain and processes information extremely well. I'm slightly more emotional, so we balance each other out. Our offices are very close and we're in each other's offices often. We are really sensitive to each other about information to make sure no one is ever caught off guard, so we make sure we're overcommunicating with each other.

JOEL LUBIN:

Everybody in our department is in real-time communication. So if somebody talks to somebody, whether it's on the phone or in an email, then everybody's responsible for making sure that information's communicated immediately to colleagues.

JACK WHIGHAM:

A lot of our conversations inside the department center on the ethos and philosophy of getting everyone working as hard and as thoughtfully and as efficiently as possible.

DAVID OYELOWO, Actor:

I've always felt that my agents are my employees. I pay them a wage whenever I work, and on that basis, they work for me and their job is to help me realize my goals. I think a lot of actors think they work for their agents; they are so happy to have an agent and give too much weight to the direction in which their agent wants their career to go. My goal every day is to outwork my agents so that they are inspired to work harder for me. I don't think there's any agent who wants to feel like they have to put dead weight on their back and try and sell it to the world.

I was at a different agency and met with CAA, specifically Joel Lubin, who I really really liked. I ended up not signing with CAA, partly because I felt it was too bright and shiny. I was concerned that all that glitters is not gold, and I was intimidated by how polished everything looked and felt. But over the next year while I was at a different agency, Joel would stay in contact with me and check in on a project I had spoken to him about that really captured his imagination, a film called *A United Kingdom.* It was a film that I had been wrestling away with for a few years, trying to get made about a beautiful interracial period love story. And it really captured Joel's imagination. I remember having a certain long conversation with him and then really taking the time to work me through the path whereby that film could get made. And with time, I became disgruntled with my current agency and ended up signing with Joel, rather than the agency, but then I watched the agency facilitate the conversations we had been having over the last year, and it was very eye-opening to me. I still believe that you sign with an agent, not an agency, but boy, when that bright and shiny thing works, it really works.

JACK WHIGHAM:

My best day was when I met my wife here. I remember the day that I first met her in the mailroom. My life is really tied to the bones of this place, and that makes sort of a cosmic connection.

JOEL LUBIN:

My best day was when Michael Cooper left WME and came over here. We are close friends who worked there together, and after a long, intense courtship, he came over. It was extremely gratifying.

On February 29, 2012, Dan Aloni suddenly exited the CAA fold. After joining the agency out of UTA in 2005, Aloni experienced several rocky relationships inside CAA that really never improved. At the time, Aloni's top client, Chris Nolan, was directing and producing big-budget projects including Inception, the Batman *trilogy, and* Superman, *and would follow Aloni to WME.*

RICHARD LOVETT:

My highest priority is culture, and our culture is defined by the way we treat each other. We prioritize our work in support of colleagues. We have each other's back, and, of course, don't work at counter-purpose with colleagues. I believe that the culture of our company is our most important differentiator; the reason our work for clients in every area is best in class. The culture of the company has a way of ejecting those who don't fit. I had many conversations with Dan, but he was never able to change his behavior.

DAN ALONI:

I left because they fired me. They tried to discredit me. They put several people I worked with under contract at the company for more money. They tried to sideswipe me.

Richard Lovett had tried to force me into running the motion picture department with Risa Gertner and Todd Feldman. I had regular meetings with them and Richard about the department. I also had a meeting with Richard every week for five years. To my knowledge, I was the only person in the motion picture department to do so. We met about management of the department: who was doing well or not, packaging movies, signing of potential clients, and the culture of the department. I was very honest with Richard repeatedly about how I felt that a lot of things weren't working. Too much favoritism from the people who were running the department. I told him that consistently for a long time.

ADAM KANTER:

I guess there are a lot of people that say he was a culture killer or didn't work well with people, but I personally never had that experience with Dan. He is a friend. I first knew him when he was at UTA. His wife and I went to high school and then college together, so I knew the personal side of him as well as the professional one. I had heard something about him not working well with others, but I don't know anything about the specifics.

DAN ALONI:

They wanted to discredit me in order to retain clients. They want you to leave the business or become a manager. They make things up about people.

KEVIN HUVANE:

One of the greatest qualities about Richard is that he always wants to see the good in people. So when someone asks for help to improve themselves, he believes you should absolutely help get them there, and he does just that. I really admire this quality that is totally free of cynicism.

DAN ALONI:

I often find myself explaining to people what happens at CAA and how it works. Richard is just a bad guy and that's really the bottom line. He used to say all the time when something good happened at the company, "This is great for the good guys." It always made me feel uncomfortable—if we were the good guys, who are the bad guys? They destroyed so many people's lives.

Patrick Whitesell had left and taken his business from CAA eleven years before me. Nobody had done that since. One of my proudest achievements is feeling I started a wave of change from CAA's dominance by being the first person to leave and take major business away. Then others wanted to follow and took all of their business. Warren Zavala, then Stuart Manashil left and took all of their clients. I feel I helped them realize they could. A trend was started.

I think what is starting to happen at CAA is similar to what happened at the old, old William Morris Agency. It is not fun when you see a lot of people who are treated poorly and management doesn't care. They really don't care. I spent so much time trying to explain to Richard the problem of what was going on in the motion picture department and how unhappy so many people were there. He ignored it.

Back in 2010, LeBron James had asked Leon Rose and CAA to hire young Rich Paul, whom James had met back in Cleveland while Paul was a teenager. For James, the move was reminiscent of what he had done years before with his childhood friend Maverick Carter. James, who was only twenty, gave Carter, all of twenty-three, the keys to managing his empire. By most accounts, Rich Paul was no charity hire but rather a solid professional, and Rose was happy to bring him into the fold.

CAA consultant William Wesley, flamboyantly known as World Wide Wes, was a close friend of Rose's and heavily involved in the recruitment of athletes as a consultant for CAA. All might have been well except Wesley and Paul operated on different circuits. Tension continued to build between the two to the point where Rose decided the ticking bomb must be defused. In London at the 2012 Olympics, Rose had Wes and Paul join him for a lunch and a frank discussion designed to clear the air, with Rose later telling colleagues he felt better about the situation. And so he did—until the night of September 12, less than one month later, when it was abruptly announced that Rich Paul was leaving CAA. Rose, shocked and hurt, had come to think of Paul not just as a protégé but as a friend and thus didn't see why Paul failed to give him warning—or even tell him personally that he'd decided to leave.

The bigger surprise would come just twenty-four hours later, when LeBron James sent notice that he, too, was leaving the agency—and would join Paul's new firm, Klutch Sports, to be based in Cleveland.

The move confirmed a shift in James's business strategy since joining the Heat. In 2011, he'd struck a deal with Fenway Sports Group (FSG), led by Red Sox owner John Henry and chairman Tom Werner, to partner with his own sports marketing firm LRMR Branding & Marketing and oversee the firm's global marketing opportunities and commercial interests. James also received a minority stake in Liverpool, the soccer club owned by FSG. According to the Wall Street Journal, *it was the first time that a professional athlete at his peak had invested in a team that in terms of prominence and prestige ranked among the most elite and formidable in the world.*

LEBRON JAMES, Athlete:

CAA and their team were amazing partners. I really appreciated everything Leon and the people at CAA did for me while I was there. Leaving CAA wasn't personal and had nothing to do with them. It didn't matter who was representing me, but when Rich was ready to start his own business, that's where I was going. First, I believe in Rich and know he is the best agent for me. He understands me, my challenges, and wants what's best for me. If Rich was in the game now and we had never met as kids, he would still be my agent. More important, I went with Rich because I am very serious about building my community. When I was twenty years old, I fired my agent and turned the business over to a few guys I grew up with. I didn't do that so I could have my crew around. Nobody convinced me to put them on payroll. I did it because I wanted to build my community. I wanted my team to show young athletes that you can build businesses. And they earned it. That if your team works as hard off the court as you do on the court, great things can happen. A young black kid from Cleveland without a college degree can be as good, or even better, at being an agent as the guy who got his law degree from Harvard. But Rich worked for it. There was never a handout and he's never rested. He grinded at CAA to learn the business. I watched him grind for years. And when he was ready to make the jump, I was 100 percent behind him.

LEON ROSE:

I helped bring Rich into the agency and supported him in his growth. LeBron decided to be loyal to his friend when Rich decided to do his own thing, and I understood that. But in the end, I'm proud of the work CAA was able to do for LeBron, and help put him in a position to achieve his ultimate goal of winning his first championship.

MICHAEL LEVINE:

We had very close relationships with Rich. Rich was someone we spent a lot of time with and always believed would be a great agent. We cared a lot about him. We understood that a young agent, to have the chance to go represent the biggest superstar in the world out on his own, was something special for him to do. We got it. My biggest issue with Rich at that moment was how he told us he was leaving and how the particulars were handled. I felt he owed Leon and us collectively a little more compassion and respect than what we ended up getting. I shared that with him directly and he seemed to understand my perspective and felt bad. I could tell, and after I explained that to him, he got it. It all happened so quickly and he was in a difficult situation.

HOWIE NUCHOW:

LeBron and Rich had their own dreams, and LeBron was going to stay loyal to a friend that he dreamed with. We understood that.

One year after the parting of LeBron James and CAA, Maverick Carter approached the agency on behalf of his client to see if there was any interest in handling the six-time all-star for television and movie opportunities—everything not covered by his NBA contract or endorsement deals. The deal would be exclusively about getting LeBron into show business.

Perhaps shockingly, CAA said no. "Oh, we'll take you back," agency executives essentially told James, "but only if we get the whole galaxy," not just limited slices of it. There was actually CAA precedent for accommodating a superstar in the *manner Carter requested for James; Real Madrid superstar Cristiano Ronaldo had just such an arrangement with the agency. But there was a major difference: Ronaldo was never a client who had walked out on CAA.*

James signed with WME the next day.

MICHAEL LEVINE:

LeBron always had his own interests outside of CAA from the very beginning. We weren't LeBron's off-court marketing agency, which meant LeBron was a different type of client than Dwyane Wade or Chris Bosh.

Both CAA and Rich have had great runs in basketball. I am most comforted by the fact that Leon has been able to thrive as much as he has since then. He is a man of honor and dignity, and lives by a special code in the way that he treats people in his circle.

CAA Sports made an initial foray into European soccer in 2009 when it became involved with international athlete and property representation, along with corporate consulting and media rights, but the big move occurred on October 1, 2012, when CAA Eleven, a Swiss-based subsidiary of CAA, was awarded the contract over dozens of other companies to sell broadcast rights for the latest cycle of UEFA's national team competitions—the 2016 UEFA European Championship Qualifiers, along with the 2016 UEFA European Championship, and the European qualifiers for the 2018 FIFA World Cup. The UEFA deal garnered much attention. Previously, the organization had only sold off rights to matches individually. Now, for the first time ever, they centralized the media and the sponsorship rights to hundreds of matches. Those broadcast rights could be extraordinarily lucrative given the sport's global footprint. A match between Germany and France isn't just sold in those two countries but to territories around the world, and if you wanted to show that game in Argentina, South Africa, Japan, or even the United States, then your network and your money were headed to CAA. The deal called for CAA to take the risk on overhead, in exchange for a range of commissions (roughly between 3 and 5 percent) based on revenue performance. Recently, the agency was given even more inventory to sell, and CAA's commissions from the deal are already in the tens of millions.

DAVID O'CONNOR:

Charlie Stillitano and I got us into the soccer business. We started out advising two big clubs on marketing and sponsorship advisory work: FC Barcelona and Chelsea football club. Those were relationships that I developed. We started an event that is now the International Champions Cup, which is touring European soccer teams in the off-season in the summer. But really what it did is it got our feet wet in the international soccer business and got us relationships with all sorts of people. That led to one of the biggest successes of the company, something that I was spearheading and intimately involved with, which was when we created CAA Eleven. CAA Eleven is a separate company, but it is majority owned and controlled by CAA, and CAA gets a lion's share of the revenues. We won the competition to manage all of the sponsorship, advising, and media rights around all of the national team play for Europe as governed by UEFA. So it's the Euros, Euro qualifying, and World Cup qualifying for Europe, it's Russia, it's Eastern Europe, it's Western Europe; all of the big federations like England, France, Italy, Spain, Russia, Germany are governed by UEFA. And we won the competition to manage all those rights over IMG, Sport 5, and other incumbents in the international sports advisory space. We were the dark horse and came from way behind to win.

HOWIE NUCHOW:

I don't believe many in our industry thought we were going to win that. Everyone thought it was going to be either IMG or Lagadère; after all, there were fifty-three federations and Lagadère had the rights to more than twenty-five of them. So when it was announced we were the winner, it was a surprise to many. Before this, people thought we would be focused on our domestic business, but after this I think people in our industry understood we would not settle for just being a domestic business. This was a strong signal that we were going to expand to sell inventory all over the world.

DAVID O'CONNOR:

That was a big one because it really established our presence internationally. Which led to other things, including our forays into IMG and potential acquisition, neither of which happened.

HOWIE NUCHOW:

Ronaldinho at the time was the biggest soccer star in the world. Vino and I were going to Brazil in an attempt to sign him. I had never even been out of the country on business before, so the entire pursuit seemed like it would be a lot of fun.

I had just spent a bit of time with Doc before this and thought he was a great guy and it would be important to have him involved with us. To attempt to get him to join Vino and me on this trip I kept e-mailing him pictures of salsa and samba shoes, and said, "You've got to come to Brazil with us. It'll be fun." And Doc said, "Great. I'm in. Let's go." So we traveled all the way to Brazil and the meeting with Ronaldinho was supposed to be on a Monday, but Ronaldinho didn't show up until Wednesday, so we were "stuck" in Rio. I was expecting Doc to start losing his mind, and I said to Vino, "Oh my God, we brought one of the owners of the company all the way here, and the guy isn't even in the country." I said to Doc, "I feel awful about what's happening." He looked at me and said, "We're chasing the biggest soccer player in the world. This is what we do. Don't worry about it." We realized at this time, *With support like this we have a chance to do really well. These guys are the types of owners who are going to continually back our play.* To some it might seem like a silly little thing, but it was important to us.

We wound up going to Ronaldinho's house, where he was having a birthday party for his sister. So we're arriving at this massive house in Brazil, and there's security all along the driveway outside. Doc was dancing with the mother at the party and we didn't talk a stitch of business for a long while that night. We just met family members and many folks who were important to Ronaldinho and his family. At some point late into the early morning we shook hands on a deal that would allow us to sell some sponsorship for Ronaldinho.

We wound up doing a very big deal for him. His portfolio was not as big as we had thought. He had a big Nike deal, but there weren't many global deals beneath that, which was surprising to us for one of the most marketable guys on the globe. But because of Vino, Danforth, and our staff, we knew we could deliver a deal that would outsize the other deals he had beneath Nike. And that's exactly how it worked out. We got him a global deal and that was an important next step for us into the world of international soccer. We learned a lot about the soccer world through this experience with Ronaldinho and his brother.

Practically every facet of agency business between CAA and WME/IMG is hotly contested now, most definitely including the lucrative arena of popular music. Other agencies represent music clients, but these two have genuine disdain for each other, and each claims to be without peer—making competition for acts especially intense. Lady Gaga's with CAA; Adele's with WME. Springsteen and Katy Perry occupy the CAA corner; the Weeknd, Sam Smith, Selena Gomez are at WME. And so on.

The modern music agent needs to discover great talent, deliver for clients in booking a great tour, make them—to the degree that they want—an important part of the burgeoning festival circuit, and find new opportunities elsewhere, like WME did with Pharrell Williams and Blake Shelton via The Voice. *But one of the niftiest tricks a music agent can pull off, because it can be the most difficult, is to bring fresh commercial life to greats who haven't made the front pages of* Billboard *or played key venues since the dawn of digital.*

In December of 2012, Led Zeppelin became one of the year's five esteemed recipients of the prestigious Kennedy Center Honors. A black-tie'd audience of Washington celebrities, including President and Mrs. Barack Obama, cheered the reconstituted British-born band wildly as its surviving members stood in the celebrity box and took bows, alongside fellow honorees Dustin Hoffman, David Letterman, blues musician George "Buddy" Guy, and ballerina Natalia Makarova.

But it was the evening's finale that proved most-talked-about afterward (including more than 10 million hits on the Internet) when Ann and Nancy Wilson of Heart boldly tackled one of the grandest anthems in all of rock, the epochal Zeppelin classic "Stairway to Heaven," with the Wilsons surrounded by an incredible lineup of musicians—movingly among them, drummer Jason Bonham, son of Led Zep's own virtuoso drummer, John Bonham, who died tragically in 1980. High in a VIP box, the Zep's surviving members—veteran performers who'd probably "seen it all" during their numerous world tours as celebrated wild men of rock— appeared to be genuinely overwhelmed. Robert Plant even had tears in his eyes.

The evening, and all the work that led up to it, are but one example of what agents are supposed to do for their clients, and Ann and Nancy Wilson can attest to that. Their appearance onstage that night would not only lead to their being inducted into the Rock & Roll Hall of Fame, but would recharge their careers and send them back out onto the road with a better class of venues and a higher level of revenues.

ROB LIGHT:

I have had the good fortune to represent Heart, and have for a long time. We were looking for a way to gain them visibility, to help their career, and wanted to remind people of their immense talent. I read that Led Zeppelin was going to be honored at the Kennedy Center Honors and I called George Stevens [Jr.]— the producer—the next day, and said, "You have to have Heart on the show. No one sings Led Zeppelin better than Ann Wilson. No one." I must have sent them ten different emails of video clips, records, recordings. I mean I bombarded him. We kept the manager in the loop, so she knew what CAA was doing. It's what we do as agents, to find ways outside of just booking dates to help. Finally, we got a call, George said they were going to put them on, and it turned out to be one of the great moments in the history of the Kennedy Center Honors. The video clip of their performance was seen by over twelve million people. Heart has always been incredible, but I do believe that performance and George Stevens's belief helped get them into the Rock & Roll Hall of Fame.

NANCY WILSON, Musician:

We had just recently had a meeting with Rob to kind of whine, complain, and gripe about us having to do what we call "hog rallies" we've been playing—you know, county fairs. We told him, "Hey, we're choking on the dust out here! Can you find us anything a little more exotic?" And that was part of the reason he came up with the idea of us doing the Zepplin tribute. We'd done a lot of Led Zeppelin songs along the way. It was a brilliant move.

ANN WILSON, Musician:

We were out on the road and heard from our assistant that this was going to happen, and it went really fast from there. There was hardly a chance to really do much planning.

NANCY WILSON:

It was more of a seat-of-your-pants production. There were only two rehearsals, and the second one was on the actual day of the performance.

ANN WILSON:

I grew up with that song, it's in our DNA, and to sing it in that company, with the president and first lady looking on and all of those incredible famous creative people in the audience, plus of course, Led Zeppelin, was just sublime and amazing.

NANCY WILSON:

At different times in your career you think, "Ah god! We can't even seem to get arrested!" But after the Kennedy Center? We definitely got arrested. It went so viral, and the change after was really noticeable. When we went back out, we wound up adding a set of Led Zepplin songs with Jason Bonham playing and various local choirs playing with us, kind of a mini-version of the Kennedy Center. People were extremely excited about it, and that live tour did really well.

ANN WILSON:

That was definitely one of those rare moments when creativity, business, and opportunity all come together at once.

After twenty-eight years with CAA, Rand Holston took his high-profile client list (including Stephen King and Rob Reiner) to Paradigm Motion Picture's literary department, of which he is now the head. The new world order at CAA was now beyond Darwinian—no matter how long one had been with the agency. It was as if the old and bizarre William Morris quote Phil Weltman heard at his firing had been resurrected: "We put you in the computer and you came up wanting."

For many others, if you weren't fired, you could either take a severe pay cut and live with it or be told you needed to find somewhere else to go. Not everyone would be given such an ultimatum, but some elected to leave anyway. A climate of fear is rarely fun, this one being no exception, and the next few years would still see more former CAAers moving to Paradigm—among them Martin Spencer, Ken Stovitz, Bob Bookman, and Adam Kanter.

Clients were not immune. For years, the operating philosophy had become if the hill looked too high for agents to climb on a client's behalf, or if their star's luminance appeared to be fading, there seemed less and less patience in this new harsher world. Case in point: Kathryn Bigelow, the richly talented director, had a rough stretch after helming K-19: The Widowmaker, *and at a CAA motion picture staff meeting, several agents advocated for her termination. It was only after a few agents, including an almost teary-eyed impassioned Ken Stovitz rose to defend her, that Bigelow was finally issued a stay of execution. She would go on to direct* The Hurt Locker, *which won the Academy Award for Best Picture, and the wildly acclaimed* Zero Dark Thirty, *but hers was a close call.*

RAND HOLSTON:

I left CAA at the end of 2012. I was fired. After twenty-eight years, it was a surprise. I had been dedicating half my time to overseeing the CAA office in China and that wasn't a profit source for the company, so it brought my overall earnings down from previous years. It was the first and only time in my life I was ever fired and it wasn't easy. But when those things happen to you, you just have to keep going.

MARSHALL HERSKOVITZ:

They fired him, and then they took it back. They never take it back—but they took it back! Because everyone said, "You can't fire

Rand." They went back to him and said, "Okay, please stay," and he basically said fuck you to them. And that's the moment when he could have said, "Okay, I'll stay."

It became one of the most wrenching experiences of my and Ed's [Zwick] whole career. It was very, very sad. Ed and I sat there looking at each other for weeks, literally saying, "What are we going to do?" Because we loved Rand, and thought about leaving CAA because we wanted to go with him. That was the hardest decision we've ever had to make. But we felt that objectively, we were still better served at CAA than to go to Paradigm. It's just how we felt at that moment. The issue was access—access to material, but it was just so horrible. And it was so painful to tell him. I'm still friends with Rand, we call each other, we speak to each other; I give him so much credit for being willing to just not hate me for the fact that we made that decision.

BOB BOOKMAN:

They gave me a specific warning, not long after the TPG investment, and I think a lot of people got a similar warning, which was: "You're overcompensated, we're going to cut you over the next two years. The first year you're going to be cut to here, and the second year you're going to be cut to here." They said, "That will be the base, and if you perform above our expectations, you still could get more." I did still love the company, but I believed I would do better elsewhere than what they were offering.

DAN ALONI:

Under the Ovitz regime at CAA, whenever somebody was not working out at the company or they wanted to figure out how to transition them out, they got them jobs. All of a sudden, you read this person got a new job and you never knew they had been fired. It happened a hundred times. Under Lovett, as opposed to the old "let's help our colleagues out and we're all family" kind of thing, they all of a sudden would fire them and it would get announced in Deadline Hollywood while CAA would figure out how to keep the agent's clients.

JEREMY ZIMMER:

A lot of that drama and pain was passed on to people who historically had been paid great and then the management started looking around and said, "What do we need these guys for? Do we really need him?" And suddenly guys who had been there for fifteen, twenty years, who thought they were just going to be CAA lifers, were getting pushed out without a parachute.

Think about it: You're a "senior agent"; you've been living over at CAA your whole life representing a nice handful of clients, and you think they're your clients. Richard Lovett hasn't told you that you serve at his whim.

DAN ALONI:

Ovitz created a certain kind of company with CAA. Everyone worked together. It may have been a threatening environment to the outside, like to studios and other agencies, but inside, everyone clung together. And every year you could count on walking in and getting a check for more money. Then Ovitz left and the young guys took over, and it became a totally different dynamic. They tried to emulate what Ovitz did, but they couldn't. They didn't change with the times. You now have a majority of people in the motion picture department who are really unhappy. They hate it. They don't enjoy the experience, and most of them are getting paid less and less because the money is going to a select group of people. And they don't know what to do about it. They're scared.

BOB BOOKMAN:

The day that I left, David O'Connor said—maybe not even so many words—"I'm glad you got the message." And the tone in which he said it was like, *I'm really happy for you because I really didn't want you to be miserable; you got the message and you acted accordingly, great going.* That was the way I interpreted it.

I was there twenty-seven years, and it was like, "Here's your hat, what's your hurry?" And I then said to him, "Are you now going to have me frog-marched out of the building?" And he said, "Well, are you planning to leave?" And I said, "Honestly I'd like to just stop by my office and say good-bye to my assistant, and then I'd like to leave." And he goes, "That's fine."

ADAM KANTER:

I left CAA in March of 2013. It was my decision one hundred percent, and it wasn't a decision I came to lightly. It was something that had been brewing. It was the only place I had ever worked. Right out of college. Twenty-four years. I had this great office and was doing very well. It wasn't that I didn't want to be an agent anymore, I just didn't want to be an agent in that corporate environment anymore. I wanted to try something new and be in a more personal, less corporate setting.

SIMON KINBERG:

When Martin [Spencer] was leaving, it was a really, really hard decision, honestly. During that transition, for the first time since I was twenty-five when I had met Martin, I met with other agents at WME and a few other places, but I ended up staying at CAA. It felt like home to me—I had been there since I was twenty-five—and I had become familiar with one of the other agents there. They'd obviously done really well for me and by me.

Risa [Gertner] is the person there in my life now, and we talk every single day, oftentimes more than once a day. I'm not actually a particularly good deal maker; I don't understand a lot of the mechanics of the deals. I actually tend to be almost embarrassed by the deals themselves, because to be honest, I really would do this for free. So I feel it's all good.

JEREMY ZIMMER:

When they push you out of the building, you leave and you don't take any of your clients with you. You wake up and you realize, *All my clients have been distributed to all these other young agents. I'm no longer an agent. I don't own anything.*

JIM BERKUS:

There are two things I tell people to keep in mind about our business: One, your clients aren't your friends. You're a paid friend, that's different. They may love you, they may think you're a great person, but at the end of the day you work for them. They pay you money. They're loyal, but they expect you to do a job. So that can be a very hard thing sometimes. If you're a young agent, you get somebody their first gig, you love each other, you're having dinner every night, your wives are best friends, and then all of a sudden, one day something happens where they perceive that somebody else can do a better job. They love you, but somebody else can give them more opportunity. And once that happens, usually they leave. Don't ever get confused about loyalty: it may help you over some rough spots, but it's always going to be about how you perform.

Two, if you're going to run an agency or create an agency, that means you're going to be firing some people. Nice people. And that's hurtful. But that's what you've gotta do if you want to build an organization, because not everybody has the right stuff.

Nick Khan had been an agent with Broder Webb Chervin Silbermann since 2005 and continued at ICM once the two agencies merged in 2006. The firm had big plans for him, but the hungry and restless Khan didn't believe ICM was big or agile enough to provide the foundation he needed for all his plans. He left ICM for CAA on April 26, 2012. ICM executives were considerably less than pleased— particularly since they had invested a large amount of time and effort in Khan and expected him to build them a bigger and better talent representation practice for broadcasting.

NICK KHAN, Agent:

My parents were immigrants from Iran. They came over in 1964 and my sister and I were born here. My father was a salesman in Las Vegas, my mother stayed at home, and their constant message to us was "Get a good education, you won't have to work as hard as we do." So after college I went right into law school. When I graduated, I had $200 in the bank, but I knew I had to be able to take two months off and study to pass the bar. So I sent out the top of a postcard to *Wheel of Fortune* and auditioned for that show. There were 1,000 people auditioning; fortunately for me 990 of them were eighty-five years or older, and I got on the show. I wound up winning $16,500 and was able to take the bar review course and passed it. I worked as a lawyer for seven years. At first I was in federal court defending people accused of crimes. It was interesting work, but as I started getting a little older, I was noticing that instead of defending the wrongly accused inner-city kid, I was defending drug dealers.

I was now in my mid-twenties, and got a call from Freddie Roach, the boxing trainer. I had watched him fight as a kid growing up in Vegas and I had helped him in a lawsuit against his gym. And Freddie thought I did really good work on that. He called me a couple of days later—this is either 2002 or 2003—and he said, "Hey, I have a fighter, nobody's ever heard of him, who's looking for a lawyer to sue his old promoter. Would you be willing to meet him at the Vagabond Hotel in Hollywood? His name is Manny Pacquiao." So I met Manny there, became Pacquiao's lawyer, sued the then promoter, helped win that case, and met the guy working ringside for ESPN, Joe Tessitore, who then introduced me to Jim Lampley and Max Kellerman. I then started representing them, in addition to Freddie Roach, as a lawyer and transitioned to agenting.

I had worked at the old Broder agency when I was in law school and had become friendly with some of the principals there who were then at ICM, including Ted Chervin and Chris Silbermann, and pitched them on the idea of hiring me as a television agent, because at the end of the day broadcast is a television business, not a sports business. They were looking to expand their television biz and it was a really affordable deal: three years, for $150,000; $160,000; and $170,000. I thought they were being generous.

It was hard. ICM had lost a lot of clients in the talent space and the sports buyers didn't know then who that agency was, so you'd sort of have to introduce not only yourself but the agency. I called a lot of people; a lot didn't call back. I quickly realized it's not about the agent or the agency—it's about the client. If you have the client, everyone will call you back.

Steve Lafferty contacted me and told me they had heard great things about me and said, "We will give you and your clients the support you don't have at ICM," and because this was 2012, he was able to also say, "Look at the sports business we are building. You'll be tapped into a natural resource of clients as certain people segue out of basketball, hockey, football, baseball, et cetera, and they want to get into television." Then I got another call from him and he said, "Can you meet Richard Lovett in an hour? He wants to keep it private, so you can meet him at the Mosaic Hotel in Beverly Hills." I said, "Sure. Where should I meet him—in the restaurant or in the lobby?" He said, "No, just tell the front desk that you're meeting with Richard Lovett and they'll tell you where to go." When I showed up at the front desk, they gave me a room key. I walked in and there were refreshments, ice, and some snacks. Two minutes later, Richard came in and we met for about forty-five minutes. They had already made me an offer and were trying to close it. Richard said, "What do you think happens when a great agent comes to a great agency? If you think you're great, which we think you are, we believe this is the best agency in the business. Just imagine what you can do with your business and the success you will have." Afterward, he said, "Okay, let me leave first. I'm going to go out the back and you go out the front, and no one will know we met." Of course as a married man you do later have to explain to your spouse why you have a hotel room key in your pocket on a workday, but I digress.

SAGE STEELE, Sportscaster:

It took me a long time to come to the realization that I would be best represented by somebody who's part of a big agency, because

I had always wanted more of a boutiquey feel. I thought that fit my personality more. But a couple things with other agents hadn't gone well; I didn't feel like I had been properly represented. But it's a fine line. I know these top agents have a ton of clients, and when you have a handful of women at the same network with only so many jobs. At some point I believe that there always is a conflict of interest. It's unavoidable. So that was one of our big questions to him, and I think he gave us as good and as honest of an answer as he could, which was, "Listen. I'm not the one that makes the ultimate decision. I represent you. I represent Lindsay [Czarniak], Hannah [Storm], and others. I obviously will present you all to them and they make the ultimate decision." I don't think there's a perfect situation with that, and I know there are things that go on behind the scenes and private conversations that I'll never know about and it's probably better that way.

I think the way that Nick stood out to me is that I still felt like I meant a lot to him, not just as an on-air person but more important as a human being. And I need to like that person as a human being as well. My husband and I met Nick and sat down and talked to him, and the moment after Nick left our house we didn't even have to say anything. We just started laughing. It was a no-brainer. I just had to get to the point where I was okay with being with those three letters, you know?

JOHN SKIPPER:

The person I've dealt with the most at CAA is Nick Khan. He is one of the rare guys who will—at any time in the twenty-four-hour clock—respond to you. Sometimes you send him an e-mail at two o'clock in the morning because you really don't want to engage, and you get the answer back in about three minutes. There is no time that's off limits.

NICK KHAN:

The negotiations about Kirk Herbstreit's new deal hadn't been going well. Skipper had delegated the negotiation to one of his top guys. I reached out to Skipper before the Super Bowl in New Orleans and said, "We've got a problem. Do you want to sit down and talk?" And he said, "Yeah, let's meet at this dive bar in New Orleans," and we wound up drinking rum and sketching out on a cocktail napkin what the important Herbstreit deal points were. We had authorization from Kirk to close at a certain number, and then we hit that number after fifteen minutes and shook hands. Skipper gave me the cocktail napkin and said, "E-mail this to me when you have the chance. The deal is closed."

MICHAEL LEVINE:

Tebow's a really interesting example. I think when I first met him after his playoff run with the Broncos, there were some people around him who were concerned that with Jimmy Sexton as his longtime football agent, CAA Sports would have too much influence in his life if we represented all of his interests, so he made a different choice.

NICK KHAN:

I met Tim Tebow prior to him being cut by the New England Patriots. I got a call from Jimmy Sexton, who's a colleague based out of Memphis—who in my opinion is one of the top football agents in the entire space, coaching-wise, player-wise—and he had signed Tim as a player when he was coming out of Florida. When Jimmy's business was purchased by CAA, Tim became a client of CAA. He took a meeting at WME for his off-the-field representation—some individuals do split representation—and decided he was going to be represented as a player by Jimmy at CAA and WME for everything else.

MICHAEL LEVINE:

I'll own some of the fact that we mishandled our recruiting meeting. I think we took an approach that in retrospect, having discussed it with Timmy, wasn't as effective as what our competitor did. We put a large group of people in front of him because we felt there were so many things that he could do with us, instead of Timmy sitting in a room with me and Jimmy Sexton and creating a personal connection which eventually got made. But that's the approach WME took and that's how they signed him.

NICK KHAN:

After eighteen months, Jimmy set up a meeting for me and Vino with Tim. We met at the Four Seasons on Doheny; Jimmy was there and it was supposed to be a quick meeting, but it ended up going for an hour and a half and he came over for off-field representation. That was a really good day.

TIM TEBOW, Athlete:

Something that I really strive for in relationships is I try to find people who can see into me and help me to make my decisions, and I really value that in Nick, particularly when it's the whole football thing versus broadcasting. He's always been very sensitive to what I wanted and not just what was best for him. I have seen him in action a few different times and it's always been impressive. He just goes in there with a lot of boldness and I really like that.

MICHAEL LEVINE:

Our lens with Timmy is very long and our bar is extremely high. He is very special and we think he's got White House–type potential, or at least I do. I shouldn't speak for the company, but I think if he wants to be, he can be the president of the United States someday, and even though I am a Democrat, I will vote for him if he does run because he's got unique leadership abilities, a selflessness that would serve our country well, and a true drive to impact the world in a positive fashion.

Clearly for Ari Emanuel and Patrick Whitesell, merging their Endeavor agency with William Morris was simple foreplay, hardly enough to satisfy them. And so it was on December 18, 2013, WME and Silver Lake announced the acquisition of IMG for $2.4 billion, with Emanuel and Whitesell to serve as co-CEOs of *the mega-agency. It was a startlingly bold purchase given the price—an amount so lofty that CAA, ICM, and a group lead by former Fox topper Peter Chernin didn't come close to with their bids. The response to the sale focused more on the price than whether the deal made sense or not, but WME was convinced it was the ace in the deck—and that the competitive landscape would be fundamentally altered as a result.*

ARI EMANUEL:

When we took over IMG, it was a motherfucker. It's now nineteen-hour days, seven days a week, 365 days a year. You've got to want that fucking piece of bread more than the other guy. Simple as that.

When Richard Lovett heard that Patrick and I were talking to Teddy [Forstmann] and he thought we were going into sports, he got into sports, without any conception of what sports was or what to do in it. Then he picked the shittiest business in sports, the team sports business, where commissions are locked in by the guild. I mean, he's a moron. He has not done one innovative thing in the company. We're four times the size of CAA Sports. I mean, it's a joke now. It's truly a joke.

MIKE RUBEL:

We did not spend $2.4 billion to buy more revenue and head count. Our goal is not to be the biggest; it is to be the most influential, integrated company in the world, focused on our strategic priorities. It perhaps goes without saying that IMG is in a number of businesses that we do not consider important in our game plan.

MARK SHAPIRO, Chief Content Officer, WME/IMG:

CAA spends a lot of time talking about the price WME paid for IMG, but that's so foolish. It's all in the eyes of the storyteller. We had to pay what was necessary to get the fuel for this enterprise to jump to the next level. Yes, our bid was materially higher, but we didn't want a second round of bidding. We wanted to avoid a bake-off. We were confident in what the two combined assets could become. IMG actually didn't want to sell to CAA or WME. They didn't want to sell to an agency, but we prevailed anyway because the headline price was a deal they couldn't refuse.

HOWIE NUCHOW:

If they pull this off, I'll tip my hat and say, "God bless." I think it would be great for everyone.

PATRICK WHITESELL:

They went into sports the way they did because we were looking at Arn Tellem. But the more we looked at it, we saw it was a shitty business at scale with low margins. If I have a hundred football players, what does that really do for my television business or my movie business? There's no vertical integration. What we liked about IMG was that it was only 10 percent high-end representation and 90 percent assets you can actually control and own. We aren't in the sports representation business like what they're doing. We are after huge growth and a way bigger business. I couldn't sign enough actors to do what we're going to be doing this year alone with our sports business.

DAVID O'CONNOR:

I didn't want IMG at all. We thought IMG was a mess, and I was not a believer in their college business. We were unanimous in that. Richard probably overall was the greatest proponent of it but at the end of the day when we really started to look at it and really understand what IMG was, nobody wanted to do it. We were all very clearly against it at the end of the day, and happy to be out of it.

JIM COULTER:

At TPG, we're interested in whether there might be acquisitions, but we are primarily focused on internal growth. If you tack a branch onto a tree, it's never as strong as if you grow it yourself.

We could have bought IMG for sports, but growing it with Howie and Vino is a much stronger base for the future.

MIKE RUBEL:

I think the IMG situation is really instructive around some of the differences that play themselves out between WME and CAA. So when Endeavor and William Morris merged, there was aggressive financial engineering: "Let's lop off 30 percent of the less productive people." When they go and acquire IMG for the number that they acquired it at, they say, "We need to cut $150 million of overhead and then all the numbers will make sense." We're probably less hardwired to be the place to cut 30 percent of old William Morris employees and send people out on the street, or to cut $150 million of overhead, because that's mostly people.

It remains to be seen if WME can do it. Although we're certainly not as large as IMG, there's nobody doing more things at scale in the areas in which we are competing.

DEREK EILER, Executive:

One of the things we had learned in our time at IMG was that it was always about faster, faster, faster, and it was rarely about being smarter, so we felt like there was an underserved void in the marketplace. We've actually taken the opposite approach: We ask people to let us help them slow down and to build strategies for how to go to market, but with a better plan in place, instead of ready, aim, fire—or in IMG's case, fire, fire, aim.

The team of people who founded Fermata was Kit Walsh, Scott Bouyack, Chris Prindiville, and myself. We're all longtime employees of what was a successful family business that was eventually sold to IMG in 2007. We stayed at IMG for several years after, but by the end of 2011, we had all departed.

Fermata is in the consumer product licensing business for sports properties. We provide strategic counsel to universities, teams, and sports properties to help them maximize their revenue and brand positioning through consumer products. We make money as an agency by sharing in the royalties generated from sales of merchandise bearing the logos of our clients.

During our time at IMG, a lot of time was merely focused on trying to aggregate rights, trying to roll up businesses, attempting the difficult task of unifying multiple cultures, multiple corporate visions, and merging disconnected management teams. As a result, there was a lot of leadership attrition across the enterprise. Many of the clients became frustrated that they weren't getting the personalized service they once got, or that the leadership attrition led to a void in expertise, and the staff knew that every fourth quarter there would be travel freezes, cost cuts, and mandated layoffs because of missed projections. It became frustrating to many leaders to be a part of that culture when the college business was supposed to be a significant growth engine for the business.

We launched our business in 2012 and have had the honor of competing for, and winning, great client partnerships with Kentucky, Miami, Georgia, Oregon, Notre Dame, and Wisconsin, as well as many Premier League Clubs, Churchill Downs, and most recently, the PGA Tour.

We were acquired by CAA in 2015, and are fortunate to have access to CAA's culture and scale, as well as capital and infrastructure. We have focused on representing a premier set of clients, rather than trying to rebuild a massive enterprise to serve everyone. Part of our magic in the college business is that premier universities don't want to be a part of 200 other college brands. They want to feel unique. We can focus exclusively on brand-building programs that matter for the property or negotiating unique licensing deals for a single university, rather than trying to serve everyone.

MARK SHAPIRO:

We don't see CAA as competitors. They're just not. What WME is now, with IMG, is a major content media company with revenues and profits that dwarf those of CAA. We are a much bigger and bolder organization, with over $2 billion in revenue and fifty offices in thirty countries. They have some great people over there—I particularly love the guys who run their sports division—but we are just in a different league, on an entirely different global scale. CAA is still focused on being the leader amongst Hollywood agencies. WME/IMG has transformed itself into a major media company. That's not a shot at CAA, it's just the reality of where the two businesses stand now.

On October 20, 2014, CAA raised an incremental $435 million of capital via a new debt financing and increased investment from TPG. The new investment increased TPG's ownership to 52 percent, with TPG again committing to fund additional equity for capital needs. The firm's increased investment marked the first time the agency was not majority owned by its operating principals. The deal included long-term extensions for the management team and the future addition of a CFO, with Jim Burtson filling this role in July of 2015 after leaving Time Warner. Valued at around $700 million at the time of the firm's first investment, estimates of the agency's worth surpassed the $1 billion mark following the firm's second investment round.

JEREMY ZIMMER:

On the day that Richard Lovett was announcing the second TPG investment from the conference room, I was getting texts by agents there—not any of the guys who came over, guys who still work there—telling me what he was saying. That would've never happened before. You used to call the CAA agents, they'd never call you back.

JIM COULTER:

CAA is not a dominant part of our portfolio; it's not the largest investment we've made; yet it is one that has gotten a large amount of focus and care. I view myself and other TPG colleagues as partners to the leadership of CAA. I sit on the board of the company, something I don't do on many of the boards, and two of our other senior partners sit on the board as well. The reason for that is severalfold. First of all, it was clear that with CAA, there would be opportunities for substantial insights into what was happening in the content world, so it was going to be a learning experience for us with our overall platform. Secondly, this was a situation where we were partnering with guys who were peers of mine in age, and the right personal dynamics in this case are more important than they might be in other industrial situations. The people were a huge part of the business, so the people relationships were going to be a huge part of this investment. And the third reason was we knew our investment in CAA would get more attention than most investments in our portfolio. CAA is a company where the brand is even bigger than the company and therefore how we help that brand could influence potential partners, and from a publicity point of view, this is an industry that seems to have a number of reporters who wake up every morning looking to write about it.

Three or four years into our partnership, the business was making good progress, but there was an understanding the company would have more growth ahead if there were more acquisitions, and they would require additional investments. So instead of waiting for a moment when we might be evaluating a particular investment, we said essentially, "Let's solve that problem now by moving you from a minority to majority."

MIKE RUBEL:

We had a tremendous amount of growth before TPG became our partner in 2010, and have had a tremendous amount of growth since. TPG has provided growth capital that has helped us enhance our service offerings for clients and our geographic reach. TPG has been the right kind of partner. When you want to discuss strategy, they have a tremendous amount to offer. They don't focus on day-to-day operational issues, as they've witnessed the twenty years of successful operations on the part of current management.

DAVID BONDERMAN:

It's true that after the second investment we now have the right to do some things which we didn't have the right to do before, but we haven't chosen to do any of them.

DAVID GEFFEN:

They're now minority partners in the agency. I had told them they didn't have to sell it to get cash. They could have factored the accounts receivable. You understand? The history of collections in agencies is well into the 90 percent that they get paid. It's a very good business in that regard. They could've gone to any factoring company to factor the receivables and not sell anything. Now they can't set their own salaries. They can't do a lot of things that they could do before. TPG is a giant, giant company, and CAA is like a pimple on their ass. It's not a significant amount of money to them. And they now control the situation there, so they can figure out how to get their money back.

KEVIN HUVANE:

There's always been an alternative narrative, and there's always been people trying to tell our story. I can tell you that the TPG partnership has been a great one. They have never interfered with anything we have done. The reason they wanted to be in business with us is because they saw how well we've done and how well we run it.

RICHARD LOVETT:

TPG has been the great strategic partner we aimed for—even beyond our expectations—providing resources, intelligence, relationships, experience and capital to help us execute on our goals. They were attracted by our consistent category leadership, industry influence, the stability of our leadership, and the tremendous growth we've experienced, all of which is driven by a deep understanding of client needs and opportunities. They have been rocket fuel for our company, not least of which includes the capital that's been critical to our ten-plus acquisitions over the past twenty-four months, in addition to other areas of investment that add to our growth.

On a more personal level, we have mutual trust, confidence and admiration for one another and the value we provide each other. There's a chemistry that works.

RISA GERTNER:

The TPG investment hasn't affected me in any way or on any day. And let me tell you, if it's not affecting my life, it's not affecting anybody's life. Anybody who says it's affecting their life is misdirecting something else that's affecting their life. They're misdirecting the blame.

For several years, slowly, CAA had been losing its grip on at least its perceived dominance. WME's 2013 purchase of IMG meant that agency was now bigger and, some said, bolder than CAA; certainly sports was a more complicated battlefield as a result. And then another front opened with the March 31, 2015, defection of ten CAA agents to UTA, including an entire comedy bench lead by CAA veterans Gregory Cavic and Gregory McKnight, and including the highly regarded Jason Heyman, Marty Lesak. and Nick Nuciforo—who were still under contract when they departed. Among the clients taken by the defectors: Will Ferrell, Chris Pratt, Zach Galifianakis, and Ed Helms—but not, after a furious CAA effort that played to her dramatic aspirations, Melissa McCarthy. The CAA spin was they wouldn't miss the agents; they were grateful for the reduction in overhead and the years of commissions they would still hold on to for several more years, but they needed to send a signal to anyone else—inside or out—contemplating such a move in the future. It was too early to know whether the migration would ultimately be a financial win or loss for either agency, but one group of professionals was sure to cash in: the attorneys hired to sort out the legal ramifications of the defections. Within weeks, CAA was at Los Angeles Superior Court with a suit attacking "a lawless midnight raid that UTA and its co-conspirators [the defecting agents] launched against CAA in a desperate attempt to steal clients and employees." There were nearly twenty pages of accusations, bitterness, drama, and industrial-strength victimization in the CAA suit: "Months in the making, this illegal and unethical

conspiracy has resulted in a number of agents who were under contract to CAA
to brazenly and abruptly breach their contractual obligations to CAA and to in-
tentionally and deliberately interfere with CAA's existing and prospective economic
relationships with its clients."

JIM BERKUS:

The law is a funny thing. You can make all kinds of arguments. We had tortious interference with contractual relationships, all kinds of things that we could have sued them for, but in the end we decided not to. But now they're suing us. I understand, they had a contract, but the way these contracts are being interpreted these days is quite different. The irony is that the lawsuit is ridiculous. It's the pot calling the kettle black given how many people they've poached from us over the years.

JASON HEYMAN:

When I joined CAA, I started in the I. M. Pei building, which still had some of the aura of Ovitz and Meyer in the hallways. The company changed a lot over the ten years I was there. I'm not sure that a lot of the clients really know how much the place has changed.

We were the backbone of the comedy business at CAA over the past ten years. I'm proud of a lot of projects we put together— for instance, *The Hangover.* Greg McKnight had sold it as a spec to Warner Bros. We all loved it. A bunch of actors had passed on it, though, and Jeff Robinov took me to lunch one day and said, "You know, Greg [Silverman], Jesse [Ehrman], and I really believe in this movie and we're willing to make it with new talent. Who should we put in it?" We repped Ed Helms, Bradley Cooper, and Zach Galifianakis, and we thought that was a winning combination. Ed had just come off *The Daily Show,* and he had just become the new lead on *The Office.* Bradley was playing the best friend in *Yes Man* with Jim Carrey, a Warners movie, so they were seeing dailies and they liked him. For Zach's role they wanted someone else, so we had to fight. Todd Phillips had seen some of the *Between Two Ferns,* and he said, "Oh, this guy is brilliant." Todd's very smart and he got it early. Zach had to test a couple of times, but he got it, and that movie became the biggest R-rated comedy of all time.

Funny or Die—I credit that as one of our big accomplishments. I mean, that's a huge company that employs hundreds of people now. That's a massive business. It's great, and we started it from nothing.

MARTIN LESAK:

So you have that incredible beginning in the first couple of years when you drink the Kool-Aid, and you're made to feel everything is laid out so perfectly. There's a lot of talk about culture and how everyone has to treat each other. But then that starts to get stripped away, and eventually you see what the reality is.

At the time CAA was this big, very dominant place, and UTA by comparison was smaller and younger, even though we had incredible clients. As much as I think our size made us somewhat vulnerable to CAA, it was also a cultural thing. We were really more builders of clients and agents than we were poachers. Our mentality was to grow the talent and make them stars, especially in comedy, which was not an area that CAA had really excelled in. UTA was earning a reputation for comedy because the agency understood the relationships between the clients and all the opportunities that existed, and the studios were just waking up to the box office potential of comedy. It was a great time for UTA. I think CAA saw what we were building, and they made it their mission to go after it, not to create their own, but just to try to take it from UTA. So suddenly your clients are being hit on all day long and you fear that they'll eventually leave you. It's not an easy position to be in, so as much as you feel loyalty to your agency and all the opportunities that came with UTA at the time, you get worn down, and after a couple of years you find yourself starting to think, *Hey, maybe we really do have to be at this place*, out of self-preservation.

CHRIS SILBERMANN:

Jason Heyman is a very good agent. I like him, and who wouldn't want to represent Chris Pratt? Will Ferrell is one of the great comedians in our business. Those agents who left have some very good people. But you know, the world changes so quickly. In the course of six months, stars are born and stars are retired.

MARTIN LESAK:

There was definitely also a curiosity factor there. Every agent at every other agency has at one time or another wondered what it was like to work at CAA—to play for the Yankees, so to speak—to know what it was really all about, if it really was this exalted thing. I'm not sure people do that as much now, but ten years ago, if an agent said they weren't curious, it probably wasn't true. You could say they're still the Yankees, but look what's happened to that team.

MIKE RUBEL:

Over the last fifteen years, only a limited number of agents have voluntarily left CAA to work for competitors. Generally, they've been surprised by the number of their clients who have stayed with CAA rather than follow them. These departures have only ever strengthened our culture, and the company has never had a better financial year.

MARTIN LESAK:

I never understood the steady stream of Ovitz bashing. It was always weird to me because he built the company and invented the playbook that they inherited, and the principles that they hated about him are the same ones they assumed. It's like they hated what he did to the company, but even a casual observer could see they were doing the same thing. I don't begrudge them for how they ran the company. It was theirs to do what they wanted with, but in the ten years I was there, the company was making decisions that made many people question the overall direction.

The agents who were there through the Ovitz years, and the dozen or so that arrived in later years that were really in our business, are the ones who really understand the reasons that we left.

JIM COULTER:

CAA doesn't want anything to be about CAA, and they don't want to speak loud about themselves in the marketplace. So when those agents left, the dialogue in the press was controlled by the people who were leaving, who by their nature would make people want to think that they were more important than they might be, and who might want to create a narrative about why they were leaving that may or may not have been the real reason why they were leaving. And so in other words, in the absence of CAA telling its side of the story, it was just to my eye overblown in the press.

MARTIN LESAK:

What I really wanted was just to be at a place that cared about artists first and foremost, that cared about its people and culture in a real way. To me that was the whole point of being an agent. UTA really embraced us. What they are giving us is a platform that's completely focused on representing artists. And you know, if we end up winning and succeeding, we will all do wonderfully. What UTA has become is beyond impressive. The board and partners just stayed on a great track. They got rid of a lot of the bad elements, kept all the best parts, and just built around that. When you look at how big it's become, and the new building, the new offices around the world, what they stand for, it's incredible.

JASON HEYMAN:

It's so impressive what UTA has accomplished during the time I was gone. There's a lot of talk about culture in the agency business, and now I've seen firsthand the influence that different agency cultures have in representing clients. I have to say, the culture at UTA gives clients an incredible opportunity to succeed. It's a special place.

JEREMY ZIMMER:

So far UTA has benefited a lot from ICM taking private equity in and then having them take private equity out. That caused massive dislocation; we picked up five or six great agents. The William Morris Endeavor merger was unbelievable for us. We picked up five or six great agents who they literally threw out the door and they paid them for years while they worked for us. It was fucking fantastic. And then because of the CAA-TPG deals, we were able to get these twelve agents.

CHRIS SILBERMANN:

CAA's lost a lot of agents over the years. We talk to a lot of people there, and they are not happy. But some are afraid to leave. Whenever you're an agent and you move agencies, you can always lose clients. Some people there now worry about what they are going to be able to walk out of there with.

JIM BERKUS:

We're all swinging at each other, no doubt, but what's different now is that people realize you can leave CAA and your world doesn't fall apart. Very few people are afraid to leave CAA now. If you're at CAA and getting what you want, fine, but if you're not, you're going to look at other places, and there are other places to go.

JEREMY ZIMMER:

They could never seem to develop really great agents on their own. Now they've done a little better, but you think about their top people over there, most of them came from somewhere else. They haven't had as strong an ethos of developing their own people. They're consistently out trying to sign and hire good people as opposed to relying on their own internal development mechanism.

PETER BENEDICT:

There's a theory, and I think there's a lot to it, that the only agents over there who are really competent, really excellent at their jobs, are the ones who were directly touched by the guys who founded that agency. So if you hadn't worked for Mike Ovitz,

Ron Meyer, or Bill Haber, you're probably not the greatest agent who ever lived.

After three decades of dominance in late-night entertainment, David Letterman announced his plans of retirement from the Late Show *in April 2014. His final show on May 20, 2015, offered a poignant farewell to Letterman's legacy. CBS would find a successor in Stephen Colbert; Letterman was not consulted in the consideration of his replacement.*

DAVID LETTERMAN:

The last contract was for only a year. I was frightened then that I might not even be able to make it through the year. Everything had stopped being what it was and I didn't want to be the last old guy in late night. And this had been an ongoing conversation. Every time I saw Les, I would say, "You know, Les," I said, "I'm ready to go any time you need me to go." And he said, "Everything's fine. Don't worry about it. Everything's fine." And then when Jay retired, I just thought, *Oh, yeah. I'm going to be the last old guy.* So that was as meaningful to me as anything else. I just thought, *I can't be the old guy trying to keep up with the kids on late night.*

LEE GABLER:

Dave said to me years ago, "Tell me, you've got to be honest with me. You've got to tell me when you think it's time." And you know, I never said to him, "Okay, it's time to go." But the conversations were "What do you want to do?" He was talking about spending more time with Harry, his son. He was talking about spending more time in Montana. At worst it was a mutual decision. It wasn't Les picking up the phone and saying, "Dave's out." That's nonsense.

LES MOONVES:

My relationship with Dave started out a little rocky, as Dave's was with his previous bosses. But through the years, we became friends. Many things were happening in the late-night world—

Leno was gone, Jimmy Fallon came, Conan was off on Turner, Jimmy Kimmel's time slot was changing, and Dave said, "You know, I shouldn't be sitting in this chair when I'm seventy." So it wasn't like one day I picked up the phone and called him; we were already talking about this. And at a certain point in time, he said to me, "I should leave at the end of this year," but it wasn't like an announcement, it was part of a dialogue we had been having for a couple years.

LEE GABLER:

I set up a meeting with Bryan Lourd and Lafferty to represent him because I wasn't going to continue past the end of the show. When the *Late Show* ended, I sat down with Dave and said, "What do you want to do?" And he said, "I don't know," and I said, "Well, why don't we sit down with CBS and come up with a post-term deal?" And *60 Minutes* was interested in making a deal with him. *Sunday Morning* was interested in making a deal. CBS Radio wanted to make a deal. There was conversation about a lecture tour in some kind of a format that he would feel comfortable with, but it turned out he really didn't want to do anything at that point.

For all today's talk of being an "artist" or "creator" and the lofty ideas and ideals that go with it, words like "branding," "growth," and "hyphenate" may be heard just as often from the clients themselves as from their agents. For many clients, the era of the conventional career is over.

JOEL LUBIN:

We play the skill sets a little different now. Talent is still extremely valuable, it's still scarce, and we're still looking to represent the most talented creative people. But the conversation is broader than just the movie business. Our conversations are different than they were just five years ago. Our agency has diversified to support clients that have interests that can go beyond the traditional movie space.

JASON BLUM:

There's such a tradition in Hollywood of having meetings and coming up with big ideas and nothing ever happening. I've had the opposite experience with these guys.

I was very intent on not just being a movie and television production company—I wanted to expand in all different phases, and they've been involved in every aspect. CAA helped us arrange financing for our company. We have a live event division; Budweiser hired us to do a haunted house in Argentina to launch a new beer; I love books and we now have an imprint deal. We've been working on the idea of producing local language movies in foreign countries that have scary themes. We had a meeting a little over a year ago about it, and now we're already doing it in several countries. CAA has also helped us get involved with an online company called *Crypt TV*, and we also have five writers in my offices here who are releasing new scary stories on Blumhouse.com every day. There are many other areas we're involved in, and none of these things would have happened if it wasn't for CAA.

When Jennifer Lopez switched agencies, at one of her first or second meetings with Kevin Huvane, he said, "I think you need to do five things." I don't know what four of them were, but the fifth one was, "You and your team should go sit with Jason Blum," and she did, only because Kevin suggested it. Then we sat down and built this movie around her called *The Boy Next Door*, and they said, "It's okay to work for scale for this guy because if the movie makes money, you're going to get paid really well."

JENNIFER LOPEZ, Actress and Singer:

I think over the past ten or twenty years artists have realized that we do have brands, that we do have other interests. I consider myself an entertainer first, but I find so much joy in creating as a producer, creating as a clothing designer, and creating as a perfume designer. I also have a production company with writers, directors, and showrunners.

Everybody knows CAA is a full-service agency, but I don't

think anybody uses it as much as I do, in every aspect. It's crazy. All of it for me is so exciting, that you don't have to limit yourself. I have an amazing team at CAA. They believe there are no limits and that the possibilities are always endless depending on how far the artist wants to go and how hard they want to work. For me that works well, because I don't ever see limits, and I'm a hard worker.

DWYANE WADE:

We do a Brand Wade Summit where we bring all my business partners together once a year. I had told CAA my idea for this, and that I needed their help putting it together, and for the past seven or eight years, we've been doing it. They host it, and they come to it. The first year we started in a hotel ballroom; for the past two years we've taken the entire team to Turks and Caicos—that's how much we've grown. Each partner sends two representatives. Last year I think we had twelve partners, so that's twenty-four people right there, and then we've got Team Wade and my family. It's a lot of people. We spend time together on the beach and spend time bonding. Then we take a look around the room and talk about what we've done, how we're growing, and what we can do in the next year. We do it in August or September—it's always right before training camp.

CAA understands my value to them and their value to me. At this point, they're part of my family, and we work well together. We're trying to build Wade Enterprises. We're trying to build a brand from what I've been able to do on the basketball court and take it off the court. When I talk to kids about CAA, I say, "Listen, I can't say it's going to be the same for you as it is for me, but this is what I've done, these are the ways that I've used CAA, and it's been an amazing relationship for me."

EVA LONGORIA, Actress:

I think I am the one client that uses that agency the most. I use every single resource and every single department like no other client. I obviously signed with them as a TV actor and then I got a film team on board after they said, "We should do film." And then I had always wanted to produce and direct, so they quickly pushed me into the department that represents producers and directors. As a producer, I needed writers, so I said, "I need the best writers CAA has. Who are they?" And they said, "You should go and meet the literary agents." So I met the literary agents, and then I started my production company and CAA helped me get one of the largest production deals an actor's ever had at Universal. Then I remember my agent saying, "You should talk to the digital department." And I go, "You have a fucking digital department? Why haven't I met them yet?" So then I went to them and made them start building up and managing my social media and figuring out ways to have a digital imprint. They built my digital space out of my production company. And then I was doing a presentation to Comcast about diversity in television and another agent said, "We should ask the market research people to help you with that." And I said, "You guys have a market research team? Why didn't I know this?" So I called them and said, "I need every single study of what Latinos watch, what Hispanics are reading." And then for my foundation, the Eva Longoria Foundation, I always say to them, "Who are the brands you represent? I need partners and sponsorships to help with my charity work." And sure enough, they found me Target and Bank of America.

CHRISTY HAUBEGGER:

I started signing clients, which was helped by my contacts from the magazine and film businesses. When I called Shakira, she knew me. I said to Eva Longoria, "You know me, and you can trust me. You should meet with us. I'll be part of your team."

If you want to know what I really do, I try and change whose stories get told and who gets to tell them. There's your work and then there's your life's work, and I believe I get to do both. I think we're all probably going to measure our lives in terms of the impact we've had, and that's why I feel so good about what I do. I define success by the impact that I'm having on the industry. When I bring in Pitbull, who's a big music artist, I understand what he can mean in pop culture, so we worked on putting together his television deal. We've sold scripted television shows for him and a New Year's special. He could be a cross between Ryan Seacrest and Will Smith.

Right now I feel like there's inelastic demand for diverse talent and insufficient supply in some ways. So my job is to elevate these folks. And if I can get more people through the pipeline and up on this platform, through the platform of CAA, that's enormously valuable. Five years ago, Eva Longoria was not a television producer, and in the past year, she sold seven series, and every one of them has diverse lead characters. We have an amazing A-list diverse roster, with Halle Berry, Vin Diesel, Will Smith, Jamie Foxx, Salma Hayek, Jennifer Lopez, and many others.

JENNIFER LOPEZ:

We already have international licenses in most parts of the world, but when we speak to the agency, we want it to continue to grow even more. My work as an actress is a whole other facet that they speak to us constantly about. I speak to Kevin several times a week, but he's in touch with my team and other agents who are on the team in all the different departments probably several times a day. At the end of the day, it's not just building a brand that is trying to make money, but trying to make history and trying to be a part of something bigger.

MICHAEL BOLTON:

CAA is as broad and as big as you want it to be. I've had some good relationships through the years at other agencies, but I cannot say that I've ever had this kind of constant communication with agents across six or seven departments, bringing me options and talking to me about whatever it is I'm thinking about doing. "Do you want to do more TV? Do you want to do theater? Do you want to act? What do you want to do?" The next thing I know,

I'm sitting in meetings and people are basically putting different options in front of me. I'm developing several television shows, I'm developing a theatrical musical, in different stages with them. I've done four episodes of *Two and a Half Men*, which gave me a great taste of what it would be like to have my own show and show up at the set and have nine writers writing funny stuff. The Captain Jack Sparrow video that I did with the Lonely Island guys was my first experience of serious viral success, and it's had close to 150 million views. It's also multigenerational, so we have this young demographic who are huge fans, who were not even familiar with my music.

SARAH JESSICA PARKER:

For many, many, years, I had dreamt of doing a fragrance, and I went to Peter Hess, who is my commercial agent and works really closely with Kevin, and said, "What about this?" They became very involved, just as they have been with my very long L'Oréal contract. I've also had several fashion endeavors come through them.

EVA LONGORIA:

I remember when I was getting divorced, I had just left my manager at the time, I was in a very bad place in my life. And I remember going into Kevin Huvane's office and just crying. I just couldn't take one more bad thing that could happen to me. And he picked me up and said, "We're going to be with you. We're never going to leave you. We're going to be here as long as you want us to be. So let's just put your life back together." He found me my new manager; he's the one that is helping me with the producing empire I'm trying to build. Kevin for me really is this father figure. You never want him as an enemy, but you definitely want him in your corner because he's going to fight for you in every way, not just for a movie part or a TV show, but in life.

People always say that "Oh, you don't want to go to CAA because you'll get lost." And I do believe you have to navigate it in a way that benefits you. But CAA was really the only place that saw me as more than an actor, and that was important to me. They'd rather have more hyphenates—"actor-producer-director-writer"—and that's what I am for them. You can tell them anything and they go, "Okay, let's go do it." I want to be Oprah crossed with George Clooney crossed with Tom Hanks. I look at those careers and go, "I want all of those careers." I've produced a lot of documentaries, I've directed a couple of documentaries, but documentaries make no money. I have one agent who's always saying, "Stop fucking making documentaries. They make no money." It's a joke—they know that those are my passion projects. Christy Haubegger was a trailblazer within this particular community, and she has brought me deals that I would've never even thought of. When you have diversity of thought, it leads to innovation. That innovation is something that I capitalize on as I try to build my small empire.

NOAH OPPENHEIM:

I became the senior producer in charge of the first hour of *Today*, and after three years, I went to Alan and said, "I really want to make a transition over to the entertainment business." I wound up working for Elizabeth Murdoch at Reveille, did that job for two years, and then I wrote a spec script. And because I knew Alan, CAA was the first recipient. A week after I turned it in, I was sitting in Steven Spielberg's office.

ALAN BERGER:

He called me one day and said, "I wrote a script and sent it to my friend at Universal, and they like it a lot." I had only known Noah as a news producer and a reality executive. He had never told me he liked to write. He explained that he had written a script called *Jackie* about the Kennedy assassination from the first lady's point of view. I asked him to send the script over and I would get into it.

I sent the script to my associate, Risa Gertner, who read it over lunch. She called me and said she really liked it, she had talked to the executive at Universal and confirmed that they liked it, and she wanted to know who this writer was! No one in our motion picture department knew of Noah, since he had never written anything. Risa then told me she was sending the script to a number of top directors.

Everything went crazy the next day when Risa told me one of them responded right away and was interested in working with Noah on the script and wanted to meet with him. I called Noah and told him he had a director meeting in two days. This meeting had a dual effect: Noah was now a writer and Noah was now a very "hot" and unknown writer.

We decided not to release the script to anyone outside the building. Producers, studio executives, and other agents from outside CAA began to hunt down who this writer was and were desperate to get their hands on this script. And since they couldn't get it, that only increased its notoriety, and their curiosity, as to who this new writer was.

Entertainment Weekly began calling around town trying to uncover this mystery and wanted to do an article on the unknown writer and script that everyone was talking about but no one had read. Noah met with the director who was interested in producing with him, but who ultimately had a schedule conflict. Darren Aronofsky optioned the script, Natalie Portman stars in it, and it will be released in the fall.

NOAH OPPENHEIM:

I started working with CAA agents in their motion picture lit group, and they got me working on films for all the studios, including *The Maze Runner* and the *Divergent* series. I then got a call from Charlie Dixon—I know Charlie's wife—and he said, "Hey, me and my boss Jamie Horowitz just moved over to NBC, and we're overseeing *Today*. Will you have dinner with us just so we can pick your brain?" So we went to dinner, and they said, "What can we do to get you to come back to the show?" And at that point I was not immediately interested. I had a pretty thriving screenwriting career. But they kind of kept at it. Pat [Filli-Krushel, former NBC News chairman] was in California at one point and they said, "Will you have lunch with her?" So I had lunch with her. I was kind of on the fence about the whole thing—probably leaning against—and then I was supposed to fly to New York to meet with them a little bit more and Alan forwarded me a link to Page Six reporting the news that Jamie had been fired. So I figured, *All right, well, that's the end of that.* And then a couple days later, then Pat called me and said, "Well, why don't you come on board in Jamie's job?"

Making the decision whether to pause my screenwriting career, which at the time thankfully was going very well, to take an executive job, let alone an executive job across the country, moving my wife and now three children, was a huge career decision, life decision, financial decision. And I really did rely heavily on the advice and sounding board of Alan Berger in particular. I think if I asked my motion picture lit agents, they would have said they were supportive of whatever I decided, but if you put them up to a polygraph, they would have preferred I remain in the screenwriting business because it's more lucrative for both me and them, at least in the short term. But I had this relationship with Alan going back over a decade and there were many long dinners with my wife and I and Alan and his wife trying to weigh the pros and cons of the choice. I have always felt with him that he cared as much about me and my family as he did about any kind of professional goal or agency goal.

DOUG ELLIN:

One of the things that became this idiotic waste-of-time criticism of *Entourage* was that we were getting paid all of this money to use certain products. It was never true. I just always put products in that I liked, and the Escalade was one of them and a staple of the show for a long time.

DAVID MESSINGER:

Entourage was coming off air on HBO. Remember, it's on HBO, so there are no commercials, no brand integrations. But Turtle drove an Escalade and the television show was a showcase for luxury automobiles, among other things. So regardless of whether there was going to ever be any *Entourage* movie or anything *Entourage*-related again, we just loved the idea of Doug Ellin working with Cadillac. So we approached Doug and eventually became a creative consultant to Cadillac.

JAE GOODMAN:

Doug Ellin is from a Cadillac family. His dad was a Cadillac driver. He loved the idea. The relationship initially had nothing to do with *Entourage*. It was for some personal appearances, and for him to write some Cadillac content at some point down the line. In the interim, Cadillac would expose Doug to what was new with their brand and cars. For example, Doug was one of the first people outside General Motors to see the new Escalade. Cadillac also showed him a concept car called the Ciel. The Ciel has the same "suicide doors" as the '63 Lincoln Continental in the opening of *Entourage*. So Doug said jokingly, "Well, that's in the movie." And, of course, the joke back was "there is no *Entourage* movie."

DOUG ELLIN:

I wasn't even sure I was going to do a movie, to be honest with you. It was this show about these twentysomething guys living together and all of a sudden they're nearing forty. Someone over there introduced me to the GM people, said they wanted to take you to their secret headquarters where they have cars that aren't even necessarily ever coming out but are prototypes of this and that. So we went to this place in the valley somewhere, I don't remember where, and I saw this car and it literally gave me impetus to start the script. How do we top Vince? The fact that he can have a car that no one else on Earth is driving. So it was, you know, the small seed of something. So I thought, *All right*, and I started writing the script. And whatever it was, eighteen months, two years later when we started getting ready, I was like, "Okay,

GM, we're ready for the car." And they're like, "Oh, we're not making that car." I said, "What do you mean you're not making that car? I don't have a movie without that car." Because I'm really obsessive about small details. I mean, this wasn't the car that GM wanted in the movie. They wanted a car that people could go buy. And I go, "There's nothing else you can give him now. Not the most beautiful Ferrari, not anything. This is special—it's one of one, you know?"

I pleaded with them and GM was great enough—after some time, though, by the way—they said, "We'll figure it out." And they basically gave us that car. Actually, I think there's two. It's not a real car. It doesn't have seat belts. It doesn't have a real suspension. It doesn't have a real engine. I think it goes thirty miles an hour, tops. So in filming it, it was very difficult, and the guys, you know, were complaining nonstop. And I said, you know, at the end of the day it's going to be worth it, it's going to be something different, something unique, and something special to us. And everybody agreed at the end of it that it was, you know?

There was no payment or anything. I always thought somehow I would get GM to actually make that car. It didn't happen.

JAE GOODMAN:

When a first draft of the movie came in, it included a scene in which the character Ari Gold gives his star client Vincent Chase this one-of-a-kind Cadillac, the Ciel. Doug shared this scene with Cadillac, who then went to the studio, Warner Bros., to create a promotional deal around the movie. Once that was in place, we used Cadillac's initial partnership deal with Doug—which you'll recall was not at all *Entourage*-related—to create a short film that connected the end of the *Entourage* television show to the beginning of the *Entourage* movie. At the end of the television show, Ari Gold is retired in Italy. But in the first trailer for the movie, audiences would see that Ari Gold was back in Hollywood. But they'd have no idea why he was back. So, Doug wrote, produced, and directed a short film that explained why Ari Gold came back. And within that film, very naturally, was that concept car, the Cadillac Ciel. It was almost a character. The short film ran online, and 30-second promos for the short film ran on television. From a marketer's point of view, you could say that we launched two great franchises into popular culture at the same time: Cadillac and *Entourage*. Cadillac was launching their new campaign "Dare Greatly," and *Entourage* was coming back as a feature film. They complemented each other beautifully, each making the other more effective.

For many of the years following Jay Moloney's tragic death, there had been not so much four remaining Young Turks at the agency as there were three-plus-one. More and more agents inside, and keen observers outside, could tell there was less and less respect and affection flowing between three of the Turks—Lovett, Lourd, Huvane, and the fourth, O'Connor. It was as if the four were in a special room, with a secret entrance through which only Lovett, Lourd, and Huvane were then allowed to go. This segregation was often subtle, sometimes passive-aggressive—until, that is, the second tranche with TPG was completed. That's when the ostracization took a financial turn.

For the first TPG transaction, the four were reputedly in the same zip code, receiving payouts commensurate with their ownership percentage in the agency. O'Connor got about $25 million, with Lourd and Huvane closer to $30 million and Lovett slightly over this. On the second transaction, the partners cashed out the "Membership Program"—i.e., an exit benefit and net present value of salary reductions previously agreed to. It amounted to two years of compensation and so, once again, the numbers were relatively close, with each man earning approximately $20 million. But this time there was a judo chop at the end. The remainder of the proceeds was in the hands of a "Comp Committee"—reportedly just Lovett and Lourd—and this time, Lovett, Lourd, and Huvane each were granted another $20 million in discretionary proceeds. O'Connor was told he would not be getting any discretionary funds.

LEE GABLER:

They wanted Doc out when we first started after Mike and Ron left. They treated him as an adjunct and didn't respect him at all. Kevin is tied to Bryan, so as long as Bryan is there, Kevin is protected. Richard abandoned Doc a long time ago.

DAVID O'CONNOR:

I was starting to privately question my role and what else there was left for me to do at CAA. Frankly, I was getting a little bored with the movie business.

I'd intentionally reduced my client load and transitioned everybody to other agents in the office, largely because I wanted to be involved and was involved in some of the larger moves of the agency on a strategic level. I spent an enormous amount of time in sports building that division out.

So as I started to look down the road, I wasn't necessarily relishing the next three to five years. Part of it was that I was doing things separate and apart from those three guys in particular. As a result of the TPG transaction, we started Evolution Media, which is now a $500 million fund we didn't have to raise and that we didn't have to put any of our own money into. It's going to be wildly successful. That was interesting and challenging to me, and those guys didn't particularly understand it or support it.

Sports was something that Richard and Rubel were definitely interested in, but they didn't have the bandwidth to concentrate on it. I had much more time to educate myself and think about where we were going to take it. I was spending a lot more time with Howie and Vino than those other guys were, and so there became this distance between us. I got married, I started having kids and had a whole separate life with my family. Richard got married and had kids and then got divorced and had to struggle with the divorce and single parenting. Bryan's kid was older, and so he was in a different place in his life. Kevin's marriage dissolved and he came out, so his whole life changed. It was only natural that there was more distance between us.

HOWIE NUCHOW:

I was very close with Doc. Vino is also close with him. Doc spent a great deal of time with us, and it was terrific. It was one of my favorite relationships I built at the company and he was another part of why we were loving our time at CAA. Doc was the guy I traveled the most with and we became supertight as friends. There was an ease of going anywhere together regardless of how far or how difficult a meeting we were facing. Doc was one of our greatest supporters and was happy for our success.

DAVID O'CONNOR:

Richard's made an entire life out of giving everybody the Heisman. Nobody really knows who Richard is. It literally was all of us in many respects, but Richard desperately wants to be *the* guy; he's competitive and he's relentless.

Bryan is very charming, one of those people that has this magnetic quality that makes you want to be around him and want his friendship. He draws you in, and when he wants to, he can make you feel you are the only person in the room. But there is always a lot going on in his mind behind the charm. What you see and what you encounter is not always what you get.

Kevin is a really, really good fucking agent.

On June 30, 2015, David O'Connor was announced as president-CEO of the Madison Square Garden Company, leaving CAA the following month to begin his new position.

Unlike the surprise defections of a few months prior, many believed O'Connor's departure was foreseen and perhaps encouraged by old friends and fellow partners.

DAVID O'CONNOR:

I was thinking about the next act, but I always thought it wouldn't play out for several more years. I wasn't looking for anything, but this opportunity was really special. Jim [Dolan] and I had a handshake on a deal somewhere around the eighth or tenth of June, and I was very stressed out about confidentiality and secrecy with all of this because I really wanted to tell my partners before they heard anything. I was getting increasingly paranoid about it, and increasingly uncomfortable around the office, pretending I was all in, when in fact I had one foot out the door. So I had my assistant call and set a meeting with Bryan, Richard, and Kevin, and as I was leaving my office to go to that meeting, the *New York Post* called my assistant looking for comment. Someone had leaked it. I got to them before the news came out.

In the meeting, I told them, "I've been offered a job and I'm going to take it. It's in many respects a dream job for me, and I think it's the right time for all of us, as you guys well know." I didn't know how it was going to go. It could have been ugly, but it was incredible. They were happy and very supportive. They could have held me to my contract, but that was in nobody's best interest, so it all worked out.

There's no need to weep for O'Connor. In his new deal with MSG, he was awarded $40 million in stock grants to compensate for the equity in CAA that he'd left behind, vesting in just three years. His deal at MSG also came with a five-year contract, and if he serves all five, his total compensation will be around $115 million, with only a portion of that tied to stock performance.

JIM COULTER:

Doc had been a critical player in the business, particularly in birthing the sports business. The opportunity for Doc was an extraordinary one.

DAVID O'CONNOR:

After my job was announced, Ari called me, and before I could even say, "Hello," he says, "So now I've got to suck your dick for the next five years? Are you kidding me?!"

ARI EMANUEL:

Since they sold a majority of the company, a lot of people there are realizing it's not going to raise all boats. I give Mike and Ronnie a lot of credit. Even when they had all those consulting fees from Matsushita and others coming in, they made sure to share it with everyone. There was a feeling that everyone was going to be elevated financially. Now there's just too many people over there who believe it's just about those three guys. Here, Patrick and I made sure that the people who have been with us all get checks. We know we wouldn't be here without them.

JEREMY ZIMMER:

Those guys at the top took a lot of money in that TPG deal and they want to take a lot more, and fine, they should, but I think it has changed the culture. You used to call CAA agents and they would never call you back, but that's not the case anymore.

In the late 1980s and early '90s, it had often been difficult for competitors to make a case against CAA other than to say it was too big and many clients got lost in the crowd. No longer. Since the merger of William Morris and Endeavor, the upgrading of UTA, and ICM getting its managerial and financial houses in order, CAA-envy has largely dissipated. CAA can speak to leadership in many categories, but the agency's rivals—the now-massive WME and sundry smaller competitors as well—seem more than content, and each has developed their own narratives about why they are the place to be. The noteworthy result: To a degree undreamed of a decade ago, there are plenty of healthy, happy, well-dressed, and extremely well-paid agents elsewhere around town, and that says a lot.

Because of their respective sizes and positions of power, CAA and WME/IMG are often put on a level of their own. One can hardly blame observers for observing: "Let those two scorpions slug it out in a dish while we hear about some others for a change."

For years, ICM would have been the next name mentioned in a list of powerful and successful agencies, but United Talent Agency would recoil at such a prospect now. The massive defection of CAA's comedy all-stars was huge news in the industry, yet their impact on profitability remains unclear. But if even a couple of the drivers behind the departures—broad tensions inside CAA and a culture not as advertised—turn out to be shared by others inside, then UTA's gain may be a harbinger of additional, and more truly disruptive, departures from CAA. One thing that can be said about UTA—which now employs three hundred agents out of a total workforce of seven hundred and fifty—is that it has "calmed down." The drama and unsettling tenor of UTA has given way to an ambitious, aggressive business plan and a far cooler patina, symbolized by sleek headquarters replete with luxe patios and the agency's own lofty art.

ICM carved out its own niche, filling its ranks with agents who find the word "culture" in the form of mission statement uniformity to be a trifle maddening, even scary. ICM's leadership has engineered the place so that agents can serve less as team members and more as—when they want—semiautonomous entrepreneurs, creating distinct and personal ecosystems under the ICM umbrella. Horizontal imperatives are not ignored, and there is teamwork aplenty, but it's also considered acceptable if agents occasionally do their own thing. Management isn't interested in forcing behaviors that in its view might waste an agent's time and psychic energies. WME and CAA may indeed offer default cross-team functionality, but for many clients who don't want to start their own product lines, that's an answer to an unasked question. ICM agents believe they enjoy a more intimate connection with their clients, precisely because they're not sharing them with half the building. Whether or not this is a rationalization—ICM, after all, pursued IMG for a while but dropped out when the price rose into the stratosphere, and has had key departures of its own—ICM agents are more secure than they've been in a long time.

Even an agency like Paradigm, which at one point had practically disappeared from this kind of conversation, has real enthusiasm from within and a stronger bench, and has found a way, particularly in the music world, to claim prominence in certain areas.

Virtually any way you look at it, CAA now faces the most competitive climate in its forty-year history.

RICHARD LOVETT:

We have seen the same individual competitors for more than three decades. They have started new agencies, they have gotten smaller, they have merged to get bigger, they have gone out of business. In the meantime, we have been consistent in our culture and clear about our game plan and strategy. The result has been that we are the leader in all categories in which we compete. Because no one has been able to compete well in the movie area, other agencies, understandably, spend a lot of time emphasizing television as an area where they have had success. Yet CAA, by every measurement, remains the clear leader in television—in terms of client success, showrunners, executive producers, writers on series—plus, helping put together the shows that define pop culture, including the top-rated show on broadcast, *Empire;* the top-rated show on basic cable, *The Walking Dead;* and the top-rated show on premium cable, *Game of Thrones.*

DAVID BONDERMAN:

They're in a business with a very aggressive competitor in WME, which is growing rapidly through acquisition and has an entirely different risk profile. The question is, what does that do to the shape of the industry?

PATRICK WHITESELL:

What's wild to me about CAA is when I left there and Ari and I were at Endeavor, it was like a knife fight. They tried to kill us every day and we were just in the movie and television business. But once we did the WME merger, I stopped thinking about them the way we did. It used to be, "How do we beat them?" Now we don't even have to think that way.

JIM BERKUS:

There's no secret we've had some run-ins with CAA recently. We brought a bunch of people over here, and now the gloves are off. I've known Bryan Lourd and Richard Lovett forever, we have a lot of social friends in common, and it's all friendly and jocular when you're together, but there's no question we're fiercely competing with each other.

I was at the *Star Wars* premiere with my client Harrison Ford and got up to talk to another one of my clients, and by the time I turned around, Richard and Bryan were on either side of him, talking to him and laughing. I moseyed over to them and just said, "Hi, guys!"—joined the conversation and eventually they left. Harrison gave me a look when they got up . . . he knew.

ADAM VENIT:

John Boyega is the lead of *Star Wars.* He left CAA with *Star Wars* coming out to come to us. You ask, why would he do that, and it's because they fell asleep at the wheel. They weren't doing their job. They don't work as a team anymore. He was living in London where there were three or four directors there. I asked John if he had been talking to them, and he said he didn't even know the directors were there. The CAA agents never called him. Because they don't work as a team anymore, so they're not communicating. I think their time is done.

JESSICA TUCHINSKY:

It all changed. If Richard came to me when I was then an agent in 1998 or 1999 and said, "I've got a meeting this week with Tom Hanks, drop everything you're doing and give me the fifty best screenplays or the ten best movies or a list of Paramount go projects," whatever he needed for Tom Hanks that week, even though I wasn't being paid for working with Tom Hanks, I would have dropped everything I was doing for all of my clients and I would have helped Richard put together that list. That's because I was old school. If you work at CAA now and Richard asks for the Tom Hanks list, I can't imagine anyone doing it today.

ADAM VENIT:

Agenting is still a personal proposition, it's still about that connection between an agent and client, but it's much easier when you're at a powerful, successful place where you have a lot of tools. I think we have better agents now and I think we're more connected individually.

SYLVESTER STALLONE:

Adam Venit is obviously a super agent and has insights bordering on the clairvoyant. He knows what to do and how to execute it, and won't let loose of what's important until he shakes you into compliance. He's a really strong personality, so it's not anything you can ignore. He wouldn't give up on *Creed*, just wouldn't give up on me doing it and it becoming a reality. He worships Ron Meyer, and they are similar in the sense that people really like them. Some agents can come in and you actually need shark repellent. They can be really aggressive. But these two are able to be nice while also being adamant about what they're going to do for you and what needs to be done.

CHRIS SILBERMANN:

There have certainly been times when they've walked on water, but now is certainly a time when they're not walking on water. They're still a very good agency, but when we compete with them now, it's not like it was those years with Ovitz and Meyer.

SAM GORES, Agent:

The bigger an agency gets, the more it loses a bit of its focus, and then one day it ends up as just another media business. Not that there's anything wrong with that, but I have always wanted us to be about our artists, not our businesses. I believe that's our competitive edge.

What I get from our guys who used to be at CAA is that they were done there because the culture is not what it used to be. Here we don't shove a culture down anybody's throat.

DAVID O'CONNOR:

I love Ari. He's a twisted fuck, but I get a kick out of him. I sat next to him at the *Saturday Night Live* fortieth anniversary celebration and we had quite a few laughs, and I've always liked Patrick too. I was sorry to see Patrick go, but I always felt he had done the right thing for Patrick. It worked out pretty well for him.

ARI EMANUEL:

The other thing he [Lovett] did which was so great for us is that he made it "The Richard Lovett Show." Every brand of theirs has to be CAA. It's moronic. We own "Red," run by "Red," and it's called "Red." Same goes for a lot of our other businesses.

JIM BERKUS:

CAA and William Morris are bigger, but I think we're the best. We're in the personal service business, and they're in the Growing-Entertainment-Company-to-Go-Public business. So Johnny Depp, Angelina Jolie, Harrison Ford, Channing Tatum, Judd Apatow, Lena Dunham, and many other big stars and clients know they get great service and they love us. We don't spend our time worrying that they're going to be walking out the door to Bryan Lourd or Richard Lovett.

MARK SHAPIRO:

We were at a lunch with a high-level Hollywood media exec and an A-list celeb we were recruiting for representation and the actor asked, "What's the difference between these two agencies?" And I remember the media exec capturing it spot on. He said, "If you're just looking for straight representation, and what agencies have done from the beginning of time, go with CAA. They are slick and transactional and they will always cut you a great deal and leverage their wide band of relationships. But if you're looking to follow in the true Michael Ovitz way of thinking, of becoming a brand and building for a future when you may not be getting the roles you get today, and want a meaningful presence in the business for decades to come, go to WME. CAA is good at answering the phones and putting out fires if you get upset with someone, but WME will be more about creating new opportunities you haven't even thought of for yourself. They will build you a portfolio. They will put you across verticals. They will make you think differently."

CHRIS SILBERMANN:

The agents at CAA and WME are working for big corporations now; being a partner there is like being a VP at Disney. I'm just surprised agents there have surrendered to that. Most great agents have always had a fiercely independent streak. When an agency gets to that size, it becomes really difficult to manage, particularly when it comes to a basic question like "What's our common reason for being here?"

MARK SHAPIRO:

Last year, we all pitched to BMW for some of their business, and our presentations were spread out a bit, and CAA was leaving as we were pulling up, and I kid you not, they were getting in their cars and they were Mercedeses! To a BMW pitch! That's the kind of thing that would never have happened under Ovitz.

JEREMY ZIMMER:

They get punched in the nose now, and they freak out. If you punched Mike Ovitz in the nose, he would spend the rest of his life fucking killing you.

It's a very complex time right now in our industry and there are many different weather patterns happening. The theatrical movie business is changing; streaming services are evolving; and the entire underlying revenue structure is up for grabs. No one really knows how it's going to sort out.

Ever since its creation in 2006, CAA Sports has been the most divisive force on Planet CAA. Competitors think it's a disaster and loss leader; CAA and, perhaps more important, TPG, believe it to be a growth story tour de force. Even inside the agency debate has raged about whether the move toward the playing fields has been sheer strategic genius or hubristic disaster.

To the very select few at CAA who have access to the numbers, it is now not worthy of debate. For decades, television and movies were the primal forces that made CAA the most powerful and profitable agency in the business. No longer. In 2015, Sports, for the first time in the agency's history, was the agency's top revenue producer, bringing in more than $215 million. Motion Pictures, the leader in championship seasons, reportedly crept close, but failed to break the $200 million mark, with television cashing in at around $160 million.

The revenue baton had been passed.

HOWIE NUCHOW:

We had tremendous growth again this past year. Whoever says we're not succeeding is either naive, stupid, or doesn't mind lying. It's only one of the three.

Both CAA and WME/IMG are structured in ways that might have seemed outlandish a few decades ago. CAA is 52 percent owned by TPG, whose roots and primary focus lie, generally speaking, far from Southern California sunshine. WME/IMG is now on the receiving end of investments from Silver Lake, which has the largest stake in the company at 49 percent, Softbank, the Japanese media and telecommunications giant, that has 8 percent, and Fidelity Management, which has roughly 2 percent. (WME/IMG holds approximately 41 percent of the company's equity, and there are several smaller investors as well.) WME/IMG's estimated market cap is around $5.6 billion, compared to CAA's just over $1 billion, with WME boasting more than twice the workforce that CAA employs. Almost immediately after the receipt of these aggressive caches of capital, speculation intensified about which company—if either—would be going public in the near future.

The short answer is, in all likelihood, yes, and WME/IMG will probably be first.

Given their particular approaches, the ways in which each reached this point are distinctly separate. WME's bet has been audacious—picture "all in" in a game of "Hollywood Hold 'Em." Co-chairman Ari Emanuel and Patrick Whitesell play the gumption game better than most in Hollywood, and a lot of what is going to happen prior to the company filing to go public will depend on how closely results mirror their bold pronouncements. Considering their $2 billion in debt, challenges with their college licensing business, and the need to find cuts of around $75 million, it's easy to predict, however glibly, that WME/IMG will be either a grand slam or a grand flameout. Given the stakes and personalities involved, a scenario somewhere in between appears less likely.

CAA's path to a public offering seems a far more "businesslike" ploy that does not need a cult-of-personality leader capable of parting the sea. CAA eschewed the big shopping trip and went largely with a build-your-own approach, making their debt a considerably lower $600 million—an imposing sum, yet not as dramatically different from WME/IMG on a relative basis.

That lower debt, and TPG's patient profile, suggest that CAA has more time to grow before filing.

Going public will not just mean more for the agencies; it will mean potentially tens of millions of dollars for employees who have a piece of the current pie. In many cases, the equity was the result of salary sacrifices in favor of climactic potential payouts at the end. The cash compensation shift—lowering salaries so that profits look higher, then paying people off with shares—was a commitment by management saying, "Trust us, the equity is going to be worth a lot more than your cash would have been." Both agencies have been doing this for several years now, though the number of agents in such a position at WME/IMG is much higher than at CAA. If the companies don't go public soon, employees will start to question the worth of those sacrifices and the value of their equity—the kind of contemplation that can derail deals and lead to potentially surly departures.

The wild card for CAA is Evolution Media (EM), driven by Rick Hess and TPG's Bill McGlashan. Hess was involved in the creation of Evolution Media Capital (EMC) back in 2008, which operates in a more classic investment banking and advisory vein.

(Since 2010, EMC has negotiated and structured over $37 billion of sports media deals, and the decision was made in 2015 that CAA would take its equity stake in EMC to more than 90 percent. That year also saw the arrival of Stuart Epstein at EMC, who was previously CFO of NBC Universal and a partner at Morgan Stanley.)

Evolution Media was founded as a straight-on investment fund, and as it turns out, EM's primary source of capital is TPG's fund, TPG Growth, where McGlashan is founder and managing partner. That fund, with over $7 billion in assets, has invested, started, or partnered with dozens of companies, like Survey Monkey, Uber, and AirBnb, along with incubating STX Studios. EM's first venture round at launch was, in investment fund terms, a modest $100 million, but the second was north of $500 million and is currently looking at a not-so-shabby return of potentially more than three times return on investment. When former eBay president Jeff Skoll became a partner in the fund through his Participant Media, there was some dilution for both CAA and TPG, but CAA retained about 44 percent of EM.

Years ago, CAA may have been at a meeting with or crossed paths with a group that had a great idea, and walked away thinking, That's going to be big, and wished them well. EM's goal is to put an end to that, and to explore investment vehicles inside and beyond the usual Hollywood prospects. EM has already made *an investment in something called Suja Juice, and within a year of doing so, the company was bought by Coke. Sky just invested in Iflix, a streaming video service for Southeast Asia which is part of the EM portfolio, and has a significant stake in Scopely, the successful mobile gaming studio with number one hits like* The Walking Dead.

Evolution Media might just be the most significant outcome of CAA's marriage with TPG, generating more revenue from its investments than anything else on CAA's own horizon. And if and when TPG decides to take CAA public, EM could be more than just wind at the backs of the IPO. Given TPG's track record, it could be more like a hurricane.

JIM COULTER:

There are two misconceptions that I often run into regarding private equity. The first is when we go into an investment, we have a plan for how long it will be before we exit. That's absolutely not true. The second misconception is we have a three- to five-year holding period, which is definitely not the case. We're already more than five years into this, and recently made another investment we wouldn't have made if we were going to exit immediately. We have companies in our portfolio that we've been involved with for fifteen years. And with CAA, the changes in the business that I've been talking about are very long-term changes. We want to continually evolve and improve the internal workings of CAA, bring in new talent, add new disciplines, create new opportunities to deploy capital. But going public is not something that is inevitable or impossible. It is something that will present itself as the opportunities evolve. We'll see.

We bought CAA because there was immense opportunity for value, and if we create that value, it will flow our way. We are in no hurry.

DAVID BONDERMAN:

The advantages of being public are that it can be easier to raise capital; it gives you a currency if you wish to make acquisitions or provide incentives for people you want to come join your firm. It also interferes with your privacy, so there are plusses and minuses. As for going first or going second, what do they say, pioneers get arrows in their back? If you risk going first, you risk going into an industry that doesn't have a lot of public exposure, and you wind up being the target of a lot of publicity and a lot of trial and error by the regulatory authorities. On the other hand, you may get a first-mover advantage.

MICHAEL OVITZ:

The momentum has totally changed. Ari has an incredible business now. He and Patrick have close to five thousand employees producing for them across dozens of countries. CAA has gone from the dominant number one to a market where owning the film business is no longer the goal or the road to the victory stand. Today, diversification and scale create competitive advantage, and because of that, Ari is now running a worldwide company that is clearly the team to beat.

MARK SHAPIRO:

We paid a considerable price for "Miss Universe" from Trump. As you might imagine, the negotiations weren't easy. But we got through it, and we were all on board for the first WME/IMG Miss Universe pageant. Ari and I were both there that night. We met with Steve Harvey prior to the show, and during the show I was in the truck, headset on, locked in. About three quarters of the way through, Ari said to me, "This show is night and day from what it was last year. I've got to catch a flight. Let me know how the rest of it goes." Other than our site going down from an overload of on-line voters, the rest of the way was smooth. Then of course, Steve said, "Miss Colombia," and it was bedlam in the truck. To Steve's credit, he kept cool and did what he had to do, but when Steve came clean on the mistake and gave the crown to Miss Philippines, then there was also bedlam in the theater.

I called Ari from the stage to give him a heads-up. He was literally on the runway about to take off. He couldn't hear me at first;

all I could hear was him yelling to the pilot, "Don't take off yet, don't take off yet!" And then I told him what had happened. Give that report to 99 percent of the executives in our business and they would have gone directly into crisis mode, deplaned, and headed back to the theater. Not Ari. As he often does, he instantly saw it from another angle, complete with upside. He knew right away all the attention the property would receive as a result of this. I told him what had happened and he immediately said, "Fuckin' fantastic!" And hung up. Two months later, Fox extended our contract.

ARI EMANUEL:

I think we've won more than we've lost with them. But it took us about four years to get there, to get this place in shape. We're killing them now.

JEFFREY KATZENBERG:

CAA was very strong and there was a lot of great talent there. Certainly it was going to be a very different enterprise when the founders left and moved on. I think we all knew there would be great changes. But the next rung of leadership in that company was already obvious, and very, very talented, and very, very strong. And here we are, twenty years later, and look where they are.

RICHARD LOVETT:

There are really two truths about CAA. One is that CAA is simply an idea. We are a group of people who believe that the better we treat one another, the more we help each other, the more our clients will succeed and the more we will succeed. This idea defines our culture and our business plan, and drives our success. The second truth about CAA is that we are only at the beginning. I have said many times at the conclusion of our annual retreat that the agency is just getting started. We are perfectly positioned at the intersection of entertainment, sports, technology, and brands for our next chapter to be the most dynamic and exciting in our history.

BILL HABER:

I think I'm going to live to about a hundred and ten. I'm going to go down kicking and screaming. There will be nobody at my funeral because you'll all be dead.

Forty years of CAA begs a comparison between the first and second twenty. Were the earlier days golden? Days of power unquestioned, movie and television businesses humming on all cylinders, the agency itself smaller, more family-like, happiness personified? Or is now the great moment in time, given the seemingly limitless future of the content universe and the fact that the agency is into so many more businesses—and armed with TPG dollars—that they can go after opportunities even Ovitz might have had to deny himself? And while we're talking money, while it's true that many of today's CAA agents don't get the premiums on their compensation the way their predecessors in the first twenty years did, the current crowd may have the ultimate lottery ticket in its pocket if, and when, the company does indeed go public.

Time will tell.

What may be most extraordinary about CAA's history is how the agency managed to have the right people in the right places at the right times. Ovitz, Meyer, and Haber were perfectly cut out for their eras, each a great salesman in a sellers' market. They wouldn't have had the patience for today's buyers' market, nor for a world where fewer movies are made, comic book heroes have the real clout at the box office, "network" television is spread out among a thousand different channels, and the majority of those listening to music wouldn't be able to recognize a Tower Records.

Ovitz in a buyers' market is like a Porsche going forty; Meyer with a long call sheet with actresses complaining of not getting enough work sounds like a job change desperately waiting to happen; and Haber having to contend with Netflix, Amazon, and YouTube suggests a deeper required dedication to the business, one that would have had him thinking about Save the Children ten years earlier.

Had he stayed at CAA, Ovitz himself would be far, far away by now from the client services business. The company would have most certainly had an office in Silicon Valley, and probably would have been angel investors in at least some of today's current content plays such as Netflix, Hulu, or countless others. Ovitz's problem with Tele-TV and AMG (among others) was that he was too early. That would have been more of an asset than an issue for him when it came to investing in technological start-ups.

The Young Turks have proven much better suited for this age. They are more patient and more disposed to the type of diplomacy needed in today's environment. In the past decade, now Not-So-Young Turks have been able to silence critics who have charged that they never built a business (and couldn't) but merely inherited an empire from the founding fathers. Now that the agency has vertically integrated and expanded as it has, that argument has begun to fade away.

When it comes to lessons learned, however, the original leaders can take the crown. They took their bills of particulars from their days outside the helm at William Morris and built a world designed to make sure their biggest complaints—strict borders between departments, unfair compensation formulas, and a strangling pseudo-aristocratic culture—were not repeated. It just so happens that the Turks' biggest issue with their bosses—lack of transparency—still exists for many at the agency and is worthy of correction.

In 1995, CAA proved that it was stronger than any one individual, and in 2017, when the current leadership's contracts are up (part of the new TPG era), that case may have to be made yet again. For some, it is beyond ironic—given what transpired in '95—that should the Big Three leave, few (if any) know who'd take over or if a succession plan even exists. What matters now isn't just what Lovett, Huvane, and Lourd think and want; it's all about what Jim Coulter and David Bonderman want. They control the company, and their agenda, designs, and decisions will determine CAA's future more than anyone else. One wants to wish them luck, but it sure won't be easy for them to make the next forty years equal the achievements, drama, and passion of the first forty.

They were, in a word, extraordinary.

ACKNOWLEDGMENTS

More than five hundred interviews were conducted for this book, and I tried to never take it for granted when someone invited me to their home, office, or favorite watering hole, and agreed to cooperate. A ton of gratitude and appreciation goes to all who were generous with their time and who spoke openly and honestly of their careers, their colleagues, their frustrations—even, as the wisest man said, their lives, their fortunes, and their sacred honor. Although many of the interview sessions were tremendous fun, there were bound to be raw and difficult moments as well. I am doubly grateful to those who displayed the fortitude to go back and revisit events they may have preferred to leave behind.

It's fair to say management at CAA was—at least initially—much less than enthusiastic about this book. I elected to pursue the project and even closed the deal before discussing it with anyone at the agency. It was no mystery what their answer would have been if I had asked permission first. The agency is known for its penchant for privacy, as evidenced by how rarely the majority of employees speak to journalists on the record. After months of discussion even about whether to have discussions, it was uncommonly decent and generous of them to cooperate to the extent that they did. More than two dozen current agents—and the entire agency leadership—along with the partners of TPG, which now has a controlling interest, spoke with me. I will always be grateful. Executives in the entertainment industry, both past and present, are also to be thanked, as are key figures at other agencies in town, particularly those who opened doors and made their agents available.

The world of HarperCollins was new to me, but was a welcoming and supportive one from the start. Lynn Grady, Doug Jones, Michael Morrison, Beth Siflin, Liate Stehlik, and Mary Beth Thomas provided leadership and guidance. The production group at Morrow, including Mumtaz Mustafa and Leah Carlson-Stanisic, both brilliant designers, and Nyamekye Waliyaya, Shelby Peak, and Andrea Molitor, all exhibited great patience, for which I am grateful. Kelly Rudolph and Shelby Meizlik make the difficult look easy, and day in and day out, Madeline Jaffe exhibits acumen way beyond her years.

Heather Karpas and Colin Graham are always a pleasure and always come through. Annie Lee at CAA, and several of her other assistant colleagues there were gracious and truly helpful. The Special Ks—Kris Fujihara, Kristina Walker, and Kari Zirkle—make life easier. Others at agencies, studios, networks, and production companies showed hospitality that was equally appreciated.

This book was years in the making; over that time, a great support system flew in and out of the *Powerhouse* biosphere, led by Keegan Gray Hawkins and Benjamin Korman, two veritable forces of nature when it came to providing assistance. Many thanks extend to Greg Collins, Marshall Finch, Trevor Hawkins, Adam Khatib, Caroline Lazar, Daniel Locke, Tiffany Tao, Arin Segal, and Pat Walker.

There are, in addition, certain people who simply must be cited for their special support: Lori Andrew, Karen Andrews, Aimee

Bell, Jim Bell, Mark Contreras, Natalie Famous, Risa and Michael Ferman, Susan Gordon, Bill LaPoint, Josh McLaughlin, Bill Phillips, Ted Schachter, Steve Skaggs, and Michael Traeger, chief among them.

Powerhouse is at Custom House because it is Geoff Shandler's imprint. There is no doubt this new enterprise will be wrapped in success for years to come. No one deserves it more than Geoff.

This is a book rooted in the world of agents, and for more than a decade, I've been fortunate enough to be represented by the gold standard, Sloan Harris. There's nothing better than to work with someone you trust professionally—and care about personally.

Last but arguably most, the indomitable Chloe Tess Miller deserves special praise and not only because her two older siblings, Zachary and Sophie, were away at college during preparation of this book. Chloe uncomplainingly and repeatedly settled for Japanese take-out when there wasn't time for a home-cooked meal. All three of my children remain my most important audience and dearest companions.

Thank you, and good night, all.

ABOUT THE AUTHOR

JAMES ANDREW MILLER is an award-winning journalist and co-author of the #1 *New York Times* bestseller *Those Guys Have All the Fun: Inside the World of ESPN; Live from New York: The Complete, Uncensored History of* Saturday Night Live *as Told by Its Stars, Writers, and Guests,* which spent four months on the *New York Times* bestseller list; and *Running in Place: Inside the Senate,* also a bestseller. He has written for the *Washington Post,* the *New York Times, Vanity Fair,* and many other publications. He is a graduate of Occidental College, Oxford University, and Harvard Business School, all with honors.